World Shores and Beaches

This is no longer
the property of
King County Library System

FEB   2006

ALSO BY MARY ELLEN SNODGRASS
AND FROM McFARLAND

Barbara Kingsolver: A Literary Companion (2004)

August Wilson: A Literary Companion (2004)

Amy Tan: A Literary Companion (2004)

*World Epidemics: A Cultural Chronology of Disease
from Prehistory to the Era of SARS* (2003)

Coins and Currency: An Historical Encyclopedia (2003)

Encyclopedia of World Scriptures (2001)

Who's Who in the Middle Ages (2001)

World Shores and Beaches

A Descriptive and Historical Guide to 50 Coastal Treasures

MARY ELLEN SNODGRASS

McFarland & Company, Inc., Publishers

Jefferson, North Carolina, and London

Library of Congress Cataloguing-in-Publication Data

Snodgrass, Mary Ellen.
World shores and beaches : a descriptive and historical guide
to 50 coastal treasures / Mary Ellen Snodgrass.
p.   cm.
Includes bibliographical references and index.

ISBN 0-7864-1886-9 (softcover : 50# alkaline paper) ∞

1. Seashore.   2. Coasts.   3. Beaches.   I. Title.
GB451.2.S66   2005   910'.914'6 — dc22   2005014051

British Library cataloguing data are available

©2005 Mary Ellen Snodgrass. All rights reserved

*No part of this book may be reproduced or transmitted in any form
or by any means, electronic or mechanical, including photocopying
or recording, or by any information storage and retrieval system,
without permission in writing from the publisher.*

On the cover: Chersonese, Ukraine (photograph courtesy of Glenn Mack)

Manufactured in the United States of America

*McFarland & Company, Inc., Publishers
Box 611, Jefferson, North Carolina 28640
www.mcfarlandpub.com*

ACKNOWLEDGMENTS

No reference book is the work of a single author. Many people contributed to this text and its illustration by brochure, fax, photo, website, email, and telephone interview. I owe thanks to all the contributors listed below for their interest in beaches and for sharing pictures, maps, and details of habitat and history:

Julie Armstrong
Monterey County Convention and Visitors Bureau
P. O. Box 1770
Monterey, California 93942
Phone: 800-555-6290
Email: julie@mccvb.org

Cori Arthur
Northumberland Tourism
860 William Street
Cobourg, Ontario K9A 3A9
Phone: 800-354-7050
Fax: 905-372-1696
      866-401-EAST
Email: arthur@county.northumberland.on.ca
http://www.northumberlandtourism.com

Holley Aufdemorte, Media Communications
      Specialist
Myrtle Beach Area Chamber of Commerce
P. O. Box 2115
Myrtle Beach, South Carolina 29578
Phone: 843-626-7444, ext. 7218
Fax: 843-916-7216
E-mail: aufdemh@mbchamber.org
http://www.myrtlebeachinfo.com

Holly Blount, Marketing Director
Vizcaya Museum and Gardens
3251 South Miami Avenue
Miami, Florida 33129
Phone: 305-860-8451
Email: blount @vizcayamuseum.com
http://www.vizcayamuseum.org

Todd Bolen
Moshav Yad HaShmonah
D. N. Tzafon Yehudah
90895 ISRAEL
http://www.BiblePlaces.com
Email: tbolen@BiblePlaces.com.

David Bourn
Environmental Research Group Oxford Limited
Zoology Department, South Parks Road
P. O. Box 346
Oxford, OX1 3QE, U. K.
Phone and Fax: 44-01865-883281
E-mail: david.bourn@ntlworld.com
http://ergadd.zoo.ox.ac.uk/

Peter Brueggeman, Director
Scripps Institution of Oceanography Library
University of California at San Diego
9500 Gilman Drive, Department 0219
San Diego, California 92093-0219
Phone: 858-534-1230
Fax: 858-534-5269
Email: pbrueggeman@ucsd.edu
http://www.nsf.gov/od/opp/antarct/imageset/
      start.htm

Dennis Buurman
Dolphin Encounter
58 West End
Kaikoura, New Zealand
Phone: 64-3-319-6777
Fax: 64-3-319-6534
Email: info@dolphin.co.nz
http://www.dolphin.co.nz/shop/item1.htm

Acknowledgments

Andrew Buys, President
Barrington-Hall Corporation
Yachting Professionals Worldwide
2400 East Las Olas Boulevard, Suite 314
Fort Lauderdale, Florida 33301
Phone: 800-478-2029
      954-720-0475
Email: into@yacht-charters.tv
http: www.yacht-charters.tv

Carlos Velazquez Cerda, General Director
Arely Figueroa, Public Relations
Acapulco Convention & Visitors Bureau
Avenida Costera Miguel Aleman # 38-A
Fraccionamiento Costa Azul
Codigo Postal 39850
Acapulco, Guerrero, Mexico
Phone: 744-484-8555
Fax: 744-484-8134
Email: rp-ocva@acapulco.org.mx
http://www.visitacapulco.com.mx

Baldwyn Chieh
Phone: 408-247-7180
Email: baldwyn@mad.scientist.com
http://www.tri-bal.com/ecuador/fernandina.
   shtml

Manuela Tiraboschi D'Ambra
Villa Meligunis Hotel
Via Marte, Seven
98055 Lipari, Italy
Phone: 39-090-981-2426
Fax: 39-090-988-0149
Email: villameligunis@netnet.it
http://www.netnet.it/villameligunis

Bob Daniel
Toronto, Canada
http://www.rgdaniel.com/
Christopher A. Davis
Alpha Centauri's Universe (ACU)
2608 Furrs Street, Apartment 202
Arlington, Texas 76006
Email: ChristopherDavis@to-scorpio.com
http:.//www.to-scorpio.com

Suzanne Downer
Redlands, Ebford
Exeter, EX3 OQT, England
Email: Suzanne.Downer@btopenworld.com

Eddie Dunmore
118 Edgecoombe
South Croydon CR2 8AD, England
Email: eddie@eddietor.icr-uk.net

Gerald England
Twenty Werneth Avenue
Gee Cross
Hyde, Cheshire, U. K. SK14 5NL
Email: nhi@clara.net
http://www.nhi.clara.net/index.htm

David Flack
P. O. Box 6005
Honolulu, Hawaii 96818
Email: ah6hy@aol.com
http://www.qsl.net/ah6hy/kahoolawe.html

Debra Walker Flemming
Florida Division of Historical Resources
500 South Bronough Street
Tallahassee, Florida 32301
Phone: 850-245-6306
Fax: 805-245-6346

Galen R. Frysinger
Sheboygan, Wisconsin
Email: peopleandplaces1@netscape.net
http://www.galenfrysinger.com

Avis Gachet, book dealer
Wonderland Books
5008 Hickory Boulevard
Hickory, North Carolina 28601
Fax: 828-396-2710
Email: wonland@twave.net
http://www.abebooks.com/home/WONLAND/

Robert Gray
1220 South Mill Avenue
Tempe, Arizona 85281
http://home.att.net/~bgray92/dec21/ghanadec221
   .htm

John S. Guagliardo, Executive Director
Hawaii Virtual Library
P. O. Box 22687
Honolulu, Hawaii 96823
Phone: 808-292-2068
Email: John@guigliardo.cc
http://www.hawaiilibrary.com

Irma Hale
5200 North Flagler Drive
West Palm Beach, Florida 33407-2770
Email: irma@irmahale.com
http://www.irmahale.com

Alan Hodgkinson
Reckenbühlstrasse Twelve
CH-6005 Luzern, Switzerland

Phone: 41-41-210-90-74
Fax: 41-41-210-16-96
alan.hodgkinson@alum.mit.edu
http://www.softxs.ch/alan

Hans Honegger, web designer
Ballyferriter, Dingle, Ireland
Phone: 066-9159812
Email: hans@irishcrafts.com
http://www.irishcrafts.com

Niall Huggard
Killarney Lake Side Hotel and Fitness Centre
Muckross Road
Killarney, Ireland
Phone: 353-0-64-31035
Fax: 353-0-64-31902
Email: info@lakehotel.ie
http://www.lakehotel.ie

Jeffrey Jarrett
University of Rhode Island
Seven Lippitt Road, Ballentine
Kingston, Rhode Island
Email: jeff1@uri.edu
http://www.cba.uri.edu/Faculty/jarrett/page3.htm

A. Michael Jones
Island Cruise Adventure, Inc.
11602 Bos Street
Cerritos, California 90703
Phone: 562-865-7198
FAX: 562-809-7300
Email: mike@islandcruiseadventure.com
http://www.islandcruiseadventure.com

Scott King
2015 Neil Avenue
Columbus, Ohio 43210-1277
Email: ScottKing@acm.org
http://www.cis.ohiostate.edu/~sking/

Emily Lyons, Media Relations Officer
Monaco Government Tourist Office
565 Fifth Avenue
New York, New York 10017
Phone: 212-286-3330
Fax: 212-286-9890
Email: Emily@Monaco1.org
http://www.leonardo.com

Glenn Mack
Institute of Classical Archaeology
University of Texas at Austin
3925 West Braker Lane
Austin, Texas 78759

phone: 512-232-9318
fax: 512-232-9324
Email: grmack@mail.utexas.edu
http://www.utexas.edu/research/ica/

Mads Nygaard
Oddesundvej Eighteen
9220 Aalborg, Denmark
Email: mads_nygaard@hotmail.com
http://traveling.igw.uk

Daniele Pascerini
House of Wonders
Via Manzoni, Six
40121 Bologna, Italy
Phone: 39-051-234974
Email: info@houseofwonders.com
http://www.House of Wonders.com

John Pearson
Pelagic Expeditions
75 Christchurch Road
Winchester, Hampshire, England SO23 9TG
Email: gc13@dial.pipex.com
http://www.pelagic.co.uk

Theodore W. Pietsch
Department of Zoology
University of Washington
Seattle, Washington 98195
Email: twp@u.washington.edu
http://artedi.fish.washington.edu/okhotskia/
    ikip/Results/Bios/pietsch.html

Nicholas K. Rauh
Department of History
Purdue University
University Hall
West Lafayette, Indiana 47907
Phone: 765-494-4122
Fax: 765-496-1755
Email: rauhn@purdue.edu

Justin Reed
University of Washington
Seattle, Washington 98195
Email: docpeppr@u.washington.edu

Charlotte Richardson, diver-photographer
Paul Young
Eleven Michigan Drive
Hudson, Massachusetts 01749
Email: Charlotte.Richardson@hp.com

Bruce Roberts
Lighthouse Publications

3601 Meadow Drive
Morehead City, North Carolina 28557
Phone: 252-247-5436

Ian Robichaud
Basecamp International
827 Bay Street, #6
Santa Monica, California 90405
Email: webmaster@base-camp.com
http: www.halong-bay.com

Wanda Rozzelle
reference librarian
Catawba County Library
Newton, North Carolina

Mark Schumacher
reference librarian
Jackson Library, UNC-G
Greensboro, North Carolina

Tracy L. Skaggs
Rock Island, Illinois
Phone: 563-388-9111
Email: tskaggs@dcsqc.com
    refcsz@hawaii.com

Bill Snow
Bike & Barge Holland Tours
778 Lillooet Court
LaConner, Washington 98257-9610
Phone: 360-466-1627
    1-800-437-4771
Fax: 360-466-1725
Email: Tours@bikebarge.com
http://www.bikebarge.com

Patrick Sobbel
P. O. Box 1041
Mudgee, New South Wales 2850
Australia
Email: aussiesonline@ozemail.com.au
http://www.aussies-online.com

Diane Somers
Alaska Photo Library
P. O. Box 110809,
Juneau, Alaska 99811-0809
phone: 907-465-2012
fax: 907-465-3767
550 West Seventh Avenue, Suite 1770
Anchorage, Alaska 99501-3510
phone: 907-269-8110
fax: 907-269-8125
http://www.alaskaphotolibrary.org

Charles Tait
Kelton, St. Ola
Orkney, U. K. KW15 1TR
Phone: 01856-873738
Fax: 01856-875313
Mobile: 07785-220269
Email: Charles.tait@zetnet.co.uk
http://www.charles-tait.co.uk

Barry Thigpen, President
National Shag Dance Championships
P. O. Box 6767
Myrtle Beach, South Carolina 29578
Phone: 843-497-7369
Fax: 843-497-9748
Email: shagnational@sc.rr.com
http://www.shagnationals.com/

Amy Thoreau
Hotel Kasha
P. O. Box 1991
San Jose, Costa Rica
Phone: 506-750-0205
Fax: 506-750-0205
Email: lducoudray@rocsa.co.cr
www.costarica-hotelkasha.com

James A. Tuck
Anthropology Department
Memorial University
St. John's, Newfoundland A1C 5S7
Phone: 709-737-8000
Fax: 709-737-4569
Email: jtuck@mun.ca

Turkish Embassy
Tourish Counselor's Office
2525 Massachusetts Avenue, N. W.
Washington, D. C. 20008
Phone: 202-612-6700
Fax: 202-612-6744
Email: turkish@erols.com.
http://www.turkey.org

Peter Turnham, photographer
Beynes, France
http://perso.club-internet.fr/ptthome
Email: ptthome@club-internet.fr

Rafael Tuts, Human Settlements Officer
UN-Habitat
P. O. Box 30030
Nairobi 00100, Kenya
Phone: 254-2-623726
Fax.: 254-2-623715
Email: raf.tuts@unhabitat.org
Web-site: www.unhabitat.org/governance

A. G. van der Steur
Kruisstraat Three
2011 PV Haarlem, Netherlands
Phone: 31-0-23-5311470
Fax: 31-0-23-5420670
Email: antiquariaat@vandersteur.nl
http://www.vandersteur.nl

Tyron van Tonder
Anita Meijberg
Lynx Tours
Box 2031
Wavecrest
Jeffreys Bay 6330 Eastern Cape
South Africa
Phone: 27-0-42-296-0594
Fax: 27-72-237-7422
Email: tyron@agnet.co.za
http://www.doorway.co.za/ec/1368.asp

Patti Daves Tyndall, Coordinator
Department of Education
University of North Carolina at Wilmington
Wilmington, North Carolina

Viking Trail Tourism Association
P. O. Box 251
St. Anthony, Newfoundland, A0K 4T0.
Phone: 709-454-8888
http://www.vikingtrail.org
Email: info@vtta.nf.ca

George Wegmann
DiveGurus Boracay
Phone: 63-36-288-54-86
Cellphone: 63-918-919-38-30
Email: george@divegurus.com
http://www.divegurus.com/

Iris Weissen
Hans-Henny-Jahnn-Weg 53
22085 Hamburg, Germany
Phone: 49-40-226-58-322
Fax: 49-40-226-58-333
Email: iris.weissen@salaction.de

Neville Williams, Visitor Services
Sydney Opera House
Sydney, Australia
Phone: 61-2-9250-7777

Fax: 61-2-9251-3943
Email: infodesk@soh.nsw.gov.au
www.sydneyoperahouse.com

Martin C. Wilson, Publisher & Editor-
  in-Chief
VietnamAdventures.com
1877 Broadway Suite 200
Boulder, Colorado 80302
Phone: 303-449-2006
Fax: 303-449-2007
Email: martyw@vietnamadventures.com

Christopher Workman
Klingentalgraben 17
CH-4057 Basel, Switzerland
Phone: 41-78-886-7094
Email: workman@genome.cbs.dtu.dk
http://www.cbs.dtu.dk/~workman/lipari99.html

Ivy Zamudio, Sales Supervisor
Qasar Nautica
Quito, Ecuador
Phone: 593-2-244-1550
       593-2-244-6996
Fax: 593-2-243-6625
Email: Ivy@quasarnautica.com
http://www.quasarnautica.com

Interlibrary Loan

Ashland College Library, Ashland, Ohio
Belk Library, Appalachian State University,
  Boone, North Carolina
Catawba County Library, Newton, North Carolina
Clearwater Christian College Library, Clearwater,
  Florida
Dare County Library, Manteo, North Carolina
Duke University Library, Durham, North Carolina
East Carolina University Library, Greenville,
  North Carolina
Fort Worth Public Library, Fort Worth, Texas
Gaston County Library, Gastonia, North Carolina
State Library of Florida, Tallahassee, Florida
Suffolk County Community College, Brentwood,
  New York
University of North Carolina at Chapel Hill Li-
  brary, North Carolina
William F. Maag Library, Youngstown State Uni-
  versity, Youngstown, Ohio

TABLE OF CONTENTS

Acknowledgments v
Preface 1
Introduction 5
Beaches and Shores Listed by Country 9

PREFACE

The plan of *World Shores and Beaches: A Descriptive and Historical Guide to 50 Coastal Treasures* is to present unique beach settings in varied locales around the globe. Each entry begins with a topographical description and one or more contacts complete with street addresses, phone and fax numbers, email addresses, and websites if available. Entries present a variety of information that may include myths and legends, history, biography, archeology, and ecosystems. Each concludes with a summary of coastal activities available today and a list of bibliographical sources drawn from books, journals, magazines, newspapers, and websites. In addition, the bibliography details data derived from invaluable electronic sources, including Alexander Street's *Early Encounters in North America*; ABC-Clio's two-part online database, comprised of *America: History and Life*, which covers learned articles about North America, and *Historical Abstracts*, which presents parallel information worldwide from 1450 to the present; and Gale Group's *Biography Resource Center* data bank, which provides information on thousands of important people, such as oceanographer Walter Heinrich Munk, compiler of *The Oceans, Their Physics, Chemistry, and General Biology* (1942), and Princess Sayyida Salme, author of *Memoirs of an Arabian Princess* (1886). A variety of photographs rounds out the reader's impressions of coastal uniqueness.

Entries touch on the lives of such expeditioners as La Salle and pirate Henry Morgan and researchers including zoologist Theodore W. Pietsch and bird enthusiast George Archibald. They also note important published works such as biologist Edward Flanders "Doc" Ricketts and novelist John Steinbeck's *Between Pacific Tides* (1939) and Steinbeck's *The Sea of Cortez* (1941), and describe particulars of locales, including the glaciers of Beagle Channel and the National Park of American Samoa, the first U.S. national park in the Southern Hemisphere.

Bolstering the text are a number of research aids:

- An introduction expressing the significance of beaches and shores to human history, religion, philosophy, and eco-awareness.
- A listing of the 50 selected beaches and shores organized by 41 countries.
- A glossary of 87 crucial terms and environmental agencies — such as ironshore, Greenpeace, tell, polder, katabatic wind, thermal plume, and UNESCO.
- An appendix of selected literary works and films listed alphabetically by title and date, including the histories of Herodotus and Thucydides, the

1

encyclopedia of Pliny the Elder, the writings of oceanographer Jacques-Yves Cousteau, Margaret Cochrane Scott's *Birds of Paradise and Bower Birds* (1950), Donald T. Bosch and Eloise Bosch's *Seashells of Eastern Arabia* (1995), and Nathaniel Bright Emerson's incisive *Unwritten Literature of Hawai'i: The Sacred Songs of the Hula* (1909).

- A general bibliography noting broader-based funds of information, particularly Peter Kemp's *Oxford Companion to Ships and the Sea* (1988), Victoria Sandz's *Encyclopedia of Western Atlantic Shipwrecks and Sunken Treasure* (2001), and Mark D. Spalding's *World Atlas of Coral Reefs* (2001). Also helpful were Geoffrey Barraclough's *Atlas of World History* (2001), Harold A. Winters's *Battling the Elements: Weather and Terrain in the Conduct of War* (1998), Charles J. Opitz's *Odd and Curious Money* (1986), Charles E. Davies's *The Blood-Red Arab Flag* (1997), Robert Bell's *Women of Classical Mythology* (1991), Gordon East's *An Historical Geography of Europe* (1966), Noel Grove's *Wild Lands for Wildlife* (1984), Jay Robert Nash's *Encyclopedia of World Crime* (1990), and Nigel Pickford's *The Atlas of Ship Wrecks & Treasure* (1994). In addition, I drew on my own writings, especially *Coins and Currency in History* (2003), *Chronology of Epidemics* (2004), *Religious Sites in America* (2001), and *Who's Who in the Middle Ages* (2001), and on *Indian Terms of the Americas* (1994), co-authored by Dr. Lotsee Patterson. Of particular help were current publications, news sources, and academic journals, notably, BBC News, *National Geographic, Nature, African Historical Studies, Canadian Geographic, Archaeology*, and online newspapers from around the world, including the *China Daily* and the *Sydney Sun Herald*. I am also indebted to numerous Internet sites, particularly "The Ramsar Convention on Wetlands," "UNESCO," "The World Heritage List," "25-Year History of INA Research," and "Greenpeace."

The indexing is exhaustive. To aid the teacher, traveler, historian, naturalist, and ecotourist, I have singled out these elements:

- Seas and waterways—Indian Ocean, Gulf Stream, Zuider Zee, Clayoquot Sound, Labrador Current, Sea of Galilee, Boomkensdiep Channel, Roskilde Fjord.
- Cities—Acapulco, Sydney, Ushuaia, Nice, Essaouira, Stavoren, Copenhagen.
- Structures—longhouses, Les Eclaireures lighthouse, Sydney Opera House, Serapeum.
- Individuals—Grace Darling, Charlie Maxwell, Marrianne Collison Campbell, Captain James Cook, Elizabeth II of England, Harald "Blue-Tooth" Gormson, Tippu Tib.
- Archeologists—Gerrit Daniël van der Heide, George F. Bass, Torao Mozai, Hugo Graf, Sir Kenelm Digby, Helmut Schlaeger.
- Tribes—Maori, Alcaluf, Makah, Aliut, Yanyuwa, Yoruba, Bantu, Wickaninnish.
- Foods—kelp, palolo reef worm, amlou, maktak.
- Currency—cowries, *manzanilla*.
- Religions and religious leaders—Diana culture, *kahunas*, druidism, animism, Pope Leo VII, Candomblé, Iyá Nasso.
- Events—Hurricane Val, D-Day, Great Miami Hurricane, Operation Harvest, Peberrenden Blockade.
- Diseases—malaria, tuberculosis, leprosy, influenza, HIV/AIDS.
- Mythic and legendary characters—Skeggi of Midfirth, Sedna, Bran, Ygraine, Grim, Hyperborean maidens.
- Films and film makers—*The Knights of the Round Table* (1953), *Shag* (1988), *Waikiki Wedding* (1937), *Ryan's Daughter* (1969), *The Man with the Golden Gun* (1974), Louis Malle, *L'Indochine* (1992), *Rashomon* (1950), Kurosawa Akira.

- Concepts — *fa'a Samoa*, over-fishing, emigration, beach music, piracy, harems, forced labor, transportation of criminals.
- Endangered species — monk seal, Nicobar pigeon, orange roughy, red-crowned crane, bowhead whale.
- Non-profit agencies — UNESCO, International Coral Reef Initiative, World Fund for Nature, Greenpeace, World Wildlife Fund.
- Coastal activities — kite fighting, yachting, drumming, fire walking, pearling, harpooning, sand castles.
- Coastal attractions — Acatushún Bone Museum, Dragon Boat Festival, Elmina Castle, Prada Challenge for Classic Yachts, "graveyard of the Atlantic," Fungie the dolphin.

- Music — *The Brendan Voyage* (1980), "With This Ring," "Sweet Leilani," *meles*, "Under the Boardwalk," *oli*.
- Musical instruments — pahu drums, *'uli'uli*, uilleann pipes, ukulele.
- Dance — capoira, hula, Carolina shag, lambada, *samba de roda*.
- Published works — *Myths and Legends of Maoriland* (1961), "Hymn to Apollo" (ca. 690 B.C.), *The Living Sea* (1963), *Lindisfarne Gospels* (ca. 698 A.D.).

Generous cross-referencing within the text and the index enables readers to make connections between entries that, at first glance, appear to have no relation to each other, for example, Monte Carlo, Woolacombe, and Omaha Beach.

If I take the wings of the morning,
    and dwell in the uttermost parts of the sea;
Even there shall thy hand lead me,
    and thy right hand shall hold me....
I will praise thee;
    for I am fearfully and wonderfully made:
Marvellous are thy works;
    and that my soul knoweth right well.
                Psalm 139:9–10, 14

And I have loved thee, Ocean! ...
For I was as it were a child of thee,
And trusted to thy billows far and near.
              George Gordon, Lord Byron
              Childe Harold's Pilgrimage
           Canto IV, clxxxiv, 1648, 1653–1654.

INTRODUCTION

The places where sky, sea, and land come together work magic on humankind. Steady tidal rhythms unite lives with a power in the universe and drum into thought and action an awareness of nature's impact on history. A study of beaches and shores produces individual examples as unique as fingerprints, from the cliff divers of Acapulco to the Samoan herbalists of Ofu Island. In Vietnam, Halong Bay charged aboriginal imaginations with the topographical layering of coral reef, fissures and sinkholes, fjords and pebbly shingles, saltwater fens, serenely meandering sea corridors, rock spindles and bridges, and tors sculpted by wind and wave. Likewise, at Point Barrow, Alaska, the Inuit shaped their community and worship around bowhead whaling, a form of sea plunder that brought them the necessities of food and building material as well as an opportunity to share their marine bounty as an act of worship and mutual regard. In Capernaum, the daily toil of Israeli fishermen influenced Jesus's friendships and ministry, his sermons and parables, and the selection of apostles to spread his message. At Punta Espinosa, Fernandina, the life forms on one of the Galápagos Islands exhibited such a clear model of biological engineering that they influenced the scientific philosophy of English naturalist Charles Darwin, a primary thinker of the Victorian age.

Because of the melange of stimuli from sky and sea and wind, folklorists and mythographers have long set oral stories along the shore, for example, in the Greek myth of the birth of the twins Apollo and Artemis on Delos, the island that welcomed their beleaguered mother Leto. The legends of Vietnamese lovers at Halong Bay and of Richberta, grand matron of Ijsselmeer, Holland, incorporate in their narratives the interplay of human will with impersonal shifts in nature that turned one couple to stone and changed the haughty Richberta into a beggar. One of the Western world's most revered legends, the life of King Arthur, begins with a shore birth. The infant washes up on the breakers of Tintagel Head where Merlin, the wonder worker, embraces him and begins readying him for England's throne. But unlike fanciful metamorphoses and births, real events often prove stranger than fiction, for example, nature's reshaping of the Tyrrhenian harbor at Ostia, Italy, and the rapid rise and cataclysmic end of the Jamaican pirate capital at Port Royal.

Along with oral lore, human development of shores has benefited communities with sculpture, engineering marvels, and architecture expressing the heights of ambition, as found in the arrival of Hellenistic sculptors at Selinus, the dredging and restructuring of Matrah on the Gulf of Oman, the design of a SeaBus in Monte Carlo, and the repositioning of the famed lighthouse on Cape Hatteras, North Carolina. The successive builders of Alexandria, Egypt, ornamented a Mediterranean shore with the landmarks of the age — the Pharos, one of the Seven Wonders of the world, and the palace and royal compound of Cleopatra, who prized Egypt's world-class library and repository of philosophical, literary, religious, and scientific achievements. Along Biscayne Bay, Florida, James Deering, a wealthy industrialist, chose the tropical coast of Miami as the ideal spot to build Vizcaya, landscape it with palm trees and jasmine, and fill it with treasures that preserve world artistry and beauty. In Sydney, New South Wales, Australians hired Danish designer Joern Utzon to erect the Sydney Opera House, a world-famous harbor adornment topped with billowing white roofs that lift toward the sky like seagulls' wings or the sails of clipper ships that brought the island nation its first English settlers. In obeisance to the demands of the sea, planners incorporated into all these projects the natural exigencies of shore life as well as its wonders.

Beyond the creative urge, the convergence of natural elements at beach and shore has led communities and individuals to reflect on the creation of life and the worship of a divine creator. On tiny Delos, a Greek isle encircled by the Cyclades, ancient peoples erected a pilgrimage site graced with temples, statuary, and sweeping promenades leading worshippers from the surf to elevated holy places. The steady access of the Delian harbor produced a commercial center and one of the Mediterranean's busiest slave markets. Farther east, Greek colonists at the Chersonese in the Ukraine established a thriving port later developed by Prince Volodymyr, a Russian Christian, into a showplace and pilgrim magnet honoring St. Clement of Rome. In contrast to these reception centers for seekers, Dingle in Kerry, Ireland, offered St. Brendan, a Celtic monk

and visionary, a point of departure for his quest of an earthly *terra repromissionis sanctorum* [promised land of the saints]. The search led him and a handful of mariners on a remarkable act of faith — an unscripted venture into cold northern waters where the elements threatened his tiny *curragh*, a flexible round boat shaped from wood ribs and covered in oxhides and oak bark. Similarly drawn to the lure of the tides, along the shores of Kaho'Olawe, Hawaii, early Polynesian expeditioners who arrived by double-hulled canoe devoted first fruits of the sea at surfside fishing altars and, at the throne-shaped "Navigator's Chair," turned their eyes heavenward in search of constellations expressing divine guidance as they paddled over treacherous sea routes.

In addition to daring acts, shore dwellers have dedicated their artistry and activism to the smallest and weakest of animals and plants, for example, artist and biologist Rae Prosser Goodall's *Tierra del Fuego, Uttermost Part of the Earth* (1948), which contains her observations and drawings of Argentine sea life, and Wally Stone's operation of a Maori-centered ecotourism center at Kaikoura Peninsula, New Zealand. Examples of nature lovers date back as far as Aidan, the Benedictine monk of Lindisfarne, Northumberland, who devoted much of his holy vocation to the protection of wild shore beings. His model of conservation impressed a follower, Cuthbert, who retreated to a tiny coastal hermitage at a lava rock cave to receive human counselees, grow onions and barley, and befriend sea otters and wading birds. The concept of coastal volunteerism continues into the 21st century. At Jeffreys Bay, South Africa, a veterinarian, D. J. Hartley, operates an outreach to the African or blackfoot penguin, a harmless creature that regularly suffers the buffeting of coastal traffic, particularly from leaking oil tankers. Off Monterey, California, a parallel mission focuses on the sea otter, a linchpin in the coastal and deep-water Pacific ecology. A life-affirming community protects as well sea urchins, migrating birds, and monarch butterflies, all elements interwoven into one of North America's most treasured bay habitats.

In recent decades, the decline of beaches and shores like Jeffreys Bay and Monterey has forced a sobering thought on human minds — the realization that nature is finite. Fear of permanent loss has produced bold and noble acts — the shielding of beings beset by pollution, shrinking habitats, El Niño, and deliberate exploitation and acts of cruelty, carelessness, and waste. The pristine beauty of reef animals and giant tortoises on Aldabra, one of the Seychelle Islands, and the unusual biodiversity of Manzanillo, Costa Rica, where the jungle meets the sea, have inspired groups to defend global edens that can survive only through human intervention. In Clayoquot Sound, Vancouver, British Columbians have risked jailing to end the wholesale cutting of old-growth cedars, the green-topped umbrellas that shelter glacial valleys, xeric rocky ridges, salmon streams, and coastal wetlands. For the opposite Pacific shore, Lucille M. Craft, a single voice for preservation of nature, launched the Kuril Island Network (KIN), a nonpartisan, nonpolitical volunteer society that protects one of the earth's last unspoiled coastal phenomena. Farther south at Apo Reef, Filipino fishers recognize that their own greed and profligacy could destroy their homeland. In the past decade, to assure sustainable sources of income for years to come, they have ended seasons of trawling, cyanide fishing, and endangerment of offshore reefs.

Because of humanity's reverence for shores, harbors and coasts have served as the stages for ambition and acts both grand and ignoble, notably, the debasement of women and the creation of a slave emporium at Stone Town, Zanzibar, and the lively slave trade that enriched Matrah, Oman. Elmina Castle, Ghana, a monument to Portuguese depravity, saw the shackling and imprisonment of Bantu and non–Bantu as the source of income for colonial adventurers. Similar acts of cruelty and conquest dot the histories of Selinus, Cilicia; Matagorda Island, Texas; and Salvador da Bahia, Brazil. At Selinus's coastal cavern, piracy and slaving colored a sea-going settlement notorious for greed and opportunism. During the American Civil War, the fortification of Matagorda Island, Texas, required the labors of 500 slaves to heap sand into earthworks. At Salvador da Bahia, black slaves so outpaced the white populace in number that ancient West African traditions prevailed, returning in full force a demoralized people to a revival of dance, dress, celebration, and propitiation of Yemanjá at an open-air beachfront sanctuary.

The best and worst of human behaviors have altered the world's coasts with a kaleidoscope of ventures ranging from the search for a cure for cancer in American Samoa and the coexistence of Jew and Muslim in Essaouira, Morocco, to fishers' threats of kidnap and murder against environmentalists at the Charles Darwin Foundation in the Galápagos Islands. When Kublai Khan assaulted Kyushu, the gods of Japan seemed to smile on islanders at Imari Bay by sending a *kami kaze* [divine wind] to crush the invasion. Soldiers on Cape Hatteras, North Carolina, responded to an advancing enemy by dismantling the lighthouse beacon and destroying the defense post, both of which would benefit the aggressor if left intact. At Woolacombe, Devon, Allied forces chose a peaceful English strand as the training ground for D-Day. After trying out new weapons and strategies of beach assault to thwart Nazi Germany, officers and men readied for the world's greatest assault from the sea at Omaha Beach, Normandy. Following a long morning of carnage, the famed landing zone lay littered with crushed war machines and soldiers' remains as the tide carried out the unnamed dead to a sea burial.

Overall, beaches and shores offer visitors the ambiguous remains of history, from the sequential conquests of Lipari, Sicily, and Essaouira, Morocco, to the ongoing international debate over who owns Cyprus and the Kuril Islands. Off Dubai in the United Arab Emirates and Phuket, Thailand, sea workers once developed shore commerce in the harvest of pearls, an industry made obsolete by the advent of cultured pearls. At Beagle Channel, Tierra del Fuego, visitors ponder the destruction of native Americans who from prehistory lived in harmony with nature. Similarly, tourists who admire the grandeur of Fortescue Bay, Tasmania, consider the great loss of traditional waters once roamed by the Maori. For those willing to dive for knowledge, the newly formulated discipline of underwater archeology offers lessons of the past in the downed Nordic *langskipet* [longship] disclosed at Roskilde Fjord, Denmark; an ancient Greek merchantman off Cyrenia, Cyprus; and the recovered shards of the Basque whaling industry at Red Bay, Labrador. A curious remnant of the Cold War era survives in "Nukey Poo," a nuclear reactor, at McMurdo Sound, the Antarctic command post that attempted to harness atomic energy.

Despite the moral shortcomings of shore dwellers of the past, the world's beaches — the prized getaways for stressed urbanites — proffer a tempting array of possibilities: observation of the Hawaiian hula on Kaho'Olawe; Masaaki Modegi's collection of children's kites at his museum in Uchinada, Japan; shag contests at Myrtle Beach, South Carolina; sand castle contests at Woolacombe, Devon; and rigorous scuba dives off Birsay Bay in the Orkneys or along the reefs of Ofu Island, Manu'a. In addition to bird watching, beachcombing, braising fresh seafood, and locating rare shells, vacationers vary their shore visits with perusals of volcanic activity at Kraternaya Bay's "Ring of Fire" in the Kurils, a quiet kayak tour of British Columbia's Clayoquot Sound, and cruises of the world's coldest point at McMurdo Sound, Antarctica. These excursions energize the body at the same time that they restore the spirit by reconnecting the individual with primeval earth forces.

BEACHES AND SHORES
LISTED BY COUNTRY

Antarctica
McMurdo Sound
Argentina
Beagle Channel, Tierra del Fuego
Australia
Sydney, New South Wales
Brazil
Salvador da Bahia
British Columbia
Clayoquot Sound, Vancouver Island
Costa Rica
Manzanillo
Cyprus
Cyrenia
Denmark
Roskilde Fjord
Ecuador
Punta Espinosa, Fernandina,
Galápagos Islands
Egypt
Alexandria
England
Lindisfarne, Farne Islands,
Northumberland
Tintagel Head, Cornwall
Woolacombe, Devon
France
Omaha Beach, Normandy
Ghana
Elmina Castle

Greece
Delos
Holland
Ijsselmeer
Ireland
Dingle, County Kerry
Israel
Capernaum
Italy
Ostia
Jamaica
Point Royal
Japan
Imari Bay, Kyushu
Uchinada, Honshu
Labrador
Red Bay
Mexico
Acapulco
Monaco
Monte Carlo
Morocco
Essaouira
New Zealand
Kaikoura Peninsula
Oman
Matrah
Philippines
Apo Reef

Russia
Kraternaya Bay, Kuril Islands
Samoa
Ofu Island, Manu'a
Scotland
Birsay Bay, Orkney
Seychelles
Aldabra
Sicily
Lipari, Aeolian Islands
South Africa
Jeffreys Bay
Tasmania
Fortescue Bay
Thailand
Phuket Island
Turkey
Selinus, Cilicia

Ukraine
Chersonese, Crimea
United Arab Emirates
Dubai
United States
Cape Hatteras, North Carolina
Kaho'Olawe, Hawaii
Matagorda Island, Texas
Monterey, California
Myrtle Beach, South Carolina
Point Barrow, Alaska
Vizcaya, Miami, Florida
Vietnam
Halong Bay
Zanzibar
Stone Town

WORLD SHORES AND BEACHES

Acapulco, Mexico

Location

A coastal resort on southwestern Mexico's mountainous Pacific shore, Acapulco de Juárez looks out on the gracefully curving Santa Lucía Bay. Historically it was the nation's best natural anchorage for commercial trade as well as pirates and hostile insurgents. Surrounded by the Sierra Madre del Sur, the narrow strip of white sandy beach below, known as Mexico's Riviera, became a prominent magnet for annual visitors. Like Mexican fishers, many tourists prefer the compact sand of La Condesa Beach at the center of the bay. Along the sickle-shaped Caleta, natural shielding from the Pacific produces a smoother swimming area compared to Los Hornos, where surf pounds directly into the shore.

Essential to the drama of Acapulco's coastal sport is La Quebrada, a thin slot of the Pacific that pierces neatly vertical headlands and lures *clavadistas* [cliff divers]. The daredevil sport got its start from fishermen leaping into the sea to release snagged nets. Because of the unique geography of the area, cliff diving became one of Acapulco's major beach attractions in the 1940s after young Mexican boys turned the dives into a sport.

Contacts

Acapulco Convention and Visitors Bureau
Oficina de Convenciones y Visitantes de
    Acapulco
Avenue Costera Miguel Aleman No. 3111
Fracc. Costa Azul, Suites 204–205
Acapulco, GRO 39850, Mexico
Phone: 52-7-484-8555
Fax: 52-7-484-8134
http://www.acapulco-cvb.org/

Mexico Tourism Board
21 East 63rd Street, Second Floor
New York, New York 10021
Phone: 800-44-MEXICO
Fax: 212-821-0367
Email: newyork@visitmexico.com

History

According to data gleaned from petroglyphs, Acapulco has been inhabited since 3000 B.C. Long before the rise of the Aztec nation around A.D. 100, indigenous Nahua farmers named Acapulco after a thick stand of reeds. In the post–Columbian era, Cuauhtémoc, the nephew of Montezuma II and the last Aztec emperor, chose the beach site as a summer getaway. The land passed from imperial hands to Hernán Cortés, who sent Fernando Chico to reconnoiter the region on December 13, 1521. A full complement of Spanish soldiers arrived, defeated the Aztec, and tortured and hanged 27-year-old Cuauhtémoc in 1525 because he refused to reveal caches of Mexican treasure.

With Aztec resistance negated, Acapulco became a crown colony of Spain on April 25, 1528. Spanish settlers enslaved the natives and began colonizing the harbor and building ships to broaden Spain's presence in the New World and to provide a base for direct routes to China. In November 1564, Augustinian priest, astronomer, and navigator Andrés de Urdaneta sailed from Acapulco to the Philippines at the head of a royal fleet, consisting of his flagship *Capitana* and the galleons *San Juan*, *San Lucas*, *San Pablo*, and *San Pedro*. After the expedition accessed northern Pacific tradewinds, on October 3, 1565, it returned safely on the round trip from Cebú Island. The annual route loaded with treasure from Cambodia, Ceylon, China, India, Japan, and the Moluccas precipitated a commercial trade event, the Acapulco Fair of the Americas, where merchants vied for Asian goods.

On April 14, 1579, King Philip II of Spain established Acapulco's harbor as the official crown port on the Central America-to-Asia trade loop. The colonial fleet, later known as the *Nao de China* or the Manila Galleon, dealt in coffee, silver, and sugar with Iberia, and the Philippines. Continental Asian steamers made the harbor a port of call on their coast-hugging swing south from San Francisco to Panama.

A free flow of money introduced career criminals. Historian Baron de Humboldt attested that, because of Acapulco's reputation for wealth in damask, incense, ivory, jade, lacquerware, musk, pearls, porcelain, silk, slaves, and spice, the region also drew pirates. The most predatory were Welsh freebooter Henry Morgan and England's Sir Francis Drake, William Dampier, and Thomas Cavendish. The latter seized the Manila Galleon *Santa Ana* from Captain Tomás de Alzola in November 1587 in dense fog on the final leg into Acapulco. Cavendish

divested the awkward, heavily laden "flying pig" of its store of goods and gold pesos minted at Central American quarries. It was England's first and greatest assault on Spain's monopoly with Asia.

By the seventeenth century, residents of Acapulco required stout protection. In 1614, menace from Dutch Admiral Joris von Speilbergen forced Viceroy Diego Fernandez de Cordoba to design the pentagonal Fort of San Diego. Begun in 1615 on El Morro hill at the west side of the bay in what is now called Acapulco Viejo [old Acapulco], the fort and moat went into service two years later. Cordoba equipped the complex with signal fires to gather villagers to the ramparts during an attack, but the system failed to keep out the Dutch on October 24, 1624, when Captain de Witte's Nassan fleet shadowed the port in hopes of meeting up with the Manila Galleon.

Acapulco's importance to history fluctuated with subsequent events. On April 21, 1776, the fort suffered structural damage during an earthquake, but the port remained a strategic location for Mexico's navy. During the Mexican war of independence in 1815, the harbor lost its hold on commerce after the Spanish abandoned the Acapulco-to-Philippines route. However, by 1850, the California Gold Rush revived harbor traffic and improved North American demand for Mexican textiles. In the late 1800s, decline in international commerce depressed Acapulco's economy once more.

Tourism was the answer to Acapulco's flagging hopes. The financial outlook improved in the mid-twentieth century with President Miguel Alemán and Texas investor Albert B. Pullen's establishment of a casuarina- and palm-lined resort. A forerunner to seekers of fun in the sun was Edward, the Prince of Wales, who surveyed the bay during a deep-sea fishing expedition. In his wake came movie stars, wealthy entrepreneurs, and trendsetters. Extending income from hotels, tours, boat charters, and restaurants were local shellworks, candy factories, silver jewelry, and weaving. After six decades of steady cash flow, the area suffered a temporary setback on October 9, 1997, when Hurricane Pauline poured wind, rain, and mud on local homes, killing forty people.

Coastal Activities

Warm and sunny, Acapulco offers deep-sea fishing for barracuda and swordfish, bungee jumping, waterskiing, riding *broncos* [mini motorboats] and catamarans, windsurfing and parasailing, jet boating and skiing, and kayaking and canoeing. Attracting families are glass-bottomed boat excursions, moonlit cruises, swimming with dolphins, and horseback riding in the surf. At Roqueta Island, skin diving, snorkeling, and exploring rocky formations take the adventurous to the Piedra de la Hierbabuena and Piedra del Elefante reefs or to the wreck of the *Rio de Plata*, which sank in 1944. Others visit an unusual coastal religious site, the underwater shrine of the Virgen Sumergida.

Inland activities include carriage rides in horse-drawn *calandria*, duck shooting, rafting, bullfights, jai alai, tennis, and golf. Young children enjoy Papagayo Park, CICI amusement park, and the art deco aquarium, Magico Mundo Marino. History buffs favor the Cathedral de Nuestra Señora de la Soledad, an architectural treasure featuring onion-shaped domes in the Byzantine style. For nature study, both the zoo at Isla de Roqueta and the swamps at the freshwater Laguna de Tres Palos draw visitors.

A feature attraction is the cliff diving spectacle, during which exhibitionists swan dive 136 feet into a small cove that is 21 feet wide and, at low tide, as shallow as eight feet. Before making the extreme plunge either alone or in tandem, performers venerate a private shrine of the Virgin of Guadalupe. During the three-second dive, each must arch the back and launch out at least thirty feet to avoid crashing into protruding cliff sides along a drop equal to a twelve-story building. Rapid surfacing prevents contact with the rocky sea floor. Many of Acapulco's performers learned the knack from their fathers and passed the skill on to their own sons. Few have been seriously injured.

The first cliff dive takes place daily around 1:00 P.M. During four hourly plunges at night, performers extend the drama by processing up the cliff with lighted torches, which they carry during a series of exhibition dives lighted only by cones of burning newspapers that fellow divers extend from the platforms below. Performers descend at speeds up to eighty miles per hour. Absorbing the impact of their feat are incoming breakers. If divers hit outgoing rather than inbound waves, they risk pierced eardrums, broken bones and tendons, dislocated joints, and permanent injury to flesh, limbs, ribs, and spine. For reasons of safety, officials prevent amateurs from attempting the dive.

Although ritual cliff diving began in 1934, the romance of extreme sport didn't emerge until the 1950s and 1960s. Acapulco profited from the support from Swedish bandleader Teddy Stauffer, a regular performer at La Perla nightclub, and from footage contained in Hollywood movies, including Elvis Presley's *Fun in Acapulco* (1963). Publicity spawned a following for cliff diving and for photographs, posters, and videos of graceful leaps into the sea.

One native veteran, Raul Garcia, dubbed the "Captain of Acapulco Cliff Divers," completed 37,348 dives over a half century of spectacular feats. He initiated his career in 1936 at age eight by leaping from the rocky heights to retrieve lost spears. Before retiring in 1986, he regularly dived open-eyed and caught small fish. One tandem leap broke his back, but didn't hinder his recuperation and return to the cliffs. In 1998, he climbed the headland on his seventieth

Because of the unique geography of the area, cliff diving became one of Acapulco's major beach attractions (courtesy of Carlos Velazquez Cerda and Arely Figueroa).

birthday for a celebratory dive that he intended to relieve Acapulco's malaise following the devastation of Hurricane Pauline.

In 1967, Ricardo Vega Moreno won the first Acapulco cliff diving championship, which he held for eight years. A year later, Wide World of Sports began broadcasting the event globally, elevating it from an unregulated tourist attraction to a respected athletic competition. At the end of Moreno's reign, Pat Sucher became the first American to win the competition, which he snagged with five perfect scores of ten points each. In November 1996, Adele Laurent of Denver, Colorado, and Montana Miller, a five-foot-three, 26-year-old flying trapeze artist and solo circus aerialist, became two of the first female divers to hurl themselves from Acapulco's crag.

One of Acapulco's cliff-diving athletes, Dustin Webster, of Santee, California, began his career at age seventeen. He mastered multiple forward somersaults and twists from a handstand to win the Califor-

nia State Diving Title and obtained thirteen medals at global competitions. He began captaining the U.S. High Diving Team in 1989 and, five years later, set out to win the La Quebrada event and return the championship to the United States. The Mexican venue preceded an extended career for Webster, whom the media nicknamed "Pan" for "Peter Pan." In July 1999, he gained sponsorship of Red Bull Energy Drink and won both a Mediterranean Cliff Diving cup in Italy and the Red Bull diving title in Brontallo, Switzerland. In 2001, upon recovery from a smashed face after a failed dive in Italy, he advanced his program with a forward quad, four somersaults that he performed at the World Cliff Diving Championship in Lanai, Hawaii.

SOURCES

"Acapulco for the Active," *Travel Agent*, August 16, 1999.
Adams, Tim, "A Leap into the Unknown," *Guardian Unlimited*, August 5, 2001.

Altonn, Helen, "Lanai to Host Cliff-Diving Competition," *Honolulu Star-Bulletin*, August 25, 2000.

Anderson, Kelli, "Steep Thinker: Colorful Cliff Diver Dustin Webster Likes to Give His Audience a Rise When He Takes His Fall," *Sports Illustrated*, August 20, 2001, p. 18.

Beddingfield, Katherine T., "No Hurricanes, No Cholera," *U.S. News & World Report*, December 29, 1997, pp. 36–37.

Hoekstra, Dave, "A Big Leap," *Chicago Sun-Times*, November 10, 2002.

Miller, Montana, "Pleasures of the Unexpected," *Radcliffe Quarterly*, Spring 1998.

Przybys, John, "High and Mighty," *Las Vegas Review-Journal*, September 9, 1997.

Ramos, Candi, "Flying Montana," *UCLA Daily Bruin*, November 7, 1997.

Santos, Hector, "The Sacking of the Galleon *Santa Ana*," *Sulat sa Tansô*, January–February 1996.

Wilkerson, S. Jeffrey K., "Following Cortés," *National Geographic*, October 1984, pp. 420–459.

Wilson, Rhonda J., "Lively, Lazy Acapulco," *American Fitness*, November–December 1990, pp. 38–40.

Aldabra, Seychelles

Location

Aldabra is one of a cluster of 115 uninhabited islands in the Seychelles, an area that French oceanographer Jacques-Yves Cousteau called some of the "last unspoiled tropical islands on earth" (1963, p. 115). Aldabra lies off the main shipping lanes in the South Equatorial Current 420 miles north of Madagascar and 660 miles from East Africa. The island is part of a granite volcanic range that sank with the gradual reshaping of the ancient continent of Pangaea around 48,000 B.C. The island cluster developed into a mass of fossilized coral limestone topped with guano and tropical detritus rimmed in sparkling sugar sand. It spreads over 650 miles of brilliant aquamarine waters warmed by Indian Ocean trade winds.

The famed nature preserve of Aldabra, the world's largest raised coral atoll, consists of concentric ovals — a 40-mile shore ringed with a coral reef and encircling a 55-square-mile lagoon. Pierced with inlets, the atoll's broken rim consists of twelve fringing islands of sand, mangrove, and ironshore, a term for rough uplifted, sharp-edged coral and/or limestone rock that the locals call *champignon* [mushroom]. The climate remains steadily warm and humid with water temperatures at 82 to 84 degrees Fahrenheit, a suitable range to attract a host of sea creatures. The rich biodiversity of Aldabra's reef so entranced Cousteau that he called it "diver's gold" (*ibid.*, p. 117).

Aldabra's interlocking ecosystems — external coral reef and inner lagoon — offer a unique glimpse of correspondence in nature. At the atoll's bull's-eye lie small islets — Île Esprit, Île Michel, and Îles Moustiques — and umbrella-capped coral outcrops sculpted by the inrush and outflow of the tide. The largest inlet, the 100-feet deep Grande Passe, fills the center pool daily in four hours. Cold water upwelling from the deep mixes with surf to support resilient corals. At low tide, the lagoon empties through Grande Passe, Passe Gionnet, Passe Houareau, and West Channel, leaving sufficient food in the bottoms to feed an amazing assortment of mollusks, turtles, and stalking birds.

Contacts

UK Seychelles Tourist Office
Phone: 44-20-8741-6262
http://www.seychelles.uk.com

Indian Ocean Explorer
Phone: 888-437-8456
     352-401-5678
Email: info@ioexplorer.com
http://www.ioexplorer.com

History

Called *Aldabra*, a corruption of the Arabic *al khadra* [green], the island attracted Arab traders bound for East Africa. After Portuguese mariners spotted the island, it first appeared on sea charts in 1511 under the names Ilha Dara and Alhadra. It earned a more complete description in 1742 after two French seamen, Captain Lazare Picault and Captain Jean Grossin, saw a reflection of Aldabra's immense lagoon during explorations commissioned by the governor of Mauritius. Fourteen years later, France annexed the Seychelles.

Largely untouched by human visitors, Aldabra was ringed by blonde hawksbill turtles, which swam undisturbed in the shoals. Because of the island's inaccessibility and its location in the cyclone belt, it remained less visited than Mount Everest and Antarctica and is still unspoiled by human pollutants and tourism. For its large number of diverse and endemic plant and animal species, it is revered as the Galápagos of the Indian Ocean.

At a tenuous moment in its history, Aldabra attracted colonial exploiters from France and England. In 1814, the British colony of Mauritius claimed the island. Sixty years later, English biologist Charles Darwin interceded for the high-domed giant tortoise (*Geochelone gigantea*). He was fascinated by the longlived reptile because it reached maturity at age twenty and remained capable of reproducing for 130 years. With the backing of the global scientific community, Darwin persuaded Mauritius's governor to protect the tortoise habitat as one of the world's finest natural laboratories. A series of unrelated events influenced the island's future. British financier Lord Walter Rothschild leased the land to assure its safety. The sanctuary made the tortoise the world's first endangered species to receive protection. A religious mission led by Fredrik Johan Larsen Lervig

and his family, followers of evangelist Hans Nielsen Hauge, left Bergen, Norway, on November 19, 1879, with a total of 47 aboard the *Debora* to establish a Christian colony on Aldabra. However, they had to alter their plans after discovering that the French had claimed the island.

After Aldabra became a British crown colony in 1903, the twentieth century posed new threats from whalers and poachers of rare birds, fish, and turtles as well as from warfare. During World War I, a German cruiser hid in the island lagoon. In 1954, James Leonard Brierley Smith, a distinguished ichthyologist at the Cecil Rhodes University in Grahamstown, South Africa, catalogued some of the island wildlife. That same year, French undersea investigator Jacques-Yves Cousteau made an expedition aboard the dive boat *Calypso* and stopped at the atoll, which he described in *The Living Sea* (1963). Joining the voyage was 23-year-old cinema director Louis Malle, who filmed an award-winning documentary, *Le Monde du Silence* [The Silent World] (1956), which introduced outsiders to Aldabra's scenic wonders. During the Cold War, after Great Britain and the United States planned to establish a BBC relay station and military air base on Aldabra in 1964, a global outcry from conservationists scuttled the project and extended a watch over nature that Darwin had initiated during the previous century.

For the time, the region seemed safe from exploitation. In 1970, pragmatic humanist Sir Julian Sorell Huxley, a zoologist at King's College, concurred with conservationists who called the site a living history museum. He agreed that the island should be guarded for all time as an international treasure. After belonging to the British Indian Ocean Territory from 1965 to 1976, Aldabra returned to local control. Supporting the cluster's serenity and uniqueness was David R. Stoddard, a fervid ecologist with Cambridge University and author of *The*

Aldabra is an uninhabited island that French oceanographer Jacques-Yves Cousteau called one of the "last unspoiled tropical islands on earth" (courtesy of Galen R. Frysinger).

Conservation of Aldabra (1968). Out of joy in its purity, he exulted that "Aldabra is the least disturbed atoll in the world and ... the richest" (Doubilet, 1995, p. 97). For his contribution to the International Society for Reef Studies and to Aldabra's salvation, he earned the first Darwin Medal and, in 1979, an Order of the British Empire conferred by Queen Elizabeth II.

Coastal Activities

In 1980, a consortium of botanists, zoologists, and technicians from the Seychelles Islands Foundation — comprised of England's Royal Society, Orstom in Paris, the Smithsonian Institution, and the Seychelles government — assumed management of Aldabra and limited access to experts studying the environment. Annually, only 300 scientists visit Aldabra's west side, called Settlement, and retrieve data from the permanent meteorological and research stations, which

are supported with donations from the World Bank Global Environmental Facility. These ventures require traveling 700 miles on the live-aboard dive boat *Indian Ocean Explorer*, which makes its runs during peak seasons in November preceding the winter monsoon and in March before the spring dry season. The cost of visiting the island surpasses $10,000 and includes a $100 environmental charge and a $20 departure tax.

Since 1991, the Seychelles government has allowed selected school field trips, ecotourism, diving, and birding on Aldabra. Following a serious incident of coral bleaching, in 1999, *National Geographic* staff journalist and photographer David Doubilet, the author of *Light in the Sea* (1989) and *Pacific: An Undersea Journey* (1992), sailed aboard the dive boat *Fantasea II* to survey Aldabra. Accompanying him was an international team of underwater explorers, filmmakers, photographers, and writers from Australia, Brazil, England, Greece, France,

Israel, New Zealand, and the United States. Subsequent monitoring activities in 2000 and 2001 reported on the status of the marine hotspot, which governments and nature lovers value for its importance to the sea's health.

Ecosystem

A pristine biosystem, Aldabra hosts an unrivaled assortment of wildlife, including the Aldabra lily and robber crabs among the dunes, spinner dolphin schools and blacktip shark along the shore, and angelfish, bumphead parrotfish, fusilier, giant potato cod, goby, humpback and madras snapper, lizardfish, lionfish, longfin batfish, manta, rockcod, rubberlips, scorpionfish, sea goldy, surgeon fish, and wrasse that swim through its lagoon. Locked in the limestone formations are fossilized fish, shells, and turtles. Tiger cowries nest in lush, wavy sea grass; a huge clam bed thrives unharvested at one end of the atoll. Naturalists recognize Aldabra as a haven for wide-winged butterflies and moths, coconut crab, fruit bats, geckos, fist-sized spiders, pemphis shrub, ferns, and exotic tropical plants. Around 150,000 giant tortoises call the island home, making it the largest refuge for 90 percent of the surviving 200-pound reptiles in the world. When Cousteau visited the nesting grounds, he was delighted to find "tractorlike treads from the water to the dunes, where sea turtle mothers had buried their eggs in the sand" (1963, p. 124).

A bird wonderland, Aldabra is the only nesting ground of the redtailed frigatebird, the harasser of the hapless redfooted booby. The atoll also hosts the bulbul, Caspian tern, dimorphic egret, drongo, forest fody, ibis, sunbird, tropic bird, turtledove, and the endangered Aldabran warbler (*Nesillas aldabranus*), the world's rarest bird, which some fear is already extinct. Cousteau marveled at the blue and white herons that "intermingled, stalking on penciled legs, selecting a smorgasbord from dishes of water and

coral knobs" (*ibid.*, p. 124). He mused on the sweep of birds across the reef and remarked that he enjoyed "a glimpse of what the world must have been before our kind spread over it" (*ibid.*).

Of particular interest to ornithologists is the white-throated rail (*Dryolimnas cuvieri aldabranus*), a relative of the dodo and the only flightless bird found in the Indian Ocean. The atoll is the only one in the world to nurture the greater flamingo (*Phoenicopterus ruber roseus*). After a first observation of a month-old flamingo and two adults on April 13, 1995, scientists determined that the rare shorebird resides permanently in the Seychelles. Previously, ornithologists assumed that it migrated east from the African coast. Another rare sighting occurred in August 2001, a glimpse of the endangered dugong or sea cow, which once roamed the sea in herds in the 1850s and was last seen in the Seychelles in 1908.

In 1997, regional plans for a limited tour package admitted eight visitors at a time through flights from Mahe to Assumption, the Seychelles' principal island, and thence by schooner to Aldabra. Rangers assured the safety of tourists by directing them through nearly impenetrable tropical growth and across razor-sharp coral, which rose some ten feet above sea level. To house future visitors, France Albert Rene, president of the Seychelles, planned to build a Malaysian longhouse and to supply all food aboard the schooner with restrictions against transporting meals to the atoll. One problem for scientists making the journey was the possibility of marooning during bad weather on an island devoid of fresh water.

Sources

Alston, Robert, "The Natural Treasures of Aldabra," *On the Edge*, Vol. 9, Winter 2003.

Bourn, David, et al., "The Rise and Fall of the Aldabran Giant Tortoise Population," *Proceedings of the Royal Society*, Vol. 266, June 7, 1999, pp. 1091–1100.

Chown, Marcus, "The Land That Time Forgot

Opens to Tourism," *New Scientist*, Vol. 131, No. 1,780, August 3, 1991, p. 9.

Cousteau, Jacques-Yves, "Exploring Davy Jones's Locker with *Calypso*," *National Geographic*, Vol. 109, No. 2, February 1956, pp. 149–159.

_____. *Life and Death in the Coral Sea*. Garden City, N. Y.: Doubleday & Co., 1971.

_____. *The Living Sea*. New York: Harper & Row, 1963.

Diamond, David W., "Birds of the Seychelles," *Auk*, Vol. 119, No. 3, July 1, 2002, pp. 875–877.

Doubilet, David, "Journal to Aldabra," *National Geographic*, March 1995, pp. 90–113.

Gordan, Ethan, "Anything but Ordinary Expedition to Aldabra," *Skin Diver*, January 2002, pp. 48–53.

Grulke, Wolfgang E., "Aldabra: The Jewel and the Crown of the Indian Ocean," *Future-World*, July 1993.

Heywood, Karen J., et al., "Eddy Formation behind the Tropical Island of Aldabra," *Deep-Sea Research*, Vol. 43, No. 4, April 1996, pp. 555–578.

Hornsby, Al, "Expedition: Indian Ocean," *Skin Diver*, September 1999, pp. 56–62.

LaSalle, Mick, "The Compassionate Observer: Louis Malle's Films Shed Light on Humanity," *San Francisco Chronicle*, November 25, 1995, p. C3.

Mayell, Hillary, "The Line in the Sand," *Environmental News Network*, October 31, 1999.

Radtkey, Ray R., "Adaptive Radiation of Day-Geckoes in the Seychelles Archipelago," *Evolution*, Vol. 50, No. 2, April 1996, pp. 604–623.

Rainbolt, Raymond E., et al., "Greater Flamingos Breed on Aldabra Atoll, Republic of Seychelles," *Wilson Bulletin*, Vol. 109, No. 2, June 1997, pp. 351–353.

Skerrett, Adrian, "Birds of Aldabra," *Bulletin of the African Bird Club*, Vol. 6, No. 1, March 1999.

Teleki, Kristian A., and Jeanne A. Mortimer, "A New Focus on the Aldabra Marine Environment," *Seychelles Islands Foundation Newsletter*, No. 6, 2000.

Wilhelmsson, Dan, ed., "Aldabra," *Coral Reef Degradation in the Indian Ocean Newsletter*, No. 3, May 2001.

Alexandria, Egypt

Location

Situated between Lake Mareotis (or Maryut) and the south shore of the Mediterranean Sea, the cosmopolitan Egyptian port of Alexandria began humbly. Around 5.5 million years ago, the Nile River sliced into the land on its way to the Mediterranean seabed, leaving behind a deep canyon that gradually silted in. By 798,000 B.C., the basin expanded into a wet, fertile vee. About 5000 B.C., African herders of the arid desert land to the south moved into the lengthening Nile River delta in search of a respite from the heat and a source of irrigation for crops. The city emerged on the left flank of the rich delta as a superbly shaped financial, industrial, shipping, and cultural center that earned the name "Paris of the ancient world."

Egyptian engineers created a sandy ¾-mile isthmus, the Heptastadion (or Heptastadium), which forms a double harbor by connecting the city to the ancient limestone island of Pharos, site of a 400-foot stone lighthouse. Built in 261 B.C., the beacon, according to Poseidippos of Pella, was the work of the architect and engineer Sostratus of Cnidus:

> This tower, cleaving the sky straight and upright, shines in the daytime countless leagues away: and all night long the sailor who runs with the waves shall see a great light blazing from its summit. And he may run even to the Bull's Horn, and yet not miss the God of Safety, O Proteus, whosoever sails this way [Goddio, 1998, p. 64].

The lighthouse, which was listed as the last built of the Seven Wonders of the World, influenced the design of other Mediterranean beacons, notably the lighthouse at Ostia, Italy. (*See also* OSTIA, ITALY.) In *Al-Kitab ar-Rujari* [The Book of Roger] (1154), the Arabian geographer ash-Sharif al-Idrisi referred to the lighthouse before its collapse in an earthquake. On the inland side of the Heptastadion rose the Moon Gate, the western entrance to the city center, and its opposite, the Sun Gate to the east. Beyond lay a gymnasium and theater, the Great Caesarium and two ornamental obelisks, the Navalia

Underwater north of Alexandria lie a royal harbor and the remains of the dwellings of Queen Cleopatra VII. Photograph by Peter Limber (courtesy of Saudi Armco World/ PADIA).

[Docks], the Emporium or mercantile exchange, and the Apostases or magazines.

Underwater north of Alexandria on Cape Lochias, a sunken peninsula of the alluvial plain, lie a royal harbor and the remains of the dwellings of Queen Cleopatra VII Philopator [Father-loving], who was called Lord of Two Lands for her rule of Upper and Lower Egypt. Nautical expeditions launched in 1996 located reefs at the mouth of the Magnus Portus [the Great Port], a peninsula that featured the temple of Poseidon. Searchers identified Mark Antony's tower retreat, the Timonium, which stood on a single jut of land extending into the main port parallel to Cleopatra's private quarters. Central to antiquity was the royal island of Antirhodos off-shore from the city, the location of a defensive stronghold, the king's residence, and a private harbor guarding a sanctuary of Isis, the queen's personal deity. Along the coast lay administration halls, temples, and the Basileia or inner sancta of Egypt's great seaport. To the northeast was the Jewish quarter.

Contacts

The Frank Goddio Society
1100 Oneok Plaza
100 West Fifth Street
Tulsa, Oklahoma 74103-4217
Fax: 509-479-3653
http://www.franckgoddio.org
info@franckgoddio.org

History

The recovery of the royal quarter of Alexandra, Egypt, retrieved from 20 feet of silted, sewage-tainted seawater a great world port that historian Ammianus Marcellinus of Antioch called the "crown of all cities" (Goddio, 1998, p. 136). Alexandria rose from the small fishing town and fort of Racondah. Built in the 38th dynasty at the beginning of the New Kingdom, Racondah acquired two additional names — the Egyptian Ra-Kedet and the Greek Rhacotis (or Rhakotis) — and earned a reputation as a pirate enclave and largely Egyptian folk settlement.

The Greek version of Alexandria dates to 332 B.C., when the Macedonian conqueror Alexander III the Great captured Egypt from the Persian ruler Nectanebo II. The famed hero-founder placed his Macedonian stamp as well as his name on Alexandria, which he intended as a suitable harbor for his large fleet. With handfuls of meal from a soldier's kit bag, he outlined the city plan for temples, a gymnasium and theater, and an agora. Pseudo-Callisthene, Alexander's biographer writing around 100 B.C., and Plutarch, author of *Life of Alexander* (A.D. 115), explained that, because birds ate the meal, Alexander feared a bad omen. His interpreters responded that the city would feed the whole world and increase the population of travelers around the globe "just as the birds fly over the whole earth" (Goddio 1998, p. 67).

Diodorus Siculus's *Library of History* (59 B.C.) commented that Alexander continued designing his new metropolis. Before marching on to the east, he anchored it to a broad intersection of thoroughfares, one north-west and the other east-west, and drew smaller streets to fill in a grid. Leaving Greek architect Dinocrates in charge, Alexander never returned. After his death from camp fever in 323 B.C., Macedonian solders and the viceroy Cleomenes bore the general's embalmed remains to Alexandria for above-ground entombment in a gold coffin, which Strabo's *Geography* (20 B.C.) pinpointed at the intersection of the two main streets.

Until the death of the Macedonian Queen Cleopatra VII in 30 B.C., Alexandria succeeded Memphis as the ptolemaic capital of Egypt. A learning center and haven of multiculturalism and religious pluralism for Egyptians, Greeks, and Jews, it outstripped

Carthage to become the foremost Mediterranean city after Rome. Around 100 B.C., free-born citizens numbered around 300,000. To Alexandria's harbor came ships carrying the wealth of the Aegean Isles, Crete, and Phoenicia, which stevedores stored in warehouses on the western promontory of the harbor after clearance through customs houses. Outgoing cargo consisted chiefly of grain and papyrus, one of Egypt's major gifts to learning and record-keeping.

During two centuries of greatness as the rival of first Athens, then Carthage and Rome, Alexandria acquired a library of 700,000 volumes of representative literature from the early classic period, a collection ten times larger than the sum of all the books in Europe. Near the center of town at the Serapeum or temple of Jupiter Serapis, the most famous museum in the ancient world, in the palace called the Brucheum or Brucheion, in 307 B.C., antiquarians placed the original book collection instituted by Ptolemy I Soter [Savior], Alexander's former bodyguard and general and Alexandria's first able administrator. A decade later, Ptolemy I appointed as an executive assistant and tutor to the royal children Demetrius Phalerus, a student of Aristotle and former governor of Athens. Demetrius dreamed up the plan for a colonnaded museum-library. As a source of data on Egypt's trade partners, he filled the royal shelves with books on royal rule and on world customs. To extend knowledge of Judaic culture, he hired 72 rabbis and housed them at the shore to translate the Hebrew Pentateuch, the first five books of the Old Testament, into the Greek Septuagint.

Less soldier than builder, Ptolemy II Philadelphus [Brother-lover], who came to power in 285 B.C., increased the city's opulence by constructing the 450-foot Pharos lighthouse over a nineteen-year period and adding an artificial causeway or dyke from the harbor to the island on which it stood.

Over fifteen centuries, the wood-fired beacon shone some thirty miles out to sea. A vigorous urban planner and promoter of Greek colonies, Ptolemy was also responsible for extending the library and its scriptorium, which produced copies of great literature to distribute throughout the world. For advice, he retained on government pay a staff of top scientists and philosophers. He also turned Alexandria into a financial and commercial center and supplied it with shrines, royal offices and residences, pleasure gardens, and a zoo.

At a period known as the Golden Age of Alexandria, the poet and scholar Callimachus of Cyrene, who served both Ptolemy II and his son, Ptolemy III Euergetes [Well-doer], became the first *bibliophylax* [library director]. His first job was to catalogue 592,000 books for the collection, including Zoroastrian scripture and an Egyptian king list, compiled by Manetho. Callimachus's final inventory, the 120-book *Pinakes* [Tables], listed all Greek literature and accompanying author biographies under subject headings — astronomy, geometry, mathematics, medicine, and philology. Great thinkers assembled at the Serapeum's observatory and classrooms for lectures and discussions that may have included the pharaoh himself. The consortium and its library comprised a forerunner of the medieval university.

By the second half of the third century B.C., Alexandria was the region's largest urban center, a polyglot cosmopolitan and commercial nexus of the southern Mediterranean with ties to Arabia, India, Greece, and Judaea. Royal book agents amassed a later library collection, which Ptolemy III began at the Serapeum after 247 B.C. The pharaoh borrowed works from Athens of tragedians Aeschylus, Euripides, and Sophocles. He relinquished his deposit by adding the texts to his own shelves. Another version of Ptolemy's unorthodox acquisition method reported that he had scribes copy the works, kept the originals, and sent the copies back to Athens. To beef up the permanent collection, he searched all ships in Alexandria's harbor and confiscated their reading material.

The resulting well-stocked library drew to Alexandria a coterie of distinguished scholars, notably Aristarchus, Aristophanes of Byzantium, Euclid, Eudoxis of Cnidus, and a father-daughter mathematics team, Theon and Hypatia. Around 240 B.C., the engineer Archimedes accessed the library while designing the first pump, called the Archimedean screw. Subsequent library directors after Callimachus were the Homeric editor and royal tutor Zenodotus of Ephesus and Apollonius of Rhodes, a native Alexandrian and author of the *Argonautica* (ca. 245 B.C.), the epic of Jason. Forcing Apollonius out of office in 235 B.C. was the stoic scientist, cartographer, and mathematician Eratosthenes of Cyrene, who taught the royal children, inventoried the library collection, and designed star maps.

Following an era of warfare in Asia Minor and Thrace, Ptolemy IV Philopator, who came to power in 221 B.C., turned his attention from Alexandria's libraries to its dockyard, where he built luxury craft and experimental warships. After 200 B.C., when Alexandria had grown into the world's largest city, municipal engineers leveled the area, built wood cofferdams, and poured mortar platforms as bases for buildings and paving. In the next century, the Ptolemaic dynasty that Ptolemy I founded gradually lost ground to the rise of Rome. The next royal prince, Ptolemy V Epiphanes [God Made Manifest], held onto his throne from 204 to 180 B.C. through negotiations with an enemy, the Seleucid king Antiochus III of Syria. Ptolemy V maintained a nationalistic rivalry with Eumenes of Pergamum, whose library shelves began to outpace Alexandria's permanent collection. To stem Eumenes's reputation as a library builder, Ptolemy curtailed shipments of papyrus to Pergamum, forcing Eumenes's staff to invent parchment books bound from scraped hides of sheep and goats. Ptolemy V died suddenly, perhaps by poison. Nonetheless, his library prospered under the management of the Homeric scholar Aristophanes of Byzantium in 195 B.C., who extended Callimachus's shelf list. In 180 B.C., the directorship passed to the astronomer Aristarchus of Samothrace, inventor of the sundial.

Egypt and its star city declined seriously in the first century B.C. To hang onto dwindling autonomy, Ptolemy XII Neos called Auletes [the Flute-player], Cleopatra's father, paid tribute to Rome to stave off temporarily the republic's lust for empire. In accordance with the incestuous system of inter-dynastic marriage, his daughter, the last of the pharaohs, was born to her aunt-mother Cleopatra V in 69 B.C. Cleopatra was only seventeen when he died, but she possessed the skills and ambitions of a ruler. He left the throne jointly to Cleopatra and her twelve-year-old brother Ptolemy XIII, a mental defective to whom she was betrothed.

In 51 B.C., Cleopatra adopted the titles of Queen Philopator and pharaoh and reigned successfully for 21 years. In 48 B.C., after the young Ptolemy forced her into exile, she had herself rolled into an oriental carpet — Plutarch says it was a bedspread tied with a cord — for presentation to Julius Caesar at his military headquarters in the Egyptian palace. The following year, when she took the 53-year-old general for her lover, he won the battle of Alexandria by calling in the reinforcements of Mithradates from Pergamum. By accident, a flash fire spread from boats Caesar's troops were burning in the harbor to the great Alexandrian library at the museum. The flames destroyed the premiere collection of books from the ancient world.

To secure sole rule, Cleopatra influenced Caesar to exterminate her brother and ceremonial husband Ptolemy XIV, whom his officers drowned in the Nile. In 46 B.C., Caesar consulted with the city's Greek astronomers to create the Julian calendar. The next year, Cleopatra traveled to Rome with her two-year-old son, Caesar's only male child, Ptolemy XV, called Caesarion or Ptolemy Caesar. According to Lucan's *Civil War* (ca. A.D. 60), to the dismay of anti-monarchical Rome, she extended the visit amid great feasting and magnificence. She appears to have used the royal sojourn to further Caesarion's chances at unifying the ancient world.

After egalitarian Romans assassinated Caesar in 44 B.C. to halt his power grab, Cleopatra formed a relationship with the consul Mark Antony, a 36-year-old Roman cavalry commander and grandson of Rome's prominent consul Marcus Antonius. Shortly afterward, in a Roman marriage of political expediency, Antony wed Octavia, the sister of Octavian, the future Augustus Caesar. Still enamored of the Egyptian queen, Antony met Cleopatra at Tarsus in Cilicia in 41 B.C. and agreed to murder her sister Arsinoë, who stood in the way of Cleopatra's complete control of Egypt. The following year, Antony and Cleopatra produced twins, Alexander Helios [sun god] and Cleopatra Selene [moon god]. When Antony moved in with Cleopatra at Alexandria that winter, he became protector of Caesarion, whom Cleopatra had elevated to Ptolemy XV Philopator Philometor. While in residence, Antony restarted the royal book collection with works from Pergamum.

After a four-year separation while Antony attended to the invasion of Parthia and a triumph in Armenia, the famed couple reunited at Alexandria in 37 B.C. For political reasons, they turned their dalliance into a royal marriage by exchanging vows at Antioch. Cleopatra conceived a third son, Ptolemy Philadelphus, born in 36 B.C. While Mark Antony dallied at the royal palace, he excited gossip about his enjoyment of the queen's considerable sexual prowess and the luxuries of the royal compound at the East Harbor. Romans began a hate campaign against him for his adoption of oriental vices, notably authoritarianism and disrespect for Roman matrimony.

Because Antony awarded the Roman territories of Crete, Cyprus, Cyrene, Palestine, and Tarsus to his Egyptian children and intended to build a massive Ptolemaic-Roman dynasty of his own, in 32 B.C., Octavian declared war on Cleopatra. (*See also* SELINUS, CELICIA.) The first clash took place at sea. At the battle of Actium at Epirus off the Adriatic coast of Greece on September 2, 31 B.C., Antony miscalculated the sea fight against Octavian's fleet. To Rome's shame, Antony abandoned his men and withdrew in a quinquereme to follow his departing mistress, who sailed for Alexandria with sixty warships. At the beginning of the end for Antony, his men surrendered and shifted allegiance to Octavian.

Alexandria was the site of the final face-off between powers. The love affair drew to a close in 30 B.C. after Octavian's army seized the city. At Antony's private retreat, the Timonium, he slew himself Roman style with his sword. On August 10, Cleopatra, who anticipated capture and display in Octavian's triumphal parade in Rome, died from an asp bite, a suitably bizarre demise in the estimation of Roman haters of royalty and Eastern extravagance. Octavian completed the removal of rivals by having seventeen-year-old Caesarion slaughtered. Octavian's sister Octavia, though divorced from Antony in 32 B.C., reared Antony and Cleopatra's twins and young son.

With the demise of the last pharaoh, as the historian Suetonius describes in *The Lives of the Caesars* (ca. A.D. 121), Egypt passed into the Roman Empire. Christianity reached Alexandria with the arrival of Mark, one of the four gospel writers, whom pagans martyred in A.D. 62 for protesting the cult of Serapis. New to the learning center was the oratory of St. Mark and the world's first catechetical school.

Around A.D. 235, the scholar Origen of Alexandria, a student of Rabbi Hillel, restored the city's earlier reputation for scriptural study by composing the *Hexapla* [Six-Part Book], a multi-columnar comparison of the Hebrew Pentateuch, the Greek Septuagint, and Greek translations by Aquila, Symmachus, and Theodotion. As the number of Christians grew, the Roman emperors Decius, Severus, and Diocletian persecuted the opponents of paganism. In 284, when Romans put 144,000 Christians to death, the period earned the name "Era of the Martyrs." In 297, erection of a 25-meter granite monolith honored Diocletian but was called "Pompey's Pillar."

The rise of radical Christianity brought Alexandria's learning center and scriptorium to a fiery end. In 391, the Christian emperor Theodosius I ordered the city's pagan temples and its Serapeum destroyed. The fervency of Christians continued unabated over the next quarter century, resulting in the assassination of scholar and mathematician Hypatia, who directed the neo–Platonic school around A.D. 400. The most famous female educator of early Middle Ages, she taught astronomy, mathematics, music, philosophy, and rhetoric and published texts on algebra and cones. In 415, Bishop Cyril of Alexandria incited a mob to ambush her in the streets. They hauled Hypatia from her chariot into the Church of Caesarium, scored her body with oyster shells, and ripped her apart.

Archeology

Until French underwater archeologist Franck Goddio resurrected ancient Alexandria a few hundred yards off the Mediterranean shore, the temples and palaces of Mark Antony and his queen had lain undisturbed since the A.D. 300s, when an earthquake and tidal wave engulfed the royal compound. Further destruction occurred from subsequent collapse of the delta landmass,

which sank twenty feet. In the mid–1980s, Goddio studied the site from references by the poet Homer in Book IV of the *Odyssey* and from the poets Theocritus and Lucan, traveler and commentator Herodotus, first century B.C. geographer Strabo, the first century A.D. Roman encyclopedist Pliny the Elder, Roman historians Flavius Josephus and Livy, commentators Dio Cassius and Seneca, and Arrian, a Bithynian philosopher and historian of the early second century A.D. In 1987, Goddio established the Institut Européen D'Archéologie Sous-Marine [European Institute of Marine Archaeology] in Paris and prepared for his expedition by learning methods of underwater archeology and by assembling a team of oceanographers, Egyptologists, linguists, and geophysicists.

Goddio's excavation required permission from the Egyptian security force, which jealously guarded the historic site. After gaining clearance from the Supreme Council for Egyptian Antiquities to penetrate the murky harbor, in 1992, Goddio and his 35 searchers began work. They headquartered aboard the research vessel *Princess Dudu* to investigate large shapes buried on the seabed in heavy silt and sand. For three months, the ship *Kaimiloa* directed sonar and trailing magnetometers and generated a sonar scan of harbor topology. After studying the seabed profile, in June 1996, twenty divers went to work at the rate of 200 minutes of subsurface work each day for a total of 3,550 dives. Experts poured latex molds of hieroglyphic inscriptions and placed recovered artifacts in Alexandria's Roman theater for cataloging, desalination, and safekeeping.

Four years later, Goddio secured financial backing for his endeavors from Martin Hilti of the Hilti Foundation in Liechtenstein. Using sonar scanners, global positioning devices, and a nuclear resonance system, the underwater team located capitals and columns inscribed in Greek, ceramics and amphorae, vases and an oil lamp from the late 100s or early A.D. 200s, a Poseidon sanctuary, and the royal harbor of Cape Lochias. In 1997, Goddio discovered a roadbed as well as evidence that Alexander the Great landed his own craft at the pier at the island of Antirhodos before the city of Alexandria took shape. Goddio also unearthed treasures — a limestone slab holding a sphinx that resembled Ptolemy XII; an oversized white marble likeness of Hermes, messenger of the Greek gods; a white marble head depicting Antonia Minor, mother of Germanicus and Claudius; the god Agathodaimon [Guiding Spirit] in serpentine form, which protected Alexandria and its citizens; a sphinx with the head of Horus; an ibis-shaped god Thot-Hermes; a black granite bust of Augustus Caesar, Rome's first emperor; a five-meter portrait statue of Caesarion; and a statue of the Great Priest of Isis lifting a canopic jar, a container in which embalmers placed human organs extracted whole from corpses.

In addition to hieroglyphic inscriptions, the site yielded a city plan, complete with limestone pavers and a wood jetty dating to the 400s B.C. At the secluded royal harbor of Antirhodos, the team found the rigging and wreckage of a vessel rammed and sunk in port, dating from 90 B.C. to A.D. 130, the time period that saw the rise and assassination of Julius Caesar, Rome's civil war, the marriage and suicides of Cleopatra and Mark Antony, and the rule of Augustus Caesar and his successors, Tiberius and Caligula. Across the watery divide from the queen's palace, divers also located the Timonium, Antony's retreat. To display these finds to the world, in 1997, Ibrahim Darwish, director of the Department of Underwater Archaeology, proposed that Egypt create a world first — an underwater museum built of plexiglass tubes and bubbles to showcase some 3,000 artifacts *in situ*.

In April 1998, Goddio formed partnerships with the Discovery Channel to film a series on his underwater archaeological findings. Late in October, he co-published *Alexandria—The Submerged Royal Quarters* (1998), a comprehensive study of surveys, site analyses, and archaeological exploration of Alexandria compiled from data collected in over 1,000 dives. The mission moved west in 1999 to survey underwater topography and the lay of ancient shipyards. On March 14, 1999, Goddio's series "Cleopatra's Palace: In Search of a Legend" aired on the Discovery Channel to ten million viewers.

Coastal Activities

A popular summer resort built along the sixteen-mile crescent-shaped drive of Sharia al-Geish, Alexandria's city beaches are low-key, but pleasant. From the Eastern Harbor, the Corniche coastal road follows the shore and parallels a tram line that carries passengers to the Al-Montazah promontory and the beaches of Maamoura Bay. For those visitors wishing to examine ancient Alexandria, private companies offer boat dives and recreational diving tours to hunks of granite and columns jutting upward in the silted waters or to the Ras Mohammed coral reef, which is now part of a national marine park. Participants follow a harbor map of antiquities that Franck Goddio published in 2001 and peruse a new microfilm library, which UNESCO is currently rebuilding. The finished repository will house 76,000 rare documents in Arabic, Persian, and Turkish.

Next to the Eastern Harbor extends Chatby (or El Shatby) Beach, a popular spot for boating and swimming near a Roman necropolis and the Al-Shatby Gardens. Adjacent to the shore promenade, the array of colonial architecture, a Mamluk stone citadel from A.D. 470, heroic statues, and crenellated towers of Qait Bey (or Qaitbay) fortress pique historical interest. At Kom Al Dikka, the Roman amphitheatre, the only one of its kind in Egypt, and some 40,000 artifacts at the Greco-Roman Museum provide a glimpse of ancient Alexandria under a foreign power. For shoppers from many lands, sidewalk cafes, patisseries, and boutiques offer directions and prices in Arabic, English, and French.

Along the strip of elegant hotels, the Hotel Cecil with its Moorish facade overlooks the East Harbor. The Cecil claims an unbroken history of elegance and grandeur since its opening in 1929. Among past guests were England's Prime Minister Winston Churchill, Field Marshal Bernard L. "Monty" Montgomery, singer Elvis Presley, actor Omar Sharif, and English novelists Somerset Maugham and Lawrence Durrell, who resided at the hotel during his composition of the *Alexandria Quartet* (1960). During World War II, British Intelligence headquartered at the Cecil to plot the battle of El Alamein.

SOURCES

"Actual Map of the Lost City of Alexandria," *Reuters*, April 12, 2001.

"Age Shall Not Wither Her," *Al-Ahram Weekly*, November 5, 1998.

"Alexandria — The Submerged Royal Quarters," http://www.franckgoddio.org/english/projects/alexandria/.

"Ancient Secrets in Dirty Water," *Diver*, March 2002.

Bowder, Diana, ed. *Who Was Who in the Roman World*. New York: Washington Square Press, 1980.

Carr, Dawson. *The Cape Hatteras Lighthouse, Sentinel of the Shoals*. Chapel Hill: University of North Carolina Press, 1991.

Clayton, Peter, and Martin Price, eds. *The Seven Wonders of the Ancient World*. London: Routledge, 1988.

Cosentino, Mike, "Canadian Production Company Produces Groundbreaking Cleopatra Special," *Discovery Channel*, February 16, 1999.

"Egypt Considers Creating Underwater Museum," *CNN News*, November 9, 1997.

"Explorer Unveils Lost City of Alexandria," *Reuters*, April 10, 2001.

"Extraordinary Finds from the Royal City of Ancient Alexandria," *Art Brief*, No. 89, November 1, 1998.

Goddio, Franck, et al. *Alexandria: The Submerged Royal Quarters*. London: Periplus, 1998.

_____. *Cleopatra's Palace: In Search of a Legend*. New York: Discovery Communications, 1999.

Keys, David, "Ancient Alexandria Emerges from Mediterranean," London *Independent*, April 11, 2001.

Macnamara, Bronwen, and Penny Cameron, "Travellers' Tales," *International Education*, Vol. 3, No. 2, June 1999.

Meinhardt, Jack, ed. *The Origins of Things*. Washington, D. C.: Biblical Archaeology, 2002.

"Raising the Lost City of Cleopatra," *Discovery Channel*, October, 28, 1998.

Rodgers, Patrick, "To Dive For," *People Weekly*, April 12, 1999, p. 93.

"Royal District," *Egypt*, No. 16, Winter 1998.

"Ruins of Cleopatra's Palace, City Found" *Press Trust of India*, November 1, 1998.

Spalding, Mark D., et al. *World Atlas of Coral Reefs*. Ewing, N. J.: University of California Press, 2001.

"Sphinx of Cleopatra's Father Emerges from Waves," *CNN News*, October 29, 1998.

"Sphinx Yields Location of Cleo's Palace," *Guardian Weekly*, November 8, 1998.

"Sunken Treasures, Sunken Myths," *Al-Ahram Weekly*, September 27, 2001.

Theroux, Peter, "The Imperiled Nile Delta," *National Geographic*, January 1997, pp. 2–35.

"Virtual Egypt," www.virtual-egypt.com/newhtml/articles/Cleopatra's%20Sunken%20Palace2.htm.

Apo Reef, Philippines

Location

Oceania's diving mecca, the Apo Reef lies on the west central edge of the Philippines Islands in the deep blue waters between the Sulu Sea and the China Sea. The subtriangular coral atoll is comprised of Apo Island, Apo Menor, and Cayos del Bajo. North of the town of Coron on the 14,896 square mile island of Palowan in the Calamianes, the reef stretches along the Mindoro Strait, which separates the island cluster from Mindoro. The 15,792-hectare Apo Reef Marine Nature Park, which a narrow channel divides into two sandy-bottomed lagoons, encompasses extensive sealife, seagrass meadows, and shipwrecks. Because of its re-mote location, the park is accessible only by inter-island charter boat from Sablayan.

Contacts

Lorenzo O. Ordoñez
NIPA-HNGO Apo Reef Natural Park
PASU Region IV-B, Apo Reef Station
254 P. Orieta Street
Sablayan, Occidental Mindoro, Philippines
Phone: 043-711-5207

Pandan Island Resort
5104 Sablayan
Occidental Mindoro, Philippines
http://www.pandan.com/index.htm
Email: info@pandan.com

History

The steamy, fertile Philippine Islands is home to one of the world's microcosms of biodiversity. Covering 115,831 square miles, the tropical cluster's 7,107 archipelagos arose between Indonesia and China during the upsurge of volcanoes and the clash of the Eurasian and Pacific tectonic plates around 150,000 years ago. During the Ice Age, un-usual life forms—108 amphibians, 111 mam-mals, 172 birds, 1,100 vertebrates, and 12,000 plants—evolved and spread from their birthplaces to nearby islands. When the land bridges from Borneo and the Malay peninsula sank around 5,000 B.C., the Philippines lay apart from its Asian ties.

In the late twentieth century, the is-lands surrounding Apo Reef earned a repu-tation for their complete ecosystems, which contain such unique life forms as the harle-quin ghost pipe fish, Christmas tree worm, leaf fish, harlequin worm, porcelain crab, and red fin anemone fish. Apo Island boasts a ten-hectare mangrove forest, freshwater lake, coralline limestone outcrops, and rookeries for many species of sea birds and for the endangered Nicobar pigeon *Caloenas nicobarica*. The Cayos del Bajo area nur-tures the giant clam (*Tridacna gigas*), an en-dangered species that survived in local wa-ters. Because of the rarity of these animals, the reef area required crucial oceanographic and ecological studies. Despite international concern for the reef, by 1979, half of the coral cover had disappeared. Within two decades, continued unfavorable conditions had depleted two-thirds of the corals.

In the 1980s, overfishing by 100 local families depleted many food fish from Apo's waters. Faced with starvation and migration to more favorable islands, in 1984, local people, led by Jesus Delmo and the Apo Is-land Marine Management Committee, ac-cepted the aid of Silliman University in Du-maguete. The faculty dispatched two social workers and a team of marine biologists to nurture reef resources and restore a balance in nature. Two years later, the islanders agreed to halt trawling of the area and to ban human activity on eight percent of the reef. That small preserve greatly enhanced natural stocks of small fish, which drew larger fish to feed on them. By 1988, shellfish and food fish had so rebounded in quantity and size that delegations from other Philippine islands surveyed the site and studied Apo's management techniques.

To the world's divers, the Apo Reef, a forty-square kilometer atoll, became famous for dramatic drop-offs as steep as eighty me-ters and for diver interaction with gray, hammerhead, nurse and whitetip sharks. Hunter's Rock, a submerged pinnacle ten nautical miles west of Apo Island, and nearby Merope Rock drew experienced divers to challenging currents and spectac-ular undersea life. Also popular were the hulks of over thirty Japanese warships sunk during World War II, the largest concen-tration of shipwrecks in the Philippines. In 1991, organized diving began under Swiss/Czech management at the Pandan Is-land resort, developed six years earlier.

In 1995, the success of Apo islanders at rescuing the reef was obvious by the world's

Apo Reef Marine Nature Park encompasses extensive sealife, seagrass meadows, and shipwrecks (courtesy of George Wegmann).

response to the recovery of the ecosystem. From 44 nations, non-profit organizations, and development agencies came 100 delegates to Dumaguete to discuss the International Coral Reef Initiative, a global effort to save endangered and dying coral reefs. Because of the seriousness of their task, members of the Eighth International Coral Reef Symposium in Panama proclaimed 1997 the International Year of the Reef.

On September 6, 1996, a presidential proclamation declared Apo Reef—along with Apo Islands, Binanggaan, and Cayos del Bajo—a protected area. The purpose of the set-aside was the preservation of the atoll itself and the cultivation of rare shells, manta rays, yellow fin tunas and mackerels, surgeonfish, triggerfish, moray and sand eels, gorgonians and Neptune cups, sea fans, and barrel sponges. The presidential act also protected the green sea turtle (*Chelonia*

mydas) and the hawksbill turtle (*Eretmochelys imbricata*) in a turtle sanctuary and nursery on Apo Island.

Ecosystem

Nurturing the region's rugged slopes are sheltering mists, which protect the rain forest. The dripping canopy slowly fills the spongy mosses below with an unlimited supply of moisture. Flagship species thrive in the isolated ecosystem — the Isarog shrew rat, Walden's hornbill, parrots, tamarau, dwarf *carabao* [water buffalo], cloud rat, and flying fox. Amid bamboo, ferns, giant lianas, and 691 orchid species live jumping and spiny-backed spiders and the Panay cloud frog, one of the islands' ninety species of amphibians. Most unusual are the rare dwarf crocodile and peacock pheasant; the lemur-eating eagle, which demands a large habitat for survival; and the tarsier monkey, the world's smallest primate.

At present, struggling species depend on the monsoon climate. The year breaks naturally into the winter-to-spring dry season, which runs from November to May, and an intense rainy season from June to November. Divers on Palawan can expect promising weather year-round. Alerting the region of wanton devastation are persistent alarms raised by *Bandillo ng Palawan*, a pro-environment newspaper. In the lead of green-minded Filipinos are the residents of Palawan, who set the pace for the other islanders. In 1996, local greens received backup from the United Nations, which listed the Apo Reef on an international catalogue of protected areas.

Coastal Activities

Unlike densely populated parts of the Philippines, the Apo Reef, called the "rain forest of the sea," is one of the last unspoiled frontiers of the Philippines. At its most appealing in spring, the reef invites naturalists, campers, environmentalists, skin divers, and photographers to a seabed garden of 500 species of coral. Angelfish, batfish, butterfly fish, clownfish, damselfish, jawfish, lizard fish, parrot fish, puffers, red-banded wrasse, spotted harlequin sweetlips, yellow-tailed trevally, zuno, and 22 other species swim in a sparkling blue environment. The other 90 percent of Philippine offshore habitats have declined from irregular weather patterns spawned by El Niño, pollution from insect repellent and suntan oils, runoff of chemical fertilizers from farms, and cyanide poisoning and dynamite fishing by collectors who stun fish for sale to Japanese and Chinese restaurants and aquariums, leaving the coral white and skeletal or tattered from concussion.

Visitors to the diving resort take *bancas* or *bangkas* [outriggers] to the site, where ropes guard reefs from fishers. The area offers swimming on sugar-sand beaches, beach volleyball, motorbiking, kayaking, windsurfing, and wakeboarding. Below the surface, visitors can pursue quality scuba diving and snorkeling in warm seawater that bathes brain, bubble, cabbage, fan, fire, mushroom, ramose, table, and whip corals. A dazzling display of spiny lobsters, crabs, jellyfish, nudibranch sea slugs, reef fish, and sea urchins inhabits branched tunicate, waving anemones, and green fronds of seaweed. Photographers frame shots of appealing shapes, such as the star crinoid, phosphorescent plankton, and the rosy periwinkle, and make color portraits of indigenous Tagbanua, seafarers who conduct surface tours by outrigger for 75 pesos per person. Outsiders seeking a glimpse of the entire habitat from pristine seafloor to the sacred Lake Kayangan and forested limestone peaks charter light aircraft over the island's matted inclines. Those wanting a fuller examination of Palawan travel inland to the underground river and the St. Paul Subterranean National Park.

Sources

"Apo Reef Natural Park," http://www.nipa. org.ph/new-nipaweb/protectedareas/Aporeef/ Aporeef.htm.

"Apo Reef Natural Park," *ASEANbiodiversity*, January–June 2001.

Arguiza, Yasmin D., "A Tale of Two Atolls," *Business World*, June 12, 2002.

Glenn-Sullivan, E. Charlotte, and Ian Evans, "The Effects of Time-Averaging and Taphonomy on the Identification of Reefal Sub-Environments Using Larger Foraminifera: Apo Reef, Mindoro, Philippines," *Palaios*, Vol. 16.4, August 2001.

Hinrichsen, Donald, " Requiem for Reefs?," *International Wildlife*, March–April 1997, pp. 12–21.

Karlson, Ronald H., and Howard V. Cornell, "Scale-dependent Variation in Local vs. Regional Effects on Coral Species Richness," *Ecological Monographs*, Vol. 68, No. 2, May 1998, pp. 259–273.

"Mediaman to Launch Banca Tour," *Manila Bulletin*, May 30, 2002.

"Paper on Apo Reef Bags Award," *Silliman University News*, Vol. 8, No. 15, July 8, 2002.

"Philippines' DENR Faces Challenge to Conserve Protected Areas," *Asia Pulse*, May 23, 2001.

Senga, Rafael G., "Establishing Protected Areas in the Philippines," *George Wright FORUM*, Vol. 18, No. 2, 2001.

Vesiland, Priit J., "The Philippines," *National Geographic*, July 2002, pp. 62–81.

Beagle Channel, Tierra del Fuego, Argentina

Location

Slicing through the extended appendage of South America south of Patagonia, the Beagle Channel presents nature as it was during the Ice Age. The waterway, one of many crisscrossing the peninsula, courses 150 miles east-west through southern Argentina between the sharp, uneroded Andes Mountain chain to the north and the Martial Chain and the large archipelago of Tierra del Fuego to the south. Tierra del Fuego earned its name from European sightings of fires kindled to warm the nearly naked Yagán Indians and to alert other communities of the approach of boats up the channel. The provincial capital of Ushuaia on the mainland and the town of Puerto Williams on Isla Navarino, Chile, vie for the title of the southernmost community on the globe. Opposite Isla Navarino, where mountains seem to plunge into the sea, rises the world's southernmost ski slope. Less than 700 miles south lies Antarctica. (*See also* MCMURDO BAY, ANTARCTICA.)

In a land of extremes, Beagle Channel, which varies from three to eight miles wide, flows within the path of powerful sweeping winds. Its shoreline offers clear glimpses of a variety of terrains — icy-capped peaks, green valleys, a high plateau with steppe vegetation, the Garibaldi Fjord, waterfalls, and the ancient Alemania, Espana, Francia, Holanda, Italia, Martial, and Romanche glaciers. Sub-antarctic rain forest offers green havens of lichens, mosses, and stands of beech trees. The rocky *nunataks* [islets] are nesting grounds of cormorants and sea lions, which favor a granite crag known as Isla de los Lobos [Island of Wolves] for sunbathing. The western extreme of the channel splits to encircle Isla Gordon.

Contacts

Tourism Board of Tierra del Fuego
Av. Maipú 505 (CP V9410BJK)
Ushuaia, Tierra del Fuego, Argentina
Phone: 54-901-23340
Fax: 54-901-30694
Email: info@tierradelfuego.org.ar
http://www.tierradelfuego.org.ar/index-eng.htm

Dr. R. Natalie P. Goodall
Sarmiento 44
9410 Ushuaia, Tierra del Fuego, Argentina
Phone: 54-2901-422742
Fax: 54-2901-422743
Email: ngoodall@tierradelfuego.org.ar
http://www.acatushun.com/eng-fund.htm

Mythology

A Yagán myth explains the unusual shape of a fish native to Beagle Channel. In the narrative, a young native girl from Wujyasima was playing in the surf. She intrigued a sea lion, which hid and watched how she amused herself. When he approached, she, like the women of her people, dog-paddled stoutly toward the gravel shore, but could not elude her admirer. She had to cling to his neck to keep from drowning. After abandoning hope of escape, she relaxed as they progressed miles away to a rocky grotto. During their seaside life together, he brought her fish, but made no fire for cooking. She grew accustomed to eating her meals raw.

The son of the girl and the sea lion was a furry humanoid who, unlike his father,

Slicing through the extended appendage of South America south of Patagonia, the Beagle Channel presents nature as it was during the Ice Age (courtesy of John Pearson).

learned human language. From conversations with his mother, he understood her loneliness for the Yagán people and their ancestral shores. The whole family swam back toward the gravel plateau where she once lived. While the sea lion rested along the channel, the girl visited her clan and ventured east in the women's beech bark canoe to hunt sea urchins and mollusks.

While the women foraged for food, the Yagán men killed the sea lion with their lances and roasted its flesh. When the humanoid son tasted the fragrant meal, he liked the flavor of cooked meat. He held out a piece to his mother, who realized her great loss. She plucked a sea urchin from the canoe and struck the boy's head. He collapsed into the water and was changed into a *syuna* [rockfish]. The girl mourned the loss of her sea lion mate and refused to remarry. Each time she saw a *syuna*, she recognized the flattened head and piercings made by the spines of the sea urchin.

History

From 8,000 B.C., the Beagle Channel was the ancestral home of several native groups — the Alcaluf (also Alacaluf, Alcaloof, Alakaluf, or Alkaluf), the Ona or Foot Indians, and the Yagán (also Yahgán or Yámana), the most prominent along the waterway. The territory entered world cartography about A.D. 100 on the map of Greco-Egyptian astronomer Claudius Ptolemaeus, who based his drawing on reports by Egyptian sailors. However, Fuegian natives didn't enter recorded history until around 1624 following their first encounter with European adventurers. The Alcaluf, described in French ethno-archeologist José Emperaire's *Les Nomades de la Mer* [The Sea Nomads] (1955), were surf wanderers who dressed in seal skins and rowed or paddled their bark canoes among the channel islands in search of otter, seal, the llama-shaped guanaco, foxes, birds, and mollusk beds. Author E. Lucas

Bridges spoke knowledgably about their craft:

> One [canoe] measured twenty-nine feet in length and well over three feet in depth. For these the Alacaloof used not only paddles, but also oars of primitive design, with wooden row-locks... . Adventurers, both the Alacaloof and Yámanas, had passed around the Brecknock Peninsula in their canoes [Bridges, 1988, p. 61].

The nomadic Ona, an extinct nation that was once made up of the ancient Haush (or Aush) and Selk'nam (or Shelknam) Indians, were bow hunters, sea-fishers, and gatherers subsisting on sea animals, shellfish, birds, foxes, rodents, and guanacos.

The Yagán, the primary inhabitants of Beagle Channel, settled on Isla Navarino, where male hunters honed lances and harpoons and made tools from shellfish. The Yagán lived on cormorants, ducks, fish, geese, mollusks, penguins, seals, snails, wolves, and small game caught with slings and snares. Trained from birth in seacraft and swimming, their women managed ocean-going canoes, fished with lines and hooks, and kept warm by stoking fires kindled on board in turf heaped on gravel. They fed the meager flames with dried moss. They first traveled to Europe after Portuguese adventurer Pedro Sarmiento de Gamboa seized two Alcaluf at Desolation Island in 1580 and presented them at the court of Philip II of Spain.

Discovered by English sea captain Robert FitzRoy in 1830, the channel earned its name from his ship, the ten-gun brig *Beagle*. After Charles Darwin joined FitzRoy's second voyage to the channel, on January 19, 1833, the captain returned a Yagán female, Fuegia Basket, and two males, Jemmy Button and York Minster, to their homeland. FitzRoy had previously transported the four Yagáns to England to be evangelized and trained as Christian missionaries, but the grand scheme failed after a captive named Boat Memory died of smallpox and the three repatriated Yagáns reverted to native ways. On February 3, Richard Matthews, the resident Anglican in charge of the native mission, abandoned the small shore outpost and joined FitzRoy on the *Beagle* as it headed west to the Pacific Ocean.

During this fact-finding journey, Darwin showed little interest in the cultural interplay between Yagáns and the English. In the entry for January 20 in Chapter X of his journal, later published in *The Voyage of the Beagle* (1909), he remarked solely on earth study:

> The harbor consists of a fine piece of water half surrounded by low rounded mountains of clay-slate, which are covered to the water's edge by one dense gloomy forest. A single glance at the landscape was sufficient to show me how widely different it was from anything I had ever beheld [1989, p. 171].

He noted the outline of the channel's western end at Isla Gordon, where snow-capped granite mountains rose to the north to 6,000 feet, dropping lacy cataracts on the shore. He compared the magnificent glaciers to the blue of beryls and surmised in Chapter XII of *On the Origin of Species by Means of Natural Selection* (1859) that the region's icebergs may have dispersed numerous species along the remote Argentine coast.

In Chapter XI of *Voyage of the Beagle*, Darwin explained the importance of fires and foodways along Beagle Channel. The native Fuegians kept beacons lighted and heaped green branches or shrubs on the coals to generate black smoke. The flames served as heat and a means of communication similar to the smoke signals employed by North American plains Indians. Naked, primitive, and naive in their dealings with outsiders, the Yagán waved at the passing *Beagle*.

In reference to Fuegian dependence on Beagle Channel, Darwin observed that natives gathered shellfish from rocks and that "women, winter and summer, either dive to collect sea eggs, or sit patiently in their canoes, and with a baited hair-line, jerk out small fish. If a seal is killed, or the floating carcass of a putrid whale discovered, it is a feast" (*ibid.*, p. 178). The canoes were so important to channel life that they served as part-time residences. Darwin's servant, Syms Covington, produced his own journal, which detailed the skimpy dress of the seagoing natives. They wore only polished shell necklaces, white and red chalk markings on their naked flesh, and the occasional sealskin mantle around the neck or waist.

Natives of Beagle Channel declined alarmingly after the arrival of Christian ministers, gold prospectors, and sheepherders. In 1860, Anglican missionaries came to Patagonia. An English evangelist, Waite Hockin Stirling, settled on Beagle Channel nine years later at the Ushuaia log mission, founded by the Reverend Thomas Bridges and his assistant, John Lawrence. Bridges's son, Lucas Bridges, born in 1874, grew up among the mission's Ona and Yagán, learned their languages, and witnessed their gradual decline. By 1880, some 300 natives had settled permanently at the complex, which offered housing and a school.

Steadily, the native presence gave place to waves of hunters, prospectors, and land developers. After whalers and adventurers targeted the promising Patagonian coast in the 1880s, alcohol and European diseases struck a virgin soil population and reduced aboriginal tribes by nearly 99 percent. French expeditioners captured one native group and displayed them in France like caged animals. Because these canoe people formed only temporary shore communities, except for cave paintings, graves, and shell and stone workshops, they left little archeological evidence of their existence. In 1890, over 300 Croatians and newcomers from Italy and Spain colonized the channel area. Argentina created a Beagle Channel penal colony at Ushuaia that remained in use until 1947.

The late twentieth century reinvigorated interest in the Beagle Channel and its history. In 1956, citizens of the former Puerto Luisa renamed their community Puerto Williams to commemorate the centenary of the expedition of Juan Williams, who claimed the Strait of Magellan for Chile in 1856. On May 2, 1985, with the aid of mediator Pope John Paul II, Argentina and Chile ended a seven-year dispute over ownership of three Beagle Channel islands — Lennox, Nueva, and Picton — which are rich in krill, natural gas, and oil. A treaty awarded the islands to Chile and maritime rights to Argentina. Although native wishes and influence counted for nothing during the negotiations, in 1992, the 74 surviving Yagán natives of Isla Navarino demanded their ancestral rights and acknowledgement of their history and culture.

Ecosystem

Tierra del Fuego National Park, ten miles west of Ushuaia, has assured the preservation of wildlife, trees, and wildflowers indigenous to Beagle Channel. Established in 1960 on 63,000 hectares, the reserve protects the subantarctic forests of southern Argentina. It offers natural forest and mountain habitats on the Cóndor and Guanaco peaks and features ferns and mosses among ñire, notro, pickwood, and winter's wood trees and six types of beech — cherry, cinnamon, firebush, guindo, lenga or evergreen, some pocked with globules of llao-llao or Indian bread parasites and clumps of mistletoe, which locals call Chinese lanterns. Dotting the terrain are everlastings, Fuegian edelweiss, mutillas, orchids, white and yellow daisies, seapinks, and yellow violets alongside boxed-leafed barberry, native raspberries, parilla bushes, and wild celery. Boggy terrain is a source of peat and sphagnum moss and home to the chungungo, a type of otter, and to red fox and guanaco, which they value as a pack animal. The prolific Canadian beaver, inadvisedly introduced in 1948, fells hardwoods and builds dam systems along Los Castores stream.

In addition to creeks, glaciers, lakes, and ponds, the reserve is Argentina's only national park featuring a seashore. Ensenada Bay and Lapataia Bay, the ancestral home of the Yágan, offer white cauquenes or upland geese along the beaches and treks inland into deep gorges. Birders at Black Lagoon and Cormoranes archipelago look for the Austral parakeet, black-chested buzzard eagle, black-crowned night heron, black-eyebrowed albatross, Andean condor, diving petrel, hawk, ibis, kelp geese, rhea, snipe, steamer duck, thorn-tailed rayadito, and the rare Andean tapaculo. The Argentine post office featured on nature stamps the indigenous magellanic woodpecker *(Campephilus magellanicus)*, a handsome red-headed larva-eater and South America's largest bird.

Essential to the world's knowledge of varied ecosystems along the Beagle Channel area is the work of Rae Natalie Prosser Goodall, a biologist and artist from Lexington, Ohio. She began ecological studies in Venezuela while working for Mobil Oil de Venezuela. She read about Argentine rancher Esteban Lucas Bridges, the son of the Reverend Thomas Bridges, and his life among the Yagán Indians in the autobiographical *Tierra del Fuego, Uttermost Part of the Earth* (1948). In the early 1960s, Goodall married Thomas D. Goodall, great grandson of the Reverend Thomas Bridges. The couple settled on the eastern Beagle Channel at Harberton, a land-grant the Spanish issued to Thomas Bridges, where she studied native history and mapped landfalls and shipwrecks. A skilled naturalist, she identified and painted in India ink notable native flora — balsam, calafate, Christmas bush, diddle-dee, evergreen beech, firebush, green orchids, streaked maiden, and winter's bark, a peppery plant that European sailors gathered to combat scurvy.

Goodall took a keen interest in Beagle Channel's animals. Her gatherings included marine nematodes, sand dollars, sea anemones, starfish, tube worms, and sponges washed up by the tide. For both food and study, she chose razor clams, mussels, channel bullfish, plunder fish, and eels. She cleaned and analyzed the structure of butterfly shells and the skulls and skeletons of rare dolphins, porpoises, and baleen and toothed whales. Some of the dry bones she found were incorporated into the gateways and fences of local homes.

On a grant from the National Geographic Society in 1971, Goodall initiated formal botanic study of rare plants on beaches and peaks. She established a herbarium of 7,000 specimens and identified nine new species and sixty subspecies. From detailed knowledge of 500 species, she delivered papers on her beachcombings, exhibited flower drawings in Pittsburgh at the Hunt Botanical Library in Pittsburgh, and wrote *Flowers of Tierra del Fuego* (1969) and *Tierra del Fuego, Argentina* (1978).

In the latter title, Goodall summarized the forbidding nature of her Argentine home:

> So strong is the current that it could smash ships against the rocks in calm or foggy weather. Fierce southern storms could capsize boats, and no one survived in the 39 degree F. water. Only the sealers were brave enough to dare the wind, current, and rocks regularly [p. 20].

She offset the grim warning with a scientist's appreciation of the "romantic land of legend," a habitat graced by snow-capped peaks, glaciers and pristine lakes, trout streams, wildflowers, and migratory flocks of geese. With a tour guide's enthusiasm, she urged, "Come and see these and many more marvels in Tierra del Fuego. You can make your own legends" *(ibid.)*.

In 1982, Goodall began working in Ushuaia for the Centro Austral de Investigaciones Científicas [Southern Center for

Scientific Research]. From her studies of channel fauna came skeletal displays of 21 species of cetaceans and eighty species of birds at the Acatushún Bone Museum, which opened in March 2001. The Goodall residence, Estancia Harberton, the oldest Fuegian farm, became a National Historical Monument. For her devotion to science, she was inducted into the Society of Woman Geographers, Explorers Club of New York, and the Ohio Women's Hall of Fame.

Coastal Activities

Visitors to Beagle Channel tour Tierra del Fuego National Park to observe birds and mammals, camp at Lake Roca, and mountain bike along the bushy steppe. Another park site is the depot of the Train at the End of the World, located along the Pipo River and over Quemado Bridge. Passengers view Lapataia Bay, recreations of Yagán and Selk'-nam Indian camps, and Chico Pass and the De la Macarena Cascade, two panoramas favored by photographers. Before its transformation for tourist use, until 1947, the steam train transported prisoners from Ushuaia's jail to outlying sawmills for forced labor.

A favorite waterway for sailboats, kayaks, dive boats, and catamarans, Beagle Channel also draws photographers and sketchers to its photogenic Les Eclaireures lighthouse, a 74-foot red-and-white striped masonry tower called in Spanish "Faro del Fin del Mundo" [Lighthouse at World's End]. Hikers at Martillo Island visit the roosting sites of the gentoo and magellanic penguins. Landward, visitors traverse Tierra del Fuego National Park, which is recovering from a devastating forest fire. Campers and hikers take the chairlift to Martial Glacier; birders sight antarctic swallows, Magellans, steamer ducks, and penguins, which form rookeries on the rocky shore. In Usuahaia, local artists exhibit their work; archeological and historic displays are available at the End of the World Museum.

For those who favor water sport, the channel provides dolphin and orca watches and hosts excellent beds of crabs, limpets, mussels, and snails. The waters also offer prime fishing for puyen, peladilla, and róbalo. Divers explore remains of the 175-foot German packet steamer *Monte Cervantes*, bound from Hamburg for China early in 1930 with 1,117 passengers. It struck an uncharted rock at Eclaireur reef in Lapataia Bay on January 22 and sank in over 100 feet, taking with it the captain, Theodore Dreyer. When Italian salvors towed it to Ushuaia in 1954, it sank once more. Recovered items as well as relics of other shipwrecks are on display at Ushuaia's Maritime Museum.

Sources

Bridges, E. Lucas. *Uttermost Part of the Earth: Indians of Tierra del Fuego*. New York: Dover Publications, 1988.

"Darwin at Terra del Fuego," *Athena Review*, Vol. 1, No. 3.

Darwin, Charles. *The Origin of Species*. New York: Modern Library, 1993.

_____. *Voyage of the Beagle*. London: Penguin Books, 1989.

Desmond, Adrian, and James Moore. *Darwin*. New York: Warner Books, 1991.

Goodall, Rae Natalie P., "Housewife at the End of the World," *National Geographic*, Vol. 139, No. 1, January 1971, pp. 130–150.

_____. *Tierra del Fuego, Argentina*. Buenos Aires, Argentina: Instituto Salesiano de Artes Gráficas, 1979.

"Islands in the Stream," *Time*, October 29, 1984, p. 59.

Johnsston, Ian A., et al., "Latitudinal Variation in the Abundance and Oxidative Capacities of Muscle Mitochondria in Perciform Fishes," *Journal of Experimental Biology*, Vol. 200, No. 1, January 1998, pp. 1–12.

"The Journal of Syms Covington," *Australian Science Archives*, August 23, 1995.

Lindsley, Lisa, "The Beagle Channel Settlement: Vatican Mediation Resolves a Century-Old Dispute," *Journal of Church and State*, Vol. 29, No. 3, 1987, pp. 435–455.

Novak, Skip, "Cape Horn," *Sailing*, February, 1992.

Piana, Ernesto, et al., "Chronicles of 'Ona-

Ashaga': Archaeology in the Beagle Channel," *Antiquity*, Vol. 66, No. 252, September 1992, pp. 771–783.

Von Hornbostel, Erich M., "Fuegian Songs," *American Anthropologist*, Vol. 38, No. 3, July–September, 1936.

_____, "The Music of the Fuegians," *Ethnos*, Vol. 13, No. 3–4, July 1948.

Birsay Bay, Orkney

Location

Bounded by the Atlantic Ocean and the North Sea, the Orkney Islands consist of seventy low, irregular archipelagos. They lie twenty miles northeast of John O'Groats, Scotland, above the treacherous Pentland Firth and fifty miles south of Greenland. Eroded by glaciers, shrouded in mist, and pounded by surf, their makeup is chiefly igneous rock, limestone, and sandstone. Because of the rugged surface, only twenty islands are inhabited. Lush green hills are largely denuded of trees because of gales and constant westerly winds. Surviving the battering are dwarf aspen, hazel, rowan, and willow. Trout inhabit island streams; moors and peat bogs harbor a variety of wildlife.

Birsay perches on the northwest corner of the island of Mainland, also called Pomona, actually a pair of islands tethered by a slim causeway. Opposite Birsay Bay lies the Brough of Birsay, a pancake of a tidal islet offering significant prehistoric archeological digs and 140-foot cliffs overlooking pods of killer whales and puffin nesting grounds. The town of Birsay was the Old Norse capital city, called Byrgisey, which Picts settled in neolithic times. They and the Vikings who came later crabbed and lobster fished and gathered abundant limpets and whelks for shore dinners that are still a favorite among Orcadians. In addition to teeming waters, Birsay offers peat-rich heathered hills, pasturage for herding beef and dairy cattle and sheep, and small plots of land for growing oats and barley and for pig and poultry raising.

Contacts

Orkney Tourist Board
Six Broad Street
Kirkwall, Orkney KW15 1NX
Phone: 01856-872856
Fax: 01856-875056
http://www.visitorkney.com/

History

The Orkney Islands were first inhabited before 3000 B.C., when farmers from Scotland ventured by sea-going skiffs north from Caithness. In 56 B.C., Sicilian travel writer and geographer Diodorus Siculus reported the rovings of the Phoenician sailor Pytheas, who had reached Britain in 325 B.C. In Diodorus's description of the waves of Orca, he named the Orkneys the Orcades, a title repeated in the first century A.D. by Roman geographer Pomponius Mela and in A.D. 140 by the Greco-Egyptian geographer Claudius Ptolemaeus of Alexandria.

Before A.D. 100, according to the Roman historian Tacitus, the aboriginal Picts or "Painted People" settled the northern isles. The Brough of Birsay, an offshore islet reached at low tide by a causeway, was home to Christians from the A.D. 400s. For sturdy residences capable of withstanding harsh sea blows, settlers built two-story, double-walled oval stone *brochs* [drystone houses] surrounded by protective battlements. By the A.D. 600s, the Brough had advanced to a defensive stronghold.

Norsemen raided the area in the late A.D. 700s. They renamed the Orcades the *Orkneyja* or Seal Islands and established their own colonies a century later, when they developed sea trade. Some of their contributions to the region were the erection of standing stones, the molding of bronze jewelry and silver armbands for currency, and the breeding of Norwegian fjord ponies, a stocky, dun-coated, black-maned relative of the Pzrewalski that the Vikings trained to fight to the death. Norse architectural remains on the Brough of Birsay include longhouses and a bathhouse or sauna adjacent to an earl's residence. The six-foot Pictish Symbol Stone, a fragmented vertical rectangle discovered in 1935, preserved symbols of a mirror, crescent, and beast and a line of three armed nobles in long fringed tunics, with a crowned king leading the procession. Experts partially reconstructed the original at the National Museum of Scotland.

In A.D. 901, as described by an Icelandic scribe in the Norwegian epic *Orkneyinga Saga: The History of the Earls of Orkney* (1206), Harold Fairhair, king of Norway, established a semi-independent Orkney earldom. First to obtain title was Harold's forcastleman, Sigurd Eysteinsson, called Earl Sigurd I the Powerful. Norse settlers, who replaced the Picts, built turf-roofed stone houses containing benches surrounding a hearth. Islanders fished for ample cod, haddock, hake, ling, saith, and torsk and flourished at water milling. In 1064, Earl Thorfinn the Mighty, who headquartered at Birsay, erected Christ Kirk, a parish church that remained in use for nine centuries.

Central to Birsay folk history is the life of Magnus Erlendson, later St. Magnus the Martyr, a pirate who became one of the region's most respected Christian earls. In April 1117 at Egilsey, he fell victim to his envious cousin Hakon, who ordered his cook Lifolf to split Magnus's skull with an axe. Birsay parishioners received the earl's murdered remains for burial. His spirit infested the grave with unexplained lights and a curious odor and reportedly caused miraculous cures among ailing pilgrims. In 1135, when he was canonized as St. Magnus, Bishop William removed his bones to the cathedral at Kirkwall.

When the last of the Viking earls died

in 1231, the Orkney cluster passed to Scotland's Angus dynasty, which continued the coastal industry in salting and air-drying fish to supply the English army with a lightweight, easily transportable food supply. After the Orkneys endured an interim period of rule by Denmark and Norway, Scotland annexed the islands in 1472 as partial dowry for Margaret, daughter of Christian I, King of Denmark, who wed James III three years earlier. In 1540, James V establish Orkney as a Scottish county.

The power of Orkney's earls resulted in despotism and oppression of natives. In 1574, the illegitimate son of James V, Robert Stewart, received the earldom of Orkney from Mary, Queen of Scots. Stewart taxed residents of Birsay and Kirkwall to finance construction of Earl's Palace, a two-story, L-shaped courtyard castle, which he built with conscript labor at Birsey Village northeast of Birsay Bay. Patrick Stewart, his son and heir, earned the name "Black Patie" for his disdain for Birsay islanders. Until 1614, he continued demanding funds as he completed his father's grandiose project. He raised additional moneys by confiscating the wealth of pirates and charging tariffs from fishers casting their nets around Birsay. The following year, Patrick faced seven charges of treason for his illegitimate son Robert's uprising against the royal authority of James VI. The crown court ended the islands' misery by executing Earl Patrick and Robert in 1615 — the father by beheading and the son by hanging.

In a more promising era, the Orkneys took part in the settlement and exploitation of the New World. Each June in the late 1700s and early 1800s, traffic from the Hudson's Bay Company fleet bore around eighty young Orcadian recruits to the "Nor-Wast" [Canada] for jobs paying six pounds per year in lumbering, boat-building, and fur trading. Lonely men far from home formed relationships with the Cree and Métis and returned to the Orkneys with half-breed children. Most concealed their native origins.

During the two world wars, Scapa Flow at the heart of the Orkneys served the British navy as a base. At the nearly vertical cliffs of Marwick Head on the Brough of Birsay, a square tower commemorates the downing of the cruiser H.M.S. *Hampshire* at 7:50 P.M. on June 5, 1916, after striking a German mine during a fierce gale. Among the battered dead was Horatio Herbert, Lord Kitchener, the Irish hero of Khartoum, who was on a diplomatic mission to Russia. Between the wars, islanders erected an unmanned, 125-foot crenellated lighthouse on the Brough of Birsay, which offers a view of the Atlantic Ocean and flashes a white beacon eighteen miles out to sea every 24 seconds. At the onset of World War II, some 60,000 soldiers quartered in the Birsay area with an additional 40,000 sailors stationed offshore. Around 37,000 construction laborers from Ireland and 1,200 Italian prisoners of war helped to fortify the islands against Nazi U-boats.

Folklore

Surviving from the heyday of the Vikings is a complex Norse — or possibly blended Celtic and Norse — folklore. It survived from the storytelling that dominated long evenings beginning with dusk that fell around 3:00 P.M. Tales centered on the ocean and its mermaids, maned seahorses called Nuggles or Nuckelavee, hull-crushing sea worms, the Sea Mither [mother], seaweed-draped sea trows (or trolls), singing huldu or huldrefolk, and long-necked, finny sea serpents resembling dinosaurs. On the shore, amphibious creatures called selkies or seal folk (also silkies or selchies) were totemic nature figures dating into prehistory. According to island legend, they were shape-shifters who had been angels until they fell from heaven into the waves.

Selkies had magical powers: They could shed sealskins and flippers to turn into beguiling humanoids. Male selkies wandered the coasts at night like predatory rakes, seducing women with their handsome faces and deft body movements. To summon their amphibious lovers again, distraught women stood at the seashore and shed seven tears into the foam. Island males who courted selkie women pursued them to the seaside rocks where the females sunbathed. The men attempted to steal the seal-women's silvery skins to halt them from shifting back into sea mammals. Bereft of ocean-going garb, the sea maidens wandered the shore keening for their watery homeland. In 1893, Orcadian antiquarian and folklorist Walter Traill Dennison of Sanday, compiler of *Orkney Folklore & Sea Legends* (1995), wrote an article for the *Scottish Antiquary* linking the selkies to real islanders who were born with webbed hands and feet.

In 1938, a visitor to the Orkneys, Otto Andersson, the first specialist in musicology and folklore at Åbo Akademi University in Finland and author of *Finnish Folklore* (1967), recorded the ballad of "Great Selkie O'Sulkeskerry." The text drew on the sad tradition of an island woman's concealed affair with a selkie and the birth of a son to the "earthly nourris [nurse]." After the child sank into the sea with his father, the woman's human husband shot both seals, which she identified by a gold chain that the father gave his son. One version of the ballad concludes that, in token of her loss, her heart broke into three pieces.

Unlike the winsome, carnal selkies, the evil-doing Finfolk lived undersea in the magical kingdom of Finfolkaheem and summered on the vanishing isles of Hildaland and Hether Blether. Finfolk menaced the shorelines and jealously guarded their coastal territory, where they herded whales. They were so strong that they could row across the North Sea to Scandinavia in seven strokes.

Finfolk intimidated mortals by snapping trolling lines and scaring away fish.

One of the Finfolk, Finman, wandered inland to stalk settlements and snatch maidens for their consorts. Finfolk further victimized islanders by slipping the anchor stones from trawlers and floating the craft out from the shore to be dashed on rocks. To counter the pagan sea creatures' vandalism, fishers began incising the sign of the cross on sinkers and marking them with tar or chalk on their hulls. Another deterrent to finfolk pranks was a silver coin tossed into the waves to distract the greedy sea dwellers.

Coastal Activities

Birsay is a birder's paradise. Viewers and photographers focus on bird reserves and cliffside breeding grounds of 109 species, including the Arctic tern, greylag goose, green-winged teal, guillemot, kittiwake, oystercatcher, petrel, puffin, razorbill, scoter, and skua. Birsay Bay offers a nesting ground to several species — the Birsay Bay curlew, eider, plover, redshank, shelduck, and whimbrel as well as seals, who rest and sunbathe on the rocks. At Marwick Head, viewers can spot pipits, ravens, skylarks, and starlings. Inland trampers following peat cutters tracks over the wetlands and maritime heaths at the Dee of Durkadale find nesting grounds of the hen harrier, loon, merganser, merlin, reed bunting, Slavonian grebe, smew, stonechat, warbler, and wigeon, all sanctioned by the Royal Society for the Preservation of Birds. Visitors also find pleasant countryside suited to cycling, hiking, shooting, boating, sailing, scuba diving, surfing, kite flying, archery, and photography of unusually brilliant seascapes and sunsets. Fishers enjoy sea quarry as well as freshwater trout from the lochs of Harray, Hungland, and Swanney.

Historians peruse the ruins of Earl's Palace, Barony grist mills, the Kirbuster Farm Museum, and Britain's most primitive horizontal grain-grinder, called a click mill. A mounted whalebone, a commemorative of the whaling industry, stands at the Birsay headland overlooking the Brough of Birsay. At Sandside Geo south of Marwick Bay on the Brough of Birsay, restored fishermen's huts and the *nousts* where they beached their boats reflect the island's historic lifestyle.

SOURCES

Barrett, James H., "Fish Trade in Norse Orkney and Caithness: A Zooarchaeological Approach," *Antiquity*, September 1997, p. 616–38.

_____, et al., "Radiocarbon Dating and Marine Reservoir Correction of Viking Age Christian Burials from Orkney," *Antiquity*, Vol. 74, No. 285, September 2000, p. 537.

Blane, Douglas, "Village That Lay Hidden by the Sands of Time," *Times Educational Supplement*, February 5, 1999.

Bradley, Richard, "Incised Motifs in the Passage-graves at Quoyness and Cuween, Orkney," *Antiquity*, Vol. 72, No. 276, June 1998, pp. 387–390.

Bryson, Bill, "Orkney, Ancient North Sea Haven," *National Geographic*, June 1998, pp. 46–61.

Fotheringham, Keith, "Jennifer & Hazel Wrigley: Orkney Ambassadors," *Sing Out!*, Vol. 45, No. 14, Winter 2002, pp. 90–93.

Jones, Andrew, "The World on a Plate: Ceramics, Food Technology and Cosmology in Neolithic Orkney," *World Archaeology*, Vol. 31, No. 1, June 1999, pp. 55–56.

Kinlen, L. J., and A. Balkwill, "Infective Cause of Childhood Leukemia and Wartime Population Mixing in Orkney and Shetland, U. K.," *Lancet*, Vol. 357, No. 9,259, March 17, 2001, p. 858.

"A Land of Wind without Willows," *Christian Science Monitor*, May 31, 2000, p. 12.

Meek, Eric, "So That's What the Birdieman Does," *The Orcadian*, May 23, 2002.

"Moves to Preserve Whalebone Landmark," *The Orcadian*, June 22, 2002.

"News," *History Today*, Vol. 51, No. 6, June 2001, p. 10.

"A No-Show by One Boat Got Orkney's Ling Festival Off to a Chaotic Start," [Glasgow] *Daily Record*, October 25, 2002, p. 78.

"Orkney's Brochs," http://www.orkneyjar.com/history/brochs/index.html.

Phillips, Tim, and Aaron Watson, "The Living and the Dead in Northern Scotland 3500–2000 B.C.," *Antiquity*, Vol. 74, No. 286, December 2000, p. 786.

Ponnampalam, Andrew, "The Exhilarating Orkneys," *New Straits Times*, October 27, 1998.

"Record Population of 30,021 Greylag Geese," *The Orcadian*, December 12, 2002.

Shattuck, Harry, "Scottish Islands Are Terrific for Birders," *Los Angeles Daily News*, May 4, 1997.

Thorson, Bruce, "The Bay Connection," *Canadian Geographic*, Vol. 120, No. 7, November 2000, p. 98.

Towrie, Sigurd, "Orkneyjar," http://www.orkneyjar.com/

Wylie, Gillian, "Norwegian Fjord Ponies Are Living Reminder of Orkney's Viking Past," *The Orcadian*, August 29, 2002.

Cape Hatteras, North Carolina

Location

At the easternmost point on North Carolina's slender outer banks, a 180-mile string of scrub-covered sandbars framing the shore line, Cape Hatteras fronts the sixteen-mile Diamond Shoals. At a 112-degree angle, the jutting breakwater points seaward to a treacherous approach further complicated by an outer shoal some ten miles out in the Atlantic Ocean. Threaded by Highway 12, this barrier of wind-sculpted sand dunes, sea oats, wax myrtle, and sea views overlooks stretches of shoreline. Along the coast, the remains of some 100 shipwrecks emerge and disappear once more under churning shallows and shifting sands that pile up as high as 250 feet. To the west, the Pamlico Sound stretches thirty miles toward the mainland.

Offshore, a sharp turn of the Gulf Stream veers north to collide with the frigid waters of the southerly Virginia coastal current, part of the Labrador Current from Greenland. The surface conditions generate such forceful white geysers of spume and gripping undertow that even the most seasoned pilots approach with caution. So many hapless seamen have drowned off Hatteras that the northern end of the beach was named Bodie Island. Because of the danger to navigators, Cape Hatteras has had a series of three lighthouses to mark the Carolina shore and an era of rising maritime power for the United States.

Set aside by Franklin D. Roosevelt in 1937 to preserve a fragile ecosystem, Cape Hatteras National Seashore was completed in July 1953. The area, which spreads across 47 acres of Bodie, Hatteras, and Ocracoke islands, is a haven for retirees, naturalists, birders, hikers, and photographers. The preserve offers seventy miles of sandy strands and dunes, salt marshes, grassy stretches, and woodlands, home to cedar, holly, and oak, habitats of nesting aquatic birds. A favorite route for sailboats, the intracoastal waterway, which lies between the bowlike Outer Banks and the mainland, passes through the Pamlico Sound.

Contacts

Carolyn McCormick, Director
Dare County Tourist Bureau
P. O. Box 399
Manteo, North Carolina 27954
Phone: 800-446-6262
Email: dctb-info@outer-banks.com

National Park Service Headquarters
1401 National Park Drive
Manteo, North Carolina 27954
Phone: 252-473-2111

History

The first national seashore in the United States, Cape Hatteras was the home of water-oriented Algonquian-speaking tribes for some thousand years before the arrival of European settlers. Native Americans, who succumbed to smallpox, scarlet fever, and tuberculosis by the mid-eighteenth century, left behind the place names

The first national seashore in the United States, Cape Hatteras is home to the Hatteras Lighthouse, a treasured piece of Americana that guides ships past the graveyard of the Atlantic (courtesy of Outer Banks Visitor's Bureau).

Chicamacomico, Chowan, Hatteras, Kinnakeet, Kitty Hawk, Pamlico, and Roanoke and possibly Chesapeake. The narrow strip of land the Indians once inhabited lies on the eastern edge of Dare County, named for Virginia Dare, the first English child born in the American colonies.

Upon their introduction to the New World, the first European settlers delighted in deep forests of cedar, dogwood, live oak, wax myrtle, wild grapes, grasses, hollies, and yaupon, which provided materials for homes, fortifications, ship building, and crafts. Deforestation to supply local and New England shipyards with lumber for schooners thinned out the forest canopy, which shielded fragile greenery from salty ocean spray and sun. Only scrub pine could survive. As tender undergrowth withered and died, root systems destabilized the soil and exposed a sandy stretch that wind scoured into waves and dunes.

Because of unstable weather, tricky currents, fog and haze, underwater dunes, and seasonal hurricanes, the Hatteras region earned a terrorizing reputation for the downing of Spanish galleons, pirate cutters, mail steamers, and German U-boats. In the 1500s, Italian expeditioners Giovanni da Verrazano and Amerigo Vespucci surveyed the area and Sir Walter Raleigh attempted to found a permanent colony. Subsequent herders and settlers inhabited Hatteras while prospering from the boatbuilding trade. Pilots and craft tenders offered their knowledge of the shifting shoals and inlets to shipmen seeking access to the lucrative Pamlico Sound and city of Bath, North Carolina's colonial capital. The growing population increased demands on exporters to channel goods directly from Europe and the caribbean over the most direct route, by sea.

In the ensuing years since the European settlement of Hatteras, over 600 ships have foundered and sunk within sight of North Carolina, 100 of them during World War II. The first known casualty was the 160-tun *Tiger*, the flagship of Sir Richard Grenville's four-ship fleet, which sank on June 26, 1585. Spanish captains directed their annual treasure fleets from the Mexican and Central American mines up the northbound current on their way to Iberia. Nonetheless, a flotilla of seven Spanish galleons met their doom after they encountered a hurricane in 1750 as they sailed north from Cuba toward Spain. Southbound crews routed their vessels along the Virginia Coastal Drive, the colder inshore counter-current. A bottleneck at Hatteras forced southbound traffic into a narrow sea lane along the narrow Diamond Shoals, a series of parallel sandbars. Before sonar, this slim passage required skill and experience to prevent grounding.

Storms and underwater hazards were not the only difficulty for close-shore navigation. From 1703 to 1713, during the War of the Spanish Succession, also called Queen Anne's War, the pirate Edward Teach (also Tach, Thach, or Thatch), better known as Blackbeard, became the most sought criminal in the North American shipping lanes. A licensed English privateer, he sailed the *Queen Anne's Revenge*, the former 26-gun slaver called the *Concorde de Nantes*, a merchant vessel from Nantes, France. He headquartered at "Teach's Hole," Jamaica, and, with a fleet of swift schooners, robbed ocean-going ships, especially cargo and passenger vessels departing Virginia and the Carolinas' Outer Banks. To elude capture, he plied the roughest waters on the Eastern Seaboard and slipped through perpetually shifting keyhole inlets at Hatteras and Oregon to the backwaters of the Pamlico Sound, where he spent his most profitable months. Each winter, he ranged south to the sunny Caribbean to scout out likely prey until his gory death in battle at Teach Hole Channel on November 22, 1718.

To aid less predatory navigators coasting the long stretch between New England and the Caribbean, in 1789, Congress set up the U.S. Lighthouse Establishment to superintend twelve colonial light stations and to build some forty more by 1820. Supporting the formalized Lighthouse Bill of 1790 was Secretary of the Treasury Alexander Hamilton, who had courted mayhem off Diamond Shoals in 1773 at age seventeen on board the *Thunderbolt* on his way from the Caribbean to college in Boston. He is reputed to have named Diamond Shoals the "graveyard of the Atlantic." His bill acknowledged that the Carolinas possessed one quarter of the coastline shared by the thirteen original colonies and that creating a safe passage for ships was crucial to the national economy and defense.

In 1794, Congress okayed plans for an octagonal lighthouse of granite and sandstone to be erected at the dangerous Carolina corridor. General Henry Dearborn, a congressman from Massachusetts and later Secretary of War, built the structure on a wooded knoll of Cape Hatteras at a cost of $38,450. He contributed some rocks to the project and dispatched them from his native New Hampshire to the cape by barge. In October 1803, the first Hatteras lighthouse went into service and was manned by Adam Gaskins at an annual salary of $333. In the ten-by-ten-by-twelve-foot iron and glass lantern room, a blue-uniformed keeper stoked with sperm whale oil the eighteen Argand lamps, invented by Bostonian Winslow Lewis, and spread the blaze seaward twelve miles with the huge lamp's fourteen parabolic reflectors. The beacon burned 2,282 gallons of fuel per year, drawn from nine cedar cisterns filled by jobber Stephen Hussey of Nantucket, Massachusetts, at under one dollar per tun. To continue the upgrade of coastal safety for shippers and passenger vessels, in February 1806, the U.S. House Committee on Commerce and Manufactures proposed surveying the North Carolina coast from Cape Hatteras south to Cape Fear in search of new lighthouse sites.

Although welcome, the original light station had its problems. It faced daily collisions with seabirds flying into the lighthead and breaking glass and survived numerous mishaps with spilled oil, which posed a fire hazard. To the detriment of travelers, the tower, at 95 feet, was too short and its flame too weak to illuminate the shoreline. As a result, a heavy gale in 1812 forced a sloop aground, stranding four women, including a Mrs. Harris and her daughter Lydia from Hillsborough, North Carolina, on their way south from New York to New Bern. The women's only salvation was an anonymous muscular black man, who knocked out the ship's deadlights and passed the women to a life-chain of men through the breakers to a hut on the shore. The islanders' only reward was the salvage from trunks, timbers, and other flotsam left behind.

Late in 1813, the government hired Samuel Wilkins to repair the upper reaches of the tower and lighthead, which the British had damaged during the War of 1812. The Lighthouse Service augmented the tower's light in 1824 with a lightship, a secondary offshore warning vessel called the *Diamond Shoals*, anchored at thirty fathoms on the eastern rim of the most perilous undersea stretch. The lightship survived until 1827, when gale winds broke it apart and tossed its remains on Ocracoke Beach.

As the Outer Banks grew in population, Cape Hatteras earned a worse reputation for peril in 1837 after the 550-ton sidewheel steamer *Home*, en route from New York to Charleston, South Carolina, beached one mile out to sea in Racer's Storm. The hurricane set a record for deaths by killing ninety of 130 people aboard. Among the survivors were twenty passengers, twenty crew, and Captain Carleton White, who supervised the burial of twenty corpses in the sand. Because so many died for lack of life preservers, the next year, Congress enacted the Steamship Act, which charged ship owners with providing life preservers for all on board. On September 7, 1846, a gale scoured out the current Hatteras inlet and Oregon Inlet to the north, offering access from the Atlantic Ocean to the Pamlico Sound.

In 1851, Lieutenant H. K. Davenport, captain of the U.S. Mail steamer *Cherokee*, reported to authorities that Hatteras, the most hazardous point on the American east coast, needed more light. Federal authorities accepted a recommendation to raise the Cape Hatteras lighthouse another 55 feet. In 1854, engineers equipped the station's tower with a rotating lamphead fitted with a Fresnel lens, an invention named for physicist Augustin Fresnel and purchased in St. Gobin, France. As keeper William O'Neal activated a weight to engage a series of gears to turn the beacon over a twelve-hour period, the lens amplified a white flame through a webwork of prisms and magnifying glasses. The remodeling of the Hatteras station took two years and greatly improved coastal visibility by 10.5 miles out to sea. Additional work on a double keeper's quarters encouraged O'Neal's employees, H. B. O'Neal and W. B. O'Neal, to retain the lonely and demanding job of lighthouse superintendent, which demanded unstinting surveillance of the flame and shores, monitoring of the weather, removal of condensation from glass, replacement of panes broken by storms and seabirds, logging ship sightings and unusual events, and policing the grounds. An offshore floating bell beacon augmented efforts to save lives, but failed within four months, when the beacon sank.

During the Civil War, the lighthouse, the faithful sentinel of the shoals, took on greater importance to the South. Before North Carolina seceded from the Union in May 20, 1861, Brigadier-General Theophilus Holmes, the Confederate military commander of coastal defense, planned a string of batteries and forts at Hatteras, Ocracoke,

and Oregon Inlets to secure inland ports at Edenton, Elizabeth City, New Bern, Plymouth, and Washington and to defend Albemarle, the Pamlico Sound, and Carolina shipping lanes from Union attack. Guarding the shore north of Hatteras Inlet was Fort Hatteras, which white soldiers, freedmen, and slaves constructed of peat blocks and marsh grass at the northeastern access. Some 1,200 yards away stood Fort Clark, a square marsh-sod block redoubt to the west. Manning both were volunteer militia to guard the position from attack by sea or land.

Because of shipping crucial to the Southern cause, Hatteras was a strategic location as home port to privateers, blockade runners, and the Mosquito Fleet, a ragtag flotilla of small attack boats that harried Union ships. From May until June 1861, rebel forces prevented Union skippers from navigating the Carolina shore, from scuttling the civilian steamers that had been adapted into warships, and from apprehending supplies that blockade runners ferried to the Confederacy. To keep Southern lighthouses from falling to the enemy, coastal wardens extinguished over 100 towers and removed their lamps and reflectors. At Hatteras, shore patrols damaged the tower walls and snuffed out the light by removing and disassembling the lens, which they transported west in 44 pine boxes to Washington, North Carolina. A Dr. Tayloe moved the valuable glass eye by train to his plantation at Townsville north of Raleigh.

The local Confederate military successfully commandeered eight schooners, seven brigs, and one bark until Hatteras fell to the North on August 28, 1861. On that morning, Commodore Silas H. Stringham led a fleet of tug boats, four lightly armed transports, the gunboats *Harriet Lane* and *Monticello*, and five armed frigates — the *Cumberland, Minnesota, Pawnee, Susquehanna,* and *Wabash* — in a circling pattern of bombardment against weak counter-moves by Confederates at Hatteras. Major-General Benjamin F. Butler landed Union invasion forces through choppy whitecaps to the beach.

The island's defense was shortlived. The next morning, Confederate Commodore Samuel Barron decided to surrender rather than risk slaughter of a garrison by an amphibious force of 900. After the capitulation, a sketch artist for *Harper's* magazine drew the 20th Indiana regiment encamped at the tower's base. The small victory was beneficial to the Union effort and to Butler's career because it occurred shortly after the spectacular Confederate victory at the first battle of Manassas. In February 1862, Hatteras figured in the Union plan to menace Norfolk and Richmond by taking Roanoke Island in Hatteras Inlet. Called the Burnside Expedition, the siege involved Brigadier General Ambrose E. Burnside in a lopsided struggle between the Union navy and the Confederacy's ineffectual Mosquito Fleet.

In June 1862, Federal officials allocated $75,000 to reconstruct the Hatteras lighthouse. Government engineers modeled the new light stations after the Cape Lookout lighthouse and moved the Hatteras structure 600 feet north before reopening the post. Abraham C. Farrow assumed the role of keeper on September 30, 1862. For additional staff members Walla R. Jennett and N. T. S. Williams, Dexter Stetson constructed a second keeper's residence. The Lighthouse Board determined that, because of a rotting wood frame and structural damage, the original light tower was not salvageable.

One of North Carolina's most enduring maritime landmarks, the current Cape Hatteras light station received its commission from the U.S. Lighthouse Service in 1867, a year that saw the loss of both the brigantine *George E. Maltby* and the schooner *Vesta* at Hatteras in the first three months. Built by engineer Major George B. Nicholson at a cost of $150,000, the new tower re-quired 1,250,000 bricks and rose 198 feet atop the earlier structure. Securing its footing below the water table were two layers of yellow pine capped with granite slabs. The nation's highest masonry lighthouse, the finished beacon weighed 4,800 tons and stood 208 feet tall and 1,300 feet from the surf. It housed a 24-panel revolving lens made by master glassmaker Henri Le Paute of Paris, France.

The light re-entered service on December 16, 1870. Two months later, authorities dynamited the old foundation into rubble, which vanished in 1980 during a storm. Climbing 268 steps of the circular stair from the first level to the service room, watch room, and gallery to the lantern, keeper Zion B. Jennett or his assistant, Nasa S. Williams, hand-cranked the clockwork gears, which rotated weights that descended through wells in the floor at each level. The man on duty then ignited the signal, which a metal door shielded from gusts that might extinguish the flame during its dusk-to-dawn service. Despite mosquitoes, bouts of malaria, and limited rations, the keeper retained the job, which paid him $1.50 per day for round-the-clock service requiring upkeep, painting to protect ironwork from salt corrosion, and regular cleaning of sea-spray from reflectors and glass mounted along the upper balcony. Augmenting the tower's effectiveness was a lifesaving operation staffed by an athletic crew capable of boating and swimming in pounding surf.

The new lighthouse underwent seasons of change and challenge. In its third year of service, the workers created a unique barber pole striping consisting of four spirals of black on white to make the vertical surface more visible against the stark white of sandy beach. Increasing safety precautions demanded a second lightship, called *Diamond*, which the Lighthouse Service anchored securely to the seafloor. In 1874, the U.S. Signal Corps chose the island site as a weather station, which increased early warnings of approaching storm fronts. Despite these upgrades and staffing, 98 of the 134 crewmen aboard the 1,020-ton screw steamer U.S.S. *Huron* drowned on November 24, 1877, after running aground in thick fog on the way down the Carolina coast to Havana, Cuba.

Mishaps and challenges continued to plague Hatteras. In 1879, the tower sustained a direct hit by a lightning bolt. On December 22, 1884, during a killer storm, the resident life-saving crew spotted a distressed ship, the barkentine *Ephraim Williams*, bound from Savannah, Georgia, to Providence, Rhode Island, with a load of pine lumber. The shore patrol dispatched chiefs Benjamin B. Dailey and Patrick H. Etheridge and five oarsmen aboard a dory to save the nine-man crew. The rescuers earned gold medals for duty and valor. On August 31, 1886, the light station weathered an earthquake emanating from Charleston, South Carolina. To provide additional shore safety, in 1905, the Coast Guard positioned a new lightship, *Diamond Shoals No. 71*, equipped with a twelve-inch steam chime whistle and hand-operated half-ton bell, which replaced the whistling buoy anchored off the outer shoals in the 1880s.

Although shifts in the shape and width of the Outer Banks whittled away at Cape Hatteras, the lighthouse remained an essential to coastal safety. The Lighthouse Service rendered the lighthead more effective after installation of an incandescent oil vapor lamp on July 1, 1912, which boosted visibility by 66 percent. In 1918, submariners of the German navy sank the lightship *Diamond Shoals No. 71* after an attendant radioed by wireless the position of the U-boat U-104. Lightship Captain Walter Barnett and his men rowed a lifeboat safely some twelve miles to shore. In 1919, coastal erosion placed the lighthouse 1,000 feet closer to the waves; sixteen years later, after the tower's electrification, it stood only 100 feet from the high water mark, where surf lapped at the station's foundation. Ironically, the tower was more brilliant than ever, yet faced certain doom as the Atlantic chewed into the coastline.

On May 15, 1936, Captain Unaka Benjamin Jennette, one of a family of twelve lightkeepers and the last custodian of the Cape Hatteras Lighthouse, extinguished its final flame, which he and his wife, Sudie Scarborough Jennette, began tending on March 16, 1919. From 1936 to 1950, coastal authorities abandoned the brick tower to the National Park Service, resituated the beacon a mile inland to a steel tower at Buxton Woods, and installed a new 90,000 candlepower lighting system that ended the keeper's twice-daily hand winding of the gear system. The historic old tower gave valiant service to the Coast Guard as a lookout post for German U-boats, but, after the war, it met new challenges from neglect and vandalism.

By the middle of the twentieth century, when supervision of navigational devices passed to the Coast Guard, the National Park Service took charge of the Hatteras tower and its historic grounds. Following an outcry over the loss of the yacht *Nautilus* in November 1946, the Coast Guard returned the light to its original position with manpower from the Civilian Conservation Corps. Engineers installed the current 36-inch rotating duplex beacon, which circles every fifteen seconds to broadcast a radio signal and 800,000 candlepower beam over twenty miles to sea. In 1966, the spreading of 312,000 cubic yards of sand proved futile in a massive effort to replenish the eroding beach. A year later, authorities improved shore safety by removing the third off-shore lightship *Diamond* and erecting a steel "Texas" tower modeled on the flat offshore oil drilling platform. Located nine nautical miles southeast of the shore in 54 feet of water, the platform supports a computer-automated surveillance system, lights, foghorn, and radio beacon. To preserve the revered Hatteras light, in 1969, the U.S. Navy installed three concrete groins or sea walls to stabilize the beach.

Still valued for its protection of the Outer Banks, the Hatteras light continued to change with advancing technology. In 1972, electrical engineers replaced the station's earlier electric light with a revolving double 24-inch-diameter aerobeacon holding two 1,000-watt lamps, each capable of 800,000 candlepower. A photoelectric cell operated the beacon, which flashed white every 7.5 seconds to be visible for nineteen nautical miles or, under optimum conditions, over fifty miles out to sea. For all its technological advancement, the lighthouse reached a crisis point in 1980, when U.S. Senator Jesse Helms and North Carolina Governor Jim Hunt formed Save the Lighthouse Committee to study erosion. The next year, installation of the first of 5,000 branching tubes filled with gravel linked the beach to an offshore sandbar, but state officials took no chances. On the advice of a consortium of 200 architects, marine geologists, and construction engineers, officials began pressing for the repositioning of the tower farther inland, after it shed a fifty-pound chunk of its upper structure in 1984. By the mid–1980s, Hatteras became even more crucial to local people after the installation of Doppler radar at the weather station, which engineers examined for additional structural faults. A two-year scientific study determined the impact of wind and solar radiation on the future preservation of the lighthouse.

After Hurricane Emily on August 27, 1993, danger returned as high winds and seas ripped the off-shore warning device from its anchor. The Atlantic Ocean surged to within 200 feet of the lighthouse and moved another fifty feet inland within two years. The public demanded one of two options — to move the lighthouse away from the sea before the next tropical storm toppled it or to pad the shoreline with more artificial groins. In 1994, after Hurricane Gordon battered the coast and shortened the dune line, friends of the Carolina shores formed the Outer Banks Lighthouse Society to preserve beacons and to aid the National Park Service in securing buildings, artifacts, and records. On advice from the research council of the National Academy of Sciences, the National Park Service chose to relocate the tower.

Five years later, under advisement from President Bill Clinton and against the wishes of many Hatteras residents, Congress arranged to reposition the lighthouse 2,900 feet inland to escape the threat of collapse. The move to a safer site 1,600 feet from the shoreline began on June 13 and cost $11.8 million. The International Chimney Company of Buffalo, New York, set the first of seven roll beams under the structure to serve as wheels. Forced by hydraulic push jacks over crushed stone compacted into the sand, the lighthouse began inching westward four days later while sensors monitored shifts in alignment. On July 9, the tower slid safely onto a new foundation, exciting cheers from tourists, patriots, and officials who watched a treasured piece of Americana preserved for future generations. To celebrate the move, late in 2001, the Outer Banks Lighthouse Society published oral histories of the building and joined the National Park Service in sponsoring a rededication ceremony and a Hatteras Keepers Descendants Homecoming for 1,200 scions of the beacon's 38 former keepers.

Legends

Amid the lengthy history of Hatteras lie a number of pirate and ghost stories. One story relates the actions of Hatteras Jack, an albino bottlenose dolphin. In 1790, when Hatteras Inlet challenged navigators with its perilous shifting sandbars, Jack swam across the true channel, leading ship captains safely to deep waters. To call up their snow-white pilot, crew tooted foghorns. Jack emerged and, when the tide reached the full, led the way through the passage. He took time to entertain his audience by rolling and cavorting at the surface. He eventually disappeared from the region.

According to a more perplexing story, "The Ghost Ship of Diamond Shoals," on a calm dawn on January 29, 1921, a coast guard patrol at the cape sighted the *Carroll M. Deering*, a 250-foot, five-masted schooner, fully rigged with its prow grounded on a sandbar. On the return voyage of a Portland, Maine-to-Rio de Janeiro coal delivery, twenty days earlier, it had received supplies at Barbados without incident. At Hatteras, a Coast Guard boarding party found no distress signals, none of the eleven-man crew, and two lifeboats missing. Except for the ship's gray cat, there were no living beings. The bunkroom was neat and the mess laid out for a meal, which awaited service from kettles and a coffee urn on the stove.

Investigators listed as missing personal belongings of the crew, anchors, naval papers, chronometer and clock, log, and navigating instruments. Coastal authorities learned nothing more about the ship's abandonment or the crew's whereabouts. After authorities explored the *Carroll M. Deering*, the sea swept away its remains on March 4. Rumors and theories of piracy, rum-running, mutiny and murder, and a Bolshevik plot circulated with little support. On September 19, 1955, Hurricane Ione dumped the remains of the ghost schooner on Hatteras Island.

Coastal Activities

In addition to a colorful history and folklore, Hatteras Beach hosts some of the world's most varied activities — swimming, windsurfing, kitesurfing, sailing, cycling, camping, boating, shelling, birding, freshwater fishing, and saltwater surfcasting.

Standing guard over seasonal activities is the Hatteras Lighthouse, one of America's most photogenic and most painted and sculpted spots. It was named a national landmark in 1998. The National Park Service equipped the new site with access roads, parking lots, walkways, restrooms, and information areas. History buffs visit a museum in the double keeper's house to view artifacts of the U.S. Life Saving Service.

Most visitors admire the nearby monument to the first airplane flight, completed by Orville and Wilbur Wright at Kitty Hawk on December 17, 1903. The North Carolina First Flight Centennial Commission spent eight years and $6 million celebrating the state's role in the founding of aviation. Aiding the state were the First Flight Society, corporate sponsors, NASA, the National Park Service, and the U.S. Army and Air Force. To pay homage to the Wright brothers, the state launched a re-enactment of the first of their four maiden flights at 10:35 A.M. on December 17, 2003. The gala event included flyovers and display of a reproduction of the original muslin-covered plane, the Flyer.

In 2004, the Hatteras Museum mounted an exhibit of the sinking of the U.S.S. *Monitor*, the Union navy's first turreted ironclad vessel, which cost $275,000 in 1861. The *Monitor* went down twenty miles off Hatteras Point the night of December 29–30, 1862, after the Confederate ironclad *Virginia* rammed it. The low-slung ship, designed by Swedish-American inventor John Ericsson and dubbed "Abe's secret weapon," was on its way to Beaufort, North Carolina. Sixteen crewmen drowned; the tow ship U.S.S. *Rhode Island* saved 41 others. The next day, a storm plunged the *Monitor* 230 feet to the bottom.

The *Monitor*'s remains, a National Historic Landmark, came to light on March 8, 1974, about sixteen miles south of Hatteras. A Duke University dive team aboard the research vessel *Eastward*, armed with camera, television, and computer equipment, located the wreckage after months of searching. A year later, the National Oceanic and Atmospheric Administration (NOAA) oversaw plans for retrieving and preserving the propeller and shaft and the side-lever steam engine. The NOAA declared a square nautical mile surrounding the wreckage the nation's first National Marine Sanctuary.

SOURCES

Allegood, Jerry, "A Beacon for the Curious," *Raleigh News & Observer*, June 17, 1999.

Betts, Jack, "What Happened to Ghost Ship of Diamond Shoals?," *Charlotte Observer*, September 30, 2002.

Bond, Constance, "A Fury from Hell or Was He?," *Smithsonian*, February 2000, p. 62.

Bordsen, John, "Prowling with Pirates," *Charlotte Observer*, August 12, 2001, pp. 1G, 8G.

Broad, William, "Archaeologists Revise Portrait of Buccaneers as Monsters," *New York Times*, March 11, 1997, pp. C1, C9.

Butler, Lindley S., "Blackbeard's Revenge," *American History*, August 2000, p. 18.

"The Cape Hatteras Lightstation," http://www.nps.gov/caha/capelight.htm.

"Cape Hatteras National Seashore and Its Lighthouse," http://www.hatterashi.com/Cape-HatterasSeaShore.html.

Carr, Dawson. *The Cape Hatteras Lighthouse, Sentinel of the Shoals.* Chapel Hill: University of North Carolina Press, 1991.

Clancy, Paul, "The Monitor Mission," *Virginian-Pilot*, July 23, 2002.

"Clues Pointing Toward Ship As Blackbeard's Researchers '95 Percent Certain,'" *Washington Daily News*, October 30, 1997.

Cordingly, David. *Under the Black Flag.* San Diego, Calif.: Harvest Books, 1995.

DeBlieu, Jan, "The Taking of the Hatteras Light," *Southern Cultures*, Vol. 7, No. 3, 2001, pp. 8–26.

"Diamond Shoals Lightship LS-105," *Outer Banks Lighthouse Society Journal*, Winter 1997.

Dollar, C. D., "A Diamond in the Rough," *New Bay Times*, Vol. VII, No. 44, November 4–10, 1999.

Eschelman, Ralph, "Cape Hatteras Light Station," http://www.cr.nps.gov/maritime/nhl/capehatt.htm, 1998.

Freeling, Bill, "Hatteras Museum Director Hopes to Exhibit U.S.S. *Monitor* Artifacts," *Sentinel*, July 2, 2002.

Gosner, Kenneth L. *Field Guide to the Atlantic Seashore.* Boston: Houghton Mifflin, 1979.

Herndon, G. Melvin, "The 1806 Survey of the North Carolina Coast, Cape Hatteras to Cape Fear," *North Carolina Historical Review*, Vol. 49, No. 3, 1972, pp. 242–253.

Lawson, John. *A New Voyage to Carolina.* Chapel Hill: University of North Carolina Press, 1967.

Lee, Robert E. *Blackbeard the Pirate.* Winston-Salem, N.C.: John F. Blair, 1974.

"The Lost Light," *Lighthouse Digest*, October 2002.

Marden, Luis, "Search for the *Monitor*," *Historic Preservation*, Vol. 38, No. 4, 1986, pp. 32–37.

McCleary, J. R., "*Monitor's* Secrets Revealed?," *Nautical Research Journal*, Vol. 43, No. 3, 1998, pp. 139–142.

Mook, Maurice A., "Algonquian Ethnohistory of the Carolina Sound," *Journal of the Washington Academy of Sciences*, Vol. 34, No. 6, June 15, 1944, pp. 181–196, 213–228.

Moss, Bennett R., "Chicamacomico Races," *Ramparts*, Fall 1996.

Musicant, Ivan, "Hot Pursuit up the Sounds," *Proceedings, U.S. Naval Institute*, Vol. 122, No. 10, 1996, pp. 68–72.

Patterson, Donald W., "America's Lighthouse," *News-Record*, http://www. news-record.com/news/indepth/lighthouse/main.shtml#top, 1999.

Phillips, Angus, "Tall Order: Cape Hatteras Lighthouse Makes Tracks," *National Geographic*, Vol. 197, No. 5, May 2000, pp. 98–105.

Pleasant, Paul, "Cape Hatteras Light," *State*, August 15, 1966, pp. 9–10.

Redfearn, D. H., "The Steamboat *Home*," *Florida Law Journal*, Vol. IX, No. 5, May, 1935.

Shelton-Roberts, Cheryl, "Our Time Is Running Out," *Raleigh News & Observer*, February 15, 1998.

Shier, Maynard J., "Hatteras Inlet: The First Revenge," *Civil War Times*, Vol. 17, No. 7, 1978, pp. 4–11, 44–47.

Sizemore, Bill, and Catherine Kozak, "Flight Centennial Budget Takes Dive," *Charlotte Observer*, October 13, 2002, pp. 1A–10A.

Slaton, Deborah, et al., "Cape Hatteras Lighthouse: Diagnostics," *APT Bulletin*, Vol. 19, No. 2, 1987, pp. 52–60.

"Tar Heel Tales," *Trailblazer*, October 1999.

Williamson, David, "Cape Hatteras Lighthouse, 'Sentinel of the Shoals,' Saved Countless Seafarers, Reflects Nation's History," *UNC-CH News Services*, September 8, 2000.

Yocum, Thomas, et al. *Cape Hatteras, America's Lighthouse.* Nashville, Tenn.: Cumberland House, 1999.

Zeller, Bob, "Diving into History," *Civil War Times,* Vol. 39, No. 7, 2001, pp. 54–58, 60–61.

Capernaum, Israel

Location

Shadowed by the rugged hill country of northern Israel, Capernaum (also called Kefar Nahum or Capharnaum) is a ruined Palestinian town on the north central shore of the Sea of Galilee. The huge landlocked body of water lies three miles southwest of its nexus with the Jordan River. Israel's largest freshwater lake, at 700 feet below sea level, is fed by the Jordan River. The sea, which is also called Lake Kinneret (or Chinneroth), Lake Gennesaret, or Lake Tiberias, was the domain of the Roman-appointed governor Herod Antipas, who named it for the Emperor Tiberias. It supplies one third of Israel's drinking water and has traditionally nurtured the region's farming industries and rich fishing grounds. Along its coast, the border settlement of Capernaum marked the end of the tetrarchy of Herod Antipas and the beginning of the tetrarch Philip's domain. At one time, the community's prosperous harbor extended for a half mile. Today, the area contains scenic countryside, accessible beaches, and archeologically significant remains of bible times.

Contacts

Fr. Stanislao Loffreda
Studium Biblicum Franciscanum
Via Dolorosa
P. O. Box 19424
91193 Jerusalem, Israel
Phone: 972-2-6282936
    972-2-6280271
    972-2-6264516
Fax: 972-2-6264519
Email: sbfnet@netvision.net
http://www.christusrex.org/www1/ofm/sites
    /TScpmain.html

Associates for Biblical Research
P. O. Box 356
Landisville, Pennsylvania 17538
Phone: 800-430-0008
Fax: 717-892-3049
Email: ABRofc@aol.com
http://christiananswers.net/forms/abr-support.html

History

Capernaum — called Kapharnaoum by Greeks, Kfar Nahum [Nahum's village] by Jews, and Talhum or Tel Num by Arabs — lay in Upper Galilee within the kingdom of Naphtali, one of the twelve tribes of Israel. The site was occupied sporadically from 2,000 B.C., when formerly nomadic desert tribes first began to form villages. By 400 B.C., because of its strategic location on the Sea of Galilee, Capernaum entered a millennium of continuous occupation and growth.

Around 100 B.C., the multicultural settlement of Capernaum took shape with stone pavement, quays, and reinforced walls. The town arose in a sparsely populated area watered by moderate rainfall and ample springs. Evergreen oaks and cypress flourished and farmers raised dates, dyestuffs, figs, flax, grain, olives, pomegranates, walnuts, and vineyards. Along stony coastlines at historic fisheries, shore laborers set up salting sheds and warehouses to hold dried fruit and fish and other exportable goods.

The early town developed an artisanal class and produced domestic and agricultural implements from volcanic basalt. Left as proof of industry were flour mills, glass vessels, grinding wheels, lamps, mortars and pestles, olive presses, ovens, and stone bowls. The region became a trade center along an artery serving Golan, Syria,

Phoenicia, Mesopotamia, and Cyprus. According to foreign coins and imported vessels found in archeological digs, as Rome's hegemony spread over the Middle East, Capernaum also served as a government center and the locus of a Roman garrison superintended by a centurion.

Around A.D. 28, the fishing village attracted Jesus, then a young Hebrew evangelist. As the Old Testament prophet Isaiah predicted, Jesus abandoned his hometown of Nazareth after its citizens rejected him. On the journey twenty miles northeast to Capernaum, he may have taken his mother and brother James with him. Jesus lodged at the home of the strong-willed apostle Simon Peter, who had left his birthplace at Bethsaida a few miles to the east, apparently after marrying a woman from Capernaum. Matthew 9:1 reports that the fishing village became a second home to Jesus during his

adult years after Peter apparently made him a semi-permanent houseguest. Peter also shared the sizeable dwelling with his brother Andrew and with Peter's mother-in-law, whom, according to Luke 4:38–39, Jesus rid of a high fever.

Working out of his new headquarters, Jesus recruited Capernaum fishermen for the first apostles and, on the sabbath, scandalized pious Pharisees by healing a mentally ill man at the synagogue, a worship center that also served as school, law court, and common gathering place. As Jesus's ministry drew believers, Peter's one-story house developed into an *ecclesia-domus* [church-house]. In this evolving religious center, Jesus healed a leper, delivered teaching parables, and preached in the courtyard. In a nearby room, according to the second chapter of Mark's gospel, four men lowered a paralyzed man through the roof for Jesus to heal.

Shadowed by the rugged hill country of northern Israel, Capernaum is a ruined Palestinian town on the north central shore of the Sea of Galilee (courtesy of Todd Bolen).

At the beach with its 2,500-foot promenade and eight-foot seawall, Zebedee owned a profitable boat-building shop, where his sons James and John, called "the sons of thunder," earned their living (Mark 3:17). According to the Gospels, some of Jesus's other disciples also resided there and fished from the shore at one of twelve fishing anchorages along the oval coast. While associating with the amiable fishermen at Capernaum, Jesus met Matthew, one of several despised tax collectors for the Romans, and called him to join the apostles. The opening chapter of Matthew's gospel, composed around A.D. 80, recognized Jesus as Jewish royalty. The text provided much of the biography of Jesus along with sermons and sayings, notably, the Sermon on the Mount, the core of Christian beliefs.

For good reason, Galilee is called the cradle of the gospel. Jesus evangelized nearby Chorazin and prayed alone in the hills above Capernaum. He made full use of the seashore as a place to plan evangelical strategy, as a getaway from oppressive crowds expecting miracles, as a retreat to be among his apostles in private, and as a source of the group's income from some eighteen species of fish, including carp, catfish, musht, perch, and sardines. The apostles spent daylight hours on Capernaum's shore sleeping, repairing their boats, and mending nets. At nightfall, with the wind abated, they seined the evening catch, which they pulled in by drag net, hand-cast net, or more complicated trammel net, composed of interconnected layers of netting. At daylight, they sorted the catch into baskets for sale or for salting and drying to trade throughout the Roman Empire as far west as Hispania.

The contrast with Nazareth, Jesus's isolated family home, explains his reasons for relocating: Capernaum was prosperous and far enough away from Herod's nerve center at Tiberias to allow Jesus some latitude in his ministry and to encourage the enlistment of worthy followers from the town's working class. To the northwest, the Mount of Beatitudes is the traditional site of the Sermon on the Mount. As detailed in John 21:4–23, in the sea opposite Capernaum and Tabghe, Peter communed with the risen Jesus, who appeared in the flesh after his crucifixion and burial. With his former conviviality, he built a charcoal fire on the shore to cook fish and bake bread and served the disciples with humility and true affection.

Because of the importance of a shore ministry to Jesus, the New Testament gospels contain numerous coastal metaphors, notably, Jesus's offer to make his followers "fishers of men" (Matthew 4:19, Mark 1:17). At the shore, Jesus spoke the agrarian parables of the mustard seed, the sower, and the wheat and weeds, then turned to the roiling waters and calmed a gale with a simple command, "Peace, be still" (Mark 4:39). He continued on his way in the next chapter, healing the sick on the far shore and reviving a dead girl, as Mark describes in Chapter 5. From Capernaum, Jesus sent his followers out to preach and heal. As he anticipated, their efforts established the Christian faith, yet he denounced the town itself for its disinterest in his teachings.

In contrast to Jesus's annoyance with Capernaum, the historian Josephus found much to admire at the fishing coast. In Book III of *Wars of the Jews* (A.D. 76), he remarked on the sweetness of the waters of Galilee and marveled at the fruitful soil, which produced a number of types of trees. After listing fruits and nuts grown for profit, he concluded:

> One may call this place the ambition of nature, where it forces those plants that are naturally enemies to one another to agree together: It is a happy contention of the seasons, as if every one of them laid claim to this country [Josephus, 1960, p. 520].

He added that both air and water produced the climate that nurtured that fertility of the land.

A subsequent travelogue, written by

the Spanish nun Egeria in the early A.D. 360s , moves directly to architecture and the historic significance of St. Peter's home, the adjacent synagogue, shore sites where Jesus stood, his speech at the Mount of the Beatitudes, and the miracles that restored health to the sick. In this same period, according to the writings of Epiphanius of Salamis, the bishop of Cyprus in A.D. 367 and author of the *Panarion* [Medicine Chest] (A.D. 377), from the first century to the fourth, Christianized Jews inhabited the formerly Jewish town of Capernaum and welcomed Gentile pilgrims, who got the same thrill of place that excited Egeria. One religious icon is a stone carving of the wheeled Ark of the Covenant that King David brought overland to Jerusalem. An antique Roman milestone dating to the era of the Emperor Hadrian establishes the influence of Rome during the second century A.D.

Capernaum's role in the Roman Empire remained amicable. The Romans allowed the city to stand because its citizens did not join in the Jewish uprising against the Roman Empire. Ruins of a fourth-century pillared synagogue of white limestone rose over a former house of worship made of black basalt that St. Luke credits to a generous centurion. An Aramaic inscription identifies Halfu, son of Zebida, as the donor. The original site was probably the place where Jesus worshipped and preached.

The town of Capernaum remained vibrant until the Islamic conquest after 650 forced its abandonment. Rapidly, Muslim insurgents ousted Jews and Christians. Some Arabs of the Semekiyeh tribe continued to live in tents and hovels built on the site, which Bedouins and citizens of Tiberias plundered. An earthquake in 746 further blurred outlines of the town. In 1333, Jewish travel writer Isaac (or Ishak) Chelo indicated that people had not lost their interest in the biblical town. In 1537, travel commentator Uri of Biel referred to the place as Tanhum, burial place of Rabbi Tan-

hum, a revered biblical scholar. Bedouin residents altered pronunciation to Talhum, which travel journalist Michel Nau named in *Voyage Nouveau de la Terre-Sainte* [A New Journey to the Holy Land] (1668). Archeologists altered the site name further to Tell Hum.

Much neglected, Capernaum began to take shape once more in the nineteenth century. In 1894, Giuseppe Baldi of Naples purchased the synagogue and most of the ruins from local Bedouins for the Franciscan Custody of the Holy Land, a Christian reclamation effort that began in 1217 at the beginning of the Fifth Crusade. To the east side of Capernaum, the rest of the archeological site became the property of Greek-Orthodox patriarchs, who erected a church. The Arab-Israeli war of 1948 ended all local habitation of Capernaum, which became an historic relic and shrine for religious pilgrims.

Archeology

When scholars began exploring Capernaum, they found devastation topped by centuries of accumulated soil and undergrowth. In 1738, Anglican bishop Richard Pococke of Southampton, England, author of the multi-volume *A Description of the East and Some Other Countries* (1743), traveled the Holy Land and misidentified the remains of the town as Bethsaida. In 1838, Dr. Edward Robinson, a Connecticut-born biblical geographer from Union College in New York and compiler of *A Dictionary of the Holy Bible* (1833), rediscovered Capernaum and described complete desolation. Along the Sea of Galilee, he found remains of a once-elegant building that was erected on a raised platform and adorned with elaborate lintels, cornices, and capitals. The edifice turned out to be a synagogue built atop the original place where Jesus taught and included a central prayer hall with benches, foundations of bimahs [pulpits], and a niche for Torah scrolls. The site included a courtyard, porch, and a side chamber of unknown purpose.

Some 28 years later, during the Ordnance Survey of Jerusalem, Sir Charles William Wilson, an English archeologist, cartographer, and explorer, mapped Capernaum and identified two tombs. In the three-book *Description Geographique, Historique, et Archeologique de la Palestine Accompagnée de Cartes Detaillees* [Geographical, Historical, and Archeological Description of Palestine with Detailed Maps] (1868) and *La Terre Sainte* [The Holy Land] (1884), Victor Guérin, a French explorer and travel writer, remarked on the seriousness of the site's decline. Vandalism and neglect ended in 1894 after Franciscan friars bought the synagogue and most of Capernaum's remains and fenced it in.

In 1905, the Franciscans licensed archeologists Heinrich Kohl and Carl Watzinger to excavate Capernaum for the Deutsche Orient-Gesellschaft to ascertain that the site was the biblical fishing village where Jesus lived. A meticulous reclamation, led by Franciscan architect Wendelin von Menden, required a decade for the cleaning of the original worship center and excavation of the town radiating from the synagogue. The project concluded with a preliminary dig at the eight-sided church to the south, which Gentiles built over Peter's house to establish their cultural presence after they outnumbered the original Jewish inhabitants.

As a result of careful analysis and restoration of the synagogue in 1921 by Franciscan archeologist Gaudentius Orfali of Nazareth, head of the Palestine Oriental Society, historians and religious seekers acknowledged the historicity of Capernaum. They identified the town as a trading center on the Via Maris, the Beth-Shan-to-Damascus highway, from the second century B.C. It also served as a customs checkpoint, a collection site for temple taxes and for Roman levies on fishing and caravans, and a focus of New Testament lore from the first century A.D. When Orfali died in 1926, the excavation of Capernaum ceased for over four decades.

A nineteen-year examination of Capernaum began in 1968 under the direction of Virgilio C. Corbo, a Franciscan archeologist and professor of archaeology at the Studium Biblicum Franciscanum, and of Stanislao Loffreda, author of *A Visit to Capharnaum* (1972) and *Capharnaum: The Town of Jesus* (1985). In addition to studying the limestone synagogue and octagonal church, the new team began uncovering the plan of the town and located Peter's house, identified by symbols and graffiti honoring both Jesus and Peter. In 1969, Corbo and Loffreda located the basalt synagogue built by the centurion in the first century A.D. under the foundations of the fourth-century synagogue. The disclosures drew throngs of historians and pilgrims to the Sea of Galilee's north shore.

In 1978, archeologist Vassilios Tzaferis, director of the Israel Antiquities Authority and author of *Excavations at Capernaum* (1989), began a four-year dig at Capernaum and concluded that Jesus wisely chose the town for his ministry. Tzaferis focused on a site dating to the Muslim conquest of the mid-seventh century A.D., when Capernaum was abandoned. Based on graffiti, a coin hoard of gold dinars, late Byzantine and early Umayyad dynasty pot shards, and ceramic oil lamps, he established the existence of an early Muslim village now owned by the Greek Orthodox Patriarchate of Jerusalem.

Coastal Activities

Visitors to Capernaum bike around the shores, trek inland for hiking and camping, cross the water by ferry, sail, ride horseback, and photograph archeological digs. The devout journey to the Jordan River to be baptized in the waters in which John the Baptist immersed repentant Jews and his cousin Jesus. Near the end of 1999, promoters of tourism drew additional trade to Capernaum and Bethsaida by building a "walk on water" exhibition, based on a biblical incident recorded in Matthew 14: 25–33 when Jesus walked on the sea. The subsurface platform allowed pilgrims to amble along the Sea of Galilee as the Gospels claimed that Peter did when Jesus called to him.

Religious pilgrims worship at a modern church, designed by Italian architect Ildo Avetta, which commemorates the coastal motif of fish, waves, and nets. Congregants walk from Capernaum toward Tabghe (or Tabgha) a mile to the west to see the Church of the Bread and Fishes, a structure erected on the rock where Jesus offered two fish and five loaves to feed 5,000 pilgrims, as described in all four gospels — Matthew 14, Mark 6, Luke 9, and John 6. A Byzantine mosaic of loaves and fish covers a fourth-century foundation. Another site built on a rock, the Church of the Primacy of St. Peter, constructed of black basalt by Franciscan friars in 1933, honors the place where Jesus chose Peter as leader of a growing religious phenomenon.

SOURCES

"Ancient 'Bone Box' May Be Earliest Link to Jesus," *Christian Science Monitor*, October 21, 2002.

Belt, Don, "Israel's Galilee: Living in the Shadow of Peace," *National Geographic*, June 1995, pp. 62–87.

Burge, Gary M., "Fishers of Fish," *Christian History*, Vol. 17, No. 3, 1998, pp. 36–37.

"Capharnaum, the Town of Jesus," http://198.62.75.1/www1/ofm/sites/TScpmenu.html.

Cleave, Richard, "Satellite Revelations: New Views of the Holy Land," *National Geographic*, June 1995, pp. 88–105.

Davidson, Linda Kay, and David M. Gitlitz. *Pilgrimage: From the Ganges to Graceland*. Santa Barbara, Calif.: ABC-Clio, 2002.

"Did You Know?," *Christian History*, Vol. 17, No. 3, 1998, pp. 2–3.

Feizkhah, Elizabeth, "Traveler's Advisory," *Time International*, Vol. 153, No. 20, May 24, 1999, p. 6.

Ford, Peter, "Past Speaks to Present in Galilee," *Christian Science Monitor*, December 23, 1991, p. 14.

Hanson, K. C., "The Galilean Fishing Economy and the Jesus Tradition," *Biblical Theology Bulletin*, Vol. 27, 1997.

Hewitt, Marsha Aileen, "Archaeology and the Galilean Jesus: A Re-Examination of the Evidence," *Anglican Theological Review*, Vol. 63, No. 2, April 1, 2002, pp. 421–422.

"Jesus in Capernaum," *Manila Bulletin*, January 6, 2002.

Josephus. *Complete Works*. Grand Rapids, Mich.: Kregel Publications, 1960.

Kraebel, A. Thomas, "Sacred Realm: The Emergence of the Synagogue in the Ancient World," *Biblical Archaeology Review*, Vol. 23, No. 5, September/October 1997, pp. 72, 74.

Liddon, Henry Parry. *Life of Edward Bouverie Pusey*. London: Longmans, 1894.

Magness, Jodi, "The Chronology of Capernaum in the Early Islamic Period," *Journal of the American Oriental Society*, July–September 1997, pp. 481–486.

Matthey, Jacques, "Pilgrims, Seekers, and Disciples," *International Review of Mission*, Vol. 91, No. 360, January 1, 2002, pp. 120–134.

Neff, David, "Listening to the Fifth Gospel," *Christianity Today*, October 22, 1990, pp. 38–39.

"New Harbor for the Galilee Boat," *Biblical Archaeology Review*, Vol. 26, No. 3, May–June 2000, p. 16.

Nun, Mendel, "Ports of Galilee," *Biblical Archaeology*, Vol. 25, No. 4, July–August 1999, pp. 18–31, 64.

Okoye, James C., "Jesus in the Synagogue of Capernaum," *Catholic Biblical Quarterly*, Vol. 63, No. 2, April 1, 2001, pp. 343–344.

"Packaged Pilgrimages," *TravelAge West*, October 7, 2002, p. 43.

"Ports of Galilee," *Biblical Archaeology Review*, Vol. 25, No. 4, July–August 1999, pp. 18–31.

Price, Ira Maurice. *The Monuments and the Old Testament*. Philadelphia: Judson Press, 1925.

Pritchard, James B., ed. *Everyday Life in Bible Times*. Washington, D. C.: National Geographic, 1967.

"Risks and Rewards," *Newsweek*, February 25, 2002, pp. 51–52.

Rogerson, John. *Atlas of the Bible*. New York: Facts on File, 1985.

Romey, Kristin M., "Ship Ahoist," *Archaeology*, Vol. 53, No. 3, May–June 2000, p. 20.

"2,000-year-old Galilee Boat Emerges Anew," *National Geographic*, Vol. 189, No. 4, April 1996, p. 1.

Vinson, Richard B., "Jesus and the Village Scribes," *Interpretation*, Vol. 56, No. 3, July 1, 2002, p. 336.

Wright, G. Ernest, ed. *Great People of the Bible and How They Lived*. Pleasantville, N. Y.: Reader's Digest Association, 1979.

Chersonese, Ukraine

Location

The Chersonese (also Chersonesos or Khersonese) is a Ukrainian suburb two miles south of Sevastopol. Named for the Greek for "peninsula," the area is a windswept Slavic toe jutting from the southwestern Crimea westward into the Black Sea. The rocky, unarable spit of 1,500 acres is currently called the Heraklean Peninsula.

Valued as the world's best preserved and longest-lived ancient colony, the Chersonese flourished from the fifth century B.C. to the fourteenth century A.D. The region's coastal archeological dig houses some 100 registered historic sites, including burial grounds, an ancient sixty-acre *chora* [farmland] with vineyards and stone farmsteads, ruins of a Hellenistic mint with smelting furnaces and foundry, thermal baths, and the region's only Greek theater. The most valuable site of the Black Sea shores, the Chersonese contains a sixth-century A.D. Christian church once adorned with a mosaic floor, some of which survives. Atop the nave of the original structure, Christians built again four centuries later.

Contacts

The National Preserve of Tauric Chersonesos
Drevnyaya Street, One
Sevastopol 99045
Crimea, Ukraine
Phone: 38-0692-55-02-78
38-0692-24-13-01
38-0692-23-15-61
Fax: 38-0692-55-02-78
Email: info@chersonesos.org

Institute of Classical Archaeology
University of Texas at Austin
Department of Classics
WAG 123
Austin, Texas 78712
Phone: 1-512-471-0340
Fax: 1-512-471-5681
Email: asele@mail.utexas.edu

History

Details on the Chersonese derive from a second-hand account by Strabo, the Greek geographer and historian who flourished around the beginning of the first century A.D., and from Arrian, the Bithynian philosopher and historian of the early second century A.D. In their descriptions, the Crimean promontory was the ancestral home of the Taurians, a warlike tribe who lived in the neighboring mountains from 2000 B.C. In 422 B.C., during the Peloponnesian War, Dorian colonists from Herakleia Pontica (modern Eregli, Turkey) settled the city of Chersonesos with the aid of the banished islanders from the holy isle of Delos in the Greek Cyclades. (*See also* DELOS.) When the Roman encyclopedist Pliny the Elder wrote about the settlement in *Natural History* (A.D. 77), he used the name Megarika to refer to an early stage of development, then switched to Heraklea Chersonesos, the more familiar place name. As described in the *Periplous* (ca. 350 B.C.) of Pseudo-Skilakes, a Carian historian, and corroborated by coin finds, the location of the promontory proved fortuitous for Greek newcomers, who prospered from the Black Sea trade with mainland Greece in grain, gold, and slaves.

A century later, in addition to maritime trade, the colonists of the Chersonese

The world's best preserved and longest-lived ancient colony, the Chersonese is the most valuable site of the Black Sea shores (courtesy of Glenn Mack).

extended their holdings into the grain fields to the west and built an extensive agrarian economy, but conducted little trade with the Taurian and Scythian mountaineers to the north. In 336 B.C., the erection of temples to the *Parthenos* [maiden] and of a stone theater spread Hellenism to the Greek-speaking colony. The theater survived, but worship centers disappeared over time. Under a decree from Gaius Julius Caesar, in 46 B.C., the city gained internal freedom to establish institutions and courts, codify laws, mint coins, and levy taxes and duties. Crafts and manufacturing flourished, notably, roof tiles, metalwork, red-lacquered and glazed pottery, glassware, wine, and a coast-based fishing industry in the Cimmerian Bosporus supported by salt cisterns and packing sites.

During the rise of the Roman Empire and the suppression of Mithradates VI Eupator, king of Pontus in Anatolia, the Chersonese continued to prosper under the La-tinized name Chersonessus or Chersonesus Tauricus. In A.D. 140, a Roman intelligence-gathering garrison quartered at a citadel on the promontory at the periphery of the Empire. The outpost also served Rome as a place to banish criminals. The original Greek theater provided an arena for gladiatorial events that remained popular into A.D. 259.

Christianity had a profound impact on local architecture. In the A.D. 300s, when Chersonesos was renamed Cherson (or Korsun), Christian missionaries spread the new faith. By 527, Justinian I annexed the city to the Byzantine empire and permanently replaced paganism with Christianity. Shortly before 695, when Justinian II was ousted, mutilated, and exiled to Chersonesos, local pietists covered the Roman arena with a church to conceal the shameful evidence of sport killing.

Late in the Byzantine era, despite the influx of Khazars in 711, the Chersonese was a valued military outpost and trading center at the northernmost point of the empire. In 988, Grand Prince Volodymyr the Great of Kiev (or Kyiv), called Vladimir of Kiev or Kyivan Rus, investigated four religions — Islam, Judaism, Roman Catholicism, and Eastern Orthodoxy. He sealed a relationship with the Byzantine empire by marrying Anna, the daughter of Basil II, and received Chersonesus as her dowry. Because the prince abandoned paganism and was baptized into the Eastern Orthodox faith, the Chersonese earned the name "cradle of Rus [Eastern Slavic] Orthodoxy" (Romey, 2002, p. 20).

Locals, whom Prince Volodymyr ordered christened, erected an elegant church on the spot. He further endeared himself to the Chersonians by enshrining in their church the head of a Ukrainian hero, St. Clement of Rome, a martyred bishop whom pagans tied to an anchor and tossed into the sea on November 23, A.D. 1000. For its sanctification of Clement's relics, the church was called the Royal Chapel of St. Clement and observed as its major religious holiday December 8, the Feast of St. Clement, with processions and shore venerations of relics borne in a boat.

Later in the Middle Ages, the Chersonese acquired cave dwellings, hermitages, and rock cloistered monasteries. Under the protection of two fortresses, Kalamita and Cembalo, the city survived insurgent Goths, Cumans, and Huns and warded off the Mongol Tatars in 1223. Resistance failed in 1278, when Khan Nogay of Bulgaria, ruler of the Galician lowlands, rode south with his pony-mounted Tatars and sacked the city. The former bastion of Chersonesos limped into the fourteenth century by repeatedly staving off waves of steppe nomads. In 1399, the long-lived civilization ceased to exist after the Mongols' Golden Horde swept south and completely destroyed and incinerated the site.

The Chersonese remained inert under nearly two centuries of neglect until the arrival of Polish ambassador Martin Bronewski in 1595. He lauded the former splendor of the retaining wall, wharf, and towers, but the houses and church lay ruined and desolate. In 1783, Catherine the Great dispatched military engineers to survey the peninsula and determine its value. On their advice, under the Treaty of Jassy of 1792, she annexed the Crimea to guard southern Russia and established the city of Sevastopol as a military bulwark on the Black Sea. In 1799, Russian author Pavel Sumarokov noted the antiquity of the area's stones, which contrasted with the emerging fortress at Sevastopol.

The resurrection of old Chersonesos began in 1827, after Admiral Alexei Samuilovich Greig, a Scots seaman commanding the Russian fleet, hired engineer Karl Kruze to raise a memorial to Prince Volodymyr the Great on the site of his baptism. During the digging of streets, squares, cruciform and basilican churches, frescoes and mosaics, and residences, the site acquired the name "the Russian Troy" for its similarity to the Homeric archeological dig on a coastal promontory at Hissarlik, Turkey. After unearthing the floors of three Byzantine structures, Kruze recycled the foundation of one church as the basis for a new shrine to St. Volodymyr.

In 1852, after the Russian Orthodox Church founded a monastery at Chersonesos and archived artifacts of past Christian activity, the site began to draw pilgrims. A year later, the Crimean War, which allied England, France, and Turkey against Russia, halted the restoration of the city. Russian cannon battered the British Light Brigade in extensive combat that ended in 1856 with the destruction of Sevastopol. At Cherneos, a willy-nilly series of digs by treasure seekers, monks, and Count A. S. Uvarov, originator of the Russian Archaeological Society, continued for nine years. In 1861, plunder ended when the Russian Orthodox Church began construction of the Church of St. Volodymyr. After Czar Alexander II, Russia's last true autocrat, laid the first brick, the building project took thirty years.

Archeology

In 1886, Czar Alexander III realized that it was too late to stop the looting and undisciplined excavation of the Chersonese. Countess Uvarova, who characterized the site as the "Russian Pompeii," requested that the czar protect the area as a certified archeological dig. He agreed that, to save his people from ridicule as barbarians, he must maintain a scholarly, controlled project. In 1888, he founded the region's archeological museum. At the Imperial Archaeological Commission in St. Petersburg, he exhibited major finds — a Greek coin, Roman lamps, an ornate belt buckle and engraved gem from the first century A.D., household utensils, and a bronze cross from the 1200s. In 1892, he opened the Warehouse of Local Antiquities, the beginning of the Russian museum system.

Systematic excavation of the Chersonese continued until World War I. To preserve historic items, Russian curators removed them from danger in 1914. The museum director, Lavrentii Alexeevich Moiseev, guarded the dig for a decade, protecting it from invading armies. Following the Russian Revolution of 1917 and the abolition of the Christian faith under Communist dictators, pilgrimages ceased. The monastery gave place to a concentration camp, at which the victorious Reds imprisoned officers of the defeated White Army. Subsequent use of the site as a hospital for the aged and as housing for a rifle regiment resulted in years of abuse and erosion of monuments.

For reasons of national security, Chersonesos became a closed city under Communism. At the height of Soviet militarism, the Russian navy anchored the Black Sea fleet at Sevastopol and organized the secretive maneuvers of the Cold War. In 1924, Moiseev gained control of the ancient site as the official location of the Archaeological and Historical Museum of Chersonesos, unofficially dubbed the "Museum of Atheism." The Bolsheviks smartened up the warehouse of antiquities and increased their role in preservation and research. With added staff, excavators were able to increase the museum's collection, compile reports, and publish site guides.

Strife continued to dog the Chersonese into the 1940s. When war threatened Sevastopol in the late 1930s, curators once more secured the permanent collection. After the Nazis occupied Sevastopol in 1941, air strikes leveled St. Volodymyr's church and museum during the battle of Sevastopol from May 8 to July 4, 1942, when the Germans claimed 200 Red Army tanks and imprisoned 100,000 Ukrainian citizens. Remaining while Chersonesos was under the threat of machine guns and bombs was Alexander Kuzmich Takhtai, who refused to abandon ongoing archeological and historical research.

Upon the Soviet liberation of Sevastopol on May 9, 1944, restoration of the Chersonese involved recycling materials from the Church of St. Volodymyr. Curators once more rebuilt museums and exhibited treasured objects. By February 1945, the museum began admitting visitors once more. Within seven years, teams of excavators were again searching the rubble of past civilizations. In 1954, Oleg Dombrovsky made one of the most exciting discoveries by unearthing ruins of the ancient Greek theater.

For thirty years, the Chersonese flourished under a new curator, Inna Anatolievna Anatonova. Beginning in 1955, she supervised the reconstruction of outer walls and sheltered mosaics and basilicas. She added a restoration laboratory and hired a knowledgeable staff to oversee activities. By 1978, authorities proclaimed the site the Chersonesos State Historical Archaeological Preserve and organized scholarly surveys of the region. After the disbanding of the U.S.S.R. in 1991, the Ukraine government reinstated the religiosity of the ancient site by reconsecrating worship centers and passing ownership of holy ground to the Vydubytsky monastery. The National Preserve of Tauric Chersonesos displayed over 200,000 recovered artifacts.

In 1994, Joseph Coleman Carter, director of the Institute of Classical Archaeology at Austin, Texas, initiated a joint dig with the University of Warsaw and the University of Poznan in cooperation with local research teams that surveyed 400 ancient farm plots, their intersecting lanes, wells, and a Hellenistic farmstead. The work came at a crucial period in Chersonese history as urban growth, church land grabs, tourists and beach-goers, squatters and vendors, and coastal erosion threatened the integrity of the ancient colony. With the concerted effort of Carter and William Miller, former U.S. legate to the Ukraine, two years later, UNESCO added the ancient Greek colony to the World Monuments Watch List of the 100 Most Endangered Sites of World Cultural Significance. The site appeared on the list again in 1997, 1998, and 2002. To boost tourism, which would spark economic growth for Sevastopol, sponsors funded the site as an international archeological treasure and planned development of the ancient mint and display of mosaics.

Since 1996, when an influx of tourists replaced Russian military personnel at the Chersonese, excavators have surveyed mosaic floors, limestone capitals, and marble columns with votive inscriptions framing sea vistas. Likewise valuable were underwater sites that yielded clues to the past from amphorae and building ceramics. The following year, a conflict of interest arose between preservationists and Archbishop Lazar of Simferopol, who campaigned to restore the monastery in the museum's facilities, reestablish the pilgrimage center, and destroy all evidence of paganism. As archeologists explored walls, pavements, hearths, and drains of the multiplex site, called Bezymyannaya, the orthodox church dispatched a gazebo by military helicopter and lowered it to the ground to stand over the Uvarov Basilica and protect the historic site of the prince's baptism. In 1999, with funds from the city of Kiev, President Leonid Kuchma began the reconstruction of the Church of St. Volodymyr. Under a unique church and state cooperative, the state held the deed to the property, but accommodated religious ritual on holy days.

While interns from Kharkiv University, Kyiv-Mohyla Academy, and Moscow and St. Petersburg state universities were conducting investigations in summer 2000, an unforeseen dispute erupted in the orthodox church. The newly established Ukrainian Orthodox Church faced a splinter group, the Ukrainian Orthodox Church of the Kyiv Patriarchate. Pietists of the original church assembled at the Chersonese to protest the unrecognized group. Rebel chief Father Paissy led thirty monks to the former monastery to repossess them for his rogue church. When peace was restored, the following summer, President Kuchma and Russian president Vladimir Putin convened at the Church of St. Volodymyr for its reconsecration. Work continued on the one-third of the site that has been excavated until funding stalled during the collapse of the Russian economy. Despite preservation and excavation by international standards, plundering remained a constant threat. In 2002, the Chersonese museum marked a 110th anniversary.

Coastal Activities

The Chersonese boasts a unique layering of history. For tourists, historians, antiquarians, church historians, and archeologists, the area offers on-site examination of a shore community's growth from fifth-century Greece to the present. Among the many elements of the preserve are kurgans [burial mounts], tombs, megaliths, terraced farms, stone boxes, roadways, summer herders' yayly [camps], and winter quarters of steppe nomads. Under the preserve director, historian Leonid Vasil'evich Marchenko, research assistants offer tours of the museum's two buildings, ancient and medieval, which contain 200,000 exhibits. Docents explain architectural styles, religious and military elements, and the importance of the agricultural base to the economic stability of the Black Sea.

The shoreline promenade draws visitors for a variety of purposes, including swimming, sunbathing, picnicking, and photography. Over 1,000 Black Sea cruises pass the Chersonese each year. Each July 28, hundreds of members of the Greek Orthodox Church celebrate the feast of Grand Prince Volodymyr of Kiev by processing into the iron-gated National Preserve of Tauric Chersonesos and through the ruins of the Chersonese to a limestone sanctuary that overlooks the shores and harbor.

SOURCES

Carter, Joseph Coleman, et al., "The Chora of Chersonesos in Crimea, Ukraine," *American Journal of Archaeology*, Vol. 104 No. 4, October 2000, pp. 707–742.

"Chersonesos," http://www.utexas.edu/research/ica/chersonesos.html.

"Chersonesos Master Conservation Planning," www.stanford.edu/~hongweix/Chersonesos-home.html.

"Crimea: Uncovering Historical Wonders," *CNN News*, August 27, 2002.

Grinenko, Ludmila, "Rescuing Chersonesos from the Ashes," *Archaeology*, November/December 2002, p. 21.

"Natural Preserve of Tauric Chersonesos," http://www.chersonesos.org/eng/.

Romey, Kristin M., "Legacies of a Slavic Pompeii," *Archaeology*, November/ December 2002, pp. 18–20, 22–25.

Telenkov, Leonid, "Chersonesos Returns," *The Day*, October 3, 2000.

Terras, Victor, ed. *Handbook of Russian Literature*. New Haven, Conn.: Yale University Press, 1985.

Treister, Michail Jr., and Yuri G. Vinogradov, "Archaeology on the Northern Coast of the Black Sea," *American Journal of Archaeology*, Vol. 97, No. 3, July 1993.

Zubar, Vitaly, "The Sources of Christianity in Chersonesus Taurica," *The Day*, October 9, 2001.

_____, and Leonid Marchenko, "Chersonesos," *The Day*, May 15, 2001.

Clayoquot Sound, Vancouver Island, British Columbia

Location

A fount of virgin forest and rich biodiversity, Clayoquot Sound (pronounced klahk' waht) encompasses the entire western shore of Vancouver Island, British Columbia. The sound offers the vigor of the maritime shore and fjords and the quiet splendor of igneous and volcanic soil, cloud-capped mountains, glacial valleys, xeric rocky ridges, salmon streams, and coastal wetlands. When attorney and traveler Thomas Jefferson Farnham of Vermont approached the region in 1844, he remarked on the terrain:

> Owing to the dense fogs, the coast is extremely dangerous; and they render it at all times difficult to approach and navigate it. The interior of this portion of the territory is traversed by the three ranges of mountains, with the several rivers which take their rise in them, and is probably unequalled for its ruggedness, and from all accounts incapable of anything like cultivation [*Early Western Travels*, 1904, p. 77].

The island's six pristine watersheds bear the load of ten feet of moisture per year. The largest watershed along the Megin River connects the mountain crest with Shelter Inlet. On the north end of Meares Island, the extinct volcanic peak of Lone Cone looms like a sentinel over a 66-foot tree, the world's largest living cedar.

Along the strand and deep inland grows the rare temperate rain forest, a valuable part of the Great Bear Rain Forest. The perhumid habitat is home to amabilis and silver fir, balsam, lodgepole pine, red alder, red cedar, maple, Sitka and white spruce, and western hemlock. The longest-lived trees, at 1,500 years old, reach twenty feet in diameter. Standing 300 feet above the forest floor, they render two contributions to the planet's health: the preservation of the habitats of animal and plant species and the trapping of globe-warming nitrogen gas. In addition, the forest supplies indigenous people who depend on nature for food and natural resources and who value the health-giving benefits of cataracts and hot springs.

Contacts

Friends of Clayoquot Sound
Box 489
Tofino, British Columbia, Canada,
    VOR2ZO
Phone: 604-725-4218
Email: focs@island.net
http://www.ancientrainforest.org/

History

Into prehistory, the Ahousaht, Haida, Kwakwaka'wakw, and Nootka Indians resided along Clayoquot Sound in forests they revered as sacred shrines and sources of individual spirit retreats. The Nuu-chah-nulth appear to have settled the Pacific coast around 500 B.C. Succeeding generations lived along the shore in cedar-plank long-houses. They picked berries and, in wetland mounds and terraces, cultivated plantings of camas, clover, potentilla, silverweed, tiger lily, wapato, and other estuarine roots and salt marsh edibles. Native cooks steamed these foods as accompaniments to a diet that focused on salmon, which fishers harvested

from nets and weirs and from intertidal stone fish traps. Garden produce also served as trade goods, as part of the traditional bride price, and as gifts at giveaway rituals called potlatches. When natives needed cedar bark or wood for domestic projects or for carving masks or totems, they prayed to the tree's spirit, then took what they needed from the leeward side to shorten the tree's healing process.

The arrival of whites began to sap Vancouver Island as early as summer 1781, when smallpox struck a virgin soil population. Lacking suspicions of the danger faced by First Nations, late in the 1700s, Wickanin-nish of Meares Island, western Canada's most powerful native chief, led a confederation of tribes on Vancouver Island and influenced the international fur trade. Two years after his first contact with the crew of a British ship in 1788, the chief welcomed Robert Gray, an American sea captain aboard the sloop *Lady Washington*, a Massachusetts-based trader bound for China. Within the next two centuries, entrepreneurs, sealers, and lumbermen ravaged sea mammal populations, over-trapped coastal streams, and reduced Vancouver Island's old-growth forests by 75 percent.

Natives were not totally at the mercy of outsiders. American Fur Company trader John Jacob Astor lost his ship *Tonquin*, an East Asian merchantman, in Clayoquot Sound in late March 1811. The ship rode at anchor on its way to Astoria, Astor's trading post on the Columbia River estuary. After an argument between the arrogant Captain Jonathan Thorn and Chief Nookamis, Thorn humiliated and outraged the old man by tossing him overboard. Around 200 Chinook and Salish, led by Nookamis's grandson Sewish, returned by canoe and massacred the 33-man crew and the captain, who lay wounded alongside the arms store. According to an eyewitness report in Scottish-American attorney Henry Marie Breckinridge's *Journal up the Missouri*

(1811), an explosion in powder kegs and the resulting fire reduced the *Tonquin* to a blackened hulk that sank in the bay. Over a half century later, in 1864, the Ahousaht seized the British schooner *Kingfisher* and killed the crew. The British Royal Navy riposted by bombarding native villages.

One unusual arrival, Englishman Fred Tibbs, immigrated to Long Beach, Vancouver Island, in 1905 and enriched himself with fishing, sealing, and lumbering. With his wealth, he bought Tibbs Island, which he called Dream Isle. He clear-cut all trees except one tall spruce and built an estate in the shape of a miniature castle. After stripping the lone tree of its branches, he constructed a perch on top where he could sit in his chair, write verse, and gaze out on the sound. He drowned in 1921 while refueling oil lamps in the harbor.

Ecosystem

Along the northeastern Pacific shores of Clayoquot Sound and its fish-bearing streams and lakes, patches of fern and moss, bunchberry and huckleberry bushes and wild roses, larkspur and lupins, the insect-eating sundew, salal, and false azalea sprout in bogs and beneath virgin stands of trees as tall as 25-story buildings. In the rain forest's 3,000-year cycle, the death of great trees results in nurse logs, the detritus that feeds new growth. Keeping the forest floor tidy are the banana slug, fungi, and newt. The varied heights of older trees produce canopy gaps that further the spread of low species and new trees, which make up 56 percent of the forest. The resulting healthy stands are home to the black bear, cormorant, cougar, bald eagle, deer, gulls, marten, mink, otter, red squirrel, spruce hen, and wolf.

The cycle of eat or be eaten involves much of coastal life. Off-shore, where gobies, ghost shrimp, mya clams, scale worms, and pea crabs propagate, pods of orcas, seals, sea lions, and gray and humpback whales thrive in the warm Pacific waters in summer and migrate south to Baja, Mexico, to winter. Laws shelter the stellar or northern sea lion *(Eumetopias jubatus)*, the largest of the eared seals, as an endangered species but cannot protect it from its natural enemy, the orca. Also threatening the sea lion are the diminishment of herring, pollock, and salmon, which seagoing trawlers have overfished. In search of food, the sea lion eats the marbled murrelet *(Brachyramphus marmoratus)*, which the Committee on the Status of Endangered Wildlife in Canada listed as threatened, and invades coastal fish farms of southern British Columbia, where the large gray mammals are easy targets in the rifle crosshairs of angry fish-farmers.

Involvement of human residents in the coastal survival struggle turned belligerent late in the twentieth century. In spring 1993, hundreds of Canadian, European, and U.S. environmentalists blocked logging roads on Clayoquot Sound in the War in the Woods, Canada's most heated episode of civil defiance. The outburst arose in response to a five-year government grant to two timber companies, International Forest Products and MacMillan Bloedel, to conduct extensive logging in 74 percent of the contested forest. Greens had reason for outrage. During the 1990s, MacMillan Bloedel acted in bad faith by fouling the salmon-spawning waters of Winter Creek and mismanaging liquid chlorine dioxide, which the company emptied into Malaspina Strait. To make a case against further despoliation of the Clayoquot Sound area, the greens photographed the denuded Catface Range and displayed the stump of a 390-year-old red cedar across Canada and Europe as evidence of the rapid exploitation and destruction of Canada's western shores. For the rapid shrinkage of Canada's rain forest, the global media dubbed British Columbia the "Brazil of the North."

As the sagging economy worsened unemployment, especially at Uclelet village south of Clayoquot Sound, working-class white and native loggers favored clear-cutting as their only means of subsistence. They retaliated against greens by halting the procession of protesters along forest roads and by immuring Greenpeace ships in Vancouver harbor. Around 100 environmentalists forced their way into the British Columbia legislature, injuring a security guard; in May 1993, three protesters were arrested for trying to burn the Kennedy River Bridge to stymy an influx of loggers. By summer, 10,000 angry greens from around the world joined the local fray and incurred 932 arrests, including a ten-year-old boy and several elders in their eighties. Defendants charged with criminal contempt of court faced mass trials in Victoria before a judge who disdained any more altruism on behalf of trees.

A star among Clayoquot's greens was Maureen Fraser, formerly a social worker in Toronto, who settled in Tofino in the 1980s, established the Common Loaf Bakery and Cafe, and served as a town councilor. While directing Friends of Clayoquot Sound and B.C. Wild, she fought breast cancer, a life threat that caused her to reexamine her priorities. To stave off ecological disaster in her homeland, she championed the beauties of Chesterman's Beach and Lone Cone over local jobs from clear-cutting.

For eighteen years, Fraser furthered ecopolitical positions by crusading with guardians of nature. She directed global attention to an imminent threat to 1,000 square miles of virgin trees along the sound, North America's last untouched coastal rain forest. A recipient of the international Goldman Environmental Prize and appointee to the province's Central Region Board, she gained credence with both environmentalists and developers by respecting both points of view concerning the logging of Meares Island and Sulphur Pass. As a result of the board's mediation, loggers reduced their take from 600,000 cubic meters per year to less than 40,000 cubic meters.

Like Fraser, greens from Coalition for Forests, Eco-Feminists, Friends of Clayoquot Sound, Greenpeace, and Western Canada Wilderness Committee developed less vitriolic strategies. They abandoned ecoterrorism in favor of lawsuits, pressure on telephone companies and newspapers who print on Canadian paper stock, and a boycott by European paper manufacturers who buy wood products from British Columbia. Aiding greens were Pulp and Paperworkers and the Fishers Union, which favored democratic decisions concerning forest use. The contretemps rekindled into active animosity in spring 1994 when loggers protested the government's decision to preserve the forest and designate it as a park. Three years later, surveys of damage to the Clayoquot Sound rain forest established that logging was still destroying watersheds.

Ultimately, protesters lauded a break in the long-running, multi-faceted dispute between forest protectors and unemployed Canadian loggers. In October 1999, timber magnate MacMillan-Bloedel reached a compromise with Iisaak Forest Resources, a company controlled by the Nuu-chah-nulth people in alliance with Weyerhaeuser, a paper and timber conglomerate. Iisaak's general manager Eric Schroff declared the shift in power the result of years of "social cataclysm" (Chadwick, 2003, p. 117). Researchers and developers joined educators in a system of managed care and wise use of resources. In exchange for selective harvesting and removal of logs by helicopter rather than over gouged-out trails, timber companies promised jobs to unemployed Nuu-chah-nulth Indians. Another hopeful sign emerged in 2000, when Canadian Prime Minister Jean Chrétien set aside 900,000 acres as the Clayoquot Sound forest, a UNESCO biosphere reserve.

Coastal Activities

Extensive media coverage of the ecology war in Clayoquot Sound turned the area into a tourist locus. Today, the coast is a favorite of picnickers, photographers, and painters and for viewers of First Nations masks and carvings, pottery, basketry, and totem poles. Visitors come to fish, surf, storm-watch, and collect chunks of sea-weathered cedar on the beach. Strollers follow boardwalk trails or hunt for the glass balls that waves wash inland from passing Japanese fishing vessels. Children comb tidal pools for shells and odd-shaped stones and enjoy the sandcastle competition at Parksville.

Clayoquot Sound is also known for more active sport — canoeing and kayaking, cycling and mountain biking, orienteering, wilderness camping, and rock scaling. Surfers at Chesterman Beach, Cox Bay, and Long Beach relish waves over 25 feet high. Barefoot hikers and backpackers follow the bog walk or mossy trails into the rain forest. Scuba divers and snorkelers visiting old wrecks in the "graveyard of the Pacific" also swim the reefs to dig for geoduck, a large edible Pacific clam, and to photograph starfish, kelp greenlings, rockcod, wolf eels, and giant Pacific octopi. Bird watchers view bald eagles, blue herons, loons, and ospreys; naturalists join black bear tours and examine a wide variety of anemones, hermit crabs, mussels, sea urchins, and sunflower sea stars.

Whale-watching is a specialty of Clayoquot Sound. Each spring, all 20,000 of the earth's Pacific gray whales migrate down Vancouver Island on their 16,000-mile journey from Baja, Mexico, to the arctic waters of the Bering and Chukchi seas. Because the huge mammals travel along the shore, they are visible from the telescopes of viewing stations and from charter craft, floatplanes, and headlands lining the sound. Regional planners offer seventy educational and entertaining events of the Pacific Rim Whale Festival, which features seafood chowder cook-offs, art exhibits, coastal tug-of-war competitions, and the reconstruction of whale skeletons from an assortment of dry bones.

SOURCES

Bulic, Ivan, "Clayoquot Summer," *Canadian Dimension*, Vol. 28, No. 1, January–February 1994, pp. 34–36.

Capozza, Koren, "Poached Salmon ... or Sea Lions?," *E Magazine*, Vol. 11, No. 6, November/December 2000, p. 18.

Carothers, Andre, "Brazil of the North," *E Magazine*, Vol. 5, No. 2, April 1994, p. 72.

Chadwick, Charles H., "Pacific Suite," *National Geographic*, February 2003, pp. 104–127.

"Cooperation in Clayoquot," *Amicus Journal*, Vol. 22, No. 1, Spring 2000, p. 39.

Davey, Robert, "Rainforest Crunch," *E Magazine*, Vol. 6, No. 3, June 1995, pp. 19–21.

Deur, Douglas, "Plant Cultivation on the Northwest Coast: A Reconsideration," *Journal of Cultural Geography*, Vol. 19, No. 2, Spring/Summer 2002, p. 9.

Early Western Travels, Vol. 29: Part II of Farnham's Travels in the Great Western Prairies. Cleveland, Ohio: A. H. Clark Company, 1904.

Flurry, Amy, "Clayoquot Mass Trials: Defending the Rain Forest," *Amicus Journal*, Vol. 17, No. 3, Fall 1995, pp. 46–47.

Genovali, Christopher, "Beyond Clayoquot Sound," *Earth Island Journal*, Vol. 10, No. 3, Summer 1995, p. 24.

Giesecke, E. W., "The Search for the *Tonquin*: A Look into the Disappearance of the Pacific Fur Company's Settlement Ship," *Columbia*, Vol. 14, No. 2, 2000, pp. 6–11.

Goldberg, Kim, "BC's NDP Government Weds MacMillan-Bloedel," *Canadian Dimension*, Vol. 27, No. 5, September–October 1993, pp. 23–25.

_____, "Green Relief for Forest Defenders," *Progressive*, Vol. 58, No. 3, March 1994, p. 13.

Govier, Katherine, "Experiencing Eternity in Clayoquot Sound," *Maclean's*, Vol. 109, No. 28, July 8, 1996, pp. 52.

"GTE Fails to Oppose Clearcutting," *Greenpeace*, Vol. 3, No. 4, October–December 1994, p. 2.

Harkin, Michael E., "Sacred Places, Scarred Spaces," *Wicazo Sa Review*, Vol. 15, No. 1, 2000, pp. 49–70.

Haythornthwaite, Gabriel, "The Clayoquot Legacy: The Future of Environmental Activism," *Canadian Dimension*, Vol. 33, No. 1, January–February 1999, pp. 28–30.

Hoberg, George, and Edward Morawski, "Policy Change through Sector Intersection: Forest and Aboriginal Policy in Clayoquot Sound," *Canadian Public Administration*, Vol. 40, No. 3, 1997, pp. 387–414.

Lertzmen, Kenneth P., et al., "Canopy Gaps and the Landscape Mosaic in a Coastal Temperate Rain Forest," *Ecology*, Vol. 77, No. 4, June 1996, pp. 1254–1270.

Levin, Bob, "A Forest Fable," *Maclean's*, Vol. 106, No. 33, August 16, 1993, pp. 20–22.

Mackie, Richard, "The Short, Happy Life and Sad Death of Fred Tibbs," *Beaver*, Vol. 71, No. 1, 1991, pp. 43–50.

Mathes, Valerie Sherer, "Wickaninnish, a Clayoquot Chief, As Recorded by Early Travelers," *Pacific Northwest Quarterly*, Vol. 70, No. 3, 1979, pp. 110–120.

Maxwell, Jessica, "The Last Best Rainforest," *Audubon*, Vol. 96, No. 1, January–February, pp. 98–103.

Newman, Peter C., "Trees Are Renewable, But Forests Are Not," *Maclean's*, Vol. 106, No. 33, August 16, 1993, p. 44.

Nichols, Mark, "The World Is Watching: Is Canada an Environmental Outlaw?," *Maclean's*, Vol. 106, No. 33, August 16, 1993, pp. 22–27.

Owens, Patricia Ann, "Clayoquot: The Sound of Wonder," *School Library Journal*, Vol. 47, No. 5, May 2001, pp. 70.

Passoff, Michael, "Clayoquot Protests Put British Columbia on Trial," *Earth Island Journal*, Vol. 9, No. 1, Winter 1994, pp. 30–31.

Priest, Alicia, "Gentle Crusader: Maureen Fraser's Rainforest Battle," *Amicus Journal*, Vol. 19, No. 3, Fall 1997, pp. 27–30.

Randolph, Mike, "British Columbia's Last Stand," *Backpacker*, Vol. 21, No. 126, September 1993, p. 11.

"Recognition for Clayoquot," *Maclean's*, May 15, 2000, p. 27.

Samson, Jane, "British Authority or 'Mere Theory?' Colonial Law and Native People on Vancouver Island," *Western Legal History*, Vol. 11, No. 1, 1998, pp. 39–63.

"Saving the Forests for the Trees (and the Ecosystem): NRDC at Work for Our Natural Heritage," *Amicus Journal*, Vol. 16, No. 3, Fall 1994, pp. 51–52.

Searle, Rick, "Marbled Murrelet to the Rescue?," *Wildlife Conservation*, Vol. 97, No. 1, January–February 1994, p. 10.

Stefanick, Lorna, "Baby Stumpy and the War in the Woods: Competing Frames of British Columbia Forests," *BC Studies*, Vol. 130, 2001, pp. 41–68.

Stein, M. L., "Assuring Newspring Buyers about Forests: British Columbia's Premier Tells U.S. Newspaper Executives That Canadian Forests Are Being Protected and Preserved," *Editor & Publisher*, Vol. 127, No. 32, August 6, 1994, pp. 9–10.

Stokesbury, James L., "John Jacob Astor: A Self-Invented Money-Making Machine," *American History*, December 1997.

Thompson, Jill, "Clayoquot Inventories Creating False Sense of Scientific Security," *Alternatives Journal*, Vol. 23, No. 3, Summer 1997, p. 3.

"Turning Forests into Phonebooks," *Earth Island Journal*, Vol. 9, No. 1, Winter 1994, p. 28.

Cyrenia, Cyprus

Location

Situated on Cyprus, the coastal town of Cyrenia, alternately called the "jewel of the Levant" and the "jewel of the north coast," offers a deep natural U-shaped harbor. The region thrust upward from a chain of subsurface ridges and peaks of Kyrenia Range, a mountain chain nicknamed the Pentadaktylos [five fingers], which extends from Syria north to southwestern Turkey. Subsequent shifts in ownership have altered the name from the ancient Greek Kerynia, Keryneia, and Kyrenia to the modern Greek Girne. Multicultural influences derived from surroundings in the Mediterranean basin — Rhodes to the west, Egypt to the south, and Anatolia to the north.

The town of Cyrenia lies on the north shore's fertile plain, which is planted in carob, lemon, and olive groves and faces inland to fields of wildflowers, acacia, cypress, eucalyptus, and pine. Its crystal shores host amberjack, bream, dolphins, eels, grouper, squirrelfish, tuna, and wrasse and green and loggerhead turtles as well as migratory birds and the resident chukar partridge and francolin. From the docks, vessels transport local barley, citrus fruit, vegetables, wheat, and wine, sources of island income. In 1998, the Turkish government, which controls the northern part of the island, began conducting seismic exploration of offshore locations for petroleum.

Contacts

Kyrenia Ship Project
Glafkos Kariolou
Stasinou 5A Lakatamia
Nicosia, CY-2331, Cyprus
Email: glaykos11@yahoo.com
Phone: 357-99473926
        357-22691100
        357-24653110
http://www.kyreniaship.agrino.org/

History

Cyrenia is a patchwork of world domination that began with cave-dwelling hunter-gatherers in 8500 B.C. Around 7000 B.C., colonists seeking virgin forests and arable soil moved from Anatolia to Cyprus. Remains from prehistory attest to the wisdom of their move, which netted them ample fauna, including boar, deer, elephant, hippopotamus, mollusks, and wild sheep. By 4000 B.C., neolithic inhabitants began developing copper deposits, the source of a lasting coastal prosperity.

Achaean colonists founded Cyrenia in 1600 B.C. and Hellenized the shore community with Greek place names. In classic times, the region was favorable to reptiles and earned the name Ophiussa [land of snakes]. According to Lycophronas, a Euboean playwright, grammarian, and librarian employed by Ptolemy II at Alexandria around 280 B.C., the city builder Kepheas of Achaea established the city of Kerynia and founded its Kephean dynasty. The wealthy

The historic coastal city of Cyrenia, the "jewel of the Levant," provides the island of Cyprus with a deep natural U-shaped harbor (courtesy of Suzanne Downer).

port traded coastal resources for pottery, jewelry, carved ivory, and bronze figures from Anatolia, Crete, Egypt, and Syria.

Because of the volatility of the southeastern Mediterranean, especially along trade routes, the port of Cyrenia required constant vigilance. In the A.D. 800s, islanders refortified Kyrenia Castle, a Byzantine structure originally built in the A.D. 600s as a hedge against restless Islamic invaders and proselytizers from Arabia. In the late Middle Ages, St. Hilarion Castle displayed twelfth-century architecture of refectory, cellars, and dormitory common to the era's monastic complexes. As religious elements gave place to military reengineering, subsequent reinforcements produced three round towers, a stronger main tower, and a chain connecting tower to ramparts to block the harbor. Despite the improvements to defense, Lala Mustafa Pasha forced the ruling Venetians to cede the fort to Turkey in September 1570.

Archeology

In 1967, a Cypriot sponge diver, Andreas Kariolou, discovered a mud-caked Greek merchantman only a mile from the port of Cyrenia. The humble coaster, built by slave labor, lay in ninety feet of water over ten by eighteen meters of sandy sea floor choked with seaweed sod. The short-decked open ship, dating to the fourth century B.C., was outward bound with a crew of four and a twenty-ton cargo of millstones from Nisyros, 27 volcanic stone blocks for hopper-type grain mills, jars from Samos, and Rhodian wine from the eastern Aegean. The aging ship probably remained in use throughout the conquests of Alexander III the Great and sank in 288 B.C.

In the fore and aft cabins, excavators disclosed 29 basalt ballast stones engraved at Cos, seven coins from 310 and 300 B.C., and a cache of 400 amphorae in ten styles, some coated with resin to prevent leakage. Sacks

and jars carried 10,000 almonds plus beans, dried herbs, figs, grapes, olives, pistachios, casks of alcohol, jars of oil, a garlic clove, and pots of salt, the basic foods of the Mediterranean world. Some of the containers bore the encircled letters API, the stamp of port authorities certifying standard measure. In the bow were humble domestic cups, a cauldron, pitcher, lathe-turned wood bowl, fish plate, and three wood spoons, indicating the aft quarters shared by the *kybernetes* [captain] and his three seafarers.

An invaluable source of data on Greek shipping and ship building in the classical era, the fifty-foot square-rigger is one of the coups of underwater archeology. Diving from the barge named *Alasia* in honor of an ancient name for Cyprus, experts began analyzing the merchantman's hull, which workers sheathed with lead secured to the surface with bronze tacks in a failed effort to ward off shipworms. According to dendrochronologists, the wreckage, which was 75 percent preserved and lying on its port side, was built from Aleppo pine felled in 389 B.C. The vessel sank after pirates began attacking with iron spears, eight of which embedded in the planking. The absence of human remains suggests that the sailors either swam to shore or were enslaved and the ship scuttled to spare the freebooters the standard Athenian penalty of crucifixion.

Over an eight-year period, dedicated work by Michael Lazare Katzev, an art historian, and student of underwater archeologist George F. Bass, along with Katzev's wife Susan, naval historian J. Richard Steffy from Texas A. & M. University, and a research team from the Pennsylvania University Museum extricated the ship and its cargo from the seabed. By 1974, the waterlogged Kyrenia shipwreck, strengthened with polyethylene glycol and reassembled, resided safely in a museum in Kyrenia Castle under the supervision of the Cyprus Department of Antiquities and UNESCO. Exhibits of a ritual basin, an iron chisel and ingots, a wooden block and sheave for raising the yard, and 100 flat lead rigging rings that guided a cord for lifting the sail contributed to the historicity of the vessel. Publicizing Cyrenia's seafind were Michael Katzev's writings for *National Geographic*, BBC television, and a documentary film, *With Captain, Sailors Three* (1978).

In 1982, the Hellenic Institute for the Preservation of Nautical Tradition joined the Institute of Nautical Archaeology of Texas in launching a project to build, launch, and sail a model of the Kyrenia ship. At the Psaros dockyard of Perama, Greece, builder Harry Tzalas commissioned the work to carpenters who duplicated the original shell-first construction by joining pine planks with oak pegs before framing the hull with ribbing. *Kyrenia II* put to sea on June 22, 1985, and reenacted its final voyage, covering open water from Piraeus to Cyprus. The ship's seaworthiness in gale-force blows disproved earlier assumptions that Mediterranean crews were timid, coast-hugging sailors.

A second replica called *Kyrenia-Eleftheria* or *Kyrenia Liberty*, computer designed and custom-built in Limassol for Christodoulos, Avgousti & Sons, was the work of "Uncle" Tassos Andreou, the oldest shipwright in Cyprus. The model set sail in November 2002. Because Turkey controls Cyrenia, Greek authorities hired the Metsovio Polytechnic of Athens to rebuild an alternate departure point, the ancient port of Amathus, which lies underwater at Limassol. The second journey in May 2003 took on added significance because the four-man crew transported twenty-talent pieces of Cypriot copper to Greece for molding bronze medals for the 2004 Olympic games in Athens.

Coastal Activities

In addition to underwater archeologists and historians, the pleasant Mediter-

ranean port of Cyrenia welcomes tourists and offers varied attractions, including wildflower tours, gambling, and a scenic view of harbor fishing boats and yachts, tavernas, and Venetian houses. Visitors seeking quiet sunning, beachcombing, swimming, and snorkeling often move to Pente Mili, a strand five miles west of town near the Peace and Freedom Museum and unidentified soldiers monument. City tours include Christian icons at Panagia Chrysopolitissa Church, a folk art museum, and historic links to medieval crusaders and pilgrims. Excursions to the east take in Bellapais Abbey, a grand cloister built by Augustinians in 1205 and planted in citrus groves to the shoreline, and the Hazreti Omer Mausoleum, a tomb of one of the seven Muslim martyrs. Divers access the sunken remains of Salamis and the Zephyros reef, a limestone reef rich in sponges and other sea life. In July 2001, Swiss divers off the Cyrenian coast at Ayios Ambrosios added to the region's appeal after locating the wreckage of a World War II fighter plane and human remains of the RAF pilot.

SOURCES

Church, Michael, "The Republic the World Forgot," *Spectator*, Vol. 275, No. 8,733, November 25, 1995, pp. 16–17.
"Cyprus History," http://www.cypnet.com/.ncyprus/n-history.htm.
"Divers Find Sunken WWII fighter off Kyrenia," *Cyprus Mail*, July 25, 2001.
Evripidou, Stefanos, "Kyrenia *Liberty* Takes to Water," *Cyprus Mail*, November 12, 2002.
"Excavation of a Greek Shipwreck off Kyrenia," *American Journal of Archaeology*, Vol. 73, April 1969, pp. 238–239.
"Excavation of a Greek Shipwreck off Kyrenia," *American Journal of Archaeology*, Vol. 74, April 1970, p. 198.
Garzanti, Eduardo, "Actualistic Ophiolite Provenance: The Cyprus Case," *Journal of Geology*, Vol. 108, No. 2, March 2000, p. 199.
Katzev, Michael L., and Susan Womer Katzev, "Was the Ship the Victim of a Piratical Attack?," *Institute of Nautical Archaeology Newsletter*, Vol.13, No. 31, November 1986.
_____, "Resurrecting the Oldest Known Greek

Ship," *National Geographic*, Vol. 137, No. 6, June 1970, pp. 840–857.

Katzev, Susan Womer, "The Kyrenia Shipwreck," *Athenian*, March 1982.

MacLeish, Kenneth, "Cyprus under Four Flags: A Struggle for Unity," *National Geographic*, March 1973, pp. 356–383.

Martin, Douglas, "Michael Katzev, Who Raised Ancient Vessel, Dies at 62," *Seattle Times*, September 30, 2001.

Mita, Alex, "Ready to Set Sail Again," *Cyprus Mail*, September 22, 2002.

"'Ship of Kyrenia' Will Carry Bronze for Athens Medals," *Cyprus Mail*, April 20, 2002.

Steinbuchel, Caroline, "Kyrenia, a Mosaic of Cultures," *Turkish Daily News*, August 1, 1996.

Theodoulou, Michael, "Shipwreck Holds Clues to Lives of Ancient Mariners," *Christian Science Monitor*, March 29, 2001.

Delos, Greece

Location

A fourteen square mile gneiss and granite island in the Aegean Sea, Delos, called Dhilos or Dilos in modern Greek, lies southeast off Attica in mainland Greece on a strait separating its sister islands, Mykonos and Rheneia (also called Island of Hecate, Rinia, Megali Dhilos, or Greater Delos). Scrubby with juniper, lush with grass, and dotted with golden daisies, blue-purple irises, and red anemones and poppies, Delos is the smallest of the Cyclades, a ring of 56 isles and islets that appears to encircle it. At its highest point, 350 feet, Mount Kynthos, named for Cynthian Zeus, drew panhellenic pilgrims, who came to the holy precinct to honor the handsome sun god Apollo and his twin Artemis, a wildlife deity derived from Mediterranean goddess worship. For its value as a cosmopolitan center of worship, diplomacy, and commerce, in 1990, UNESCO named Delos to the World Cultural Heritage list.

Contacts

21st Ephorate of Prehistoric & Classical Antiquities

Ten Epaminonda Street
GR-105 55 Athens, Greece
Phone: 0289-22-259, 01-32-50-148
Fax: 0289-22-325, 01-32-15-897
E-mail: protocol@kaepka.culture.gr
http:// WWW Address: http://www.culture.gr/2/21/211/21121a/e211ua06.htm

Mythology

According to Greek lore, the floating island of Delos became stationary in the Mediterranean Sea as the birthing chamber of the twin deities Apollo and Artemis. The story, in true mythic form, meanders about the seduction scenarios of Zeus, a wily shape-shifter. While he pursued Asteria [star], the maiden took the shape of a quail, which he stalked by taking the form of an eagle. Fearful of heaven's most august god and desperate to maintain her virginity, Asteria turned into a floating rock and dropped into the sea like a falling star. Known as Ortygia or Adelos, the floating isle roamed much of the Mediterranean.

The insatiable Zeus next impregnated Leto, Asteria's sister. According to the "Hymn to Delos" (ca. 270 B.C.) by the Alexandrian court poet Callimachus, Hera, Zeus's wronged wife, directed her jealousy against the unfortunate girl and refused her a place to give birth anywhere the sun shone. Out of pity to the wandering mother-to-be, the island of Delos offered shelter. In Ovid's words in the *Metamorphosis* (8 B.C.): "'You are a vagrant on the land; I, on the sea,' and gave her a place that never stood still" (1986, p. 301). Out of loyalty to Leto, Zeus asked his brother Poseidon the sea-shaker to secure the floating island with four diamond pillars to the bedrock of the Cyclades. The stability that Delos acquired had special meaning in an island cluster frequently rocked by tectonic shifts.

Leto traveled easily to shore on a dolphin's back. In exchange for shelter, she promised the island that, for its kindness to

Delos, the smallest of the Greek Cyclades, drew panhellenic pilgrims to a holy precinct to honor the handsome sun god Apollo and his twin Artemis (courtesy of Greek Tourist Board).

her, it would become Greece's richest sanctuary. In the "Hymn to Apollo" (ca. 690 B.C.) by an unknown poet, possibly Kynthaios of Chios, she vowed:

> No one else will ever touch you, as you will see,
> > nor do I think you will be rich in cattle or sheep,
> > nor will you bear grain nor will you grow abundant crops.
> But if you have a temple of Apollo the far-shooter,
> > then all men will gather here and lead hecatombs [animal offerings],
> > and the boundless savor of sacrificial fat will always rise up,
> > and you will feed those who dwell on you from the hand of a foreigner, since you do not have rich soil
> [Shelmerdine, 1995, p. 65].

Thus blessed, the island received godly honor and Leto's prediction that "octopuses will make their lairs on me and sleek seals their homes untroubled with no people near" (*ibid.*, p. 67).

At the foot of Mount Kynthos, Leto, one of the most celebrated maternal figures in mythology, crouched in labor on soft grass. With the aid of the attendant Hyperborean maidens, sometimes identified as Arge and Opis, Leto gave birth under a sheltering olive or palm tree at the shore of a small lake. The firstborn infant was Artemis, goddess of chastity, wild animals, and the hunt. Nine days later, Leto, with the aid of her new daughter, produced a second child, Apollo, the many-splendored god of light, creativity, healing, prophecy, music, poetry, law, and truth.

Concerning the island's future, Apollo concurred with his mother and showed his gratitude by designating Delos his holy precinct. As the island progressed from a faceless rocky dot in the Mediterranean to a center of holiness, its name altered from Adelos [invisible] to Delos [visible]. Local people honored the god of light with the first fruits of their harvests. The Augustan epic poet Virgil relocated some of the sanctity of the shore in Rome by directing Aeneas to the Delian oracle for directions to the site where he would found a new homeland for the wandering Trojans. In Book III of the *Aeneid* (19 B.C.), Rome's literary epic, Aeneas falls as a suppliant before the echoing shrine, from which Apollo's voice directs him to a new homeland:

> O [Trojan] people strong to endure, the land
> That cradled first your race, from whence you sprung,
> That land shall take you to her joyful breast
> On your return. Seek for your ancient mother.
> From there the house of Aeneas and the sons of his sons
> And all that are born from them shall hold dominion
> Over the whole earth [1961, p. 55].

With proper piety and sacrifice of two bulls and two lambs, Aeneas withdraws from the welcoming harbor to obey the god's directive.

As the "Hymn to Apollo" describes, the typical visitors to Delos, arriving by ship like Aeneas and his crew, saw "the grace of all and [took] pleasure in his heart" (Shelmerdine, 1995, p. 71). At gorgeous ceremonies, priests in long flowing robes officiated while their families received honor from attendees at the contests in "boxing and dancing and song" (*ibid.*). Also revered among Delians were the island's symbols — the quail, the holy lake, the palm tree that shaded the twins' mythic birthing, the tombs of Arge and Opis, and Eileithyia, goddess of birth, who aided Leto in her labor and swaddled the newborn Apollo.

History

For over two millennia, the mystic isle of Delos has borne a reputation for sanctity. First inhabited by Carians of Asia Minor around 2800 B.C., the island was originally called Ortygia or Quail Land. It gained its connection to the cult of Leto from Ionians who colonized the shores around 1000 B.C. The immigrants made Delos headquarters of an amphictyonic league of maritime nations. As a religious capital, Delos unified pan–Ionian members in the common performance of pious duties and in a sacred truce that kept the peace. Historians characterize the evolution of panhellenism as a people's progress from barbarism to the acme of Greek social and intellectual life.

At the Apollonia, a festival also called the Delia, participants focused worship on the magic number seven and propitiated Apollo on the seventh of each month to shed his warmth and light on grain fields and vineyards. In his honor, out of the horns of sacrificial animals, the devout built a magnificent altar on Delos at the long, narrow sanctuary of the bulls, one of the seven wonders of the ancient world. Each year, the religious elect presented the god with a gold corona, a symbol of the sun's rays. Maidens danced down the long central hall. At the end of the annual observance, a banquet hosted by Delians concluded the gathering.

The islanders outfitted their shore with a sacred harbor, dug a holy lake for the convenience of temple geese and swans, and built gymnasia for ritual exercise dedicated to Apollo. In the 600s B.C., the Homeric hymns described the cult, which involved games, horse racing, dancing, ritual, and pilgrimages. Every four years on the seventh of *Thargelion* [May], Apollo's birthday, the religious isle became a folk center and locus for the Delian Thargelia Festival. In addition to entertainments, food, and worship, the event included a beachfront trade fair, which was a favorite of Ionians.

As pilgrims arrived by boat, they sang choral anthems to the gods and processed up the sacred way to the holy of holies. Participants maintained the traditional rhythms and unfoldings of the *geranos* [crane dance],

a maze-like Cretan ritual that the Greek hero Theseus had introduced to the accompaniment of harps to celebrate Ariadne's safe landing at Delos after a bold escape from the Minotaur in the underground labyrinth of Crete's Knossos Palace. The dance appears in Chapter XVIII of Homer's *Iliad* (ca. 750 B.C.) in a scenario inscribed on Achilles's new shield:

> A dancing floor, like that which once in the wide spaces of Knossos
> Daedalus built for Ariadne of the lovely tresses.
> And there were young men on it and young girls ...
> dancing and holding hands at the wrist [p. 391].

Homer adds that, while observers watched, women in light robes and men in tunics danced with light, intricate steps in crisscrossing rows. Dance historians surmise that the spiraling pattern of steps survive on painted pottery and murals depicting a winding line dance imitating the back-and-forth ritual of the crane's mating. The choreography is the foundation of the Greek tsakonian dance, which is performed to a slow, deliberate five-part rhythm of 1, 2, 3, 4, pause.

In *The Life of Greece* (1939), historian Will Durant remarked on the harmony and glory of Delian festival days:

> A seventh-century hymn describes the "women with fine girdles," the eager merchants busy at their booths, the crowd lining the road to watch the sacred procession, the tense ritual and solemn sacrifice in the temple, the joyous dances and choral hymns of Delian and Athenian maidens chosen for their comeliness as well as their song, the athletic and musical contests, and the plays in the theater under the open sky [p. 131].

Athens honored Apollo's birthday with an embassy borne to the island in a sacred ship and with the suspension of all execution of felons. The interval coincided in 399 B.C. with the incarceration of Socrates, who gained a brief reprieve from the death penalty for committing sacrilege in his lectures to young Greek students.

Notables from the ancient world involved themselves and their art in the ritual sails to Delos. Around 750 B.C., the poets Hesiod and Homer took part in a poetry contest "stitching a theme in new hymns" (Shelmerdine, 1995, p. 88). In the "Hymn to Apollo" (ca. 690 B.C.), one of the oldest in the collection of Homeric Hymns, the author, possibly identified as Kynthaios of Chios, describes a competition for which Delian maidens sang in honor of Apollo, Leto, and Artemis and concludes with an heroic narrative. On another mission, in 513 B.C., the mathematician-philosopher Pythagoras, a devotee of Apollo the healer, traveled to Delos to attend and seek healing for the dying Pherekydes of Syros, his mentor and friend.

Though isolated and pledged to holiness, Delos was an independent city-state that lay amid a swirl of political maneuvering. In 550 B.C., Polycrates of Samos seized the Cyclades, but symbolically blessed and secured Delos by chaining it to nearby Rheneia. With the rise of Athens under the power-hungry tyrant Pisistratos, Delos's image changed. In 543 B.C., representatives from Attica obeyed a Delphic oracle calling for the cleansing of Delos by removing old tombs, a psychological strategem that stripped Delians of their earthly heritage. Another power-seeker, Darius of Persia, arrived in 490 B.C. According to the Greek historian Herodotus, Darius rendezvoused on the island with the Athenian traitor Hippias. Darius made his obeisance at the island sanctum and burned incense to Apollo before setting out for the battle of Marathon, Persia's great defeat at the hands of the Athenians.

In *The Peloponnesian Wars* (ca. 400 B.C.), the historian Thucydides records that, after the Greco-Persian Wars in 478 B.C., Delos held economic and political importance as the bank vault of the Delian League, a maritime alliance that headquartered its treasury in the temple of Apollo in care of Athenian archons [magistrates]. Aristides the Just, the Athenian chief and league organizer, collected an annual assessment of 460 talents, paid in cash or in vessels donated to the fleet, which numbered 200 warships. During annual on-site meetings, representatives of member states in Greece and Asia Minor discussed how best to pool resources and military might to ward off Persia. When an earthquake shook the sacred isle for the first time in Hellenic memory, people interpreted the event as a portent requiring expert investigation. In a tense scenario, the Greeks anchored their fleet at tiny Delos harbor and consulted the oracle before risking all against the Persians.

Tensions between Delians and the pompous Athenians erupted in heavy punishment of the small island and its people. Athens again denigrated Delos in 454 B.C. by transferring the treasury to the Acropolis in Athens. When Apollo appeared to punish the city with a plague for its disrespect, Athenians stripped the island of its humanity by forbidding births and deaths on the premises. Because of the sanctity of the grounds, Delos received no more human remains for burial and dispatched its dying citizens and parturient women to Rheneia for care. A rival to the Delian religious festival grew up at Ephesus. In 422 B.C., Athens demoralized Delians a third time by banishing them to Anatolia and the Chersonese and by slaying their leaders. (*See also* CHERSONESE, UKRAINE.) Within a year, the persecutors allowed expatriates to return to Delos.

In later centuries, the tiny island of Delos passed from despot to despot, yet maintained its piety. In 413 B.C., Nicias, a glory-seeking Athenian leader, extended a gilded bridge from Rheneia over the strait and onto Delos's sacred way. As described by the biographer Plutarch, Nicias personally led hymn-singing entourages over the bridge and into the presence of Apollo. After Nicias set up a brass palm tree to the god, Apollo responded by upending the tree in a strong wind.

Under the Spartans, the island was free of Athenian cruelties. In the 300s B.C. during the conquests Alexander III the Great, the Delian Festival became the most popular in the Mediterranean for its cosmopolitan offerings of music, drama, and sport. In celebration of free trade, islanders built new shrines and maintained an open port that controlled the east-west flow of commerce in grain, oil, wine, and wood. In 200 B.C., Philip V of Macedon curried favor with Apollo by erecting a portico over the island's main road. This thoroughfare directed embassies and processions from their arrival at the shore to the holy of holies.

At this time, Delos, known as the slave emporium of the Mediterranean, processed coffles from as far east as China and India, north from Thrace and Europe, and south into Africa. The heavy merchandising of refugees, captives, prisoners of war, and the kidnap victims of Cilician pirates survived a revolt of 130 B.C. (*See also* SELINUS, CILICIA.) Slaves passed in and out of the auction site in huge numbers. In *Geography* (20 B.C.), the cartographer Strabo claimed that, after a major war, as many as 10,000 captives exchanged hands in a day before setting out with their new masters from the harbor to posts ranging from concubine, housemaid, cook, and nanny to mine drone and galley rower.

In 166 B.C., Rome denied Delos the independence it had enjoyed after the dissolution of the empire of Alexander III the Great by passing the island back to Athenian control. Two decades later, the island bobbed back into power as a commercial nexus in competition with Rhodes. To the sacred precinct, the Romans contributed their own *lares* [household gods] and trade guilds and built an agora. As commerce bur-

geoned, islanders constructed new docks and harbor markets. Phoenician Jews added their religious slant to the island with a synagogue built around 100 B.C. By the end of the millennium, the seaport numbered 25,000 citizens from a variety of ethnicities.

The island reached a nadir in 88 B.C. after Mithradates VI of Pontus sent General Menophanes on a sacking mission. In punishment of the island's loyalty to Rome, the general slew 20,000 Delian males, sold women and children into slavery, confiscated treasures, and left the land mass barren. In the year before Lucius Cornelius Sulla reclaimed the island, the void welcomed pirates who thrived on coastal raids. The Emperor Hadrian tried to resurrect Apollo's cult, but Delians were broken, scattered, and hopeless. Upon the rise of Christianity, Theodosius the Great banned paganism on Delos, where a Christian enclave supplanted the former devotees of Apollo. During the Middle Ages, when commerce passed to other locales, Delos continued to languish, serving Venetians and Byzantines as a source of marble blocks and islanders as pasturage for goats.

Archeology

Delos lost some of its treasure to the Renaissance Venetians and Romans, who plundered freely and incinerated some works in lime kilns. A royal pirate, Sir Kenelm Digby (also Kenelme Digbie), a court favorite and privateer for Charles I of England, made a voyage of thievery on August 28, 1628, when he stole part of Apollo's temple. Beginning in 1873 and concluding in 1914, excavation by l'École Française d'Athènes [French School of Athens] disclosed the thriving quays, homes, marts, statuary and mosaics, theaters, sanctuaries, and Doric temples of Delos's golden age. The digs revealed the temple of Dionysus with its holy friezes and phalli erect on pedestals facing a temple of Aphrodite and Hermes, which skirted a marketplace. Additional sites enshrined religious exotica — the Syrian love goddess Atargatis, the Samothracian underworld gods, the Egyptian divinities Isis and Serapis, and the Phoenician Astarte and Baal.

Stretching from the Sacred Harbor, the Sacred Way consisted of a paved boulevard for holy processions into the western shrine or east to the temple Lion Terrace, named for stylized statues of five rampant, open-mouthed lions. There, priests received votive offerings from the Hyperborean Maidens, devotees of Artemis. Pilgrims from much of the Mediterranean world crowned their heads with garlands and brought oxen to sacrifice at the structure, which may be the oldest temple from the pre–Hellenic era. At the shrine of Iris, the rainbow goddess, devotees brought dried figs and wheat cakes sweetened with honey.

Antiquarian Maurice Holleaux, author of *La Grèce et les Monarchies Hellénistiques* [Greece and the Hellenistic Monarchies] (1921), gained funding from Joseph Florimont, le Duc de Loubat, to excavate at the water's edge a residential district that had hosted the artisans responsible for the island's beauty. In 1932, Kazimierz Michalowski, professor of classical archaeology at Warsaw, published a report on the Delos excavations. To brighten the close arrangement of lanes and homes, islanders established a system of oil lamps, which reposed in niches along the way to illuminate the footsteps of pedestrians. Toward the Delian theater, which seated 5,500 viewers, columned houses of rich financiers, merchants, and shipping magnates displayed expensive mosaic flooring. The grandest, the House of the Dolphins and the House of the Masks, offered indoor water systems, Rhodian peristyles, stuccoed walls, and high-ceilinged sleeping chambers.

Coastal Activities

A fount of Mediterranean history and open-air museum of art and architecture, Delos is long known for its photogenic views and historic panorama. One of the region's most famous writers, English novelist Lawrence Durrell, thwarted island security by bribing a boatman to leave him overnight on Delos. As Durrell described in *The Greek Islands* (1978), a beachside tryst at the Bay of Phourni with his wife began with a moonlight swim and a prowl of the silent Delian ruins.

The island has also become an escape from local pleasure centers devoted to cruising, sailing, snorkeling, and diving. Pilgrims continue the age-old treks to the sacred precincts. Marble, tufa, and granite surface present smooth images steadily weathered over time from salt air and spray and reduced from their original sharp outlines. A museum initiated in 1904 exhibits the famed Delian marble lions as well as funerary statues, grave monuments, ceramic pots and figurines, jewelry and masks, glass vials, and plaques and mosaic tiles. According to marine archeologist Nicholas K. Ruah of Purdue University, who snorkeled the Delian harbor in 1981 with oceanographer Jacques-Yves Cousteau, much history, art, and architecture remains to be excavated on the seaward approach to Delos. Into the 21st century, the Greek government guards the treasure from damage and plunder until native teams can begin work.

SOURCES

"Delos," http://icdweb.cc.purdue.edu/~rauhn/roman_places.htm#del.

"Delos Lions to Be Moved," *Athens News*, October 28, 1999.

Dougherty, Sarah Belle, "A Key to Ancient Greece," *Sunrise*, August/ September 2000.

Duchene, Hervé, "Delos et Marseille," *Provence Historique*, Vol. 42, No. 169, 192, pp. 519–535.

Gawlikowski, Michal, "Kazimerz Michalowski (1901–1981)," *Acta Poloniae Historica*, Vol. 45, 1982, pp. 297–298

Hall, Roland, "Unnoticed Words and Senses from Sir Kenelm Digby," *Notes and Queries*, March 1999, 21–22.

Homer. *The Iliad*. Chicago: University of Chicago Press, 1951.

Ovid. *Metamorphoses*. Cambridge, Mass.: Harvard University Press, 1986.

Shelmerdine, Susan C. *The Homeric Hymns*. Newburyport, Mass.: Focus Books, 1995.

Thucydides. *The Peloponnesian Wars*. New York: Washington Square Press, 1963.

Virgil. *The Aeneid*. New York: New American Library, 1961.

Dingle, Ireland

Location

Sixty miles west of Killarney and Tralee in southwestern Ireland at Europe's westernmost point, Dingle is a sheltered, photogenic seaport of County Kerry. The Dingle Peninsula is the northernmost and smallest of four parallel rocky appendages reaching into the Atlantic Ocean. Warmed by the Gulf Stream, the frost-free region is a deeply creviced tract of limestone and sandstone softened by lush green grass. From early times, prehistoric Irish turned the natural resources into the country's largest display of rock art.

Tucked into the underside of a rugged sliver of land thrust into the ocean, the town of Dingle lies on a shallow harbor accessed through a slender channel that is 35 feet deep and 310 feet wide. The fish- and lobster-rich waters provide ample stock for traditional sea pies. An appealing countryside draws visitors to sandy beaches along the bays, gentle heather-decked hills, freshets and cataracts from rugged rock formations, and a variety of arctic alpines, bluebells, foxgloves, fuchsia, greater butterworth, loosestrife, meadowsweet, montbretia, primroses, and St. Patrick's cabbage. For its unspoiled beauty, the country earned honors as one of *National Geographic's* top ten scenic areas.

Unlike the Hiberno-English east coast, which came under English domination in the twelfth century, County Kerry is located on the Celtic fringe "beyond the pale" of Anglo-Ireland and its collision of languages (McCrum, 1986, pp. 166, 168). Because of its ties to the past, the county is one of the Gaeltacht or Irish-speaking areas of the island's rural west. Local people still adhere to the storytelling, folkways, open-air dancing, and spirituality of their ancestors and daily converse in Gaelic, the first Indo-European tongue used in the British Isles.

Contacts

Claire Galvin, Marketing Director
Dingle Peninsula Tourism
Cooleen Dingle, County Kerry, Ireland
Phone: 353-66-51000
Fax: 353-66-51991
Email: dingle@tinet.ie
dingle@eircom.net
http://www.dingle-peninsula.ie/index.html

Early History

Dingle was first inhabited around 8000 B.C. by mesolithic hunter-gatherers, who netted and spearfished the coast for congers, haddock, mollusks, thornback ray, tope, and wrasse and foraged farther inland for hazelnuts. More experienced aborigines snared gannet and guillemot, trapped hare, and bow-hunted for wild pig and red deer. By 5700 B.C., locals were pasturing cattle and later added sheep and goats to the agrarian system. Settlers left behind passage tombs and hilltop cairns as well as shards of pottery and rhyolite tools and weapons. Excavations of a Stone Age site at Ferriter's Cove near Ballyferriter unearthed the earliest seasonal settlement of Dingle's beachcombers. By 2500 B.C., additional stone monuments, ritual circles, burial mounds, and petroglyphs displayed an emerging artistry beyond mere subsistence. In subsequent centuries, artisans crafted intricate

At Europe's westernmost point, Dingle is a sheltered, photogenic seaport that earned honors as one of *National Geographic's* top ten scenic areas (courtesy of Hans Honegger).

hair ornaments, armlets and collars, earrings, bronze vessels, and gold boxes.

Around 500 B.C., Iron Age Celts, who migrated north from Western Europe, built *dúnta* [ring forts] and *dina* [hill forts] at Caherconree and Faha, established a Druidic system of religion and education, and erected monuments to Celtic gods. Ogham stones bearing Irish script may have indicated land boundaries of farmers and detailed their patrilineal descent as a thorough identification of each landowner. After St. Patrick brought Christianity to the Irish around the mid–400s A.D., a colony of monks set up stone hermitages on the barren rocks at the Skellig Islands off Dingle Peninsula. Local people sanctified healing wells and organized pilgrimages to sacred destinations. One traditional pilgrimage took locals up Mount Brandon on the last Sunday of July to honor Lughnasa, a Celtic god of harvest and plenty. Late in the sixth century, the yearly trek advanced from Celtic ritual to the reverence for St. Brendan the Voyager, who reputedly climbed the hill to look to the west for an earthly *terra repromissionis sanctorum* [promised land of the saints].

Legend

A migrating visionary and the patron of Kerry, St. Brendan the Voyager, who was born on Dingle Peninsula around A.D. 484, became a medieval saint and popular mythic figure. After education by St. Ita of Killeedy, his spiritual mother, at her boy's school in Limerick, he was ordained a friar in A.D. 512. He spent the remaining 65 years founding monasteries along the Shannon River and on the Aran Islands. The most famous is Clonfert, a prominent abbey and school in County Galway that housed 3,000 monks and remained in service into the sixteenth century.

According to local lore, for forty days, Brendan refused to stay put in a monastery and moved about the Christian cosmos to religious sites in Wales and Scotland. Led by a vision toward his most amazing journey, he fasted in three-day segments, then gathered 33 mariners to depart from Dingle Bay in 539 in search of an earthly haven. As described in the epic of his journeys, Brendan "pitched his tent on the top of a mountain that extended far out to sea, in the place that is called Brendan's seat [on the Dingle Peninsula]" (Baldrick, 1965, p. 36). His crew built a *curragh*, a supple round boat formed of wood ribs and covered in "tanned ox-hide stretched over oak bark" (*ibid.*). Before setting sail on the summer solstice, he stood at the Dingle shore and blessed the harbor.

The twelve-year journey took Brendan's company to Iceland, Wales, Brittany, Iona, and the Hebrides before reaching Newfoundland, which the saint identified as paradise. Highly stylized details of Brendan's voyage suggest that the saint's crew followed prevailing winds and encountered identifiable phenomena — sea mammals, volcanic islands, the warm Azores, icebergs, flying fish, the sluggish Sargasso Sea, even

Eskimo. Known as the Irish discoverer of America, Brendan espoused a distinctly Christian purpose for his gadding — the search for the Holy Grail, the chalice from which Christ's disciples shared sacramental wine at the Last Supper. Upon return to Dingle, Brendan died soon after rejoining his monastic cell.

From emerging legends of St. Brendan came ballads, poems, and two long *imrama* [voyage tales], *Navigatio Sancti Brendani Abbatis* [The Navigation of St. Brendan the Abbot] (ca. A.D. 700) and *Vita Brendani* [Life of Brendan] (ca. A.D. 900). Both were anonymous, the latter written during Ireland's Golden Age of Christianity and scholarship. Translated into Middle English, French, German, Italian, and Flemish and read by navigator Christopher Columbus, much of Brendan's seafaring lore appears to be a fusion of Christian legend with the *Imram Brain* [Voyage of Bran] (A.D. 600s) and with the Christian romance *Imram Curaig Mailduin* [Voyage of Maelduin's Boat] (A.D. 700s), the story of the Celtic navigator Maelduin.

In the mid–1970s, adventurer and film-maker Tim Severin, a veteran retracer of the journeys of Jason, Odysseus, Sindbad the Sailor, Marco Polo, Genghis Khan, Robinson Crusoe, and Ahab, captain of the fictional whaler *Pequod*, began pondering the truth behind the Brendan stories. (*See also* MATRAH, OMAN.) Severin built a *curragh* from local timber to which he lashed tanned oxhides with thongs. He fitted the craft with a steering oar and hired four crew members to accompany him. Upon their departure on May 17, 1976, they accustomed themselves to the unusual rhythmic motion of the round boat, which undulated with the waves like a living being.

Severin located Brendan's island stepping stones by hopping from Scotland to the Hebrides and Faroes and west over ice-packed stretches to Iceland, Greenland, Newfoundland, and Nova Scotia. A mid-ocean repair required the crew to lean over the side in pitching seas to patch a rip in the leather. After traversing 3,500 miles, the crew reached Peckford Island off Newfoundland on June 26, 1977. From the astonishing journey, composer Shaun Davey took inspiration for a musical suite, *The Brendan Voyage* (1980), which features traditional reels on the uilleann pipes.

In 1978, Severin captured the adventure in a book, *The Brendan Voyage*. Of the departure point at Dingle, Severin mused:

> This was Saint Brendan's own country, the Dingle Peninsula of County Kerry and the farthest point of Ireland reaching out into the Atlantic, a place where the sweep of green hills and moorlands ends in the blue-grey ocean, and the air is so clear that one almost has a sense of vertigo as the land seems to tilt toward the distant horizon [pp. 17–18].

Severin noted that the Irish refer to the saint as Brandon, the name for a creek, bay, point, headland, village, and a holy mountain, the site of a pilgrimage on Saint Brendan's Day. For a touch of saint's luck, local fishers typically stow a vial of holy water on their boats. Severin enhanced onboard luck by painting his sails with the Celtic cross.

Post-Celtic History

As European trade grew, Dingle continued to prosper. In the 1100s, the Normans introduced feudalism and the building of walled towns in imitation of model communities in Europe. The Fitzgeralds and the Rices established Dingle, which dominated maritime commerce in southwestern Ireland. From the busy harbor, pilgrims sailed for Santiago de Compostela, a holy site in Spain. Ships bearing trade goods coasted along the Atlantic shore of France as far south as Iberia.

In 1585, Queen Elizabeth I sanctioned Dingle and paid £300 for a protective wall, but the arrival of the Spanish Armada to the

English Channel in September 1588 interrupted the completion of the town's incorporation. Some of Spain's ships sailed around Dingle Peninsula, where four were wrecked. The worst hit was the 945-ton Basque-built armed troop transport *Santa Maria de la Rosa*, vice-flagship of the fourteen-ship Guipuzcoan squadron and captained by Martin de Villafranca. Aboard were two Genoans, Francisco de Martiato and his son Giovanni.

The recycled merchantman grounded during a storm on September 10 and broke up in the swift currents that swirled by the Blasket Islands before sinking in 110 feet of water. The captain's son, Giovanni de Martiato, the lone survivor, swam to Dingle, where Dominick Rice, commander of an English garrison, and merchant James Trant arrested him. In 2001, playwright David P. O'Sullivan of Minneapolis, Minnesota, produced a play about the incident, *The Interrogation of Giovanni de Martiato*.

In 1607, King James I completed the official sanctioning of Dingle by issuing a charter and granted commercial privileges under crown law. Town builders encircled the space with a wall and gates, thus creating a distinct division between urban and rural dwellers. Like the rest of Ireland, Dingle suffered the same peasant uprisings, flight of Irish aristocrats, and English landlord system. As a result of starvation and disease during the Potato Famine of 1846–1847, the population dropped by half. In an unprecedented exodus, many starving Kerryites fled to the United States, forming the nation's first non–Protestant immigrant wave.

In February 1969, the filming of MGM's *Ryan's Daughter*, an historical romance directed by David Lean, involved many locals as extras and sources of details. Set in fictional Kirrary, the story of the marriage of a barkeeper's spoiled daughter (Sarah Miles), characterizes her boredom with a fusty Dingle schoolmaster (Robert Mitchum) and a risky affair with a British soldier (Christopher Jones). The love plot meshes with the foiled plans of Irish revolutionaries. The film earned Oscars for John Mills and cinematographer Freddie Young and Oscar nominations for Sarah Miles as lead actor and Gordon K. McCallum for sound. In March 2000 on the thirtieth anniversary of the film, a local festival featured rambles, storytelling, a stage version of the film, and a reunion of the cast, including Miles, who returned to Dingle to hobnob with locals who had worked on the picture.

Ecosystem

Dingle has developed a dolphin culture because of one mammal, Fungie, the world's longest-known association between a human community and a solitary dolphin. A lively twelve-foot, 500-pound bottlenose *(Tursiops truncatus)*, he arrived through the narrow channel in early 1984 and made the port and adjacent Slaidín Cove his home waters. Lighthouse keeper Paddy Ferriter began observing the animal's escort service for Dingle's fleet of fifty fishing boats. By August 1984, the Ministry of Marine Manager Kevin Flannery entered the extroverted bottlenose into official marine records as the harbor's volunteer pilot.

Cavorting about Dingle harbor, the perky dolphin fed on garfish, trout, pollock, even squid. Easily identified by the pattern of scars on his fins, he earned his name from a fisherman nicknamed Fungus for his scraggly beard. From "Fungus's dolphin," he was eventually dubbed Fungie. Central to Fungie lore are the comments and records of Brian Holmes and Sheila Stokes, who made a hobby of swimming with Fungie and introducing him to human swimmers, divers, sailors, canoeists, kayakers, and windsurfers.

Fungie managed to avoid propellers as he chased in the wake of vessels, offered pollock to swimmers, encircled kayakers, retrieved lost diving masks and flippers, and prodded divers and scuba tanks with his beak. His activities drew dozens of excursion boats from the Dingle pier carrying tourists, ecologists, and cetacean watchers eager to observe, photograph, and swim with Fungie and pose by his statue at the Dingle marina. As media reporters spread his story in 1987, some declared that he had a mate. Authors began commenting on Dingle's star mammal, notably diver Ronnie Fitzgibbons, author of *The Dingle Dolphin* (1988), and Seán Mannion, who wrote *Fungie, Ireland's Friendly Dolphin* (1991). In his sixteenth year in Dingle, Fungie showed the tooth-rake marks commonly resulting from flirtations with females. By 1995, he joined a pod of dolphin pals at the harbor mouth and, in his seventeenth year in the port, swam with Dony, a dolphin known on the Blasket Islands.

On February 2, 2002, Dingle suffered from an oil spill when the ninety-foot, 180-ton Spanish fishing vessel *Celestial Dawn* was blown against the rocks and grounded at 7:30 P.M. on its way through the harbor mouth near the lighthouse. Wedged into rocks by bad weather, the diesel-powered trawler listed on its starboard side amid floating wreckage. As raw winds and rough seas continued along the Kerry Coast, the 10,296 gallons of oil in the hold threatened scallop beds and sea birds and mammals. Because rescue craft failed to reach the *Celestial Dawn*, eight hours after the wreck, winchman Peter Leonard and an Irish Coast Guard helicopter team from Shannon airlifted the ten Spanish crewmen clinging to the starboard rail and transported nine of the men to a Tralee hospital for treatment of hypothermia.

Dingle residents feared for Fungie's survival if the bottlenose should ingest fuel leaking from the trawler. Immediately, local officials of the Dingle Harbour Board began the massive job of monitoring leakage, stringing absorbent booms to contain the oil, scheduling air monitoring of pollutants, and planning for clean-up and reclamation

of animals. Dr. Simon Berrow of the Shannon Dolphin and Wildlife Foundation reported that Fungie surveyed the area for a few days, then instinctively removed himself to safety from the oil spill. At the direction of Geoff Livingstone, chief of operations for the Irish Coast Guard, officials ordered hot-tapping equipment from Holland to drill into the *Celestial Dawn*. Mainport Company of Cork and the Smit Tak salvage group siphoned off forty tons of diesel fuel. On March 5, 2002, a salvage barge from Scaldis in Belgium lifted the wreck by crane and took it to the Continent for scrap.

Coastal Activities

Still picturesque and inviting, Dingle offers a number of shore activities, including water sports, kayaking, canoeing, shore fishing, *curragh* racing, and sailing west to Ventry Bay, Slea Head, or the Blasket Islands. Naturalists enjoy birding among a wide range of shore and coastal species — choughs, egrets, hoopoes, gannets, kestrels, ouzels, peregrines, and wagtails. Drivers prefer a car tour of the O'Connor Pass and Brandon Mountain, which overlooks the peninsula's northern coast. Rambling and pony trekking are popular sports farther inland, where the ambitious hiker or rider can choose among the Three Sisters, three headlands west of Dingle, or visit the stone *clocháns* [beehive huts] at Mount Eagle or camp at Dingle Bay. For religious historians, exploring the unmortared stone church known as Gallarus Oratory reveals the piety of Ireland's earliest Christians. Other visitors follow Pilgrims' Way from Ballyferriter to Ballinloghig to follow the route of ancient seekers past Riasc (also Reasc or Reask), a fifth-century stone monastery that remained active for 700 years.

Additional sites intrigue tourists. At the Freshwater Experience, a fifteen-acre shore theme park, staff recreated an authentic *crannog* [shore dwelling] as well as a working trout farm and wildfowl reserve counting among its twenty species black swans, Hawaiian geese, Mandarin ducks, and rheas. The site displays an Ogham stone, a wedge tomb, and a stone circle. Mara Beo, Dingle's Oceanworld, which opened in 1996, features an aquarium overlooking the Dingle Marina. The aquarium displays 100 species of West Kerry sea culture and Ireland's only shark tank and rare fish, which are often stranded along the peninsula. A thirty-foot underwater tunnel displays creatures in their habitat; a touch tank invites children to experience sea life with their hands. A history section exhibits facts about the voyages of St. Brendan the Navigator and artifacts from the Spanish Armada.

SOURCES

Baldrick, Robert, et al., eds. *Lives of the Saints.* Harmondsworth, Eng.: Penguin Books, 1965.

Bardon, Jane, "Are Ireland's Friendly Dolphins at Risk?," *BBC*, July 17, 2002.

Conniff, Richard, "Ireland on Fast-Forward," *National Geographic*, September 1994, pp. 4–31.

Darrike, "Relevant Nautical History," http://www.webschooner.com/gnm/library/index.html.

Harrison, John, and Shirley Harrison. *Ireland.* Chicago: Rand McNally, 1982.

Hickey, Donal, "Fungi 'Too Slick' to Be Caught Up in Oil Spill," *Irish Examiner*, February 9, 2002.

Lawyer, John E., "Three Celtic Voyages," *Anglican Theological Review*, Vol. 84, No. 2, April 1, 2002, pp. 319–343.

Lewis, Lionel Smithett, "The Celtic Church," *St. Joseph of Arimathaea at Glastonbury.* London: James Clarke, 1955.

Mac Donough, Steve. *The Dingle Peninsula: History, Folklore, Archaeology.* Dingle: Brandon Book Publishers, 1993.

Martin, Colin, "Guns of the Armada," *British Archaeology*, No. 64, April 2002.

Meaney, Dolores, "Saints of County Galway," http://www.galwayonline.ie/welcome/history/history2/saints.htm, 1998.

Moreton, Cole, "A Flipping Miracle," *London Independent*, February 19, 2000.

Rutter, Jon, "They Sailed in an Oxhide Ship," (Lancaster, Pa.) *Sunday News*, April 9, 2000.

Severin, Tim. *The Brendan Voyage.* New York: McGraw-Hill, 1978.

"Some Individual Natural Disasters and Catastrophes," http://www.btinternet.com/~mike.ferris/l2002events.htm.

"St. Brendan and His Irish Monks," (London) *The People*, July 21, 2002.

Steves, Rick, "Dingle Peninsula," *International Travel News*, September 1999, p. 111.

_____, "Doing Dingle Town," *ABC News*, March 4, 2000.

Dubai, United Arab Emirates

Location

Formerly one of the Trucial States, Dubai (or Dubayy) lies tucked into the southwestern shore of the Persian Gulf beyond the Hajar Mountains, where Bedouin herders once tended flocks of camels and goats. Dubai joins Abu Dhabi, Ajman Sharjah, Fajairah, Ras al Khaimah, and Umm al Qaiwain to comprise a confederation known as the United Arab Emirates, the world's most stable Arab entities. The second in size and population, the rectangular land mass of Dubai lies on the Shindhaga Peninsula and borders on Abu Dhabi and Al-Shariqah. In addition to mountains, oases, and sand dunes, the terrain also contains salt marshes, mudflats, lagoons, graveled strands, offshore islands, and reefs. Fossilized roots, reeds, burrows, crocodile and turtle skeletons, and mollusk and ostrich shells attest to past periods when rainfall was much higher and desertification less advanced.

For its coastal location, Dubai is known as the Venice of the East and the gateway to the Persian Gulf. The seacoast consists of 45 miles of soft white beach outlining the perimeters of parks and luxury hotels. An S-shaped waterway called the Creek runs six miles inland and divides Dubai town from Dayrah, the commercial center. From a humble fishing enclave touching on a desert extending south beyond the

Tropic of Cancer, the metropolis developed into a world-class port city valued for its tolerance and cosmopolitan, progressive attitude toward expatriates. The environs contain 90 percent of the emirate's citizens, most of whom live in high-rise apartments, townhouses, and upscale villas.

Contacts

Dubai Commerce & Tourism Promotions Board
P. O. Box 594
Dubai, United Arab Emirates
Phone: 009714-511600
Fax: 009714-511711
Email: info@dubaitourism.co.ae
http://dubaitourism.co.ae/www/main/content.asp

Gary Geulner, Chairman
Dubai Natural History Group
P. O. Box 9234
Dubai, United Arab Emirates
Phone: 971-4-313-321, ext. 500
Fax: 971-4-313-371
Email: neilc@emirates.net.ae

Pearl Diving

From as early as 5000 B.C., the oyster and its hidden pearl determined the prosperity of desert dwellers who migrated to Dubai's gulf shores. Herders entered the Juma valley near the fortified village of Hatta and colonized the coastal region after 2000 B.C. with nondescript fishing and pearling villages. Divesting themselves of a desert lifestyle, the newcomers initiated new trades in fishing, pearl extraction from oyster shells, net weaving, and ship building. To protect pearling craft from seawater, builders rubbed heavy oils into the hulls.

Pearling was seasonal work limited to the summer months from June to September, but offering the chance of instant wealth from an auspicious find. After the *nukhadha* [captain] hired men for a voyage,

they returned home before embarking to deposit their advance pay to feed families during the long separation. Crews of twenty divers — some former African slaves, indigent Arabs, Baluchis, and Persians — resided for up to four months aboard wooden dhows or battils, buoyant, double-ended craft that they stocked with water, rice, dates, dried fish, ballast stones, and rope. Families approached the Dubai harbor and raised the *al nofe* [black flag], a shore signal that the pearl dhows had departed. Historian Charles E. Davies reports in *The Blood-Red Arab Flag* (1997) that the women sang marine laments, "Have mercy, have mercy oh Sea! ... Bring them [safely] back to us, as they hoist their jib-sails" [p. 23].

The pilot navigated the pearling dhow by sun, constellations, land bearings, and the color and depth of the ocean and quality of the seabed. As Davies described the craft in motion:

> The lateen is a grand pulling sail, and the dhows sail handsomely in their own conditions. There is nothing clumsy about them, though their fish-oiled hulls smell abominably and their underwater bodies are preserved by a mixture of tallow and lime, rubbed on by hand and renewed quarterly [p. 19].

Powered by a triangular sail, the pearling craft advanced to oyster beds along the shores of the shallow, warm-water gulf, which is not a true cold-water ocean basin like the Gulf of Oman.

From ancient times, pearling technique was uncomplicated, but hazardous and physically draining. Before submerging, divers pinched their nostrils shut with turtle shell clips and donned thick gloves and diving suits that protected them from rough oyster shells and jellyfish stings. Around their necks, the divers slung oyster baskets before tying stones to their feet to pull them rapidly to the sea floor. In clusters of oysters, they selected up to ten for harvesting, then tugged the rope to signal their diving

For its coastal location, Dubai is known as the Venice of the East and the gateway to the Persian Gulf (photograph by Jeff Harris, courtesy of Saudi Armco World/ PADIA).

mates to hoist them up. The unlucky suffered short careers in diving from lung and skin diseases, hemorrhaging, emphysema, and perforated ear drums. To ease fears of the exhausting, life-threatening dives, *dhow* teams made up pearling chants and rowing songs and patterned steps to dance during celebrations of their safe return to port.

When *dhows* reached workable sites at sea, the diving spread out over daylight hours. Thirty times each day, divers plunged up to fourteen fathoms and remained underwater around ninety seconds per dive. They took no nourishment between breakfast and dinner. After each plunge, they heaped the rugged shelled bivalves on deck until the entire crew returned at evening to pry them open with their knives and deposit pearls in the captain's sea chest. Because the shells lay in a common pile, no one knew who located the richest finds.

In a wage-less system, all divers shared in the final tally when the captain traded the results of the voyage with coastal dealers for cash. Each crew member gambled on the odds of one pearl per 10,000 oysters. If the advance exceeded the returns, divers remained in the captain's debt through subsequent voyages. A good catch and high prices at the bazaar could free a diver from a life of rigorous undersea toil and set him up with a date grove or prime land at an oasis. As the dives increased the wealth of the community, more desert dwellers migrated to Dubai to work as oarsmen for a half share or divers for a full share.

History

The earliest tribal control of Dubai involved the seizure of coastal dominance of the fish and pearl markets. Some eight miles south of the port, after A.D. 650, Umayyads, an early Islamic dynasty, ousted Persian invaders and established a caravan outpost, which thrived at a juncture of east-west

trading routes. From Baluchistan, the Indus Valley, and Mesopotamia, Dubai's merchants imported sacks filled with fragrant cardamom, cinnamon, clove, dried fruit, incense, and nuts. The Umayyads dispatched the goods in merchant *dhows* to India and China. On the ships' return, owners sold in local *souks* [bazaars] and exported to European cities rich cargoes of Asian porcelain, precious stones, and silks.

In the Middle Ages, control of the Persian Gulf centered to the east of Dubai at the north end of the Gulf of Oman. In the 1200s, the kingdom of Hormuz, an Iranian island on the Strait of Hormuz, controlled Arab commerce from India, China, and Africa. In 1514, Portuguese adventurers seized the strategic strait, built a fort at Julfar near Ras al-Khaimah at the southern end of the Persian Gulf, and taxed the gulf trade, milking it of profits. Despite the competition, Dubai steadily prospered. In 1580, an Italian adventurer commented on the importance of fishing and pearl diving to the coastal economy.

As the British presence in the Persian Gulf grew around 1766, the city of Dubai got its start. In the early 1800s, the sea rock–and–lime Al-Fahidi Fort, the center of government, housed the ruler's family, served as a prison, and guarded the Creek from invaders. With the aid of the British navy, in 1809, Dubai and other seagoing economies began combating piracy based at Ras al Khaymah. As one English viceroy described the situation:

> There were constant trouble and fighting in the Gulf; almost every man was a marauder or a pirate; kidnapping and slave-trading flourished; fighting and bloodshed went on without stint or respite, no ship could put out to sea without fear of attack; the pearl fishery was a scene of annual conflict; and security of trade or peace there was none [*ibid.*, pp. 9–10].

The mission took a decade to complete because Qawasi Arab pirates stayed on the move to prey on extensive shipping lanes that reached east to India and west into the Red Sea. To end the pirate juggernaut, the British assembled flotillas and placed occupation troops in ports.

Until 1833, the Bedouin of Abu Dhabi dominated Dubai. The city gained independence after 800 clan members of the Bani Yas pearling clan advanced to the coast from the Liwa oasis to the south. Led by Maktoum bin Butti, founder of the Al-Maktoum dynasty, clan members freed the emirate from Bedouin control and created a viable state. Rejoicing in liberty, citizens threw off Qawasim pirates as well as the plots of envious sheikhs. In 1835, the emirate allied itself with Britain by accepting a maritime truce. City authorities increased commerce by removing taxes and duties on foreign trade and by offering the harbor as a port for British steamers.

The twentieth century saw a shift in Dubai's source of income. By 1900, the city controlled banking, barter, and harbor commerce, which centered on exported pearls. In a period when pearling supplied 95 percent of the emirate's income, the Creek harbored *abras* [water taxis] and 335 teak trading *dhows* from which divers retrieved the gems and sold them as far away as India and East Africa. In old Dubai, wealthy merchants built comfortable residences along the Creek in the Bastakiya district and cooled them with square *barjeels* [windtowers], which directed sea breezes through burlap panels into living quarters. Prosperity waned after the Japanese cultured pearl, first marketed by Mikimoto in the 1890s, replaced Arab pearls in the lucrative jewelry market.

By 1929, Dubai's pearl-driven economy crashed. The collapse idled oarsmen and divers, bankrupted sea captains and merchants, and plunged Dubai into the "Great Depression." To survive, entrepreneurs shifted from pearl marketing to gold. In the 1950s, Sheikh Rashid bin Saeed Al Maktoum, a visionary city planner called the "Father of Dubai," helped to reshape the port into a gulf coast gold-trading center. At this point in port history, merchants dispatched small tenders offshore to larger seagoing craft to load and unload cargoes of fish, grain, herbs, dates, woven mats, and small arms too heavy or bulky for Dubai's sand-choked Creek.

After the discovery of oil in 1958, Dubai's harbor traffic increased, calling for the construction of the Al Maktoum Bridge. In 1966, the city profited from the discovery of oil to the west at the seabed field of Fath (also Fateh or Fatta). Almost overnight, Dubai developed into the busiest port on the globe. The ambitious emirate joined Qatar in establishing the *riyal* as their currency unit. In 1967, Rashid dredged the Creek of silt and erected steel walls and pilings to create the deepwater port of Jebel Ali, the world's largest artificial harbor.

In 1971, the British abandoned Dubai to native government. Under the guidance of Sheikh Rashid, the city became a founder of the United Arab Emirates. Rashid enabled the Creek to receive larger cargo vessels and to control 70 percent of United Arab Emirate imports and exports. Within months, city officials opened a new harbor, Port Rashid, which was comprised of thirty berths for large vessels. In 1973, the emirate substantially increased its financial base with three twenty-story oilfield tanks holding a total of 1,500,000 barrels. Local people referred to the bottom-heavy shapes as Dubai's three pyramids.

Dubai's growth hinged on a sizeable flow of currency. To honor the past, government financiers chose a new national monetary unit, the *dirham*, an historic Muslim coin derived from Parthian coinage from before 200 B.C. The coin commemorated Arabs who distanced themselves from Hellenism and Zoroastrianism to become a Muslim theocracy. With an eye to the future, emirate entrepreneurs invested the new *dirhams* heavily in modernization, communication, education, a supertanker drydock, and an international airport.

Offering access to the whole Middle East, Dubai remains a mercantile center, where the merchant class has shucked off the tribal identity of medieval times and currently influences international policy, service supply, urban planning, and culture. The nation prospers from free gold trade as well as from aluminum smelting and a natural gas plant. Ambitious Brits, Indians, Iranians, Pakistanis, and Filipinos hustle alongside native Arabs in trading with Arabs, Indians, Iraqi, Irani, Somali, and Yemeni. In Arabic, English, Farsi, Malayalam, and Urdu, keepers of booths and shops in the city *suqs* or bazaars offer deals in gold jewelry, clothing, leather goods, textiles, perfume, fish, and vegetables. Because of the liberal nature of the city's Sunni Muslim creed, residents have escaped the harsh anti-female fundamentalism of other Arab nations and offered tourists and business consortia a welcoming climate in which to relax and do business.

Ecosystem

To enlarge the emirate's economic base, Dubai authorities have beefed up their interest in ecotourism. In 2002, Hamdan Al Shaer and a team of marine scientists investigated coral reefs of the Jebel Ali Marine Sanctuary, which lies over eighty square miles of the Persian Gulf between Jebel Ali and Ras Ghantoot. The consortium initiated a coral-monitoring program as a preliminary to organizing tourism and diving, species collection and identification, and sources of seafood. Applying information gleaned from satellite data and acoustic seabed mapping, the team studied coralline algae, crabs, diverse corals, sea urchins, and snails and determined how a fragile ecosystem could coexist with the region's vital sea trade, oil exploration, and drilling.

In 1993, Sheikh Mohammed bin Rashid, a bird fancier, established the Khor Dubai Wildlife Sanctuary on the upper end of the Creek. At any given moment, 50,000 birds resided in fifty hectares of tidal mudflats along a shallow lagoon, a habitat of the mudsnails, worms, bivalves, and crabs that waders eat. Serious birders obtained passes to glimpse and photograph the migratory avocet, citrine wagtail, desert wheatear, flamingo, great white egret, hoopoe, Pacific golden and gray plover, bar-tailed and black-tailed godwits, spotted eagle, and broad-billed and curlew sandpiper. Requiring more patience and luck were the rare black-crowned finch lark, chestnut-bellied sandgrouse, crab plover, Hume's wheatear, purple sunbird, and socotra cormorant. For comparison, naturalists ventured into the Hajar Mountains to study habitats favored by the desert lark, desert whitethroat, house bunting, lappet-faced and griffon vulture, and the spotted, short-toed, and Bonelli's eagle.

Coastal Activities

Dubai offers more variety than the usual big-city entertainments. At Deira on the north shore and Bur Dubai on the south, tourists access shops by the Al Maktoum bridge and Al Shindagah undersea tunnel, which connects the two sites. Visitors enjoy haggling with shopkeepers over the prices of antiques, cookware, jewelry, spices, and rare seashells. Strollers tour the restored palace of Sheikh Rashid, Islamic art and architecture in Sheikh Saeed's nineteenth-century residence, and facsimile pearling villages displaying artisans weaving and shaping pots. Some tourists gather for Dubai Folklore Society performances of the traditional *liwa*, a dance introduced by East African traders to drum and flute accompaniment, or the Bedouin *ayyalah*, a stylized battle dance performed by two facing lines of male performers to drums and tambourines and the cheers of women.

Outdoor activities in Dubai draw the adventuresome to scuba diving in quiet ocean waters at three major sites — Dara, the Cement Barge, and the Hannan. Currently, the government is pursuing the building of artificial reefs to boost ecotourist interest in sponges, corals, algae, and barracuda. Along the strand, beachcombers can go shelling for cockles, cypraea cowries, and sea urchins.

Appealing to families with children are fireworks over the ocean, air shows, *dhow* cruises, and the Dubai International Kite Festival, the first in the Middle East, which began in 1998 during the annual shopping festival. The beach show features multiple, maneuverable, oversized, and inflatable models as well as trick kites and character shapes, such as Bert and Ernie from *Sesame Street*. Entrants have come from Arabia, France, Italy, Japan, New Zealand, and the United States. Naturalists opt for observing the Arabian wolf, barbary sheep, chimpanzee, deer, desert and mountain gazelle, Gordon's wildcat, gorilla, hyaena, mongooses, reptiles, scimitar-horned oryx, Siberian and Bengal tiger, and water buck at the Dubai Zoo, the oldest on the Arabian peninsula. Its animal population also features an aviary of migratory flamingoes, herons, and parakeets.

Sports fans can play golf and tennis, watch cricket matches, shoot trap, fish from piers, or go deep-sea fishing in the gulf for the local hammour, barracuda, shark, and sailfish. Other options are to swim, water-ski, windsurf, sail, jog, or play beach volleyball at Al Mamzar Beach Park or Jumeirah Beach Park. Strollers tour Creekside Park gardens or Hatta, a village in the Hajar Mountains ringed by red iron sand dunes, wadis, and foothills. Desert safaris offer Arab barbecues, sand-skiing, motocross, go-karting, wadi exploring, rock scaling, flying, and camel and horseback rides. Spectators enjoy pigeon and camel races and the Dubai World Cup, the world's richest horse race.

History buffs favor the Islamic design of the Jumeirah Mosque and restored nineteenth-century housing along the creek. At the Dubai Museum, located in the former Al-Fahidi Fort, visitors examine ancient weaponry and *dhows* and peruse alabaster, jewelry beads, funerary and household ceramics, and copper artifacts and pearls from the historic Qusais tombs dating to 2000 B.C. The museum's two water world exhibits recreate the life and work of pearl divers and display the grading sieves, weights, and scales of gem merchants. A large facsimile of a souk recreates the bartering of early Arab residents in fish and pearls.

SOURCES

Al Qadi, Salahudin, and Suchitra Bajpai Chaudhary, "Traditional Dances Reveal the Soul of Arabia," *Gulf News*, October 23, 2000.

Al Tekriti, Waleed, Yassin, "Archaeology in the UAE — The Fourth and Third Millennium B.C., *El Ain Bulletin* 20, July 1983.

Belbin, Catherine, "The Pearl of the Gulf," *International Herald Tribune*, May 20, 2002.

Block, Robert, and Daniel Pearl, "Much-Smuggled Gem Aids al-Quaida," *Wall Street Journal*, November 16, 2001.

"The Blood-Red Arab Flag," *American Historical Review*, Vol. 104. No. 4, October 1999.

Bond, Constance, "Islamic Metalwork at Freer Gallery," *Smithsonian*, October 1985, p. 225.

Burdett, Anita L. P. *Records of Dubai, 1761–1960.* London: Archive Editions, 2000.

Davies, Charles E. *The Blood-Red Arab Flag.* Exeter, Devon: University of Exeter Press, 1997.

"Discover Dubai," http://www.dubaitourism.co.ae.

"Dubai Means Business," *Leadership*, May 2001.

"Dubai Zoo Gifts Animals," *Inter Press/Global Information Network*, September 27, 2002.

"Global Experts to Study Dubai Coral Reefs," *Inter Press/Global Information Network*, September 6, 2002.

Glueck, Grace, "The Nature of Islamic Ornament, Part 1: Calligraphy," *New York Times*, April 24, 1998, p. B32.

Hecht, Jeff, "Global Experts to Study Dubai Coral Reefs," *New Scientist*, August 3, 2002.

Joyce, Miriam, "On the Road Towards Unity," *Middle Eastern Studies*, Vol. 35, No. 2, 1999, pp. 45–60.

Kennet, D., "Excavations at Al Sufouh, a Third Millennium Site in the Emirate of Dubai," *American Journal of Archaeology*, Vol. 128, No. 1, January 1998.

Murray, Stanley, "Dubai: The Pearl of the Gulf," *International Herald Tribune*, April 14, 2000.

Reif, Rita, "Islamic Calligraphy Makes a Statement," *New York Times*, December 16, 1990, p. H48.

Riegl, Bernhard, "Reef Sites: A New Reef Marine Reserve in the Southern Arabian Gulf—Jebel Ali," *Coral Reefs*, Vol. 17, No. 4, 1988, p. 398.

Said, Rosemarie J., "The 1938 Reform Movement in Dubai," *Al-Abhath*, Vol. 23, No. 104, 1970, pp. 247–318.

Sayegh, Fatma al-, "Merchants' Role in a Changing Society: The Case of Dubai, 1900–1990," *Middle Eastern Studies*, Vol. 34, No. 1, 1998, pp. 87–102.

"Seashell Exhibition Tells UAE's Seafaring History," *Khaleej Times*, August 7, 2002.

Elmina Castle, Ghana

Location

Originally, the nation of Ghana spread 500 miles beyond its current border to the north across wooded hill ranges between the Niger and Senegal rivers. Europeans arrived, advanced into the Ankobra Valley, and set up trading outposts in the coastal plain. While exerting three centuries of control, they protected their backs with a line of forts erected at ten-mile intervals along a gently curving Atlantic beach.

Elmina Castle, the first of these forts, evolved into an historic coastal city situated between Cape Coast and the port of Sekondi-Takoradi some 100 miles southwest of Accra, the nation's capital. From a high hill, the defense post overlooked the Gulf of Guinea, the source of its income from fishing. Along the sandy, rock-strewn shore in the hot afternoons, local people beached dugouts under coconut palms, where women sold local dishes and men hawked fresh fish and metal sculpture.

The whitewashed trader fort, bolstered with thick, artillery-proof walls and sturdy turrets, stood on a peninsula near the village of Aldeia das Duas Partes on a rocky spit at the Benya River lagoon. The structure bore the name of St. George, Portugal's patron saint. The maritime trading empire grew rich on the export of African ivory and gold from alluvial veins along the Prah River and between the Ankobra and the Volta rivers. Ore exports, which supplied ten percent of the global demand for gold, became the source of the name Gold Coast. In the 1800s, the slave trade that supplanted other commodities in importance channeled 30,000 black Africans per year through Elmina's confines, turning the fort into a slave factory.

Contacts

Ghana Tourist Board
P. O. Box 3106
Accra, Ghana
Phone: 233-21-222153
Fax: 233-21-231779
Email: gtb@africaonline.com.gh
http://www.africaonline.com.gh/Tourism/info.html

History

Ghana's coast is rife with the kind of history that engenders an ache for the miseries of the past. In A.D. 1240, the epic hero Sundiata was the Ghanian king who controlled the Wagadugu kingdom. After its merger with Mansa Musa's Mali empire, a flourishing trade extended from the Songhai, Hausa, and Kanem-Bornu peoples along the Volta River to the coastal savannas. For currency, locals developed the *manilla*, an anklet, C-shaped bangle, or torque money shaped from iron, brass, or copper and named from the Portuguese for "little hand."

The Portuguese were influenced by an impulse to explore to the south, grab part of the West Indies spice trade, map sea routes around Africa to China, and evangelize the black animist. In 1420, Infante Dom Henrique, called Prince Henry the Navigator, established himself as Master of the Order of Christ and launched expeditions to seize Morocco and to colonize and establish sugar plantations at Madeira, the Canary Islands, and the Azores. Henry's caravels advanced on Africa's west coast as far as Sierra Leone.

Enslavement followed rapidly on the Portuguese itch for expansion. (*See also* ESSAOUIRA, MOROCCO.) In 1441, two fortune hunters, captains Antao Gonçalves and Nuno Tristao, sailed to Cape Bianco and negotiated with local authorities for gold dust and ten black slaves. They returned from a second expedition in 1443 with 235 slaves. Three decades later, Portuguese sea captains began a profiteering partnership between Ghana and Europe, swapping alcohol, beads, brass pots and *manillas*, cowries, iron bars and knives, firelock muskets and minie balls, horses, linens and silks, mirrors, schnapps and rum, tobacco, and wheat for African gemstones, gold, hides, ivory, mahogany, pepper, salt, sugar, wax, and thousands of slaves. To supply gold ore to the Lisbon mint, the entrepreneurs extended their range by bartering inland with the Akan, Commany, Efutu, and Wassaw.

To protect themselves in Africa, the Portuguese vigorously fortified the coast, turning cannon into their salvation against retaliatory blacks and pirates. On December 12, 1481, Juan II of Portugal dispatched Don Diego d'Azambuja with 500 soldiers and a team of 100 crafters to build the first permanent European enclave on the Gold Coast at Elmina, a medieval fort modeled on the military architecture of the Italian Renaissance. The workers imported prefabricated timbers and flagstone for a moated defense with curtain wall. Called São Jorge da Mina or St. George of Elmina Castle of the Mine, it was Portugal's Ghanian headquarters, the first of a string of 43 shore defenses protecting African gold, 33 of which were located in Ghana.

In addition to warehousing gold shipments, Elmina Castle's ramparts encircled a grim, windowless dungeon matrix cut from stone for the storage of slaves, whom kidnappers trapped in the interior, shackled by leg and neck, and hustled mercilessly over jungle trails. Below stairs, keepers turned a profit by crowding slaves 200 per cell. The dazed prisoners, mostly aged sixteen to thirty, stood in their own excrement, which gradually padded the floor several inches over a two- to three-month incarceration. Many died of hunger, despair, infections, malaria, and yellow fever. Rebels were starved, whipped, tortured, and chained to cannonballs or slain outright to halt incipient mutinies.

Above the dungeon, the overlords ate and drank well, gambled, and caroused in luxury. Those black females who appealed to the governor passed through the women's holding pen to his quarters above for sexual exploitation. In addition to a parade of concubines, staffing for the colonial governor required a fort manager or factor, clerks, keeper of stores, a surgeon and pharmacist, stonemasons and carpenters, a cooper, a few priests, and a garrison of soldiers.

In 1486, the castle formed the nucleus of a small walled city, where the two cultures communicated in Portuguese creole. Farther inland, to finance their hegemony, the Portuguese brokered a deal with the Congolese monarchy to funnel Bantu and non–Bantu slaves to the coast. In the midst of Elmina's oppressive slave conduit, a religious element appeared in 1503 with the erection of a chapel to Santiago [St. James], which remained in service parallel to slaving for 93 years. In the shadow of a Christian handhold on Africa, buyers could choose an ivory tusk for one *manilla* or a slave for eight to ten *manillas*.

Inside iron gratings in a damp, unlit atmosphere, Elmina's slaves awaited transport down a tunnel and shoreward through a small slit in the wall, the "door of no return," to square-rigged transatlantic vessels beached 100 yards away. Chained foot to head in fetid holds, slaves journeyed across the infamous Middle Passage to world flesh markets in New Orleans, Charleston, Jamestown, and Baltimore or south to Barbados, Jamaica, Recife, Salvador da Bahia, Rio de Janeiro, and Buenos Aires. (*See also* PORT ROYAL, JAMAICA; SALVADOR DA BAHIA, BRAZIL.) From the auction block, slaves were transported to sugar, rice, cotton, and coffee plantations that had already killed off native American press gangs.

The envious Dutch set their sights on Elmina Castle's prosperity and waged a doomed war against Portuguese Governor Dom Cristovao de Melo throughout the winter of 1606–1607. With the development of competition between Catholic Portugal and Protestant Denmark, England, Netherlands, Prussia, and Sweden for the lucrative North American slave trade, a more determined power struggle arose for Portugal's coastal monopoly. After an earthquake weakened the security of Elmina in 1615, a decade later, the Dutch tried once more to take the fort. Ironically, the salvation of the Portuguese were the African allies who fought off invaders.

On August 29, 1637, the Dutch finally ousted the Portuguese from Ghana by capturing Elmina Castle. Like the pious Portuguese, the new dominators added a Catholic chapel, the first in sub–Saharan Africa. After enlarging Elmina with timber and brick imported from Amsterdam, they secured their holdings by erecting Fort Conradsburg — later called Fort St. Jago — on Santiago Hill overlooking the shore defense. Under Dutch management, slavers trafficked through Elmina at the rate of 1,000 human captives per coffle, all destined to a life of servitude.

In the late 1600s, Africans began to stir and reach for their own destiny. The restless Akan of Akwamu competed for trade along routes reaching from Dahomey to eastern Ghana. At the fall of Akwamu, the Ashante unified in the African forest and reached out to enfold the Banda, Bono, Dagomba, and Gonja peoples. Overcome by the Denkyera kingdom, the region and its prosperous trade center at Elmina Castle fell temporarily to new ownership until the Ashante regained power in 1701.

In 1703, Elmina's Dutch governor sought permission from the crown to give up gold and concentrate only on slave trading. Ghanians profited from complicity with African kings and traders who were eager to capture and sell black slaves on a free-market basis to the rich English, who transported their goods to England's New World colonies. Thus, the Gold Coast rapidly altered into the Slave Coast, where powder and shot from Europe increased the number of prisoners of war. Adding to traffic in human beings was an efficient social culling system that rid black society of criminals, debtors, delinquents, mental defectives, and tribal outcasts by turning them into a profitable commodity. Total sales mounted from 10,000 slaves annually in the 1620s to 25,000 per year in 1675.

In an insatiable buying frenzy of human cargo, by 1700, colonial American markets had absorbed 1,494,000 slaves. In 1730, Rademacher, director of the Dutch West-Indian Company, reported to the motherland:

> The Gold Coast has now virtually changed into a pure Slave Coast. The great quantity of guns and gunpowder which the Europeans have brought there has given cause to terrible wars among the kings, princes, and caboceers [middlemen] of those lands who made their prisoners of war slaves. These slaves are bought at steadily increasing prices. Consequently, there is now very little trade among the coast Negroes except in slaves [Anquandah, 1999].

The flesh mart reached its height in the 1780s with an average of 78,000 slaves imported annually to the Western Hemisphere.

Consequently, the Gold Coast lost population at the rate of twenty percent or about 9,400 people per year. Within a century, the number of exported slaves mounted to a total of 5.2 million, omitting a standard loss of fifteen percent from injury, suicide, and disease.

By 1750, English, Danish, and Dutch fortifications rose in number to forty. Their seacoast locations simplified African trade, which had previously relied on lengthy and expensive overland routes from Sudan. These stout European outposts held off attempts by France, Germany, and Sweden for a part of Ghana's seaboard wealth. The boost to the Ghanian economy, coupled with new technology in armaments and tools, altered the region's traditions. At the end of the 1700s, the Ashante pressed into Ghana under the aegis of Western Europeans along the coast to profiteer alongside whites.

After 1804, the wealth of Ghana began to pall as gold commodities weakened and Denmark, England, and the Netherlands banned trade in black African flesh. After George Maclean, the British merchant-governor of the Gold Coast, led British traders inland to guard the Fanti from internal predations, England assumed control of the trader forts, purchased Denmark's coastal rights, and, in 1872, added Elmina to the British colonial empire. Because England prevailed as a sea and commercial power and took responsibility for developing business and mining, Ghana threw off the age-old Ashante menace. By 1901, colonial powers broke Ashante's strength permanently and guided Ghanians toward a republican government and court system. The success of cacao plantations as well as lumbering and manganese mining reinvigorated the economy, made more efficient by upgraded roads, rail lines, and harbors.

Outdated as an Atlantic coast guardian, Elmina Castle, the oldest European structure in sub–Saharan Africa, passed through various incarnations—a World War II training camp for the West African Volunteer Force, a police academy, then a tourist attraction and archeological site. On March 6, 1957, the Gold Coast dropped its colonial name to become Ghana. In 1972, UNESCO named Elmina Castle a World Heritage Monument. In 1985, Kenneth G. Kelly of the University of South Carolina and Christopher R. DeCorse, an anthropologist with Syracuse University and author of *An Archaeology of Elmina: Africans and Europeans on the Gold Coast, 1400–1900* (2001), conducted a dig of the Elmina area to locate pre-colonial cities and to investigate trade shifts during Ghana's colonial history.

Coastal Activities

Afro-American visitors choose Elmina Castle as a holy shrine to their cultural forebears. On pilgrimages to Ghana's shores, Westerners tour the dungeons and holding cells and relive the terror of being herded into a courtyard for stripping, inspection, random violence, and pricing. Strollers climb Fort St. Jago to get a better view of Elmina's construction. The lighter-spirited absorb African atmosphere by attending the July fish festival and Panafest—the Pan-African Festival—and by bartering for carved wood animals, jewelry and metalcraft, and kente cloth garments and table linens. Some visitors immerse themselves in patio barbecue, bamboo music, drama, folklore and trickster tales of Anansi the spider, and the Ghana National Dance Company; others study genealogy and exhibits at the Cape Coast Castle Museum, which narrate the story of coastal trade from stone implements and earthen figurines to gold and slaves.

Elmina Castle offers a respite for the tourist. For the devout beachgoer, canoeing, surfboarding, and jet-skiing make the most of the Atlantic breakers. Side trips to

Kakum National Park introduce ecotourists to a scrap of Ghana's semi-deciduous rain forest, which has receded by ninety percent from its original acreage. From towers, trails, and seven plank-and-rope skywalks slung 100 feet above the hardwood canopy, visitors survey and photograph the antelope, baboon, bushbuck, flying squirrel, forest hog, leopard, monkey, and wild ass. Forty large mammalian species coexist with 600 indigenous butterflies and 300 types of birds, including the bateleur, black bee-eater, emerald cuckoo, blue cuckoo-shrike, gonolek, kingfisher, malimbe, sunbird, turaco, and white-crested and pied hornbill. A more active perusal of Ghana's forest entices others to camp and track forest elephants.

SOURCES

Anquandah, Kwesi J. *Castles and Forts of Ghana*. Paris: Atalante, 1999.

Anthony, Ted, "Ghana, Land of Contradictions," *Augusta Chronicle*, November 22, 1998, p. 10.

_____, "Visit to Slave Castles of Ghana Evokes Guilt and Beauty for Tourists," *Seattle Post-Intelligencer*, February 4, 1999.

"The Artistry of African Currency," http://www.nmafa.si.edu/exhibits/site /manillas.htm.

Barfield, Deborah, "A Journey to the African Motherland Is Both Painful and Education," *St. Louis Post-Dispatch*, June 21, 1998.

Billings, Malcolm, "Ghana's Slave Castles," *History Today*, Vol. 49, No. 8, August 1999, p. 2.

Bruner, Edwin M., "Tourism in Ghana: The Representation of Slavery and the Return of the Black Diaspora," *American Anthropologist*, Vol. 98, No. 2, June 1996, pp. 290–304.

Burch, Bob, "Ghana: Ecotourist's Paradise," *African Business*, October 1997, p. 23.

Eltis, David, "The Volume and Structure of the Transatlantic Slave Trade: A Reassessment," *William and Mary Quarterly*, Vol. 58, No. 1, January 2001.

Finley, Cheryl, "The Door of No Return," *Common-Place*, Vol. 1, No. 4, July 2001.

"Ghana: A Museum Development Project," *Commonwealth of Associations Museum Bulletin*, No. 5, December 1998.

Henige, David P., "Kingship in Elmina," *Cahiers d'Etudes*, Vol. 14, No. 3, 1974, pp. 499–520.

Norton, Graham, "Ghana's Crumbling Heritage," *History Today*, Vol. 45, No. 10, October 1995, pp. 2–3.

Palmer, Colin, "African Slave Trade: The Cruelest Commerce," *National Geographic*, September 1992, pp. 62–91.

Perry, James A., "African Roots of African-American Culture," *Black Collegian*, October 1998.

Schildkrout, Enid, "Kingdom of Gold," *Natural History*, Vol. 105, No. 2, February 1996, p. 36.

Tibbles, Anthony, "TransAtlantic Slavery," *Antiques*, June 1999.

"Trading with Europeans," http://educate.si.edu/resources/lessons/siyc/currency /essay5.html.

Essaouira, Morocco

Location

A coastal pleasure center northwest of Marrakesch, Essaouira (pronounced eh' sah . wee' rah) is a well-preserved example of an eighteenth-century planned city. Peaceful and ethnically diverse, it is situated on the south central coast of Morocco on a treacherous sea channel. The city arose on the elevated peninsula that, in time of heavy seas, becomes an island. From a rocky outcropping, it looks out on the Atlantic Ocean from a gently curving, hook-shaped bay.

From medieval times, outsiders came to Essaouira's coast to play backgammon in its relaxing, intimate cafes and to taste fresh catches of sardines, prawns, squid, and sea urchins. Fishing families cooked the traditional Moroccan cuisine at the shore on braziers. Farther inland, Berbers settled their extended families in suburban *douars* [villages], where they preserved a distinct lifestyle and spoke their native language.

The white-walled port currently prospers from fishing, crafts, boat building, and light industry, but less from tourism, which is still underdeveloped. The constant wind and clean shallow water make the beach a favorite for windsurfing and family gatherings. The coastline stretches over eight miles of white sand featuring an island bird sanctuary, sandarac and argan trees, oak and juniper forests, and gorse-lined dunes at Cap Sim, all elements that UNESCO sanctioned on March 16, 2002, for a World Heritage site.

Contacts

Embassy of Morocco
1601 21st Street, NW
Washington, D. C. 20009
Phone: 202-462-7979
Fax: 202-462-7643

Moroccan Consulate General
Ten East Fortieth Street
New York, New York 10016
Phone: 212-758-2625
Fax: 212-779-7441

Tourism in Morocco
http://www.tourism-in-morocco.com

History

Essaouira exemplifies the open-mindedness of a coastline frequented by many ethnicities and religions. Established by the Phoenicians in the 1300s B.C., the rudimentary coastal city thrived as a trading center with the Berbers, who controlled the trans–Saharan commerce of North Africa. The Phoenicians merchandised flasks and amphoras, red-slip plates, engraved vases, and oil lamps. From 1000 B.C., the coastal strip was a pirate enclave. As described by the traveler Hannon in the brief Greek manuscript *Periplus of Hannon* (ca. A.D. 900s), the settlement passed to Carthage after explorer and colonizer Hanno, king of Carthage, visited Essaouira around 500 B.C. with his fleet of fifty ships and 30,000 colonists. Archeologists have located remains of the Carian fortress he built on the shore to protect Carthaginian trading posts.

Others also captured Essaouira, which

From medieval times, outsiders came to Essaouira, Morocco, to play backgammon in its relaxing, intimate cafes and to taste fresh catches of sardines, prawns, squid, and sea urchins (courtesy of Rafael Tuts).

seemed little changed by the passing parade of foreign tenants. The Romans gained a foothold after they sacked Carthage in 146 B.C. Around A.D. 100, Juba II, king of Mauretania, added to the city's industry by building a dye factory. As described in *Natural History* (ca. A.D. 77), a Roman encyclopedia compiled by Pliny the Elder, harvesters extracted the purple colorant from the *Murex trunculus* and *Murex brandaris*, small spiny sea snails or whelks that thrived on the small archipelago across from Essaouira's beach. To make the dye, workers exposed yellow fluid from the shell to light and stabilized it with urine to produce a shade known as Tyrian or royal purple, a rich crimson favored for the ceremonial border on senatorial togas.

With the creation of Islam in the 600s, Saracens seized Morocco and controlled all of North Africa around 700. Unlike more virulent Muslim communities, the people of the region remained loyal to the faith, yet established a reputation for religious tolerance. Two centuries later, the citizens named their town Amogdoul [well-protected] in honor of a Berber magnate, Sidi Mogdoul, who became their patron saint. They honored his tomb a few kilometers away from the town center.

Late in the fifteenth century, Essaouira received Sephardic Jews fleeing the Spanish Inquisition, which ousted Jews and Muslims from Iberia in 1492. This act of charity toward the stateless instituted one of the Islamic world's most honored open-door traditions. Essaouira created a welcoming environment that aided both Arabs and Jews to coexist without suspicion or animosity, to maintain their cultural identities, yet, to share customs, dress, and cuisine. The populace grew to one-third Jewish and supported commerce and thirty synagogues, where worshippers intoned Andalusian-Sephardic songs.

In the late 1400s, when England, Portugal, and Spain vied with Moroccans to control North Africa, the Portuguese chose Essaouira as a military outpost and commercial center and renamed it Mogdoura or Mogador. On its shores emerged a free port trading in African gold dust, ivory tusks, and negro slaves. In 1506, Manuel I, the king of Portugal during its golden era of voyages and expansion, engaged architect Diego d'Azambuja, builder of Elmina Castle in Ghana, to establish a coastal fortress, Castello Real. (*See also* ELMINA CASTLE, GHANA.) The defense site was necessary to protect the newcomers from Arab and Berber attacks. Despite these precautions, by 1541, local traders recaptured their home from the Portuguese. In 1577, the fame of the region drew English navigator Sir Francis Drake for a visit. To assure the welfare of the port, in 1628, Moulay Abdelmalek rebuilt the crumbling coastal fortress.

After Morocco developed its interest in the outside world, in 1760, the ambitious Alouite sultan Sidi Muhammad ibn Abdullah held captive French architect and surveyor Théodore Cornut, a student of French military engineer Sébastien le Prestre de Vauban. The sultan forced Cornut to lay out a formal plan based on Moorish fortress towns of the Middle Ages and resembling the French port of Saint Malo, Brittany, city of the corsairs. Essaouira's sculpted architecture whitewashed, then outlined in ochre and red and shuttered in bright sea blue blended French boulevard influences with Portuguese and Berber basics.

The sultan wanted a compact gated city to rival Agadir to the south. He instructed Cornut to incorporate both defense and the Mellah, a commercial center in the northeast of town which the sultan populated with Moroccan Hebrew brokers, called "the king's Jews." As the sultan commanded, Cornut's new town center complemented the cross-shaped *Skala du Port* [ramparts of the port], overlooking anchorage for the royal navy. When the new buildings, walls, and streets were complete, the sultan set up consulates and encouraged additional trade by marketing the products of tanners, artisans, painters, and sculptors. In 1765, he named the city Essaouira from the Arabic *al Souirah* [the wall] and, a decade later, established a mint near the mercantile center, which controlled forty percent of Moroccan trade with Europe.

In the 1800s, Essaouira, the port city for Timbuktu, developed into Morocco's main port, the only North African harbor open to Europeans. Local people prospered from trade with British, Danish, Dutch, French, German, Italian, Portuguese, and Spanish merchants in local sardines and African gold, sugar, sea salt, and ostrich feathers. To assure public health during international exchange, European medical authorities forced the city's government to oversee stringent rules against the importation of cholera and other communicable diseases spread by the return of Muslim pilgrims on their annual haj to Mecca. Each year in September, Jews from around the globe made pilgrimages to the Jewish cemetery and site of a shrine to a Hebrew saint, Rabbi Chaim Pinto, a bible scholar and fabulist and one of the revered Wise Men of Morocco. Attesting to the ease of human relations, Jews continued to worship in their synagogues and even offered Torah readings in Arabic.

International unrest weakened Essaouira's hold on North African trade. In 1844, after Abd al-Kadir established an Algerian resistance to foreigners, the French shelled the city. To draw more European visitors, Essaouira remained a tariff-free port into the 1900s, when the wharves housed both British and Moorish vessels. Under protection of the French, in 1912, officials changed the city's name back to the medieval Mogador, but maintained the open-door policy that made the region the Arab world's most Judaic settlement. A thriving middle class of silverworkers and artisans relieved pockets of poverty created by refugees from less prosperous regions.

During World War II, once more opened its port to the unfortunate. King Sidi Mohammed inveighed against the Vichy French for deporting Jews into Nazi hands for extermination in death camps. Ethnic tensions throughout Europe forced Essaouira to extend its role of multinational peacemaker by welcoming 300,000 Jews in flight from the Nazis. On November 8, 1942, during Operation Torch, General Dwight D. Eisenhower landed a convoy of U.S. troops at Essaouira and established an allied base in Morocco.

The return of peace restored the creativity and laid-back philosophy of Essaouira. By 1956, when local people reverted to the original Moroccan name of Essaouira, the city once more offered tourists a melange of Andalusian, European, and Melhoun music and cuisine. Into the 1950s, a stream of movie stars sought the exotic coastal atmosphere, where Orson Welles filmed *Othello* (1952), winner of a Grand Prix at the Cannes Film Festival. The lure for famous people — novelist Madame de Staël, fabulist Antoine de Saint-Exupéry, and playwright Tennessee Williams — continued with the arrival of hippies and rock stars, notably, the Rolling Stones, Cat Stevens, and Jimi Hendrix.

After a decade of work toward salvaging the crumbling ramparts, in 1996, a consortium of ecologists discussed how to protect Essaouira from salinization of aquifers and from beach erosion. They conceived a restoration plan to preserve the historic medina at the city center and built a breakwater to weaken and deflect the pounding waves. After making emergency repairs to the seawall, city authorities relocated poor families residing nearby, established green swards and recreational areas, and upgraded sanitation. To preserve the city's history, planners rehabilitated the port fortification and the old Danish consulate.

Folklore

According to Moroccan legend, Bilal, a black slave from Guinea, saved Lalla Fatima Zahra, one of the four daughters of the trader Khadijah and her husband, the prophet Mohammed, whom Fatima, his favorite child, nursed during the last months of his life. After Mohammed's death on June 8, 632, she sank into despair and wailed into the night, longing for "Allahu akbar" [God is great], the first words of the Adhan, the Muslim call to prayer. Bilal played the crotales, a pair of iron castanets, and used incantatory folk methods of relieving Fatima's life-threatening melancholia. Upon recovery, Fatima founded the Shiite branch of Islam and was proclaimed one of Islam's four perfect woman.

In recognition of the importance of music to ethnotherapy, each June, citizens of Essaouira celebrate a festival of world music. On the Lila of Derdeba [the Night of Healing], the Gnaoua (or Gnawa), black ancestors of Guinean slaves, celebrate their Afro-Islamic roots. Troops of robed performers called "brotherhoods of Gnaoua" process, play crotales and the *sintir* [lute], sound the *tbel* [barrel drum], and sing and dance. To cure the sick, in an all-night mystic ceremony, performers chant a seven-part ritual, call on the *mlouk* [supernatural], burn incense, and re-enact the healing musical trance that purged Fatima of an evil spirit.

Ecosystem

Essential to the region around Essaouira is the thorny argan or Moroccan ironwood, an evergreen tree and a doughty survivor of thin soil, heat, wind, and drought. Long-lived, but gnarled, the argan reaches some 35 feet in height. It provides branches low enough to extend leaves and fleshy green date-like fruit to browsing goats and sheep. The animals excrete the fruit pits, saving herders the trouble of removing the rough shells.

Over the centuries, processing the argan fruit generated a family business among desert dwellers. After opening the pits, Berber women roasted and ground the argan nut, which resembles the almond. Through a lengthy process similar to the making of olive oil, they added warm water to make the dark reddish oil float, then patiently extracted the nut-flavored arganine oil to serve on salads or couscous. They pounded the nut meats to produce *amlou*, a fatty brown paste eaten at breakfast as a dip for bread and mixed with honey by Berber cameleers during long treks over the Sahara.

The oil had a number of other uses. It was an ingredient in skin preparations, aphrodisiacs, soaps, and cosmetics. As a medicine, the oil soothed outbreaks of chicken pox and acne, stretch marks, and the arthritic joints and dry skin caused by advancing age. The versatile oil was also valued as a lamp fuel. Argan wood heated stoves and could be carved into inlaid chests and boxes, domestic utensils, implements, and plows. The argan's shady canopy sheltered small animals; deep roots protected the harbor town from soil erosion and desertification.

Coastal Activities

Visitors to Essaouira come for the quiet and cleanliness of the Moroccan shore and the peace of courtyard lodgings. At the modest market, crafters sell intaglio mosaics, chess sets and salad bowls, jars of spice, carpets, and filigree lamps crafted from cedar, ebony, lemon wood, thuja, and walnut wood. The Sidi Mohamed Ben Abdellah Museum, founded in the residence of a former pasha, preserves stringed instruments, costumes, jewelry, fiber work, marquetry, and weapons from the days of the sultan. Galleries offer canvases by local painters Nourredine Alioua, Fatima Ettalbi, and Mohammed Tabaland and pieces by stone sculptor Mohammed Bouada.

Activities suited to personal interests and hobbies are in great supply. Nature lovers enjoy strolling the dunes and watching the barbary partridge, brown-throated sand martin, black-headed bush shrike, or the endangered Eleanor's falcon, which is found at the harbor's bird sanctuary, at Ksob Wadi south of town, or at their breeding grounds on the Île de Mogador, once called *iles purpuraires* [the purple isles] for the dye-bearing murex shells. Photographers frame the architecture, arched windows, and city gates — the Bab Sbaâ and Bab Doukalla — before moving on toward the traditional shipyard and crenellated walls of the ramparts, punctuated by seventeenth-century bronze cannon guarding the shore and adjacent archipelagos. More athletic visitors camp on shore to surf, sail, fly surf, funboard, and windsurf in the ceaseless wind. In June 1999, the region involved participants from England, France, Germany, and Hawaii in free style, high jump, and speed surfing at the World Fly Surf Championship.

SOURCES

"Ancient Medina of Essaouira to Be Officially Proclaimed World Heritage," *Friends of Morocco Newsletter*, March 2002.

"Argan," *Australian New Crops Newsletter*, July 10, 1998.

Bezzaz, Mohammed Amine el, "Les Debuts de la Reglementation Sanitaire du Pelerinage Marocain a la Mecque," *Hespéris-Tamuda*, Vol. 22, 1984, pp. 67–77.

Fabricant, Florence, "Latest Oil in American Pantry Is Argan Oil from Morocco," *New York Times*, January 3, 2001.

Gardener, Ian, "Out on the Town: Essaouira, Morocco," *Geographical*, Vol. 73, No. 8, August 2001, p. 95.

Harnik, Eva, "In a Moroccan Tizzy: A Cool Side Trip," *World and I*, March 2001.

MacLeod, Scott, "The King and I," *Time*, May 28, 2001.

Moussouris, Yorgis, and Alan Pierce, "Biodiversity Links to Cultural Identity in Southwest Morocco," *Arid Lands Newsletter*, November/December 2000.

"Music-Morocco: Gnawa Celebrates African Roots," *Inter Press Service*, June 29, 2001.

Nizar al-Ali, "Fight to Save Rare Endangered Tree," *One World*, November 1998.

Paskoff, Roland, "Le Rempart Historique d'Essaouira," *Mondes et Cultures*, Vol. 59–60, No. 3-4, 1999–2000, pp. 64–67.

Schmitz, Philip C., "A Research Manual on Phoenician and Punic Civilization," *Journal of the American Oriental Society*, Vol. 121, No. 4, October 1, 2001, p. 623.

Schroeter, Daniel, "Anglo-Jewry and Essaouira, 1860–1900," *Jewish Historical Society of England*, Vol. 28, 1981–1982, pp. 60–88

Spritzer, Dina A., "'Party Line' Aside, Moroccan Jews, Arabs Find Mutual Respect," *Travel Weekly*, Vol. 54, No. 81, October 12, 1995, pp. 14–15.

Tuts, Raf, "Awakening of a Coastal Town: Localizing Agenda 21 in Essaouira," *UN Chronicle*, March–May 2001, p. 58.

"The Voyage of Hanno, King of the Carthaginians," http://www.jate.u-szeged.hu/~gnovak/f99htHanno.htm.

Zwingle, Erla, "Morocco," *National Geographic*, October 1996, pp. 98–125.

Fortescue Bay, Tasmania

Location

The heart-shaped island of Tasmania, Australia's only island state, offers spectacular mountain scenery, a valuable wilderness, rain forests, and lakes. For this reason, the island is comprised of more government-operated preserves than any other state. Some 35 miles east of Hobart, the sheltered white-sand crescent of Fortescue Bay lies on the southeast coast of Tasman Peninsula among tall gum trees within the Abel Tasman Forest Reserve. Curving south along Fortescue Lagoon and opposite Canoe and Bivouac bays, the bay extends eastward within a somber arm of sea cliffs, the highest in the Southern Hemisphere.

In view of the automated lighthouse rising 250 feet from Tasman Island, the glaciated coastline is washed by clear, tranquil waters rich in food fish — abalone, crayfish, king crab, mackerel, oyster, rock lobster, scallop, shrimp, and mako and white shark. The World Heritage Area protects 20 percent of the island's treasured environments. In early 1994, when the crew of the French research vessel *L'Atalante* studied the seabed south of Tasmania for the Australian Geological Survey Organisation, divers found seamounts hosting additional life forms. Where currents met near extinct volcanoes some thirty million years old, plankton and other sea food fed an array of animal life.

Contacts

Tasmanian Parks and Wildlife Service
Tasman Peninsula
Port Arthur, Tasmania 7182
Phone: 61-0-3-6233-6191
Email: interps@dpiwe.tas.gov.au
www.parks.tas.gov.au

Forestry Tasmania
79 Melville Street
Hobart, Tasmania, 7000
www.forestrytas.com.au

History

Humans from Australia first arrived on Tasmania by 38,000 B.C. Around 23,000 B.C., survivors had to adapt to unpredictable changes in climate. By 8000 B.C., during the last ice age, rising seas permanently separated the aborigines from Australia, causing them to develop a unique culture apart from Australia's native people. Tasmanians lived unclothed except for the charcoal and oil skin rub and ochred hair that distinguished them from the mother island's populace.

The sea nourished the island's aborigines. They inhabited bark hovels near teeming shores, where hunter-gatherers dived for abalone and lobsters and gathered shellfish. They made seasonal treks to plentiful hunting and gathering grounds, where they clubbed possums. These survival methods

sufficed until the arrival of Europeans cost the aborigines their traditional haunts.

On November 24, 1642, Dutch adventurer Abel Janszoon Tasman, an employee of the Dutch East India Company, first glimpsed Tasmania while exploring Australia and the South Pacific with two ships, the *Heemskerk* and the *Zeehaen*. His intent was to map a sea route to Chile. For extensive South Seas explorations, he earned the rank of commander, yet disappointed the firm by failing to locate rich lands. For the next 214 years, the island was called Van Diemen's Land after Anthony Van Diemen, the governor of the East Indies who dispatched Tasman on the fact-finding mission.

The French and English were the next to show interest in the South Pacific. In 1772, explorer Marc-Joseph Marion du Fresne and Julien Crozet sailed to Tasmania aboard the *Mascarin* and *Le Marquis de Castries*, followed a year later by Tobias Furneaux of Portsmouth, England, who captained the *Adventure* for the British and charted Tasmania's eastern and southern coast. As head of the *Esperance* and *Recherche*, on April 23, 1792, Joseph Antoine Bruni, Cavalier d'Entrecasteaux, a French naval commander from Aix-en-Provence, led a lengthy exploration. He left his name on the d'Entrecasteaux channel on the island's southern tip, but died of dysentery and scurvy on July 21, 1793, off New Guinea and was buried at sea. In 1798, British surgeon George Bass and Royal Navy navigator Lieutenant Matthew Flinders sailed near Tasmania through a strait named for Bass. Discovery of the passage lessened travel time from the Cape of Good Hope or from India to Sydney by seven days. By circumnavigating the land mass, Flinders established that Tasmania was an island.

In 1802, under the aegis of the Emperor Napoleon, French navigator Nicholas Baudin sailed to the South Pacific on a cartographic mission with the corvettes *Le Geographe* and

Le Naturaliste. Traveling among scientists on the forty-month expedition were 25-year-old artist Nicolas-Martin Petit and 22-year-old painter and taxidermist Charles-Alexandre Lesueur of Le havre, who produced the most useful on-site reproduction —1,500 accurate watercolor drawings of the region's unusual animals. Ravaged by dysentery, malaria, scurvy, and snake bite, the expeditioners collected 60,000 dried specimens of plants and 40,000 of animals. About 2,500, notably, the emu, kangaroo, koala, platypus, wallaby, and wombat, were unknown to the French. Lesueur allotted his specimens to the Empress Josephine and the Jardin des Plantes. His watercolors first appeared in print in the multi-volume *Voyage de Decouvertes aux Terres Australes* [Voyage of Discoveries of Australian Lands] (1807), published three years after co-author Petit's sudden death. After Lesueur's appointment to curator of the Muséum d'Histoire Naturelle du Havre in 1845, he hung many drawings and paintings on public display.

While Baudin's men cruised and studied the island, the British were actively colonizing Tasmania with transported criminals, whose punishments consisted of isolation from society at a rocky land where they performed intense forced labor. (*See also* SYDNEY, NEW SOUTH WALES.) Between 1830 and 1877, England dispatched around 12,500 convicts to labor in mines and logging camp and reside in silent cells. In public, prisoners maintained silence and appeared among free citizens in hoods and masks to conceal their identities.

By 1840, the European population topped 57,000 as Hobart welcomed traffic from whalers and sealing crews at ports constructed by convict labor. After the cessation of penal colonization in 1852, the rapid decline of aborigines resulted in part from the sexual slavery of native women. Authorities relocated dispossessed natives to Oyster Cove on Flinders Island in the Bass Strait, where they pined for home and died of hunger, European diseases, and despair. By 1876, Tasmania was occupied solely by immigrants, who valued natural resources and the sandy bays of the southern coast.

Fortescue Bay made headlines on November 8, 1915, when the S. S. *Nord*, a 1,057-ton, 290-foot cargo steamer, sank at 2:00 A. M. at the base of a cliff. On the way to Hobart from Melbourne with 12,000 cases of fuel, the vessel ran afoul of a sou'wester that forced it onto uncharted Needle Rock between the Hippolytes, twin off-shore isles. The captain tried to limp into Port Arthur, but lost steam when in-gushes of seawater extinguished the coal fires under the boilers. The wreckage settled in 120 feet of water with its keel pressed to the sandy bottom.

Ecosystem

The spectacular underwater habitat of the Tasman Sea derives from the warm water of the continental shelf and the updrifts of colder water from the ocean floor, which sinks away over 3,000 feet. Feeding the panorama of sea life are abundant plankton amid waving sea whips, feathery gorgonians, sea dragons, anemones, salpa and other tunicates, long spined sea urchins, and orange and yellow sponges. Anchored to a sandy, rocky bottom, forests of giant string kelp *(Macrocystis pyrifera)*, which writer and illustrator Jeannie Baker featured in the children's book *The Hidden Forest* (2000), stretch nearly 100 feet in length. Among clouds of shrimp, divers photograph elephantfish, lobsters, seahorses, Ziebell's handfish, saw and white shark, barber and butterfly perch, seastars, weedfish, fur seal, skates, sculpins, and venomous red velvet fish.

A lure to experienced divers in Fortescue Bay is Cathedral Cave, one part of a sea-cavern network. In an area known for caprices of weather, cave diving requires calm days for maximum safety. Bright corals and sponges mark dim chambers that lure light-avoiding creatures from some 300 feet below. In 1988, discharge of contaminated ballast tanks introduced undaria *(Undaria pinnatifida)*, a heavy brown macroalga that grows one centimeter per day in its native Japan Sea. Although the Japanese value it for fresh and dried food and for healing outbreaks of herpes, its rapid growth and invasion of reefs compromised the ecosystem, reducing visibility for divers, infesting marinas and boat hulls, engulfing reefs, entangling and sinking buoys, and forcing some forms of sea life to feed elsewhere. The Tasman-Nelson Regional Pest Management Strategy organized divers to hand-pluck fronds of the opportunistic pest from the water and add them to compost heaps.

Coastal Activities

Visitors to the rugged south Tasmanian coastline enjoy hiking, fishing, sailing in protected anchorage, swimming, camping at Fortescue Lagoon, and observing the elephant seal, dolphin, and right whale. Beachcombers collect cone shells and starfish; birders sketch or photograph the albatross, gannet, gull, muttonbird, penguin, petrel, and tern. The region also features heartier adventure — shallow diving, sea-kayaking, spelunking, hang gliding, walking the Cape Hauy trail, and climbing the three dolerite pillars, Candlestick, Moai, and Totem Pole. These rugged sea cliffs reach up to 1,000 feet and test the most experienced climbers.

Some beach-goers prefer scuba-diving to the wreckage of the S. S. *Nord* or exploring the Lanterns, a mile-long string of rocks at the end of Cape Hauy, a distinctive landmark. From the cape's vantage point, visitors can look far north to Schouten Island off the Freycinet Peninsula. Others choose seaplane flights over the bay for sightseeing and photography. To enjoy clean air and scenic wonders in unspoiled settings, some travel inland to Fortescue Bay's camp-grounds or Oyster Bay Pines, visit the mountains by rail, or choose bushwalks or self-driving tours in Cape Pillar State Reserve, Pirate's Bay, Waterfall Bluff, or the Abel Tasman Forest Reserve.

SOURCES

Bavendam, Fred, "In Search of the Ziebell's Handfish," *International Wildlife*, November–December 1996, pp. 52–57.

"Beautiful Scenery Is Accessible to All," *Travel Trade Gazette U. K. & Ireland*, May 7, 2001, p.46 .

Brace, Matthew, "Trek Tasmania," *Geographical*, September 2002, pp. 87–89.

Cooper, Russell, et al. "GFS, a Preparation of Tasmanian *Undaria pinnatifida* Is Associated with Healing and Inhibition of Reactivation of Herpes," *BMC Complementary and Alternative Medicine*, Vol. 2, February 17, 2003.

Croft, Fiona, "Safe Havens to the East," *Offshore Yachting*, December 2000, p. 52.

Diamond, Jared, "Ten Thousand Years of Solitude," *Discover*, March 1993, pp. 48–57.

Doubilet, David, "Beneath the Tasman Sea," *National Geographic*, January 1997, pp. 82–101.

Firth, Jeremy, "Down the d'Entrecasteaux Channel," *Offshore Yachting*, December 2001, pp. 48–52.

Foster, Catherine, "Lush Tasmania Is Australia's Counterpoint," *Christian Science Monitor*, November 2, 1995.

Fuller, Errol, "Voyage of a Painter," *Natural History*, April 1998, pp. 12–14.

Gussie, Grant, "Two Wrecks," *Calquarium*, Vol. 41, No. 6, February 1999.

Holden, Peter, "Tasmania, with Tea and Scones," *Insight on the News*, April 24, 1995, p. 30.

James, Jamie, "The Edge of the World," *Atlantic Monthly*, March 2000, p. 32.

Johnson, Katherine, "Deep Discoveries," *Ecos*, April–June 1998, pp. 14–19.

Jones, Lisa, "Tasmania Wildness Unbound," *Buzzworm*, July–August 1992, pp. 71–75.

Obendorf, David, "Fortescue Bay," *Tasmanian Conservationist*, No. 279, December 2001.

Porch, Nick, and Jim Allen, "Tasmania: Archaeological and Palaeo-ecological Perspectives," *Antiquity*, 1995, pp. 714–732.

Pyper, Wendy, "Running with Bugs," *Ecos*, July–September 2002, pp. 29–31.

Roy, Barb, "Trekking Tasmania," *Diver*, June 2001.

Sanderson, Craig, "Looking After Fish Habitats," *Fishing Today*, February 20, 2000.

_____, "Wakame—Long Spined Sea Urchin," *Fishing Today*, March 20, 2002.

Sayle, Murray, "Primal Planet," *Conde Nast Traveler*, August 2001, pp. 56–56–70.

"Tasmania the Exotic Apple That's Now Tempting U.S. Tourists," *Sydney Morning Herald*, July 20, 2002.

Thompson, Jo-Ann, "Joseph Antoine Bruni Chevalier d'Entrecasteaux," *Stamps*, December 11, 1993, p. 323.

Halong Bay, Vietnam

Location

Halong Bay is a natural marvel—a clean, tranquil stretch of the South China Sea pocked with 1,969 limestone and schist peaks and hidden freshwater lakes. Geologically diverse, the green karst islets and sheer pinnacles resulted from seabed erosion over 1,650 square miles of a limestone plateau beneath the aquamarine waters. Lying along 135 miles of coastline in northeast Vietnam, the bay blends the geographical backdrops of coral reef, fissures and sinkholes, fjords and pebbled beaches, saltwater bogs, serenely meandering sea corridors, rock spindles and bridges, and tors sculpted by wind and surf. The shore, now a popular resort, is known for shifting mists that add gray, mauve, olive, and teal hues and impart sparkle from changes in natural light. The rocks winnow and echo evocative wind sounds that complement the elaborate folklore and sailors' tales of a sea *tarasque* [monster], all human interpretations of natural phenomena.

Contacts

Vietnam National Administration of Tourism
80 Quan Su, Hoan Kiem
Hanoi, Vietnam
Phone: 84-4-8224714
Email: vnat@vietnamtourism.gov.vn
http://www.vietnamtourism.gov.vn/

Mythology

Natural shapes in Halong Bay suit tales of the supernatural. Vietnamese folklore tells of the supreme jade emperor who dispatched a dragon family, symbols of nobility and justice, to swoop down from the sky and protect Vietnam from northern invaders. During the battle, the thrashing of a dragon's tail split mountains and produced Halong Bay. The dolomitic outcrops arising in the Gulf of Tonkin were pearls and jade-green gems that the dragon spit as ammunition. Local convention supplied names for the formations—Dragon, Driftwood, Frog, Incense Burner, Man's Head, Fighting Roosters, Sail, and Teapot. The beauty of the bay served Vietnamese artists with a limitless source of inspiration.

Two romantic settings—Trinh Nu [Virgin Grotto] and Trong [Male Grotto]—commemorate the story of a fisherman who had to pledge his daughter as sex slave to a wealthy Mandarin overlord. Because she loved another man, she reneged on her father's oath. The overlord banished her to a bay island, where his soldiers left her to die of exposure and starvation. Her corpse turned to stone. When her lover rowed out to the bay to find her, a gale forced him to a nearby island. In the distance, he glimpsed the cold, hard outline of his love's body and flowing hair and sank onto the shore, where he, too, turned to stone. Pilgrims visited the romantic sites to leave fruit, incense, and coins and pray for true love.

Another mythic explanation of limestone formations describes the ornately figured Thien Cung [Heavenly Palace Grotto], a cave hidden by thick woods. Because May [Cloud] appealed to the Dragon Prince, he won her love. They courted and married at the heart of the grotto. The nuptial ceremonies, set at vertical organ pipes under the central "roof of heaven," broke into the frolics of fairies and scenes of guests, fish, birds, and wedding flowers. The

Halong Bay, Vietnam, is a natural marvel — a clean, tranquil stretch of the South China Sea pocked with 1,969 limestone and schist peaks and hidden freshwater lakes (courtesy of Mads Nygaard).

seven-day ceremony and its rituals supposedly marked the fossilized surface of the cave walls. When the wind blew, the grotto echoed with the beat of a wedding drum.

The longest cave, Quang Hanh [Tunnel Grotto], opens at low tide to reveal colorful stalactites and Ba Co [Three-Girl Shrine]. The images of three girls traveling by sea resulted from their retreat to the cave to escape a storm. Because they were unaware that the grotto flooded at high tide, they drowned. Kindly gods changed them into water sprites, whom fishers propitiated to guard them as they cast their nets and rowed home with loads of seafood.

Mythic explanation of local pearls derives from the legend of My Chau, a traitor to King An Duong Vuong after she revealed to her lover the location of a magic arrow at Co Loa citadel in Hanoi. When enemies seized the stronghold, the holy tortoise informed the king of her betrayal. My Chau and her father fled to the coast. After the king overtook and killed her, he grieved for his country's disaster and killed himself. My Chau's husband also despaired and drowned himself in a well. Where the victims' blood spilled into the sea, oysters produced abundant oversized pearls, the source of local income from pearl diving and oyster farming.

History

"Vinh Ha Long," a name meaning "bay of the dragon's way to the sea," is part of the historic Gulf of Tonkin, where Communist leader Ho Chi Minh spent his summers. According to archeological evidence, the waterfront saw the emersion of agrarian and piscatory communities at Cat Ba Island, Dong Mang, Soi Nhu, Thoi Gieng, and Xich Tho. In 1938, a French archeological team headed by Swedish geologist and author Johan Gunnar Andersson, founder of the Museum of Far Eastern Antiquities in Stockholm, made a thorough study of Halong culture at Cai Beo Cave. Subsequent digs of seventeen sites in 1972, 1973, and 1981 unearthed stone implements, axes and chisels, graters, terra cotta artifacts, prehistoric shells, human teeth, and bones of boar, deer, and goat to indicate that inhabitants populated the region around 5000 B.C.

Halong Bay once hosted rebels, bandits, and pirates, who receded into the mist from pursuers and hid out in grottoes and caves. Fishing families connected their boats to create free-form villages. They dived for oysters and lived at sea without need of beaching their craft. Shore dwellers domesticated wild flora, producing lumber from 118 species of trees and medicines from sixty herbs, including bacson palm, chodoi, kimgiao, lathao, traily, and vanuoc. They climbed sheer cliffs to gather sea swallow nests, the source of a healing broth.

Sequential invasions caused the Halong culture to huddle at the foot of the mountains along the bay, forcing them to think up unique treacheries against their enemies. In A.D. 938, Ngo Quyen grouped ironwood stakes on the bed of the Bach Dang River to impale the armada of the South Han dynasty. In A.D. 981, King Le Dai Hanh successfully reprised the battle plan when the Song advanced on the bay. In 1917, the emperor Khai Dinh visited Dau Go [Driftwood Grotto] to honor the memory of Tran Hung Dao, a legendary warrior who applied the trick a third time. To protect a riverbed from an invasion of Kublai Khan's 300,000 Mongols, in 1287, Tran tipped bamboo stakes with steel and positioned them below the waves. At low tide, the Chinese general O Ma Nhi found his vessels impaled and sunk by the thrice-clever ruse.

It is obvious to locals and visitors alike why Halong Bay is worth saving. In 1468, while the beloved poet-emperor Le Thanh Tong toured the bay, he halted at Bai Tho [Poem Mountain]. The loveliness of the view over Halong Bay inspired his verse, which he ordered a calligrapher to engrave on the slope. In 1729, Lord Trinh Cuong added his own poem, the first of six additions to the mountainside treasury of writings. Out of deep appreciation for the bay's natural beauty, modern novelist Nguyen Ngoc described it as God's workshop, where nature sculpted timeless stone art with the natural powers of sea and wind.

The Halong mountain range remained crucial to the Vietnamese in the twentieth century. On August 8, 1961, American bombers targeted the bay during their first raid of the Vietnam War. In the mid–1960s, American planes crashed on the cliffs, where radar uselessly caromed off rocky surfaces. Medical forces set up a hospital at Hungson Cave in Cat Ba Island as a hedge against falling bombs. During this turbulent period, the island developed into a symbol of hope and stability — a national park that became a haven of natural beauty during the lengthy, brutal conflict. In 1991 and 1992, contemporary artist Geoff Lowe of Melbourne, Australia, visited Halong Bay and created drawings and gouaches of the region on linen. Later, his expanded realism of jungle, landscapes, shrines, and wooded settings earned exhibits in Hanoi and Saigon.

Coastal Activities

Declared a UNESCO World Heritage Site in 1994, Halong Bay's stone islands form one of Vietnam's focal attractions, which survived undeveloped until 1997. Among scenic wonders are Hon Dua [Praying Buddha], Sung Sot [Awe-inspiring Grotto], and Tam Cung [Three Palace Grotto], all examples of the bay's natural imagery locked in stone. Cinematists tapped its beauties for local backdrops, notably, for Regnis Warnier's *L'Indochine* (1992), Oscar winner for best foreign film, which the Paradise Film Company set at Hon Oan Island, fictionalized as L'ile du Dragon. A decade later, investment increased tourism in 2002 with the building of a beachfront hotel complex.

Visitors to Bai Chay Beach, a windward resort, swim and snorkel in isolated beach coves, row or kayak alone or in tandem, and hire tourist junks for a languorous glide through Halong Bay. The more adventuresome fish, climb and delve into stalactites and stalagmites, and photograph Buddhist shrines erected in the caves. Some choose a torchlit guided excursion through tranquil waters and listen to the retelling of age-old myths about fossilized images that have left their unique prints on each grotto and spire. History buffs explore evidence of the China trade route to the old port of Van Don, the red brick lighthouse of Ngoc Vung Island, and the site of naval battles at the Bach Dang River. Children enjoy a circus and a dugong and porpoise show at the 3,000-seat shell-roofed arena; adults opt for relaxing on an artificial beach at Halong City or for golfing, gambling, and collecting the region's rare shells.

The curious visit Cat Ba island and national park by ferry or hydrofoil and photograph boar, chamois, hedgehogs, macaques, red-buttocked monkeys, dolphins, and seals. Birders seek the caocat, cuckoo, hawk, honeysucker, hoopoe, and hornbill. Tropical groves of casuarina, fica, and mangrove trees are roosting sites for migratory shorebirds. Of particular interest is the Cay Kim Gao tree, the source of magic chopsticks said to turn from tan to black if they touch poisoned food.

SOURCE

Boren, Milly, "Kayaking among Dragons," *New York Times*, May 10, 1998.

"Cac Dao Vinh Ha Long Cultural and Historical Site," *Sourcebook of Existing and Proposed Protected Areas in Vietnam*, February 19, 2001.

Diep Dinh Hoa, "New Findings on Zhang in the Phung Nguyen Culture," *South Pacific Study*, Vol. 17, No. 1, 1996, pp. 83–102.

Green, Charles, "Geoff Lowe," *Artforum International*, Vol. 32, No. 4, December 1993, p. 93.

"Halong Bay Island Transformed," *Asia Africa Intelligence Wire*, September 2, 2002.

James, Jamie, and Russell Ciochon, "Voyage to Vietnam," *Archaeology*, Vol. 46, No. 4, July–August 1993, pp. 48–50.

Pritchard, Chris, "Beauty and the Beast," *Business Traveller Asia Pacific*, November 2001, pp. 54–57.

"Star Cruises Operates Additional Ship to Halong Bay," *Asia Africa Intelligence Wire*, November 19, 2002.

"Taiwanese Investors Up the Ante in Halong Bay Resort," *Asia Africa Intelligence Wire*, September 9, 2002.

Thich Vien Thanh, "Beating a Path to Happiness," *Vietnam News*, February 16, 2002.

Ijsselmeer, Holland

Location

Originally a Rhine-fed freshwater lake that the Romans called Flevum Lacus, Ijsselmeer was once northeastern Holland's shallow influx of the North Sea known as Almere [Great Sea] or the Zuider Zee [South Sea]. To sailors, the strip of shoreward dunes was thin; the inlet posed difficult sailing beset by fickle, unpredictable winds. Through human intervention, the inlet was reincarnated a second time with the closure of the sea's access, leaving as its main replenisher the Ijssel River. Mudflats and bogs line the shore, where reclaimers of the flood plain score the land with ditches and heap the soil into protective dikes and levees. In land over ten feet below sea level, retaining walls formed of rocks, rubble, and brush and planted with Kwelder grass keep silt from washing into the channel. The sprouting surface became pasturage for sheep and welcomed a wide variety of shore and migratory birds.

Today, the ongoing process of heaping of earth and rock creates more land for development and building. To protect the lowlying tracts from rising salinity, pump stations continually eject seawater. As water levels drop, the former lake and sea become archeological hunting grounds rife with the remains of Holland's ocean-front towns and sea-going past. With history literally tramped underfoot like a nautical graveyard, scientists and historians resurrect from the muck and loam of Holland's wet heart the bones of indigenous mammals and birds as well as the hulks of downed ships, barges, and planes.

Contacts

Nederlands Instituut voor Scheeps
Oostvaardersdijk 01-04
8242 PA Lelystad, Holland
Phone: 31-0-320-269700
Fax: 31-0-320-269750
Email: info@archis.nl
http://www.archis.nl/html/nisa/index.html.

Tourist Information Office
Noord Five
8711 AA Workum, Holland
Phone: 0031-515-54-1300

Legend

According to a Dutch legend about the Zuider Zee, the city of Stavoren, which was founded around 500 B.C., developed into a flourishing port during the rise of the Hanseatic League, a trade consortium formed by north German towns. Stavoren traded peat and salt with England, France, and Scandinavia until the municipality vanished, just like the region that the sea inundated during the Middle Ages. The cause of the catastrophe was the foolishness of a rich, pompous berger named Richberta, the *Het Vrouwtje van Stavoren* [Lady of Stavoren], the widow of a successful merchant and fleet owner. To flaunt her wealth and beauty, she was hosting a feast when a seafarer arrived. He marveled at the prosperity and luxury of Stavoren, where even door knobs were wrought from gold. To hear more flattery, she invited him to dine. He followed Asian customs by asking for bread and salt. Servants ignored his odd request and offered him sumptuous courses.

After dinner, the outsider, like the wandering Odysseus, told of his travels. Central to the stories was the transitory nature of human fortune, a theme that sobered the festive diners. Richberta regretted welcoming the intruder because his tales depicted the wealthy as doomed to a host of personal and economic disappointments. On a tour of her home, the stranger admired the mansion, but regretted the absence of the earth's noblest treasure. To her questions, he refused to identify the item and soon took his leave.

Richberta dispatched a state fleet and instructed the admiral to locate earth's most valued treasure, which she intended to flaunt before envious rivals. He sailed east and west without success. When a leak spoiled the bread stored in the hold of one ship, the crew went hungry. The admiral recognized that gems and precious metals were worthless when people lacked bread. He applied his conclusion to the tales of the stranger at the feast and realized the true meaning of "earth's noblest treasure."

At the grain depots in Gdansk, Poland, the admiral filled his fleet with wheat and sailed home to Stavoren. Richberta questioned his enterprise and learned that the mission had resulted in the purchase of common stores. In a fit of anger, she commanded a servant to toss the grain into the North Sea. When the poorest citizens learned the fate of the unwanted wheat, they crowded around Richberta's mansion to beg her to rescind the order. She ignored the ragged petitioners, even women who knelt and raised their empty hands to her for succor.

After the servant jettisoned bags of wheat into the sea, Stavoren's poorest citizens cursed Richberta and prayed that God would avenge their loss. She pulled a gold ring from her finger and tossed it into the surf with a promise that the ring would return to her hand before she should fall into misfortune. To her dismay, the sea proved her nemesis. Within days, she sliced into a meal of white fish and discovered the ring inside it.

That year, the grains sprouted on the sea floor, tangled in seaweed, and choked Stavoren's harbor. Richberta's fleet sank; trade came to a halt. The people of Stavoren lapsed into poverty and blamed their proud patroness for the town's ill luck. After they drove her out of town, poverty forced her to beg for food. Cursed among humble people, she wandered until she died of exhaustion and hunger. One night, the sea flooded the dunes and buried the town. Sailors of the Zuider Zee declared that they could glimpse the haughty towers of Richberta's town still rising from the seabed. They named a harbor sandbar *Vrouwenzand* [Lady's Sand] in honor of the greedy, self-important Richberta. Standing in Stavoren is a statue of the proud woman with an uplifted hand to her forehead as she looks out to sea.

According to a second legend, the submerging of Dutch villages covered a treasure in gold along the Zuider Zee. Before the engulfing of Etersheim, an affluent town during the Spanish occupation of Holland, false accusations linked Dirk Smit, the wealthiest burger, with the disappearance of two Spaniards. After the Spanish executed Smit and his wife, villagers spread rumors that the couple left a fortune in gold guilders and ducats buried in the doomed town.

Survivors of the flood prowled the region, but found no gold. Decades later, an iron crate turned up 350 yards from the coast. The lucky finder was astonished to locate goldpieces inside. Within weeks, a fisherman netted a gold ring even closer to the shore. Each find padded the treasure tale and fanned the hopes that more gold would surface.

History

The region around the freshwater lake of Ijsselmeer between the Ems and Rhine rivers was the ancestral home of Frisian tribes since 3000 B.C., when they ousted resident Celts. Axheads and a flint sickle from the early Bronze Age in 1500 B.C. attest to the growing technological skills of residents. In the pre–Roman era, the Frisians put to sea in narrow, shallow-draft oak vessels propelled by a single sail and rowed by up to thirty oarsmen. After increasing the cargo capacity of their ships, between A.D. 500 and 800, Frisians advanced along the coast in search of trade in metals, woven goods, and wine.

Others of the Frisian nation farmed the rich land, which they heaped into mounds to protect the soil from flooding by the sea. In Book IV of his *Annals* (A.D. 109), the Roman historian Tacitus called the spot *Flevum* (or *Flevo*). His text speaks of a fortress that Roman expeditioner Nero Claudius Drusus established during a Frisian uprising in A.D. 23 to defend the approach from the North Sea. Drusus increased Roman penetration of northern Europe by digging a canal connecting the Rhine with the Yssel River to speed inland raids. As related by Pliny the Elder, early Imperial Rome's encyclopedist, the Roman *Classis Germanica* [Germanic Fleet] patrolled the shores as far east as the Rhine estuary.

Roman development of the Zuider Zee was considerable. Legionaries erected the *Nigrum Pullum* [Black Marsh] fort in A.D. 47 and established quays, landings, and a boatworks that produced fishing boats and troop transports for the next 133 years. According to a find made in the late 1700s by surgeon Rutger Paludanus of Hoorn, an amateur archeologist and author of *Oudheid en Natuurkundige Verhandelingen* [Antiquity and Physical Treatises] (1766), the Romans may also have built a road that the Zuider Zee later covered.

In the early Middle Ages, Flevum, a prosperous land, was ripe pickings for Viking shore raiders. The area deteriorated after a flood opened sea channels into the lake in 1170, engulfing sand dunes as well as whole towns and villages in a shallow, gale-plagued lake. The incursion formed a deep eighty-mile saltwater gulf called the Zuider Zee, created the Boomkensdiep and Marsdiep channels, and left above water the West Frisian islands of Ameland, Engelsmaplaat, Schiermonnikoog, Terschelling, Texel, and Vlieland, collectively known as the West Frisian Islands. Another flood in 1287 drowned 80,000 victims; in 1421, the loss to flooding was 8,000. In the sixteenth century, the Dutch began reclaiming a half million acres of their lost lake and turned the resulting dry land into fertile farms.

The approach of a Spanish fleet near Enkhuizen in winter 1573 illustrates the difficulty of navigating the inland waters of the Zuider Zee. When the surface froze, pack ice immobilized the invading ships. The Dutch surprised the Spaniards by launching a cavalry charge across the ice. The capture of Spanish ships by land forces, called the battle of the Zuider Zee, was the rare sea battle fought with cavalry tactics. The victory preceded Holland's Golden Age, a maritime domination of shipbuilding and exploration that spread over the seventeenth century.

In 1920, technology improved for the revitalization of the former Zuider Zee. On May 28, 1932, the previously untameable saltwater bay ceased to exist. The Zuider Zee Works Department divided the inlet into two parts — the saltwater Waddenzee, a shallow sound beyond a seventeen-mile barrier to the north, and Ijsselmeer, a freshwater lake created inside the dike. A heavy seawall, the Afsluitdijk [closure dike], built of glacial boulder clay, rubble, and sand and capped with basalt and concrete, joined Friesland to the province of North Holland. At the same time, the new barrier locked out the saltwater of the North Sea and Waddenzee. Gone were tides and unruly waters that flooded out farming. At the dike at Den Oever, a statue of Cornelis Lely honors the visionary engineer and minister of public works who conceived the project, but died three years before its completion. His name survives in the town of Lelystad and in the Lely Pumping Station at Medemblik, where electric pumps remove water from polders.

The draining of the region revealed a half million acres of land divided into five regions — Wieringermeer Polder, Noordoost Polder, Eastern Flevoland, Markerwaard, and Southern Flevoland. The government identified five arable tracts of flatland called polders, which produced fields of rye, fruit and vegetables, flowers, and pasture grass. Raised hillocks called terps supported greenhouses and urban expansion. Carrying in fresh water were the IJssel, Vecht, and Zwatewater rivers, which rinsed salt from the former sea bottom. Itinerant teams of *polderjongens* [polder men] tended to the constant surveillance of reclaimed land and repaired dikes, levees, and roads. The addition of locks and drainage sluices protected with weighted brushwood pads encouraged another source of revenue, barge traffic from the Rhine River. To profit from the job of clearing underwater weeds, harbor teams cut kelp from the shallows, collected it in nets, and dried it for use as mattress stuffing. Horse-drawn carts scored the beaches as shell-seekers harvested seashells to be ground for fertilizer.

In World War II, Nazi Germany invaded Holland on May 10, 1940. Near the end of the war, the German high command called for the breaching of the dikes to prevent the Allied army from advancing to free the starving Dutch. Military agents carried out the plot on April 17, 1945, by bombing the dikes. At war's end, the Dutch were liberated, but face flooded polders. By 1950, they once more drained their sub-sea level land and erected a new dike from Lelystad to Harderwijk and a second barrier from Harderwijk to East Flevoland.

Archeology

As the water level receded, the former Zuider Zee turned into the world's most valuable ship graveyard. Dutch government agencies began excavating over 435 shipwrecks along with fishing ports, trading harbors, shipyards, barges, and planes that crashed in the reclaimed land. Under the supervision of Gerrit Daniël van der Heide, director of the archeology division of the Ijsselmeer Polders Development Authority, discoveries typically occurred after farmers plowed up wooden blocks and ironware along with well-preserved equipment, cargo, and human remains. Of interest to anthropologists and historians were personal effects — maps and sextants, prisms and decklights, eggs, grain, tanned leather, pots and pans, jugs and mugs, plates and goblets, utensils, clay pipes, dominoes and toys, shoes, uniforms and clothing, even the wood clapper wielded by a medieval leper to warn the healthy of his approach. Among valuable discoveries were the prow of an elm-log canoe from 5000 B.C., a channel ferry that went down in a gale about 1440, a 99-foot *waterschip* [fish transport vessel] and human skeleton from the 1600s, a spritsail barge or ferry from 1650, a storm-swamped coal barge from 1825 that housed a family with two small children, and the *De Zeehond* [the Seal], a small sea-going vessel carrying a load of bricks that capsized in 1886.

Salvors who recovered items and ships' hulls deposited these shards of history at the *Nederlands Instituut voor Scheeps* [National Institute for Ship and Underwater Archaeology] or the Rijksmuseum of Ship Archeology in Amsterdam, where advanced preservation systems keep fragile materials from disintegrating. Under the direction of Henk van Veen and Sybe de Jong, biologists studied pollen, plant matter, and the layers of silt covering each find to determine the climate conditions of the period. Dendrochronologists helped to pinpoint the date by identifying trees by location and growing period when they were cut for lumber to build the ships. Additional details came from coins and clay tobacco pipes, which were frequently incised with historical images.

In 1953 at Gilze-Rijen Airbase, the Salvage and Recovery Service of the Royal Netherlands Air Force began concentrating on the excavation of wartime plane wreckage, an operation begun during World War II by the German Luftwaffe. Within four years, the drainage process lowered water levels so far that aircraft were visible, but the ground too boggy for the retrieval of heavy metal frames. Under Operation Harvest, on May 11, 1960, the service located the British combat turbojet *Gloster Meteor*, the world's first fighter jet. Near war's end, it intercepted V-1 missiles, but entered air combat after the Allies had destroyed most of the Luftwaffe. The Meteor's remains were the first of 28 planes salvaged and identified over the next 17 years, including two B-17s and a British Hudson downed on July 6, 1944.

Ecosystem

The land around Stavoren offers fresh- and saltwater habitats covering established natural harbors, lowlands, fens, salt marshes, alluvial reedbeds, sandy beaches, and dunes. Despite increased human pollutants from beachgoers and boat traffic, pondweed, hornwort, yellow water lilies, eel, bream, pike, roach, ruff, smelt, and water fleas continue to thrive in inland waters within the seawall. However, the status of the seaward side of the wall is more problematic. Fresh water from the Ijsselmeer Dam has poured into the Waddenzee from outlet sluices near Den Oever, Enkhuizen, Kornwerderzand, and Lelystad since the 1960s, reaching current levels of 5,000 cubic meters per second.

Under stringent water management programs, ejection occurs at ebb tide, with sluices remaining closed during flood tide and inclement weather. According to data collected by the Netherlands Institute for Sea Research, the ocean environment has declined in salinity and has gained more chlorides, nitrates, and phosphates from farmland runoff. Hydro-ecologists have discovered that the shift in water quality promotes algae blooms and alters the number and type of plankton, the food source for sea mammals and endangered coastal birds such as the cormorant, pochard, goosander, tundra swan, and heron, which also thrive on water plants, smelt, perch, and zebra mussel.

Inland, farms located below sea level require constant monitoring. Because the drained tracts settle as the water table sinks, farmland needs protection from an influx of saltwater that would end the polder's production of food. The Dutch have developed sophisticated technology for altering diked land with arable fields and for shielding precious crops from inundations of the sea by erecting seawalls and by pumping saltwater into canals. These measures proved fruitless during a 1953 gale that destroyed ramparts against the North Sea and killed 2,000 residents.

In 1995, pump stations worked at maximum capacity after a flooding river forced 200,000 flatlanders to flee along with their livestock. Shielding the Dutch from future seasonal floods, sea storms, and unforeseen rampages were new strategies implemented by the National Institute for Coastal and Marine Management to combat the challenges of global warming and rising levels of the North Sea and Rhine River. In addition to stronger levees, the government designated sections of pastureland to serve as temporary storage ponds and selected additional tracts to revert to forest and fen preplanted in trees and shrubs that can survive sodden turf. Other possibilities under consideration include floating farms similar to the ancient Mexican system of chinampas.

Coastal Activities

In Flevoland, Europe's youngest province, outdoor activities invite bike tours, cycling and skating on designated pads, barging, picnicking, picture-taking from the ferry, beachcombing, shelling, and camping. Naturalists and bird fanciers find rich territory for surveying the bittern, bluethroat, buzzard, falcon, gadwall, goldeneye, goosander, Horsterwold hawfinch, marsh harrier, owl, osprey, pipit, pochard, scaup, sea eagle, shrike, smew, tit, twite, tufted duck, and wryneck. At the 13,000-acre Hoge Veluwe National Park, once the estate of industrialists Helene Müller and Anton Kröller, the nation built its largest nature reserve and bird sanctuary. The park's woods, moors, swamps, and sand drifts also harbor badgers, feral sheep, red fox, roe and red deer, and wild boar. At Harderwijk, families with children enjoy the dolphin, porpoise, ray, seal, and walrus water show at the Dolphinarium, Europe's largest sea mammal park, which doubles as a rescue center for stranded or distressed sea creatures.

Fishing and eeling are important parts of the economic resurgence of the former Zuider Zee. On Ijesselmeer, eels, perch, and pike flourish in waters that once hosted cod, herring, and saltwater plants and mammals. Along the shallows, water sports tempt vacations to enjoy boating, cruising, windsurfing, sailing, and regattas. In winter, ice skaters dot the frozen lakes and canals. An historical tour calls for a water cruise of the sea's former outlines, a climb to the top of the Hoofdtoren [harbor tower] for a panoramic view, and a visit to the outdoor Zuider Zee Museum Village at Enkhuizen. Within the folk exhibits, 130 buildings and workshops reconstruct the lifestyle of Ijsselmeer when the basin's water came from the sea, four-bladed windmills produced power for pumping water and grinding grain, and traders grew rich on deals made with the East India Company. Costumed residents reenact the chores of stitching sails, twining rope, weaving rush baskets and nets, and smoking cod, eel, and herring. Built on the site of a pepper importer, the indoor Binnenmuseum offers eleven sailing vessels, recreations of whaling voyages, and memorabilia from the region's sea-centered lives and commerce.

SOURCES

Bemrose, John, "Battle Diary: From D-Day and Normandy to the Zuider Zee and VE," *Maclean's*, Vol. 107, No. 23, June 6, 1994, pp. 56–57.

Billings, Malcolm, "Landlocked Shipwrecks," *BBC News*, January 7, 2001.

Borah, Leo A., "Some Odd Pages from the Annals of the Tulip," *National Geographic*, September 1933, pp. 321–343.

Fradin, D. B. *The Netherlands*. Chicago: Children's Press, 1983.

Gould, Donald, "Draining the Zuider Zee Uncovers a Boneyard of Ancient Ships," *Smithsonian*, Vol. 4, No. 12, 1974, pp. 66–73.

Harrington, Spencer P. M., "Fine Wine & a Piss-Poor Vintage," *Archaeology*, Vol. 53, No. 6, November/December 2000.

"Historic Dutch Site Cleans Up," *Engineering News-Record*, March 2, 1998.

Knight, E. G. *The Falcon on the Baltic*. London: Hart-Davis, 1951.

Kruisinga, J. C. M., "A New Country Awaits Discovery," *National Geographic*, September 1933, pp. 293–320.

van der Heide, G. D. *Zuyder Zee Archaeology*. Brussels: The Hague, 1956.

Walker, Bill, "Life along the Zuider Zee," *Travel & Holiday*, June 1985, pp. 59–61, 73–74.

Winerip, Frank, "Memorial Day: Ohio Vet Put to Rest Years Later," *Dayton Daily News*, May 28, 1996.

Woodard, Colin, "Netherlands Battens Its Ramparts against Warming Climate," *Christian Science Monitor*, September 4, 2001.

Imari Bay, Kyushu, Japan

Location

A fishing, manufacturing, and commercial port northeast of the China Sea and west of the Inland Sea, Imari Bay prospers between the Higashi Matsu-ura-hanto and Kita Matsu-ura-hanto peninsulas. The harbor lies in a circle of the tall volcanic Kyushu Mountains, the source of Imari's soothing, healing hot springs. The island, which is Japan's most southerly land mass, enjoys a warm, humid climate common to the semitropics. Lying on the Arita River south of Nagasaki, the natural curve of the Imari gulf joins the islands of Fuku and Taka to form a tight-necked harbor that is the breeding ground of the helmet crab (also horseshoe or king crab).

The port of Imari once supported an enclave of Japanese pirates, who ravaged shipping routes on the Yellow Sea and the Pacific Ocean. Commerce in ceramics from ten kilns relied on the kaolin clay deposits that ringed the city and supplied the tables of the shoguns and the imperial court with fine tableware. Nearby Akita produced a greater store of earthenware goods at its 150 kilns and shipped them from the Imari gulf. From the seventeenth century, Imari dispatched ships that furthered an interchange between Japan and the outside world. In March 1980, the city expanded its technological ventures with a power plant fueled by a conversion of ocean thermal energy, the first such experiment in clean, renewable energy in Japanese history.

Contacts

Japanese National Tourist Organization Tenth Floor, Tokyo Kotsu Kaikan Building 2-10-1, Yurakucho, Chiyoda-ku, Tokyo 100-0006
http://www.jnto.go.jp/eng/JNTO/whats_jnto/index.html

History

Imari is situated on the archipelago of Kyushu, where Japan was first inhabited and where Jimmu (or Jinmu) Tenno, the "divine warrior," the first of the fourteen legendary emperors, established power in 660 B.C. Imari Bay is an historic site of one of Japan's most memorable victories over invaders. The conflict arose during an era of progress, when Japan saw the rise of its mercantile class, who prospered from trade with China and Korea. Strengthening stability for islanders was the Joei Code of 1232, which outlined the social structure for tenured farmers, religious houses, artisans, merchants, and a warrior class known as *samurai*. The era also saw the growth of Buddhism and a religious fervor that developed into Japan's age of faith.

In 1268, Japan's development drew the interest of Chinese imperialists, an international crisis that the fiery evangelist Nichiren had predicted in 1260. Using Chinese technology, Kublai Khan, the grandson of Genghis Khan, intended to tap Japanese wealth and to restore China's prestige in Asia. Kublai Khan began his quest with a letter to the regent, Hojo Tokimune, a valiant warrior-king and Zen follower. Hojo ignored written threatens and pursued a ruthless militarism later called *bushido*, the Way of the Warrior. According to legend, the khan retaliated by engineering the second of two drives, the world's largest seaborne assault. For troops, he commandeered men from the Sung dynasty in southern China and from Koryu, the Korean vassal state to the southeast.

The Mongol invasion began with seven weeks of land fighting followed by atrocities committed against islanders. To the dismay of Kublai Khan's naval commander, Fan Wenhu, a typhoon developed east of the Philippines and moved northwest toward China. Although the Japanese had only coastal fishing vessels as defense, a mighty 75 mile-per-hour wind saved Japan from the attackers, who were largely destroyed by nature alone. On August 15, 1281, the Mongol fleet of 4,400 warships, history's largest sea invasion force, collapsed after 4,000 ships sank in Imari Bay. Grateful island priests called the lucky storm a *kami kaze* [divine wind].

When the Mongol officers pulled away ahead of the storm, they left ships tethered by roped planking to allow soldiers free movement throughout the flotilla. The strategy caused the storm-tossed ships to lurch into each other and into the rocks. As the wreckage choked the bay, men drowned in huge numbers. Those who swam to Imari met Japanese swordsmen, who immediately dispatched all the living on the beach. The total loss to the khan was 100,000 men.

Archeology

In 1980, divers located wooden remains of Kublai Khan's fleet, sunk six feet deep in the soft muddy sea floor down a declivity at a depth of eighty feet. The bay began yielding proof of the armada's location after fishers netted pottery pieces, porcelain cups, and the bronze engraving seal of a Mongol commander. Investigating the site was Torao Mozai, an engineer at Tokyo University and father of Japanese underwater archeology. Using sonar, he sighted a morass of shattered timbers from seventy wrecks, the residue of a terrifying typhoon. From the detritus at Imari, his team retrieved rice-grinding stones, a bronze Buddha dating to the 1100s, pieces of red leather armor, and a Mongol helmet. Cha Yun of the South Korean Embassy attested to the importance of Mozai's find by proposing a joint survey of the recovered items that impact both nations' histories.

At Tokonami harbor off Takashima, a subsequent project underwritten by the Kyushu Okinawa Society for Underwater Archaeology in 1988 substantiated the finds in Imari Bay. Archeologist Kenzo Hayashida, the society's director, focused on a single plank-hulled warship, which was discovered in October 2001. Measuring 230 feet long, the ship relied on iron fasteners to secure its keel and a one-ton red oak-and-granite anchor 23 feet long to secure it to the ocean floor. Divers retrieved the mast step, a ceramic bowl, three wood anchors and anchor stones, rope, human bones, and food stored in jars as well as a cache of spear and arrow points, crossbow bolts, sabers, swords, a helmet, and six black-powder earthenware *tetsuhau* [bombs], one packed with iron shrapnel. During analysis of the finds, scientists housed them at the Takashima Museum of Folk History and Culture.

In the estimation of James Delgado, executive director of the Vancouver Maritime Museum, the Mongol warship was twice the size of its European counterparts and more technologically advanced. With a rudder, layered planking over the hull, and watertight bulkheads, the ship was unusually resilient, maneuverable, and strong for its size. Delgado particularly admired the thick-walled ceramic bombs, which extended the range of the Mongol arsenal with projectiles hurled by catapult. The total picture of the khan's armada proves that he had progressed from land-based assault to naval attack mode and had mastered Chinese technology, which advanced the capabilities of world warfare.

Coastal Activities

In addition to its historical significance, Imari bears name recognition among porcelain lovers, who value the fine hard-paste china made from the 1600s to the 1800s and shipped by the Dutch East India Company from Imari Bay to tony houseware boutiques throughout Europe. The styles of Imari or Arita porcelain varied over time into three distinct groups. The oldest, Ko Imari, derived from Korean technology and bore a bright background and typically Chinese patterns over the whole surface. Ko ware featured silvering or gilding of its main motifs — chrysanthemums, peonies, pines, bamboo, plum blossoms, and dragons. It was the ko style that influenced European baroque and rococo art.

The middle group, Kakiemon, replaced chalky white with a pale ivory background and added asymetric designs that German potters replicated as Meissen ware. The last style, spare, elegant Iro Naboshima, was the presentation ware designed for the tables of feudal lords, shoguns, and emperors. Because of the elitism connected with upper-crust dinnerware, manufacturers guarded the secrets of its origins.

To locals, Imari is also the home of movie director Kurosawa Akira. An artist of international fame, he conceived the classic film drama *Rashomon* (1950), winner of an Oscar and a Golden Lion award. In 1990, the city opened a 1.5 billion-yen memorial museum to Kurosawa on an incline overlooking Imari Bay. Dedicated to his life and works, the museum's collection attests that he was the first filmmaker to earn the nation's Order of Culture, presented in 1985, and the first to receive an honorary Oscar for lifetime achievement, which he accepted in 1990.

Visitors to Imari enjoy fine seafood and the Kurosawa cinema museum as well as the Akira Kurosawa Studio, which exhibits costumes, a film digest, trophies, personal effects, and the director's handwritten manuscripts and memos. In October, the annual Imari Tontenton, one of Japan's feistiest traditional battle festivals, reenacts the past each November at ten city venues. Along the Imari-gawa River delta, competing teams bearing mikoshi shrines deliberately crash into each other and attempt to remove shrines lodged in the river bed. The purpose of the staged set-to is to bring prosperity and luck to the people of Imari. The event precedes an internatnional hot-air balloon fiesta at nearby Saga in late November.

Most outsiders travel to the tourist center of Arita eight miles away, where they can view pottery making. At Imari Ceramics Hall, tourists dip into enamel paints to draw patterns on porcelain. They learn the history of Imari pottery at the Arita Ceramics Museum and purchase from an array of styles and patterns at the 25 shops at the Arita Ceramics Wholesale Complex. The first week in April, china collectors swamp the Imari Spring Ceramics Fair, a prelude to the Arita Porcelain Fair later in the month and into May. The latter event, Japan's largest, brings together 750,000 buyers and sellers at 650 stalls and shops.

SOURCES

Bhaskaran, Gautaman, "Kurosawa Museum Planned at Imari," *The Hindu*, October 16, 2001.

Delgado, James P., "Relics of the Kamikaze," *Archaeology*, Vol. 56, No. 1, January/February 2003, pp. 36–41.

Dodd, Jan, and Simon Richmond. *Japan: The Rough Guide*. London: Penguin, 1999.

Hiwatari Mitsunori, "Most Imperious Imari," *Fingerpost*, February 2001.

"Kublai Khan's Fleet Reported Found by Japanese," *New York Times*, December 14, 1980.

Murdoch, James, and Isoh Yamagata. *The History of Japan*. Kobe, Japan: Chronicle, 1903.

Nelson, Bryn, "Anchoring the Kamikaze Legend," *Newsday*, December 17, 2002.

Ruel, Timothy, "The Beauty of Imari," *Honolulu Star-Bulletin*, February 24, 2000.

Suzuki, K., et al., "C Dating of Wooden Anchors and Planks Excavated from Submerged Wrecks Located at Takashima in Imari Bay," *Proceedings of the Japan Academy*, September 2001, pp. 131–134.

Winters, Harold A. *Battling the Elements: Weather and Terrain in the Conduct of War*. Baltimore: Johns Hopkins University Press, 1998.

Jeffreys Bay, South Africa

Location

On the 800-mile eastern curve of Africa's southern shore southwest of Port Elizabeth, the beach city of Jeffreys Bay lies in a diverse coastal zone marked by sandy shore, dunes, river estuaries and bogs, floodplains, indigenous coastal forest, and slopes rising into the cape mountains. Located between the deltas of the Kabeljous and Seekoei rivers, the town occupies prime land along the Gamtoos and Kromme rivers and features southeast Africa's largest dune field. Since the 1960s, the broad, safe white-sand beaches, super tubes and curls, temperate winters, and mild summers have turned the former fishing village into "Jay Bay," a youth paradise. To the delight of the surfer, inland from a reef formed of misshapen volcanic rock, where the warm Indian Ocean waters collide with the cold Atlantic, the southwesterly two- to thirty-foot rollers consistently pound the beach. An otherwise nondescript coastal town, Jeffreys Bay bears the distinction of being the landing site of the surfer's ideal curl, the perfect wave.

Contacts

Mariza Muller, Tourism Officer
Jeffreys Bay Tourism Bureau
P. O. Box 460
Jeffrey's Bay, 6330, South Africa
Phone: 27-0-42-2932588
Fax: 27-0-42-2932227
Email: jbay@ilink.nis.za
http://www.gardenroute.co.za/jbay/jb-home.htm#billabong

Jeffreys Bay Penguin Rehabilitation Fund
P. O. Box 309
Jeffreys Bay, 6330, Eastern Cape, South Africa
Email: jbaypenguin@hotmail.com
http://www.geocities.com/jeffreysbaypenguin/

History

From prehistory, Jeffreys Bay has had a working-class aura. Around 118,000 B.C., San hunter-gatherers, called Bushmen, ancestors of modern *homo sapiens*, settled cape land known as Kouga. In the middle Stone Age, rock artists adorned sites in the Klasies River estuary with petroglyphic images drawn from nature. Succeeding waves of nomadic herders and cultivators passed through the region without making any significant change to the landscape. Later, agrarian Hottentot or Khoikoi plowed fields, fenced in pasturage, and thrived on fish and seafood and on trade in cowries, a pre-coinage form of money.

Early in the eighteenth century, natives of the bay suffered a tragic retreat. In May 1713, Dutch entrepreneur, historian, and cartographer François Valenty composed *Description of the Cape of Good Hope; with Matters Concerning It* (1726), in which he recorded the onslaught of smallpox in a virgin-soil population:

> The Hottentots died in their hundreds. They lay everywhere on the roads. Cursing at the Dutchmen, who they said had bewitched them, they fled inland with their kraals, huts, and cattle in hopes there to be freed from the malign disease [*Reader's Digest Illustrated History*, 1994, p. 45].

In the northern interior, indigenous tribes recoiled from the pocked refugees and murdered some when they first halted their flight. The dispirited Hottentot ceded their ancestral fields to the Dutch and abandoned coastal life for inland farming and herding.

At a strategic point on Africa's southernmost reach, the shore was not long without settlers. The British arrived in 1820 at the height of the Kaffir Wars, a confrontation between Afrikaners and the Xhosa. The losers were the Xhosa, whom European newcomers forced away from the South African Coast. The region proved fruitful to entrepreneurs. Founded in 1849, the town of Jeffreys Bay grew from a utilitarian fishing colony known for calamari to a trading center, established in 1894. However, while European colonists thrived, the region's black natives maintained one of southern Africa's highest rates of unemployment.

Prosperity came from unexpected

sources — surfing and tourism. By the late 1960s, American and Euorpean hippies took over the strand and established the surf dynasties of Billabong, Country Feeling, and Rip Curl. Within the decade, South Africa sponsored the first global surfing championship and fostered the world's most respected water-sport athletes. Declared a city in 1968, Jeffreys Bay incorporated Aston Bay, Kabeljous-on-Sea, and Paradise Beach to become a sizeable vacation mecca, retirement resort, and home of the Billabong Pro surfing competition. Rapidly, Australian experts outpaced Hawaiian and South African participants.

In 1999, when 59 athletes competed at the annual Jeffreys Bay competition, a minor flap arose between Christians and multiculturalists over the use of ten traditional Xhosa *sangomas* [healers] in the blessing of the ocean. Based on respect for nature gods, the ceremony parallelled similar indigenous propitiations of the sea at surfing events in Australia, Bali, Hawaii, and Tahiti. Instead of accommodating ancient animistic prayers and sacred dancing, authorities removed the blessing from the program.

Ecosystem

The seas around Jeffreys Bay are habitats of the cowrie, a freckled gold or yellow and brown olive-shaped shell which was at one time the world's most widely used primitive currency. In the late Middle Ages, Islamic Africans traded in metal rings and bars as well as cowries. Financiers set prices in cowries, for example, 25 for a chicken, 500 for a goat, and 2,500 for a steer. Grouped in combinations, a *rotl* [necklace] was standardized at 32 cowries and five strings at 160 shells. Ten bunches or 1,600 shells equalled a head of cowries. Because of the acceptance of the monetary unit and the ease of its exchange, bay shell seekers prospered on cowries, which circulated in Angola, Benin, Cameroon, Congo, Dahomey, Ethiopia, Ghana, Ivory Coast, Mozambique, Nigeria, Tanzania, Togo, and West Africa.

Into the twentieth century, the cowrie remained valuable for its beauty and collectability. According to local shelling expert Denis Harper Kennelly, honorary conchologist of the East London Museum and author of *Marine Shells of Southern Africa* (1969), the *Cypraea citrina*, a gray cowrie, ranged along the cape shores, but was not found alive. Three other shell varieties, the *Cypraea capensis, Cypraea edentula,* and *Cypraea fuscodentata,* were less common, but had been sighted alive in the maws of large fish. Offshore, the rare and valuable yellow and chestnut *Cypraea* (or *Cypraeovulva*) *fuscorubra,* a gently curving pearly beige gastropod, was harder to locate because it favored deep water.

In addition to mollusks, shellfish, seals, sea turtles, and marine birds, the Jeffreys Bay region harbors one of the globe's few convergences of all seven biomes or vegetation types. The ecosystem shelters small mammals and 120 bird species, including the African or blackfoot penguin (*Spheniscus demersus*), also called the jackass penguin for its braying voice. A fragile, two-foot-high carnivore unique to the shores extending from Namibia to Southern Natal, the flightless penguin breeds on offshore islands and lives on sardines, anchovies, crustaceans, and squid. Until the passage of laws in 1919, scavengers killed and rendered the bird for its valuable oils and robbed its nests of guano, which they sold for fertilizer. In addition to loss from egg harvesting, the penguin often succumbed to poachers and hunters, coatings of oil, tangling in fish line, or choking on cigarette filters, plastic foam and shopping bags, or bottle tops. The species, which numbered 1.5 million in 1900, began decreasing in population in the 1950s to 300,000. It dropped to 240,000 in the late 1970s and to an early 21st-century count of under 100,000, when environmentalists began to fear its extinction.

Jeffreys Bay produced a pro-penguin savior. In 1983, a veterinarian, D. J. Hartley, set up an office near the beach and began treating injured or ailing birds. His practice grew so rapidly over the next decade that neighbors pressed him to move the busy bird hospital from the residential area. In 1995, after the media publicized Dr. Hartley's huge task and the plight of cape penguins, the Eastern Cape Nature Conservation established the Seekoei Nature Reserve and penguin rehabilitation center, which opened in May 1996. At the rate of up to sixty patients at a time, workers diagnosed sick birds with an endoscope, dosed them with antibiotics and vitamins, scrubbed pollutants from their bodies, stitched up shark bites, and hand-fed them with pilchards, their favorite meal. Until they were ready for release into the wild, the patients remained at the center for three to 52 weeks.

The African penguin still faces threats to its survival. Devastating to the species are catastrophes resulting from heavy ocean-going traffic of oil ships, trawlers, and tankers, the chief sources of petroleum pollutants. Unless volunteers can remove oil and sludge from plumage, the birds are stripped of insulation and waterproofing and can no longer ply the seas to hunt food. In addition, overfishing, plastic refuse, and the ravages of El Niño continue to reduce the bird's main source of sustenance. Most doomed penguins die of toxicity, low birth weight, starvation, septicemia, or hypothermia.

In late June 2000, volunteers from around the globe converged to save 40,000 African penguins after a Panamanian oil carrier, *The Treasure*, sank off Cape Town on June 23. At a pivotal time in the bird's reproductive cycle, sticky bunker oil produced a 1,100-ton slick along South African beaches and into the core of the bird's feeding and breeding grounds. The unique South African bird responded to conservation efforts, funded by the International Fund for Animal Welfare and the World Wildlife Fund. In all, workers secured 23,000 struggling, biting birds for cleaning, medication, and feeding on fish and vitamins. Of that number, 95 percent survived the toxic coating and release back into the wild. The University of Cape Town set up a banding and tracking program to determine how readily the spunky birds recovered and mated. Results were encouraging for a program that attempted to rescue so large a number of penguins at one time.

Coastal Activities

In addition to the cowrie, tasty calamari, and the African penguin, Jeffreys Bay offers surfing heaven. The beach lures the water sports aficionado to pleasant days of swimming, snorkeling and spearfishing, body- and wind-surfing, sand-boarding, paragliding, sailboarding, and surfing, which reaches its climax in July with the world champion Billabong Pro Surf Festival. The Jeffreys Bay Surf Museum at the Instep Shoe Shop exhibits newspaper and magazine articles on the sport as well as a collection of historic surf boards. Adults opt for sailing, trail hiking, horseback riding, motorcycling, caravanning and camping, and canoeing as well as games of tennis, bowling, golf, shopping for leather and seashell crafts, and shore dining at a floating restaurant. Rock angling, and deep-sea fishing produce prize catches of baardman, blackmail, dageraad, elf, grunter, kob, leerfish, poenskop, ray, roman, shark, and steenbras. Scuba divers of Eastern Cape estuaries find small mollusks, musselcrackers, stumpnose, and jellyfish among soft corals at depths ranging from 35 to 160 feet. By dive boat, the adventuresome can explore the wrecks of the H.M.S. *Osprey*, a steam-driven screw gunboat that foundered in a storm on May 30, 1867, or survey the scattered remains of the British steamer *Cape Recife*, which sank in fog on February 20, 1929, on its way to Cape Town.

Scientists have their own reasons for visiting Jeffreys Bay. The naturalist can dolphin-watch, observe the Southern right whale, and trek over the Kabeljous Estuary and Nature Reserve to view cormorants, fish eagles, flamingos, gulls, red knobbed coots, and shrike. Biologists study aloes, protea, orchids, iris, and shrubs in the unique fynbos family of flora, and collect conch, cone, cowrie, harp, nautilus, and pansy shells from the ample supply washed up on the beach. A four-day shell festival each September and the Jeffreys Bay Shell Museum housing over 600 of the world's bivalves, cephalopods, chitons, and gastropods promote beachcombing and shell art from South African and Indo-Pacific specimens.

SOURCES

"The Artistry of African Currency," http://www.nmafa.si.edu/exhibits/site/manillas.htm.
Boroughs, Don, "A Battle for a Wild Garden," *International Wildlife*, May/June 1999.
Carlton, James T., "Introduced Marine and Estuarine of North America," *Journal of Shellfish Research*, Vol. 11. No. 2, 1992, pp. 489–505.
Cohen, Mike, "Tanker Spill Endangers Africa's Largest Penguin Colonies," *ABC News*, June 29, 2000.
Cull, Patrick, "R9-million Kouga Cultural Centre a Symbol of African Renaissance," *Jeffreys Bay Herald*, December 21, 2002.
Hosking, S. G., and M. du Preez, "Valuing Water Gains in the Eastern Cape's Working for Water," *Water SA*, Vol. 28 No. 1, January 2002.
"The Incredible Rescue of the African Penguin," *Africa News Service*, September 7, 2000.
Jugens, Andre, "Blessing That Created Waves at Surf Contest," *South Africa Sunday Times*, July 4, 1999.
Kennelly, D. H., "*Cypraea fuscorubra* Shaw, 1909," *The Cowry*, Vol. 1, No. 4, August 15, 1962.
_____, "The Range of *Cypraea citrina* Gray," *The Cowry*, Vol. 1, No. 5, March 1, 1963.
_____, "The Range of Three South African Cypraeidae," *The Cowry*, Vol. 1, No. 3, February 1, 1962.
"Leo Africanus: Description of Timbuktu," *The Description of Africa*, http://www.wsu.edu:8080/~wldciv/world_civ_reader/world_civ_reader_2/leo_africanus.html.
Reader's Digest Illustrated History of South Africa. Capetown, South Africa: Reader's Digest Association, 1994.
"The Truth and Reconciliation Commission," *ANC Daily News*, February 23, 1999.

Kaho'Olawe, Hawaii

Location

Hawaii's smallest island, Kaho'Olawe is a frog-shaped land mass at the south center of the eight-island chain along the 'Alalakeiki Channel, which separates it from Maui. Formed by volcanic action, Kaho'Olawe island lies in the lee of Haleakala, a 10,023-foot volcano on Maui eight miles to the east that blocks hard-driving Pacific rains and leaves much of Kaho'Olawe's central upland dry and dusty. The island's rocky coastline was the site of numerous shipwrecks, particularly at Kuia Shoals.

The 48-square mile, 27,000-acre island of Kaho'Olawe originally supported moss and gnarled ohia and wiliwili trees on a wavy grassland, but currently lacks ample fresh water to support farming or permanent habitation. Revered as the "Southern Beacon," Kaho'Olawe is the spiritual homeland of native Hawaiians who make pilgrimages to seek healing and consolation at its 2,000 archeological sites. The land began undergoing a physical and religious renaissance in 1994, when the U.S. military returned it to local control after a half century of desecrating the land with bombing and gunnery practice.

Contacts

R. Keoni Fairbanks, Executive Director
Kaho'Olawe Island Reserve Commission
811 Kolu Street, Suite 201
Wailuku, Hawaii 96793
Phone: 808-243-5020
Fax: 808-243-5885
http://www.kahoolawe.org

Revered as the "Southern Beacon," Kaho'Olawe is the spiritual homeland of native Hawaiians who seek healing and consolation at its 2,000 archeological sites (courtesy of David Flack).

Mythology

As described in animistic Polynesian lore compiled in David Kalakaua's classic compendium *The Legends and Myths of Hawaii* (1888), the powers of nature created Papa, the earth god, and Wakea, the sky. Beneath them in importance were the creator and organizer Kane, the builder and warrior Ku, the shark god Kalahiki, and Lono, the divine canoeist and fertility god governing earthly elements and creativity. Lono was equally skilled at surviving wind and sea and at reciting epic poetry. It was he who first came to Kaho'Olawe and landed at Kealakekua Bay, the "Pathway of the Gods" (Theroux, 2002, p. 11). With island clay, he shaped earthlings. After living among the new beings and competing with them in athletic contests, he retreated to the sky. At sixty shrines, Hawaiians propitiated his beneficent powers and control of the harvest.

Early Hawaiian islanders, the offspring of eastern Polynesian sea rovers, called Kaho'Olawe their *piko* [navel or landmark] and dedicated it to Kanaloa, the nature god who ruled the sea. At Honokoa Bay, an early islander named Ai'ai erected *ko'a* [fishing shrines] and constructed a holy mound, the island's first beachfront altar. On its central *akua* [sacred stone], fishers offered up their morning catch as well as gifts of shells, mollusks, and coral. Twentieth-century Lono worshippers prayed that the heavenly governor of the elements could once more green up the scarred land and welcome back fish, terns and tropic birds, healing herbs, and native food plants. In token of past traditions, activists erected the traditional Hawaiian *hale* [residence] and scheduled seasonal ceremonies demonstrating island respect for nature.

History

Around A.D. 1000, Kaho'Olawe became a Polynesian *wahe pana* [religious site] called Kohemalamalama 'o Kanaloa. At Moa'ulaika, a peak 1,444 feat high, island priests summoned the congregation with a bell stone. From the vantage point, the congregation gazed out on Maui, Moloka'i, and Lana'i; from sighting slabs and stone *ahu* [cairns], they viewed constellations and whale pods. Young men developed seamanship and celestial navigation as well as fishing and *he'enalu* [surfing], an indigenous sea sport. Artisans raised fish shrines and inscribed petroglyphs with fishhooks, humanoid shapes, and island nature deities. Mourners interred their dead *kahunas* [priests], *kakpuna* [elders], and *ali'i* [tribal leaders].

By A.D. 400, the island gained 150 semi-permanent settlements along the shore at holy springs. For purification and the preparation of the individual for worthy tasks and rituals, islanders turned to the sea to bathe and ready the spirit for holy duties. Sacred singers formulated *meles* [songs] and *oli* [chants] that commemorated the birth of the Pacific isles, complex symbols and deeds, and a dynasty of chiefs. Rock carvers adorned Moa'ulanui with images of coastal animals, athletes, and dancers. At Pu'u Moiwi, a hillock rich in basalt at Kaho'Olawe's center, one of Hawaii's largest prehistoric stone workshops, islanders quarried celts to make into *koi* [adz], their basic wood-shaping tool.

By 1150, Kaho'Olawe had become the educational center of the Hawaiian islands. At a sacred point, islanders named a throne-shaped rock the "Navigator's Chair." From this commanding view of the sea, barefoot priests clad in customary white loincloths taught young men the rudiments of astronomy, current directions, cloud and wind interpretation, and navigation of the 'Alalakeiki Channel. These basics served crews on the long ritual voyage to Kahiki or Tahiti, a general term for Polynesia, home of the *ka po'e kahiko* [people of old]. Around 1600, Kaho'Olawe gained a permanent

agrarian colony. Island fishers erected a fish shrine at Kamohio Bay and used the sheltering cliffs as a place for the carving of seashell, tortoise, and wood fishhooks.

The terrors of the colonial era forced Hawaiians into social and cultural retreat. They sought seclusion for religious ceremonies and stowed sacred objects and idols where disapproving Christian missionaries could not find and destroy them. In 1826, newcomers made the north shore areas of Kuheia and Kaulana into a prison for exiled felons. Three decades later, herders leased the entire island, dug rock-lined wells, and destroyed the natural growth of sweetgrass by raising more cattle, goats, and sheep than the land could support. In August 1881, according to an article in the *Hawaiian Gazette*, stockman William Cummings reported a total of 2,000 goats and 1,000 sheep populating Kaho'Olawe.

Island healing lore proved inadequate to Hawaiians as whites and Asians brought new diseases from the outside world. With the voyages of Captain James Cook and Captain Jean-François Galaup de La Pérouse, the late 1700s inflicted on natives a fate shared by many of the indigenous people of North America — scarlet fever, pneumonia, tuberculosis, and venereal disease, which Hawaiians called *ka'oka'o* [red rot]. Explorer Captain Louis Claude Desaulses de Freycinet, a physician and author of *Voyage autour du Monde* [Voyage around the World] (1839), arrived in 1819 and identified rampant ophthalmia and scabies. In 1835, Chinese laborers on sugar plantations imported *Ma'i Pake* [Chinese sickness], the Hawaiian name for leprosy. In 1848, influenza, measles, and pertussis killed 40,000 or 27 percent of the native population. In spring 1853, a crewman aboard the American trader *Charles Mallory* introduced smallpox, a scourge so terrible that Hawaiians retreated from white settlements, missions, and harbors and hid themselves from contamination. After the docking of the freighter *Nippon Maru* from Hong Kong at the Pacific Mail pier in October 1899, leprosy swept the entire island chain, killing natives three times more frequently than whites. As a result, Kaho'Olawe was depopulated.

In 1913, John F. G. Stokes, curator of Polynesian Ethnology at the Bernice Pauahi Bishop Museum, mounted an archeological dig at Kaho'Olawe's Kamohio Bay, where he located an early model of a carved wooden *ki'i* [idol]. His team identified styles of fishhooks and the coral knives and files used in their manufacture. Along with workshop equipment, the site bore signs of cookery — the remains of fish meals, firesticks and charcoal, and calabashes. The dual nature of the beach site was obvious in the assortment of bundle offerings, kapa or tapa [bark cloth], and religious statuary carved from echinoderm, sandalwood, and stone. Before their removal to the museum, Kamohio Bay artifacts suffered loss from a rockslide.

Kaho'Olawe fell to its lowest point in 1920, when the United States military restricted the acreage and set up artillery training and ordnance practice. After the U.S. entered World War II on December 8, 1941, the marines and navy drilled on the island to prepare for their invasions of Iwo Jima and Okinawa. At the sandy beach at Honokanai'a, the navy staged amphibious landings. The island sustained torpedo launches, trial bombing runs, and strafing as the ships and planes of the third and seventh fleets obliterated reefs and petroglyphs, washed two millions tons of topsoil onto low-lying historic sites, and flattened the soil into unarable hardpan. In June 1965, the navy stirred Hawaiians to action with the last straw — a mock atomic blast, which gouged out a fifty-meter crater called Sailor's Hat and opened a fissure that drained the water table into the sea.

Organizers Emma DeFries, Barbara Hanchett, Lani Kapuni, Clara Ku, Mary Lee, and Rose Wainui led acts of civil dis-

obedience and protested loudly enough to win over the media. In the late 1900s, freedom fighters Noa Emmett Aluli, George Helm, healer Harry Kunihi Mitchell, his nephew Kimo Mitchell, and storyteller Charlie Maxwell, all members of the Protect Kaho'Olawe 'Ohana [extended family], demanded native Hawaiian rights to revive indigenous worship on the sacred isle. They charged the U.S. Navy with desecrating an ancient altar and holy grounds with bombs and live-fire munitions. During protracted demonstrations, Helm and Kimo Mitchell disappeared, presumably drowned.

The repatriation of the tortured remains of Kaho'Olawe began in 1976, when islanders made an initial pilgrimage. Some recalled an ancient prophecy that the seventh generation of Hawaiians would recapture the wisdom of the island's early settlers. The transformation of the target zone required location and removal of ordnance before worshippers could lay permanent claim to the land. In 1980, protesters gained a partial victory after the U.S. Navy agreed to a limited clearing of island debris. Five years later, the National Register of Historic Places acknowledged the island as official holy ground. Under military direction and protection, 5,000 Hawaiians lovingly revived sacred centers and held seasonal worship rites. In 1990, the U.S. military abandoned the site, leaving it to island governance.

In its recent reincarnation, the island became a cultural preserve, where traditionalists pass on nature lore, beliefs, chants, and dances. The devout instituted an official healing of the tormented island by offering coral at Mua Ha'i Kapuna. According to Mayor James Kimo Apana of Maui, the transformation from bomb run to cultural preserve benefits Hawaiians on several levels:

> Our helicopter companies are getting work. People are buying supplies, people are being employed, people are growing plants to be

replanted on the island. There is a lot of economic value. More than money to the community, the cleanup of Kaho'Olawe brings healing and makes the country whole [DiPietro, 2001, p. 1].

To clinch the deal, on May 7, 1994, a conveyance ceremony on Maui in sight of Kaho'Olawe presented a seaside sounding of the conch and ceremonial drumming as leaf-cloaked *nakoa* [warriors] guarded 700 viewers with upraised spears.

Ecosystem

To restore Kaho'Olawe's former ecological balance, a massive cleanup began with a sifting of the land and offshore slopes and reclamation of hiking trails and campsites. Work progressed on a $400 million budget granted by Congress over a ten-year period. Some 300 people journeyed daily to their jobs hunting unexploded bombs, tamping trees and shrubs into holes, cultivating healing herbs, and heaping stone dams to halt erosion. Essential were Hawaii's "canoe plants," the species that Polynesians imported from the southwestern Pacific: taro, mulberry, kava, candlenut, banana, coconut palm, wild ginger, sweet potato, and breadfruit. Each night, sixty volunteers remained behind to guard the work site and its solar- and wind-powered generators.

The task of upgrading Kaho'Olawe was complex. In 1992, Hawaiian native plant and endangered species specialist Rene Sylva proposed the cultivation of hau, mesquite, and naupaka trees and the creation of windbreaks along with revegetation using curative herbs, edible flora, and rare tropicals, particularly *puakala*, the native poppy. For the sake of offshore schools of ehu and onaga, laws prohibited diving and fishing. The gradual restoration of health to the land, reefs, and shores welcomed the return of green sea turtles, jellyfish, monk seal, and spinner dolphin as denizens of the *ahupuaa*

[self-contained ecosystem]. In Sailor's Hat Crater, shrimp, snails, and red tubeworms thrived in a landlocked body of water that displayed the salinity and tidal fluctuations of an ocean-fed lake.

The target date of 2004 for reforestation and sustainable environment and for revival of native religion displayed the earnestness of lawmakers, who designated the island and its shores two miles out to sea as the Kaho'Olawe Island Reserve. Offshore at Kanapou Bay, a *kai kapu* [marine sanctuary] welcomed large fish and *mano*, the mythic shark named Kamohoali'i who guided aborigines on their voyage to Hawaii and made a home in cliffside caves. In 1995, Nelson Foster published *Kaho'olawe: Na Leo o Kanaloa*, a vivid picture book and tribute to the island's resilience and to the people who believe in its ancient value as a homeland and natural habitat.

Dance History

Essential to the return of Hawaiian beliefs and worship is the hula, a religious interpretive dance that once graced the pavilions and halls of nobles and royalty before islanders had a written language. The dance was introduced by the goddess Hi'iaka or Laka, who gestured and chanted to soothe her fiery sister Pele, goddess of volcanoes. In the words of ethnologist Nathaniel Bright Emerson: "The wave-beaten sand-beach was her floor, the open air her hall. Feet and hands and swaying form kept time to her improvisation" (1965, p. 8).

For its connection to island mythology, procreation, courtesy, and protocol, hula study and performance were sacred. Privileged students favored by Hi'iaka learned the art at a *halau* [training center], a worship center where the gods resided in a *kuahu* [altar] adorned with fresh greenery and sweet-scented blossoms. Performers dressed in ceremonial garb — the *malo* [tapa loincloth] for men and the raffia or ti *pa'u* [skirt] for bare-breasted women — and danced barefoot to maintain contact with the earth's energy. Binding them closer to sea and shore were whale bone, shell, and shark tooth anklets and bangles and coronas and leis woven of fragrant bougainvillea, plumeria, and stephanotis interspersed with tropical foliage.

The substance of the dance was an idyllic celebration of the mythic past when deities lived on the islands in harmony with humans. Interwoven with the movements were imagination, philosophy, history, incantations, sensual emotion, and longings common to the mortal spirit. Viewers absorbed allegorical elements, poetry, drama, and the lore of remote antiquity. Unlike modern social dance, performances were never informal or indulgent. Rather, hula belonged to the trained practitioner whose accomplishment resulted from training in godly song and classic dance and from respect for religion, taboo, and ritual.

The clash of cultures in the nineteenth century weakened folkloric dance as an integral part of Hawaiian genealogy, worship, and literature. In the 1820s, the arrival of puritanic missionaries from New England resulted in a wave of ethnocentric moralizing and proselytizing. Tight-lipped evangelists stripped Hawaiians of their Maori-Tahitian language, native idols, and indigenous dances in order to make them Christians. The newcomers disapproved of naked flesh and insisted that islanders cover their bodies American style in shirt and pants for men and high-necked, long-sleeves dresses called *mu'umu'us* [mother hubbards] for women. When Queen Ka'ahumanu accepted Christianity in 1830, she abandoned native temples and stone statues and forbade native dance. Those who cherished hula as a spiritual ceremony retreated to rural spots to teach succeeding generations what their ancestors had treasured.

In 1874 under Hawaii's jovial last king,

David Laiamea Kalakaua, known as the "Merrie Monarch," islanders renewed their dedication to ritual dance and embraced its slow, flowing grace as a symbol of Polynesian roots. In his words, "Hula is the language of the heart and therefore the heartbeat of the Hawaiian people" (Hale, 2002). Select troupes enacted 260 chants and hulas for his coronation. In 1909, Nathaniel Bright Emerson, a missionary's son born on Oahu and educated at Harvard Medical School, introduced the outside world to true spiritual island dance and oral history in *Unwritten Literature of Hawai'i: The Sacred Songs of the Hula*, a thorough compendium and glossary he compiled for the Smithsonian Institution. He described the dance as "a religious service in which poetry, music, pantomime, and the dance lent themselves, under the forms of dramatic art, to the refreshment of men's minds" (Emerson, 1965, p. 12).

Into the twentieth century, hula moved away from its holy, folkloric origins. As Europeans and Americans influenced performances, they became more melodic and employed more types of accompaniment than the original drum and chanting voices. Songs such as Bing Crosby's "Sweet Leilani" (1937), movies like *Waikiki Wedding* (1937), television and nightclub comedy routines, and island tours trivialized the dance as sweet island coquettes in motion or lascivious paganism, the erotic dance of an ignorant race.

Coastal Activities

Currently, Kaho'Olawe's resurgence has reintroduced Hawaiians to their native traditions. Some stand at the waterline and pray or chant as the sun sinks into the Pacific or intone island melodies on the bamboo nose flute. Others nurture delicate vines and shrubs in earth that has grown dry, cracked, and hostile to living things. The venturesome learn how to pilot sea-going craft on planned voyages aboard double-hulled canoes. Budding healers learn fig- and fruit-based dietetics, herbal cures, and traditional massage and curative technique.

On the island's clay dance courts, master dance coaches assemble students to impart the sensuous undulations and dramatic posturing set to chant and stringed instruments, notably, the ukulele and steel guitar. While dancers stand, sit, kneel, or recline, percussionists and rhythm keepers employ 'ili'ili [stone castanets], tall pahu drums, 'uli'uli [gourd rattles], double gourd drums, bamboo sticks, and calabashes to establish a precise pattern of motion. To a swaying, at times spirited melody, the movements mime Hawaiian history and wars, epic narratives, creation myths, and values in unvarying gestures of hand, head, torso, and legs.

Students learn to pay homage to sea gods, extol heroes and chiefs, and encourage the fertility of nature and islanders. With gesture, posture, and rhythm, polished, synchronized dancers express aloha [love], malama [tenderness], and kokua [compassion]. Youngsters learn the basics of character — mahalo [respect], kupono [honesty], kuleana [duty and service], pono [righteousness], and ha'aha'a [humility]. All Hawaiians reacquaint themselves with hu'eu [humor], malu [strength], ahonui [patience], mahao'o [wisdom], and 'oia'i'o [truth].

Each winter for the past two decades, Kaho'Olawe islanders have observed the traditional harvest with a three-month propitiation of Lono, the farmer's god. The agricultural ritual begins with the arrival of the rainy seasons at the rise of makali`i [Pleiades]. During twelve weeks of rest, feasting and drumming, and sports events, the island stores up energy for the following growing season. At select spots, native stewards erect lele [ritual platforms] to hold ho`okupu [offerings] to Lono — calabashes of spring water and meals of 'awa [a bitter kava drink], bananas, black coconut, bread-fruit, ki-wrapped pork sides of black pigs, lama wood, redfish, and sweet potatoes. At Hakioawa Bay, they conduct rituals at temples, a thatched communal hut, commemorative platforms to island ancestors, and a rocked-edged pa hula [dance platform].

The festival concludes in January with a Polynesian purification and thanksgiving celebration, which begins with a tone blown on the pu trumpet, made from the conch or Cassis cornuta shell. Celebrants view a processional bearing a sixteen-foot carved stone twined in ferns and bark cloth and topped with feathers. The kahunas store sacred objects and load a wa'a'auhau [ceremonial koa canoe] with ti-wrapped ho'okupu [offerings] of pork and taro. With farewells from the shore, the canoe glides down the strand at Kealaikahiki Channel into the Pacific and back to the Polynesian fount of Kahiki.

SOURCES

Aluli, Noa Emmett, and Davianna Pomaika'i McGregor, "Maike Kaimaike Ola, From the Ocean Comes Life," *Hawaiian Journal of History*, Vol. 26, 1992, pp. 231–254.

Biondo, Brenda, "Turning a Bombing Range into a Spiritual Homeland," *Christian Science Monitor*, December 31, 1998, p. 4.

"Bishop Museum Exhibit Highlights Sacred Island," *Travel Weekly*, February 12, 1996, p. 58.

Bowman, Sally-Jo, "The Way Back," *Sierra*, Vol. 77, No. 5, September–October 1992, p. 28.

Bushnell, O. A. *The Gifts of Civilization: Germs and Genocide in Hawai'i.* Honolulu: University of Hawaii Press, 1993.

Command, Bobby, "Kaho'Olawe Use Plan," *Planning*, April 1997, pp 12–13.

DiPietro, Ben, "Base Camp Manager Brings Home-Feel to Island," *Pacific Business News*, February 9, 2001, p. 5.

_____, "Businesses Clean Up on Kaho'Olawe," *Pacific Business News*, February 9, 2001, p. 1.

_____, "Race Against Time and Money to Clear Island," *Pacific Business News*, February 9, 2001, p. 4.

Emerson, Nathaniel B. *Unwritten Literature of Hawaii.* Rutland, Ver.: Charles E. Tuttle Company, 1965.

Enomoto, Catherine Kekoa, "Hula Is More Than Dance steps," *Honolulu Star Bulletin*, April 16, 1998.

_____, "My Turn," *Honolulu Star-Bulletin*, March 18, 1997.

Foster, Nelson. *Kaho'olawe: Na Leo o Kanaloa*. Honolulu: Ai Pohaku Press, 1995.

Gomes, Andrew, "Protection of Archeological Sites Lies in Hands of Cultural Surveys," *Pacific Business News*, September 22, 1997.

Hale, Constance, "The Hula Movement," *Atlantic Monthly*, July–August 2002, pp. 166–168.

"Hawaiian Sacred Sites and Power Spots," http://www.psience.net/sites, 1999.

Hurley, Timothy, "Environmental Restoration of Kaho'Olawe to Proceed," *Maui News*, June 20, 1997.

"Interview with Charlie Maxwell," *Pacific Connections*, September/October 1996.

"Island remains in Navy Hands despite Protests," *Navy News & Undersea Technology*, August 28, 1989, p. 7.

"Kaho'olawe Island Cleanup Approved," *Superfund Week*, November 19, 1993, pp. 4–5.

"Kaho'Olawe Mahakiki Overview," http://www.brouhaha.net/ohana/makahiki.html.

Kalakaua, David. *The Legends and Myths of Hawaii*. Rutland, Ver.: Charles E. Tuttle Co., 1972.

King, Serge Kahili, "Kahuna and Hawaiians," *Aloha International*, http://www.huna.org/html/hunahaw.html.

Kubota, Gary T., "Kaho'Olawe Going Back to Native Foliage," *Honolulu Star-Bulletin*, July 3, 1997.

_____, "Kaho'Olawe Planners Vote for Fishing Ban," *Honolulu Star-Bulletin*, May 23, 1997.

MacDonald, Peter, "Fixed in Time: A Brief History of Kaho'Olawe," *Hawaiian Journal of History*, Vol. 6, 1972, pp. 69–90.

McAllister, J. Gilbert. *Archaeology of Kahoolawe*. (monograph) New York: Kraus Reprint Co., 1973.

Merrill, Christopher, "A Little Justice in Hawai'i: Kaho'Olawe Lives!," *Nation*, September 5, 1994, pp. 235–236.

"Military Wants Access in Hawaii; Focus of U.S. Dispute Is over Use of 27,000-Acre Island for Practice Shooting," *New York Times*, December 20, 1990, p. A15.

Miller, Corki, and Mary Ellen Snodgrass. *Storytellers*. Jefferson, N. C.: McFarland, 1998.

"Navy Agrees to a Partial Cleanup of Hawaiian Island," *New York Times*, December 7, 1980, p. 31.

Omandam, Pat, "Fallen Warriors," *Honolulu Star-Bulletin*, August 11, 1998.

Schmitt, Robert C., and Carol L. Silva, "Population Trends on Kaho'Olawe," *Hawaiian Journal of History*, Vol. 18, 1984, pp. 39–46.

Skow, John, "In Praise of the Goddess Pele," *Time*, August 24, 1987, p. 67.

Stasack, Edward, "First Direct 14C Ages on Hawaiian Petroglyphs," *Asian Perspectives: the Journal of Archaeology for Asia and the Pacific*, Vol. 35, No. 1, Spring 1996, pp. 51–72.

Theroux, Paul, "Hawaiians Reclaiming Their Culture," *National Geographic*, December 2002, pp. 8–18, 24–41.

Torres, Nohea, "Kaho'Olawe," http://gohawaii.miningco.com/gi/dynamic/offsite.htm?site=h ttp://leahi.kcc.hawaii.edu/~dennisk/

Kaikoura Peninsula, New Zealand

Location

Emerging from two parallel rocky declivities of the snow-capped Kaikoura Range, the Kaikoura Peninsula took shape along South Island's northeast shore in 178,000 B.C. The first headland emerged when the earth's crust forced limestone and silt from the sea floor into a craggy outcrop that reached alpine heights. The land mass, scored by the Clarence River, stretched straight down into the sea at a drop of 22,000 feet to an abyss known as Kaikoura Canyon. A narrow coastline supported an active involvement of human settlers with sea creatures, including seventeen species of dolphins and whales.

Because of the merger of a subtropical ocean current with a subantarctic flow, the canyon supported rich phytoplankton and zooplankton, the food of large sea mammals. Along the Hikurangi Trench, a subsurface canyon scored the continental shelf and provided a habitat for anchovy, grouper, lobster, and shark. The deepwater lair hosted the giant squid (*Architeuthis*), a sea beast that has haunted the minds of ocean-going crews from prehistory. In recent times, the small fishing village of Kaikoura on the Marlborough coast some ninety miles north of Christchurch became the world's prize spot for an ecologically sound interaction between humans and cetaceans.

Contacts

Kaikoura Information & Tourism
Kaikoura Visitor Centre, West End
Kaikoura, New Zealand
Phone: 64-3-319-5641
Fax: 64-3-319-6819
Email: info@kaikoura.co.nz
http://www.kaikoura.co.nz

Mythology

Led by the beneficent *mata-mata* [whale], Polynesian island explorers carved whale symbols on their *takatimu* [outriggers] and found their way to New Zealand. As characterized by Auckland-born mythographer and publisher Alexander Wyclif Reed, author of *Wonder Tales of Mao-riland* (1956) and *Myths and Legends of Mao-riland* (1961), the aboriginal Maori claimed the cluster. Their mythos accounted for the Kaikoura Peninsula's birth as the spot where the demigod Maui paused to shape North Island from sea floor muck. To assure that the land would prosper, deities took the shape of whales to swim in the bay and observe humankind. The calls of the whale reassured the Maori that the gods were ever near, protecting Oceania.

In Maori lore are oral histories of the hero Kupe, the discoverer of New Zealand. Upon leaving the Maori homeland of Hawaiki, he reached a cloud-topped sea paradise that he named Aotearoa, the Land of the Long White Cloud. To take possession, he used whalebone weapons to defeat Te Wheke Muturangi, the great octopus that ruled the shore.

According to one adventure tale, the whale-riding hero Paikea traveled New Zealand's coast on the back of Tohora. After

New Zealand's Kaikoura Peninsula became the world's prize spot for an ecologically sound interaction between humans and cetaceans (courtesy of Dennis Buurman).

his canoe capsized, he escaped drowning by summoning his sea-going transport with a magic call. Natives named the jut of land he found Kaikoura [meal of crayfish]. In acknowledgement of Maori lore, natives adorned canoes and storage houses with whale symbols. Crafters used whale bone to shape combs, clubs, cloak pins, fishhooks, and talismans. Islanders kept alive the myth of the whale rider by assigning the title to heroes of each succeeding generation.

History

Moa hunters from the Cook and Society islands first accessed the coastal wildlife of Kaikoura, New Zealand, around 1100. Legends name the first hero-explorer as Kupe, who arrived in A.D. 950; two centuries later, Toi, a second canoeist, completed an epic voyage. Permanent habitation dates to 1350, when migratory Melanesians in seven canoes originating east of New Guinea arrived in their splendid single-log *waka* [canoes], some reaching 100 feet in length. The Maori took pride in these early settlers by naming individuals who headed island genealogies and by reciting a proverb: "I shall never be lost, for I am a seed sown from Rangiatea" (Powell, 2003, p. 41). Perhaps the first settled region of New Zealand, Kaikoura has known a series of Polynesian tribal enclaves, beginning with the Waitaha nation and continuing with waves of immigration by the Ngati Mamoe and Ngai Tahu, the dominant aboriginal nations. To avoid the extreme cold of the mountains, bands of agrarian colonists settled at fortified *pa* [villages] near the shore to farm and gather ample abalone, cod, mussels, and other crustaceans as well as seals, moa birds, and their eggs.

Late in the 1600s and early 1700s, Anglican and Wesleyan missionaries and traders from the outside world impacted Maori life by introducing European economic, religious, and social concepts. To the

people's detriment, the new arrivals brought unknown viruses and bacteria and sold guns that encouraged violence and warfare. English navigator James Cook, captain of the *Endeavour*, observed the region in February 1770, when 57 rowers in double canoes pushed off from the shore to return the stares of English sailors. Two decades later, natives encountering an English ship produced *tikotiko toto* [bloody feces], possibly a symptom of dysentery. Sickness worsened into epidemic flu, which islanders treated with plunges into the sea to reduce fever. More loss of life followed the spread of pertussis, scarlet fever and measles among island children and enteritis and typhoid fever among all Maori.

From the early 1800s, European hunters targeted the fur seal of South Island for its warm brown pelt, used in making coats and hats. In 1824, one party of sealers amassed 80,000 skins. After surveying the shores from around 1830, in February 1840, the English made New Zealand a British crown colony by settling the Treaty of Waitangi with the Maori, who hastily relinquished their fishing rights under a promise of fair treatment. Greedy outsiders bought ancestral lands from unwary islanders and tricked and cheated other Maori out of their holdings.

White Europeans colonized Kaikoura in 1843, beginning with Alexander Robert Fyffe, a sea captain from Perthshire, Scotland. He established Waiopuka, New Zealand's first whaling station, with the help of a partner, John Murray, and with whaler Jacky Guard and his wife Betty and their two sons. The community-based economy, boosted by forty employees from Australia, Great Britain, France, Germany, Hawaii, India, and North America, required spotters on pinnacles to watch for whale spouts and flukes. They alerted harpooners and native and immigrant crewmen, who put to sea in whaling boats, killed their catch, and hauled it ashore for carving, removal of baleen, and rendering oil from blubber in coastal try-pots. The company profited from trade in spermaceti, used in candles and ointment, and ambergris, an ingredient in perfumes.

At an ancient Maori site, Robert Fyffe erected a permanent dwelling amid piles of whale skeletons and diversified his investment in 1846 by initiating shipping and goat and sheep herding. After the capsize of his ship, the *Fidèle*, he drowned in late April 1854 while transporting whale oil to Wellington on the southern tip of South Island. His cousin, George Fyffe, managed the whaling station, set up farming north of the bay, and sided the original whalebone cottage with lath and plaster and named it Fyffe House.

In 1860, the Maori attempted to drive off white insurgents, but their effort was too little too late. The arrival of Mormon missionaries in the 1880s resulted in greater weakening of tribal tradition and customs. Swift changes in island survival continued in the early 1900s, when influenza and the smallpox epidemic of 1913 drastically reduced the Maori, a virgin-soil population that lacked immunity to European diseases. Aggressive whaling of cows and calves soon exhausted the cetacean population and ended traditional dependence on coastal harvests after the whaling industry crumbled in 1920. The Fyffe name remained at Mount Fyffe Run and the Fyffe House customs station as tributes to the first white explorers and entrepreneurs.

Because of the rugged country and fingers of river that cut settlers off from the interior, Kaikoura remained bound to the shore and to sea travel. Coastal storms along the Pacific made transport hazardous and wrecked numerous ships. By the mid-twentieth century, engineering had solved overland travel problems with bridges, roads, rail lines, and tunnels, thus eclipsing the era of sea dependence. In place of sealing and whaling, local people earned a living from dairying and farming, sheepherding, cray-fish canning, lime processing, and marine biological research. To preserve the environment, New Zealand ended sealing in 1946; to halt the threat to whales, in 1964, the government closed its last whaling station. Adoption of the Marine Mammal Protection Act of 1978 shielded sea life as a part of the Southern Hemisphere Whale Sanctuary.

At a low ebb in Maori history and economy, in 1989, Kaikoura underwent a cultural renaissance with the restoration of their commercial fishing rights. Native islanders took on a new approach to whaling with the introduction of ecotourism and excursions to pods of gray-skinned sperm whale, the world's largest toothed whale. At the Ngai Tahu *marae* [ceremonial courtyard] at Takahanga, natives began teaching the aboriginal language, farming and forestry, and conservation methods to protect dwindling whale populations.

Central to aboriginal appreciation of sea animals was the interlinking concepts of *maori* [life force] and *mana* [power], the sharing of godly gifts between earthlings and nature. As science writer John Patterson summed up in an article for *Ecologist*, reverence for life bound the Maori to respect for individual beings:

> Although the *mana* of a creature might be thought of as simply being its importance, that would be an over-simplification. *Mana* also relates to unity, to the connectedness of each thing with all other things. No creature has *mana* on its own. Its *mana* relates as much to its interrelations with other creatures as to its individual character and activities [1999, p. 229].

To illustrate *maori* and *mana*, the Maori instructed their children to examine their place in the natural world and encouraged them to leave the sea as clean and wholesome as they found it.

At the heart of the regenerated Maori world view was *mata-mata*, the whale, symbol of bounty. Once more, the luck-bringing beast boosted the outlook for natives, who drew outsiders to a time-honored mythic view of sharing the planet with sea creatures and maintaining a balance in nature. Visitors glimpsed the majestic flukes and left-sided blowhole and observed how the animal used deposits of spermaceti for sounding and diving to depths of 3,000 feet. Refreshing with its vistas of mountain and sea, the region continued to attract vacationers and naturalists, who also studied the antics of the bottlenose, dusky, hectors, and southern right dolphin.

In 1998, the National Geographic Society organized an expedition to follow whales into the offshore trench. The purpose was to locate the giant squid (*Architeuthis dux*), an elusive creature that grows up to 75 feet long. The eight-armed, two-tentacled cephalopod was a central feature of Jules Verne's *20,000 Leagues Under the Sea* (1873), which most readers categorized as fiction. Remains of the squid have washed up on the coast or been trapped in trawling nets, but not studied in the wild. Led by marine invertebrate zoologist Clyde F. E. "Dr. Squid" Roper of the Smithsonian Institution, the team applied scientific equipment — sonar, robot submarine, hydrophones, and deep water cameras fitted with squirt tubes of liquid bait — to the quest of one of the sea's great mysteries. By logging, tracking, and dissecting the squid, into early 1999, they added to the world's knowledge of deep-sea life.

Coastal Activities

At Kaikoura Bay, the variety of coastal activities lures visitors to seal swimming, surfing, sailing, diving, canoeing, rafting, and dragon-boat racing, an exuberant sport imported from Hong Kong. The town's specialty is boating on the year-round Maori Whale Watch, Kaikoura's homegrown industry and largest employer. Operated by Maori enthusiast Wally Stone, the tours gather and depart from the Whaleway Sta-

tion, a recycled train depot. From there, tourists board coastal vessels to witness dolphin pods and humpback, killer or orca, pilot, and sperm whales, which have thrived from proper sea management and rebounded to a population of 400,000 whales. To assure the coastal health, local spotters monitor underwater noise and pollutants for danger to animals or for stress on the environment. For nurturing anti-industrial whaling and sustainable tourism, the company has earned an international commendation from the Pacific Asia Travel Association, a British Airways honorarium, and the Green Globe Achievement Award for distinguished tourism.

In addition to whale watching, nature offers numerous activities to ecotourists. Some choose undersea photography of barracuda, dogfish, eels, lantern fish, ling, blue and mako shark, octopus, squid, and tuna. Others take helicopter flights over rocky shores for filming the rare colonies of silvery brown fur seals and the breeding grounds and habitats of a huge variety of birds — albatross, dotterel, gannet, heron, mollyhawk, oystercatcher, penguin, petrel, seagull, shearwater, stilt, tern, and wrybill. Inland adventures intrigue tourists to horse trek, join forest tramps, tour caves, motorbike, and ski and to study the fauna of the interior — the bellbird, creeper, falcon, fantail, black-eyed gecko, grebe, kea, morepork, scaup, giant skink, tomtit, weta snail, and wood pigeon. Artists prefer the natural backdrops for sources of murals, carving, and painting. Each October, Kaikoura aficionados return for the annual Seafest to enjoy food, music, and shore sights.

Sources

Allen, Thomas B., "Deep Mysteries of Kaikoura Canyon," *National Geographic*, June 1998, pp. 106–117.

"Arrival of the Ship Collingwood," *New Zealand Times*, July 12, 1876.

Blake, Patricia, "Sacred Treasures of the Maoris," *Time*, September 24, 1984, pp. 50–51.

Brunton, Ron, "Beef-Eaters Have No Right to Stop Whale Hunt," *Courier Mail*, August 4, 2001.

Clark, Geoffrey R., "Maori Subsistence Change," *Asian Perspectives*, Vol. 36, No. 2, Fall 1997, pp. 200–219.

Day, Alison, "Chastising Its People with Scorpions," *New Zealand Journal of History*, Vol. 33, No. 2, October 1999, pp. 180–200.

"A Harpoon in the Side," *Time International*, Vol. 156, No. 22, December 4, 2000, p. 49.

Hicks, David, "People of Wood," *World and I*, Vol. 15, No. 12, December 2000, p. 174.

Lange, Raeburn, "Indigenous Agents of Religious Change in New Zealand," *Journal of Religious History*, Vol. 24, No. 3, October 2000, pp. 279–295.

Momatiuk, Yva, and John Eastcott, "Maoris: At Home in Two Worlds," *National Geographic*, October 1984, pp. 522–541.

Moon, Paul, and Sabine Fenton, "Bound into a Fateful Union: Henry Williams' Translation of the Treaty of Waitangi into Maori in February 1840," *Journal of the Polynesian Society*, Vol. 111, No. 1, March 2002, pp. 51–63.

Mutu, Margaret, "Maori Issues," *Contemporary Pacific*, Vol. 14, No. 1, Spring 2002, p. 220.

Newton, Douglas, "Maoris: Treasure of the Tradition," *National Geographic*, October 1984, pp. 542–553.

Patterson, John, "Mana: Yin and Yang," *Philosophy East and West*, Vol. 50, No. 2, April 2000, p. 229.

_____, "Respecting Nature: The Maori Way," *Ecologist*, Vol. 29, No. 1, January–February 1999, pp. 33–38.

Powell, Eric A., "Searching for the First New Zealanders," *Archaeology*, March/April 2001, pp. 40–47.

Purdue, Carla, "An Assessment of Critical Periods and Possible Cold Injuries Associated with Prehistoric Life in Murihiku," *Archaeology in New Zealand*, Vol. 45, No. 3, September 2002, pp. 201–214.

Tapsell, Paul, "Marae and Tribal Identity in Urban Aotearoa/New Zealand," *Pacific Studies*, March–June 2002, pp. 141–171.

Underwood, Grant, "Mormonism, the Maori and Cultural Authenticity," *Journal of Pacific History*, Vol. 35, No. 2, September 2000, p. 133.

Webster, Steven, "Maori Retribalization and Treaty Rights to the New Zealand Fisheries," *Contemporary Pacific*, Vol. 14, No. 12, Fall 2002, pp. 341–377.

"Whale Watch," http://www.whalewatch.co.nz/.

Kraternaya Bay, Kuril Islands

Location

A 750-mile arc of over thirty islands between Hokkaido, Japan, and the Kamchatka Peninsula, Siberia, the Kurils (or Kuriles) lie west of the Okhotsk Sea and east of the Pacific Ocean on the region's "Ring of Fire." Windswept and largely uninhabited, the islands rise from 100 volcanoes that extend 10,000 feet under the sea. The region bears the name of the Ainu or Kur, Japan's aborigines.

The terrain varies widely from land to sea. At least one-third of the Kuril Island peaks are still active. A variety of grasses top steep inclines some 1,000 feet above the bay. To the east, the Kuril Trench is an undersea depression reaching 34,000 feet deep through a progression of undersea terraces. A cold, wet island chain, the Kurils experience monsoon rains, and snow as well as typhoons, tidal waves, and earthquakes. Further inhibiting human habitation is a heavy fog generated by the clash of air currents from the warm Pacific and frigid Okhotsk Sea.

Adding to the rigorous landscape are environmental extremes — glaciers, cataracts, boiling lakes, gaseous vents, and magma-heated waters. At the volcanic spring in the breeched crater known as Kraternaya Bay, steam, gases from fumeroles, and yellow sulfur scum engulf the coast, where seawater oxidizes noxious sulfur fumes into sulfides. Underwater eruptions through seafloor vents warm the waters to 100 degrees Fahrenheit, sixty degrees higher than the island's shoreline. Within the shallow basin far from human pollution, anomalous sea life entices biologists to study natural adaptation to nature's extremes.

Contacts

Lucille M. Craft
Kuril Island Network
4-44-13 Izumi
Suginami-ku, Tokyo, Japan 168-0063
Fax: 3315-6820
Email: kurilnature@gol.com
http//www.kurilnature.org

Kurilsky State Nature Reserve
Email: magnoliya@sakhmail.sakhalin.ru

History

The inaccessible Kuril Island chain was originally settled by the Ainu, bushy-bearded hunters, fishers, and trappers who spoke the Kurile language, lived in pit dwellings, and worshipped the bear. They designated the volcanic spring at Ushishir, an island at the center of the Kuril chain, as sacred ground, where would-be priests propitiated the gods by tossing in chunks of wood incised with ciphers. On the southeastern shore at Kraternaya Bay, the priests conducted shamanic initiations. Only the toughest survived three days on log platforms erected over toxic fumes arising from a vigorously boiling volcanic crater heated by subterranean magma. The Ainu respected successful initiates as priests capable of combating any disaster or evil.

In 1643, Dutch navigator Martin Heritzoon de Vries reached the Kurils. A century later, Russian expeditioner O. Argunov and others studied the north end of the chain to determine how to exploit indigenous fish, crabs, and the *Phoca vitulina stejnegeri* seal. Under Tsar Peter the Great, in the 1690s, Russian interest in seizing the archipelagos increased. Explorer Ivan Cherny arrived on Yankich Island at the center of the chain in 1769. At Kraternaya Bay, one of the earth's more desolate coasts, he was the first to record the effect of sulfur on puffins, which flew over the submerged volcanic crater and stewed in the boiling broth. In his words:

> At night, young puffins flying toward the sea over these springs often fall in the

Within a shallow basin far from human pollution, anomalous sea life of Kraternaya Bay entices biologists to study natural adaptation to nature's extremes (courtesy of Lucille M. Craft).

water, overcome by the heat and sulfur fumes. The poor birds stew there, and soon only their feathers are seen in the water ... the air is charged with sulfur, and fierce heat belches forth from the land in loud bursts [Propp & Tarasov, 1989, p. 28].

Explorer and navigator Morekhod Gerasim Izmailov reported to the government on the lifestyle and rituals of Kuril aborigines called Tungu. In the same period, Japan began a similar reconnaissance of the southern Kurils under the leadership of Admiral Kondo Juzo (also Kondo Morishige), a respected scion of Toyko samurai. He mapped the area as though the Kurils belonged to Russia.

Despite Russia's unofficial claims of ownership, Japan seized the most liveable Kuril Islands to the south in 1855 under the Treaty of Shimoda. Under the agreement, Russia divided the Kurils between Iturup and Urup at the Vries Strait, giving Japan Iturup and Kunashir. From 1872 to about 1889, Henry James Snow, author of *In Forbidden Seas* (1910), hunted the islands for sea otters. Twenty years after the Shimoda agreement, under the Treaty of St. Petersburg, all the chain returned to the Japanese, who traded Sakhalin for the right to fish, hunt, and mine sulfur from the Kurils.

In September 1943, the Kurils figured in the Japanese defense line, which extended south to the Bonins, Marianas, and Carolines, to western New Guinea, the Sunda Islands, and Burma. At the end of World War II three weeks after Japan's surrender, Soviet dictator Joseph Stalin organized an amphibious invasion of the Kuril Islands coordinated with land and air forces. Although Japan had not been at war with the Soviets, the Yalta Conference gave the Kurils to the Soviet Union as of September 1945. The decision had the backing of U.S. President Franklin D. Roosevelt. Three years later, Stalin engineered the expulsion of 17,300 Ainu and Japanese Kurilites to Hokkaido and established September 3 as Liberation Day. The Soviet military garrisoned forces on the islands during the Cold War. To curtail Soviet expansion of a strategic perimeter and the placement of missiles along the Sea of Okhotsk and the use of the Kurils as a naval and submarine base, the United States, represented by Secretary of State John Foster Dulles, shifted its position from support of Russian claims to backing the Japanese.

As both Japan and Russia industrialized, their interest in the Kuril Islands intensified. For nationalistic and economic reasons, Japan refused to reconcile itself to the loss of the isles they call *Chisima* [Thousand Islands] or the Northern Territory, comprised of the Habomai Islands, Shikotan, Iturup, and Kunashiri, the isle that protrudes into Hokkaido only seven miles from land. Nostalgically, they mourned:

> We had everything we wanted.... It was a perfect garden. It was a complete balance of sea and rivers and mountains and harbors. The winters were mild. And we even rode wild horses on the cliffs above the sea [Crump, 1987, p. 59].

The Japanese valued the boiling lakes as potential sources of energy and mineral spas. Central to the international dust-up was the worth of the Kuril hardwood forests and fishing grounds, one of the world's richest sources of sockeye salmon and its roe and of pollock, flounder, squid, sea urchins, crabs, clams, shrimp, and scallops, all Japanese delicacies.

The centuries-old animosities inhibited island development and stymied regional accord. Japan began publishing maps in 1969 that featured the islands as a legitimate possession. Japanese merchants limited trade with the Russian fishers of Kunashir, who prized Japanese cars and fresh produce, two commodities in short supply on the Kurils. In October 1994, an earthquake in the Kuril Islands caused an easing of international tensions after the Russian military helped to airlift 1,359 islanders to safety and deliver 310 tons of aid.

In the 21st century, the worth of the Kuril Islands grew from a strategic, economic, and political landbase to global interest in preservation and exploitation of a natural wonder. To evaluate coastal resources, physicist Victor Suetin of Moscow joined divers in perusing a volcanic crater to determine the quality of the water. He reported:

> The air was heavy with sulphurous fumes, hot gases spurted from fissures in the rocks, and the water boiling near the shore was covered by a black volcanic foam. Descending into this natural witches' cauldron, we took samples of the soil at the bed of the volcanic lake, sampled the water and the gases, and measured the temperature at various depths [Aksyonov & Chernov, 1979, p. 38].

He was so taken with the churning sea broth in the crater that he declared, "It was a dive I shall never forget" (*ibid.*).

After considerable study, Russia established the Kurilsky State Nature Reserve to protect one of the earth's few unexplored habitats and stands of virgin forest. Most endangered were sea otters and seals that inhabit the chain's ample kelp beds. In addition to Kunashir's gold veins, the island of Iturup proved most valuable to Russian metallurgists for its deposits of rhenium, a rare earth metal and one of the densest elements. The silvery-white, extremely hard ore is used in fountain pen nibs, heat sensors, catalysts, electrical components and contact points, and thermocouples.

Ecosystem

The ecosystem of the uninhabited parts of the Kuril Islands is virtually pure because of the chain's largely untrammeled natural development over seventy million years. As Japanese wetlands declined at a rapid rate, breeding grounds shrank. International Wildlife encouraged the fostering

of endangered birds, which the Japanese revere by picturing them at temples and shrines and on sake bottles, jets, and wedding kimonos. A tradition dating to the 1950s begins annually in late fall, when farmers spread corn kernels to feed long-legged waders over the winter. In 1992, Russia allowed Japanese ornithologists to investigate the crane's Kuril habitat.

Environmentalist Sergey Sheveiko, former project director of the Far East Ecological Department and associate of the Climate Institute in Washington, D. C., earned recognition from the United Nations in 1992 for proposing turning the desolate Kurils into a world marine park. He foresaw the island chain as a home to rare mollusks, fish owls, Steller's sea eagles, tufted puffins, guillemots, and stormy petrels, all endangered wildlife. Central to his concept was the protection of marshy nesting and feeding grounds of the migratory red-crowned crane, a magnificent dancer and trumpeter that both Russia and Japan hope to save from extinction.

Much of late twentieth-century interest in the Kurils focused on less eye-catching wildlife. In 1985, an American team from the Institute of Marine Biology exited the Siberian port of Vladivostok on the way to Kraternaya Bay on Ushishir Island, a five-square mile archipelago where plate tectonics govern the bursts of lava from the seabed. Divers Michael V. Propp and Vitaly G. Tarasov, both associates of the Institute of Marine Biology in Vladivostok, observed volcanic activity and gauged its effect on wildlife. In a circular bay that opens to the sea at a narrow gap, they mapped fumaroles and gasohydrothermal vents, the remaining grumblings of a volcano that erupted in 8000 B.C. and separated a single volcano into Raponkich and Yankich islands. The volcano's last activity occurred in 1710, 1769, and 1884.

From dives into shallows, the two scientists examined fissures from which volcanic heat issued into the bay and identified diatoms, plankton, tuba anemones, cyanobacteria, archaebacteria, and photosynthesizing algae, the source of the bay's food chain. Subsequent surveys by the institute produced data on the unusual organic habitat and the 150 species that populate it. The identification of bay life added new species to oceanography—red and white sea cucumbers, large anemones, and some previously unknown clams. These discoveries shed light on invertebrate zoology and evolution on a coast where all life copes with a challenging environment. In 1987, designation of Yankich Island as a nature preserve helped to guarantee a unique habitat worth exploring for its glimpse of the biota that thrived on earth during its volcanic stage of development.

In September 1991, Theodore W. Pietsch, a zoologist at the University of Washington, proposed the International Kuril Island Project, a cooperative survey of animal life that teamed Americans with Japanese experts from Hokkaido University and scientists from the Russian Academy of Sciences. In July 1994, a team of 23 collaborators made a trial expedition aboard the *Professor Bogorov* in hopes of obtaining funding from the National Science Foundation for a five-year project. Because of the dire conditions on the island, rather than camp on the shore, they had to live aboard the research vessel. They departed the site the following June with more new species—nine aquatic insects, twenty spiders, ten mollusks, and nine freshwater fish, which cataloguers at the universities of Washington and Michigan identified.

Protection of the Kurils appears to have fostered the red-crowned crane. In 1996, a Nova Scotian bird enthusiast, George Archibald, a co-creator of the International Crane Foundation in Baraboo, Wisconsin, located a nest of the elusive wader among tall weeds. Despite a thaw in chilly Russo-Japanese relations, Russia refused to allow the Japanese to band the birds or to conduct field studies, population counts, or the training of rangers to protect the environment and ward off poachers and conditions causing disease.

Coastal Activities

Interest in preserving the Kuril habitat has spawned the Kuril Island Network (KIN), a nonpartisan, nonpolitical volunteer society launched by Lucille M. Craft, an American freelance journalist and photographer living in Japan. The group, which formed unofficially in 1998 and established itself the following year, raises public awareness of the importance of pristine shores to world ecology. By drawing attention to the Kurils through multilingual articles, nature comic books for children, lectures, website, and educational symposia, members have helped to preserve native flora and fauna from poaching and wanton exploitation by loggers and miners.

The purpose of KIN's concerted efforts is to foster bird life in the Pacific Basin and to maintain the Kurils as a control for ecologists studying old forest growth and endangered species. KIN supports mobile squads of rangers on foot and in power boats and encourages ecotourist expeditions to the islands by island ferry or flights from Hokkaido for backpacking, canoeing, photography, and birdwatching. Drawing visitors are Chinese peacock caterpillars and butterflies, dragonflies and leaf rollers, bark beetles, flower and crane flies, teeming fish and mollusks, 200 bird species, and 800 kinds of trees, grass, and plants.

SOURCES

Aksyonov, Andrei, and Alexander Chernov. *Exploring the Deep*. London: Collins, 1979.
Craft, Lucille, "Dangerous Reporting," International Wildlife, May 1999.
_____, "Divided by Politics, United in Flight," *International Wildlife*, May–June 1999.

_____, "Eagle on the Edge," *International Wildlife*, September 2000.

Dodd, Jan, and Simon Richmond. *Japan: The Rough Guide*. London: Penguin, 1999.

Elleman, Bruce A., et al, "A Historical Reevaluation of America's Role in the Kuril Islands Dispute," *Pacific Affairs*, Vol. 71, No. 4, 1998–1999, pp. 489–504.

Gallicchio, Marc, "The Kuriles Controversy," *Pacific Historical Review*, Vol. 60, No. 1, 1991, pp. 69–101.

Hara, Kimie, "New Light on the Russo-Japanese Territorial Dispute," *Japan Forum*, Vol. 8, No. 1, 1996, pp. 87–102.

Harmer, George A., "Islands of Dispute," *Military Review*, Vol. 62, No. 6, 1982, pp. 12–18.

Hesse, Stephen, "Poachers, Politics Threaten Japan's Eden," *Japan Times*, August 23, 2001.

Hill, Fiona, "A Disagreement between Allies," *Journal of Northeast Asian Studies*, Vol. 14, No. 1995, pp. 3–49.

Horne, Mari Kuraishi, "The Northern Territories: Source or Symptom?," *Journal of Northeast Asian Studies*, Vol. 8, No. 4, 1989, pp. 60–76.

"International Kuril Island Project," http://artedi.fish.washington.edu/okhotskia/ikip/index.htm.

Kim, Roy U. T., "Warming Up Soviet-Japanese Relations?," *Washington Quarterly*, Vol. 9, No. 2, 1986, pp. 85–96.

Ladigin, Alexander, "Fire, Ice, and Eagles," *Natural History*, Vol. 103, No. 2, February 1994, pp. 26–33.

Lasserre, Frédéric, "The Kuril Stalemate: American Japanese, and Soviet Revisitings of History and Geography," *Journal of Oriental Studies*, Vol. 34, No. 1, 1996, pp.: 1–16.

Latyshev, I. A., "Reactionary Nationalist Tendencies in the Policy of the Ruling Circles of Japan," *Asia Quarterly*, Vol. 1, 1973, pp. 3–16.

Morton, Louis, "Crisis in the Pacific," *Military Review*, Vol. 46, No. 4, 1966, pp. 12–21.

Murai, Tomohide, "The Problem of Japanese-Soviet Relations: Japan's Northern Territories," *Asian Profile*, Vol. 12, No. 5, 1984, pp. 457–463.

Narasimha Murthy, P. A., "The Kurile Islands in Japan's Relations with the Soviet Union," *India Quarterly*, Vol. 20, No. 3, 1964, pp. 281–311.

Nester, William, "Japan, Russia, and the Northern Territories," *Third World Quarterly*, Vol. 14, No. 4, 1993, pp. 717–734.

Nikiforov, S. M., "Allozyme Variability of the Sea Urchin *Strongylocentrotus droebachiensis* in an Area of Volcanic Hydrothermal Vent," *Biologiya Morya*, Vol. 27, No. 6, 2001, pp. 438–445.

Pala, Christopher, "Russian Emigrants Tread Water off Japanese Bay," *Insight on the News*, December 12, 1994, pp. 15–17.

"Poached Salmon," *Eat Magazine*, July 2001.

Propp, Michael V., and Vitaly G. Tarasov, "Cauldron in the Sea," *Natural History*, Vol. 98, No. 8, August 1989, pp. 28–33.

"Rich Natural Heritage on Disputed Isles," *Japan Times*, October 18, 1999.

Shesl, Alexander, "Iturup — Treasure Island of the Kurils," *Moscow News*, February 11, 1999, p. 7.

Shulkin, V. M., "The Hydrothermal Influence on Metal Scavenging in the Coastal Areas," *Oceanology*, Vol. 35, No. 3, December 1995.

Stephan, John J. *The Kuril Islands: Russo-Japanese Frontiers in the Pacific*. Oxford: Clarendon Press, 1974.

Stone, Richard, "Academy Fights to Maintain Research in the 'Wild East,'" *Science*, May 31, 1996, pp. 1259–1260.

"World Park Proposed for Kuril Islands," *National Parks*, January–February 1992, p. 15.

Lindisfarne, Farne Islands, Northumberland

Location

In the North Sea off the northeastern tip of England at the village of Beal, the rugged Farne (also called Fearne or Fern) Islands consist of 28 black dolerite isles and islets and numerous small reefs. Only fifteen of the islands are visible at high tide. At Staple Island, the Pinnacles comprise the island cluster's highest rock columns. Clustered around Staple Sound, they lie only 1.5 miles from Bamburgh on the Northumberland coast, where they are exposed to the wind scouring and heavy seas. For all their forbidding barrenness, they appear to have been inhabited from as early as the Stone Age.

A treacherous stretch surging with rip tides and tricky currents and given to gales and fog, the area has accumulated the remains of many ships that failed to navigate the jagged rocks and thick patches of kelp. There are two lighthouses; only the inner island group offers safe anchorage. During a 5.5-hour window of safety from tides, a causeway leads to the ax-shaped Holy Island, site of Lindisfarne Castle, which rises above the sharply jutting Beblowe Crag. The shore's natural resources have fostered human inhabitants, who netted salmon, hunted rabbits, fermented mead, gathered kelp for fertilizer, bored for coal, quarried limestone, and extracted lime. In response to local love of wildfowling on dune, mudflat, and salt marsh, the British government chose the island for the Lindisfarne National Nature Reserve.

Contacts

Northumbrian Association
P. O. Box 78
Hexham, Northumberland, England
Email: info@northumbrianassociation.co.uk
http://www.northumbrianassociation.co.uk
    /contact.html

Lindisfarne Castle
Holy Island
Berwick-upon-Tweed TD15 2SH England
Phone: 01-289-389-244
Fax: 01-289-389-349

History

The windswept Farne Islands, the cradle of Christianity, has a long history of benevolence and wildlife protection. Inhabited by mesolithic nomads from 8000 B.C., the main island suited hunter-gatherers for its variety of fish, fowl, and shellfish. With the emergence of stable settlements, Lindisfarne, which the Celts called Metcaud or Metgoit, was first mentioned around A.D. 800 in the Welsh monk Nennius's history as the site of a siege in A.D. 575. It altered under the Saxons to Lindisfaronaea or Lindisfarne, literally "water island," perhaps reflecting the name of a stream or channel.

When the Normans came in 1066, they chose a pious designation with Insula Sacra, Latin for "holy island," a place-name that took hold in official references.

Lindisfarne's holy confines developed into the Christian capital of the north. Free of human distractions, the land mass provided a natural retreat for religious contemplation and solitude. The first hermit of the Farnes was St. Aidan, an Irish prelate whom King Oswald made his missionary to Iona to convert heathen Northumbria. In A.D. 635, Aidan advanced to bishop of Lindisfarne Abbey, a Benedictine cloister where he built a wood church and huts in which to lodge his monks. From Lindisfarne school came missionary priests to evangelize northern Britain into the 700s.

Aidan revered nature. When he could avoid riding horseback, he chose to walk to be close to God's creation. He took as a personal ministry wild animals, which he protected from hunters. His religious house followed the injunction of St. Benedict in offering hospitality to all comers, whether pilgrims or stray cats. Chief among the human refreshments were hot drinks of herb tea and mead brewed on the grounds from wild honey. At Aidan's death on August 31, 651, his monks buried him in the island cemetery. After the erection of the Church of St. Peter, his successor, Bishop Finán, reinterred Aidan's remains to the right of the altar.

Aidan continued to influence religion and nature after his death. Upon receiving a vision of the abbot the night of his demise, Cuthbert of Lindisfarne, a seventeen-year-old Anglo-Saxon shepherd and nature lover, resolved to become a monk. After he survived an outbreak of plague, he replaced Boisil, the prior at Melrose, Scotland, who died of the scourge. At the demand of the Synod of Whitby, Cuthbert gave up obedience to Celtic rites to embrace Roman Catholic ritual and, at age 29, become an itinerant evangelist to the pagan Northumbrians.

For his zeal, he earned the nickname "the fire in the north."

Like Aidan, Cuthbert advanced to the post of prior at Lindisfarne, where he disciplined monks with stern rule and asceticism. His outreach focused on the underclass and on plague victims, with whom he could commiserate. One of the world's first wildlife conservationists, for twelve years, while he preached throughout Northumbria, he modeled the tender care of seabirds by nurturing eider ducks and allowing them to nest beneath his church altar. The ducks became known as St. Cuthbert's ducks, elided in time to Cuddy's ducks.

To achieve spiritual purity, in A.D. 676, Abbot Cuthbert retired to a silent, lonely hermitage seven miles offshore in a lava rock cave on the tiny isle of Inner Farne. As explained by the historian Bede, England's main chronicler of the Middle Ages:

> The Farne lies a few miles to the south-east of Lindisfarne, cut off on the landward side by very deep water and facing, on the other side, out towards the limitless ocean. The island was haunted by devils; Cuthbert was the first man brave enough to live there alone [Baldick, 1965, p. 95].

After driving away evil spirits, Cuthbert built a round dwelling cut from rock. By prayer, he summoned a spring of fresh water to the waterless islet and used the pleasant gush as a source of cooling foot bathes for visitors. By a second miracle, the sea washed up wood in the exact length he needed to build a shed. In seclusion, he grew barley and onions and befriended sea otters and the wading birds that fed on sea life in the teeming estuaries.

In 684, King Egfrid named Cuthbert bishop of Lindisfarne, where the old man earned a reputation for succoring the poor during service lasting two years. Only months before death in his early fifties, he returned to the quiet cell on Farne Island to commune with God. He died on March 20, 687, when Edbert succeeded to the post of abbot. Cuthbert's relics stayed in demand by pilgrims, whom the brethren segregated by gender. While women waited in an adjacent chapel, men could view and touch the sacred artifacts to obtain cures. The wealthy left a cache of treasure to Lindisfarne in precious metals, jewelry, ivory, and fabric and fine needlework.

During the Golden Age of Northumbria, Cuthbert's monks followed his pious example by manning a scholarly scriptorium that produced the intricately illuminated *Lindisfarne Gospels* (ca. 698), one of the period's outstanding Christian manuscripts of the Vulgate and a pinnacle of Celtic art. Bishop Eadfrith of Lindisfarne, England's first known artist, illuminated the 258 vellum pages in Hiberno-Saxon style. The monks dedicated the work to God, St. Cuthbert, and the island's saints. The book is revered for its merger of classical, Byzantine, Celtic, and Anglo-Saxon influences in elaborate calligraphy amid ornamental capitals, colored knotwork, spirals, mazes, braiding, and animal patterns, particularly birds and dogs. Originally, it bore the artistry of Ultan, a Scots priest who adorned the books; Bishop Aethelwald, who bound the pages; and Billfrith, a hermit who constructed a *cumdach*, a protective metal casing to contain and preserve the text. A glossary of the gospels from the late 900s is the first biblical text produced in the English language.

Lindisfarne altered significantly in the eighth and ninth centuries. The Venerable Bede, the father of English church history, attested that Bishop Finán completed the see with an oak-beamed church roofed with split reeds and made it a center of spirituality, evangelism, and learning unparalleled in English Christendom. Vikings raided the holy ground in 793, the official beginning of the three-century Viking era and the first of a series of sackings and plunderings in the British Isles that targeted wealthy monasteries. In 875, Danish raiders burned the abbey, killed the island's inhabitants, and, after eight years of constant battery, forced the church's abandonment of its offshore religious house. Having protected the *Lindisfarne Gospels* and secured Cuthbert's remains in a crypt known as Cuthbert's Cave, the monks fled inland with the jeweled text and his body. After eight years of wandering, in 883, the brethren established a permanent home at Chester le Street priory in Durham.

The golden era of Holy Island ended with the decline of Celtic monasticism and the desolation of a holy site left to nature. Nonetheless, elements of spirituality survived, emanating onto the mainland. Because of reports of miracles and prophecies, Cuthbert, the beloved wonderworker of Britain, became Northern England's most revered saint. Because of his ministry to fishing communities, local people celebrated his kindness and referred to fossilized crinoid seashells on the shore as St. Cuthbert's or Cuddy's beads. In Canto II, Verse XVI of the poem *Marmion* (1808), romance writer Sir Walter Scott claimed that Cuthbert sat at an anvil on Hobthrush Island hammering out rosary beads centered with crucifixes:

> ...On a rock by Lindisfarne
> St. Cuthbert sits and toils to frame
> The sea borne beads that bear his name.
> Such tales had Whitby's fishers told,
> And said they might his shape behold,
> And here his anvil sound:
> A deadened clang — a huge dim form
> Seen but and heard when gathering storm
> And night were closing round.
> But this, a tale of idle fame,
> The nuns of Lindisfarne disclaim
> *[Marmion]*.

Pilgrims treasured the beads; sailors chose the hermit as their patron; monks from Durham frequented his cell. His hermitage, renamed Holy Island in 1082, experienced a brief renaissance when church architects replaced the old priory with an arched Norman-Benedictine structure built of sand-

stone. Offshore, Inner Farne lured mystics and pilgrims, whom monks welcomed to Fishehouse, the small stone guest cottage that Cuthbert built alongside the stone jetty.

Surviving from Cuthbert's occupancy is the priory site beneath the remains of the late eleventh-century structure and a late fourteenth-century chapel. After 1255, the abbot at Durham decided to end the island's reputation as an empty hermitage by posting two Benedictine friars to Cuthbert's old cell. A century later, reconstruction of the prior's residence and the addition of a barbican and five guns produced a hybrid monastery fort. In 1500, Thomas Castell, Prior of Durham, added Pele Tower to St. Cuthbert's church as a barracks for monks. In 1888, Sir William Crossman, owner of Holy Island, excavated Celtic structures, including a medieval chapel, sandstone grave markers, and some mortared walls and foundations that may be the remains of an oratory.

The saint's monument at Lindisfarne drew pilgrims until it was destroyed in 1541 during the dissolution of monasteries ordered by Henry VIII when he defied the Vatican by creating the Church of England. In an era fraught with Scottish border raids, island architecture shifted from monastic to military and governmental. In 1543, Tudor defense architects hauled stones from the priory as materials for a garrison fort housing a 24-man defense team. In the former church, they stockpiled munitions.

The union of England and Scotland under James I in 1603 lessened the need for a military outpost at Lindisfarne. As border surveillance eased, in 1613, the Earl of Dunbar pillaged the priory's lead roof and bells. To his dismay, the ship on which he loaded the loot sank off Holy Island with a great loss of life. The downed vessel was not the first. Captain Robin Rugg, governor of Holy Island, reported that local people regularly retreated to Cuthbert's cell to pray when ships were in danger. With a wry twist, he explained that they were not praying for rescue but for a shipwreck for them to despoil.

In the late seventeenth century under Charles II, coastal authorities recycled the Lindisfarne fort into a lighthouse. Subsequent lighthouses established the interest of the British crown in preserving northern shipping lanes. In 1776, a coal and wood-burning beacon at the top of a 43-foot tower illuminated the sea around Inner Farne. By 1809, the primitive system gave place to a revolving beacon that engineers automated a century later. Without need for a keeper and his family, the site was deserted.

Farne Island lights performed a necessary service to the channel. In 1826, William Darling settled his family at Longstone Island north of Lindisfarne to tend the Longstone Light. On September 7, 1838, his 23-year-old daughter Grace became a British hero for initiating a rescue of five crew and only four of sixty passengers of the luxury paddle steamer *Forfarshire*. During a storm, the ship was bound from Hull for Dundee, Scotland, when it foundered on the western edge of Big Harcar after a boiler failure and sank. Grace Darling and her father rowed the nine shivering survivors to the lighthouse to tend them until they could be transported to the mainland three days later. Preserving Grace's memory are books and poems, a museum, her grave on the mainland at Bamburgh, and a lifeboat, the *Grace Darling*, maintained by the Institute of Shipwrecks.

In 1902, publisher Edward Hudson, founder of *Country Life*, and editor Peter Anderson Graham rediscovered Holy Island. After scaling the wall of Lindisfarne Castle, they conceived a plan for reclaiming the abandoned structure. Architect Sir Edwin Landseer Lutyens rebuilt the structure as a private residence for the Hudson family's summer holidays. Although the castle lacked electricity and central heating, it offered the Hudsons unlimited views of the sea and of Bamburgh Castle on the opposite shore plus a beach for swimming and building sand castles and ample territory for wading, lobster potting, sailing, and birding. In 1912, horticulturist Gertrude Jekyll designed a small walled garden for the site on the original castle grounds at a former sheep pen. She chose belladonna, delphinium, geraniums, gladioli, helianthus, and lobelia — vivid colors and shapes to contrast the typically spare island landscape. In 1944, a subsequent castle owner, Sir Edward de Stein, passed the property into the national trust as a model of historic English gardening.

Ecosystem

Because of St. Cuthbert's love of maritime creatures, Lindisfarne became the world's oldest bird sanctuary. As the English crown's first nature reserve, the island cluster survives untouched primarily because of the activism of Lord Edward Grey of Falloden, a former Secretary of State for Foreign Affairs, who proposed sheltering unique island life. Since 1925, the British National Trust has designated the island group as the preserve and breeding grounds of some 140,000 birds and 8,000 gray seals. In addition to natural nesting grounds among sheer cliffs, in the outlying lowlands, surface whinstone, a fine-grained igneous basalt, weathers from wind and rain. The thin layer of soil the whinstone generates above the striated dolerite supports a unique group of shallow-rooted wildflowers, herbs, and grasses — bugloss, daisy, dock, elder, nettle, parnassus grass, primrose, purple sea rocket, ragwort, scurvy grass, silverweed, sorrel, and thrift. The island produces a unique orchid, a marsh helleborine, which arises from strappy leaves on a long stalk.

Today, the island cluster welcomes 150 avian species per year, notably the bunting, cormorant, eider ducks, fulmar, guillemot, herring gull, kittiwake, mute swan, oyster-catcher, peregrine, pipit, puffin, razorbill, redshank, ringed plover, sandpiper, scoter, shag, shelduck, skua, swallow, varied terns, whooper swans, and wrens. In addition, the islands and their shoals shelter the Atlantic blenny, conger, killer whales, octopi, wolf fish, cod, ling, and wrasse. Insecta include two main butterflies, the grayling and the fritillary. Gray seals favor Nessend rocks, where they gather on pleasant days in groups of forty. For the protection of the ecosystem, Brownsman Island is closed for bird breeding; only Inner Farne and Staple Island are open to visitors.

Coastal Activities

Tourists, pilgrims, and historians enjoy the Farne Islands for their austerity and colorful past. Photographers and naturalists access miles of clean, uninhabited beaches and climb rocks in search of nesting areas and puffin colonies. A drive across the causeway at low tide allows for a tour of the castle on Holy Island. Hikers enjoy scaling Beblowe Crag, a conic rock at the island's center. Although St. Cuthbert's cell is currently uninhabited, some 50,000 visitors annually seek the peace and sanctity of the monk's former hermitage. Along Pilgram's Way, a series of poles marks the approach to the holy site. In addition to a priory museum, tours include St. Aidan's Winery and the Museum of Island Life and Visitor Centre.

Offshore, experienced divers favor the Farne Islands for the variety of seabed wreckage, which is largely reduced to rubble, plates, ribs, and boilers. In rigid inflatable boats, they gather shellfish and photograph gray seals. The remains of a French steamer, the 1,100-ton *St. Andre*, is located off Crumstone, where it sank in 1908 after a collision with submerged rock in dense fog. It bore a load of wrought iron bound from Caen, France, for Grangemouth, Scotland. One of the most popular dives, the re-mains of the *Forfarshire*, lies some six miles southeast of Holy Island.

At Gun Rocks, cannon and cannon balls mark a kelp-draped wreck site dating to 1700 but otherwise unidentified. Off Beadnell and Seahouses, the 8,000-ton supply ship *Somali* remains upright in about 100 feet of water. The flagship of a convoy, it exploded, broke in half, and disappeared after Heinkel 111 bombers struck it on March 27, 1941, on its way to Hong Kong. At Knivestone Reef, the wreckage of the 5,753-ton German steamer, *Abessinia*, the largest in the Farne Islands, offers a habitat to anemone, coral, seals, and sponges. The ship, built in 1900, sank on September 3, 1921, after hitting Knivestone Rock. To the northeast at Whirl Rocks, unidentified wreckage may be the remains of the *Jan Van Ryswick*, named for a nineteenth-century Dutch poet. In the opposite direction off Longstone, divers explore the *Chris Christenson*, a 1,491-ton Danish steam merchantman grounded under German artillery fire on February 16, 1915, on its way from Aarhus to Newcastle. South of Blue Caps, the 740-ton steamer *Britannia* lies strewn some ninety feet all the way to the nearest reef after breaking up on the rocks.

SOURCES

Baldick, Robert, et al., eds. *Lives of the Saints.* Harmondsworth, Eng.: Penguin, 1965.
Cartwright, R. A., and D. B. Cartwright. *The Holy Island of Lindisfarne and the Farne Islands.* Vancouver: David & Charles, 1976.
Caws, Ian, "Lindisfarne," *Month*, Vol. 31, No. 6, June 1, 1998, p. 218.
Donnelly, Rachel, "Lindisfarne Gospels Return to Their Roots," *Irish Times*, October 19, 2000, p. 12.
Foley, W. Trent, "Suffering and Sanctity in Bede's Prose Life of St. Cuthbert," *Journal of Theological Studies*, April 1999, p. 102.
Lane, N. Gary, and William I. Ausich, "The Legend of St. Cuthbert's Beads: A Palaeontological and Geological Perspective," *Folklore*, Vol. 112, No. 1, April 2001, p. 65.
Lewis, Lionel Smithett, "The Celtic Church,"

St. Joseph of Arimathaea at Glastonbury. London: James Clarke, 1955.

Mairson, Alan, "Saving Britain's Shore," *National Geographic*, October 1995, pp. 38–57.

Marmion: A Tale of Flodden Field, http://www.geocities.com/poeminister/introcanto1.htm.

"A Northern Holy Grail," *Economist*, Vol. 346, No. 8,050, p. 48.

"So You Want Seals," *Diver*, January 2000.

Lipari, Sicily

Location

The largest of the Aeolian Islands, Lipari is a group of seven volcanic archipelagos — Alicudi, Filicudi, Lipari, Panarea, Salina, and Vulcano — and five islets — Basiluzzo, Bottaro, Dattilo, Lisa Bianca, and Lisca Nera. The Lipari cluster consists of mountain tops jutting upward from a semicircular aeolian volcanic arc submerged in the Tyrrhenian Sea off the northeast coast of Sicily and extending nearly 225 miles west toward Calabria, Italy. Accessible to Messina, Milazzo, Naples, and Palermo by ferry or hydrofoil, the main island of Lipari rises some 3,600 feet from the sea floor and has served as the Aeolian civic and religious center for 6,000 years.

The island of Lipari extends outward from Mount Chirica, from which fumaroles of hot groundwater spew upward like geysers. Comprised of cube-shaped houses, the city spreads north and south to the Marina Lunga and Marina Corta inlets, where pirates once beached their craft and fishermen anchored boats and brought their nets ashore for repair. In terraced fields, farmers raised vegetables that made the island self-sustaining and planted almond trees and caper shrubs, figs, olives, and vineyards. At the natural fortification that looms over the shore, a parade of conquerors has held sway for some six millennia. Today, a lack of fresh water forces residents to import their stock from Sicily.

Contacts

Lipari Travel Board
Corso Vittorio Emanuele 202
98055 Lipari, ME
Phone: 090-9880095
Fax: 090-9811190

Museo Archeologico Eoliano
Via del Castello
98055 Lipari, ME
Phone: 090-9880174

Mythology

Called Lipara or "Glorious" by the ancients, Lipari was the home of Aeolus, a pious man who became king of the winds. The myth appears to have emerged from the annual spell of cold, dry weather from the Tyrrhenian coast and the subsequent emergence of the African scirocco, a warm, humid air stream rising from the south. As characterized in Valerius Flaccus's *Argonautica* (1st century A.D.), the region terrorized sailors for its unpredictable currents:

> Zephyros [the West Wind] and Notus [the South Wind] of the night-dark pinions with all the sons of the Storms, and Eurus [the East Wind] his hair dishevelled with the blasts, and tawny with too much sand; they drew the tempest on, and in thunderous advance together drive the curling waves to shore, and stir not the trident's realms alone, for at the same time the fiery sky falls with a mighty peal, and night brings all things beneath a pitchy sky [Aiolos].

Such dire descriptions of Aeolia in ancient Mediterranean literature summarized the sailor's pervasive fear of death from the sudden unleashing of natural elements.

To stabilize extreme variances in weather, Aeolus took possession of the Aeolian Islands and headquartered at Lipara, called Aeolia, a mythic "floating island" walled by bronze. At the command of the Greek goddess Hera, he confined air currents in island caves to keep them from

The largest of the Aeolian Islands, Lipari has served as a civic and religious center for 6,000 years (courtesy of Manuela Tiraboschi D'Ambra).

overpowering earth and sea. When summoned by any Olympian deity for a change in weather, he pierced the cliffside with his spear to allow a gale to emerge, then he corked the site to halt the flow of air. The wind god benefited humankind by looking into the embers for signs of arising storms and by teaching seafarers how to rig their vessels with sails.

In his steamy hideaway, Aeolus lived secluded and content with a wife and twelve children and served the gods as confidant. The family idyll came to an end after his six sons and six daughters began mating within the family. According to Homer's *Odyssey* (ca. 850 B.C.), the gods, mainly Hera and Poseidon, rivals for wind control, squabbled over whether Aeolus deserved a place at the Olympian table. Zeus respected the dutiful wind-keeper so thoroughly that, at Aeolus's death, the god placed him on a throne in the cave of winds rather than send his spirit to live among the wraiths of mortals in Tartarus.

During Odysseus's ten-year voyage home to Ithaca from the Trojan War, he left the underworld, sailed past Circe's isle and the Symplegades or clashing rocks before moving north toward Scylla and Charybdis at the Strait of Messina. He experienced the call of the Sirens, which may have been located at Naples, Italy, or at Faro, Sicily, then sailed beyond the Planctes (also Planktai or Wandering Rocks), another name for the Lipari Islands. When he approached them, he faced the strong pull and backwash of a whirlpool, which the ancients personified as Charybdis, a deadly female monster. To the south of Lipari, Scylla, a twelve-foot, six-headed she-monster, bared fangs and barked in menace from a cavern. In sight of the coast of Lipari, Odysseus chose to combat Scylla for snatching six of his mariners in the jaws of her six heads. In vain, he strove with the beast, then turned his ship south, leaving his hapless men in Scylla's clutches.

Aeolus, who may have been the original warden of the winds or his grandson, entertained Odysseus and his crew for a month on Aeolia, which Book X of the *Odyssey* describes as a "sea-cradled fastness, within a bulwark of invincible bronze from which the cliff falls sheer" (1956, p. 136). Before the famed mariner left for the final leg on his journey to Ithaca, Aeolus gave him an oxhide bag of all winds except for the west wind, which would gently direct Odysseus's ship home. Over a ten-day sail, Odysseus kept the bag tied, but his men, suspicious that their captain might be hiding secret treasure, opened the bag shortly before the ship beached at Ithaca.

The sudden released of so strong an air current blew the ship back to Aeolus's kingdom. The wary king of the winds refused to intervene a second time because he realized that Odysseus labored under a curse from deities of great power. Aeolus thundered, "Get off the island instantly, you vilest thing alive! Am I to make a habit of maintaining and fitting out one whom the gods hate? ... Out! out!" (*ibid.*, p. 138).

History

First inhabited by emigrants from Sicily, in neolithic times around 4000 B.C., Lipari, called the "first-born of Italian cities," offered a natural fortification that has remained viable for 6,000 years (Piccalomini, 1991, p. 55). The island first prospered in the Bronze Age as an artisanal center of lithoid products, beginning with black and white liparite or obsidian, a sharp volcanic glass, and expanding to pumice, which buyers used in tanning, construction, coating, and abrasives. Because of its location, harbor, and natural resources, the island passed through the hands of sequential invaders, beginning with outlanders from Greece and including waves from Carthage, Rome, Arabia, the Ottoman Empire, Norman France, Sicily, and Aragon.

According to Book III of the Roman encyclopedist Pliny the Elder's *Natural History* (A.D. 77), the current name derives from King Liparos, the island's first true monarch, who succeeded the mythic Aeolus and established a stronghold and a town. The story of Liparus derived from Ausonian immigrants who emigrated from Campania in lower Italy in the 1400s B.C. When the Greeks sanctioned the departure of settlers to Sicily and southern Italy from 750 to 550 B.C, the newcomers created Magna Graecia [Greater Greece], a series of autonomous states that served the motherland as trading posts. These Greek colonists named Lipari "Melingunis" for its gentle climate.

Because Lipari displays the most complex volcanic activity of the Aeolian group, its mythos permeated Greco-Roman literature with stories of unspeakable perils. Ovid's *Metamorphoses* (A.D. 8) described the site as smoking with sulfurous fumes and, in Book XVI, renarrated Odysseus's attempt to return home with Aeolian winds in a bag. Book I of Virgil's *Aeneid* (19 B.C.) declared that the volcanic peaks of Aeolia echoed with the growling of the pent-up winds.

Despite the rumble of the volcanoes, from the sixth century B.C., as far east as Crete, Liparians made the most of their natural resources and exported pumice and liparite, which they quarried from two outflows, Rocche Rosse and Spanarello.

The congregation of Mediterranean pirates generated rapid demographic and economic change among the Aeolian Islands. Only Lipari had the natural fortification of cliffs and a high plateau to stave off invaders and support a stable citizenry. In 570 B.C., late in the colonial era, pirates from Cnidus set up an island commune financed by loot seized from merchantmen sailing the Straits of Messina. As described in *Library of History* (59 B.C.) by Diodorus Siculus, residents drew lots and autocratically separated their citizenry into land dwellers and seafarers. Civil authorities parceled out the land to farmers, who raised crops in terraced patches. At the crescent-shaped shoreline, fishing crews lugged catches of swordfish from their ships. To assure fairness, the citizenry distributed fish, fruits, and vegetables equally to all islanders.

In 408 B.C., Lipari passed temporarily into Carthaginian hands after its capture by Himilcon, a noted sea rover. The islanders had to scrape together blood money to free themselves once more from invaders. Around 393 B.C., when Liparian shipmasters again ruled the Tyrrhenian Sea, they captured a Roman vessel and stole a large golden urn. Because it was sacred to Apollo, Timasiteus, the Liparian chieftain, made the sailors return their loot to its rightful owners.

In spring 260 B.C., Lipari fell to Gaius Cornelius Scipio, commander of a Roman fleet of seventeen warships. Hannibal, the Carthaginian admiral, rapidly dispatched a fleet of twenty ships from Panormus in northern Sicily under Boodes, who seized Scipio's fleet, the commander himself, and his sailors. As Carthage increased its grip on Rome, from 258 to 257 B.C., the shores of Lipari were constantly roiled by the power struggle.

The Romans learned from their defeat that they needed a new ploy. They invented boarding methods and trained the world's first marines. The island passed to Rome after unprecedented civil destruction during the First Punic War in 252 B.C. Razed and depopulated, the former battleground became the Roman legal system's locus for exiled citizens. After Admiral Marcus Vipsanius Agrippa seized the island from Pompey the Great in 36 B.C., the Romans turned the land into a naval base and built a traditional *decumen* or main street. The island served Rome's varied governmental and punitive needs. When the Emperor Caracalla needed a suitable prison for his wife Plautilla and her brother Plautius in A.D. 205, he chose Lipari as the place of banishment.

During fourth century A.D., Christians dominated Lipari. Around 500, they made the island the depository for the relics of St. Bartholomew, one of Christ's twelve apostles. Lipari became a popular destination for pilgrims seeking miracles and cures. As the Roman Empire entered the last phase of its decline, Vandal raids ended Roman interest in the island. When Rome fell to outsiders, in 543, the Ostrogoth king Totila and his invaders established Lipari as their own island naval base and remained it for nine years until their defeat by Belisarius, commander in chief under the Byzantine emperor Justinian I.

Christianity enjoyed nearly three more centuries of control before Saracens radiating from Islamic strongholds overran Lipari. The attack of Muslims was so devastating in 839 that the island was virtually deserted. Some Greco-Roman columns and capitals with bird, leaf, and monster motifs weathered Saracen attacks. Surviving monks collected the desecrated relics of St. Bartholomew and removed them to Sicily for safe keeping. Muslims held Lipari until 1061, when the Norman French invaded and rid it of sacrilege.

To re-establish Christianity in the region, the Normans designated the island as a holy see and built a Benedictine abbey and a palace for the bishop's residence. A square cloister, established in 1083 by Abbot Ambrogio, encircled a garden, a common adjunct to healing centers dependent on herbs. After Roger II of Sicily acquired a vast navy and fortified the stronghold around 1150, the church rebuilt Lipari's cathedral and abbey. Into the 1300s, Sicilian monarchs and the Angevins of Naples vied for the Aeolian Islands. In 1340, Robert I of Naples ruled Lipari. From Alfonso V of Aragon, in 1479, the island cluster passed to Ferdinand II of Aragon.

When a Tunisian pirate, Ariadeno Barbarossa (also Kaireddin, Kair-ed-Din, or Khayrad-Din), a red-bearded Barbary brigand, laid siege in July 1544, he succeeded at capturing the citadel, sacking the monastery, and burning most of the buildings. He enslaved the island's 9,000 citizens, one of the turning points in Lipari's turbulent history. It took the combined sea-clearing of Britain's Admiral Horatio Nelson and the French to end piracy in the Mediterranean and restore normal folk life. Ironically, under dictator Benito Mussolini, Italian fascists returned the island to its original Roman use, as a detainment center for political prisoners.

Archeology

Archeologists — particularly Mediterranean specialist Luigi Bernabò Brea of Genoa, author of *Sicily before the Greeks* (1957), and his colleague, Madeleine Cavalier — have elucidated the complex layering of cultures on Lipari. They discovered late neolithic red earthenware created from 3000 to 2500 B.C., evidence of the Diana Culture that extended over Italy, eastern Sicily, and the Aeolian Islands. Further investigation disclosed layers of a community on Lipari dating to 1700 B.C. Scientists were astonished to discover that, in the 1600s B.C., builders produced a Mycenean cupola, an architectural detail that proved Liparians were influenced by the advanced culture of Mycenae.

At the island acropolis, the Diana District Archeological Park and the Aeolian Archaeological Museum, which Brea established at the bishop's palace in 1954, draw historians and the curious, who survey geologic exhibits, data from underwater archeology, and an array of axes, hatchets, and tools dating from the Stone Age into the Iron Age. From the Greek era are votive and funerary theater masks in the comic and tragic mode, all contemporary with the playwright Menander. The ceramic faces feature painted complexions, eyes, and lips and variant clay textures to indicate features and hair. In the same cache was a stone dedicated to Aeolus around 750 B.C. A sizeable necropolis of 1,300 tombs produced grave goods from the 700s B.C.— earthen sarcophagi, stone and brick burial chambers, tile-covered Hellenistic graves, bowls and figured crematory urns, and bronze Roman oil lamps. Additional finds include bowls, figurines, vases, and various other shapes of painted terra cotta from 500 and 400 B.C. The cache of ceramics displays the finest of Siciy's Hellenistic plastic arts.

The museum displays treasure from a Greek merchant vessel that capsized and sank off Capistello, Lipari, opposite the island of Vulcano around 300 B.C., carrying with it black burnished pottery and amphorae corked and sealed with pine tar resin. Lost on a steep declivity over 170 feet deep, the wreckage remained undisturbed under another shipwreck, the *Posidonia*, until the discovery of the Greek ship in 1966 by coral divers. During the underwater exploration, archeologists Hugo Graf and Helmut Schlaeger, director of the German Archeological Institute of Rome, died in diving accidents that appeared to curse the Lipari underwater site.

In the decade before the American Institute of Nautical Archaeology and the Sub

Sea Oil Services began a two-year expedition with diving bell and mini sub, looters robbed the shipwreck. The remains, covered in simple planking, contained an anchor, fishing weights, lead bars, and some cargo still arranged vertically in the hold. Divers surfaced with terra cotta plates, goblets, drinking bowls, water carafes, and 100 amphorae stamped with their Greek places of origin, including Bion, Chares, and Euxenos. Those amphorae still tightly corked appear to have carried Sicilian *garum* [fish sauce], a strong-flavored, strong-smelling processed fish-pickle made from salt, vinegar, parsley, wine, and sweet herbs to produce a thick condiment paste essential to the diet in Bithynia, the Far East, Greece, and Rome.

Additional artifacts at the Lipari museum derived from the workshop of the *pittore di Lipari* [Lipari painter], who lived from around 300 to 270 B.C. The unknown artisan produced hundreds of pieces in hazel brown, notably, distinctively figured craters [drinking bowls], two-handled cups, and polychrome lidded urns made of terra cotta mixed with the island's unique kaolin clay. Focusing on women, wedding scenes, the afterlife, and the Dionysus cult, the painter produced mythic scenes of red-brown figures enhanced with light blue, lilac, orange, white, and yellow applied after he fired the pieces in a kiln. The Lipari painter initiated a school of polychrome earthenware that survived until the arrival of Roman insurgents in 252 B.C. From the Roman era remain glass, ceramics, grindstones, ingots, and the ever-present amphorae from numerous coastal shipwrecks.

Most photogenic of Lipari's sites is a Greek castle surrounded by walls and a defense tower raised in the 1200s alongside additions completed by the Spanish in the 1500s. Visitors to the complex also view the neo-baroque San Bartolomeo church inside the castle compound, which required reclamation after the pirate Barbarossa attacked

in 1544, and the episcopal or bishop's palace that Ruggero II the Norman erected in 1084. A portcullis and embrasure guarded the tunnel at the Norman gate. Among the worship centers inside the compound are Chiesa dell'Addolorata, a baroque facade from the 1500s leading to wood altars and gilded stucco; Chiesa Santa Caterina and Santa Maria delle Grazie from the late 1600s; and Chiesa dell'Immacolata, a smooth-fronted church erected in 1747. The museum also summarizes island history and archives data on historic trade routes over which islanders sold obsidian and pumice. In addition to an antique acropolis, ruins of a Roman sweat bath suggest leisure activities of centuries past.

Coastal Activities

Lipari's sights feature a wealth of historic and natural beauty. Ponente Beach offers surf fishing, castle and volcano climbing, cavern exploration, bicycling, and water sports, including scuba diving to underwater pumice caves. Sailboats and excursion craft travel to nearby Vulcano or to Stromboli, the most famous of the Aeolian Islands for its volcanic activity. In 1976, local people added an open-air theater in Greek style for evening performances.

Researchers value visits to the island for access to archives that date back to 1544. Historians favor remains of Roman thermal baths and a Mycenean sauna built over a spring at San Calogero. Some seek information on social philosopher Carlo Rosselli, a famed anti–Fascist exile who shared wretched conditions with 400 other prisoners and used his nineteen-month immurement on Lipari from 1928 until his escape in July 1929 as an opportunity to write *Socialismo Liberale* (1930), a disputation on the sources of Fascism and its impact on labor and the Italian Socialist Party.

SOURCES

"Aiolos," http://www.theoi.com/Kronos/Aiolos. html.

Ancona, Gabriella, "The Norman Cloister of Lipari," *Sikania*, No. 11, November 1998.

Curtis, Robert I., "Food Technology in the Ancient Urban Context," http://www.stlcc.cc. mo.us/fv/users/mfuller/aia/papers/curtis/curtis.html, 1997.

Giuffrida, Antonino, "Lipari e Suoi Archivi," *Rassegna degli Archivi di Stato*, Vol. 31, 1971, pp. 94–102

Gore, Rick, "When the Greeks Went West," *National Geographic*, November 1995, pp. 2–37.

Homer. *Odyssey*, trans. T. E. Shaw. New York: Galaxy, 1956.

Malone, Caroline, and Simon Stoddart, "Editorial," *Antiquity*, Vol. 73, No. 380, June 1999.

_____, "Editorial," *Antiquity*, Vol. 75 No. 289, September 1, 2001, p. 459.

Nishimura-Jensen, Julie, "Unstable Geographies: The Moving Landscape in Apollonius' Argonautica and Callimachus' Hymn to Delos," *Transactions of the American Philological Association*, No. 130, 2000, pp. 287–317.

Ovid. *The Metamorphoses*. Cambridge, Mass.: Harvard University Press, 1977.

Piccolomini, Manfredi, "Home of the Wind King," *Archaeology*, Vol. 44, No. 3, May–June 1991, pp. 54–55.

"Pirates, Parasites, and Population," UNESCO *Courier*, October 1987, p. 23.

Simeti, Mary Taylor. *Pomp and Sustenance: Twenty-Five Centuries of Sicilian Food*. New York: Alfred A. Knopf, 1989.

Van der Heyden, A. A. M., and H. H. Scullard, eds. *Atlas of the Classical World*. New York: Thomas Nelson & Sons, 1959.

Virgil. *The Aeneid*. New York: New American Library, 1961.

Manzanillo, Costa Rica

Location

An isolated Afro-Caribbean village ten miles east of Puerto Viejo in southeastern Costa Rica, Manzanillo lies in the southern Caribbean near the Panama border. Dotted with coconut palms, the community, accessed by an old logging road, occupies a coastal point of Talamanca Canton and Límon Province, the nation's least populated sector. In a region where the jungle meets the sea, the land earns the name "rich coast" for the untrammeled beauties of nature and the world's widest variety of life forms in so small an area. At Mona (or Monkey) Point Island, old coral reefs rise nearly 100 feet to form a plateau. Offshore in calm waters, coral reefs at Mona, Manzanillo, and Uva points parallel twelve miles of sandy lava and white beach that earn the praise of honeymooners, ecotourists, and nature photographers.

To the southeast, Gandoca Beach is 5.5 miles of steeply sloped black sand reaching the Sixaola River and the border of Panama. Constantly reshaped by waves, tides, and storms, the strand enwraps Gandoca village, a Spanish-speaking enclave of immigrants and refugees from El Salvador, Honduras, Nicaragua, and Panama. A lagoon in the Rio Gandoca estuary harbors oyster beds, a spawning ground of tarpon, and the region's only red mangrove.

Farther inland, the Gandoca National Wildlife Refuge preserves world-class wilderness suited to nature walks and photo safaris under tall groves and thick, shady understory. The reserve guards endangered species as well as primary tropical rain forest, rare bromeliads and orchids, and a pristine reef. Jungle trails lead past marshland and into lowlands, savannah, the sedimentary rocks of the Banano River, and hill country. To the south stretch 400 acres of herbaceous swamp featuring cat claw, black stick, and aquatic plants.

Contacts

Earl Junier, Ministry of Environment and Energy

Apdo. 1077-7300

Limón, Costa Rica

Phone: 506-754-2133

Fax: 506-754-2133

Email: aclaca@sol.racsa.co.cr

http://www.rainforest-alliance.org/programs/cmc/newsletter/apr99-2.html

Ecosystem

Manzanillo is an important part of Costa Rica's immense biodiversity, which encompasses four percent of earth's total species of flora and fauna. To assure the survival of tropical rain forests and offshore reefs, the nation has designated ten percent of its terrain as protected areas. One of the nation's poorest regions, the southeastern corner draws indigent *campesinos* from less stable Latin American countries to a valuable and diverse ecosystem that spreads from Mount Chirripo to the Caribbean shoreline and beyond to the nation's only coral reef. Crucial to the survival of the ecosystem is the education of newcomers in the preservation of nature.

The focus of Costa Rica's conservation effort is Manzanillo's 22,000-acre forest-ocean preserve, created in 1985 and covering about twenty square miles of jungle and nearly eighteen square miles of sea floor. Its selection is the result of decades of activism by the Asociación de los Nuevos Alquimistas, founded by American fish ecologist William O. McLarney and supported by the New Alchemy Institute of North Carolina, a nonprofit organization promoting ecologically derived forms of agriculture, aquaculture, housing and energy, and landscapes that harmonize with nature. Unique to the nature preserve are a rare cativo stand and coastal plains thickly forested in caobilla trees, red and yellow heliconia, and sea grape. The dense growth is home to the cayman, crocodile, green iguana, howler and capuchin monkeys, otter, peccary, spider monkey, curré, great curassow, and paca or agouti. Heavy with epiphytes, ferns, lichens, and moss, the preserve is home to the basilisk lizard, boa, coral snake, fer-de-lance, poison dart and tree frogs, and viper and to 358 bird species, notably, the broad-billed motmot, brown pelican, collared aracari, frigatebird, kingfisher, red-capped manakin, red-lored amazon parrot, sul-phur-winged parakeet, toucan, lineated woodpecker, and harpy and hawk eagles. Common to the less humid outer fringes are mahogany and sajo and holillo palms, the feeding ground of tapirs.

Offshore, warm, sheltered waters rich in plankton and lush with turtle grass and seaweed nurture a natural clam bank and some 45 species of coral, including brain, fire, lettuce, sheet, and star varieties. Traveling from shore in dugouts and pangas, divers glimpse angelfish, blue parrotfish, damselfish, hydroids, lobsters, sea cucumbers, sea anemones, sea urchins, sponges, Venus sea fans, white shrimp, and West Indian manatee. Swimmers interact with dolphin, which appear naturally friendly. To assure their safety, the Asociación Pro Delfínes de Talamanca [Talamanca Dolphin Foundation], a non-profit nature organization, studies the Atlantic spotted dolphin (*Stenella frontalis*) and monitors the tucuxi dolphin (*Sotalia fluviatilis*) and its social interaction with the bottlenose dolphin (*Tursiops truncatus*). The protective agency also promotes awareness of animal habitats and research into behaviors altered by ecotourism.

In addition to sheltering rare dolphins, Manzanillo is the south Caribbean's most valued nesting ground for green, hawksbill, loggerhead, and leatherback sea turtles, a threatened species. The world's largest sea turtle and one of the earth's most ancient reptiles, leatherbacks have survived 100 million years, outliving the rise and fall of the dinosaur. Reaching up to ten feet in length, the turtles feed on jellyfish and soft-bodied creatures. Leatherbacks attain reproductive maturity after age ten. Each spring between early March and May, they arrive at Manzanillo to lay sixty to 125 eggs in each of some 1,000 nests. Hatchlings appear by mid–May.

Until 1980, the turtles' coastal habits were largely unknown to the outside world. Local people, who coexisted with them, harvested their eggs in limited numbers for food. The turtles began to suffer after the onset of poachers, who snatched the eggs for sale as aphrodisiacs and threatened the animals' survival. Now, night patrols of the Sea Turtle Conservation program assure the safety of nests and the viability of young as they crawl toward the sea.

Birds began receiving their share of attention in fall 2000, when Manzanillo started Central America's first raptor migration monitoring program. During a three-month period, volunteers of the Bribri tribe from the Kekoldi Indian Reserve observe the behaviors and habitats of some 1.3 million migrating raptors, one of the world's largest bird populations. For the quality of jungle life and its numerous rare species, the refuge was declared a Ramsar site under an international convention protecting wetlands of global importance. In August 2002, the area's biomonitoring won the Equator Prize for its protection of a World Heritage Site.

Coastal Activities

Visitors come to Manzanillo for its serene waters and opportunities to swim, kayak or canoe, snorkel, surf, and ride horses on an uncrowded beach. At nearby Hot Salsa Brava, powerful waves invite surfers. Offshore, deep-sea and fly fishers vie for bonefish, kingfish, mackerel, snook, tarpon, and wahoo. Naturalists pursue inland trekking, beachcombing, butterfly- and whale-watching, dolphin tours, birding, and identification of indigenous wildflowers, particularly the anthurium, canna, devil tongue, hibiscus, and pink flower. A favorite stroll to Punta Uva reveals a natural arch through which the sea gushes.

Scuba divers and snorkelers enjoy the region's clearest waters at the 150 dive sites of Manzanillo's barrier reef, called Long Shoal. Within the multi-hued coral wall, caves and canyons invite exploration and photography of sea turtles, bull sharks, dolphins, cubera snapper, flamingo tongues, lobsters, and squid. In addition to oversized barrel sponges, divers can cruise wavy patches of grass to view french grunts, midnight parrotfish, and queen triggerfish. Night dives access a different habitat — an undersea fantasy of phosphorescent creatures that make their own light.

A select group comes to Manzanillo to learn. The World Wildlife Fund and the Toledo Institute for Development and Ecology funds training of farmers and guides to enhance their understanding of environmental stewardship, permaculture, and sustainability. Unique opportunities result from the Permaculture Trail project, which schedules classes in forest rehabilitation and ecologically sustainable jobs in sylvan gardening and pattern planting, fruit production, aquaculture, and ecotourism. At the eighty-acre Punta Mona Permaculture Center, participants in hands-on labs learn how to cultivate a diverse garden of non-invasive medicinal herbs and spices, organic vegetables and tubers, rice paddies, lianas, shrubs, and such tropical trees as bamboo, cacao, coconut, and native fruits. Student interns acquire the skills for interpretive trail guiding and demonstrations.

SOURCES

"Asociación ANAI," http://www.anaicr.org/ index.html.

Brockett, Charles D., and Robert R. Gottfried, "State Policies and the Preservation of Forest Cover," *Latin American Research Review*, Vol. 37, No. 1, January 1, 2002, pp. 7–40.

"Cahuita and Laguna Gandoca, Costa Rica," http://www.unesco.org/csi/pub/papers/cortes .htm.

Campbell, Lisa H., et al, "Community-Based Conservation Via Global Legislation?," *Journal of International Wildlife Law & Policy*, March 22, 2002.

Chacon, Didiher, "Asociacion ANAI in Costa Rica," *Marine Turtle Newsletter,* Vol. 67, 1994, pp. 19–20.

"Costa Rica," *Caribbean Update*, Vol. 15, No. 12, January 1, 2000, p. 4.

Cromie, William J., "Operation Green Turtle," *U.S. Naval Institute Proceedings*, Vol. 92, No. 12, 1966, pp. 58–69.

"A Directory of Wetlands of International Importance," http://www.wetlands.org/RDB/Ramsar_Dir/CostaRica/cr005D02.htm.

Dulude, Julie, "Oil Exploration Protested," *Tico Times*, December 10, 1999.

Frazier, J., "Resolutions of the 21st Annual Symposium on Sea Turtle Biology and Conservation," *Marine Turtle Newsletter*, Vol. 93, 2001, pp. 24–30.

Godwin, Chloe, "Pura Vida," *Catalyst*, Fall 1998.

"News and Notes," *Cutting Edge*, Vol. 6, No. 2, April 1999.

"Tarpon Fishery Gets Recreational Boost," *Salt Water Sportsman*, Vol. 62, No. 12, December 2001, p. 46.

Villa-Lobos, Jane, "Talamanca Biological Corridor," *Biological Conservation Newsletter*, No. 110, June 1992.

Matagorda Island, Texas

Location

One of a chain of five barrier islands created by natural sea action around 3,000 B.C., Matagorda Island, stretching southwest to northeast, lies between the Gulf of Mexico and Espiritu Bay in Calhoun County east of Lavaca, Texas. Edged in fifteen-foot sand dunes and covered with cactus and mesquite, mangrove shrubs, twining goatsfoot morning glory, stretches of sea purslane and beach fimbry, and swamps tufted with marshhay cordgrass, paspalum, bluestem, sea oats, and saltgrass, the land mass deflects strong sea winds, rip tides, and currents from the Texas mainland. The resulting 250-foot swath of beach appeals to vacationers, water sports enthusiasts, fishers, and naturalists.

Because the barrier islands lie in the path of seasonal hurricanes, Matagorda's backbeach remains dynamic, shifting as sand washes into the channel and spits of land pile up along the shore. Although lacking in fresh water, the island, ranging in width from one to four miles, offers a 38-mile shoreline and 32 miles of crushed shell road. For ecotourists and historians, the island is a favorite nature reserve, a lookout site for the endangered whooping crane and migrating monarch butterflies, and the location of an antebellum lighthouse still in operation.

Contacts

Matagorda Island State Park
P. O. Box 117
Sixteenth Street and Maples
Port O'Connor, Texas 77982
Phone: 361-983-2215
http://www.tpwd.state.tx.us/park/matagisl/matagisl.htm

Wildlife Diversity Program of Texas Parks and Wildlife
3000 IH-35 South, Suite 100
Austin, Texas 78704
Phone: 800-792-1112, ext. 7011
http://www.tpwd.state.tx.us/monarch

History

Matagorda Island was a domain of the nomadic Karankawa (also Carancahua), paleoindians who harvested berries, roots, and edible plants and thrived on turtles, flounder and red drum, blue crabs and brown and white shrimp, and coquina clams they dug along the shores. Armed with red cedar longbows and accompanied by dogs, the bay dwellers also hunted turkeys, rabbits, and deer. They stored food in clay pots waterproofed with asphaltum, which washed up from petroleum deposits on the sea floor. They built frame huts covered with skins or thatched with grass mats and fronds and traveled by dugouts hollowed from logs. During seasonal migrations, they traded pigmented conch shells to plains tribes for buffalo robes. The Karankawas' peripatetic lifestyle ended with the arrival of Europeans, who wiped out Texas shore Indians by 1850.

The first outsider to sail and map the Texas shore was Alonso Álvarez de Pineda, commander of a Spanish expedition in 1519. Later expeditioners — Spanish author Álvar Núñez Cabeza de Vaca, French pirate Jean Lafitte, and French explorer René Robert Cavalier, Sieur de La Salle, and his crewman Henri Joutel — faced formidable Karankawa braves tattooed about the face and chest and coated in alligator fat and sand. Spanish explorer Juan Cortez cruised the region in 1793, but declined the island's fierce infestation of mosquitoes. In his writings, he declared Matagorda a purgatory.

As Karankawa natives dwindled in number, white entrepreneurs and farmers supplanted them. In 1839, the town of Calhoun served the channel as a short-lived customs station. Two years later, planter J. W. Byrne sowed Matagorda Island in long-staple sea island cotton, an experimental crop. The following year, Zachary Taylor erected Fort Washington on the southeast shore overlooking the gulf. By 1850, Matagorda Island and the town of Saluria at Pass Cavallo on the northern tip comprised a total citizenry of 120 whites and 44 slaves, whose livelihood depended on schooner and ferry traffic between the island and the Texas mainland.

In 1852, the Murray and Hazlehurst Company of Baltimore constructed a 57-foot cast-iron lighthouse to secure the passage of vessels along the Gulf Intercoastal Waterway and to guard the approaches to Indianola and Port Lavaca. The tower occupied seven and a half acres of land belonging to Thomas Jefferson Chambers, who earned the property in 1834 from the Mexican government in lieu of salary for his services as a superior court judge. Upon the first kindling of a signal flame on December 21, the light began illuminating maritime transport of local goods and needed supplies, which enabled settlers to survive in the harsh Texas environment. The first beacon, striped black, red, and white, was a favorite of photographers and weekend watercolorists. Seven years later, the coastal authority raised the original structure 25 feet to a total of 92 feet and added a revolving Fresnel lens to maximize the beacon's reach out to sea.

During the Civil War, Matagorda Island was the location of Fort Esperanza, an earthwork defense on the leeward side that lay in sight of traffic along the inland channel, but out of cannon range of Union gunboats plying the gulf. In December 1861, a work crew of 500 African slaves under the command of Confederate Colonel R. R. Garland, heaped sand into earthworks twelve feet high and fifteen feet thick to defend the south end. In addition to log supports and an overlay of shellcrete, a blend of sand with pulverized seashells, the soldiers fortified their beach redoubt with rifle pits, trenches, and trip-wire mines.

In mid-war, Union General Nathaniel Prentiss Banks, a lackluster appointee of President Abraham Lincoln, advanced on Matagorda to seize the stronghold, halt surveillance of Cavallo Pass, and disrupt the South's slender thread of trade with Mexico in cotton and salt. During a gale on November 19, 1863, Banks's forces, including the 15th Maine, was advancing by ferry from St. Joseph's Island when a Confederate major requested a parlay at Cedar Bayou. The major violated the truce by firing on the sergeant who met him at the channel. Banks's men shot the rebel major, who crawled into Matagorda's dunes and died.

Facing nine Confederate cannons, 8,000 Union forces continued by a fleet of two-masted yawls toward Matagorda. Backed by gunships, they engaged Confederate troops on November 29. The confrontation of Yank to Reb at a ratio of sixteen to one was hopeless. Before fleeing the Union onslaught, under orders of General John Bankhead Magruder, Captain John Brackenridge's Confederate cavalry disabled the fort's cannons with spikes in the vents, detonated powder magazines, broke iron plating off the lighthouse, and buried the Fresnel lens in the sand.

The large body of Union troops overwhelmed Matagorda's resources. To survive the cold winter without additional supplies, Union invaders slew the island's wild cattle for food and flayed the hides to dry as covers for rifle pits. From Matagorda Island, Union raiders made inland forays on Indianola and Lavaca. Passage along the inland waterway was tricky, needing an insider's knowledge of shifting inlets and sandbars. After two river steamers, the *Matamoros* and *Planter*, grounded offshore, their crews had to fuel boilers with coal, driftwood, and siding from cabins to force the boats back into the channel.

By spring 1864, on orders from General Ulysses S. Grant, the island occupation force departed for more valuable territory in Louisiana, leaving Matagorda Island and its damaged lighthouse and keepers' graveyard to Texas rebels. At the end of the war, the lighthouse remained dark after U.S. coastal authority replaced it with a makeshift three-story wood tower.

During Reconstruction, the town of Saluria sank to 100 residents, the hearty souls surviving both yellow fever and the depredations of advancing and departing armies. Still facing the forays of nature, the Matagorda lighthouse began to list. In 1868, Fort Esperanza lost its eastern ramparts to a gulf storm and gradually eroded with the tide.

On September 1, 1873, the original lighthouse went back into service after officials repositioned it 1.5 miles inland from the advancing Gulf of Mexico. Engineers refurbished the structure to prevent swamping. The beam passed through a modern Fresnel lens made by L. Sautter and Company of Paris. By 1882, oil lamps gave place to incandescent kerosene-lit fixtures. In 1943, the military once more considered the island a strategic post for observation towers and plane spotters. Four years after World War II, the Strategic Air Command maintained the U.S. military's hold on the island. With wars in the past, in 1956, Matagorda's lighthouse cast its first automated electric beam onto peacetime traffic in the gulf.

Archeology

When 42-year-old French expeditioner René-Robert Cavalier, Sieur de La Salle, discoverer of the Great Lakes, set sail for a last mission in 1685, he intended to explore the Mississippi Delta to halt the spread of Spanish control over prize territory. He traveled under the aegis of Louis XIV, who approved his plan to claim the estuary for France and to set up river forts to ward off both Indians and the Spanish. The four ships and 300 passengers included 100 soldiers, artisans, craftsmen, six missionary priests, and a dozen women and children.

The royal fleet was nearing the Gulf of Mexico in late summer 1685 when crew and passengers experienced near-fatal thirst after water casks ran dry. The pilots' map reading and performance may have suffered from dehydration and replacement of drinking water with brandy and wine. Adding to their difficulties in late September was the loss of the supply ketch *Saint-François*, which Spanish pirates captured. Off Cuba, two ships tangled in a squall and lost anchors, but continued toward the Gulf of Mexico in November.

Thrown 500 miles off course into Spanish territory, in the first weeks of 1686, La Salle's captain and crew anchored off Matagorda Island and ventured inland, where Indians attacked and killed some of the French. Thirsty soldiers drank brackish water and sickened; one ate a prickly pear for the moisture inside and died from throat injuries caused by thorns. In addition to illness, injuries, and death among the men, La Salle lost two ships. Off Matagorda Island, the eighty-foot shallow-draft *La Belle*, a six-gun, 65-ton longboat, ran onto a sandbar during a January gale. It was a small frigate, a gift of Louis XIV to La Salle, but valuable to the expedition during excursions on the inland waterway. Some crewmen drowned while attempting to escape by raft.

Author Robert S. Weddle, fellow of the Texas State Historical Association, described in *Wreck of the Belle, the Ruin of La Salle* (2001) how the hulk appeared to Spanish salvor Enríquez Barroto on April 4, 1687:

> A "broken ship," she lay on the bottom with a sharp list, her prow underwater, her deck awash.... Out of control in a howling north wind, she had struck the bank stern first; her bow anchor, dragging, served only to turn the ship, so that the rudder and sternpost gouged into the bank and kept the poop deck above water [p. 1].

The much larger supply ship *L'Aimable* grounded in an inlet near Cavallo Pass in February. Only the 34-ton man-o'-war *Le Joly* made it back to France.

After the loss of *La Belle*, six Frenchmen were able to locate a canoe and rejoin La Salle. His makeshift plans to build Fort St. Louis in Victoria County, Texas, as a shelter for 180 survivors foundered because of depletion of forces from smallpox, poisonous snakes, hunger, and Indian attacks. On the way north to Canada to seek help, the expedition ended with La Salle's murder at the hands of disgruntled expeditioners. They wearied of his arrogance, poisoned his food, and finished him with a shot to the head. Because only fifteen of the original party members survived, researchers of Texas history leaned heavily on one primary source, Henri Joutel's *Journal of La Salle's Last Voyage, 1684–1687*, published in New York in 1906.

After seventeen years of sea probes to locate wreckage of the French fleet, the Texas Historical Commission, led by archeologist J. Barto Arnold of the Institute of Nautical Archaeology and the Nautical Ar-chaeology Program at Texas A. & M. University, launched a magnetic survey of Matagorda's waters in summer 1995. On July 5 on his fourth dive, Chuck Meide, a student at Florida State University, recognized the uniqueness of a cannon with handles in the shape of dolphins. Salvors lifted the crusted barrel and transported it to Corpus Christi Museum of Science and History for identification and preservation. In 1996, discovery of the sunken *La Belle* along with skulls and the complete skeleton and finger ring of a middle-aged French crewman made real for Texans their state's role in global exploration. The completion of a steel cofferdam helped speed the mapping and reclamation of the remaining one-third of the *Belle's* hulk and contents, a task that ended in May 1997.

Scholars ranked the find off Matagorda as the most significant in North America. Preservers spent $5.5 million protecting over a million artifacts retrieved from the eighty chests and barrels in the hulk. Among the seventeenth-century treasures were 600,000 glass beads and brass bells for trade with Indians, pewterware, porcelain china table service, a brass colander and nested pots, a cauldron, ceramic medicine jars, a lucky coin and crucifix, a cobbler's last for shaping leather shoes, coiled rope, casks, axes, dividers, and a sword hilt. The inventory summarized for historians the outfitting of French vessels for trips to New World colonies down to military needs for four bronze cannon, lead shot, and muskets.

One set of pewter plates bore the initials of Sieur Le Gros, an officer who was bitten below the knee by a rattlesnake while hunting birds on Matagorda Island on Easter Sunday. He received no treatment from Duhaunt, the military surgeon. Three months later, Le Gros's wound putrified, forcing Duhaunt to amputate the leg. After three days of terrible pain, In September 1685, Le Gros died.

Exhibition of items from the sunken

La Belle encouraged Texas tourism. Over a four-year period, Glenn Grieco of the Nautical Archaeology Program at Texas A. & M. University completed a 1:12 scale model of the *La Belle* illustrating the original Spanish shipbuilder's command of the latest technology. In 1998, controversy arose over display of the *La Belle's* artifacts. Matagordans wanted possession of their offshore treasure; state officials preferred a museum in Austin. The Texas Historical Commission settled the dispute by dividing artifacts and displaying some at the Bob Bullock Texas State History Museum and the rest at museum near Matagorda Bay.

Ecosystem

The Matagorda Island State Park and Wildlife Management Area conserves a diverse habitat on 43,893 acres comprising shores, a saltwater lake, wetlands, and prairie. Sheltered by the State of Texas, the U.S. Fish and Wildlife Service, and the U.S. Department of the Interior, the island is home to badgers, coyotes, javelinas, jackrabbits, raccoons, and white-tailed deer. After the reintroduction of the endangered aplomado falcon in 1996, it began nesting in 1999. In addition, the island affords glimpses of the endangered Texas horned lizard, rare whooping cranes, clapper rails, crested caracaras, egrets, grackles, herons, ibis, meadowlarks, peregrine falcon, piping plovers, brown and white pelicans, sandpipers, and yellow-breasted chats. In the marshland, alligators thrive along with the diamondback rattlesnake, sand wasp, speckled king snake, western coachwhip, and wolf spider. Offshore, the waters are home to Portuguese man o' wars, sharks, and stingrays and offer gulf-side sightings of bottlenosed porpoises and dolphins and five of the world's eight sea turtle species.

Entomologists favor the island for its diverse butterflies, including blues, brushfoots, emperors, fritillaries, gossamers, hairstreaks, heliconians, leafwings, monarchs, satyrs, skippers, snouts, sulphurs, swallowtails, and whites. Like migratory birds, the eastern-migrating monarch breeds east of the Rocky Mountains along the Canada-U.S. divide and, with the advance of winter weather, travels south through the coastal Texas flyway along the Sierra Madre Oriental. By late October, monarchs reach their overwintering haven in central Mexico, where up to six million occupy a single acre. After mating in mid–March, they begin the return flight toward Canada. The Texas Monarch Watch, sponsored by the Wildlife Diversity Program of Texas Parks and Wildlife, collects data about butterfly migrations, recording when and where the insects breed and how availability of milkweed for food and shifts in weather impact their arduous life cycle.

Protecting the eco-structure on land and offshore presents difficulties in an area devoid of permanent residents. In the 1950s, coastal storms robbed the island of sixty percent of its tidal flats, which returned to wetlands, seagrass beds, and open sea. In 1979, environmentalists plugged the passage at Cedar Bayou to ward off contamination from an off-shore an oil spill. The Texas Parks and Wildlife Department designated the site as an official fish pass and regulated its protection. A year later on the night of August 9–10, Hurricane Allen swept south Texas and partially cleared the inlet of obstruction; dredging completed the job in 1988.

Human hands powered a cleanup of garbage left by polluters. In October 2000, the Texas Natural Resource Conservation Commission and Texas National Guard spearheaded the removal of 600 drums and barrels of toxic waste dumped illegally on the beachfront. Among the pollutants were corrosive solvents, herbicides, pesticides, and petroleum. The campaign may be only a temporary stay for island habitats. Nine miles from shore, the Bellwether Exploration

Company operates five gas wells in geopressurized sandstone. Seabed charts of petrochemical explorers hint at more deposits off the southwestern shore, which could increase fuel shipping the additional threats to Matagorda.

Coastal Activities

A tranquil retreat, Matagorda Island is also a locus of history excursions and hearty outdoor adventures. Cut off from the mainland, the slender island, which has been a national nature reserve since 1986, allows access only by ferry, charter boat, or kayak and limits arrivals to 100 at a time. Campers in the area enjoy exploring trails, collecting oysters, beachcombing and shelling, wading and swimming, snorkeling, and bird watching for black-necked stilts, killdeer, roseate spoonbills, and black-shouldered kites. Botanists identify some of the 500 varieties of flowering plants along the Texas shore, which include goldenrod, Indian blanket, and seaside gerardia, a bloom common to prairies and salt marshes and easily exterminated by toxic substances.

The glory of Matagorda Island is its variety of natural wonders. A favorite annual event is the annual migration of the monarch butterfly, which sends thousands fluttering into island roosts from spring and fall flights varying from 500 to 2,000 feet high. More active sports invite biking, backpacking, surfing, diving off Penrod Reef, and offshore shrimping, crabbing, and sport fishing on the sheltered north shore and at Pringle inland salt lake for flounder, mullet, redfish, speckled trout, and whiting. Offshore and near oil rigs, spearfishing and deep-sea fishing feature the gulf's array of dolphin, jackfish, kingfish, ling, marlin, red snapper, sailfish, tarpon, and wahoo.

After collecting $1.2 million to rescue the Matagorda lighthouse, restorers rekindled the antebellum tower on December 31, 1999, at a New Year's Eve party held at the U.S. Coast Guard station at Port O'Connor. The 125-year-old conical light tower required new window panes in the lantern room, replacement of the concrete base, repaired plating, sandblasting and paint, and construction of catwalks, fences, information center, and walkways. In its refurbished state, it flashed a beacon every ninety seconds that ranged sixteen miles out to sea. Southern historians and Civil War buffs plan a restoration of trenches and rifle pits, rebuilding of Fort Esperanza, display of artifacts, and posting of signs and photos to describe occupation by Confederate and Union troops. History tours inform visitors of the importance of the small sliver of sand to past events.

Sources

Arnold, J. Barto, III, "The Texas Historical Commission's Underwater Archaeological Survey of 1995, and the Preliminary Report on the *Belle*, La Salle's Shipwreck of 1686," *Historical Archaeology*, Vol. 30, No. 4, 1996, pp. 66–87.

Ashcraft, Allan C., "Sea Island Cotton in Texas," *Cotton History Review*, Vol. 2, No. 3, 1961, pp. 147–151.

Baker, T. Lindsay. *Lighthouses of Texas*. College Station, Tex.: Texas A. & M. University Press, 1991.

Baldauf, Scott, "A Turf War in Texas Builds over Historic French Shipwrecks," *Christian Science Monitor*, April 8, 1998.

"Bellwether Completes Well," *Oil Daily*, Vol. 46, No. 61, April 1, 1996, p. 2.

Brewster, Charles, et al., "Finding Off-Structure Geopressured Gas Accumulations in U.S. Gulf," *Offshore*, Vol. 59, No. 1, January 1999, pp. 114–117.

Cabrillo, Juan Rodriguez. *Spanish Exploration in the Southwest, 1542–1706*. New York, N. Y.: Charles Scribner's Sons, 1916,

Castañeda de Najera, Pedro de. *Spanish Explorers in the Southern United States, 1528–1543*. New York, N. Y.: Charles Scribner's Sons, 1907.

Conway, David, "Floundering along the Texas Coast," *Gray's Sporting Journal*, April–May 2001.

"Enron Reveals Significant Gas Find at Matagorda," *Oil Daily*, No. 9, 227, March 29, 1989, p. 8.

Givens, Murphy, "Forts and Fortified Places," *Corpus Christi Caller-Times*, July 14, 1999.

_____, "The Forts of Corpus Christi," *Corpus Christi Caller-Times*, July 14, 1999.

Henry, William Seaton. *Campaign Sketches of the War with Mexico*. New York: Harper & Brothers, 1847.

Leduc, Adrienne, "Dear Sieur de La Salle," *Beaver*, Vol. 79, No. 2, 1999, pp. 8–12.

"Lighthouse Restoration Projects under Way," *Corpus Christi Caller-Times*, July 2, 2000.

"Matagorda Lighthouse to Shine Again," *Corpus Christi Caller-Times*, December 31, 1999.

McAlister, Wayne H., and Martha K. McAlister. *Matagorda Island: A Naturalist's Guide*. Austin: University of Texas Press, 1992

McCorkle, Rob, "Mission at Matagorda," *Texas Parks and Wildlife*, February 1999.

Nelson, Jay T., et al., "Nutritional Value of Winter Foods for Whooping Cranes," *Wilson Bulletin*, Vol. 108, No. 4, December 1996, pp. 728–739.

Petrovich, Sandra M., "Robert Cavalier, Sieur de La Salle's Adventures of French Colonial Policy," *East Texas Historical Journal*, Vol. 36, No. 2, 1998, pp. 35–41.

Reinert, Patty, "Explorer's Shipwreck Discovered," *Houston Chronicle*, March 2, 1998.

Richardson, Alfred. *Wildflowers and Other Plants of Texas Beaches and Islands*. Austin: University of Texas Press, 2002.

Roberts, David, "Sieur de La Salle's Fateful Landfall," *Smithsonian*, April 1997.

"Shipwreck Not Part of LaSalle Fleet," *Abilene Reporter-News*, August 6, 1998.

Thomas, Les, "Matagorda Island's Piece of Paradise," *Southern Living*, Vol. 27, No. 7, July 1992, pp. 14–15.

Todhunter, Andrew, "Diving into the Wreck," *Preservation*, Vol. 48, No. 4, 1996, pp. 60–65.

Turner, Allan, "La Salle Shipwreck Yields Skeleton," *Houston Chronicle*, November 7, 1996.

"Union Invasion of Texas Part 4 of 4," *Corpus Christi Caller-Times*, November 27, 2002.

Weddle, Robert S., "La Salle's Survivors," *Southwestern Historical Quarterly*, Vol. 75, No. 4, 1972, pp. 413–433.

_____. *The Wreck of the Belle, the Ruin of La Salle*. College Station, Tex.: Texas A. & M. University Press, 2001.

Wolff, Linda Hetsel. *Indianola and Matagorda Island, 1837–1887*. Austin, Tex.: Eakin Publications, 1999.

Woodard, Will, "An Island in Time," *Backpacker*, Vol. 28, No. 5, June 2000, p. 108.

Matrah, Oman

Location

An ancient trading nexus at the Gulf of Oman, the modern deep-water port of Matrah (also Mutrah or Muttrah) in the Sultanate of Oman is a coastal jewel of the Arabian Peninsula. In a torrid zone along a 1,000-mile coastline, the city lies on the underside of the peninsula, a position that earned it the name "hermit of the Middle East." Built west of the capital on the eastern cusp of a coastal crescent overlooking the Arabian Sea, Matrah is the twin of Muscat, which is two miles away. The pair form a commercial-governmental metropolis that contrasts inland population centers, which are landlocked, arid, and largely rural.

At the meeting of the Arabian Gulf, Indian Ocean, and Mediterranean Sea, Matrah flourishes from October to mid–April from Austrian, British, Dutch, French, German, Italian, and Swiss tourists seeking a respite from the winter on wide white-sand shores. Encircled in black rocks and decked with scarlet, yellow, and orange bougainvillea, the horn-shaped crescent, called the corniche, plunges deep into the Mediterranean. The harbor city is home to prosperous merchants, ship-builders, and fishers who capitalize on the wealth of the sea. At the *dhow* harbor, the city hosts a long-lived fish *souq* [market], where turbaned clerks spread tarps on the ground and heap fresh catch of grouper, snapper, tuna, shark, and kingfish for shoppers to peruse. A camel caravan depot also offers fish to residents of the interior plus welcome mangoes and figs, bananas and apricots, large clusters of black and green grapes, and pearls for jewelry crafting.

Matrah's residential section is the oldest in Oman. With subtle embellishments to a boxy style that evolved over millennia, urban architecture expands on the crenellated desert forts and on square mud-brick huts of desert dwellers. To combat stifling

An ancient trading nexus of the Gulf of Oman, the modern deep water port of Matrah is a coastal jewel of the Arabian Peninsula (photograph by Tor Eigeland, courtesy of Saudi Armco World/ PADIA).

summers, citizens built stark-white homes along the shore of the Persian Gulf with high ceilings, screened verandahs and balconies, and open atria to welcome sea breezes. A shift in the economy to tourism forced Omanis to examine threats to their domestic serenity. The government now battles rising soil salinity, oil spills dirtying the beach, and water resources badly strained by aquifers drained by diesel-powered pumps rather than the traditional wooden bucket.

Contacts

Embassy of the Sultanate of Oman
Chancery
2535 Belmont Road, NW
Washington, D. C. 20008
Phone: 202-387-1980, ext. 81
Fax: 202-745-4933
http://www.worldrover.com/country/oman
_main.html

History

Oman, originally called Magan, once was peopled by tribes from Saudi Arabia, Bedouin herders and stock dealers, and ambitious cameleers working caravan strings across the Arabian deserts. At the coast, star-guided navigation reached such heights after the advent of sailing in 3000 B.C. that the Gulf of Oman was dubbed the "cradle of navigation." From early times, commerce enriched the port, from which ships bore frankincense, a fragrant gum resin, to Egyptian temples, Greek and Roman markets, and the Jewish Temple in Jerusalem.

Serious trade in metal dates to 2200 B.C., when Omani traders exported copper to Sumeria. Under King Abi Sin, from 2029 to 2006 B.C., outgoing craft bore diorite and copper from local smelters and returned with malabar wood and spices from India, ivory and leather from Africa, oil and grain from Mesopotamia, and silks and pottery from China. In the 500s B.C., as reported by the Greek historian Herodotus in *The Histories* (ca. 450 B.C.), the great Phoenician sailors of Tyre originated on the Omani Gulf coast. By the seventh century A.D., when Oman embraced Islam, the commercial beachfront dominated sea routes and became a prime market for the Indian Ocean slave trade. (*See also* STONE TOWN, ZANZIBAR.)

In 750, Oman took on its current characteristics — an isolated Arab state east of the mountains and deserts that separate it from Islamic cultural centers. From Omani ports, local sailors ferried both goods and Islam to East Africa, China, Indonesia, Malaysia, the Maldives, and the Philippines. Inland routes carried overland trade into the Asian interior. The prize location at the entrance to the Persian Gulf made Matrah a strategic gulf warden of incoming and outgoing traffic and a locus of slaving and shipbuilding. The Omani claim the first Arab to enter China, Abu Obeida bin Abdulla bin Al Qasim, who reached the Far East in 750.

Outsiders brought new iniatives to Matrah. In 1000, Persian colonists expanded Oman's herding and agrarian productivity by digging the subterranean *falaj* [irrigation system] along a series of mountain water sources. The gush of fresh water enabled settlers to raise date palms, which provided the Omani with a staple fruit. The trees were so valuable that families registered them and passed them to daughters as a part of dowries. In the 1400s, the Hindu Bhattias migrated to Matrah from Sind, bringing new trade partnerships. They remained a significant financial and mercantile force in the Persian Gulf and Indian Ocean for over four centuries.

In 1507, Afonso de Albuquerque, a Portuguese adventurer, seized the strategic shoreline from Muscat to Matrah and enabled his successors to hold sway for 143 years. In 1650, the Ya'rubid dynasty recovered the ports and advanced them into commanding naval centers. Prized for its beauty and convenient location, the region began flourishing in the 1700s with the rise of a Bedouin merchant culture enriched from trade in cloves and other spices, herbs, and perfumes. A new wave of Portuguese opportunists in 1737 resulted in twelve years of domination until the Al Bu Sa'id dynasty took permanent control.

Oman survived significant change in the nineteenth Century, when influences from the West altered medieval attitudes dating to tribal times. Sayyid Said bin Sultan, called Said the Great, came to the throne in 1803 and stabilized the country during a 53-year reign. In 1833, the Omani government extended friendship to the United States. By mid-century, relationships with the U.S. and England spelled the end of the slave trade and an economic downturn until trade initiatives replaced former earnings from the sale of black Africans. In 1895 and 1915, the imam sparked tribal uprisings against Muscat and Matrah. In 1920, the British brokered a long-lived peace and secured the autonomy of Sultan Taimur ibn Faysal, who remained in power until 1932.

Under the despotic hand of Sultan Said bin Taimur, in the 1950s and 1960s, Oman retreated into its former insular state, which cut off contact with the outside world. The ambitious fled the country to seek education and jobs in less oppressive Arab states. When Suzanne Marie Adele Beauclerk, the Duchess of St. Albans, wrote a travelogue of the region in 1980, she titled the work *Where Time Stood Still: A Portrait of Oman*, a reflection of Sultan Said's backward government. Constant immurement changed in 1964, when the country, still ruled by an absolute monarchy, exploited wealth from oilfields that were discovered at the rim of Rub 'al-Khali to the west. Oil officially went into production in 1967 at Mina Al Fahal, reaching a rate of over 800,000 barrels per day.

As they had for centuries, the Omani peasantry remained uncomplicated, ill-informed, and largely ignorant of such Western luxuries as bicycles and sunglasses. Their unenlightened existence ended under Said's son, absolute monarch Sultan Qaboos bin Said Al Said, an energetic young ruler educated in England. He used aid from the British to overthrow his father and seize the throne on July 23, 1970. Complete control took another five years.

Under Qaboos's vibrant rule, the nation quickly developed from third world squalor to upscale modernism. In 1971, Oman joined the Arab League and the United Nations. Rather than ally with the Organization of Arab Petroleum Exporting Countries (OPEC), in 1981, Qaboos helped five other members found the Gulf Cooperation Council. Because his country's oil reserves were predicted to run dry by 2010, the progressive sultan diversified exports to include liquefied natural gas, copper, coal, and electricity and instituted rapid change to elevate his people in outlook and expectation.

During Oman's renaissance, Qaboos welcomed Western tendencies toward secularism and such un–Islamic notions as family planning. He promoted a high degree of literacy, a 3,500-mile asphalt-and-gravel road network, a modern telephone link to the rest of the world, immunization and quality health care at fourteen new hospitals, education at 370 new schools, and domestic conveniences. To lure outside investment, he advertised no taxation, low-interest loans, government-built factories, and modest rents. His clever management won seventy companies to the Matrah-Muscat area producing batteries, cement, vegetable oil, machines and machines parts, electronics, and jeans. In addition, he encouraged excavation of off-shore mineral deposits in pillow lava, ancient plumes of molten rock that quickly hardened into undersea columns.

By the 1970s, Oman opened the nation's first hotels, built new jetties at Port Qaboos in Matrah, and enticed outsiders to sample the city's famous hospitality. The piers were deluged by freighters from Hamburg, Kobe, London, Rotterdam, and Singapore. In 1980, the sultan celebrated a decade of reform by supporting a re-creation of the voyages of legendary merchant-adventurer Sindbad of Sohar. On November 23, Irish navigator Tim Severin and a twenty-man crew retraced the historic Arab sea routes aboard the hand-sewn *Sohar*, formed of aini wood held together with 15,000 bundles of string stripped from coconut husks. After departing Muscat harbor and crossing the Indian Ocean, Severin called at ports in India, Sri Lanka, and Sumatra and traverse the Malacca Strait. At the end of a 6,000-mile voyage, the *Sohar* arrived at Singapore in February 1981.

Oman's setting proved valuable to travelers seeking an alternative to beach sites in the Caribbean and South Pacific. From the outset, the Omani encouraged only beneficial outsiders by banning an influx of poor immigrants from Jordan and Palestine and by issuing limited work visas to 400,000 low-wage laborers from Bangladesh, India, Pakistan, the Philippines, and Sri Lanka. As Matrah's milieu developed multicultural influences, the Omani kept their identity by marrying only within their tribal society and dressing in traditional garb: women chose colorful shawls and veils; men wore the traditional dishdasha, sash, and silver-sheathed *khanjar* [daggar], a ceremonial adornment expressing masculinity.

In the 1990s, the Omani reclaimed their weathered beach through dredging and pier-building. With much of the shipping resituated at a container freight harbor at Salalah, Matrah began growing into a coastal resort complete with date palm–lined highways, acacia-decked villas, and sixty hotels. In 2001, a wise government continued to control development by opening the Sultan Qaboos Grand Mosque to tourists and banning discos and trivial entertainments along the shore. To maintain a contented laboring class, the government also oversaw workers' residences and recreation venues and battled the infestations of prostitutes, thieves, and con artists that thrive on the world's shores.

Today, the world-class Omani Al Bustan Palace Hotel and international hotel chains feature gardens, tea lounges, Indian and Persian jewelry boutiques, and luxurious accommodations that include air conditioning. To meet demands for water, the country provides a system of water tankers that distributes fresh supplies. Along winding city streets and against dwellings, tourist *souqs* scented with burning frankincense invite browsing. Male clerks dressed in traditional long-sleeved robes and sashes display silks and linens, bronze *dallah* [coffeepots], Baluchi yogurt snacks, forty varieties of dates, squash and melons, prawns, and Omani perfumes and rosewater. By 2005, the country intends to offer seaside resorts suited to family vacations, notably, an ocean liner tied up at the Matrah dock and offering rooms.

Under a progressive preservation program of the Ministry of National Heritage and Culture, five national institutions research Oman's past. At the Oman Centre of Traditional Music, visitors can access an extensive recording collection of 130 types of classic desert music plus 23,000 photos and 580 audiovisuals. Songs extend from Bedouin and mountain melodies to fishing songs and sea chanties. The House of Omani Heritage displays artisanal crafts for sale, notably metal goods, baskets, woven rugs, and wood carvings. At the Traditional Medicine Clinic, which the sultan established in 1988, outsiders can seek free treatment with plant remedies dating to ancient times.

Coastal Activities

Moneyed tourists arriving by plane and ocean liner find a tolerant Islamic nation that permits alcoholic beverages and avoids the violent fundamentalism and religious police found in more conservative Arab nations. Visitors divide their time between swimming and sunning on crystal waters, jogging, camping, picnicking, windsurfing, water-skiing, pedal-boating, birding, and playing seaside games of beach checkers, which requires only pebble markers and a rectangle sketched in the sand. The shores are famous for their shells, such as the spiky orange *Thais mancinella*, the beautifully sculpted *Distorsio reticulata*, the creamy yellow *Cypraea talpa* with lustrous black mantle, the finely whorled *Rhinoclavis sinensis*, and the rare *Terebra thomasi* and *Generalis maldivus* cone shells. One variety, the *Cymatium pileare aquatile*, is found under rocks at low tide; another, the *Conus inscriptus*, was located 200 feet off Matrah's shore.

Dr. Donald T. Bosch and Eloise Bosch have combed Oman for undocumented mollusk species. Donald Bosch, a medical doctor trained at the State University of Iowa and in the U.S. Army medical corps, collected and cataloged 1,000 types for a standard reference work, *Seashells of Eastern Arabia* (1995), illustrated with line drawings and photos of mollusks. In an earlier text, *Seashells of Oman* (1982), the Bosches remarked on the beauty of "conchological treasures" from the Arabian Peninsula (p. 10). They added that, in ancient times, prize specimens as well as common cowries and iridescent *Haliotis mariae* returned with travelers from Egypt, Pompeii, Rome, and Athens. Among the most prized is the finely spiraled *Telescopium telescopium*, which is almost always found dead.

Some Matrah beach-goers watch *dhow* races or move inland to gamble at camel races on the hard desert floor, examine Martian meteorites, hike *wadis* [dry river valleys] and floodplains, and climb dunes and rock formations of mountains that jut upward from the shoreline. The Muscat aquarium displays indigenous saltwater species.

The Bait al Falaj, a military museum that once housed a garrison, contains weapons, uniforms, vehicles, and relics of a long history of shore defense. Farther west, the Oman Museum displays Islamic architecture, shipbuilding, and fort construction and summarizes 5,000 years of Omani history.

Along the curved shore, fishermen row their woven *shashas* [boats] in search of sardines to dry for camel feed and fertilizer. Beyond, the royal palace and the Jalali, Matrah, and Mirani forts link beach leisure to a lengthy and heroic past. Set on a hill above the beach, Matrah Fort, the most prominent of a string of thirteen fortifications, features six imposing towers. Built in 1558, the outpost was the work of a Portuguese visionary, perhaps sea captain Rui Freire de Andrade. Under Sultan Said bin Sultan al Busaidi, the ramparts served as a seat of government. Jalali (also Fort de Sao Joao) and Mirani oversee the southeastern portion of the crescent-shaped beach. Completed in 1551, they once protected the region from attack by sea. After a Turkish onslaught, in 1588, the Portuguese remodeled Jalali, which later served Oman as a prison.

Visitors enjoy a variety of local treats, including a climb of the 100 steps of an ancient watchtower to view the harbor. Some choose a noontime rest at the Matrah bazaar, the best in the region. Of its treasures, the Duchess of St. Albans wrote:

> The Matrah *souq* with its constant clatter, its lively, incessant bustle and its smells is probably much the same as it looked two or three thousand years ago. The narrow streets are neither paved nor cemented.... The milling throng is constantly being squashed and flattened against the walls by little donkeys [1980, pp. 14–15].

Her testimony highlights the specialty streets that feature spices, baubles, tailoring and shoemaking, even plastic goods.

Shoppers plunder the stalls for handmade local items, notably loomed rugs and colored kimah hats stitched with flower shapes. Jewelry crafted medieval style from silver and gold is a major attraction, whether key chains, hair clasps, pendants, paired toe and finger rings, or the heavy *hirz*, a neck adornment containing bangles and a compartment holding protective scripture from the Koran. Talismanic rings are a traditional bride gift, usually presented ten at a time and made of silver to ward off sickness and the evil eye.

Other visitors sample the Al Dhakhiliya festival of oases in late winter or explore banana plantations and lime groves, newly planted mangrove reserves along the coast, mountain oasis villages, and refurbished castles and forts. Celebration of Eid al Adha [the pilgrimage to Mecca] introduces visitors to an Islamic holy day that involves prayers, distribution of alms to the poor, shared meals of spiced meat and rice, aromatic coffee with sweets, and family get-togethers. Young women display new clothes and paint hands and feet with arabesques and complex geometrics in brown or black henna.

Ecosystem

Divers are often surprised to find sparkling waters around the crescent beach for year-round snorkeling, guided tours, observing fifteen species of dolphin and whale, and underwater photography of coral-lined fjords. Coral reefs, like undersea limestone gardens, possess a rich ecosystem similar to tropical rain forests in diversity of flora and fauna. Oman's waters host 75 species of coral, some in centuries-old colonies. In 2002, the government launched the Coral Reef Management Plan and a clean-up program to secure off-shore diving habitats. More adventuresome swimmers off Matrah peruse blue holes, coral heads, and precipitous canyon walls. The scenic ocean floor is most alive from September to June with 1,500 species of fish and crustaceans, including moray eels, butterfish, snapper, lobster, grouper, anemone, parrotfish, sponges, blue box fish, sea urchins and slugs, lionfish, golden cardinals, clownfish, frog fish, starfish, seahorses, and black-tip sharks.

In Omani's offshore diving areas, the ancient sea turtle thrives after being hunted for seven millennia and continues to nest at Ras al Hadd, laying up to 160 eggs per clutch. A strict policy of habitat protection has preserved swimmers' access to seven endangered species of sea turtles, including the greenback, hawksbill, leatherback, loggerhead, and Olive Ridley turtle. Surviving for over 185 million years, sea turtles once shared the area with dinosaurs and currently inhabit thick undersea groves, seaweed, and seagrasses thick with shrimp, snails, barnacles, crabs, and pearl oysters.

SOURCES

Abdullah Al Khamyasi, Saleh, "The Saga of a Maritime Legend," *Oman Observer*, July 27, 2002.

Abercrombie, Thomas J., "Oman: Guardian of the Gulf," *National Geographic*, September 1981, pp. 344–395.

Allen, Calvin H., Jr., "The Indian Merchant Community of Masqat," *Bulletin of the School of Oriental and African Studies*, Vol. 44, No. 1, 1981, pp. 39–53.

Azzi, Robert, "Oman, Land of Frankincense and Oil," *National Geographic*, February 1973, pp. 205–230.

Bhacker, Redha, and Bernadette Bhacker, "Diggin in the Land of Magan," *Archeology*, Vol. 50, No. 3, May/June1997.

"A Boom in Resorts beside Oman Seaside," *Oman Observer*, June 25, 2001.

Bosch, Donald, and Eloise Bosch. *Seashells of Oman*. London: Longman, 1982.

Curtiss, Richard H., "Oman 1972–1992: A Personal Reminiscence," *Washington Report*, December/January 1992–1993, p. 42.

_____, "Once Inaccessible Oman Has Become Winter Vacation Choice for Europeans," *Washington Reports*, March 1999, pp. 64–74.

"The Dilmun Civilization," *Washington Times*, March 21, 2000.

Duchess of St. Albans. *Where Time Stood Still: A Portrait of Oman*. London: Quartet Books, 1980.

"Elixir of the Jabals — Rosewater on Al Jabal al Akhdar," *Oman Observer*, April 30, 2001.

George, Ebby Chacko, "Dhakhiliya Festival to Showcase Essence of Arabia," *Oman Observer*, February 20, 2002.

James, Viju, "A Ring for Each Finger," *Oman Observer*, November 4, 2001.

Kamoonpuri, Hasan, "Dive and Explore Omani Waters," *Oman Observer*, November 5, 2001.

_____, "Mangrove Afforestation Project," *Oman Observer*, August 6, 2001.

_____, "Oman Achieves Yet Another feather on Its Cap," *Oman Observer*, March 6, 2002.

_____, "Protecting and Promoting Marine Environment," *Oman Observer*, May 24, 2002.

_____, "Scenic Coasts Put Up Spectacular Views," *Oman Observer*, June 11, 2001.

Khalfan, Maryam, "Tradition Adds Flavour to Eid," *Oman Observer*, February 22, 2002.

"Non-Muslims Allowed to Visit Grand Mosque," *Times of Oman*, July 25, 2001.

Prabhu, Conrad, "Preserving the Vibrant Heritage of Oman," *Oman Observer*, August 25, 2001.

Qaiser, Ziana, "Add a Dash of Henna to Colour Your Celebrations," *Oman Observer*, February 22, 2002.

Range, Peter Ross, "Oman," *National Geographic*, May 1995, pp. 112–138.

Segal, Ronald. *Islam's Black Slaves: The Other Black Diaspora*. New York: Farrar, Straus and Giroux, 2001.

Shaji, Aruna, "The Call of the Sea!," *Oman Observer*, February 17, 2002.

_____, "Legendary Voyage," *Oman Observer*, February 18, 2002.

_____, "Oman a Haven for Rare Turtles," *Oman Observer*, December 14, 2001.

_____, "Rainforests of the Sea," *Oman Observer*, December 21, 2001.

"Voyage," *Courier International*, November 26, 2002.

McMurdo Sound, Antarctica

Location

A 92-mile inlet of the Ross Sea in the far southern reaches of the Pacific Ocean, McMurdo Sound is the site of Antarctica's largest community. In the shadow of Mount Erebus, an active volcano, the harbor lies on the southern shore of Victoria Land at the rim of the Ross Ice Shelf, a frozen mass larger than the state of Texas. Tinged with ice fog, the blue-white expanse reaches to the horizon. Breaking the sameness are pressure ridges and sastrugi, waves, hummocks, and snow drifts created by fierce winds. Icebergs and bergy bits that break away obey the Antarctic laws of contraction and expansion.

The setting is a glimpse of the last ice age. Forty million years ago, the island continent supported stands of conifers and beech, low vegetation, reptiles, marsupials, and dinosaurs. Now, in an environment where ice covers 98 percent of the surface and surrounding waters, the silent, indifferent tundra is both hyper-arid and hyper-cold, stripped to sandy fingers and rocky spurs by merciless katabatic or downslope winds that turn snow and sheets of ice into lethal weapons. The frozen totality equals three-quarters of the world's fresh water, but the continent's streams thaw for less than six weeks per year. In rare upsurges in temperature, the Onyx River flows from Lower Wright Glacier into nearby Lake Vanda, which is in Wright Valley 45 miles northwest of the bay.

Contacts

Denise Landau, Executive Director
International Association of Antarctica Tour
    Operators
P. O. Box 2178
Basalt, Colorado 81621
Phone: 970-704-1047
Fax: 970-704-9660
Email: iaato@iaato.org
http://www.iaato.org/contact_iaato.html

History

Earth's only unowned land mass, Antarctica became a global crossroads in 1820, when Estonian expeditioner and naturalist Baron Thaddeus von Bellingshausen, English sealer Edward Bransfield, and Connecticut-born sea captain Nathaniel Brown Palmer sighted the frozen continent after sailing their wood ships through Drake Passage in the South Atlantic Ocean. Early seafarers venturing to Antarctica valued the area for abundant colonies of Adélie penguins, which they rendered for oil. Sir James Clark Ross, a London-born explorer and commander of the H.M.S. *Erebus* and *Terror*, discovered the Ross Ice Shelf and McMurdo Sound in January 1841. He remained in the area until September 1843 to map the coastline and conduct tests for the Royal Society, for which he earned a fellowship. The expedition earned him a knighthood from Queen Victoria.

In subsequent years, McMurdo Bay has served research teams as an access to inland mysteries. Because the peninsula offered solid ground and harborage for ships, navy hero and explorer Robert Falcon Scott of Devonport, England, piloted the *Discovery* to McMurdo on January 21, 1902, to investigate the South Pole. He named the land for King Edward VII. After surveying the region from a hot-air balloon, Scott pitched camp at Hut Point on Ross Island in 1904. On his return to England, his narrative, *The Voyage of Discovery* (1905), became a bestseller. He made a last trek to the region in 1913 aboard the *Terra Nova* and died en route, leaving a two-volume journal, *Scott's Last Expedition* (1913), which Leonard Huxley edited. Scott's building and its laboratory and provisions survive as an historic monument to early exploration.

On January 1, 1908, Irish expeditioner Ernest Henry Shackleton arrived at Mc-Murdo Bay and, the next month, scaled Mount Erebus. In addition to national acclaim, he earned a purse of £20,000, a gold medal from the Royal Geographical Society, and knighthood from King Edward VII. At the beginning of World War I, Shackleton returned to Antarctica aboard the *Endurance*, which was disabled by pack ice and

At McMurdo Sound, Antarctica, rookeries of penguins enjoy the spare blue-white expanse that reaches to the horizon (courtesy of Irma Hale).

sank on November 21, 1915, stranding the crew. After harrowing experiences, the captain led a rescue party on August 20, 1916, and retrieved his men. In 1921, he mounted a third expedition with the intent of crossing Antarctica, but died of a heart attack in 1922 and was buried near a whaling depot.

Despite tales of starvation, shipwreck, rogue icebergs, and physical depletion, ambitious nations chose McMurdo Sound as one of several sites for scientific research in meteorology and ecology and the staging point from which expeditioners penetrate the frozen continent. After the U.S. Navy established a military presence in December 1955 on the bare volcanic rock of Hut Point Peninsula on Ross Island, 200 Seabees constructed the first McMurdo station to serve "Operation Deep Freeze." Over a half century, it expanded to a complex of 100 structures that consist of laboratories, dormitories, radio shack, power plant, warehouses, wharf, harbor, helipad, and Williams Field, an airport offering 6,000-foot hard-ice runways on sea and shelf ice. During the brief Antarctic summer, 1,200 residents inhabit the complex — four times the number that stay through the winter.

Aiding the growth of scientific understanding of Antarctica was the cooperative spirit of governments that shared research efforts and their outcomes. After the establishment of the first U.S. outpost during the International Geophysical Year of 1957–1958, additional data accrued on aerology, climatology, geography, glaciology, and oceanography, providing the world with data on subatomic particles, meteors lodged in ancient ice shelves, ice movement, wind circulation, the polar atmosphere, plate tectonics, hydroacoustics, upper atmosphere physics, and the growth and pattern of volcanic eruptions. Among notables contributing to world knowledge of Antarctica was Austro-American geophysicist Walter Heinrich Munk, the world's most respected oceanographer, who, in 1963, measured

ocean swells generated in Antarctica by calculating fluctuations with pressure-sensing probes placed on the ocean floor. (*See also* MONTE CARLO, MONACO.)

In 1960, the navy built an antarctic nuclear reactor, a portable, medium-output model nicknamed "Nukey Poo." In 1962, its first year of operation, the equipment incurred a flash fire on October 7, but remained functional until 1971 without achieving adequate electricity output for the base. In 1968, the 196-man Detachment ALFA staffed the reactor through the winter. From the personnel stationed at subsequent military outposts came the first Antarctic natives, eight children born between 1978 and 1983.

In 1985, British scientists Joseph Farman, Brian Gardiner, and Jonathan Shanklin from the British Antarctic Survey at McMurdo Bay discovered a rise in lake levels resulting from a hole in the ozone layer, a shield in the atmosphere filtering out ultraviolet solar radiation before it reaches earth. The loss resulted from gases emitted by chlorofluorocarbons and other man-made coolants and aerosol propellants. Among the living things damaged by harmful rays were plankton and krill, a shrimplike crustacean already seriously depleted by commercial fishing. Researchers determined that a decrease in these basics of the food chain threatened the survival of fish, penguins, pinniped seals, and whales living in the Southern Hemisphere. By 1992, the ozone hole had spread over Tierra del Fuego, Argentina. (*See also* BEAGLE CHANNEL, TIERRA DEL FUEGO, ARGENTINA.)

To support scientists in environmental research, the U.S. Coast Guard stationed the *Polar Star* and the *Polar Sea*, the world's most powerful non-nuclear icebreakers, alternately at the Arctic Circle and McMurdo. Currently, laboratories on board accommodate the work of twenty scientists and technicians per voyage to investigate geology, oceanography, and sea-ice physics. The icebreakers use both gas and diesel turbines to ram frozen port waters to create a turning range for the freighters and tankers that provision the outpost. Crew of the Coast Guard vessels explore the sound with surf and survey boats, a landing craft, an inflatable Zodiac, and two three-passenger helicopters.

Ecology

McMurdo Bay is home to the Weddell and leopard seals, nematodes, spiny crabs, octopi, anemones, starfish, bristle worms, dragonfish, eelpouts, rockcod, skates, orcas, blue and minke whales, nudibranch, and sponges. Albatrosses, cormorants, gulls, petrels, and skua fly over land where bacteria, blue-green algae, fungi, lichen, and yeasts inhabit the crystalline layers within rocks. At the end of the twentieth century, scientists, one-third of whom were female, were beginning to evaluate data from the port's biosystem, which lacks insects, vertebrates, and vascular plants. Some considered McMurdo's environment a glimpse of how life ended on Mars and began on Earth. Others were more concerned with temporal despoliation, such as the Russian overfishing of squid and the pollution of the bay with human wastes and detritus from laboratories, cruise lines, and military vessels.

Response to decline in Antarctica's environment was swift and technologically advanced. In 1992, at the prompting of Vice President Al Gore, seventy scientists formed the Environmental Task Force and began sharing aerial photography, instrumental readings, and reports from military vessels essential to analysis of such issues as natural disasters and changes to the ecosystem. In this same period, the National Science Foundation (NSF) sponsored non-governmental study groups. In 1993, the NSF sent high school teachers on a project involving measuring temperature patterns at the Taylor ice dome. The NSF also fostered astronomical observations by the Center for Astrophysical

Research, a consortium dispatched by eight universities, two institutes, and two corporations to observe electromagnetic waves emitted by cosmic clouds, galaxies, and stars.

In an ecosystem that has remained largely unaltered over millennia, ongoing observation of nature includes study of crystal-clean air, the cleanest on earth, as well as krill populations, the heaps of moraine left by outlet glaciers, and coal and other minerals. Newcomers are dazzled by the aurora australis or southern lights, a phenomenon caused by the sun's energy impacting earth's gases, creating colorful rays that magnetic fields draw to the north and south poles and reduce to a greenish glow. Investigation of nutrient-deficient dry valleys focus on McMurdo's terrain of thin soil, snowpack, sandy gravel, bedrock, ephemeral creeks, the East Antarctic Ice Sheet, and iced-over lakes Bonney, Hoare, and Fryxel.

Parallel to scientific exploration, over the second half of the twentieth century, commercial developers studied McMurdo Sound as a potential airport-hotel-ski lodge vacation complex, but tempered their optimism under the strictures of the Antarctic Treaty of 1959, by which thirteen signatories recognized the area's uniqueness and foresaw the endangerment of a fragile ecosystem from exploitation or military use. Because of the absence of liquid water, life-sustaining nutrients, and light, the land supports few biota beyond seasonal production of plankton, viruses, bacteria, algae, protozoans, and rotifers, disk-shaped freshwater invertebrates that move by thrashing their cilia. Most at risk are rookeries of the Adélie, chinstrap, emperor, gentoo, and macaroni penguins, which, like baleen whales, subsist primarily on ocean krill. To assure the future of ocean denizens large and small, in 1982, the 45 signers of the original global treaty extended its protection to the sea around Antarctica; nine years later, a treaty addendum banned mineral exploitation in favor of pure scientific study.

Even with concerted efforts of the scientific community, Antarctica has not escaped serious threats to the environment. The fears of conservationists came true on January 28, 1989, after the *Bahia Paradiso*, an Argentine transport/cruise vessel, followed erring navigation charts, grounded, and incurred a thirty-foot gash in its side. The double-hulled vessel sank off Palmer Station west of McMurdo, spilling 68 percent of 250,000 gallons of diesel fuel. A fifteen-mile slick cost scientists a source of pristine ocean waters and killed krill and hundreds of cormorants, giant petrels, penguins, seals, and skuas. Dr. Polly Penhale, an NSF program manager, reported the skuas disoriented and their chicks dead; cormorant hatchlings suffered internal bleeding; limpets died, leaving kelp gulls without food. In October of that year, Australian and French minerologists startled other nations by announcing their intent to explore mining the McMurdo area's minerals. In addition, decades of accumulated waste built up from the U.S. station at McMurdo have soiled the harbor with the same variety of hydrocarbons, coliform bacteria, toxic chemicals, fuel drums, defunct vehicles, and scrap metals that taint ports in warmer climes. In January 1992, Greenpeace opposed but did not stop the NSF from incinerating a chemical dump at the McMurdo Station to rid it of insulation, construction debris, and asbestos, a hazardous air pollutant.

McMurdo Sound made news in 2000 when the Ross Ice Shelf calved B-15, an iceberg the size of Connecticut. As the immense expanse floated into shipping lanes, radar and satellites charted its progress. By November 2000, the single berg had disintegrated into four huge chunks, one blocking the entrance to McMurdo Bay. Reporting events was the *Antarctic Sun,* a new bimonthly dubbed the world's southernmost newspaper, which separated from government involvement on March 13, 1998.

Into the 21st century, it reported news of the sound's environment, select population of scientists, military personnel, and support staff.

Coastal Activities

Antarctica is no longer a forbidding continent, but its stark atmosphere, extremes of cold and foul weather, and lack of fresh milk, meat, eggs, fruit, and vegetables can induce fits of temper, depression, and alcohol abuse by those posted at McMurdo for military reasons or research. For staff restricted to laboratories of McMurdo's "MacTown" for scientific study, email and the Internet provide news and sources of information as well as training in foreign language, a favorite pastime. Support staff also arrange costume parties and offer lessons in dance and pottery-making, aerobics, bowling, and gymnastics. In calm weather, the outdoors offers exploring by helicopter and skidoo, birding, ice diving, and hiking up Observation or "Ob" Hill.

Ecotourism has expanded the number of people who travel to Antarctica, particularly after the collapse of the Soviet Union and the leasing of Russian research vessels to tour organizers. By summer 2001, over 15,000 tourists visited the frozen continent, generating a growth rate of 500 percent. Hardy skiers, bush pilots, astronomers, ice fishers, divers, and photographers are among the expeditioners who pay tens of thousands of dollars to vacation in Antarctica. In addition, cruise lines carry thousands of less adventuresome tourists annually along the shores of McMurdo Sound. In 1992, the complex extended the Pegasus site, its first year-round airstrip for wheeled planes, which should increase the number of people venturing south to McMurdo Sound.

SOURCES

Burns, Jennifer M., and Gerald L. Kooyman, "Habitat Use by Weddell Seals and Emperor

Penguins Foraging in the Ross Sea, Antarctica," *American Zoologist*, Vol. 41, No. 1, February 1, 2001, pp. 90–98.

Fountain, Andrew G., et al. "Physical Controls on the Taylor Valley Ecosystem, Antarctica," *BioScience*, Vol. 48, No. 12, December 1999, p. 961.

Gelatt, Thomas S., et al., "Molecular Evidence for Twinning in Weddell Seals," *Journal of Mammalogy*, Vol. 82, No. 2, May 2001, p. 491.

Hodgson, Bryan, "Antarctica: Land of Isolation No More," *National Geographic*, April 1990, pp. 2–47.

Horgan, John, "Are Scientists Too Messy for Antarctica?," *Scientific American*, Vol. 266, No. 3, March 1993, pp. 22–23.

Johnson, Heather, "Winter Wonderland Learning," *Training*, Vol. 38, No. 10, October 2001, p. 22.

Joyce, Christopher, "Asbestos Found in Antarctic Waste Dump," *New Scientist*, Vol. 130, No. 1,764, April 13, 1991, p. 12.

Kiernan, Vincent, "The Far Frontier," *New Scientist*, Vol. 150, No. 2,025, April 1996, pp. 32–35.

Lopez, Barry, "Informed by Indifference," *Whole Earth*, Spring 2000, p. 50.

Lyons, W. Berry, et al., "History of McMurdo Dry Valley Lakes, Antarctica," *Geology*, Vol. 27, No. 6, June 1999, pp. 527–530.

Mastro, Jim, "Oasis under the Ice: Exploring the Surprisingly Rich World Hidden beneath the antarctic Ice," *International Wildlife*, November 21, 1997.

McKnight, Diane M., et al., "Dry Valley Streams in Antarctica: Ecosystems Waiting for Water," *BioScience*, Vol. 48, No. 12, December 1999, p. 985.

McNeeley, James S., "Deep Freeze Diary, 1968," *U.S. Naval Institute Proceedings*, Vol. 96, No. 3, 1970, pp. 50–57.

Mervis, Jeffrey, "Panel of Scientists Helps Open Lid on Secret Images," *Science*, Vol. 286, No. 5,437, October 1, 1999, p. 34.

Monastersky, Richard, "Antarctic Pollution: How Bad Is It?," *Science News*, Vol. 143, No. 15, April 10, 1993, p. 234.

Moorhead, Daryl L., et al., "Ecological Legacies: Impacts on Ecosystems of the McMurdo Dry Valleys," *BioScience*, Vol. 48, No. 12, December 1999, p. 1009.

Nash, J. Madeleine, "Cracking the Ice," *Time*, February 3, 2003, pp. 50–55.

Nordwall, Bruce C., "Antarctica's First Year-round Runway," *Aviation Week & Space Technology*, Vol. 156, No. 16, April 22, 2002, p. 47.

Parfit, Michael, "Timeless Valleys of the Antarctic Desert," *National Geographic*, Vol. 194, No. 4, October 1998, pp. 120–135.

Price, Dick, "A Hole in the Ice," *IEEE Expert*, Vol. 10, No. 6, December 1999, pp. 20–22.

Priscu, John C., et al., "Carbon Transformations in a Perennially Ice-Covered Antarctic Lake," *BioScience*, Vol. 48, No. 12, December 1999, p. 997.

_____, "Life in the Valley of the 'Dead,'" *BioScience*, Vol. 48, No. 12, December 1999, p. 959.

Rivkin, Richard B., "Seasonal Patterns of Planktonic Production in McMurdo Sound," *American Zoologist*, Vol. 31, No. 1, Spring 1991, pp. 5–16.

"Russia's Ice-breaker Cruising Antarctic with Passengers," *ITAR/TASS News Agency*, January 10, 2001.

Sharp, Bill, "Ice Boxes," *HP Professional*, Vol. 5, No. 9, September 1991, pp. 54–57.

Smith, Roff, "Frozen Under," *National Geographic*, Vol. 200, No. 6, December 2001, pp. 2–35.

Sorenson, Alia, "Former Nuclear Plant Is a Relic from a Futuristic Past," *Orlando Sentinel*, February 12, 2003.

"State-size Iceberg Grinds toward Antarctic Shipping Lanes," *Christian Science Monitor*, September 28, 2000, p. 14.

Stone, Gregory S., "Exploring Antarctica's Islands of Ice," *National Geographic*, Vol. 200, No. 6, December 2001, pp. 36–45.

"Summer on Ice," *Christian Science Monitor*, March 7, 2000, p. 18.

Sweitzer, James S., "The Last Observatory on Earth," *Mercury*, Vol. 22, No. 5, September–October 1993, pp. 13–18.

"Tracking Rogue Giant Icebergs from the Skies," *New York Times*, November 28, 2000.

Van Wey, Nate J., "Antarctica — The Ultimate Summer Institute," *Physics Teacher*, Vol. 33, No. 5, May 1995, pp. 280–281.

Virginia, Ross A., and Diana H. Wall, "How Soils Structure Communities in the Antarctic Dry Valleys," *BioScience*, Vol. 48, No. 12, December 1999, p. 973.

Walker, Zachariah, "Antarctic Adventure," *Ostomy Quarterly*, Vol. 36, No. 4, Summer 1999, p. 37.

Wilkes, Owen, and Robert Mann, "The Story of Nukey Poo," *Bulletin of the Atomic Scientists*, Vol. 34, No. 8, 1978, pp. 32–36.

Monte Carlo, Monaco

Location

Located on an escarpment of the southern Alps on the Riviera di Ponente or west end of the Côte d'Azur [French Riviera], Monte Carlo is western Europe's one-of-a-kind playground. The region enjoys a pleasant Mediterranean climate, limited rainfall, subtropical flora, excellent fishing, top-drawer yacht anchorage, and engaging scenery, where the wealthy, powerful, and fashionable gather. At only 0.73 of a square mile, the principality of Monaco is the world's second smallest state after the Vatican. It affords visitors spectacular views from rail lines and highways that skirt orange and lemon groves, olive trees, vineyards, and fields of lavender and other flowers grown for the fragrance industry.

Since the mid-nineteenth century, Monte Carlo, the capital of the Grimaldi family's independent state, has drawn 1.5 million tourists a year to its beaches, gaming tables, shops, and marinas. Only nine miles east of Nice and five miles west of Italy, the city capitalizes on the allure of Europe's prize coast. At the highest point, the royal palace in Monaco-Ville, called Le Rocher [the Rock], looks down from a crag that is home to a cathedral, government offices, and a world-class oceanographic museum and sealife research center. Along the port at La Condamine, casinos, a saltwater therapy clinic, yacht basins, and luxury hotels and boutiques selling goods by Bulgari, Cartier, Chanel, Dior, Escado, Hermes, Piaget, Valentino, and Yves St. Laurent further the city's reputation as a getaway for the rich and trendy.

Contacts

Cindy Hoddeson, Director of Convention
    & Incentive Sales
Monaco Government Tourist Office

Monaco Ville, Monaco
Phone: 800-753-9696
          212-286-3330
Fax: 212-286-9890
Email: travelagent@monaco1.org
          c.hoddeson@monaco1.org
http://www.monaco-tourism.com

Musée Océanographique de Monaco
Avenue Saint Martin
Monaco Ville, Monaco
Phone: 377-93-153600
Fax: 377-93-505297
http://www.oceano.mc/fr/index_flash.html

History

Monte Carlo's beginnings date to Ligurian settlers known as Monoïkos, one possible source of the place-name "Monaco." Phoenician colonists, who settled the shore in the 1100s B.C., fortified the natural harbor, and remained for over 500 years. The Greeks sanctified the stretch as the Port of Herakles, named for their semi-divine strongman. Rome held sway into the Christian era, when the Islamic Saracens seized the coastal area. In the A.D. 800s, they built ramparts on the headland, a natural defense from enemies and pirates.

The Grimaldi dynasty, the principality's only ruling family, received power from Holy Roman Emperor Otto of Brunswick in 1191. The Genoese kings established themselves in 1297 with François Grimaldi's bold capture of the rocky headland and affirmed their power in 1304 with the crowning of Rainier I. Through a series of ambassadorial arrangements and concessions, the dynasty clung to power under the aegis of France, Spain, Sardinia, and Nazi Germany. Only in 1792 following the French Revolution did the royal line waver, but it regained the throne in 1814 with the ousting of Napoleon.

Monte Carlo changed significantly in 1856, when Prince Carlo III built the famed

Located on an escarpment of the southern Alps, Monte Carlo is western Europe's one-of-a-kind playground (courtesy of Andrew Buys).

Place du Casino and the steep seaside town that bears his name. To bring in rich French gamblers, he initiated steamer routes to Nice, later replaced by a railway. Such famous visitors as dancers Isadora Duncan and Rudolf Nureyev, shipping magnate Aristotle Onassis, painters Pablo Picasso and Henri Matisse, actors Greta Garbo and Errol Flynn, composer Cole Porter, auto maker Gianni Agnelli, the Duke and Duchess of Windsor, film producer Jack Warner, statesman Winston Churchill, and writers Scott and Zelda Fitzgerald added glamour to basic sunning, beach picnics, and moonlight sails. The filming of James Bond movies in the casino — *Casino Royale* (1967), featuring David Niven and Peter Sellers, and *Goldeneye* (1995), starring Pierce Brosnan as agent .007 — spread the cachet of the region. The public also identified Monte Carlo with Princess Grace,

Philadelphia-born film star and wife of Prince Rainier III until her death in 1982.

In a clean, superbly policed atmosphere, elite visitors to the city window-shopped while strolling along pink granite sidewalks and stopped in at the lavish Hermitage or Hotel de Paris for lunch. Splendid yachts the equal in luxe of nearby pastel mansions hugged the coast and glittered by night. Mobile partiers alternated locales from on-deck to such palatial villas as Stavros Niarchos's Château de la Croe and Onassis's Château de la Garoupe at nearby Cap d'Antibes, France. On January 8, 1997, Monégasques feted the longevity of the Grimaldis' 700-year rule with a ten-month bash beginning with a Catholic mass and Te Deum, a ballet, a harbor show of coastal history, a musical on the life of Pablo Picasso, and the unveiling of a statue of dynasty founder François Grimaldi.

Ecosystem

The beauty of Monte Carlo rests on local appreciation for the Mediterranean's historical prominence and ecological balance. In 1902, the unearthing of a fragmented *Cassis rufa* shell at the Grotte du Prince, one of the Grimaldi Caves of Monaco, revealed a paleolithic treasure that previously surfaced only at the Aden coast and the Indian Ocean. The cream-to-pink carnelian shell turned up during an excavation that archeologist Le Chanoine Villeneuve began in 1895. Because the cave mouth gradually silted in, seventy feet of detritus covered five hearths built by Neanderthals and secured a stratified view of flora and fauna. Historians pondered why and how the shell had been transported in the early Stone Age. A prehistoric form of currency from around 48,000 B.C., the shell, later housed at the Musée d'Anthropologie Prehistorique de Monaco, may have traveled far through a series of human exchanges or barters.

To establish the importance of shells, birds, fish, and plants to Monaco's future, the government declared 1992 the "Year of the Environment." The seven-day World Symposium on the Migration of Birds and the International Hydrographic Conference convened at Monte Carlo at the Oceanographic Museum, an architectural gem rising grandly above the coastline. It offered participating ecologists and naturalists biological specimens, a self-sustaining coral reef at the research lab, a weather station and seismological observatory, and a sizeable oceanographic library to aid in the international war on water pollution. To the public, the institute exhibits an aquarium, 350 species of fish, a 65-foot-long skeleton of a whale that museum founder Prince Albert I harpooned, and a model of the prince's marine lab aboard his yacht *Hirondelle II*, named for the swallow. The institute also archives the equipment of diver, environ-

mentalist, and film maker Jacques-Yves Cousteau, who directed the museum from 1957 to 1988.

Monte Carlo continued its commitment to the environment in 1992 with the addition of the SeaBus, the world's first acrylic-hulled submarine. Its excursions offer an adventure in tourism that glimpses underwater biota at 130 feet through transparent viewing windows. Powered by a silent, nonpolluting electric engine, it accommodates 45 passengers on a panoramic tour that departs from quayside at a recycled railway station in La Condamine, the main harbor. On day and night tours, the SeaBus reveals natural and artificial reefs, simulated shipwrecks, and living fish and undersea plants.

On November 25, 1999, for the sake of endangered cetaceans, Monaco joined France and Italy in a treaty establishing the Northern Hemisphere's first whale sanctuary. Spread from the Gulf of Genoa on the Ligurian coast east to the Côte d'Azur and south to the Balearic isles of Corsica and Sardinia, the 32,424-square mile reserve monitors land-to-sea pollution and protects large sea animals, including sea turtles and thirteen species of dolphin and whale. A research program informs the public about the life of the whale and its environmental and reproductive needs and the policing of tourism, fishing, oil tankers, and toxic discharge and run-off. Claude Martin, director of the World Wildlife Fund, predicted that other countries would join the effort to preserve marine animals and their habitats.

Monaco pursued its sea ecology drive by creating the Prince Albert I Medal, issued biennially by the International Association for the Physical Sciences of the Oceans for a lifetime of service to the environment. The honorarium carries the name of a Monacan prince who served in the French and Spanish navies and who, in 1919, founded an oceanographic wing of the International

Union of Geodesy and Geophysics. In August 2001, Prince Rainier III presented the medal to Austro-American geophysicist and oceanographer Walter Heinrich Munk, coauthor of the classic text *The Oceans, Their Physics, Chemistry, and General Biology* (1942) and *Ocean Acoustic Tomography* (1996).

The choice echoed Monaco's long history of ecological stewardship. For 61 years, Munk aided the Scripps Institution of Oceanography at the University of California and taught new generations of sea scientists. Working with Norwegian oceanographer Harald Ulrik Sverdrup, Munk formulated a method of predicting surf conditions and a curriculum for training military meteorologists to assist the Allied amphibious landings in North Africa and Normandy during World War II. (*See also* OMAHA BEACH, FRANCE.) He invented instruments for measuring ocean circulation, waves, and tides. Only ten miles from ground zero, he aided the military by quantifying ocean disturbance resulting from atomic weapons testing at the Bikini Atoll in the South Pacific on June 30, 1946, and by locating the source of long ocean swells spreading from the Indian Ocean to the Pacific. In 1959, he founded the Institute of Geophysics and Planetary Physics in La Jolla, California. In his late seventies, Munk applied ocean tomography to the study of global warming. Over a lifetime of dedicated service to humankind, he chaired the Ocean Studies Board of the National Academy of Sciences and served Vice President Al Gore's environmental task force and the board of the Monterey Bay Aquarium Research Institute. (*See also* MONTEREY, CALIFORNIA.)

Coastal Activities

Currently, Monte Carlo boasts a variety of pastimes and entertainments — the Ballet Russe de Monte Carlo, Opera de Monte Carlo, Monte-Carlo National Orchestra, Museum of Prehistoric Anthropology, Napoleonic Museum, and a cactus garden and zoo. Among the usual trappings of a coastal resort, the city offers deep-sea diving, helicopter rides, hang-gliding, discos, terrace lunches, and late-night games of baccarat and roulette. In addition, local event organizers host an international television festival, dog show, firework festival, Red Cross gala, and circus festival.

Monte Carlo's pilgrims venerate the tomb of Saint Dévote or Devota, Monaco's patron and guardian of sailors, and join in an annual torchlight procession and blessing followed by the ceremonial burning of a boat. The ritual reenacts the attempted theft of relics of the saint, a revered Corsican whom the Roman Emperor Diocletian persecuted and martyred in A.D. 303. On Good Friday, the Venerable Brotherhood of the Black Penitents of Mercy processes along the Stations of the Cross. On June 23–24, an annual bonfire and open-air festival and dance honor St. John the Baptist, who baptized Jesus in the Jordan River at the beginning of his ministry.

Monte Carlo earns a separate identity as a sports haven, which hosts prestigious international events as well as Prince Albert's wheeled bobsled races on the promenade. In a limited edition book, *Le Passion Bleue* (2002), the Yacht Club de Monaco collected photos of 140 classic craft that have participated in the Prada Challenge for Classic Yachts, an annual regatta. The city is home to an International Sporting Club and two world-famous car races, the International Monaco Grand Prix and the Monte Carlo Rally. The latter is a three-day race begun in 1929. To a packed assemblage, Formula One racing cars accelerate from zero to 100 miles per hour in under three seconds and travel over 907.5 miles. The race progresses through Provence over fifteen stages. Two-person teams cover dry asphalt, cliffside turns, blind corners, falling rock, and mountain passes made perilous by snow and ice.

One seaside pleasure unique to the city is Les Thermes Marins de Monte Carlo, a $27-million thalassotherapy spa that opened in 1995. Sparkly with chrome, glass, mirrors, and marble mosaic walls and balustrades, the 20,000-gallon thermal baths rise above the remains of an early twentieth-century spa that German bombers destroyed in the 1940s. Clients swim in therapy pools, relax in seaweed baths, and unkink under jets spouting heated salt water free of chemical additives. To revive the respiratory system, some indulge in mineral-rich inhalants and scented oil massage; others prefer algae and dried sea mud wraps or fasciotherapy, a deep-muscle massage that frees the body from stress.

At the Port of Monaco, a U-shaped harbor receives ocean-going vessels in 434 berths. To keep pace with the Riviera's demand for space, at a cost of $251 million, the government is restructuring its strategically located port with a 160,000-ton floating breakwater and a jetty capable of handling cruise liners. At Port Hercules the annual Monaco Yacht Show features 65 superyachts and a trade show of 26 sailing vessels. The most technologically advanced craft from some twenty countries offer such amenities as teak decking, jacuzzis, advanced galley appliances, satellite communication systems, super-fast tenders, and pocket submarines.

Sources

Alper, Joseph, "Munk's Hypothesis: A Slightly Mad Scheme to Measure Global Warming," *Sea Frontiers*, Vol. 37, No. 3, June 1991, pp. 38–44.

"Bikini," *Newsweek*, July 1, 1946.

Biggs, Melissa E., "The Royal Riviers," *Town & Country*, June 1997, p. 55.

Clarke, Jay, "Famous Casino Is Overrated, But Other Sites Win Over Visitors to Monaco," *Knight Ridder*, December 8, 1997.

Conniff, Richard, and Jodi Cobb, "Monaco," *National Geographic*, Vol. 189, No. 5, May 1996, pp. 80–95.

Davis, Matt, "The 70th Monte Carlo Rally," *Motor Trend*, June 2002, pp. 110–112.

Edmondson, Jolie, "A Queendom by the Sea," *Forbes*, September 23, 1996.

Esterhazy, Louise J., "Louise Does Monaco," *W*, May 2002, p. 218.

"The Full Monte Carlo," *Travel Trade Gazette U. K. & Ireland*, May 1, 2000, p. 35.

Geracimos, Ann, "In Monaco, Spa Springs from the Sea," *Washington Times*, March 22, 1998, p. 1.

Guider, Elizabeth, "Fest Ups the Ante: Monte Carlo Event Expands Slate and Date," *Daily Variety*, March 6, 2002, p. 8.

Hayden, Bryan, et al., "Dating the *Cassis rufa* Shell from the Mousterian Levels of the Grotte du Prince, Monaco," *Antiquity*, Vol. 67, September 1993, pp. 609–612.

"Keeping It in the Family," *People Weekly*, January 27, 1997, p. 113.

"Monaco," *Conference & Incentive Travel*, May 8, 2002, p. 71.

"Monaco," *Incentive*, September 2002, p. 87.

"Monaco of the Moment," *Town & Country*, May 2000.

"Monaco's 700th Birthday Bash," *Maclean's*, January 20, 1997, p. 53.

"Monaco Talks Set to Revive Sporting Ties," *Asia Africa Intelligence Wire*, August 2, 2002.

"Monte Carlo TV Festival: The Remake of a Sequel," *Video Age International*, June–July 2002, pp. 1–2.

Mount, G., "The Men Who Built the Bank at Monte Carlo," *History Today*, Vol. 41, No. 10, October 1991, pp. 32–37.

Neil, Dan, "Whispering through Monte Carlo's Curves," *New York Times*, October 20, 1999.

Paris, Sheldon, "Monaco's History Dates Back to the Phoenicians," *Stamps*, May 13, 1995, p. 17.

"A Piece of the Rock," *Travel Weekly*, March 8, 1993.

"Principality Steps Up Its Efforts to Curb Pollution, Save Wildlife," *Travel Weekly*, May 11, 1992, p. 23.

Sixeas, Virginia M., "Whale of a Place," *Environment*, January 2000, p. 4.

Theodoracopulos, Taki, "Goodbye to All That," *National Review*, March 1, 1993, pp. 64–65.

Thompson, Mark, and John F. Burns, "Monaco," *New York Times Magazine*, May 12, 2002.

Trease, Norma, "2002 Monaco Yacht Show the Best Ever," *Dockwalk*, October 2002.

"Walter Heinrich Munk Biography," http://scilib.ucsd.edu/sio/archives/siohstry/munk-biog.html.

Yam, Philip, "The Man Who Would Hear Ocean Temperatures," *Scientific American*, Vol. 272, No. 1, January 1995, pp. 38–39.

Monterey, California

Location

The historical city of Monterey, one of California's coastal resorts and artist enclaves, borders the Pacific Ocean 100 miles south of San Francisco. The region lies west of the Gabilan Mountains and seventy miles east of the massive two-mile deep Monterey Canyon, the nation's largest undersea crevasse, home to soft mushroom corals, eelpouts, luminescent hatchetfish and viperfish, mysid, pom pom anemones, peppermint gorgonians, sea whips, and spotted ratfish. Blessed with marine resources, the city of Monterey is tucked into the south end of the bay between Castroville to the north of the crescent and south Pacific Grove on the point of the bay.

In *The Universe Below* (1997), William J. Broad exulted that Monterey Bay lies at an auspicious intersection of currents and winds:

> An enormous canyon cuts the continental shelf in two, bringing deep water remarkably close to land. The canyon is so close that erosional forces at its tip keep nibbling away at the old pier at Moss landing, located at the bay's midpoint [p. 202].

He noted the role of Monterey in nurturing a vast slice of sea life. In addition to channeling the mainland's toxic silt far out to sea, the canyon promotes the growth of kelp and rich nutrients that feed plankton, fish, and marine mammals. A great tide pool tips the peninsula. In its basin, the onrushing sea brings in anemones, hermit crabs, mussels, limpets, octopi, shrimp, snails, and starfish to nestle among waving algae, barnacles, and nudibranches.

At the heart of Monterey City is an eight-block strip affectionately known as Cannery Row, which extends from the Coast Guard Pier to Hopkins Marine Station. The area appeals to vacationers and naturalists for its cliffs, sandy beaches and dunes, surface canopy of kelp, and stands of cypress and pine, which Spanish explorer Juan Rodriquez Cabrillo first glimpsed when he reached the bay on November 17, 1542, and named it *La Bahia de los Pinos* [Bay of Pines]. Today, the region hosts one of the world's most creative aquariums.

Contacts

Julie Armstrong
Monterey County Convention and Visitors
    Bureau
P. O. Box 1770
Monterey, California 93942
Phone: 800-555-6290
Email: julie@mccvb.org

Monterey Bay Aquarium
886 Cannery Row
Monterey, California 93940
Phone: 831-648-4888
       831-648-4800
http://www.mbayaq.org

History

In prehistory, Monterey Bay flourished in one of North America's most beautiful and flourishing natural habitats. Around 22,000 sea otters thrived on abalone, crab, mussels, octopi, sea urchins, snails, and squid and ranged along the shores from Baja California north to Oregon, providing paleoindian hunters with pelts as early as 17,000 B.C. From 500 B.C., the Costanoan (also Costenos or Ohlone) netted seabirds, gathered shellfish and mollusks, and trapped and speared eels, salmon, steelhead trout, and sturgeon. At Achasta Village near present-day Monterey City, they dwelt in conical homes shaped from fern, grass, and tule around a pole structure, where they roasted the meat of sea lion and whale in earth ovens. They traded their bounty with the Miwok and Yokut, using as money abalone and mussel shells, clamshell beads,

The historical city of Monterey, one of California's coastal resorts and artist enclaves, is blessed with ample marine resources (courtesy of Julie Armstrong).

dried abalone meat, olivella shells, piñon nuts, acorns, cinnabar, obsidian, and salt.

On December 16, 1602, explorer Sebastian Vizcaíno captained a fleet — the *San Diego, Santo Tomás*, and the frigate *Tres Reyes*— to Monterey Bay to claim it for Spain. He named the place for Mexican viceroy, Don Gaspár de Zúñiga y Acevedo, Count of Monte Rey, but the land remained in the hands of native tribes. In the 1740s, Russian fur hunters followed the trail of expeditioner Vitus Bering, a Danish navigator whom Tsar Peter the Great dispatched to further Russian colonialism and expand trade. Bering scouted the coasts of Alaska's Kuril and Aleutian chain and pushed south to California's Farallon Islands. He targeted sea otters for their valuable pelts, containing the densest underfur of any mammal, which is ten times thicker than human hair.

Nearly 230 years after Cabrillo located the bay and almost 170 years after Vizcaíno conferred its name, Catalonian expeditioner Gaspar de Portolá and Franciscan evangelist Father Junípero Serra of Majorca sailed up California's coast aboard the *San Antonio* and reached Monterey on May 24, 1770. They founded a city, the Catholic mission of San Carlos Borromeo, and, on June 3, outlined a royal presidio. Serra, the master planner, was called the Apostle of California for envisioning a string of 21 missions and a campaign for Christianizing area aborigines, later known collectively and pejoratively as the Mission Indians.

Under exploitation by Catholic fathers, the Costanoan, who had reached an estimated headcount of 10,000 by the mid–1700s, suffered a two-century decline that eventually reduced them to 200. Contact with Europeans hastened the demise of their religion, language, and customs and threatened them with extinction. Under the lash of Spanish fathers and soldiers, most of the indigenous Indians helped to build the mission and the fort. Others fled to the interior to escape proselytism until Father Junípero Serra forced their return. Within crowded, unhygienic missions, they died off at an alarming rate.

As the Spanish flourished, Monterey became California's capital in March 1776, when Captain Juan Bautista de Anza of Sonora, the first European to map a land route from Mexico, led 200 colonists and their domestic livestock up the Anza Trail, later called *El Camino Real* [the King's Highway] from Sonora to the Monterey mission. While Spaniards rapidly dispossessed Indians to make the city a social, military, and political nexus, depredations continued at sea. Uncontrolled northern sea otter harvesting continued until 1799, when Tsar Paul I sponsored the Russian American Company, a semi-official corporation regulating the fur trade in Alaska and the Pacific-Northwest. After Alaska's killing fields played out, the hunting crews moved south along the North American coast to California, where they picked the habitat clean by the 1830s.

Deregulation again threatened the sea otter's survival in 1867 after the United States purchased Alaska from the Russian government. By the early twentieth century, persistent hunters from America, England, and Russia had reduced the animal population to a little over 1,000. In 1911, the International Fur Seal Treaty's ban on trapping saved the sea otter from extinction. At that time, only thirteen otter colonies survived.

On March 19, 1938, Californians cheered the plucky sea otters that suddenly resurged at Bixby Creek south of Monterey Bay near Big Sur. About a half mile from the shoreline, females once more began sleeping in tight, kelp-draped formations called rafts while males withdrew to bachelor quarters on the outer rim of their territory. The kelp fronds kept them from drifting out of formation while they lolled on the Pacific. At their busiest, they followed the daily task of harvesting up to forty sea urchins, which fed a high metabolism that kept them warm.

In 1968, Margaret Wentworth Owings, an activist from Berkeley, California, formed the Friends of the Sea Otter (FSO), a pressure group that successfully countered hostile fishers and derailed a legislative bill allowing hunters to shoot sea otters. The FSO shaped public policy, educated citizens on the interconnectedness of ecology, and trained volunteers for an oil spill response team. Additional protection from the 1972 Marine Mammal Protection Act and an Endangered Species Act the following year enabled the otters to build their number at the painfully slow rate of five percent per year. The limited growth resulted from low birth rate and deaths from acute emphysema and fungus. In all, the sea otters could depend on protection from the state of California and from American, Canadian, and Russian wildlife laws. They remained on the endangered list until they could produce a headcount of 2,650 for three consecutive years.

At a tenuous point in Monterey's otter saga, in 1972, the animals recolonized the bay. Thirteen years later, nature writer Marianne Riedman, an employee of Monterey Bay Aquarium, and marine ecologist James A. Estes of the University of California at Santa Cruz began monitoring sixty tagged otters by telescope. They concluded that otter behaviors often contribute to violent deaths. During mating, males clamp down on female noses, a fierce hold that can lead to fatal infection or death from trauma or drowning. The animals' territorial struggles also result in the kidnap of pups by males, who thrive on food extorted or stolen from females anxious to retrieve their young.

Monterey's nature advocacy provoked coastal business leaders. The fishing industry protested protection of the sea otter, which competed for precious mollusks, the source of income for coastal fishers. In 1986, Congress ameliorated a standoff between conservationists and fishers by declaring the shore south of Point Conception a no-otter zone. The Federal Wildlife Service attempted to increase the animal's chances of survival by moving 140 of the California population to San Nicolas, an island seventy miles west of Los Angeles. San Nicolas once sustained a sea otter population until Russian hunters exterminated the species through overhunting. The experiment recolonized only 25 otters. In 1993, federal authorities stopped rounding up stray otters for return to San Nicolas and stopped policing the no-otter zone.

That same year, President George Bush stemmed a mounting ecological disaster on California's scenic coast by establishing the Monterey Bay National Marine Sanctuary, a 4,024 square-mile sea habitat protected from offshore oil rigs, overfishing, commercial shipping, dredging dumps, and untreated sewage. At the time, seven on-going marine study centers armed with roving seafloor vehicles and high-tech methods of analysis focused attention on biota dependent on seamounts and thermal plumes. The retrieved data elucidated gaps in knowledge about the habitats of fish, marine mammals, and seabirds and highlighted threats to the health of the Pacific Coast ecosystem.

Despite high-tech monitoring, in the mid–1990s, the sea otter's range shrank to the California shore from Santa Cruz south some 150 miles. Protecting them was the California Sea Otter Game Refuge, which extended from Monterey south about 65 miles. By 1995, naturalists counted 2,400 surviving sea otters, who remained vulnerable to hyperthermia, killer whale and shark attack, and storms at sea as well as to ambush by hunters, gillnetting, and competition from sea urchin fishers, who sold their catch as well as abalone and urchin roe to the Japanese. By 2002, otter colonies radiated out from Monterey Bay only as far north as Pescadero Point and south to Point Conception.

More insidious were pollutants, particularly oil spills and chemical wastes. California's legislature remanded tankers to shipping lanes farther from land, stopped off-shore oil rigs from drilling in the otter habitat, and forbade farmers from creating a toxic runoff with chemical fertilizers and pesticides. To ward off a catastrophe like the 1989 spill of the *Exxon Valdez*, which killed 5,000 Alaskan otters in Alaska's Prince William Sound, Californians designed a rehabilitation center at Santa Cruz to rescue, cleanse, and reclaim oily animals from a deadly soup.

Ecosystem

The sea otter (*Enhydra lutris*), a member of the weasel family and a resourceful saltwater cousin of the river otter, exemplifies the land-based, carnivorous mammal repatriated in the sea. The otter appeared on the Pacific Coast of North America in the Pliocene era three million years ago. Lively and appealing in its antics, it lies on its back to propel a grizzled reddish-brown body through the water in back-front undulations and paddles with small forelegs and broad webbed flippers at back. With its paws, it grubs for sea urchins, which tend to overrun and strip the sea floor of its forty-foot greenery, leaving the coast unprotected from currents and tides.

Like primates, sea otters receive a conscientious upbringing because, without proper tending and education, the young are susceptible to many dangers. Mothers give birth annually from December to February and feed their three-to-five-pound pups on milk that contains six times the fat of human breast milk. The heat generated by fat metabolism protects the animal, which lacks the body-warming layers of blubber found in seals and whales. Because the sea otter is the only mammal other than primates to gather and employ tools, the mother must demonstrate how to plump up fur to insulate the body with air bubbles and how to find a flat rock to use as a base on which to pound hard mollusk shells to release the chewy meat. A breakdown in otter training condemns pups to certain collapse and death from cold and hunger.

Because the death of a female sea otter often leaves the young vulnerable, compassionate marine biologists at Monterey Bay Aquarium maintain a program of parenting orphaned pups. Round-the-clock care begins with bottle-feeding and rehydrating babies, grooming their thick fur, and monitoring body temperature. To simulate the fatty milk of lactating mothers, veterinarian Tom Williams created a nutritious cocktail of chopped clams and squid in a slurry of cod liver oil, half-and-half, vitamins, minerals, and saline solution. More crucial to the pups is a six-months series of lessons in survival, such as diving, foraging on the seabed of the museum's Great Tide Pool, overturning rocks and reaching into crevices to grub for food, and cracking shellfish open against a rock that the otter tucks into a pouch at the foreleg for safekeeping. Like mother otters snatching children from play, museum divers force the pups to pay attention to the full-time job of staying alive.

The healthy babe, returned to the wild with a radio transmitter under its pelt, wears a contented grin on its face as it gnaws shellfish, forcing its lips away from the spines of urchins and the raw edges of mollusk shells. The act of feeding the body sufficient calories requires each neophyte to consume the equivalent of a quarter of its body weight per day. Consequently, females spend 43 percent of their time foraging for themselves and their pups; males, who take no part in rearing a family, devote 38 percent of their time hunting food. To remain afloat in the Pacific, the pups constantly cavort and roll in the waves and clean their fur to spread skin oils and create the bubbles that insulate them from cold currents.

Into the 21st century, Monterey's sea otters continued to decline in number. In 2000, the California otters again lost ground at the annual rate of five percent. In February 2001, necropsies pointed to parasites from untreated sewage and from the infectious feces of bobcats, cougars, and house cats. In spring 2001, a census of the sea otters of central California revealed 2,161 animals. Enlarging the threat to Monterey's fragile coastal ecology was a shift in federal oil spill protection after President George W. Bush upped the licensing of offshore drilling platforms by 180 percent. French oceanographer Jean-Michael Cousteau warned that further decimation of the sea otter population could shift the ecological balance beyond repair, costing California its lush kelp forest and all the sea life that flourishes within.

Coastal Activities

The health of Monterey Bay ensures the area's tourism, which has increased in spring 2000 with the scheduling of visiting ships from Crystal Cruises, Princess Cruises, and Royal Caribbean. A protected environment welcomes the migrating birds and monarch butterflies that draw outsiders to walk the hillsides and to photograph wildflowers at the U.S. Navy dune restoration area. In town, a glimpse of past wildlife survives in Kris Swanson's *Grizzly*, a public sculpture of a large brown bear that once flourished in the area. Hearty kayakers paddle over the Monterey Bay National Marine Sanctuary to observe harbor seals and sea lions and otters; divers enjoy one of the world's most popular undersea landscapes. Landlubbers board harbor cruises to watch whales as they migrate from Mexico. Biking, jogging, and skating at Shoreline Park offer more vigorous sport. Along the shore, others choose from skim-boarding, hang-gliding, trekking, and launching sailboats from the marina.

A favorite spot, Cannery Row, was once frequented by Nobel Prize-winner John Steinbeck, who studied marine biology before electing writing as his life's work. His novel *Cannery Row* (1945) glimpses the heyday of the coastal food business, which played out in the 1950s from the overfishing of sardines. In the novel's introduction, he immortalized the Row as:

> a poem, a stink, a grating noise, a quality of light, a tone, a habit, a nostalgia, a dream. Cannery Row in the gathered and scattered tin and iron and rust and splintered wood, chipped pavement and weedy lots and junk heaps, sardine canneries of corrugated iron, honky tonks, restaurants and whore houses, and little crowded groceries, and laboratories and flophouses [p. 1].

Today, the beachfront features the lab of his pal, pioneering marine biologist Edward Flanders "Doc" Ricketts, owner of Pacific Biological Laboratory and co-author of a classic textbook, *Between Pacific Tides* (1939), and of Steinbeck's *The Sea of Cortez* (1941). Visitors revere Ricketts as the biologist who helped to wed life study to ecology. The remainder of the street encompasses art galleries, scenes from the sardine fishing industry that once thrived at Monterey, and the Maritime Museum and History Center, which features a five-ton, 1,000-prism Fresnel lens, which once lighted the coast from the Point Sur Lighthouse.

The Monterey Bay Aquarium, a 3.3-acre preserve costing $60 million, opened in October 1984 and became one of the world's prime sea exploratoria. Built into a rocky crag, the facility overlooks a tidewater pool and incorporates an amphitheater and patio with free telescopes, from which viewers can observe dolphins, lounging seals, and porpoises. At 100 glass tanks, visitors witness the interdependence of 571 species of plants and animals, some of which feed on nightly influxes of larvae, plankton, and seaweed spores. In 1993, aquarists added a one-million-gallon tank, which stands three stories high to increase viewing space. Twice daily, divers clean the windows and feed fish from squirt bottles filled with anemone mash. A living exhibit, "Myster-

ies of the Deep," presents video footage of the *Ventana*, an unmanned robot submarine, on an undersea expedition begun in 2000; an auditorium presentation, "Exploring Monterey Canyon," coordinates maps, video, and still photography to explain the interrelation of living things and their impact on human life.

For its accessibility and ingenious design, the museum is a tutorial marvel. Thirty interactive exhibits allow children to investigate the Splash Zone, a touch pool that introduces the Coral Cove and the Rough, Rocky Shores habitats, and to familiarize themselves with tropical sharks, a giant clam shell, starfish, sea cucumbers, and a penguin colony. A favorite with youngsters is the lifestyle of sea otters and information on how the Sea Otter Research and Conservation (SORAC) program protects coastal animals. An exhibit on vanishing sealife focuses on the hardships faced by green sea turtles, hammerhead sharks, and tuna. In addition, a "Seafood Watch Chart" enlightens visitors on the availability of farmed catfish and tilapia, mahimahi, and wild Alaskan salmon and warns that the American lobster, Chilean seabass, orange roughy, swordfish, tiger prawn, and white shrimp are endangered following uncontrolled harvesting. A 25-foot window added to the million-gallon Outer Bay environment in 2001 displays bluefin and yellowfin tuna, bonito, pot belly and tiger tail seahorses, soupfin shark, and sunfish and promotes public awareness of the importance of ocean stewardship.

Sources

Barnes-Svarney, Patricia, "Where Research and Diatoms Bloom," *Sea Frontiers*, Vol. 39, No. 3, May–June, pp. 16–17.

Benz, Carl, "Evaluating Attempts to Reintroduce Sea Otters along the California Coastline," *Endangered Species Update*, Vol. 13, No. 12, December 1996, pp. 31–35.

Broad, William J. *The Universe Below*. New York: Simon & Schuster, 1997.

Burnside, Mary Wade, " $3 Mil Monterey Bay Aquarium Exhibit Makes a 'Splash,' Set for Five-Year Run," *Amusement Business*, August 28, 2000, p. 21.

Cabrillo, Juan Rodriguez. *Spanish Exploration in the Southwest*, 1542–1706. New York, N. Y.: Charles Scribner's Sons, 1916.

"California's Monterey Bay to Receive Three Cruise Ships in 2002," *Knight Ridder/Tribune Business News*, February 26, 2002.

Carey, John, and Fred Bavendam, "The Sea Otter's Uncertain Future," *National Wildlife*, Vol. 25, December–January 1987, pp. 16–20.

Childs, Marquis, "A Novel Aquarium Depicts the Story of Monterey Bay," *Smithsonian*, Vol. 16, June 1985, pp. 95–100.

Clark, Jamie Rappaport, "Overview of the Legislative Mandates and the Agencies Responsible for Implementation of Southern Sea Otter Protection under the Endangered Species Act," *Endangered Species Update*, Vol. 13, No. 12, December 1996, pp. 26–28.

Cohn, Jeffrey P., "Understanding Sea Otters," *BioScience*, Vol. 48, No. 3, March 1998, pp. 151–155.

Cousteau, Jean-Michael, "New Home for Sea Otters, Kelp Forests," *Skin Diver*, Vol. 50, No. 9, September 2001, p. 22.

"Diseases Cited in California Sea Otter Deaths," *Endangered Species Update*, Vol. 11, No. 6–7, April–May 1994, pp. 19–20.

Donathan, David, "Diving the Monterey Bay Aquarium," *Skin Diver*, October 1993, p. 23.

Dybas, Cheryl Lynn, "In the Sea, No Fish Is an Island," *BioScience*, Vol. 52, No. 2, February 2002, pp. 124–127.

"Expedition to Explore Remarkable Deep-Sea Mountain," *Ascribe Higher Education News Service*, May 8, 2002.

Faurot-Daniels, Ellen, and Donald C. Bauer, "The Role of Friends of the Sea Otter in Resource Protection," *Endangered Species Update*, Vol. 13, No. 12, December 1996, pp. 47–49.

Garshelis, David L., et al., "Otter-Eating Orcas," *Science*, Vol. 283, No. 5,399, January 8, 1999, p. 176.

Gordon, David George, "The Incredible Sea Otter Rescue," *National Geographic World*, May 2002, pp. 22–25.

Hecht, Jeff, "Local Heroes of Monterey's Marine World," *New Scientist*, October 23, 1993, pp. 40–41.

Lee, David N. B., "Bad News for Sea Otters," *Wildlife Conservation*, Vol. 103, No. 1, January–February 2000, p. 14.

Lowry, Cindy, "Otter Despair," *Earth Island Journal*, Vol. 17, No. 2, Summer 2002, p. 11.

Marsh, DeLoss L., "Otters Learn Survival Skills from Surrogate Mothers," *Sea Frontiers*, Vol. 36, No. 1, January–February 1990, pp. 22–27.

McRae, Michael, "Earth's Last Frontier," *Life*, March 1, 1999, p. 65.

Mestel, Rosie, "Seamy Side of Sea Otter Life," *New Scientist*, Vol. 141, No. 1,913, February 19, 1994, p. 5.

Mintchell, Gary, "Monterey Bay Aquarium Reels in the Perfect Automation Solution," *Control Engineering*, November 2000, p. 28.

Rayl, A. J. S., "Researchers Focus on Sea Otter Deaths," *Scientist*, Vol. 15, No. 4, February 19, 2001, p. 17.

Scully, Jessica M., "Canyon Channels Toxic Soil Far Out to Sea," *New Scientist*, Vol. 174, No. 2,342, May 11, 2002, p. 18.

"Seafood Watch Campaign Expands," *Seafood Business*, Vol. 20, No. 9, September 2001, p. 10.

"Sea Otter Victory," *Earth Island Journal*, Vol. 15, No. 2, Summer 2000, p. 9.

"Slick Publicity, Slack Science," *Economist*, Vol. 312, No. 7,617, August 26, 1989, p. 68.

Steinbeck, John. *Cannery Row*. New York: Viking, 1945.

Stuller, Jay, "Don't Rock the Kayak: The Paddling Is Easy on Monterey Bay," *Travel & Leisure*, Vol. 23, No. 5, May 1993, pp. C1–C2.

"Twilight Mysteries," *U.S. News & World Report*, March 15, 1999, p. 52.

Vogel, Gretchen, "Migrating Otters Push Law to the Limit," *Science*, Vol. 289, No. 5,483, August 25, 2000, p. 1271.

Watson, John F., and Terry L. Root, "Why Southern Sea Otters?," *Endangered Special Update*, Vol. 13, No. 12, December 1996, pp. 4–5.

Wilkinson, Todd, "Marine Mystery," *National Parks*, March 2000, p. 20.

Willis, Monica Michael, "Make the Right Choice," *Country Living*, Vol. 23, No. 3, March 2000, p. 70.

Wolkomir, Richard, "The Fragile Recovery of California Sea Otters," *National Geographic*, June 1995, pp. 42–61.

Myrtle Beach, South Carolina

Location

A popular vacation and travel spot on the Atlantic seaboard, Myrtle Beach, South Carolina, is a sea community adjacent to freshwater and tidal marshlands, where welcome sea breezes relieve tropical humidity. The gently sloped Atlantic coastal plain, which covers two-thirds of the state, produces moss-draped cypress, gum, live oak, magnolia, and palmetto palm forests that fringe the shore. Set along an agricultural belt famous for truck farming, the coast was once fertile farmland until its abandonment in the late 1800s. In the next century, landowners turned from rice, soybeans, tobacco, peanuts, peaches, and melons to recreation, homesite development, and tourism.

The beach, which takes its name from the wax myrtle tree, was enriched by a prosperous seventeenth-century rice-growing culture that spread over the low country along with the enslavement of black African laborers. (*See also* ELMINO CASTLE, GHANA.) Incorporated in 1938, the Myrtle Beach community covers half of a sixty-mile crescent-shaped coastline of sandy shores that form the Grand Strand. The term also pinpoints the most frequented stretch, which reaches from Little River to Murrells Inlet, the state's most popular destination for South Carolinians and visitors and a world mecca for the shag, a Southern dance phenomenon.

Contacts

Holley Aufdemort, Communications
Myrtle Beach Chamber of Commerce
1200 North Oak Street
Myrtle Beach, South Carolina 29577
Phone: 843-626-7444
Fax: 843-916-7216

Email: info@mbchamber.org
http://www.mbchamber.com

Society of Stranders
P. O. Box 37690
Rock Hill, South Carolina 29732
Phone: 888-SOS-3113
        888-767-3113
Email: rwhisen686@aol.com
http://www.shagdance.com

Dance History

An original Southern American phenomenon born of urban rhythm & blues, the term "beach music" originated on the Carolina coast in the 1930s. The Carolina shag was an outgrowth of the Charleston and collegiate shag. It appealed because, in comparison with jitterbug, it was smoother and more romantic, required less space to perform, and was less strenuous for partners to master. Shag flourished at Myrtle Beach, a vibrant working-class and middle-class getaway where white teens from racist cities could hear popular black music on club jukeboxes. They carried it home with them to fraternity parties, parking lot sock hops, and teen canteens across the South.

Demand for Afro-American music created the right atmosphere for development of an idiosyncratic gliding dance. Growing apart from livelier big band swing in the American northeast, the Carolina shag appropriated such basic steps as the brush, crossover, Cuban step, hook, shuffle, spin, turn, and twinkle or sugarfoot, a little twist step with a crossover similar to a light tap step. Dancers performed regularly at the Myrtle Beach pavilion during World War II. The relaxed choreography suited swing band music and white groups performing fancy footwork on the sand in the style of blacks. As beach towns flourished, the dance endured, elevating to fame the names of performers Jackie McGee, J. J. Putnam, and Charlie Womble.

A popular vacation and travel spot on the Atlantic seaboard, Myrtle Beach, South Carolina, welcomes sea breezes that relieve tropical humidity (courtesy of Holley Aufdemorte).

In the second half of the twentieth century, beach music became an integral part of Carolina partying folkways. Along the Grand Strand, the shag flourished over the 1950s and 1960s with the easy steps of hip guys in ducktails and pegged pants and their dates in sweater sets, poodle skirts, and loafers. Shagging took for its theme song the Drifters' "Under the Boardwalk" (1964), a perennial jukebox oldie. Beach music gatherings favored a mix of slow and moderate tempos and a variety of themes — the Dominoes' lustful "Sixty Minute Man" (1951), Jackie Wilson's melancholy "Lonely Teardrops" (1959), the Four Tops' sincere "Baby, I Need Your Lovin'" (1962), Barbara Lewis's soulful "Hello Stranger" (1963), Smokey Robinson and the Temptations' cheerful "My Girl" (1964), and the Platters' teen favorite "With This Ring" (1967). The smooth, connected partnering of beach dancing spread inland to state universities, north along the Virginia shore, and south down the Atlantic coast of Georgia and Florida.

In the 1970s, four small towns — Windy Hill Beach, Crescent Beach, Cherry Grove Beach, and Ocean Drive Beach, nicknamed "O. D." — joined to form the commercial resort known as North Myrtle Beach. In a holiday atmosphere, shagging to beach music emerged from a contemporary deluge of hard rock. Unlike more frenetic body movements, beach dance offered a more refined, sophisticated form of touch dancing. It remained a DJ favorite and a suitable adjunct to disco. Elevated to history by the Embers' "I Love Beach Music" (1977), the form grew from folk style to cultural icon in the 1980s, when awards honored beach dancing at Myrtle Beach, gubernatorial candidates used beach tunes for campaign theme songs, and young people vied for trophies at National Shag Dance Championships. In 1984, the South Carolina legislature named the shag the state dance.

Shagging gained formal structure in 1980, when aficionados formed a Society of Stranders to perpetuate beach music, shag dancing, and traditions of the Carolina coast. The group began celebrating beach life at a Spring Safari and Fall Migration plus monthly parties. The dance energized gatherings for the fall Carolina Heritage Festival and the summer Sun Fun Festival. A nostalgic teen film, *Shag* (1988), pictured the glory of beach fun from 1963 with an all-girl fling at the Sun Fun Festival, featuring beer, flirting, a beauty parade, and shagging. That same year, Kevin Costner and Susan Sarandon introduced curious young teens to the shag in the cult classic baseball film *Bull Durham* (1988), which revived touch dancing as an essential to romance.

Late in the century, tutorial videos and dance studios began teaching shag steps. Their audience was an uninformed generation eager to embrace the mystique of baby boomer dancers from the mid-twentieth century. In 2003, Coastal Carolina University at Conway, South Carolina, added beach music to its curriculum as an integral folk element of the South Carolina coast. Assisting with authentic details was beach music performer Billy Scott, chairman of the Beach Music Association International.

Coastal Activities

Although the shag is a focus at the Carolina shore, vacationers at Myrtle Beach never lack for a variety of activities, including a string of restaurants offering favorite local dishes — salt-and-pepper catfish, oysters, and popcorn shrimp served with iced tea, hushpuppies, fries, and cole slaw. For dancing and music, Shag fans haunt the dance clubs along North Myrtle and Ocean Drive Beach. For children, in addition to water slides, a spring kite-flying festival, and goony golf, the Myrtle Beach Pavilion Amusement Park added the Hurricane, the 3,800-foot-long roller coaster that rises 110 feet. For more daring beach-goers, parasailing gives a bird's eye view of the Grand Strand.

The glittering, over-developed region also features surf-casting, pier fishing, tennis courts, golfing at over 100 courses, canoeing and kayaking, carnival rides, cruising on a stern-wheeler, coastal campsites, the Myrtle Beach Speedway, and shopping malls. To the south, the strand offers Huntington Beach State Park for camping, hiking, and birding for brown pelicans on the marshes. Art lovers favor Brookgreen Gardens, billed as the world's largest outdoor sculpture garden. Historians prefer the Hampton and Hopsewee plantations and the Palmetto Trail, which ends at McClellansville, a scenic fishing enclave.

Sources

"Beach Music Goes Academic," *Charlotte Observer*, November 26, 2002, 5B.

Fannin, Michelle, "James Brown May Sing at Beach Music Day," *Tribune News*, April 9, 2002.

Gibbons, Ann, "What's the Sound of One Ocean Warming?," *Science*, Vol. 248, No. 4851, April 6, 1990, pp. 33–34.

"The Grand Strand Is Open for Business," *Business North Carolina*, May 2001, p. 56.

Grelen, Jay C. "Shag's Fat Cat Keeps Memories of Faded Era," (Myrtle Beach) *Sun News*, October 13, 2002, p. C1.

Guier, Cindy Stooksbury, "Carolinas Attract 73 Million Tourists," *Amusement Business*, March 20, 2000, p. 20.

Hendrick, Bill, "The Fine Art of Enjoying the 'New' Myrtle Beach," *Atlanta Journal and Constitution*, May 7, 2000, p. K20.

Hodges, Jim, "Beach Music Official Becomes Popular Sound of South Carolina," *News Tribune*, March 28, 2001.

Kimes, Kent, "Beach Music May Shag into Classroom," (Myrtle Beach) *Sun News*, November 25, 2002, p. C1.

_____, "Return of Shag," (Myrtle Beach) *Sun News*, September 13, 2002, p. 4.

_____, "Shag and More," (Myrtle Beach) *Sun News*, October 25, 2002, p. 4.

Klepper, David, "Celebrating All Things Carolinian," (Myrtle Beach) *Sun News*, October 27, 2002, p. C2.

Mariscotti, Marisa, "Myrtle Beach: The Insider's Guide," *Dance Spirit*, September 2001.

Nickens, T. Edward, "The Jitterbug Met R&B," *Smithsonian*, September 2000, p. 16.

Ross, Alice, "Myrtle Beach," *Travel America*, November 2000, p. 46.

Selingo, Jeff, "North Myrtle Beach, the World's Widest Beach?," *Wilmington Morning Star*, August 25, 1996.

Ofu Island, Manu'a, American Samoa

Location

The three Manu'a Islands, a Polynesian triad known as American Samoa, are the most southerly of U.S. territorial possessions. They extend into the southwestern Pacific Ocean between Hawaii and New Zealand. A rugged black atoll formed over seven million years by clashing tectonic plates, Ofu angles northwest of Ta'u, the chief island, along a narrow channel and covers only three square miles. Ofu is so close to Olosega, the third island, that the two appear as one.

Most of Ofu's human habitation has occurred at the coastline, which is comprised of porous basalt, clay loam, and fine coral sand. Less accessible are steep-sided volcanic peaks that have remained dormant since 1911. A constant cloud drifts overhead from fertile old-world rain forests derived from African and Asian stock. A soft, misty fog enshrouds the peaks and falls back to the white, palm-edged shore in gentle, refreshing cascades. Ringed by narrow coastal plains, the island is surrounded by some of the Pacific's healthiest barrier reefs, called the "rain forests of the Ocean" for their complex ecosystems.

Contacts

American Samoa National Park
Pago Pago, American Samoa 96799
Phone: 011-684-6337082
Email: NPSA_Administration@nps.gov
http://www.nps.gov/npsa/

Pacific Island Support Office
Box 50165
300 Ala Moana Boulevard
Honolulu, Hawaii 96850-0053
Phone: 808-541-2693
808-541-3696
Email: melia_lane-kamahele@nps.gov
http://www.nps.gov/gis/metadata/npsa/con
    tours.html

Mythology

According to native storytelling, a highly developed Polynesian art form, Ofu

In American Samoa, Ofu Island is surrounded by some of the Pacific's healthiest barrier reefs, called the "rain forests of the Ocean" for their complex ecosystems (courtesy of Tracy L. Skaggs).

is the sacred center of the universe and the cradle of Polynesian civilization. The island is the spot where Tagaloalagi, the creator and supreme ocean god, separated sea and sky from rock and earth. In an idyllic setting, he shaped the first islanders, Luao and Luavai, forebears of a sturdy, large-bodied race. They evolved a unique *fa'a Samoa*, the Samoan way, which honored God, the *aiga* [extended family], and *faiga* [friendships].

With the first peppery drink squeezed from the tranquilizing kava root *(Piper methysticum)*, the creator initiated the *'ava* ceremony, a formal exchange of sentiments on spirituality and ancestry between male dignitaries. The ritual quaff, swallowed in one gulp from a polished coconut shell chalice, symbolized the island's life force and powers of regeneration. The initial sharing of the kava drink preceded servings of island largesse — bananas, breadfruit, creamy coconuts, fish, papayas, suckling pigs, yams, and taro, the staple crop that generates food for fried chips, greens, baked or boiled roots, and a grated dessert.

Among newly created animals, a day-flying fruit bat *(Pteropus samoensis)*, called the *pe'a vao* or flying fox, was sacred. It became so integral to island lore that young men displayed its stylized shape in elaborate *tataus* [tattoos], an art brought to Samoa from Fiji by the mythic conjoined twins Taema and Tilafaga. Because of their unique duality, tattoo artists observed a strict symmetry and harmony of design that conferred ceremonial significance and protected warriors like armor. In keeping with traditions, only tattooed males could participate in religious dance companies, where graceful movements of hand and arm expressed the bird in flight and the wave approaching the shore.

To make the triangular images, tattoo artists worked for weeks at the painful process of inserting the soot of burned candlenuts mixed with oil into skin designs across the torso and legs. For tools, the tatooist employed traditional wooden and bone awls, boar's tusk, or turtle shells containing up to twenty needles. Peripheral implements consisted of the sausau or palm leaf mallet, the tu'i or pestle for grinding pigments, the ipulama or dye cup, the tuluma or implement pot, and the autapulu, ausogi'aso tele, ausogi'aiso laititi, and aumogo, all types of tattooing combs. The lengthy ritual, concluding with the adornment of the navel, incorporated friends singing encouraging songs and the observance of gender-based taboos. The completed patterns suggested the circular flight of the bat, which island religion interpreted as a harbinger of recurrent life cycles.

History

Ofu probably received its first human inhabitants around 2000 B.C., when Melanesian islanders sailed east in double-hulled canoes from Southeast Asia via Fiji and Vanuatu. Lacking the "flat earth" theory that inhibited Europeans, Pacific canoeists, dubbed the "Vikings of the sunrise," attempted courageous journeys. Polynesian navigators made the Manu'a cluster a base and explored islands within the Polynesian triangle, which extends from Hawaii to New Zealand and Easter Island. Their example in myth, legend, chant, and song remains so powerful to Manu'ans that, during Independence Day celebrations each June, islanders hold the fautasi race in which teams row longboats in the style of their ancestors.

Traces of early Manu'ans exist in ceramic and stone on the islands south central shore. Upon its emergence in European geographies, the island of Ofu was a latecomer to world maps. It was discovered in late summer 1722 by Dutch sailor Jacob Roggeveen, admiral of the ships *African Galley, Eagle*, and *Thienhoven*. According to Karl Friedrich Behrens's *Histoire de l'Expedition de Trois Vaisseaux* [History of an Expedition of Three Vessels] (1737),

Roggeveen was on his way west from Chile to locate an exploitable southern continent for the Dutch West India Company. Because he recorded Ofu's location incorrectly, the Island remained free of European influence until the arrival in 1768 of French adventurers and cartographers Louis-Antoine de Bougainville and Jean-François Galaup de La Pérouse. To honor island canoe crews, Bougainville named the central Polynesian cluster Navigators' Islands. Later arrivals introduced waves of influenza, pertussis, mumps, measles, and dysentery, which decreased the island population and perplexed chiefs, who had no preventatives or treatments for European diseases.

Although the island cluster drew a steady stream of trading and whaling vessels, religion made a more lasting impact on Ofu than commerce. In the 1830s, traders and John Williams, an agent of the London Missionary Society, arrived aboard the schooner *Messenger of Peace*, the source of a deadly outbreak of influenza. His work among the unchurched required the first transcription of Samoan words to spread Christianity. Ultimately, the outsiders triumphed in turning a pagan sea culture into the Bible Belt of the South Seas. Williams recorded the transformation in the immensely popular *Narrative of Missionary Enterprises in the South Sea Islands: With Remarks upon the Natural History of the Islands, Origin, Languages, Traditions, and Usages of the Inhabitants* (1837), which went through several printings. Samoans maintained traditional dance, fire walking, and tattoos, but, by the 1870s, were fully proselytized by Catholic, Congregational, and Mormon evangelists. Zealous islanders launched their own mission drive to Melanesia.

America gained its place in Polynesian affairs by surveying the Samoan islands in 1839 under the leadership of scientist and sailor Charles Wilkes, head of the United States Exploring Expedition of 1838–1842. As commander of a fleet comprised of the *Peacock, Porpoise, Relief, Seagull,* and *Vincennes* and equipped by Congress, he sought new and uncharted whaling grounds and initiated a thorough exploration of Samoa. On March 2, 1872, Richard Worsam Meade, commander of the U.S.S. *Narragansett,* arranged with Chief Mauga for the establishment of a Samoan coaling station.

At the turn of the century, an international agreement of neutrality between America, Britain, and Germany awarded the Manu'a Islands to the United States as an unincorporated territory and location of a naval base. The strategic location proved valuable to the U.S. military, which stationed 20,000 soldiers, including members of the 2nd Marine Brigade, on the islands during World War II to prevent a Japanese takeover. The site proved valuable to communications links to the U.S. Pacific Fleet in early 1942 before the battle of Midway on June 4–7, the turning point in the Pacific war. In 1975, the Army Corps of Engineers returned for a peace-time mission, the construction of an artificial breakwater at Ofu Harbor, which hurricanes Ofa and Val pummeled in 1990 and 1991.

Archeology

In the 1970s, scholars began to doubt the montage of oral histories that explained the Polynesian canoe voyages across Oceania. Cobbled together from thin tissues of history and legend was a description of the Lapita culture, a Melanesian people from islands east of New Guinea. They dispatched colonists in 200 B.C. to eastern Pacific island clusters, reaching Fiji by 900 B.C. Over eleven centuries, these waves of ocean-going explorers advanced to the Society Islands and Rapa Nui, swung north from A.D. 300 to 600 to the Marquesan and Hawaiian chains, and veered south from the Cook Islands in A.D. 1200 to New Zealand, the final Melanesian landfall.

In summer 1986, Terry L. Hunt, an

anthropologist and paleo-environmentalist at the University of Hawaii, and Patrick Vinton Kirch, director of the Hearst Museum of Anthropology, excavated the beachfront To'aga Archeological Site and located stone, coral, bone, and shell fragments of adzes and abraders. Evidence of creative manufacture survives in fishhooks shaped from the *Turbo setosus* shell, pierced shells strung for jewelry, and remains of pottery that islanders either imported or made on Ofu. Coastal people subsisted on dogs and pigs, fish, sea urchins and mollusks, turtles, birds, and island plants. In deep pits, they fermented breadfruit, the island staple.

During subsurface study the following year and in 1989, researchers from the universities of Hawaii and California at Berkeley traced the wanderings of prehistoric islanders through an analysis of basalt adzes and flakes, items of daily utility and trade that passed from mainland Asia to Tonga and Samoa and on through the Polynesian diaspora to the Cook Islands, Tahiti, Hawaii, and Easter Island. Hunt and Kirch coauthored two texts on their digs, *The To'aga Site: Archaeological Investigations at an Early Polynesian Site in the Manu'a Islands, American Samoa* (1993) and *The Historical Ecology of Ofu Island, American Samoa* (1997).

Ecology

A biological wonderland, Ofu exudes the heady scent of wild ginger. Paogo or pandanus trees and bird's nest fern draped in lianas and decked in air plants and orchids rise above lichens and mosses that are soft underfoot to the bushwalker, hiker, and climber. Naturalists survey the rare toothbilled pigeon and the flying fox bat or fruit bat, which takes off in a tight fold and extends to three or four feet of wingspan. Revered as the mythic sentinel of the forest and pollinator and seed sower of island plants, the indigenous bat sank to near ex-

termination and became a *cause célèbre* for American intervention and conservation. Because the animals are easy daylight quarry from poachers, an international treaty protects the bats from both hunting and exportation.

In 1988, the creation of the National Park of American Samoa, a 10,500-acre reserve, produced two firsts — the first U.S. national park in the Southern Hemisphere and the nation's first contract-based park leased from nationals. The new entity encompasses sixteen percent of territorial land and fifteen percent of the island cluster's shoreline. The region's paleotropical flora is found nowhere else in the U.S. park system. The opening of the facility piqued interest, especially among conservations, but boosted island tourism to only 5,000 visitors per year.

Unique to the reserve is protected land that reaches from the shore over 35 acres of the Pacific sea floor. Under a complex cultural tenure system, Manu'ans maintain rights to natural resources for making mats and *fale* [open shelters], to shelling and fishing, and to food plants grown on established farmland. Islanders may also gather the curative herbs used in *fofo*, their folk medicine. Of particular efficacy are jatropha leaf for fever, ficus or banyan bark for dysentery, bottle gourd for stomach upset, moso'oi for asthma, red bentgrass for wounds, canna or hoya for swelling, and polo leaf for sunstroke. Applying these plants are skilled faith healers who study medicinal plants from ancient sing-song tradition and who learn the art of massage through woman-to-woman apprenticeships with practitioners.

One curative, the bark and wood of the mamala tree (*Homalanthus nutans*), traditionally treated hepatitis and yellow fever and holds out hope for an anti–AIDS drug. Harvard-trained American ethnobotanist Paul Alan Cox, a former Mormon missionary and professor at Brigham Young University, began studying the mamala in 1984 in hopes of finding a cure for cancer, the disease that killed his mother. Funded by the National Science Foundation Presidential Investigator Award, his project took him to Samoa in search of local faith healers and their plants. In his words, "I see ethnobotany — the study of the relationship between people and plants — as the key to the preservation of this vast collection of species as well as a pathway to halting many diseases" (Hallowell & Cray, 1997).

After lengthy field study, Cox collected 74 likely specimens of plants used in island poultices and infusions and shipped them to the National Cancer Institute for analysis. The most promising extract was prostratin from the mamala, a substance that appears to shield human cells from infection by the HIV virus. Shortly after his research showed positive results, islanders considered selling logging rights to hardwoods in their ancient rain forest in exchange for cash to build a village school. Cox launched a pay-back of the lease with his own money and donations and saved the trees. To assure islanders of income, he developed skin-care products from local botanical extracts. Manu'ans were so charmed by his gracious attitude and commitment to the island's well being that they named him Nafanua after an ancient protective warrior goddess.

Coastal Activities

The few ecotourists who venture to Ofu's national park each year enjoy an edenic world wrapped in curling vapor, shadowed by tree fern, and echoing with the call of the white-tailed tropic bird. No trails or signs direct enjoyment of the inviting interior. Naturalists observe the Pacific boa, banded snake eels, geckos, skinks, and green sea turtles. From August to November, spotters watch migrating humpback whales. Overhead, flights of the brown booby, frigatebird, honeyeater, lorry, noddy, petrel,

shearwater, fairy tern, and tropic bird loop above the shoreline, a favorite locale for kayaking. On the southern beach, scuba divers and snorkelers float among mushroom and staghorn coral alive with the bladed alogo, damselfish, manini, octopi, pone, puffer fish, skipjack and yellowfin tuna, and unicornfish, the most eye-catching of the bay's 890 piscatory species.

Once or twice each year, Samoans enjoy an island treat — hunting the shores for the palolo reef worm (*Eunice viridis*), a sixteen-inch marine annelid called the "caviar of the Pacific." The worm lives in the hard substrata of the coral shore. After breaking in half on "worm night" during the neap tide a week after the full moon in October or November, which is spring in the Southern Hemisphere, the palolo's lower portion rises and spawns at the water's surface. The mass reproductive process emits a salty smell and a brown foam of sperm and ova that floats on the sea. To catch the choice morsels, islanders arise before dawn and wade into the surf to net the worms with cheese cloth for stone-baking, frying, or eating raw.

SOURCES

"Agreement Will Share Profit from AIDS Drug with Samoan Healers," *Virus Weekly*, January 8, 2002, p. 8.

"American Samoa: Country Profile," *Asia & Pacific Review World*, September 6, 2000.

"American Samoan Island Feeling Neglected," *BBC Monitoring Asia Pacific*, July 17, 2002.

Anderson, Atholl, "The To'aga Site: Three Millennia of Polynesian Occupation in the Manu'a Islands, American Samoa," *Journal of the Royal Anthropological Institute*, Vol. 1, No. 4, December 1995, pp. 838–839.

Ayres, William S., "The To'aga Site: Three Millennia of Polynesian Occupation in the Manu'a Islands, American Samoa," *American Antiquity*, Vol. 60, No. 3, July 1995, pp. 583–584.

Bower, Bruce, "Polynesian Tools Tout Ancient Travels," *Science News*, March 2, 1996.

Chadwick, Douglas H., "The Samoan Way," *National Geographic*, July 2000, pp. 72–89.

"Corals That Tolerate High Temperatures," *Center for the Study of Carbon Dioxide and Global Change*, January 30, 2002.

Cox, Mary, "Friend of the Forest: Pe'a Vao," *Odyssey*, Vol. 10, No. 2, p. 20.

Craig, Peter, "Natural History Guide to American Samoa," http://www.nps.gov/npsa/book/index.htm.

Deihl, Joseph, "Kava and Kava Drinking," *Anthropological Quarterly*, Vol. 5, No. 1–4, 1932, pp. 61–68.

Hallowell, Christopher, "Rainforest Pharmacist," *Audubon*, Vol. 101, No. 1, January 1999, p. 28.

_____, and Dan Cray, "Seeking Answers in Ancient Rain-forest Remedies Is a Life's Work for the Plant Hunter," *Time*, Fall 1997, pp. 16–21.

Kirch, Patrick V., "An Ancestral Polynesian occupation Site at To'ago Ofu Island," *Archaeology in Oceania*, Vol. 25, 1990, pp. 1–15.

_____, and Terry L. Hunt, "Historical Ecology in the Pacific Islands: Prehistoric Environmental and Landscape Challenge," *Geographical Review*, April 1998.

Luders, David, "Legend and History: Did the Vanuatu-Tonga Kava Trade Cease in A.D. 1447?," *Journal of the Polynesian Society*, Vol. 105, No. 3, 1996, pp. 287–310.

Merewood, Anne, "A Park in the Pacific," *Sierra*, Vol. 77, No. 1, January–February 1992, pp. 16–17.

O'Meara, Donna, "Samoa," *People, Places, and Cultures*, Vol. 18, No. 9, May 2002, pp. 607.

"Pacific Islands Were Hardly Paradise," *USA Today*, Vol. 129, No. 2,663, August 2000, p. 14.

"Polynesians with a Purpose," *Discover*, Vol. 17, No. 6, June 1996.

Powell, Eric A., "Searching for the First New Zealanders," *Archaeology*, March/April 2001, pp. 40–47.

Smith, S. Percy, "Kava Drinking Ceremonies among the Samoans," *Journal of Polynesian Society*, Vol. 29, No. 114, June 1920, pp. 1–21.

Steadman, David W., et al., "New Species and Records of Birds from Prehistoric Sites on Niue, Southwest Pacific," *Wilson Bulletin*, Vol. 112, No. 2, June 1, 2000, p. 165.

Stevens, Charles J., "Historical Ecology in the Pacific Islands," *Journal of Political Ecology*, Vol. 6, 1999.

Stover, Merrily, "Individual Land Tenure in American Samoa," *Contemporary Pacific*, Vol. 11, No. 1, Spring 1999, p. 69.

"Tropical Paradise," *National Parks*, January–February 2001, p. 54.

Webb, Virginia-Lee, "Picturing Paradise," *USA Today*, Vol. 125, No. 2,614, July 1996, pp. 68–75.

Weisler, Marshall I., and Patrick V. Kirch, "Interisland and Interarchipelago Transfer of Stone Tools in Prehistoric Polynesia," *Proceedings of the National Academy of Sciences of the United States*, Vol. 93, No. 4, February 20, 1996, pp. 1381–1385.

Willis, Monica Michael, "The Plant Detective," *Country Living*, Vol. 21, No. 1, January 1998, pp. 18–19.

"Worn with Pride: Celebrating Samoan Artistic Heritage," http://www.oma-online.org/worn_with_pride_02.html.

Omaha Beach, France

Location

In northwestern Normandy, Omaha Beach lies east of Utah Beach and the Vire River along the Calvados coast, also called the Côte de Nacre [Mother-of-Pearl Coast]. Strong channel winds buffet the 100-foot bluffs, which overlook the flat hard-sand strand below. The beach faces the English Channel, the deep-water separation between England and the European continent that the French call La Manche [the sleeve]. From high cliffs, five passages offer outlets to the beach. Farther inland, the coastal towns St.-Laurent, Vierville, and Colleville face the Seine Bay nine miles northwest of Bayeux and northeast of Isigny.

Because of its lengthy shallows and reefs, the Normandy coast favored the D-Day landing of Allied forces on June 6, 1944. Along the six-mile stretch, the military focused on a 7,000-yard landing zone scored at intervals with parallel runnels. Because the shore led up to a wide expanse of coarse gravel shingle and a steep embankment already fortified by the Germans, forces struggled to take cover and to drive tanks and vehicles over loose rock. In the high ground beyond, spotty dunes, marshland, and tufts of high grass ringed the bluffs. Beyond the war's most dramatic combat zone lay a paved road, villas and stone houses, orchards and trees, and the infamous hedgerows that stymied the motorized advance into German-held territory.

Contacts

Brett A. Phaneuf
Institute of Nautical Archaeology
P. O. Drawer HG
College Station, Texas 77841-5137
Phone: 409-845-6694
Fax: 409-847-9260
Email: Brett@ocean.tamu.edu
       ina@tamu.edu
http://ina.tamu.edu/

Musée Memorial d'Omaha Beach
Rue de la Mer
14710 St. Laurent-sur-Mer, France
Phone: 02-31-21-97-44
Fax: 02-31-92-72-80
http://www.musee-memorial-omaha.com
Email: contact@musee-memorial-omaha.
       com

History

Omaha Beach, the aboriginal home of Celts, was once known as Salvador, a name that evolved into Calvados. Belying the peace of pastures and rolling farmlands is a long history of European hostilities acted out in northern Normandy. In 56 B.C., the area fell to Caius Julius Caesar, the Roman commander-in-chief who turned it into a Gallic province answerable to Rome. Passed to the Merovingian Franks in the A.D. 200s, the area belonged to the Neustrian kingdom, which carried on a protracted territorial war with Austrasia. By the 700s, the shores were a battleground of Viking raids on the Carolingian monarchy.

The Northmen who settled northwestern France were called Normans and their land, Normandy. The ambitious William, Duke of Normandy, launched an invasion over the English Channel on October 14, 1066, and killed King Harold II. Ruled by English kings, Normandy returned to local custody in 1144 after Geoffrey Plantagenet, the Count of Anjou, seized the area. The rich property, called the Angevin, passed to his son Henry II until Philip II Augustus annexed it for France in 1204. In 1259, the formal surrender took shape as the Treaty of Paris.

The back and forth struggle between England and France passed Normandy to the English early in the Hundred Years' War, but England lost the territory permanently on April 15, 1450, after a great defeat of Sir Thomas Kyriel at the battle of Formigny. By 1468, the land was an autonomous French province. One distant clash resulted in the offshore foundering of a warship of the Spanish Armada at Omaha Beach in July 1588, when England defeated Philip II's famed flotilla of 130 ships, a mass of 8,000 sailors similar in scope to the D-Day landing of 1944.

The Allies long anticipated D-Day in months of planning under command of Lieutenant Colonel Paul Williams Thompson, who won a Distinguished Service Cross. (*See also* MONTE CARLO, MONACO; WOOLACOMBE, DEVON.) The assault was the final face-to-face confrontation with invasive Nazis, a coordinated knockout blow that General Dwight David Eisenhower, supreme commander of the Allied expeditionary force, called Operation Overlord. The purpose of the strike at northern France was to prepare the way for an easterly plunge into Nazi Europe. The allies intended to end World War II by driving the Germans out of ill-gotten territory as far south as Greece and as far east as Poland and Romania. To combat the Allied push, Field Marshal Erwin Rommel, the German commander, employed engineer Fritz Todt to beef up coastal defenses by pocking hillside with bombproof pillboxes and blockhouses, locating machine-gun nests above the shoreline, constructing barriers and hull-piercing steel hedgehogs in the shallows, digging trenches for mortar emplacement, and submerging undersea barbed wire and acoustic and magnetic mines.

Omaha Beach was the largest of five landing zones chosen for the invasion of Nazi-occupied France and included Gold, Juno, Sword, and Utah beaches. To prepare the way, in April, the British Special Operations Executive ferried Anglo-French spy Violette Bushelle Szabo to Normandy by Lysander aircraft. She parachuted to Normandy and, under the code name Louise, infiltrated the German coastal defense. She then slipped safely back to England to report on likely snags to a beach assault. She returned to Limoges, France, on D-Day to supervise the French Resistance against the Reich Panzer Division, a phalanx of tanks that was motoring toward Omaha Beach to counter the invasion. Following her shootout with German soldiers, the Gestapo captured, tortured, and fatally shot 23-year-old Szabo through the throat at Ravensbrück concentration camp six months after D-Day.

In addition to spy missions, thousands of reconnaissance fliers determined how to block Luftwaffe support for the German coastal defense. About 48 hours before D-Day, advance submariners in 45-foot X-boats traversed the channel and hid in church spires from which to flash colored lights to the approaching armada. The Allies delayed the invasion for 24 hours because of bad weather. Preceding the predawn action at low tide under overcast skies on June 6, 1944, were night flights to Sainte-Mère-Église by the U.S. 82nd and 101st Airborne, which winged as low as thirty feet from the ground to knock out bridges over the Loire and Seine rivers. Thus, the night fliers prevented German troops from reinforcing the beach, which was obviously more territory than the overextended Reich could defend. Simultaneously, British commandos disabled Nazi communications and seized bridges over the Orne River and Caen canals.

On the night that forces massed for the invasion, minesweepers led the way as 1,000 Royal Air Force bombers struck Normandy's shore to neutralize gun emplacements that faced incoming Allied troops. Only ten minutes before the landing, offshore Hawker Typhoon fighter planes began pelting bridges, trains, tanks, armored cars, and light ships with a hail of three-inch unguided air-to-surface rockets. They struck the startled Germans at a strong point, the *Widerstandsnest* [resistance nest] 62, a major obstacle to the Allies manned by only 35 German gunners.

Meanwhile, the Allied high command amassed 73,000 Americans and 83,000 British and Canadian troops for a total of 156,000—the world's largest invasion armada. Of the total, 23,500 parachuted or flew to France; the other 132,500 entered from the sea. The target of allied troops, Omaha Beach was an American code name. On military maps, the shoreline from the Orne delta to the heavily infiltrated Cotentin promontory split at center, with Americans moving west under the direction of Lieutenant-General Omar N. Bradley, who assaulted the beachhead along with his men. The eastern sector was the target of the British and Canadians under General Sir Bernard Law "Monty" Montgomery. Quartered into Fox Red, Fox Green, Easy Red, and Easy Green sectors, the beach suffered its worst battering from high seas and a relentless pounding from crack German forces of the 352nd and 716th divisions. The combined effects jeopardized the invasion.

Naval, air, and amphibious forces relied on 10,000 planes and Operation Neptune, a ship-to-shore troop transport led by Admiral Sir Bertram Ramsay. Delivery of forces coordinated 4,126 landing craft, 1,200 warships, 804 transport vessels, 300 minesweepers, pontoon rafts called rhino ferries, amphibious trucks, and varied LSTs (Landing Ship Tanks), LCVPs (Landing Craft Vehicle Personnel), LCPs (Landing Craft Personnel), LCTs (Landing Craft Tanks), LCIs (Landing Craft Infantry), and LCFs (Landing Craft Flak). From the amassed vessels, some of the Army's toughest soldiers spilled out in rapid order, accompanied by *Collier*'s war correspondent Ernest Hemingway and combat photographer Robert Capa, who landed with the first brutal wave. Following the thirty-minute air bombardment, rank upon rank half-swam, half-waded into the fire-swept shallows with no cover and plunged or crawled up the beach against a merciless barrage.

Activity along Omaha preceded the drive of the U.S. First Infantry, which crossed from Weymouth and Portsmouth, England, in an easterly direction. Loaded with sixty to ninety pounds of battle gear, each soldier headed for shore in eighteen-knot winds at 6:30 A.M. Each thirty-man section of infantry consisted of rifle teams, bazooka and wire-cutting teams, flame-throwers, demolition experts, a 60mm mortar team, and one officer. The Sixth Naval Beach Battalion of 363 men survived at sixty percent original strength. Covering the columns wading through vigorous breakers were the five-inch guns of destroyers and battleships serving as floating artillery with a range up to seven miles away.

The U.S. Fifth Army faced near disaster from seasickness, the soporific effect of motion sickness pills, panic, and the sight of slaughter ahead. Of the 741st Armored Battalion's 32 amphibious tanks, only five lumbered out of the sea. Their radioed warning of hazardous conditions saved the men and tanks of the 742rd Tank Battalion. The Allies had to improvise to stay alive while capturing the strand. In daylight, infantry advanced on an enemy well dug in after months of preparation and beach fortification. Heavy artillery fire from the cliffs left dead and wounded strewn in the surf

and in the sand. Some men drowned in the advancing tide, which reduced the wide strand to a sliver. The smell of dismembered GIs tainted the sea air as subsequent waves in full battle dress leaped over the dead to press on. General Omar Bradley was so alarmed by the carnage that he began scrambling to withdraw and try again at a safer landing point.

At a terrible cost, D-Day proved effective. The plan to sweep over the German coastal defense was complete by nine A. M. Until afternoon, a traffic snarl on the shore prevented the British from moving southeast toward Caen, where a German Panzer division blocked the massed drive that would liberate western France from fascism. By late afternoon, surviving machine-gunners at *Widerstandsnest* 62 surrendered, although snipers continued to run the tangle of communication tunnels to delay the Allied victory. Along the cliffs of Omaha Beach, while Seabees directed traffic, medics doctored suffering men who awaited evacuation to aid stations, Red Cross tents, and field hospitals.

Losses didn't end on D-Day. At dawn on June 7, one of the largest troopships, the U.S.S. *Susan B. Anthony*, struck a mine amidships and sank east of Omaha Beach. The 2,000 men aboard the "Susie" survived and joined an uninterrupted stream of Allied troops to shore. Within two days of the assault, 200 landing craft and numerous heavy artillery were lost at sea or disabled on Omaha by heavy German resistance. Nonetheless, by June 16, a total of 300,000 men and 35,000 vehicles had made landfall on Omaha and Utah beaches, the beginning of the end for Nazi Germany.

American memorial services have kept alive the heroics of D-Day. On June 6, 1984, President Ronald Reagan stood at the U.S.-French cemetery to deliver a eulogy to England's Queen Elizabeth II, French President François Mitterrand, and other dignitaries, visitors, and families. Reagan reminded survivors that General Omar Bradley called every member of the invasion force a hero. A decade later, some 30,000 survivors of the conflict celebrated the fiftieth anniversary of the D-Day landing. Welcomed to the gala event by President Mitterrand and eighteen heads of state, participating veterans waded ashore, dropped from planes in parachutes, wept, cheered, and relived the turning point of the war.

At the Normandy American Cemetery near Omaha on July 7, 1994, President Bill Clinton led survivors in honoring over 9,000 comrades killed in a "savage place" (Clinton, 1994). He commented on their youth and willingness to defend democracy. Soberly, he noted:

> They were the fathers we never knew, the uncles we never met, the friends who never returned, the heroes we can never repay. They gave us our world. And those simple sounds of freedom we hear today are their voices speaking to us across the years [*ibid.*].

He stressed that D-Day started the fifty-year liberation of Europe that ended with the collapse of Soviet Russia.

Numerous first-person memoirs captured the pathos and glory of the Allied capture of Omaha Beach. Among the reflective, a naval cartographer, Lieutenant William Allison Bostick, a veteran of the 1943 invasion of Sicily, had been on hand at Omaha Beach for D-Day to draw two official landing charts. Amid chaos, he took the time to sketch the blanketed remains of 1,000 corpses that mortuary crews gathered and laid out in decent order. At a distance, more dead floated with the tide.

An 81-year-old former flight nurse, 2nd Lieutenant Evelyn Kowalchuk of the U.S. Army Air Corps, joined the 1994 reunion as one of 25 nurses in the 818th squadron who each staffed a C-47 alone. She recalled landing on D-Day plus one on perforated steel planks laid out on the sand near hundreds of white crosses. She com-

mented on the torso wounds, amputated limbs, frostbite, and the smell of blood from horribly maimed men. She treated them with morphine and blood transfusions, a technology in its infancy. Under makeshift conditions, she winced from whirls of beach grit from propellers and barely closed the door before the first of three airlifts took off for its two-hour flight to England. Planes carrying 42 casualties each flew under 5,000 feet to spare gaping chest wounds resulting from what Kowalchuk termed a "mean war" (Conley, 1994).

Archeology

D-Day left a jumble of war souvenirs in France. In 1970, a scrap-iron dealer, Jacques Lemonchois of Port-en-Bessin, Normandy, received a license from the French government to plunder undersea relics off Normandy's beaches. Declaring his profiteering legitimate, he battled historians and veterans with claims that he had a right to strip mementos as salvage. An international flap arose among survivors and families of dead sailors and soldiers who risked all at the D-Day landing. The Normandy Veterans Association labeled Lemonchois's cynicism a disgusting sacrilege.

Nonetheless, the profit-grabbing salvor continued operating his crane to retrieve parts of bottles, ships' bells, deck guns, tanks, Jeeps, and LSTS and more personal items, including wallets, helmets, field kits, shell cases, and rifles, which he sold or displayed in his museum, Musée des Épaves Sous-Marine du Débarquement [Museum of Underwater Wrecks of the Invasion]. Lemonchois also led divers on tours of World War II's detritus. Opponents of his rogue diving and grave-stripping operation clamored for the French government or the United Nations to pass the same protective laws that govern historic combat zones in England.

In 1999, Project Neptune 2K, a two-year archeological expedition of the Institute of Nautical Archeology (INA) at Texas A. & M. University, studied the war relics of Omaha Beach, where ninety vessels sank during the Normandy landing. The Aggie project began a race against gradual erosion of the site and the necessary removal of wrecks from shipping lanes. Conducted in 100 feet of water, the effort was a significant link between the university and a D-Day hero, Ranger leader James Earl Rudder, an Aggie alumnus who became university chancellor in 1959. He made history once more by turning an all-male school into a co-ed facility.

Led by Robert Neyland and Brett A. Phaneuf, INA participants applied once top-secret charts and maps plus geomagnetic counter-imaging and sonar to a study of the Normandy seabed. The area was still potentially hot with unexploded ordnance that fishermen dropped onto naval wrecks to rid them of two hazards, bombs and snags. Off shore, the INA team activated a remote-operated vehicle (ROV) to spot thirteen Sherman tanks and 25 World War II wrecks, including LCTs, a Rhino barge, and a Higgins boat, the main carriers of troops and tanks. Additional data from tidal charts and beach currents shed light on the natural forces at work during the landing that caused many units to drift east of their designated target zone. The purpose of the INA team's location and identification of cargo-laden ships, artillery, and equipment was the preservation of an underwater combat site for history.

From mid–May to June 30, 2000, the Aggie team, sponsored by a Texas Sea Grant, the Discovery Channel, and the British Broadcasting Corporation in cooperation with the Naval Historical Center's Underwater Archaeology Branch, set to work laying out research grids of a quarter of the historic landing area. Analysts examined and photographed a weak spot in Allied planning — 27 amphibious Duplex Drive or DDs, the boxy diesel-powered tanks of the 741st Armored Battalion that didn't survive the choppy surf on D-Day. Some of the sunken 35-ton hulks, which were launched over three miles out to sea, were less than a mile from their expected landing. Analysts determined that engineers intended the awkward tanks for launch in mild white-caps, but six-foot high seas swamped them like bobbing toys. The tanks drifted on the current to the east and took the brunt of the sea's power abeam at the weakest point in their sides.

Phaneuf's attempt to protect and catalog elements of the D-Day landing immediately piqued public interest, particularly in the navy's role in the massive off-shore operation on D-Day. He was able to explain why the advance stalled during the early morning at Omaha Beach. For relatives of navy heroes reported killed or missing at sea, the INA study honored men who received little of the adulation accorded the strike force. In October 2001, Phaneuf presented "Uncovering D-Day: Project Neptune 2K," a lecture on his correlation of the undersea archaeological excavation with historical and technical aspects of the invasion. On June 6, 2001, "Deadline Discovery" aired on the Discovery Channel, complete with photos of the bones of vessels that have survived a half century in the murky channel. A new segment aired on June 5, 2002, entitled "D-Day Beneath the Waves," featuring combat film footage, battle reenactments, and interviews with German and Allied veterans.

Coastal Activities

Because D-Day was a brief human effort, the shoreline returned to normal after the last soldier strode inland and ambulance crews retrieved the wounded and dead. Tides leached away bloody stains. Sea birds circled over the surf; wildflowers bloomed again on the headlands. Solid evidence of the great military engagement at Omaha Beach was limited to bunkers on the headlands and battered hulks on the sea floor.

As a reminder to history, the name "Omaha" attached permanently to the peaceful strand once called Calvados. Currently, although sea and land tours are numerous, few people disturb the quiet or even set foot on near-sacred ground that is devoid of commercialism. Among the sand dunes, a mass of craters, some up to three feet wide, attest to an aerial bombardment that preceded the Allied landing. Munition dumps, trenches, and bunkers remain from the German beach defense. Offshore, barriers and a concrete tank carrier lie submerged in the shallows.

Historians, photographers, patriots, and families of World War II military heroes flock to Omaha Beach to study the most fully reported decisive battle in world history. Between St. Laurent and Vierville, tourists visit the Musée Memorial d'Omaha Beach at the very spot where soldiers disembarked from landing craft. People from many nations examine German and Allied uniforms, medals and badges, weapons, and military equipment and vehicles. Mannequins posed in combat readiness demonstrate the tensions and exertions of warriors. Outside the museum, an American 155mm. "Long Tom" howitzer and a Sherman tank model authentic invasion artillery.

A focus of D-Day memorabilia is Ranger Monument, a tall granite stele atop the 100-foot crag and concrete bunker at Pointe du Hoc, which overlooks the sea. Dedicated by the French to Lieutenant Colonel James Earl Rudder and to his 225-man 2nd Army Ranger Battalion, the monument attests to the loss of 140 "Rudder's Rangers" who died in the path of six German howitzers encased in concrete. After weeks of rehearsing at Woolacombe Bay, Devon, the rangers were the only force trained for a suicide mission — to silence the Germany artillery nest and secure the sheer cliffside and

a stretch of thirty acres. The once disputed turf became a peacetime memorial to ranger grit.

A little over a mile west among Austrian pines, French tamarisk, and sea buckthorn, the American Military Cemetery covers 172 acres and displays perfectly aligned Carrara marble markers for 9,386 American dead on the spot where the allies triumphed over the enemy. The fallen came from all fifty states of the Union, Washington, D.C., Canada, England, and Scotland. Of the total, 307 were unidentified, 33 were brothers, two were father and son, four were female, three were posthumous Congressional Medal of Honor recipients. Amid elm and cypress, the Garden of the Missing posts the names of 1,557 Americans carried away on the tides. A reflecting pool, colonnade, and bronze statue sculpted by Donald de Lue honor American youth. At the entrance to a green sward filled with casualties killed within hours of each other, the lintel poses the inscription "Mine Eyes Have Seen the Glory of the Coming of the Lord" from Julia Ward Howe's Civil War–era "Battle Hymn of the Republic." A German burial site fifteen miles away holds the remains of 21,000 war dead.

SOURCES

Allen, Thomas B., "Untold Stories of D-Day," *National Geographic*, June 2002, pp. 2–37.

Ambrose, Stephen E. *D-Day June 6, 1944: The Climactic Battle of World War II.* New York: Touchstone, 1995.

Bass, Richard T. *Spirits of the Sand: The History of the U.S. Army Assault Training Centre.* Exeter, Eng.: Lee, 1992.

Bernage, George. *Omaha Beach.* Thionville, France: Heimdal, 2002.

Cawthon, Charles, "On Omaha Beach," *American Heritage*, Vol. 34, No. 6, 1983, pp. 49–64.

Clinton, Bill, "Remarks by the President at U.S. National Cemetery above Omaha Beach ," http://www.hatemonitor.org/pres_activity/clinton/us_national_cemetery.html, 1994.

Conley, Jay, "D-Day Behind the Scenes," *Roanoke Times*, May 20, 2001.

"D-Day Memorial Creators to Receive Legion of Honor Awards," *Associated Press*, October 5, 2002.

Fussell, Paul, "The Other Side of War," *Atlantic*, February 1997.

Jones, Tim Kilvert. *Normandy: Omaha Beach*. Havertown, Pa.: Casemate, 1999.

Lewis, Adrian R. *Omaha Beach: A Flawed Victory*. Chapel Hill: University of North Carolina Press, 2001.

Marshall, S. L. A., "First Wave at Omaha Beach," *Atlantic*, November 1960.

"Medal Round," *Texas Monthly*, May 2001, p. 46.

"Naval Secrets of D-Day Landing Emerging from Coastal Depths, As Archaeologists Continue Omaha and Utah Beach Survey," *Science Daily*, June 25, 2001.

Omaha Beachhead. Washington, D.C.: War Department, 1945.

Phaneuf, Brett, "D-Day, the Untold Story," http://www.bbc.co.uk/history/archaeology/marine_dday_underwater_01.shtml.

_____, and Robert S. Neyland, "Neptune 2K: The Underwater Archaeology of D-Day," *Under Water*, March/April 2001.

Sharp, Drew, "Lesson of Omaha Beach Hits Home," *Detroit Free Press*, July 26, 2002.

"Tania Gets the Medal," *London Daily Herald*, May 3, 1950.

"The Tanks That Didn't Land on D-Day," *BBC News*, May 30, 2002.

"This Is the Army, Mr. Jones," http://www.lynchburg.edu/historyctr/chronicle/ww2_2.htm.

Viegas, Jennifer, "Underwater Footage Reveals D-Day Wreckage," *Discovery News*, November 21, 2002.

"War Sea Graves Pillaged," *London Daily Mirror*, November 2, 2000.

Zoccola, Mary, "Using New Technology to Document the Wreckage of the Normandy Invasion," *Wavelengths*, December 2001.

Ostia, Italy

Location

A coastal village of northwestern Latium near Lazio, Italy, Ostia Antica, Rome's vestibule and emporium, was originally built along the Tyrrhenian Sea. It was named from the Latin *os* [mouth] because it served as a defensive outpost guarding the estuary of the Tiber River. Arising over salt-pans, swamps, and sandy stretches, the town lay west of Rome at the end of the Via Ostiensis or Ostian Way and shared the fortunes of its host city.

After a lengthy period of wars, the prosperous port developed into the *horreum* [warehouse] district of Republican and Imperial Rome, the nerve center that lay fourteen miles to the east of the sea. During the Republic, the town received *navicularii* [sea transports] that ferried in grain to feed the growing Mediterranean area and Rome's ambitious and widespread army. After 27 B.C., Ostia changed once more into a cosmopolitan center that interspersed people of many nations, races, and religious beliefs.

As the delta eroded and silted in, Ostia was newly situated four miles inland. Because sandbars inhibited water traffic, the harbor lost its steady influx of ships from Alexandria, Cagliari, Carthage, Narbonne, Porto Torres, and Sabratha. The warehouse complex, which no longer stored sacks of grain, fell to ruin. Broad highways altered the ancient traffic pattern that once flowed from Rome to the coast by dirt road or river barge. The Tiber changed course and became impassable by deep-draft vessels, thus diverting loading and warehousing to deeper seaports.

Contacts

Ostia Antica Ruins
Viale dei Romagnoli
717 Ostia, Roma
Phone: 39-06-32810
         39-06-56358036
http://www.ticketeria.it/ostiaruins-eng.asp

Ministry of the Cultural Activities and Heritage
Archaeological Superintendency of Ostia
Via dei Romagnoli 717-00119
Phone: 06-56358099
Fax: 06-5651500
Email: ostia.scari@agora.stm.it
http://itnw.roma.it/ostia/scavi

History

According to Roman legend compiled by Livy, author of *Ab Urbe Condita* [From the City's Foundation] (ca. A.D. 14), Ancus Marcius, fourth of the city's fabled kings planned Ostia around 620 B.C. As shown by archeological evidence, however, the city's foundation seems to date to 338 B.C., when Rome defeated the Etruscans and Volsci and mastered the sea. The harbor for the emerging Mediterranean power demanded a rectangular fort to guard the west coast approach from marauding Gauls. During Roman wars with the Veii and the people of Anzio, the beach settlement provided a vital link for communications and goods shipped up the river. In 278 B.C., Carthage anchored its navy at the harbor while aiding Rome in conquering Pyrrhus, a Hellenistic conqueror from Argos.

Within two years, the former citadel of Ostia had become a humble settlement. It recurred in history in summer 260 B.C., when a huge new armada of 100 quinqueremes and thirty triremes sailed from Ostia to fight the growing menace of Carthage, which vied with Rome for domination of the Mediterranean. In 217 and 212 B.C., Ostia handled convoys loaded with military provisions and supplies posted to garrisons in Hispania and received badly needed Sardinian and Sicilian grain. In 211 B.C., the proconsul and general Publius Cornelius Scipio made the port a departure point for thirty quinqueremes in a doomed attempt to hold off Hannibal.

Ostia was Rome's first maritime colony. As of 150 B.C., commented historian Polybius, the rough fort and dockyard became a town and warehouse center with gridded streets. Planners laid out the standard rectangular *castrum* [military camp] as a coast guard station centered by a cross of straight streets leading to four gates in the tufa block walls. The port flourished as a salt production site supplying much of central Italy.

Succeeding wars kept Ostia in a state of metamorphosis. After the Roman general Gaius Marius sacked Ostia in 87 B.C., the Senate turned it into a navy base protected by a 1.5-mile city wall that Lucius Cornelius Sulla erected after 83 B.C. Despite ongoing fortification, Cilician pirates infiltrated the port and swamped the Roman fleet in 67 B.C., obliging Gnaeus Pompey to accept the Senate's command to sweep the sea of brigands and freebooters. In the time of Julius Caesar, the port needed excavation and harbor re-engineering. The biographer Plutarch explains that Caesar was assassinated before putting into action a plan to "clear the coast at Ostia of all the hidden rocks and shoals that made it unsafe for shipping and to form ports and harbors fit to receive the large number of vessels that would frequent them" (1959, p. 231).

As Rome shifted its governance from republic to empire, Ostia expanded from simple piers and homes to a brick and concrete market complex. The transport of granite, marble, and porphyry from Asia Minor, Greece, and North Africa to Rome's imperial remodeling projects increased dockside activity. Like Rome, the evolving port metropolis ran out of room to expand and began scaling upward from the typical *domus* [one-story house] with *insulae* [apartment complexes], the typical mercantile class high-rises constructed by improved building techniques. After the rise of Augustus Caesar, his propagandist Virgil authored the *Aeneid* (19 B.C.), which glorified the workaday atmosphere of Ostia as the site where the Trojan hero Aeneas made landfall when he discovered Latium.

Made convenient by communal baths, dyeworks and *fullonicae* [laundries], a municipal senate and basilica, and the tufa-and-brick Augustan theater, the city center lay along a highway. It arose across a series of bridges beyond the Isla Sacra, a necropolis where rich families buried bodies in chamber tombs and the poor enurned the

Ostia Antica, Rome's vestibule and emporium, was the warehouse district of Republican and Imperial Rome (courtesy of Justin Reed).

ashes of cremated loved ones, leaving the neck of the burial *amphora* [storage jar] open to receive ritual libations. Scattered throughout a hive of workshops were stevedores and divers, bakers, knife grinders, hardware sellers, rope dealers, tanners, and shoemakers. A multicultural mix of travelers, foreign traders and merchants, soldiers, customs inspectors and duty agents, stock managers and actuaries, and residents passed among the inns and bars and in and out the Marine Gate.

Outsiders arriving in Rome imported a wide range of devotional styles and a demand for shrines, altars, and temples suited to exotic deities. As Rome prospered during the first years of the empire, at Ostia's temples, newcomers pursued the worship of Vulcan, the Bona Dea, Venus, the Dioscuri, and Hercules. Demand for new divinities added the Persian soldier's god Mithras, cel-

ebrated with ritual bull slaughter, and the Egyptian cults of Serapis, Isis, Attis, and Cybele, Phrygia's Magna Mater, whom worshippers adored through self-flagellation and ecstatic dance. During Tiberius's reign, he re-emphasized the city's Roman origins by building the Temple of Roma and Augustus, who had advanced from emperor to godhead.

Ostia remained on the rise with explosive growth. Furthering Rome's economy, the massive colonnaded Forum of the Corporations dealt in drugs, fish, fur, gold, grain, ivory, melons, mirrors, oil, silk, and wood. During Caligula's reign around A.D. 40, city planners added an aqueduct and ferry service. Because of heavy silting, any goods from vessels moored at Ostia had to be offloaded onto cumbrous river transports for sailing or towing, an expensive and time-consuming maneuver requiring the concerted efforts of mules, oxen, and slaves. In A.D. 52, the Emperor Claudius came to power during a serious grain shortage. Two years later, he developed the most up-to-date artificial port in the empire as a conduit to feed the city. As a hedge against periodic flooding, the port gained two moles, and a four-tiered lighthouse that, according to the biographer Suetonius, was modeled on Alexandria's Pharos. [*See also* ALEXANDRIA, EGYPT] Upon the emperor's death, his successor Nero completed the refurbishment in A.D. 54.

The improved imperial harbor was capable of handling huge loads of imported Egyptian grain, North African olives and oil, Asian spices and balsam, and wine from Gaul and Hispania. Unfortunately for Rome, previous warnings from engineers proved the project flawed and the investment risky. The surf pounded Claudius's jetties, limiting access. The historian Tacitus's *Annals* (A.D. 109) chronicled the sinking of 200 corn vessels at anchor during a storm in A.D. 62. Sea traffic had to divert from the blocked Tiber Mouth to Puteoli farther south along the Campanian coast.

Though compromised by nature, Ostia's port remained in constant service into the second century of the Roman Empire. Trajan, the fabled *Optimus Princeps* [best prince], further ennobled himself by digging a canal, called the *Fossa Trajana* [Trajan's ditch], connecting the city to an artificial river harbor built of seven-ton blocks of travertine. He modernized the north side of the harbor by constructing a double highway to a new hexagonal drydock on the inner side of Claudius's wharves. Trajan's addition featured dockside warehousing and a world-class naval reception center with numbered berths capable of holding 200 seagoing freighters. From his efficient inner harbor, merchants exported fine Italian wines, *garum* [fermented fish sauce], pottery, and metalware. Increased business and immigration generated

a populace of 50,000 citizens; large slave gangs of stevedores staffed quays bustling with riverfront trade.

Prosperity enabled public-spirited citizens to adorn the city with plazas, altars, public baths and a twenty-seat latrine, and *thermopolia* [food bars]. Artists and architects added inscribed frescoes, travertine cornerstones and porticos, fountains, courtyards, and statuary. Apartment dwellers inhabited concrete and brick-veneered multistory complexes as tall as six levels and adorned their ten- and twelve-room flats with wall paintings, murals, inlaid marble, and polychrome mosaic paving laid by artisanal guilds from the Via Marmorata. The city took on new names, beginning with Portus Romanus [the Roman port], Portus Urbis Romae [port of the city of Rome], and Portus Ostiensis Augusti [Augustus's Ostian port] and shortening to the simplified Portus. After A.D. 117, Hadrian, the expansionist, supplied the luxurious Baths of Neptune completed in A.D. 133 and added mundane warehouses, granaries, and a company of *vigiles* [firemen] to protect tall buildings, ground-floor *tabernae* [shops], shipyards, and highly flammable grain supplies. Hadrian left his successor, Antoninus Pius, to complete a modest pantheon and a capitolium honoring Juno, Jupiter, and Minerva and possibly housing the city's treasury and archives.

Upon the port's decline during an economic downturn in the A.D. 200s, building shifted from warehousing and piers to upscale housing. Within a century, the arrival of Jewish workers, merchants, and moneylenders created the demand for an *archisynagogos* or congregation leader, Plotius Fortunatus, and the addition of a sizeable ocean-front synagogue with Torah shrine, the first Jewish worship center constructed in the West. Italian archeologist Maria Floriani Squarciapino, director of the Department of Antiquities of Ancient Ostia, unearthed the remains in 1961–1962 and first described the structure in *La Sinagoga di Ostia* (1964).

The worship center had to coexist with paganism and Christianity, an emerging faith. Christian ferment was obvious on the coast from the religious writings of Marcus Minucius Felix, who set at Ostia the passionate apologia *Octavius* (ca. A.D. 245), one of the first Christian literary monuments. During the persecutions of A.D. 269, Ostia welcomed the burial of early Christian martyrs Aurea and Cyriacus. In A.D. 388, Christians added the Constantinian basilica honoring John the Baptist and saints Peter and Paul, a Christian church at the Marine Gate, and the tomb of Monica, mother of St. Augustine of Hippo, who resided in the city in the months following her son's conversion.

As barbarians pressed around Rome in the A.D. 400s, both the economy and residents of Ostia dwindled because of the impossibility of defending the city from attack and from encroaching malaria, a more insidious adversary. The pagan poet Rutilius Namatianus, author of *De Reditu* [The Return] (A.D. 417), noted the sad state of a former Roman boomtown, with its broken water pipes and heaped rubble. After its abandonment, the city remained a ghost town until A.D. 830, when Pope Gregory the Great erected a fortified town, Gregoriopolis, upriver as a defense against invaders and pirates. When Saracens attacked Ostia in A.D. 847 in a prelude to the sacking of Rome, Pope Leo IV formed a coalition of navies from Amalfi, Gaeta, and Naples and defeated the insurgents in a grand victory celebrated in fresco at the Vatican by the painter Raphael.

In the mid–1480s, when forces from Genoa, Naples, and Pisa besieged and looted Ostia, Pope Julius II hired Florentine architect and engineer Baccio Pontelli to erect a huge brick *castellum* [defense tower], one of the world's first modern forts. After the digging of the Fiumicino canal in 1613,

domestic builders and scavengers used ancient Ostia as a convenient marble and stone quarry. Renaissance sculptors cut costs by recycling choice blocks for projects.

Frequent flooding preserved Ostia by steadily engulfing its 170 acres in muck. The city's value as a glimpse of ancient Roman life did not emerge until the 1810s, when Pope Pius VII launched excavations of the site, which belonged to the Vatican. In 1909, experts made a scientific study of the city's growth. Under scholarly excavators Giuvonni Becatti, Italo Gismondi, Dante Vaglieri, and Alessandro Q. Visconti, investigation and reclamation continued during the first half of the twentieth century. The site burgeoned in 1939 during Guido Calza's unearthing of 600,000 cubic yards of soil from whole blocks of the Imperial Forum and the disclosure of seventy acres of the original city. He restored tesserae of old mosaic flooring, reinforced painted walls, and lifted fallen balconies, ceilings, and columns into their original positions.

Coastal Activities

Currently, Ostia retains its mercantile reputation in part from activity at the Mercati Generali, which bears boxed fruit and vegetables over the Via Ostiense to stall markets in Rome. Tourism flourishes in Ostia Antica's streets, where sixty percent of the ancient domestic and commercial architecture has been excavated. At the National Museum of Ostia, antiquarians, archeologists, and tourists visiting the Tyrrhenian shores view carved bas reliefs, sarcophagi, portrait busts, terra cotta nymphaea, and 600 sculptures and sacred objects retrieved from digs. The Museo delle Navi [Museum of Ships] reprises the construction of warships that patrolled the Tyrrhenian Sea as well as the sailing equipment and supplies of food and water loaded onto the fishing skiffs and fluvial barges that carried goods into Ostia Antica and up the Tiber to Rome.

Since 1916, a coastal resort three miles southwest of ancient Ostia has drawn picnickers and city families to the Lido di Roma, the soft, inviting brown beach that stretches parallel to Leonardo da Vinci Airport. At the shore, which is a short train ride from the city, thick maquis growth protects the sand from erosion. The strand offers standard tourist fare, including ice cream bars and patisseries, a square wharf and promenade, Cineland multiplex entertainment center, discos, and a tropical aquarium. More active amusements range from camping and birding in the surrounding greenwood of a state nature preserve to seaplane races, an annual airshow, judo and kung fu championships, and a windsurfing championship each August. From the coast, ferries and hydrofoils take visitors to the Pontine Islands of Ponza, Ventotene, and Zanone.

SOURCES

Clayton, Peter. *Treasures of Ancient Rome*. New York: Gallery Books, 1986.

Dal Maso, Leonardo B., and Robert Vighi. *Archeological Latium*. Florence, Italy: Bonechi, 1979.

Gessert, Genevieve S., "The Fasti Ostienses and the Forum of Ostia," *American Journal of Archaeology*, Vol. 105, No. 2, April 2001, p. 284.

Hale, William Harlan, ed.-in-chief. *The Horizon Book of Ancient Rome*. New York: Doubleday & Company, n. d.

Koloski-Ostrow, Ann Olga, "Talking Heads: Interpreting the Paintings in the Terme dei Sette Sapienti at Ostia," *American Journal of Archaeology*, Vo.. 105, No. 2, April 2001, p. 261.

Laird, Margaret L., "Imaging a History of Seviri Augustales at Ostia Antica," *American Journal of Archaeology*, Vol. 105, No. 2, April 2001, p. 284.

Plutarch. *Lives of the Noble Romans*. New York: Dell, 1959.

Runesson, Anders, "The Oldest Original Synagogue Building in the Diaspora," *Harvard Theological Review*, Vol. 92, No. 4, October 1999, p. 409.

Van Der Meer, L. Bouke, "Travertine Cornerstones in Ostia Antica: Odd Blocks,"*American Journal of Archaeology*, Vol. 106, No. 4, October 2002, pp. 575–580.

Watts, Donald J., and Carol Martin Watts, "A Roman Apartment Complex," *Scientific American*, Vol. 255, December 1986, pp. 132–139.

White, L. Michael, "Reading the Ostia Synagogue," *Harvard Theological Review*, Vol. 92, No. 4, October 1999, p. 435.

_____, "Synagogue and Society in Imperial Ostia: Archaeological and Epigraphic Evidence," *Harvard Theological Review*, Vol. 90, No. 1, January 1997, pp. 23–58.

Phuket, Thailand

Location

A lightly hilled island off southwestern Thailand on the Malay Peninsula along the Andaman Sea, Phuket is both a popular resort and seaport. It was alternately known to Malays as Ujong Salang [Cape Salang] and to European expeditioners as Junkceylon or Jonkcelaon, a name derived from cartographer Claudius Ptolemy's *Geographia* (ca. A.D. 150), in which he referred to the cape of *Jang Si Lang*. Currently named for the Malay *bukit* [big island or hill], the island lies in the way of equatorial sea breezes, which cool stilted fishing villages that dot the coastline.

Phuket is blessed by nature. Mangrove swamps enrich islanders with crabs, fish, prawns, and shellfish; the sea provides wealth from pearl fishing beds. Harbors receiving rice and manufactured goods export charcoal, coconut, cultured pearls, fish, lumber, pepper, and rubber. The most valuable resource, tin, Thai workers dig from gravel pits or dredge from the seabed. Since the 1970s, when outsiders discovered Phuket, tourism began outpacing tin mining and luring miners into coastal employ.

Contacts

Tourism Authority of Thailand
1600 New Phetburi Road
Makkasan, Rachathewi
Bangkok 10310, Thailand

Phone: 66-2250-5500
Fax: 66-2250-5511
Email: assist@tat.or.th
http://www.tat.or.th/about/index2.htm

History

In prehistory, Phuket was the home of Semang pygmies and the nomadic Chao Nam sea gypsies, who paddled log houseboats along the shore while they spearfished and searched for shellfish and the sacred sea turtle. Exploiters valued Phuket from the Stone Age for the veins of tin that lie close to the island's surface. Pirates called Saliteers followed in the wake of tin entrepreneurs to rob ships of valuable ores. In early recorded history, sailing charts listed the island as a waystation for becalmed crews and a handy source of caulking, firewood, hides, and fresh water.

Hindu explorers and sailors from India settled Phuket around 100 B.C., marking the territory with worship sites sacred to the god Vishnu. By the 1500s, the island was part of Siam's Ayutthayan realm and its emerging faith in theravada Buddhism. When Malays seized the island, they left Laksamana of Quedeh in control. The enslaved islanders bided their time, then repossessed their land in a fierce night-time raid. The Malays were so deceived by the seemingly mild-mannered Thais that they fled by dawn, leaving behind sacks of plunder. In 1626, the Dutch established a coastal station on the island. A century later, European traders and Chinese emigres engulfed the population.

According to Thai legends from the 1780s, at the death of island governor Phraya Pimonkhan, his widow, Khunying Chan (also Kunying Jan), the granddaughter of the Sultan of Quedah, realized the menace of offshore powers. When the Burmese threatened in early April 1785, the queen and her sister, Khunying Mook, mustered an army of women. Lacking weapons, they daubed sticks with tar and deceived their enemy into believing they were heavily armed. The all-female army achieved victory on March 13. As a result, Siam's King Rama I decorated the women for heroism.

Upon the arrival of Sir Francis Light of Suffolk, England, an agent of the British East India Company and captain of the British trader H. M. S. *Country Ship*, the heroine Chan match-mated the handsome sailor with a local beauty named Martina Rozells, the Siamese-Portuguese Princess of Quedah. With the queen's assistance, the newlyweds set up a prosperous enterprise at Suffolk House and reared five children. In May 1786, England named Captain Light as the island's superintendent. Historically noteworthy was his eldest son, William Light, founder of Adelaide, Australia. In 1809, the Burmese made one last attempt to seize Phuket. After a major failure, in 1810, they withdrew.

Ecosystem

In the past two centuries, entrepreneurs have extracted wealth from Phuket by methods that increasingly endangered the ecosystem. In the late 1880s, tin mine owners employed 30,000 Chinese and Malaysian immigrants in virtual slave labor to unearth valuable veins. Tin mining and cultured pearl farming continued to stir dreams of wealth into the twentieth century. The greedy turned to push nets and dynamite and cyanide fishing and to trawlers that indiscriminately trapped hatchlings and killed dolphins and sea turtles.

By the 1990s, islanders were beginning to embrace ecologically sound policies as good for the planet as well as for the preservation of local resources. In 1997, the Muslim Ao Goong Fisher Folk Society fought off new-wave commercial tiger prawn farms that bulldozed around eighty percent of mangrove forests to clear land for artificial ponds. Angering the island greens were farm managers who compromised the environment by spreading pesticides and clogging waterways with breeding farm waste that tainted drinking water, polluted coconut groves, and killed fish in the bay. In a system of participatory restoration, villagers established a patrolled sea life preserve extending from the shoreline three miles out to sea.

Replacing exploiters with ecotourism, Phuket's residents marketed their region's clean waters and pristine shores. High on the list of photogenic spots is Phangnga Bay. In a gently flowing current, saltwater has carved unique rock formations and hollowed out caves and grottoes in limestone islands and shaped stalactites and headlands as tall as 950 feet. Sea turtles nest near protected mangrove swamps on a nine-island group called Similan at the Ao Phangnga National Park, where the James Bond classic *The Man with the Golden Gun* (1974) was filmed. Tourist accommodations include upscale hotels as well as habitat-friendly grass-thatched huts and live-aboard houseboats. Only ten weeks after a tsunami struck on December 26, 2004, the tourist trade resumed full operation.

Coastal Activities

Visitors to Phuket enjoy canoeing to caves and grottoes, boating and cruising, motorcycling, windsurfing, sailing, and cable waterskiing along with inland elephant trekking, cliff climbing, mountain biking, monkey shows, ox-carting, and Thai boxing. While bats circle in the late evening sky in search of insects, languid moonlight tours of Phangnga Bay pass stilted fishing villages, the landmark crag of Khao Tapu, and prehistoric calligraphy along Khao Khian [Written Mountain]. In the 140 acres of Phuket FantaSea, a Kamala Beach theme park, families can view elephants and buffaloes, a tiger, colorful birds, and a troupe of 500 dancers. At a variety of venues, serious birders can survey some of Thailand's 925 species, which include the flowerpecker, flycatcher, hornbill, kingfisher, reef egret, and whimbrel.

Along Patong Beach, power-snorkeling using oxygen from a shore compressor introduces neophyte divers to anemones, crabs, lobsters, nurse sharks, octopi, parrot fish, puffers, rays, and sea turtles on the red coral-laced sea bottom. More adventurous scuba divers explore the waters, canyons, and rocky pinnacles of Richelieu Rock, Shark Point, and the Burma Banks, home to the bannerfish, barracuda, batfish, cuttlefish, fusilier, ghost pipefish, glassy sweeper, gorgonian, harlequin shrimp, horse-eye jack, Moorish idol, seahorse, snapper, and surgeonfish as well manta ray and silvertip and whale shark.

Nature tours suggest a wide range of possibilities, such as orchid farms and a reptile and butterfly reserve. Excursions to off-island pearl farms demonstrate the deliberate injection of irritants into pearl shells to cause the exudation of pearlescent fluid around each object. Experts monitor the layering process and remove the finished pearl for grading and sale. At the Phuket Seashell Museum, naturalists enjoy 2,000 specimens featuring oversized pearls, fossil gastropods and nautiluses, trilobites, sedimentary rock, giant clams, vase and volute shells, turbans, and other rare beachcombing from Phuket and Thai waters.

SOURCES

"Andaman's Amazing Anemones," *Benjarong Magazine*, Vol. 5, No. 11, September 2002.

Ehrlich, Paul Charles, "Violence Erupts in Thailand over Phuket Tantalum Plant," *American Metal Market*, Vol. 94, June 26, 1986, p. 5.

"Exotic Nightlife or Isolated Beaches," *Travel Trade Gazette UK & Ireland*, October 18, 1999, p. 51.

Falkus, Malcolm, "Labour in Thai Mining: Some Historical Considerations," *Asian Studies Review*, Vol. 20, No. 2, 1996, pp. 71–95.

Greenwald, Jeff, "Thailand's Phuket Island," *Islands*, July/August 1986, pp. 42–63.

Ismailji, Saifuddin, "Onboard the Asian 'Titanic," *PSA Journal*, Vol. 66, No. 4, April 2000, p. 19.

"More Trouble in Paradise," *Time*, July 7, 1986, p. 41.

Peters, Ed, "Detour," *Time International*, Vol. 156, No. 25–26, December 25, 2000, p. 8.

"Phuket FantaSea to Be 'Rising Star' of Thailand," *Hospitality Foodservice*, April 1999.

"Siamese Seas," *Skin Diver*, Vol. 49, No. 8, August 2000, p. 70.

Skinner, Cyril, "The Interrogation of Zey a Suriya Kyaw," *Journal of the Siam Society*, Vol. 72, No. 1–2, 1984, pp. 59–76.

Wiesmann, Elke, "Fisher Folk Fight Back," *Habitat Australia*, Vol. 25, No. 1, February 1997, pp. 36–37.

Zoltak, James, "Thailand's Dino Park to Open in December," *Amusement Business*, Vol. 108, No. 42, October 14, 1996, p. 29.

Point Barrow, Alaska

Location

The northernmost city and promontory of the continental United States, Point Barrow lies on a treeless tundra on a north slope that embraces a harbor of the Chukchi Sea at its confluence with the Beaufort Sea. Along the coast lies a major migration route of sea mammals, the life's blood of the indigenous Inuit. Lacking firewood, gardens, and building materials, Point Barrow's 4,500 natives subsist on sea creatures and birds. Inhibiting hunting is the wintry water, which chokes with ice all but 41 days of the year and opens to barge traffic only in August.

Key to the Inuit culture is the white-chinned bowhead or Greenland whale *(Balaena mysticetus)*, named for the white eye ring on its long curved head. The great migratory ocean beast, one of the earth's most vocal sea animals, emits a variety of bugling, grunting, and groaning and mimics the trumpet of elephants on the whale's journey about the North Atlantic and Arctic oceans and along the northern shores of Russia, Scandinavia, Greenland, Baffin Bay,

the Northwest Territories, and Alaska. The adult's fatty flesh renders 6,000 gallons of oil, more than any other cetacean. Out of respect for the whale's uniqueness, in Chapter VII of *On the Origin of Species by Means of Natural Selection* (1859), English naturalist Charles Darwin called the bowhead "one of the most wonderful animals in the world" (1993, p. 285).

Contacts

Diane Somers
Alaska Photo Library
P. O. Box 110809,
Juneau, Alaska 99811-0809
Phone: 907-465-2012
Fax: 907-465-3767
550 West 7th Avenue, Suite 1770
Anchorage, Alaska 99501-3510
Phone: 907-269-8110
Fax: 907-269-8125
http://www.alaskaphotolibrary.org
Email: diane_somers@dced.state.ak.us

Mythography

The Makah of Point Barrow celebrate a 1,500-year-old food-sharing ceremony derived from centuries of survival based on the whale, the creator's favorite animal. As explained by Inuit myth, God so cherished the whale that he enshrouded the sea with mist in spring so he would not witness the annual killing and butchering. Mythographer Susan Feldman explains the dichotomy of life for humans and death for whales in an animistic tale, "Sedna, Mistress of the Underworld," which Stith Thompson incorporated in *Tales of the North American Indians* (1929). In the story, Inung, an Alaskan Inuit, lived alone with Sedna, his daughter. The fulmar, an arctic sea tern, lured her from the shore to the icehouse of a duplicitous lover, who was really a dog disguised as a man.

The elopement brought sorrow to

Key to the Inuit culture of Point Barrow, Alaska, is the white-chinned bowhead or Greenland whale (courtesy of Diane Somers).

Inung, who dwelt in solitude. By the next year, the grieving father had readied for the hunt. After killing the fulmar, Inung retrieved Sedna. On the voyage home to the Alaskan shores, seabirds keened their grief at the death of the fulmar. They generated sympathetic waves in the sea, which threatened to swamp Inung's frail canoe.

To restore unity with the elements, Inung threw Sedna to the sea as a propitiatory gift to angered sea deities. When she grasped the gunnels of his craft, he struck out one of her eyes with the paddle and sliced away her fingertips with a fishing knife. As the tips dropped into the waves, they changed into whales. More chopping at Sedna's bloody hands produced ten more portions of her fingers, which altered into seals.

Sedna's sacrifice saved Inung. The seabirds concluded that Sedna was lost at sea and halted their pursuit. After beaching his craft, Inung restored her to their shore hut against her will. One-eyed and finger-less, she stoked her resentment and trained the family dogs to chew away Inung's fingers and toes in retaliation for wrongs done to her body.

Ritual

Point Barrow's aborigines who listened to the story of Sedna attached the myth to the lore that formed their cosmic vision of a universe controlled by *tuungaq* [animal spirits]. They intoned chants and formulaic incantations to soothe earth's spirits and heal their ailments. Ritual ordered Inuit men to sea in 26-foot skin umiaks (or *umiaqs*), which Inuit women shaped and sewed. As the winter moon grew full, the paddlers purified themselves in fresh streams and pools. To harden bodies for the spring chase, they scrubbed at their flesh with bundles of nettles and hemlock boughs. As they approached sanctification for the hunt, they swore off sexual intercourse and other pleasures, fasted, and steeled their courage by swimming in the sea in imitation of the mighty *agvik* [whale].

The Inuit favored the bowhead whales (*Balaena mysticetus*) because it was easily tracked and predictable in its movements. Each March, when pods of the doughty "rocknosers" migrated from the Bering Sea into the Arctic Circle on their way to the Beaufort Sea, the Inuit readied for the epic pursuit, which began at Point Barrow in August and extended to late October. After a crewman received a symbolic dream of a whale, in response to the sacred vision, the eight-man teams pulled their umiaks down the beach into the waves. They carried along lucky amulets to suspend from the masts and loaded canteens of food and water, bailing cans, sealskin floats or drags, coiled sinew fishlines, and sixteen-foot harpoons tipped with honed mussel shell. Paddling away from the strand with prayer and vigilance, the oarsmen began to stalk the eighty-ton, sixty-foot mammals.

Lookouts watched for schools of fish escaping the whale's mouth and awaited the emergence of the great humped back, a rolling forward thrust, and water and air spewed from the blowhole. Maneuvering to the left, seven men at the oars positioned the umiak and steadied its approach while the eighth man wielded the harpoon. After he made a killing thrust, the crew marked the area with floats as the coil of sinew spooled out. At a crucial point in the drama, the dying beast could tow them for days into fog-bound waters far from shore. Floats helped to slow and tire out the animal and also attached to the boat to prevent capsizing.

The chase continued as long as the whale was strong enough to fight death. Bled dry of its life fluids, it died near the surface. To keep it afloat, a volunteer leaped from the gunnels to overlap the great lips and stitch them tight, forming a huge ball around the whale's last gulp of air. During the turmoil created by the thrashing tail,

native oarsmen continued to steady the umiak and to toss floats to any men unseated by the battle. On the way back to Point Barrow, the hunters could hear folk songs and drumming. As the victorious crew drew their prey on the shingle, ritual keepers filled the blowhole with eagle down. Beach worship consisted of additional ritual, sea blessings, and storytelling honoring whalers, Point Barrow's heroes. In community gatherings, villagers danced in imitation of Alaskan animals and the shaman acted out instructive scenarios.

History

Seafaring Alaskans of Point Barrow have hunted whales for some twelve millennia. As explained by one theory of the aboriginal settlement of North America, Asiatic travelers crossed Beringia, the former land tether tying Alaska to Siberia over the 56-mile Bering Strait, and continued down the Pacific coast and as far south as Tierra del Fuego, Argentina. Like their Chukotka cousins of southeastern Siberia, the newcomers to North America depended on sea life for food. Around 4,000 B.C., paleoindians left flint tools at Cape Denbigh on Norton Sound that proved to archeologist Louis Denbigh that the area's first settlers were hunters.

Living in underground sod huts, the Tareumuit, the first Point Barrow residents, developed a complex society. They used Asian-style clayware from around 3,000 B.C. and added to their stores oil lamps, slate implements, and burins, the pointed styluses with which they etched their goods. From subsistence on caribou, they advanced to open-sea hunting in A.D. 800 and extended their red-meat diet with the flesh and oil of sea creatures. To secure huge sea mammals for food, they developed the Thule lifeway based on open-boat fishing. Each boat carried a toggle-ended harpoon, a fishhook that secured the prey with a safety latch attached to the snell. By A.D. 1,000, the Point's residents developed dog sleds to link growing settlements and built two-passenger kayaks for ice-hunting and the 25-man umiak for large-crew whaling.

On a treacherous expanse of shore, Point Barrow's residents honored whaling as the central function of their hunting-gathering society. They valued sea beasts as the source of body-building oils, which gave them strong limbs and courageous hearts and promoted sea captains and their wives to positions of leadership. Even "stinkers," decaying carcasses trapped under ice, were valuable for their edible skin.

When British explorer and Royal Naval Captain Frederick W. Beechey visited the region in 1826, he named it for British geographer Sir John Barrow of Lancaster, secretary of the British Admiralty. Barrow promoted the arctic expedition of Sir James Clark Ross, Sir John Franklin, and Sir John Ross. In addition to the naming of Point Barrow, Cape Barrow, the Barrow Strait, and Barrow's goldeneye duck bear the name of Barrow, who founded the Royal Geographical Society in 1830. In 1889, the U.S. government began building the Point Barrow Refuge Station, a manned outpost intended to aid sinking vessels or whaling crews threatened by arctic gales. When the idea failed, the government passed along its altruistic concept to the Pacific Steam Whaling Company in 1896 only months before a serious shipwreck.

Late 19th-century whalers intruded on the established Alaskan shore life by firing black-powder charges through shoulder guns and stripping whale carcasses of oil for lamps and bone and ivory for corset stays, skirt hoops, knife handles, and trinkets. Into the early 1900s, ceremonial whaling gave place to whaling-for-hire, a commercial job held by intruders among the arctic's northern maritime peoples. After gas and kerosene began encroaching on the use of whale oil as fuel for lamps, in 1908, the

manufacture of flexible steel replaced whale bone as a raw material and ended the heyday of commercial whaling.

Point Barrow took on strategic importance to the Allies during World War II, when the U.S. Naval Arctic Research Laboratory posted researchers to the beach vantage point. In 1947, the government opened the Barrow Arctic Science Station as a strategic observation point that involved as many as 300 scientists to study such basics as fluctuations in precipitation, vegetation, and ice floes and the influence of bodies of water on climate. By 1959, the Inuit of Point Barrow sought formal incorporation as a city, which enriched itself on the proceeds from natural gas deposits and oil wells. Tourism put Point Barrow on the map after promoters arranged whale-watching excursions. On October 3, 1963, a freak storm struck the Point, ruining government quonset huts and laboratory equipment and destroying 32 village residences.

Modernization of Point Barrow did not destroy early folkways. During Senate hearings on the Marine Mammal Protection Act in May 1972, the Eskimo, Aleut, and Indians defended their ceremonial whale kills. A citizen, Martha Aiken, posed a rhetorical question to the panel that met at Nome, Alaska: "If our livelihood and diet of centuries are taken from us, what's the use of being called an Eskimo? What's the use of trying to recapture our Eskimo culture, which is fast dying anyway?" (Morgan 1973, p. 354). David Stone, a hunter from Point Hope, explained that loss of ocean mammals to the Eskimo would equate with the decimation of buffalo to plains Indians. The pleas proved insightful to government officials, who exempted the Aleut, Eskimo, and Indian from protective legislation.

In response to technological advances in sea fishing, Point Barrow natives updated their ritual. To protect the endangered gray whale *(Eschrichtius robustus)*, traditional hunters voluntarily placed the mammals under protection, a position mandated by the 39-member International Whaling Commission. However, natives pointed out to the press that if they gave up whale meat entirely, their demands on caribou would soon deplete the species. In 1977, local citizens began studying the hunting tactics of outsiders whose money-based killing diminished the bowhead whale to the point of extinction.

The following year, spokesman Eben Hopson, the mayor of the North Slope borough, chairman of the Inuit Circumpolar Conference, and spokesman for the Alaska Eskimo Whaling Commission, explained to a London audience the importance of the bowhead to Inuit survival:

> He is the most alert to environmental danger, and the least tolerant of intrusion or environmental insult. The bowhead will not wait around to be threatened by an oil spill. He needs only to be insulted to make him deviate sharply from his traditional routine. We don't want anything to happen to disturb bowhead migratory routes because our villages are located along these routes. If the bowhead migrates elsewhere because of insulting offshore oil and gas operations, our villages will disappear. Without the bowhead whale, Barrow would not exist [Hopson, 1978].

Filled with sensitivity to the plight of the whale and to the people who depended on it, his speech won sympathies for the Inuit traditions of Point Barrow.

The whale's importance to Barrow natives remained in world headlines. To reiterate their dedication to the ancestral lifestyle, in October 1983, the Alaskan legislature chose the whale as the state mammal, a ceremonial gesture that unified local people against the destruction of their traditional sea spirit. In October 1988, a coordinated rescue party joined the National Guard, oil industrialists, the Russian military, and environmentalists to free three whales trapped in ice.

In 1994, whales rebounded from near extinction. In celebration of Inuit heritage, the Makah of Cape Flattery near Seattle, Washington, petitioned the International Whaling Commission for license to bag four gray whales per year. After the Marine Mammal Protection act exempted the Inuit from the ban on whaling, natives launched fall and spring hunts of whales for food or other non-commercial use. During the presidency of Bill Clinton, he and Vice President Al Gore honored the Treaty of 1855, which extended unlimited whaling privileges to the Makah, who became the nation's only sanctioned whalers. Joyfully, on May 22, 1999, the Makah anticipated a ritual hunt that made national headlines.

The Makah precedent aided Point Barrow natives in restoring their whale-hunting traditions. As of August 2002, Eugene Brower, a representative of the Alaskan Eskimo Whaling Commission, reported to the International Whaling Commission that whale meat again constituted nearly seventy percent of the native diet. Celebration of Inuit whaling produced a northwestern Alaskan renaissance called the *Inupiat Ilitqusiat* [the Spirit Movement], a cultural and religious regeneration by a renewal of ties to Inuit heritage. During the annual whale migration up the Pacific coast, like Great-Grandfather Wilson Arnold, Grandson Greig Arnold and his son, the namesake of Wilson Arnold, mapped out a series of coastal activities to uplift Point Barrow's indigenous people. The season was a blend of traditional whaling and careful supervision of the wealth of the Arctic Sea and of the means of killing, which, under the Weapons Improvement Program, reduced the pain the animals feel.

On the shore, hunters brought out primitive sea craft and harpoons that had been essentials during the elders' childhood. After natives took to sea in skin-covered wood boats, the revival of animism resurrected ties to the elements. Whale hunting was once more a focus of native religion and the social order of the circumpolar world. During a season of cooperation, tribesman Daves Sones reported on the building of traditional cedar longhouses for singing and feasting on holidays and at weddings. As the unemployed found jobs and native families held reunions, the celebration of the kill climaxed in the sharing of meat and blubber.

Coastal Activities

Outsiders come to Point Barrow on the Chukchi Sea to witness whaling as well as polar bears on pack ice, dance performances, migratory flights of birds, and the midnight sun, a period when the day fails to darken into night. The beach offers guided tours, orienteering and camping, tundra touring, dog-sledding, snowmobiling, kayaking, and recreational flying. Landmarks include a whalebone arch, the whalebone jaw at the entrance to the Inupiat Heritage Center, and the Wiley Post–Will Rogers Memorial, which notes the crash of their Lockheed plane in 1935.

Nurse and writer Elise Sereni Patkotak, author of *Parallel Logic: A Barrow Memory* (2002) and winner of a writing award from the Alaska Press Women, described the convergence of Point Barrow's natives at the beach, where the whale ceremony is kept private from tourists and the media. To assure the proper spirit, all participated in prayers, thanksgiving, and controlled dismemberment of the whales, which offered not only meat and oil, but tooth and bone for religious carvings. Meat carvers began with the removal of flukes, blubber, and fatty maktak [or muktuk], a nutritious source of vitamin C in a land poor in fruits and vegetables.

In addition to enough meat to feed seventy people for a year, slaughterers valued the delicate, brushlike plates of baleen. The fine fringe filters gaping mouthfuls of water to trap meals of small Arctic crustaceans called *Calanus* copepods at the rate of 50,000 per minute. Whaling participants hauled the valued plates up from the shore on *komatiks* [sleds] for distribution to widows and the elderly and awarded prize slices to the valiant whaling captain and his crew. Recyclers shaped baleen into mammal traps, bird snares, baskets and buckets, toboggans, and drums; oil extracted from blubber heated homes, fueled lamps for light and heat, and baited fox traps. Officials set aside substantial chunks of the best meat in ice cellars beneath the permafrost for serving at Thanksgiving, Christmas, the after-Christmas Messenger Feast, and *Nalukataq*, the spring whaling festival and blanket toss. The few Point residents who disdained the ceremony received no meat, baleen, or oil.

Sources

Adams, Jacob, "Office of the President," http://arcticcircle.uconn.edu/ArcticCircle/ANWR/asrcadams.html.

"Archeology of the Tundra and Arctic Alaska," http://www.nps.gov/akso/akarc/arctic.htm.

Bock, Paula, "Caring: This Is the Gift," *Seattle Times Magazine*, December 21, 1997, pp. 8–13, 22.

Bockstoce, John, "Arctic Castaway: The Stormy History of the Point Barrow Refuge Station," *Prologue*, Vol. 11, No. 3, 1979, pp. 153–169.

_____, "The Point Barrow Refuge Station," *American Neptune*, Vol. 39, No. 1, 1979, pp. 5–21.

"The Bowhead Whale," http://www.geobop.com/Eco/AK6.htm.

"Bowhead Whales," *Beringia Natural History Notebook Series*. Washington, D.C.: National Audubon Society, September, 1992.

Britton, M. E., "U.S. Office of Naval Research Arctic Research Laboratory, Point Barrow, Alaska," *Polar Record*, Vol. 13, No. 85, 1967, pp. 421–423.

Carpenter, Les, "Inuvialuit Bowhead Harvest," *Inuit Whaling*, Inuit Circumpolar Conference, June 1992.

Chance, Norman A. *The Inupiat and Arctic Alaska*. New York: Harcourt Brace, 1990.

Clebsch, Edward E. C., and Royal E. Shanks, "Summer Climatic Gradients and Vegetation near Barrow, Alaska," *Arctic*, Vol. 21, No. 3, 1968, pp. 161–171.

D'Oro, Rachel, and Don Hunter, "Rescuers Lift

142 Whalers off Ice," *Anchorage Daily News,* May 19, 1997.

Ellis, Richard, "Leviathans of the Deep," *Los Angeles Times Sunday Book Review,* August 5, 2001.

Feldman, Susan, ed. *The Storytelling Stone.* New York: Laurel Books, 1965.

Fox, Mike, "The Inuit Case for Whaling," *BBC News,* May 24, 2002.

Freeman, Milton M. R., et al. *Inuit, Whaling, and Sustainability.* Walnut Creek, Calif.: Altamira Press, 1998.

Gragg, Larry, "The Port Royal Earthquake," *History Today,* September 2000, p. 28.

Hall, Charles Francis. *Life with the Esquimaux.* Rutland, Ver.: Charles E. Tuttle Co., 1970.

Hooi, Alexis John, "Alaskan Upbraids Whaling Commission, Japanese," *The World Paper,* August 1, 2002.

Hopson, Eben, "Hopson's Address to the London Press Corps," http://www. ebenhopson. com/papers/1978/London.html, June 1, 1978.

Hume, James D., and Marshall Schalk, "Shoreline Processes near Barrow, Alaska," *Arctic,* Vol. 20, No. 2, 1967, pp. 86–103.

Huntington, Henry, "Alaska Eskimo Whaling," *Inuit Whaling,* Inuit Circumpolar Conference, June 1992.

"Japan Blocks Indigenous Whaling," *BBC News,* May 23, 2002.

Jarman, Lloyd, "Floats on Post-Rogers Lockheed," *American Aviation Historical Society Journal,* Vol. 37, No. 1, 1992, pp. 38–41.

Kofinas, Gary, "Subsistence Hunting in a Global Economy: Contributions of Northern Wildlife Co-Management to Community Economic Development," *Making Waves,* Vol. 4, No. 3, August 1993.

Kristof, Emory, "The Last U.S. Whale Hunters," *National Geographic,* March 1973, pp. 346–353.

Lauffenburger, Julie A., "Baleen in Museum Collections: Its Sources, Uses, and Identification," *Journal of the American Institute for Conservation,* Vol. 32, No. 3, 1993, pp. 213–230.

Lowy, Joan, "Politics: Global Warming Threatens Alaskan Villages," *Nando Times,* May 5, 2001.

Marquette, W. M., and H. W. Braham, "Gray Whale Distribution and Catch by Alaskan Eskimos: A Replacement for the Bowhead Whale?," *Arctic,* Vol. 35, No. 3, September 1982, pp. 386–394.

Mastny, Lisa, "Coming to Terms with the Arctic," *World Watch,* January 2000, p. 24.

Mauer, Richard, "Unlikely Allies Rush to Free 3 Whales," *New York Times,* October 18, 1988, p. 8.

Morgan, Lael, "Ocean Mammals Are to Us What the Buffalo Was to the Plains Indian," *National Geographic,* March 1973, pp. 354–355.

Mowat, Farley. *The Polar Passion: The Quest for the North Pole.* Toronto: McClellan & Stewart, 1989.

Murdoch, John. *Ethnological Results of the Point Barrow Expedition.* Washington, D.C.: U.S. Bureau of American Ethnology, 1892.

Nicklin, Flip, "Bowhead Whales, Leviathans of Icy Seas," *National Geographic,* August 1995, pp. 114–128.

Oswalt, Wendell H., "Technological Complexity: The Polar Eskimos and the Tareumiut," *Arctic Anthropology,* Vol. 24, No. 2, 1987, pp. 82–98.

Patkotak, Elise, "Fall Whaling Main Attraction in This Community," *Heartland,* September 29, 1996.

"Remote Areas of Alaska," *Monkeyshines on America,* January 1989, p. 34.

Ritter, John, "Way of Life Could Fade with Whale Population," *USA Today,* October 4, 1999, 6A.

Rosenblatt, Roger, "Looking at Them Looking at Us," *U.S. News & World Report,* November 7, 1988, p. 8.

Rossiter, William, "The Makah Whaling Dance," *Whales Alive!,* Cetacean Society International, January 1997.

"Science Improves When Archaeologists Work with Locals," *Frontiers,* January 1997.

Shelden, Kim E. W., and David J. Rugh, "The Bowhead Whale, *Balaena mysticetus:* Its Historic and Current Status," *Marine Fisheries Review,* 1995.

Simon, Jim, "Whale Hunt Throws Tribe into Risky Waters," *Seattle Times,* March 13, 1998.

Warburton-Lee, John, "The Final Frontier," *Geographical,* Marcy 1, 2000, pp. 62–66.

Wells, Robert D., "The Naval Arctic Research Laboratory," *U.S. Naval Institute Proceedings,* Vol. 95, No. 9, 1969, pp. 39–45.

Westneat, Danny, "Makah Whaling OK'd," *Seattle Times,* October 23, 1997.

_____. "Whales Die, a Culture Lives," *Seattle Times,* October 13, 1996.

Williams, Brian, "Should the Makah Tribe Be Allowed to Resume the Hunting of Grey Whales?," *MSNBC News Forum,* January 1997.

Port Royal, Jamaica

Location

Port Royal is a West Indian harbor and fortified town in southeastern Jamaica built on a slender twelve-mile palisado or sandspit shaped like a sinuous dragon or the letter J. The hook, which was once a separate cay, offers prime anchorage in a deep sheltered harbor that is the seventh largest on the globe. The island setting consists of miles of sandy beach lapped by the warm Caribbean waters within sight of the Blue Mountains. Inland, sand dunes, mangrove, and thin cactus add texture to the narrow curve of land that wraps around a deep, peaceful lagoon.

A mid-seventeenth-century commercial success, the area, guarded by six forts, overlooked the Caribbean's main shipping lanes and profited from trade in sugar, rum, and African slaves. When pirates headquartered at the port, it earned a reputation for lawless, licentious, and wicked behavior. Because of the swift demise of Port Royal in a devastating earthquake, nature transformed it from a sinful city to one of the most valuable offshore historical preserves in the Northern Hemisphere. The late twentieth century advanced a forgotten disaster zone to a prime tourist enclave and cruise, ferry, and dive-boat destination.

Contacts

Anthony King, Manager
Jamaica Tourist Board
801 Second Avenue, Twentieth Floor
New York, New York 10017
Phone: 212-856-9727 or 800-233-4JTB
Fax: 212-856-9730
Email: jtblibrary@jamaicatravel.com
http://www.jamaicatravel.com/

History

Around A.D. 600, Port Royal became an Arawak fishing site called Xaymaca, which flourished at the mouth of a deeply arced natural port. In 1493, the unsuspecting natives died at a horrendous rate from European diseases borne by Christopher Columbus and his crew. Bartolomé de las Casas, a Dominican friar and historian and author of "Memorial on Remedies for the Indies" (1518), grieved that the disease seriously reduced the populations of Hispaniola, Cuba, and Jamaica.

In 1647, yellow fever struck the island during high importation of West African slaves. Historian and mapmaker Richard Ligon, author of *A True and Exact History of the Island of Barbadoes* (1657), blamed black islanders for spreading the disease across Jamaica, Cuba, Guadeloupe, Saint Kitts, and the Yucatán peninsula of Central America. Unlike black Africans, whites lacking immunity and enjoying high living and indulgence in rum died in large numbers. Because New England's port authorities suspected Jamaicans of harboring the fever, they rejected ships from Port Royal before they could dock.

Following their seizure of the island of Jamaica from Spain, the British established the town in May 1655 at the heart of the Caribbean. To secure it, the military built Fort Cromwell or Passage Fort at the tip of the landmass. Lacking soldiers, Governor Edward D'Oyley recruited Tortuga privateers Bartholomew Roberts, Roche Brasiliano, John Davis, and Edward Mansveldt (or Mansfield) for a *de facto* army by issuing letters of marque allowing piracy against the Dutch and Spaniards who menaced the island.

Coinciding with Port Royal's establishment, islanders encountered a double disaster. Along with 1,000 islanders, hundreds of British soldiers died of a yellow fever epidemic at a rate of twenty per day. Because black Africans bore a natural immune to the fever, the slave population remained stable while white headcounts dropped dramatically. When a hurricane washed away part of the sandspit that same year, the English were so intent on maintaining their island headquarters that they filled the gap with derelict hulks and smoothed over the top with sand.

In 1660, after Charles II trounced the Puritans and restored the English monarchy, the new Jamaican town was formally named Port Royal and the palisades, Fort Charles. Traveler and map publisher Richard Blome, the author of *A Description of the Island of Jamaica and Barbados* (1672), visited Jamaica in 1678. He described the harbor as around three leagues wide and amply supplied with deep-draft anchorage to accommodate a 1,000-ton ship. Because of the convenience of the harbor and its nearness to Caribbean traffic, Port Royal grew faster than any other English colonial settlement, reaching 7,000 inhabitants within three decades.

In the late seventeenth century, according to island historian Charles Leslie, author of *A New History of Jamaica* (1740), Port Royal gained a reputation as the wealthiest harbor city and trading center in the Caribbean. Using the port as headquarters, between 1655 and 1661, some twenty buccaneers, like the Mediterranean pirates of Cilicia, looted around sixty settlements and towns at the rate of ten raids per year. As the Spanish treasure flotilla made its annual crossing from the Gulf of Mexico through the Caribbean Sea to Spain, privateers picked off ships in twos and threes or more to rifle for chests of gold and silver coins intended for the royal treasury. The money returned to Port Royal and enriched an economy unequalled in the New World colonies.

Of the city's inhabitants, around half engaged directly in illicit goods. In an economic era governed by bribery and barter, such freebooters used their swag as spendable cash. Through local merchants, pirates exchanged for goods and services jewels, exotica, gold bouillion, silver ingots, and newly minted *pistoles* and pieces of eight stolen from Spanish treasure ships. The most notorious of the lot put in at Port Royal for a rest from sea plunder to drink, gamble, patronize brothels, stock up on goods, and deck themselves in leather, wool hats, and gaudy finery befitting pillagers of the Spanish Main. Threats of punishment did little to stem pirate excesses. In 1679, the secretary of Jamaica's governor wrote to an official in England of a foiled attempt of the Royal Navy to capture a blatant no-good, who escaped, retrieved his vessel, and continued his predations.

Sir Henry Morgan, one of the most brutal of the era's plunderers, called Port Royal home. The son of Robert Morgan, a farmer and herder in rural Llanrhymney outside Cardiff, Wales, he was born in 1635 and took to the sea in late childhood as ship's boy, the standard beginning for a career sailor. Embarking from the port of Bristol, England, he gained experience for a decade and apprenticed with Sir Christopher Myngs around 1655. When Myngs accrued 1.5 million gold coins in loot, he shared enough with his crew to pay for Morgan's first ship.

Enrolled in the Puritan army of Oliver Cromwell, Morgan enlisted under General Robert Venables and was posted as a freebooter to Barbados at the height of Caribbean piracy. In 1663, Morgan commanded part of Myngs's armada, a ship formerly captained by Edward Mansfield. Rapidly, Morgan enriched himself while partnering with Jackman & Morris, predators along the shores of Central America. Boosting Morgan's position in the Caribbean was his inheritance from an uncle, Edward Morgan, lieutenant governor of Jamaica. Henry Morgan also profited socially and politically by marrying his cousin, Edward's daughter Mary Elizabeth.

During the Second Anglo-Dutch War, the British Royal Navy licensed Morgan from 1665 to 1667 to victimize England's enemies at sea. At Puerto Príncipe, Cuba, he fleeced locals of 50,000 pieces of eight, the coins that circulated so widely in the colonial Americas that they became legal tender. His most blatant heist was the sacking of Puerto Bello, Panama, where he amassed 250 million gold pieces along with a stock of silver plate, gemstones, weapons, bolts of silk, spices, ale and rum, and African slaves. When his fleet put in at Port Royal, Jamaicans gave him the seventeenth-century equivalent of a ticker tape parade. His renown reached new heights in 1668, when Morgan, aboard his French flagship *Satisfaction*, overran the ramparts of Maracaibo, Venezuela, where he loaded his galleys with treasure. He killed off a rival, Captain Manuel Pardal, who sheltered in Cuba, then returned to Port Royal at the head of 35 galleons manned by 2,000 buccaneers.

Morgan proved useful to Governor Thomas Modyford as a spy and sea warden. In 1669, in flight from Admiral Alonso de Espinosa and three Spanish frigates of the Windward Armada, Morgan met ill luck off St. Domingue in the explosion and sinking of his flagship *Oxford*. He recouped his former strength on January 9, 1671, when he and 460 crewmen seized the Panama colony, Spain's coiner of the realm. Morgan's party edged up the Chagres River by canoe from the Castle of San Lorenzo to burn and pillage Panama City. When his men returned to Port Royal on May 31, local fans cheered him for carting along 600 Spanish captives and for leading a train of 175 mules laden with 750,000 doubloons.

At age 37, Morgan's prospects dimmed after he was arrested under the orders of Charles II, who capitulated to island leaders claiming that pirates were both a civic nuisance and bait for Spanish reprisals. By pleading his value to British interests in the Caribbean and especially at Port Royal, Morgan appeased the king with new strategies to guard Jamaica against the same type of predations that Morgan had wreaked on

Panama. By age 39, he was exonerated, proclaimed a patriot, and knighted for his service to English colonies in the Caribbean. As admiral of the Jamaican fleet, in 1674, he continued to rise in importance to the Crown, which appointed him Deputy Governor of Jamaica.

Morgan was a familiar figure at Port Royal, where he boasted and drank among local profligates at harbor rumhouses. In retirement, he had the gall to style himself an island planter, militia captain, and opponent of piracy, which the island government banned in 1678. He continued to harass the upright British hierarchy and expired of alcoholism and dropsy on August 25, 1688, in Lawrencefield, Jamaica. His death produced nostalgia in islanders who remembered Port Royal in its prime. The old pirate's funeral concluded with cannon fire from the battlements and interment at the palisades, known as Morgan's Fort.

In the late 1680s, Port Royal vied with Boston, Massachusetts, as the most prosperous colonial city. South Jamaican harbor traffic consisted of over 200 vessels traveling to and from Cartagena and Havana to deal in lumber, cloth, indigo and other dyestuffs, liquor, food, sugar, and cocoa. The sumptuous lifestyle of Port Royal's 4,000 residents extended to successful entrepreneurs and planters who enjoyed opulence and self-indulgence, including sizeable gangs of slaves imported from west Africa. [*See also* ELMINA CASTLE, GHANA.] Some functioned as housekeepers, innkeepers, chefs, and trusted valets; most, however, performed the menial dray labor common to docks and warehouses.

From continued prosperity, the town developed into a densely packed metropolis of 2,000 multi-storied buildings covering 51 acres. As of 1692, the non-slave populace consisted of courtesans, merchants, bankers, and artisans working in wood, brick, leather, cloth, felt, rope, glass, paint, iron, and precious metals. In addition to legitimate citizens, over 1,000 privateers ignored the anti-piracy law and continued to anchor at Port Royal, which admirers called the Caribbean's storehouse and the treasury of the Indies. Magistrates enriched by trade with brigands winked at the law by maintaining a relaxed attitude toward felons who were generous and congenial so long as the rum flowed free.

Jamaica's pirate capital came to a swift, cataclysmic end. On June 7, 1692, at 11:43 A.M., after a calm, dry morning, an earthquake turned Port Royal's sandy base into quicksand. Most of the shops, hotels, and streets on 33 acres of the privateers' home port slid into the bay as the sea floor swallowed up the "Sodom of the universe." When the tremors ceased, the buildings remained obscured in the near-perfect vertical state in which they sank. In addition to brothels, casinos, taverns, and rum dives, the loss extended to churches and bell towers belonging to Catholics, Anglicans, Puritans, Presbyterians, Baptists, Quakers, and Jews.

The catastrophe produced 5,000 casualties. As three tsunamis struck the sandspit, concussion and drowning killed over 2,000 immediately. The remaining 3,000 perished as a result of injuries and contagious disease. Ministers immediately categorized the disaster as God's rebuke to thieving undesirables and an omen to Port Royal authorities and collaborators against shady, quasi-legal dealings with brigands and cutthroats. Rescuers found bodies afloat in the bay alongside corpses shaken from their graves by tidal waves. In the spirit of Spanish Main, looters thronged residences and warehouses in search of salvageable goods. An outraged Anglican clergyman reported that harbor lowlife stripped the dead down to their gold buttons and lopped off fingers to free gold rings, then set out on a binge of drinking and wenching. The resulting pious interpretation declared sin dens such as Port Royal a natural target of God's wrath.

Jamaicans attempted to rebuild Port Royal along its original plan, but had less than half the acreage on which to erect harbor buildings. Measuring one-half by one-quarter miles, the port continued to house the British West Indian Navy, but commerce moved east to Kingston on higher, more substantial ground at the other end of the arcing bay. A fire in 1703 and a hurricane in 1722 ended Port Royal for good. As of 1774, the site contained around 100 homes, but offered none of the vice and shore amusements that once enticed the likes of Sir Henry Morgan. Like other world harbors, the port city continued to suffer serious blows, notably, the ship-borne yellow fever and cholera epidemics of 1860, and smallpox the following year.

Archeology

Undersea archeologists have retrieved goods and treasure while exploring the sunken main wharf and whole city blocks that survive intact. Their salvage attests to the lavish lifestyle paid for in gold and goods, the wages of piracy in what was once America's most prosperous English city. In the 1980s, Dr. Donny L. Hamilton of the Institute of Nautical Archaeology at Texas A. & M. University organized a study of the remains, beginning at the intersection of Queen and Lime streets. Findings substantiated eyewitness claims that the earth literally engulfed whole structures in the wet sand in which they were built without tipping them off their foundations. Because of the swift vertical plunge into sand and silt, a surprising number of ceramic goods, Chinese porcelain, and kaolin clay smoking pipes were unharmed.

According to underwater research, thirteen acres of seventeenth-century Port Royal survives, in some respects, without a brick out of place, even in cobbled flooring. Diving in fifteen-to-thirty feet of water, salvors have worked in sandy, silt-filled waters with air lifts, which vacuum away centuries of debris, and with water dredges, which inhale muck to spit out items for identification and study. Among their discoveries were one-third of the sunken ship *Belle* and a bottle containing a pickled cricket. At the university's Conservation Research Laboratory, staff secured waterlogged artifacts in water-soluble wax and wax polymers. Subsequent analysis of ceramic remains attests to a sizeable influence from West Africa, particularly Ghana, but none from Caribbean Indians.

Coastal Activities

Jamaica's travel bureaucracy, led by Robert M. Stephens, president of Pragma Consultants and Caribbean Travel & Tours, has capitalized on old Port Royal with numerous harbor projects costing $50 million. Cruise ships and a ferry ply the water alongside the historic restoration of Kingston and Port Royal, which began in January 1995. Photographers snap pictures of buildings designed in the early 1600s, including St. Peter's Church, a ring of six forts, Chocolata Hole Bay, and the Giddy House, a gunnery supply shed that the earth's upheaval tilted at a 45-degree angle. Bay locations invite amateur scuba divers to visit the underwater streets of the Caribbean's renowned Pompeii. Plans call for costumed parades, a reconstructed naval hospital and African-Jamaican pavilion, Fort Rocky Entertainment Centre, a royal dockyard, and an underwater museum revealing old Port Royal in its glory.

At a distance from Port Royal, additional motoring and cycling excursions offer the inland sights of Kingston, including Devon House, the Bob Marley museum, harbor sound and light shows, the National Maritime Museum in Greenwich, and nearby Fort Charles, Jamaica's oldest surviving structure, which sank 3.5 feet during the earthquake of 1692. One vastly changed landmark, Gallows Point, was once the execution site for "Calico Jack" Rackham, Charles Vane, and other pirates, whom authorities left hanging in chains at Gun Cay as a warning to budding criminals. In addition to nature and biking trails, paddle boats, and a cactus garden, visitors also venture offshore by excursion boat to Lime Cay and Manatee Cay, where stretches of sand foster snorkeling, scuba diving, kayaking and canoeing, shelling, and beachcombing.

SOURCES

Baratta, Amy, "Jamaican Investors Are Working to Lure Ships to Kingston," *Travel Weekly*, August 4, 1994, pp. C26–C27.

Burnard, Trevor, "The Countrie Continues Sicklie: White Mortality in Jamaica, 1655–1780," *Social History of Medicine*, Vol. 12, 1999, pp. 45–72.

Carroll, Cathy, "Jamaica Approves $58.6M Development Plan for Port Royal," *Travel Weekly*, May 14, 1998, p. 16.

Cordingly, David, "Pirates and Port Royal," *History Today*, May 1992, p. 62.

Eaglesham, Barbara, "Time in a Bottle," *Odyssey*, February 2000, p. 18.

Gragg, Larry, "The Port Royal Earthquake of 1692," *History Today*, Vol. 50, No. 9, 2000, pp. 28–34.

Hamilton, Donny L., "The Port Royal Project: History of Port Royal," Nautical Archaeology Program, College Station, Tex.: Texas A. & M. University, College Station, June 1, 2001.

Kelleher, Terry, "Pirate Tales," *People Weekly*, August 25, 1997, 18.

Kruszelnicki, Karl, "And the Earth Did Swallow Them Up!," *New Scientist*, December 21, 1996, pp. 26–29.

Link, Marion Clayton, "Exploring the Drowned City of Port Royal," *National Geographic*, February 1960, pp. 151, 158–182.

Major, Brian, "Port Royal Calls," *Travel Agent*, February 23, 1998, pp. 100–101.

Meyers, Allan D., "West African Tradition in the Decoration of Colonial Jamaican Folk Pottery," *International Journal of Historical Archaeology*, Vol. 3, No. 4, 1999, pp. 201–223.

Paris, Sheldon, "Sir Henry Morgan: Pirate or Patriot?," *Stamps*, June 17, 1995, p. 3.

Pearson, M., and David Buisseret, "A Pirate at Port Royal in 1679," *Mariner's Mirror*, Vol. 57, No. 3, 1971, p. 303.

Smith, K. C., "Jamaica's Enduring Heritage," *Archaeology*, January–February 1992, pp. 73–75.

"Subsea Recovery," http://www.subsearecovery.com/ssr.html.

Thomas, Mary Elizabeth, "Quarantine in Old Jamaica," *Caribbean Studies*, Vol. 4, No. 4, 1965, pp. 77–92.

Treaster, Joseph B., "Divers in Jamaica Sift Ruins of Pirate Town Destroyed in 1692," *New York Times*, August 21, 1984, p. C3.

"UNESCO Urges the Americas to Join the Underwater Heritage Convention," *UNESCO Press*, June 13, 2002.

Weston, John, "Sir Henry Morgan," http://www.data-wales.co.uk/morgan.htm.

Zahedieh, Nuala, "The Merchants of Port Royal, Jamaica, and the Spanish Contraband Trade, 1655–1692," *William and Mary Quarterly*, Vol. 43, No. 4, 1986, pp. 570–593.

Punta Espinosa, Fernandina Island, Galápagos Islands, Ecuador

Location

A province of Ecuador located on the Equator in the eastern Pacific Ocean, the Galápagos Islands lie 621 miles west of South America. The group, covering 3,093 square miles, consists of thirteen large islands, six small archipelagos, and 42 islets. Naturalist Charles Darwin described their configuration: "The currents of the sea are rapid and sweep between the islands, and gales of wind are extraordinarily rare; so that the islands are far more effectually separated from each other than they appear on a map" (1993, p. 541).

The Galápagos group appears to have developed nine million years ago from basaltic lava exuding from shield volcanoes and took its current shape around five million years ago. It hosts some of the world's most unusual endemic fauna and flora that have adapted to craters, sheer cliffs, and arid lava slabs. An array of natural wonders highlights Isla Fernandina, an unpopulated land mass of 425 square miles. Once called Narborough Island, Fernandina lies at the convergence of three tectonic plates — the Cocos, Nazca, and Pacific — in the western curve of Isabela Island.

Of the entire cluster, Fernandina is the youngest, farthest west, and most unspoiled by human contact. On a hotspot called the Galápagos Platform, Volcon La Cumbre, Fernandina's 4,900-foot black-shield volcano, retreats behind a fine mist during the July-to-December cool season, triggered by the cold Humboldt Current. La Cumbre's collapsed crater, which arose at a mantle plume around 698,000 B.C., exudes gases from the fumaroles on its unvegetated slopes. Punta Espinosa, a narrow lava-flow peninsula on the island's northeastern shore, displays the resilience of biota to a habitat both harsh and constantly shifting in threats to life.

Contacts

Roslyn Cameron
Department of Institutional Development
Charles Darwin Research Station
Isla Santa Cruz, Galapagos
Email: cdrs@fcdarwin.org.ec
http://www.darwinfoundation.org

History

The Galápagos Islands were known to the Chimu and Inca in pre–Columbian times, when adventurers guided balsa rafts from the South American coasts in search of new fishing grounds. The cluster entered world geography books and maps on March 10, 1535, after the arrival of Tomás de Berlanga of Valladolid, the bishop of Panama and director of Dominican missions in Cuba, Hispañola, Jamaica, and New Spain. He accidentally discovered the island group while he journeyed from Panama on an investigatory mission concerning military atrocities in Peru. Forced on the Galápagos shore by strong currents, he lost two

At Punta Espinosa in the Galápagos Islands, some of the world's most unusual endemic fauna and flora have adapted to craters, sheer cliffs, and arid lava slabs (courtesy of Bob Daniel).

crew members and ten horses before he could escape.

The bishop used his marooning as an opportunity to examine nature. He studied huge tortoises on the coast and named the islands *Las Encantadas* [the Enchanted] for their magically shifting undertows. Berlanga produced the first written description of Galápagos birds, giant tortoises, and shore armies of algae-eating marine iguanas, the only lizard that has adapted to dependence on the sea. In his unflattering dispatch to King Charles V of Spain, the bishop commented on the islands' lack of fresh water and their god-forsaken stony surface. As his initial contact revealed, the islands remained uninhabited because of their unarable soil and lack of mineral resources and water. Science writer Barry Lopez, co-author of *Galápagos* (1989), echoed the bishop's thought in his assessment that the islands were "inhospitable, deserted stone blisters in a broad ocean, harboring no wealth of any sort." (p. 8)

In Bishop Berlanga's wake came voyagers, whalers and sealers, and pirates and smugglers fleeing the possessive Spanish and English navies, who gave the islands English names commemorating royalty, statesmen, scientists, vessels, and a traitor. Whaling captains used Fernandina's nearness to Isabela as a blind into which they could herd whales for easy slaughter. The Flemish engraver and cartographer Abraham Ortelius of Antwerp, father of the modern atlas, added the islands to the 53 maps in his best-seller, *Theatrum Orbis Terrarum* [Atlas of the Lands of the Earth] (1570). He labeled them *Insulae de Galápagos* [Islands of Saddles], which compared the island tortoises to leather saddles.

Around 1685, William Ambrose Cowley, an English cartographer and navigator aboard the *Batchelor's Delight*, charted the region from personal observation. Cowley's fellow adventurer, pilot and surveyor William Dampier, issued a popular description of the islands' habitat in *New Voyage*

Around the World (1697), followed in 1700 with M. de Beauchesne-Gouin's terse summation that no place on earth was more frightful. In 1712, British privateer Woodes Rogers, author of *A Cruising Voyage Round the World,* proved more bemused than dismissive. Instead of recoiling from the harsh terrain, he puzzled over the origin of the great tortoise, a question that remained unanswered until the studies of English naturalist Charles Darwin.

An undiminished stream of visitors to the Galápagos began the depredations that rapidly altered island wildlife. Cowley, sperm whale hunters, and other voyagers valued island tortoises as a reliable source of fresh meat and fount of up to three gallons of oil each. Ship's provisioners could store turtles alive in their holds for a year, then slaughter them on deck for cooking and rendering. From 1811 to 1883, human predators reduced the tortoise count by 16,000, extinguishing four of fifteen species. Settlers from Ecuador altered the balance of nature by introducing cats, dogs, donkeys, goats, pigs, and black rats, which gobbled vegetation and feasted on Sally Lightfoot crabs, bird and reptile eggs, and tender hatchlings.

Aboard the ten-gun brig *Beagle,* 26-year-old Darwin, the island cluster's most famous explorer, left England in December 1831 in hopes of corroborating his assumptions that nature did not produce a stable family of flora and fauna. After calling in at ports along South America's coast, he rounded Tierra del Fuego, sailed north, and arrived at the Galápagos Islands on September 17, 1835. [*See also* BEAGLE CHANNEL, ARGENTINA.] In Chapter X of his journal, later published in *The Voyage of the Beagle* (1909), he ventured a personal reaction to lava-base archipelagos: "The age of the various beds of lava was distinctly marked by the comparative growth, or entire absence, of vegetation. Nothing can be imagined more rough and horrid than the surface of the more modern streams" (*ibid.,* p. 270).

He summarized his impression of the group's "workshop appearance" by comparing it to iron foundries in Staffordshire.

Over five weeks, Darwin investigated Albemarle (Isabela), Brattle (Tortuga), Champion, Charles (Floreana), Chatham (San Cristobal), and James (Santiago). He collected specimens of thousands of endemic species, including grasses, ferns, and cacti as well as their fossilized precursors. In his writings on natural selection in the landmark *On the Origin of Species by Means of Natural Selection* (1859), he noted:

> Here almost every product of the land and of the water bears the unmistakable stamp of the American continent. There are 26 land-birds; of these, 21, or perhaps 23, are ranked as distinct species and would commonly be assumed to have been here created, yet the close affinity of most of these birds to American species is manifest in every character, in their habits, gestures, and tones of voice [1993, pp. 537–538].

His text describes the giant tortoise, iguana, flightless cormorant, fur seal, and penguin and their adaptation to changes in the food supply and environment. Most intriguing to him was the wide variety of finches, which fed on native prickly pear. Darwin found the songbird adapted differently in shape and beak formation on each island, thus proving his contention that animals have an in-born method of changing to suit alterations to their environment.

Contact with the islands increased as traffic through the Panama Canal channeled more ships from the Caribbean to South America's northwestern coast. When American novelist and sailor Herman Melville observed the Galápagos cluster, he composed *The Encantadas or Enchanted Isles* (1854), an unflattering series of diatribes that stressed the region's desolation and reptilian inhabitants. As negative in his evaluation as Bishop Berlanga, Melville compared the solitary isles to piles of cinders and an abandoned graveyard and described

Fernandina's relationship to Isabela as "[lying] in the black jaws of [Isabela] like a wolf's red tongue in his open mouth" (1986, p. 90). Calling them cursed and "Apples of Sodom," he lambasted the group as rainless, ruined deserts cracked by drought (*ibid.*, p. 73). He experienced volcanic rumblings and observed fiery illumination against the night sky, which resembled the chimneys of a glassworks. Whereas Darwin found abundant life, Melville encountered hellish lava formations, distorted trees, wiry shrubs, the hiss of iguana, and the incessant railing of the frigatebird.

A century after Darwin's momentous voyage and the publication of his writings, the government of Ecuador agreed with his findings and set aside much of the island cluster as one of the world's unique wildlife preserves. Mainlanders concurred and joined the push for conservation. During World War II, the United States used Baltra island as an airbase, which developed into a regional airstrip. In June 1946, public outcries against the American presence ended any ideas the U.S. might harbor about turning the archipelagos into a permanent naval base.

In the last half of the twentieth century, the future of the islands as a nature preserve seemed certain. In 1959, the Charles Darwin Foundation, with the support of UNESCO and the World Conservation Union, founded a research station at Puerto Ayora on Santa Cruz at Academy Bay. Among their many duties, staff raised giant tortoises to a size where they could survive in the wild. In response to conservators' success, in 1968, the Ecuadorian government earmarked ninety percent of the island group as Galápagos National Park, which included a visitors site at Fernandina. In 1979, UNESCO listed the Galapagos Islands as a Natural Patrimony of Humanity.

In 1977, geophysicists and oceanographers employed the minisubmarine *Alvin* to study an undersea ridge off the Galápagos

Islands, an area west of Fernandina that the U.S. Navy mapped with sonar. A mile and a half down, scientists located bacteria-rich warm-water springs, fresh lava, and lush biota previously unseen by human eyes. A reading of temperatures found the hydrothermal vent community to be bathwater temperature. Smoke from the vent registered at over 700 degrees Fahrenheit. In this unusual undersea atmosphere, the variety of life ranged from shrimp, lobsters, anemones, clams, mussels, crabs, and fish around the warm vents to the *Riftia pachyptila* tubeworm living in partnership with bacteria. Diver John Corliss of Oregon State University was so impressed with the unique deep-sea habitat that he called it the "Garden of Eden" (Broad, 1997, p. 107).

Fernandina's fragility suffered from human predators in the twentieth century. The island lost its last giant tortoise in 1906, when California-born ornithologist and ethnographer Rollo H. Beck on an expedition for the California Academy of Sciences slaughtered the last adult male to conduct experiments on its carcass. In the mid–1990s, the rise in tourism, particularly island-to-island vessels, left in doubt the future of the pristine islands that once knew no human inhabitants.

Ecosystem

The Galápagos Islands are rated the world's best dive destination, best fish life habitat, and healthiest marine environment in the Indo-Pacific area. Their primeval beauty has awed some of the great naturalists. When French diver and oceanographer Jacques-Yves Cousteau arrived aboard the *Calypso* in 1972, he described "an equatorial paradise — enchanted isles where, far from the domain of man, strange and marvelous animals lived side by side in peace" (1973, p. 17). In *Three Adventures* (1973), he particularized how molten rock shaped Punta Espinosa into an "amphitheater above the level of the sea, with circular tiers, ... the favorite spot of the penguins and of a colony of small sea lions" (*ibid.*, p. 65). At the rugged point, he found the coastline covered in marine iguanas basking in the sun. In the estimation of nature writer Peter Benchley, Cousteau's evaluation was correct. Benchley concluded, "Over the past 150 years [the Galápagos chain] has contributed incalculably to our understanding of our origins, our existence, and our destiny" (1999, p. 8).

On Fernandina, the crater of La Cumbre has erupted ten times since 1813. When it spews melted rock, the lava wipes out all life in its path, including birds flying through toxic gas. Molten rock resurfaces the long, irregular shore of Punta Espinosa, its only visitor landing site, with a new layer of black rock, where marine iguanas absorb the equatorial sunshine to raise their body temperatures. In 1968, Fernandina's caldera sank to 3,000 feet and generated waves of earthquakes, which unsettled its lake, reshaped once more the island's ashy lava field, and altered wildlife habitats. When the volcano erupted again on February 8, 1995, the outburst lasted for ten weeks, subjecting the island to a new feeding of natural nutrients from sea organisms and bleached algae churned up in heavy surf. As Darwin theorized, living things followed the principle of natural selection as the weak died out, leaving the strong to repopulate the island. French vulcanologist and photographer Maurice Krafft, author of *Volcanoes, Fire from the Earth* (1993), rephrased Darwin's theory in anthropomorphic terms: "Sometimes the Earth destroys her own creations, only to better rebuild them" (De Roy, 1995).

Today, Fernandina's lava slabs and warm waters, designated off-limits to hunters and fishers, are home to cormorants, dolphin, frigatebirds, green turtles, lava and swallowtail gulls, manta and sting rays, sea lions, sharks, and pods of orcas. Penguins carried north from Antarctica on the Humboldt Current flourish in the lava caves on Fernandina, but are thinner and less furry than the Antarctic species because of the island's warm equatorial climate. One of the most prolific plants that relieves the austere crevices of the island's volcanic slopes is the unique brachycereus or lava cactus, a stubby yellow paintbrush that grows in clumps protruding from rocky crevices.

The habitat is far from safe. The harvesting of sea cucumbers *(Isostichopus fuscus)* off Punta Espinosa and poaching of cormorants and penguins provoked a constant patrolling of Fernandina's waters and search for poachers' harvesting camps and drying operations farther inland. The International Union for the Conservation of Nature reported that poachers were snagging some 150,000 sea cucumbers per day in mid–1995, a rate that would devastate the species by 1998. In an article for *Audubon*, science writer Bruce Stutz stated that brazen fishers camping on Fernandina burned trees to steam sea cucumbers before drying and shipping them to Asian markets to be sold for as much as $60 per pound, some twenty times what fishers made from other species. During the "Sea Cucumber War," resentment grew in fishers, who saw resources as the playground rich American scientists and tourists. A face-off pitting conservationists against fishers and tour operators erupted in September 1995 with island vigilantism, molotov cocktails, death threats against the director of the Charles Darwin Research Station, and ominous schemes to kidnap and kill tourists and animals.

Nature, too, has made its onslaughts against Fernandina. In 1982, the formation of the El Niño weather phenomenon along the Ecuadorian shore quadrupled the island's number of rainy days and raised the sea temperature over three degrees and the usually mild air temperature over two degrees. Navigation became chancy and road travel, drinking water, and electrical power compromised. The verdant overgrowth of herbs, bromeliads, and climbing lianas left the island's national park inaccessible in places and increased the populations of rats and stinging fire ants. Root rot attacked scalesia trees and giant cacti.

Environmental changes disrupted the nesting of the albatross, booby, and penguin. The shift in temperature and rainfall produced a huge increase in finch and mockingbird populations, increased plants that feed insects and reptiles, and decreased the headcounts of the marine iguana, booby, and sea lion. At Punta Espinosa, the flightless cormorant temporarily disappeared, as did fish, porpoises, and whales. A recurrence of El Niño in 1997 forced the Cromwell and Peru currents deeper. The shift increased rains and raised sea temperatures by five degrees. As a result, the destruction of algae and plankton starved thousands of marine iguanas and reduced Fernandina's sea lion population. Underwater, divers found bleached coral and fewer barnacles, clams, tubeworms, and plankton, the basis of the ocean food chain. That same year, the Metropolitan cruise line established the *Fundacion Galépagos-Ecuador*, a conservation effort that joined Galápagos National Park, the Charles Darwin Foundation, and the World Fund for Nature in cleaning trash from beaches and introducing ladybugs to fight plant scale.

In December 2001, four months after the Sea Shepherd Conservation Society charged shore patrols with coddling poachers, UNESCO named the Galápagos Islands a World Heritage Site, Ecuador's third designated site. On January 18, 2002, a 140,000-gallon spill of diesel fuel and sticky bunker oil from the Ecuadorian tanker *Jessica* struck the harbor on Isabela opposite Fernandina, rousing world conservationists to action within hours. The spill set off alarms from strict preservationists who had long warned of the dangers of residential growth, tourism, commercial fishing, poaching, and lax monitoring of passing fuel tankers. Although volunteers quickly contained the spill, Fernandina's marine iguana population dropped by 60 percent.

Coastal Activities

Ecotourists, sailors, birders, naturalists, and photographers rate Punta Espinosa high on their list of shores, in particular for the sandy beaches that blend black lava and shell fragments. There are generous sightings of flightless cormorants, boobies, cow and eagle rays, flycatchers, indigenous hawks, blue and striated herons, oystercatchers, turnstone birds, short-eared owls, yellow warblers, shearwaters, and some 850,000 pairs of Galápagos penguins, the world's northernmost penguins. Swimmers enjoy beach tidepools, which harbor green turtles. Kayakers and scuba divers have close encounters with hammerhead and silky sharks, triggerfish, salema, bigeye jacks, and dolphin pods.

Visitors to Punta Espinosa develop a personal relationship with the Galápagos. Passengers on live-aboard dive boats and nature cruises discover that fur seals are brave enough to dance around skiffs and touch snorkelers; in view of hikers and bikers, sea lions give birth on the sandy strands. High above the shore, a crater lake centered with a smaller crater and another lake draw the most vigorous trekkers, birders, and rock climbers. Spelunkers press through mangrove thickets ringing the volcano crater to traverse underground lava tubes, long tunnels left empty when lava flowed through them on the way to the sea. Like Darwin, outsiders discover the rhythms of nature that rule a vibrant, ever-changing land.

Sources

Alten, Michelle, "A Tale of Three Boobies," *International Wildlife*, January/February 1998.

Beecher, Jonathan, "Variations on a Dystopian Theme: Melville's 'Encantadas,'" *Utopian Studies*, Vol. 11, No. 2, 2000, pp. 88–95.

Benchley, Peter, "Galápagos: Paradise in Peril," *National Geographic*, Vol. 195, No. 4, April 1999, pp. 2–32.

Broad, William J. *The Universe Below.* New York: Simon & Schuster, 1997.

Butler, Declan, "Galápagos Tortoise Disease 'Contained,'" *Nature*, Vol. 383, No. 6,598, September 26, 1996, p. 290.

"The Chicken and the Banana," *UNESCO Courier*, February 1994, p. 37.

Cousteau, Jacques-Yves. *Three Adventures.* Garden City, N. Y.: Doubleday & Co., 1973.

Darwin, Charles. *The Origin of Species.* New York: Modern Library, 1993.

_____. *Voyage of the Beagle.* London: Penguin Books, 1989.

De Roy, Tui, "The Day the Earth Blew," *International Wildlife*, September/October 1995.

_____, "Life in the Shadow of Death," *Geographical*, Vol. 74, No. 5, May 2002, pp. 20–24.

_____, "Such Innocent Isolation," *International Wildlife*, November/ December 1998.

Desmond, Adrian, and James Moore. *Darwin.* New York: Warner Books, 1991.

Doubilet, David, "Galápagos Underwater," *National Geographic*, Vol. 195, No. 4, April 1999, pp. 33–39.

Emory, Jerry, "Up the Volcano," *Runner's World*, Vol. 25, No. 9, September 1990, pp, 84–87.

Estes, Gregory, et al., "Darwin in Galápagos: His Footsteps through the Archipelago," *Notes and Records of the Royal Society of London*, Vol. 54, No. 3, 2000, pp. 343–368.

Fitter, Julian, et al. *Wildlife of the Galápagos.* Princeton, N. J.: Princeton University Press, 2002.

"Galápagos," *Rodale's Scuba Diving*, Vol. 11, No. 4, May 2002, p. 100.

Gordon, Bonnie Bilyeu, "Roaming the Galápagos," *Sea Frontiers*, Vol. 42, No. 1, Spring 1996, pp. 6–7.

Heppenheimer, T. A., "To the Bottom of the Sea," *American Heritage of Invention & Technology*, Vol. 8, No. 1, 1992, pp. 28–38.

Hitching, Corinne, "Wild Encounters," *Geograpical*, Vol. 74, No. 6, June 2002, pp. 90–93.

Larson, Edward J., "Pursuits & Retreats," *Atlantic Monthly*, Vol. 289, No. 1, January 2002, p. 108.

Lidz, Franz, "Tiptoeing Through the Galápagos," *Sports Illustrated*, Vol. 91, No. 9, September 6, 1999.

Lopez, Barry, "Life and Death in Galápagos," *North American Review*, Vol. 274, No. 2, June 1989, pp. 8–13.

McEwen, Alec, "The English Placenames of the Galápagos," *Geographical Journal*, Vol. 154, No. 2, 1988, pp. 234–242.

Melville, Herman. *Billy Budd and Other Stories.* New York: Penguin, 1986.

Merlen, Godfrey, "The Orca in Galápagos: 135 Sightings," *Noticias de Galápagos*, No. 60, December 1999.

"Oil Spill off Galapagos Islands Threatens Rare Species," *CNN News*, January 22, 2001.

Raeburn, Paul, "Walking in Darwin's Footsteps," *Business Week*, May 14, 2001.

Salwen, Peter. *Galápagos: The Lost Paradise.* New York: Bantam, 1990.

Stimac, Jim, "The Strangest Place on Earth," *Earth*, Vol. 7, No. 2, April 1998, pp. 72–76.

Stutz, Bruce, "The Sea Cucumber War," *Audubon*, Vol. 97, No. 3, May–June 1995, pp. 16–17.

Tasch, Paul, "Geology and Zoology — A Symbiosis: Darwin's *Beagle* Voyage and Galápagos Experience," *Earth Sciences History*, Vol. 4, No. 2, 1985, pp. 98–112.

Thurston, Harry, "Last Look at Paradise?," *International Wildlife*, May/June 1997.

"Troubled Waters; The Galápagos Islands," *Economist*, July 13, 2002.

Red Bay, Labrador

Location

On the foggy southern shores of Labrador on the strait of Belle Isle, the New World's first commercial venture flourished at Butus (also Boytus), the whaling headquarters now called Red Bay. Located 400 miles from St. John's, Newfoundland, the bay lies west of Quebec on the shallow offshore shelf known as the Grand Banks, where the Gulf Stream mingles with the cold, berg-bearing Labrador Current. One of the world's richest sources of codfish, the bay is sheltered from sea gales by Twin Islands and Saddle Island.

In the sixteenth century, the Red Bay region became the world's whaling capital for the Basques, the first European fishermen to venture to the New World. During the first global oil boom, the shores accommodated the region's largest whaling operation and Canada's first industrial complex, which extended down the St. Lawrence Seaway.

On the foggy southern shores of Labrador on the strait of Belle Isle, the New World's first commercial venture flourished at the whaling headquarters called Red Bay (courtesy of Parks Canada).

Whalers chose Red Bay for its nearness to the bowhead whale, which traveled only Arctic waters, and to the slow, steady right whale, which swam to the ice-strewn Bay of Fundy and the Gulf of Maine. The Basque success at the international whale oil trade was a major impetus to Europe's colonial expansion.

Contacts

Red Bay National Historic Site
P. O. Box 103, Rocky Harbour
Red Bay, Labrador
Canada A0K 4K0
Phone: 709–920–2142
         709–920–2051
         709–458–2417 (off season)
Fax: 709–920–2144
         709–458–2059 (off season)
Email: redbay_info@pch.gc.ca
http://www.parcscanada.gc.ca

History

Red Bay has earned its designation of Site of National Historic Significance, bestowed by the Historic Sites and Monuments Board of Canada. The shore area has been inhabited since around 7000 B.C., when paleoindians settled the shores of Labrador. Later influxes of Innu and Beothuk brought residents to waters teeming with fish. They left behind quartzite flakes and biface tools, evidence of ingenuity and diligence. After early Inuit settlers migrated to Red Bay around 2000 B.C., as stated in Moravian records, they followed whaling rituals as an essential of their shore culture.

European exploration altered the pattern of whaling at the same time that it exterminated native people by the importation of unknown diseases to a virgin soil population. Before 1500 and perhaps as early as 1300, Basque and Breton fishers set out from the Bay of Biscay in the Pyrenees between France and Spain and reached Labrador, which they called Terra Nova, Latin for "new land." The seagoing Basque had been whaling since A.D. 700. They customized the whaling boat and invented systemized harvest from pods migrating near their home grounds. In the 1500s, François Sopite Zaburu lessened the labor of beaching and stripping blubber by building rendering cookers on deck of whaling vessels and storing the oil in wood tuns. Profits were steady, but pursuit of quarry took the Basque farther from Europe as the annual migratory routes bore pods to the north Atlantic during summer months.

In 1412, Basque whalers reached Iceland, an arctic venture that prefaced voyages to North America. They left few records of their routes because they guarded maritime expansion to protect new fishing grounds from competing crews. By 1517, Basque fishers followed the whalers and set up a cod fishery in Labrador and Newfoundland. They avoided the ravages of scurvy, a curse of the seagoing man, by eating cod roe, a valuable source of vitamin C. The whalers' traffic over the Atlantic soon rivaled a parallel exploitation of the West Indies by the Spanish fleet known as the *Carrera de las Indias* [Indies Route].

Although historic details are lacking, shards of evidence attest to the lure of Canada for Western Europeans. By the time French expeditioner Jacques Cartier surveyed the eastern shores of Canada in 1534, he found French fishing trawlers in an island port. The barren shore led him to remark that Red Bay was *la terre que Dieu donna à Cayn* [the land God gave Cain] (Tuck 1985, p. 55). From 1540 to 1610, hundreds of Basque immigrants from their pre-teens into their forties proved less picky than Cartier by invading the twelve whaling harbors in Labrador's Grand Bay. With a positive outlook, they sought work and adventure as they hunted whales along southern Labrador and northern Quebec.

The resident Basques, called *Terre-Neuviers* [new-landers] in French, preferred Red Bay, the island's largest whaling port. In early summer, the right whale migrated through the Strait of Belle Isle, coming temptingly close to seamen at Red Bay. In October, the Basques anticipated the fall migration of the bowhead, a more profitable catch that produced forty barrels each. Some resided on board ships as watchmen;

others lived in sod hovels at the tryworks or along the coast at small hearths sheltered by rocky outcroppings and tent-like coverings made from tarp cloth and the skin and baleen of whales. Whalers earned 33 percent of the return, leaving 25 percent for the ship's owner and 42 percent for the outfitter. In their eagerness to prosper, within a half century, they may have reduced the whale population in Labrador's waters by 20,000.

The money did not come easy. Each year, around 1,000 whalers, some as young as eleven years old, based at Red Bay. They signed on for shares of around fifteen voyages that took them into whale migratory paths to kill and ferry back the huge bowhead and right whales. Their work involved manning a *chalupa* (also shallop or shaloupe), the forerunner of the Nantucket whaling boat. Of its sturdiness, Robert Grenier, chief of marine archeology for Parks Canada and the Department of Indian and Northern Affairs, remarked, "The Basques designed a boat that could beat the waves and get through the surf whatever the conditions" (Vincent 1998, p. 55).

The whaler's work was labor intensive and life threatening. After pursuing and locating the kill in Red Bay, the six Basque crewmen attached a drogue or sea anchor to their lines and hung fast to the expiring catch until they could finish it with lance thrusts. The job of landing a large whale could take as many as five *chalupas*, which towed the unwieldy carcass to shore for processing. If the men had to row through the strait after dark, they searched the shores for signal beacons lit at coastal stations to guide them home.

Crucial to the whaling industry was the craft of the cooper, who assembled, sealed, and repaired 55-gallon *barricas* [casks] out of oak and beech staves cut and shipped in tight bundles from western Europe. Employing iron wedges, planes, augers, drawknives, adze heads, vises, a scriber, and croze blades, the cooper followed a spiral drawn on the outside of the staves and held each barrel in a tight round of twenty split alder hoops secured with willow withes. Barrels cut in half made cooling tubs in which oil extractors poured hot whale oil into water for rapid cooling. The cooper ferried the casks from his smithy to galleons anchored in the harbor, which served as floating warehouses until the company accumulated enough oil to make profitable a voyage to Spain. From there, distributors sold oil stocks to jobbers in Flanders, Bristol, London, and Southampton.

At cutting-in piers at each whale oil center, flensers balanced on floating whale carcasses, which they streamlined by removing flippers and tail. With long parallel cuts, the men began stripping sections of blubber for processing. Workers passed each chunk of whale meat by winch to a stone tryworks or rendering furnace set up under a shed roofed with overlapping red clay tile transported from Spain as ship's ballast.

At one thirty-foot shelter built over a stone-lined firebox sunk four feet into the ground, laborers cooked whale flesh in six copper cauldrons, stoking the flame with logs, whale skin, and oily scraps. The rendering operation released a marketable oil, leaving behind scraps of copper from ruined pots and a hard black granular crust of burned blubber on stone walls. From the cauldrons, men ladled the bright oil into casks for shipping. Pay for each ship's crew ranged from five tuns of oil for a sailor to six times that amount for a sea captain.

By the 1560s, some 1,000 laborers worked the five-month season to produce 25,000 gallons of oil per week. From Labrador, the oil galleons carried their cargos on month-long journeys across the Atlantic to Europe. On the way east, ships weathered the perils of the ocean that included tricky currents and icebergs. Of the fifteen or twenty galleons at anchor, most set sail before fall, when an iced-in harbor kept remaining crew members in Red Bay for the entire winter. One such winter oc-

curred in 1574, when ice decreased productivity, forcing the price of whale oil up by 50 percent.

In June 1565, Simon and Domingo de Echaniz chartered the *San Juan*, a Basque *naos* [galleon], the slow-moving workhorse craft of both New World colonists and the whaling industry. Owned by Ramos de Arrieta y Borda of Pasajes de Fuenterrabia, Spain, it encountered unusually bad luck. As it eased from moorings in fall 1565 on the journey to Iberia, an Arctic windstorm suddenly struck the harbor and forced the oak hull into rocks, leaving its remains exposed above the waterline. Analysis of its wreckage proved that the craft was no match for hard-driving seas, which ripped open the keel some ninety feet from land. The wreck constituted the world's first oil spill.

Crew of the *San Juan* survived, but the investor lost 1,000 casks of whale oil. By 21st-century standards, the cargo of oil, used in lamps, lubricants, pitch, soap, fabric sizing, and pharmaceuticals, was worth the equivalent of $6,000 per cask for a total of $6 million. Salvors from *La Concepcion*, captained by the *San Juan's* outfitter, Juanes de Portu of San Sebastián in the Canary Islands, helped to reduce losses. With grappling hooks, they recovered usable sails, cables, and casks of wine, cider, and sea biscuit along with around half the 1,000 casks in the hold.

Documents from Red Bay illuminate the hazards of life at an isolated whaling station, which included unforeseen shifts of weather like the storm that destroyed the *San Juan*. On June 22, 1577, Juan Martinez de Larrume signed his will in the town of Orio at Red Bay. Bedfast with a debilitating illness, he settled medical and personal debts and displayed the piety of Iberian Catholics by requesting holy rites, a memorial service, and Christian burial at the local Church of Saint Nicolas. Another example of preparedness is the will of Joanes de Echaniz, a Basque whaler who completed his last testament at sea on December 24, 1584.

His death coincided with a major decline in Labrador whaling about the time that King Philip II demanded 130 galleons and 8,000 crew to man the Spanish Armada, which made a disastrous attempt at attacking England in July 1588.

Apparently, the Labrador whaling industry dwindled from lack of men, ships, and capital. After Red Bay's abandonment early in the seventeenth century, whalers moved to Spitzbergen on an archipelago in northern Norway, where cetaceans were so plentiful along fjords and islands that Dutch, English, German, and Spanish crews killed 1,059 in 1697 alone. The old Red Bay whaling station served codfishing crews and fur traders, who exploited two lucrative industries of Canada's early colonial history. In 1705, French sailor Augustin le Gardeur de Tilly, Sieur de Courtemanche, explored the region and found some 3,000 carcasses and the skulls of at least ninety enormous whales that the Basques left in one spot.

Red Bay lost its edge in the global whale oil market and receded into a less profitable, but steadier and safer fishing port. In the 1850s, residents gave the bay its current name, which reflects the color of surrounding bluffs. Late in the nineteenth century and into the twentieth, Sir Wilfred Thomason Grenfell, an English surgeon associated with the Royal National Mission to Deep Sea Fishermen and author of *Vikings of Today; or, Life and Medical Work among the Fishermen of Labrador* (1895), established a medical mission, hospitals, orphanages, and schools along the coast. In 1896, he founded Newfoundland's first fishing cooperative on the site of the defunct Basque whaling station.

Archeology

In 1977, Selma Huxley Barkham of Quebec, a great-granddaughter of English scientist Thomas Huxley and an historical geographer, collaborated with Robert Grenier and James Alexander Tuck, head archeologist at the Memorial University of Newfoundland, to survey Red Bay harbor. Barkham began her search in 1965 while working for the Canadian government, then resettled in the Burgos provincial archives in Oñate, Spain, to survey notarial documents. While supporting her family by teaching English, she learned to read Basque and devoted a decade to shuffling through court papers and wills, insurance policies, maritime contracts, and mortgages to pinpoint twelve Labrador whaling ports.

In one glimpse of the past, one of the earliest rutters or *routiers* [pilot's sailing directions] — *Voyages Avantureux* [Adventurous Voyages] (1579) by Basque sea captain Martin de Hoyarsabal — surveyed New World journeys in the 1560s and 1570s. The text proved that Red Bay was the historic Butus, also spelled Buitres, Buttes, and Buytes. From stacks of yellowed documents, Barkham gleaned ship, captain, and crew names as well as yearly kill and other cargo of whaling vessels. In 1980, the resulting project earned Barkham a gold medal from the Royal Canadian Geographical Society.

A six-year, 14,000-hour marine archeological study, the Red Bay Project, set a precedent as the most thorough examination of Canadian history. Heavy offshore concentrations of whale bone along Red Bay attest to Labrador's role in the Atlantic whaling industry. On the leeward side of Saddle Island, digs located eight whale-processing plants, two cooperages, a graveyard, and a lookout to sea. A ninth oil refinery on Penney Island to the north and additional whale bone dumps contribute to the assumption that Red Bay prospered as a whale-processing center.

Author James Tuck worked for eight seasons at Saddle Island under the sponsorship of the National Museums of Canada and Memorial University of Newfoundland to summarize the progress of archeological digs that employed sixty people. Aided by archeologist-diver Peter Waddell, designer of heated wet suits, the team at Red Bay worked in zero-degree water to locate such readily identifiable items as a porringer of majolica, a highly decorated polychromatic form of ceramic tableware made in Spain. The dig turned up three Basque galleons, a forty-foot tender or intercoastal commuter vessel called a pinnace, and four smaller whaling vessels. One of the four, a 25-foot *chalupa*, went down in the sinking of a whaler. Trapped on the starboard side, the small seagoing craft enlightened restorers to the *chalupa's* design, materials, and workmanship.

In summer 1978, a major find, the wreckage of the *San Juan*, occurred at a depth of thirty feet. The three-masted, ninety-foot vessel, weighing 700 tons and carrying some 300 tons of cargo, lay flattened on the channel floor from the pressure of winter ice. The oldest New World shipwreck north of the tropics, the remains were intact, presenting historians with the first merchant class vessel of the period for analysis. Covering the timbers was an easily removable skin of fine silt and heavy kelp. Among the detritus within or near the prefabricated frame and its flooring were items preserved by the intensely cold water — baskets, barrel cants and staves, ballast stones, nails, dowels, adze, axe, knife, harpoon, sandglass, wood reel, capstan, hemp rope, swivel gun, anchor, and a compass. Personal items included a straw mattress, utensils and plates, and the leather shoes of a crew member.

In 1983, the recovery of a charred second galleon led archeologists to conclude that it caught fire at sea. Among the treasure located in its remains was a brass astrolabe. Diver Marianne Stopp surfaced with an unusual relic — a portrait of a galleon carved on a timber. Dendrochronological study of the planking and wood stored on board provided a clearer estimation of the date that workers felled Spanish oaks to built the ship. From its dimensions and from rubber casts as well as from plans and drawings of period ships, builder Marcel Gingras began constructing a scale model of the hull in pearwood.

On land, archeologists found coins, pocket knives, a Venetian-style drinking glass, a majolica condiment or medicine jug, and wood rosary beads, along with the ubiquitous red clay roof tiles from sleeping quarters at a terraced commune. Because of the whalers' use of building material from their homeland, searcher Selma Barkham remarked in an article for *Canadian Geographic:*

> [The Basques] were not only the first large scale *exporters* of Canadian produce to London, Rouen, Antwerp and Seville, but they were also the first large scale *importers* for the construction of buildings in Canada [1978, p. 19].

On the channel islands off Red Bay, bones left over from meals as well as iron nails, a monogrammed harpoon head, coiled rope, and a wood tally stick proved that whalers lived at shore campsites in full view of migrating whale pods.

At 62 shallow, stone-marked graves in an island cemetery, in 1982, researchers recovered the skeletons of two young boys and 138 adult males, presumably those killed in the course of whaling, drowned at sea, or dead of disease or exposure at their Red Bay whaling stations while ice-bound during the winter. Remnants of Inuit scavengers suggested that, when the Basques sailed home in fall, local Indians gleaned leftovers of the desolate camps throughout the winter, leaving behind bow and arrows, slate harpoon tips, chert drill bits, and seal bones. In 1993, researchers hoped to apply medical observations and DNA testing to human remains to learn more about the origin and fate of the Beothuk.

Coastal Activities

Visitors to the National Historic Site of Red Bay, Labrador, can observe a detailed study and recreation of Canada's whaling industry. Since July 1, 1998, a visitor's center has displayed a fully excavated *chalupa*, which marine archeologist and historian Charles E. Moore, author of *Traditional Fishing Boats of the West Coast* (2002), analyzed from pieces of the original keel and frame, planking, mast holes, thwarts, and gunnels. At the central lab in Ottawa, conservators photographed, treated with waxy polyethylene glycol, freeze-dried, and re-assembled the craft, which they bolted with brass fasteners painted black to emulate the original wrought iron nails. The five-day, 2,000-kilometer return journey to Red Bay began with careful packing in a custom-built aluminum cradle to support the fragile rowboat.

In addition to the *chalupa*, the center displays recovered clothing — a knit cap, cape, jacket, blue wool pants, two shirts, wool stockings, and leather shoes with ties, the only sailor's clothing surviving from the 1500s. The garments clad corpses buried in a bog, where acid conditions preserved fibers. Tours to Saddle Island cover the remains of tryworks and the whaling graveyard. Locals also scour the area, selecting whalebone for sled runners and chunks of red clay tile for chalk and for the basis of paint. Appropriately, at the community center in the town library, Red Bay citizens exhibit the skeleton of a 450-year-old right whale along with other bones extracted from the coast.

SOURCES

"Archaeology of a Sixteenth-century Basque Whaling Boat," http://parks canada.pch.gc.ca/parks/newfoundland/red_bay/english/history2_e.htm.

Baker, Melvin, and Robert H. Cuff, "'Down North': A Historiographical Overview of Newfoundland Labrador," *Newfoundland Quarterly*, Vol. 88, No. 2, Summer/Fall 1993, pp. 2–12.

Barkham, Selma, "The Basques: Filling a Gap in Our History between Jacques Cartier and Champlain," *Canadian Geographic*, Vol. 96, No. 1, February–March 1978, pp. 8–19.

_____, "The Basque Whaling Establishments in Labrador 1536–1632," *Arctic*, Vol. 37, No. 4, 1984, pp. 515–519.

_____, "Finding Sources of Canadian History in Spain," *Canadian Geographic*, Vol. 100, No. 3, 1980, pp. 66–73.

_____, "Two Documents Written in Labrador, 1572 and 1577," *Canadian Historical Review*, Vol. 57, No. 2, 1976, pp. 235–238.

_____, and Robert Grenier, "Divers Find Sunken Basque Galleon in Labrador," *Canadian Geographic*, Vol. 97, No. 3, February–March 1978, pp. 60–63.

"Discovery in Labrador: A 16th-Century Basque Whaling Port and Its Sunken Fleet," *National Geographic*, July 1985, pp. 40–49.

Fagan, Brian, "Basques of Red Bay," *Archaeology*, September–October 1993, pp. 44–51.

Grenier, Robert, "The Basque Whaling Ship from Red Bay, Labrador," *International Symposium on Archaeology of Medieval and Modern Ships*, 2001, pp. 269–193.

_____, "Excavating a 400-year-old Basque Galleon," *National Geographic*, Vol. 168, No. 1, July 1985, pp. 58–67.

Jerkic, Sonja, "Burials and Bones: A Summary of Burial Patterns and Human Skeletal Research in Newfoundland and Labrador," *Newfoundland Studies*, Vol. 9, No. 2, 1993, pp. 213–234.

Laxalt, Robert, "The Indomitable Basques," *National Geographic*, Vol. 168, No. 1, July 1985, pp. 69–71.

Page, Denis, "Red Bay Whaling Galleon," *Skin Diver*, April 1989, pp. 34–35.

Pope, Peter. *Ships and Navigation in Atlantic Canada in the 16th Century*. Torbay, Newfoundland: Nova Scotia Department of Tourism and Culture, 1992.

Proulx, Jean-Pierre. *Basque Whaling in Labrador in the 16th Century*. (monograph) Ottawa: Canadian Parks Service, 1993.

"Red Bay, Labrador," http://www.ucs.mun.ca/~k15djy/intro.html.

Sanger, C. W., and A. B. Dickinson, "Newfoundland and Labrador Shore-Station Whaling: Overexpansion and Decline, 1905–1917," *Northern Mariner*, Vol. 10, No. 4, 2000, pp. 13–38.

Taylor, J. Garth, "The Arctic Whale Cult in Labrador," *Etudes/Inuit/Studies*, Vol. 9, No. 2, 1985, pp. 121–132.

Théorêt, Marc, "Découverte d'un Galion au Labrador," *Diving*, Vol. 7, No. 4, May 1979.

Tuck, James A., "Unearthing Red Bay's Whaling History," *National Geographic*, Vol. 168, No. 1, July 1985, pp. 50–57.

Vincent, Mary, "Ancient Whaler," *Canadian Geographic*, November–December 1998, p. 55.

Zulueta, Julian de, "The Basque Whalers: The Source of Their Success," *Mariner's Mirror*, Vol. 86, No. 3, 2000, pp. 261–271.

Roskilde Fjord, Denmark

Location

A long probing finger of the Baltic Sea, Roskilde Fjord extends 45 miles north from Isefjord and lies due west of Copenhagen, Denmark, and penetrates the north end of Sjaeland [Zeeland] Island. Covering extensive submerged eelgrass meadows, the waters produce algae, phytoplankton, and seagrasses. As explained by Saxo Grammaticus's *Gesta Danorum* [Deeds of the Danes] (ca. 1185) and by *Hralf's Saga Kraka* (ca. 1100s), an Iceland legendary saga, the shallow, wind-swept estuary was the Viking heartland. It took its place-name from "Hroar or Ro's *kilde* [spring]," a spot once owned by the mid-sixth century Viking founder Ro.

The city of Roskilde, once Denmark's capital and religious center, grew into one of the metropolises of northern Europe and celebrated its 1,000th birthday in 1998. Since its eclipse by Copenhagen at the end of the Middle Ages, Roskilde became a university town, county seat, and rail center. Today, it manufactures machinery, leather, pharmaceuticals, and distilled goods and cures bacon and other meats. The region is a tourist haven known for its cathedral, royal burial sites, fishing grounds, woodlands and beaches, and a world-class museum collection of preserved Viking ships.

Contact

Tourist Bureau of Roskilde
Roskilde-Egnens Turistbureau
Gullandsstraede 15, Postboks 637
4000 Roskilde, Denmark
Phone: 45–46–35–27–00
Fax: 45–46–35–14–74
Email: info@destination-roskilde.dk
http://www.destination-roskilde.dk/

Frederikssund Tourist Information Centre
Havnegade Five A
Denmark 3600, Frederikssund
Phone: 45–47–31–06–85
Fax: 45–47–31–36–74
http://www.frederikssund-tourist.dk

Vikingeskibsmuseet Museum
Strandengen, DK-4000
Roskilde, Denmark
Phone: 45–42–35–6555
Fax: 45–42–32–2115
http://www.mac-roskilde.dk.

Legend

Roskilde (or Roeskilde) became a holy city because it was the residence and burial site of Danish kings. During the A.D. 600s, King Hrolf Kraki ordered his ironmaster to forge an all-conquering sword. Similar to the Arthurian Excalibur, the sword took on a name, Skofnung, a personality, and a reputation for achieving great victories for Hrolf. When enemies loomed, the anthropomorphic sword shuddered at taunts and shrieked to be loosed from its scabbard. Because Hrolf's subjects feared the battle-keen weapon, they added it to the king's burial treasure and buried it with his remains and grave goods in the royal vault at Roskilde. The sword's reputation grew, influencing the combat passages of *Hrolf's Saga*.

In the late A.D. 900s, the Danish *Landnamabok* [Book of Settlements], first printed in 1688, reported that Skeggi of Midfirth won a lottery that allowed him to pillage Hrolf's tomb and seize the invincible Skofnung from the king's bony fist. The desecrator valued the cold killing edge and followed legendary injunctions to protect the hilt from the sun's rays and from the unworthy eyes of females. Because of these taboos,

The city of Roskilde, once Denmark's capital and religious center, boasts a world-class museum collection of preserved Viking ships (courtesy of Frederikssund/Hornsherred Turistbureau).

Skeggi was unwilling to lend Skofnung to his friend and fellow warrior Cormac. Because Cormac continued to plead, Skeggi allowed him the use of Skofnung, but Cormac was unable to draw it from its scabbard.

Skofnung remained a treasured possession passed from father to son. The *Laxdaela Saga* (ca. A.D. 1245) claimed that, in the early 1000s, Eid, Skeggi's son, inherited the sword. Eid responded to the death of his own son, Skeggi's grandson, by arming the avenger Thorkel Egjolfsson with Skofnung for an attack on the outlaw Grim. However, Thorkel betrayed Eid by befriending Grim.

Thorkel and Grim became fellow warriors. With Skofnung in hand, Thorkel thrived in combat and brandished his weapon as though he owned it. As told in Chapter LVI of the saga, on his voyage to Broadfirth on Maundy Thursday around 1026, he was shipwrecked and drowned along with his warriors. A shattered timber in which Skofnung was imbedded washed up on Easter morning at an island named Skofnungsey. Thorkel's son Gellir retrieved the weapon, which he claimed for himself. In old age, Gellir went on a pilgrimage to Rome, gained atonement and inner peace, and returned to Roskilde to die. The Danes passed the 300-year-old sword to its rightful owner by reinterring it with King Hrolf. Modern weapons makers devoted evolving technology to copying the famous sword.

History

Roskilde was once a heavily populated center of Danish might, which grew from A.D. 800 to 1100 in tandem with Viking dominance of sea lanes and distant shores. For three centuries, kings post raiders along the fjord. The restless warriors set out west to Northumberland and south to North Africa and wrested control of coastal peoples. In a display of Norse manhood, they spurned sails in favor of oars, an extension of arm power into the sea. In 1986 a short distance inland from the fjord, Danish archeologist Tom Christensen, curator of the Roskilde Vikingeskibshallen [Viking Ship] Museum, began a two-year excavation of a huge Viking hall that may have been the headquarters of these sailors and the era's Nordic royalty.

The intersection between Viking might and Christianity generated great change in Roskilde. In A.D. 940, the warrior-king Harald "Blue-Tooth" Gormson began his 45-year reign on the fjord. He introduced literacy and record-keeping to the Danes. Through his friendship with Belgian evangelist Poppo of Stavelot, the nation abandoned paganism and embraced Christianity as the Danish state religion. Harald provided the first wooden worship center, the site on which the medieval Roskilde Cathedral was built.

When Harold's ambitious son Sweyn (or Svein) I Forkbeard overthrew and banished the king, Sweyn developed a ferocious reputation. Unlike his pious father, he learned sailing from a Viking master and, in 1013, amassed an armada to direct against England's Ethelred the Unready, whom Sweyn also exiled. The third in the royal dynasty, Canute (or Knut) II the Good, took the throne during a seafarer's ceremony at which his sailors acclaimed his reign. From Roskilde, Canute swept across Scandinavia, overwhelming the fleets of Sweden and Norway. He became the first ruler to unite England, Denmark, and Norway into a single realm.

Archeology

In the 1960s, the discovery of five wood vessels in Roskilde Fjord at Skuldelev produced a stir among historians. The location of the Viking ships was not news to Danish skippers, who began finding medieval salvage in 1898. The widening of the fjord mouth in 1924 unearthed a keelson or mast step in the seabed wreckage, which preservers housed in the National Museum. Diver Jan Uhre added to the cache of Viking oddments in 1953. Three years later, sport divers Hartvig Conradsen and Age Skjelborg became the first to report a section of

hull framing, which lay at 6.5 feet. Local lore erroneously identified the wreckage as one of the ships of Margaret I, who ruled centuries later, from 1376 to 1412. In 1957, Olaf Olsen and Ole Crumlin-Pedersen, director of the Centre for Maritime Archaeology, led a study of the wreckage for the National Museum and, using dendrochronology or tree-ring dating, correctly placed the hulks in the Viking era.

Recovery of the historic ships began with the erection of a cofferdam in summer 1962 and steady excavation, which continued until 1969. Studied under the supervision of naval specialists, the single-masted ships emerged from myth into reality. Just as ancient sagas had described, the Nordic *langskipet* [longship] was designed lean and lethal and built clinker-style or with overlapping pine and oak planks pegged together with metal rivets. Each ship glided on curved hulls, a technology dating to the early 1000s. As explained by Yale-trained archeologist John R. Hale of the University of Louisville, the Vikings crafted the *langskipet* at a ratio of six to one — so long and thin that it could prowl inland channels.

The Roskilde find dated to the late Viking era, when design called for great Nordic ships seating oarsmen at thirty rowing benches. Numbered one through five, the recovered hulks demonstrated a variety of styles:

• Number one, a 45-foot, 24-ton *knarr* or *hafskip* [cargo vessel], a standard oceangoing workhorse, put to sea around 1030. Built in Norway of pine, fir, oak, and lime, this vessel held thirty tons and was capable of journeying across the Atlantic on Viking explorations of Iceland, Greenland, and Vinland, a Canadian landfall. After extensive wear, the ship was replanked with oak.

• Number two, a slender 100-foot oak warship derived from shipworks near Dublin,

Ireland. The shipwright used locally felled timber and a design ratio of seven to one, a long, narrow craft that held up to 100 warriors and thirty rowers.

- Number three, a weathered 46-foot oak *karv* [merchantman], held six oarsmen. It put to sea around 1070 as a local coaster intended to hold some five tons of goods from trade along Danish shores and the Baltic Sea.
- Number four, a thin, 55-foot, thirteen-oar ash, oak, and pine warship or troop carrier bore a striking edging — Viking shields lashed to the gunwales. Out of king-mandated *Leidang* [duty] to national defense, Danish peasants built the thirty-man craft around 1030 at a ratio of seven to one. Local seagoing militia maintained the ship, which remained in the king's service for the call to war — the dispatch of a runner bearing a symbolic arrow. After heavy use, some three decades later, the ship underwent extensive repair.
- Number five, a 35-foot pine-planked and oak-keeled fishing vessel or ferry, the smallest of the five, which builders completed in Norway.

The five ships were additives to the Peberrenden Blockade, a strategic stone barrier that protected the fjord and its trade from the deep-draft vessels of invaders. At the inlet's narrows, defenders stripped the aging ships of their rigging, loaded them with boulders, and scuttled them — three after A.D. 1070 and two for reinforcement after A.D. 1100. Low water temperatures slowed the disintegration of the wood. Preserved at the Roskilde Museum, today, the five ships serve as models for replicas that allow modern shipwrights to use Viking tools — ax, plane, awl, drawknife, chisel — to duplicate early carpentry and help sailors to relive the sailing conditions experienced in the Middle Ages.

In 1996, when the museum staff commissioned a waterfront building to hold the five ships, dredgers of the harbor were startled by the disclosure of nine more hulks. These included a 119-foot *drekar* [dragon boat] or troop carrier, the longest Viking craft ever excavated, which Danish archeologists unearthed in September 1997. The craft held 100 crewmen and 37 rowers. Through dendrochronology, experts linked the craft to lumber cut in A.D. 1025, during the reign of Canute II the Good. Ole Crumlin-Pedersen deduced that the lightning-swift warship, the largest class of Danish strike vessel, sank in a gale.

Coastal Activities

On historic ground once claimed by Europe's most feared sea raiders, visitors can enjoy beaches, horseback riding, cycling, sailing, cruising, and boating. Culture seekers enjoy Viking drama and the award-winning summer music festival, a late–June banquet of big band, folk, jazz, orchestral, and rock music that has thrived for over a quarter century. At reed beds, salt meadows, and along shores and creeks, bird enthusiasts trek near veritable bird roll call — the coot, cormorant, dunnock, goldeneye, graylag goose, grebe, heron, linnet, mallard, moorhen, osprey, pochard, red kite, redshank, shelduck, shoveler, siskin, skylark, smew, teal, tufted duck, wigeon, and yellowhammer.

For the antiquarian, Roskilde is a trove of Viking, medieval, and renaissance lore. Historians peruse the Lejre open-air museum of prehistoric life, Ledreborg Palace, and Roskilde Priory, built in 1560 to accommodate pious women in a refined, luxurious manse. The sea-minded access Denmark's National Museum to study the culture of a seafaring people and examine the five Nordic ships housed at the Roskilde ship museum. At the museum's harbor, replicas of the ships allow individuals to grip the oars and imagine the task of maneuvering medieval ships along the fjord and out to sea.

Aiding in the reclamation of ancient artifacts is the Roskilde Fjord Gruppen, a coterie of scuba enthusiasts that excavates finds in cooperation with Danish museums. From April to November, the divers aim to locate tools, bones and antlers, flint blades, and wood domestic remnants of the *Konge-mosekulturen*, the prehistoric era after 6400 B.C. The divers work from a dory and extend their nets into likely locales, such as the site at Blak island, which they explored from 1989 to 1993. Their underwater archeology yielded a human jawbone that may have been the refuse of cannibal meals dumped into a kitchen midden.

SOURCES

Byock, Jesse, trans. *The Saga of King Hralf Kraki.* London: Penguin, 1998.
"Denmark Honors Tourism in Scandinavia," *Stamps,* Vol. 251, No. 11, June 10, 1995, pp. 1–2.
Hale, John R., "The Viking Longship," *Scientific American,* February 1998.
Osborn, Marijane, "Two-Way Evidence in Beowulf Concerning Viking-Age Ships," *ANQ: A Quarterly of Short Articles, Notes, and Reviews,* Vol. 13, No. 2, Spring 2000, pp. 3–6.
Rayburn, Kevin, "Genius and Terror on the High Seas," *University of Louisville Magazine,* Winter 1999.
The Secret Arts. Enchanted World series. Alexandria, Va.: Time-Life, 1987.
"Viking Museum in Denmark," *Sunset,* Vol. 171, August 1983, p. 38.

Salvador da Bahia, Brazil

Location

Salvador da Bahia lies on the northern horn of the deep Todos os Santos [Bay of All Saints] of Bahia, a deep natural harbor that is the cultural and spiritual heart of Brazil. The capital, fourth largest, and most Africanized city, Salvador claims the second largest African population after Nigeria.

Heavily coastal in orientation, the city looks out on fishing crews and sailboats plying the Atlantic Ocean. On the eastern extreme of the Recôncavo, the shell of land that encircles the bay, Salvador stands as the gateway to calm inner waters and a guardpost against invaders.

History

On his way west from Lisbon to India, Portuguese navigator Pedro Álvares Cabral was the first European to explore Brazil. Named admiral of a fleet of thirteen caravels, in early March 1500, he accepted the charge of Manuel I to follow the route of Vasco da Gama and to establish commerce with nations to the west. Traveling southwest, Cabral landed at Porto Seguro, Brazil, on April 22, 1500. He sent one of his ships back to Portugal to inform the king of a significant landfall at a land Cabral called Vera Cruz [true cross], a pious place-name later changed to Salvador [savior]. Eighteen months later on All Saints' Day, November 1, 1501, merchant-explorer Amerigo Vespucci, an Italian sailing from Lisbon for the Portuguese crown, arrived at the bay.

The reports of Brazil's rich coastline spurred settlers to build communities at the bay. At the behest of Joaõ III, later expeditioners followed Martim Afonso de Sousa, Brazil's first colonizer, and settled the deep inlet at Bahia in 1531. Eighteen years later, 1,000 newcomers, led by Tomé de Sousa, a gentleman soldier, chose Salvador, the cradle of Brazilian civilization, as the new nation's original capital and coastal defense point against the Dutch and French. Accompanying the first wave of colonists were Jesuit missionaries who set about converting Indians to Christianity. Within two years, the Catholic hierarchy created the diocese of São Salvador da Bahia.

At the price of a wave of miseries — smallpox, plague, and hemorrhagic dysentery — by 1560, the city of Salvador began developing its greatness. Jesuit chronicler Antonio Serafim Leite, compiler of *Monumenta Brasilae* [Monuments of Brazil] (ca. 1560), described how aborigines fled contagion in the *aldeias* [mission compounds]. Those who were too sick to run received makeshift treatment from missionaries, who peeled away corruption from legs and feet with scissors and washed the live flesh to remove disease.

As tribes thinned out from the scourge, Marshall C. Eakin, author of *Brazil, the Once and Future Country* (1997), explained the high loss of indigenous laborers and their replacement by black Africans:

> Starving and sickly Indians staggered into the colonial settlements begging for food and work. With the breakdown of barter, the difficulties of fighting both Indians and Jesuits, and the rising demand for labor on the sugar plantations, the Portuguese began to look for an alternative to native labor [p. 18].

The cheapest and most expendable choice were black Africans, whom Portuguese slavers captured on the Gold Coast and bound into coffles of sugar cane workers. [*See also* ELMINA CASTLE, GHANA.] Arriving from Angola, Congo, Ghana, and Mozambique in 1570, the first Africans, called *Negros Bantos* [black Bantus] began rapidly replacing less hardy Indian press gangs.

Heavy sea traffic altered Salvador da Bahia into a major Portuguese port — second only to Lisbon — for the receipt of slaves and the exportation of diamonds, dyes from the *pau do brasil* tree, gold, and sugar. The importation of Africans for the auction block rapidly altered the bay's racial makeup and inspired the pious to greater acts of Christianizing the heathen. The Catholic Inquisition arrived in 1618; six years later, the city fell temporarily to pirates, but, within the year, returned to Portuguese control. In 1700, as smallpox once more swept Angola, slavers cut their risks by importing new labor forces solely from Benin, Nigeria, and Togo. Because half of all the world's slavers sold their human cargo in Brazil, the black African and mulatto population burgeoned to four million.

After the first permanent European residents settled *Vila Velha* [Old Village] on an inner beach, later European arrivals built similar inland dwellings sheltered by bluffs and free of strong Atlantic winds and ocean undercurrents. While forts, piers, and warehouses developed along the shore for over three centuries, *donatários* [landholders] chose the tall bluffs for government offices, estates, boutiques, and permanent mansions and villas. The separation of high and low country produced a division of ethnicity and social class, with African tastes, patois, and rhythms dominating the waterfront.

Into the nineteenth century, West Africans enriched Salvador with their labors and established an ethnic base of some 80 percent of the populace as compared to around 20 percent Europeans. The hardiest of imported black slaves jumped ship at Salvador and moved inland to *quilombos*, black outlaw communities that drew additional runaways from mines and farmsteads. By 1850, when the slave trade was outlawed, some 3.6 million African slaves had passed through the port of Salvador to wealthy plantations growing coconuts, coffee, sugarcane, and tobacco. Clandestine slaving continued for another two decades, extending local ties to the homeland, Western Africa. Although flesh peddling ceased, Brazil underwent protracted slave ownership until the liberation of blacks in 1888, the last human emancipation on the globe. Because of the imbalance of land ownership, the disparity between white profiteers and black laborers placed less than 5 percent of the population over the remaining 95 percent.

Ritual

As a legacy of slavery, Salvador was long a center of African sensuality and ecstatic worship, marked by trances and possession by *orisha* or *orixa* [spirits]. According to folk history, in the early 1800s, Iyá Nasso, a freed Afro-Brazilian woman, imported Caboclo Candomblé, an Afro-Brazilian variant of voodoo and Santería that placed women in positions of power and authority. Nasso erected Engenho Velho (or Casa Branca), the first Candomblé *terreiro* [temple]. After seven years of ritual study in Nigeria, Nasso's daughter Marcelina rose from temple maiden to high priestess, called Mother of the Saints. On journeys from the motherland to Bahia, other religious Africans became go-betweens and ferried to Salvador additional liturgy, charms and spells, cures, and methods of divining. Many independent dirt-floor temples sprang up in pious communities, where female priestesses danced themselves into frenzies, then dressed and acted the part of the West African divinity that possessed them.

To discourage rebellion, government officials allowed Afro-Brazilians to congregate, worship, and dance Yoruban style the capoira, a stylized hand-to-hand combat that slaves cultivated as an outlet for rage at their captors. These gatherings prolonged an African mindset in blacks and slowed acculturation to European tastes, attitudes, and religious beliefs. Blacks felt more at home with their intimate spirit world than with the lifeless plaster saints and gods that the Catholic Church displayed in niches.

To escape persecution by missionaries and officials, who denounced African-style worship, slaves appeased the Roman Catholic hierarchy by syncretizing their gods with Christian divinities and saints. Covertly, Orishans transformed Oxala, god of beneficence and purity, into Jesus and propitiated Ogum, their ancient war god, during the feast of St. George. They turned Xango, the wilderness spirit, into St. John the Baptist and worshipped Omulu, the god of smallpox, in the guise of St. Lazarus the leper. Stealthy church-goers wore crucifixes

along with colorful African beads and talismans and promoted Catholic lay brotherhoods and sisterhoods as a mask for their true religion. Such accommodation of Portuguese overlords allowed blacks to perpetuate the age-old Nigerian cult of Candomblé while simultaneously adding powerful white gods to their original pantheon.

Like their African-American cousins, who shouted and gyrated with the spirit in Protestant revival services, Afro-Brazilians expressed the Candomblé faith by manifesting the presence of deities and incorporating godhood into their flesh. At transcendent moments, congregations drummed, clapped, sang, and tapped their feet to rhythmic chants as the spirit permeated the human community. Barefoot dancers acted out Yoruban legends and performed sacred motions beseeching the goddess for blessing and healing. Some practitioners, unable to choose between loyalties to past and present, followed both Candomblé and Catholicism.

Generally more easygoing than Spanish inquisitors and overlords, Portuguese officials nonetheless banned public practice of Candomblé in the early 1800s. African *orisha* worship remained underground until 1970, when the old-country faith burst into popularity as an element of black identity. Salvador's animists began asserting their African origins, opening temples to visitors, and organizing street and beach processions and rituals. Each year on New Year's Eve and on February 2, tens of thousands of black Bahians dressed in white and blue and congregated at Todos os Santos to celebrate the pagan festival of Yemanjá (also called Iemanja, Iyá, Janaina, Queen of Aioká, Yemaja, and Ynaê), a protective mermaid and mistress of the seas and fresh flowing waters.

A cleansing, sustaining orisha, Yemanjá represented energy, balance, and a feminine duality that brought the gentle tropical seasons as well as typhoons and death on the deep. As a nature goddess, mother of waters, and consort of fishers, she orchestrated winds, tides, and storms. Imported along with black Yoruban slaves from Benin and Nigeria, she shared in the fate of West Africans as they were borne over the middle passage from the Bight of Benin to slave auction houses in Brazil, Cuba, and Puerto Rica. To cultivate Yemanjá in a Roman Catholic state, black devotees identified her with the Virgin Mary, a deity of fertility and maternity. Yemanjá became the creator of life for giving birth to most of the other deities in the West African pantheon.

On the annual women's festival night, the climax of a seven-day Carnaval, much of the Salvador beachfront became an open-air sanctuary to Yemanjá. At the shoreline, celebrants shot fireworks, drummed uninterrupted heart rhythms, and danced with exaggerated gestures representing the motions of the sea. Other celebrants lit candles before images of Yemanjá at the water's edge or bore offerings to deposit in the waves while expressing hope for good fortune.

At the upscale Rio Vermelho Beach, an artists' colony adjacent to Salvador's tourist section, the annual festival turned the strand into Yemanjá Beach. A flotilla of boaters intoned Yoruban prayers to Yemanjá as they upended baskets in which to drop bright flowers, melons, fragrant soap and cologne, liquor, cigarettes, bangles, and combs and mirrors and deposited the gifts in the surf. If the baskets traveled out to sea, the faithful knew that the goddess had accepted them and would provide a profitable year for fishers. If not, each participant had to choose a more appealing method of wooing the mother of the waters.

Coastal Activities

Called the Brazilian New Orleans for its colorful festivities, Salvador offers a variety of experiences. Its highrises mark the Port of Barra, a lively beach center that ex-

tends east to Farol da Barra, site of a lighthouse and of sheltered pools, a favorite wading spot for little children. The sea stronghold, Fort São Marcello, guards the marina. Because Barra's waters are polluted, beachgoers sun, but don't swim or surf. The best water sport is offshore at Itaparica Island and along the northern coast. Traveling along the Green Line highway, tourists relax on the sandy shores at Praia do Forte and observe wildlife preserves for the TAMAR [Tartaruga Marinha] Project, which have ensured the survival of endangered giant sea turtles since 1982.

At the historic district of Pelourinho, named for the pillory or whipping post on which overseers lashed and tortured recalcitrant slaves, UNESCO declared the cobbled streets and baroque dwellings and churches a world treasure. The heart of the historic district is the slave-built Rosário dos Pretos Church. Before emancipation, out of some 300 churches, Rosário was the only religious house that accepted black worshippers. For festival-goers, the best time of the year is Carnaval, the pre-lenten holiday held in February or March, which anticipates the austerity and dietary taboos of the pre–Easter season with revelry. Less commercialized than the heavily orchestrated parades and street dances in New Orleans and Rio de Janeiro, Salvador's Carnaval offers extensive nightlife, tableaux by the Ballet Folklorico de Bahia, and *blacos* [street singers], performing to *trios eléctricos* the lambada and *samba de roda*, the Yoruban national dance.

Sources

Amado, Jorge. *Bahia de Todos os Santos*. Sao Paulo, Brazil: Martins, 1956.

Aufderheide, Patricia, "True Confessions: The Inquisition and Social Attitudes in Brazil at the Turn of the XVII Century," *Luso-Brazilian Review*, Vol. 10, No. 2, 1973, pp. 208–240.

Bellos, Alex, "Girl of 10 in Line to Lead Brazilian Religion," *Manchester Guardian*, August 14, 2000.

Bernhardson, Wayne, et al. *South America on a Shoestring*. Hawthorn, Victoria: Lonely Planet, 1994.

Cobb, Charles E., Jr., "Bahia, Where Brazil Was Born," *National Geographic*, August 2002, pp. 62–81.

Eakin, Marshall C. *Brazil, the Once and Future Country*. New York: St. Martin's Press, 1997.

Palmer, Colin, "African Slave Trade: The Cruelest Commerce," *National Geographic*, Vol. 182, No. 3, September 1992, pp. 62–91.

Rotella, Sebastian, "In Brazil, a Threat to Fusion of Religions," *Los Angeles Times*, August 8, 1998, p. A18.

Schubert, Guilherme, "O Desmembramento das Dioceses do Brasil," *Revista do Instituto Histórico e Geográfico Brasileiro*, Vol. 316, 1977, pp. 152–169.

Walker, Sheila S., "Africanity vs. Blackness: Race, Class and Culture in Brazil," *NACLA Report on the Americas*, Vol. 35, No. 6, May/June 2002.

_____, ed. *African Roots/American Cultures: Africa in the Creation of the Americas*. Lanham, Md.: Rowman & Littlefield Publishers, 2001.

Selinus, Cilicia, Turkey

Location

A major port during the classical era, Selinus (also Selinos), now known as Selinti, Turkey, lies south of the appealing fishing town of Gazipasa (or Gazipasha) in a region formerly known as Cilicia. The coastal strip, not to be confused with the Sicilian colony of the same name, appears to have been occupied from 600 B.C. After the discovery of iron ore and the development of iron smelting and tool and weapon manufacture, the region, under the Hittite name Kizzuwadna, was long under Assyrian rule. As an imperial possession of Rome, the province of Cilicia covered the southern shores of Asia Minor and ranged inland from the Anatolian coast up the steep slopes of the Amanus and Taurus mountains.

Built on a triangular jut of seashore in a flat river valley, the city of Selinus occupied a shore frequently jarred by earth tremors. It took shape on an impregnable upthrust of rock that rises above hidden coves and sea crevices that served pirates as hideouts. In addition to shocks and quakes, the site suffered heat, humidity, and challenges to health from coastal swamps and lagoons that gave the region an unsavory reputation. In its favor were narrow coastal plains supporting stands of cedar, a prime source of lumber for shipbuilding.

Contacts

Turkish Tourist Office
821 United Nations Plaza
New York, New York 10017
Telephone: 1-212-687-2194
Fax: 1-212-599-7568
Email: ny@tourismturkey.org
http://www.tourismturkey.org
www.turkey.org/intro.html

History

The region around Selinus, called Kue in the Old Testament, was a rough buffer state lacking its own monarchy. Claimed by the Hittites, rulers of a vast stretch of empire from Mesopotamia to Syria and Palestine, the shore community offered rich alluvial farmland and pasturage, the source of horses for King Solomon's purchasing agents. The trading agreement mentioned in I Kings 10: 28–29 names the going price of 150 silver shekels for a horse.

Helpless to alter their quandary, Selinians experienced centuries of warring imported by outsiders. In 557 B.C., King Neriglissar (also Nergal-shar-usur) of Babylon, the son-in-law of Nebuchadnezzar and a brazen usurper, campaigned against Piriddu. In a vicious bid to control eastward trade routes, Nerglissar burned Selinus all the way to the harbor. In the winter of 334–333 B.C., Alexander II the Great of Macedon carried his campaign along the coast and out-manned local chieftains, who

The city of Selinus received historical notice from Pliny the Elder as a haven of trans–Mediterranean pirates (courtesy of Eddie Dunmore).

foolishly attempted to shut their gates and refuse him provisions for his march to the East.

Like all of Cilicia, the city of Selinus lost its tribal edge through Hellenization, which replaced Assyrian influence and brought sculptors and coiners to impose a Greek identity on an Asian shore. The city received historical notice in Pliny the Elder's encyclopedia *Natural History* (A.D. 77), Pliny the Elder and in Claudius Ptolemy's *Geographia* (ca. A.D. 150). As described in Plutarch's *Lives* (A.D. 115), the coastline became the haven of trans–Mediterranean brigands. The pirate headquarters flourished for a century beginning in 139 B.C. in a virtual free zone that spread from Phaselis in Lycia west to Dianium, Spain. In his text on Pompey, Plutarch noted:

> The power of the pirates first commenced in Cilicia, having in truth but a precarious

and obscure beginning, but gained life and boldness afterwards in the wars of Mithradates [VI], where they hired themselves out and took employment in the king's service [1959, p. 260].

Thriving both as thieves and mercenaries, outlaws like Chief Zenicetes made useless captives walk the plank, offered more appealing kidnapped victims for sale at dockside, forced the best laborers into slavery at pirate ship-building harbors, and retained for ransom those with rank or promising lineage. Professional slavers called in at the coast to trade oil and wine for captives and merchandised them at the flourishing slave auction houses on the duty-free island of Delos. [*See also* DELOS.]

After over a century of freebooting, Cilician pirates took advantage of Rome's civil strife and inattention to coastal waters to prey upon merchants at sea and to plunder islands and seaports at will. Plutarch commented on the brigands' organization:

> Diverse arsenals, or piratic harbours, as likewise watch-towers and beacons, all along the sea-coast; and fleets … well manned with the finest mariners, and well served with the expertest pilots, and composed of swift-sailing and light-built vessels adapted for their special purpose [*ibid.*].

So ostentatious were the pirates that they decked out their craft with gilt masts, purple sails, and silver oars and feasted and danced along the shore. Plutarch estimated corsair fleets at 1,000 vessels and charged them with looting 400 cities, despoiling residents, burning ships, and desecrating temples.

The lawless Cilician coast drew Roman attention in 102 B.C., when the loss of notable citizens and ships' cargoes to pirate bands became morally intolerable as well as financially crippling to the Republic. To foster badly needed grain supplies to the army, the Roman navy, led by the praetor Marcus Antonius, suppressed brigandage and, in 100 B.C., earned for himself a public triumph. In 67 B.C., Gnaeus Pompey the Great, backed by Senate decree and a fleet of 500 ships, divided the Mediterranean into sixteen strike zones and set out to end piracy. He required only forty days to wipe out the remaining buccaneers, disband their rogue brotherhood, and seize ninety ill-gotten warships. The few outlaws who escaped to Cilician hideouts he scoured from their dens. He shaped the area into a province and, nine years later, added to its domain the island of Cyprus.

Lacking interest in the area around Selinus, Rome governed the Cilician coast from Syria, a territory more suited to administration and military control of a long, ragged shoreline. The harbors served as a receiving point for Roman provisions and as an exporting station of fruit, olives, timber, wheat, and oil and wine, dispensed in locally made koan-styled or pinch-handled amphorae [storage jars]. After the triumvir Mark Antony, grandson of Marcus Antonius, presented Cilicia to his paramour, Queen Cleopatra of Egypt, in 32 B.C., she exploited the coast for timber to build a navy by which she and Antony intended to rule the eastern Mediterranean. [*See also* ALEXANDRIA, EGYPT.]

Under the ineluctable thumb of the Roman Empire, Selinus, at its historic peak, took the name Trajanopolis in honor of Trajan, the ambitious emperor. He sheltered along the coast on his way home from a successful campaign in Mesopotamia begun in fall A.D. 114. Already weakened by combat wounds, an earthquake at Antioch in December A.D. 116, and Jewish rebellions, the 64-year-old emperor wept that he lacked the strength to outpace Alexander the Great and to impose law and order on an ungovernable coast. Trajan suffered a stroke in Syria and died at Selinus on August 8 or 9, A.D. 117. His survivors dispatched his ashes to Rome in a gold urn for burial under a memorial column; a cenotaph at Selinus marked his death in Asia Minor.

After the city of Selinus merged with Isauria, from the A.D. 400s, the coastal community declined in importance. In the 700s, the rise of Islam weakened Cilician chieftains and returned the area to piracy and lawlessness. Disease and poverty diminished the citizenry to the poorest of Anatolia. Under the rule of the Emperor Constantine VII Porphyrogenitus, author of *De Administrando Imperio* [On the Governance of the Empire] (950), the city shrank to a nondescript seaside town.

Archeology

Selinus remains in ruins, which offer glimpses of a porticoed quayside market, aqueduct, cisterns and two-story public bath, burial ground, and theater. Using advanced electronic survey equipment, terrain studies, and satellite maps, from 1996 to

2000, archeologists Jason DeBlock, Michael Hoff, and Rhys Townsend — under the supervision of Nicholas K. Rauh, a history professor at Purdue University, and LuAnn Wandsnider of the University of Nebraska at Lincoln — studied the ancient city as part of a survey of 35 miles of coast. The project, funded by the National Science Foundation and the American Research Institute in Turkey, encompassed small sites and additional ancient cities — Antiochia, Iotape, Kestros, Laertes, Lamos, and Nephelion. After the combing of six urban sites and seventy rural locations, searchers found few artifacts from the pirate era and Hellenic Greece and even fewer that linked Selinus to the Phoenicians of the late Bronze Age, to Greeks from Kos and Rhodes, and to subsequent pirate habitation. The absence of evidence suggests that the region was sparsely populated and largely undeveloped. It made an appropriate lair for sea predators traveling light and fleeing justice in an unscripted cat-and-mouse pilfering of the civilized Mediterranean world.

The archeological team was successful in unearthing ceramic, stone, and metal evidence of farmsteads and communities and of the Roman fortification of Selinus. The team excavated remains of a Roman citadel at the Selinus acropolis rising on a coastal crag some 1,000 feet above the shoreline. Workers deduced that standard Roman structures topped sites of earlier military outposts and terracing. Historians identified dressed stone blocks mortared with limestone cement for maximum strength. Within the keep, they found native rock shaped into an *odeion* [council house]. The main fortification linked to outlying *castella* [watchtowers] and to heavily protected Roman villages.

Coastal Activities

No longer a haven for pirates, conquerors, or exploiters, Selinus lies along the Turkish Riviera, a pristine shore frequented by cruise liners and private yachts. Visitors, like the residents of ancient times, value the offshore waters for their beauty and the Roman ruins for their historic value. The athletic tourist enjoys swimming, snorkeling, parasailing, jet skiing, boating and sailing, and diving and deep-sea fishing tours and chooses seaside cliffs for scaling and the Yalandunya and Korsanlar caves for spelunking. The splendid crags, pastures, cataracts, a crystal cave, hidden coves, and beaches, both sand and pebble, suit photographers, painters, and hikers.

Selinus offers some of the best in Turkish wildlife. In 2000, the region joined other Mediterranean countries in protecting its endangered species, the *Monachus monachus* monk seal, one of the world's six most threatened animals, and the giant *Caretta caretta* or loggerhead sea turtles, which move up the shore from May to October to lay eggs. Both animals hover near extinction because of loss of the quiet rocky shores they inhabit and because of pollution, noise, over-fishing, poaching, and deliberate slaughter. Ecotourists and naturalists observe olive and citrus groves, wildflowers and herbs, birds and fish, and geological formations thrust up by tectonic plates. Inland, motorcycles and bus tours take visitors to rivers for rafting or to mountain peaks for a full view of the historic shore.

SOURCES

Calik-Ross, Ayse, "Roman Sculpture from Excavations and the Museum in Tarsus," *American Journal of Archaeology*, Vol. 105, No. 2, April 2001, p. 282.

Hall, Hines H., "The Turkish Conundrum: French Diplomacy and the Occupation of Cilicia," *Proceedings of the Annual Meeting of the Western Society for French History*, Vol. 24, 1997, pp. 198–210.

"Hellenistic, Roman, and Byzantine Settlement Patterns of the Coast Lands of Western Rough Cilia," *Antiquity*, Vol. 75, No. 288, June 2001 p. 426.

Hoff, Michael, and Rhys Townsend, "The Urban

Landscape of Western Rough Cilicia," *American Journal of Archaeology*, Vol. 105, No. 2, April 2001, p. 272.

King, William H., "Settlement of Armenians in Eastern Cilicia," *Armenian Review*, Vol. 24, No. 3, 1971, pp. 32–36.

LeTallec, Cyril, "De la 'Legion d'Orient' a la 'Petite Armenie,'" *Gavroche*, Vol. 18, No. 105–106, 1999, pp. 19–23.

Mutafian, Claude, "La Cilicie Turquifiee par la France," *Historiens et Géographes*, Vol. 83, No. 336, 1992, pp. 151–160.

Niemeier, Wolf-Dietrich, "Archaic Greeks in the Orient: Textual and Archaeological Evidence," *Bulletin of the American Schools of Oriental Research*, May 1, 2001, p. 11.

"Pirates in the Bay of Pamphylia," http://www.clarku.edu/research/access/vpa/townsend.shtml.

Plutarch. *Lives of the Noble Romans*. New York: Dell, 1959.

Raban, Avner, "The Sailing Study Tour to Cilicia and Northern Cyprus," *RIMS Newsletter*, No. 27, December 2000.

Rauh, Nicholas K., "Rough Cilicia Regional Archaeological Survey Project," *Near Eastern Archaeology*, Vol. 62, No. 1, March 1999, pp. 54–55.

_____, et al., "Amphora Production in Western Rough Cilicia," *American Journal of Archaeology*, Vol. 105, No. 2, April 2001, pp. 298.

"The Sea Turtles' Struggle for Survival," *Turkish Daily News*, September 4, 1998.

Stone Town, Zanzibar

Location

Separated from the Swahili Coast by a 22-mile stretch of the Indian Ocean, Zanzibar is a sweet-scented coral, limestone, and sandstone island that was once the trading center of East Africa. It lies opposite the mainland and forms the eastern segment of Tanzania. Africa's largest coral isle, Zanzibar and its northern sister Pemba split from the motherland at least 5.3 million years ago. Both islands developed a palm-dotted topography graced by a hot, humid, but breezy tropical climate.

Stone Town, the antique section of Zanzibar Town, lies on a jutting triangular promontory peopled with a cosmopolitan mix. Ample monsoon rains feed evergreen forests and water clove and coconut groves and farmlands producing rice, cassava, yams, chilies, and citrus fruit. Settlers once made the island a pirate capital, warehouse site, and the hub of the Africa-to-Asia slave trade. In 1963, Zanzibar merged with Tanganyika to create the independent state of Tanzania, which took its name from the first syllables of the two names.

Contacts

Zanzibar Tourist Corporation
P. O. Box 216
Malawi Road
Zanzibar Town, Zanzibar
Phone: 259–232–344
Fax: 259–233–430

History

Home to seafaring merchants, Zanzibar displays an organic melding of Arab, European, and African customs and languages that is unique to Eastern Africa. The island's early history derives from recorded contacts with Assyrian, Phoenician, and Egyptian sea captains. First settled by Bantu from the African mainland, the island, called Unguja, appealed to Persian colonizers, who began arriving in A.D. 701 By the A.D. 800s, the Baghdad caliphate was purchasing slaves from Zanzibar. In A.D. 975, Abi Ben Sultan Hasan of Shiraz built the first coastal community. Under Persian influence, islanders called themselves Shirazi.

Two years later, Arab settlers joined the influx of Persians and renamed Unguja "Zinj el Barr" [Land of Black People]. Among the outsiders from Arabia was the legendary Sindbad the Sailor, who frequented ports along the Indian Ocean. The slave trade from the continent became a long-standing business for Omani Arabs.

Once a commercial center of East Africa, Stone Town, Zanzibar Town, was a pirate capital and hub of the Africa-to-Asia slave trade (courtesy of Daniele Pascerini).

Kidnapped from Bantu tribes in Kenya and Tanzania by the Nyamwezi (also Yeke) of Lake Tanganyika, black captives passed to Arab slavers, who transported them tightly packed in lateen-rigged dhows and merchantmen across the watery divide. [*See also* MATRAH, OMAH.]

Amid loud, contentious deal-making, black slaves went on display at the coastal market of Bagamoyo and at Zanzibar, the largest slave-trading house in the East. In a lively money-making atmosphere, Omani and Afro-Arab middlemen bid for the pick of the lot to train as house servants, sex workers, bearers, miners, salt makers, soldiers, and pearl divers. In contrasting the treatment of these laborers to slaves bought and worked by Christians, Ronald Segal, author of *Islam's Black Slaves: The Other Black Diaspora* (2001), noted that Islamic slavers were consistently humane and more amenable to emancipating slaves. As a caution against hasty generalizations, Segal

added, "Individual Muslims have been among the most ferocious slavers in history" (p. xi).

During an expansionist period for European colonizers, the Portuguese settled Zanzibar after expeditioner Vasco da Gama accidentally discovered East Africa in 1498 while searching for a route to China. Zanzibar became the first Swahili trading site under dominance by Portugal. In 1503, a Portuguese sea captain, Ruy Luourenco Ravasco, menaced the island with offshore cannon fire. He kept up the barrage against Stone Town until the sultan agreed to Portuguese blackmail, a yearly tribute of 100 miticals or 460,000 reis.

Headquartered at Zanzibar, Ravasco set up a series of raids on ships from the Swahili coast and slaughtered high-ranking Muslims while adventurer and Catholic zealot Afonso de Albuquerque obliterated mosques. Two years later, Admiral Francisco d'Almedia led a flotilla of eleven warships to fan out from Stone Town and seize more territory for Portugal. For 190 years, Portuguese newcomers redirected commercial profits from the Arabs. After Arabs once more seized Zanzibar in 1698, they established an island garrison in 1710 at a fort built atop Portuguese residences and chapel. The conquerors set up an island oligarchy headed by Arabs, who became the political, economic, and social elite.

To supply the harbor with stevedores, palaces with a security force of eunuchs, and Arabian date plantations with laborers, Arab traders initiated an immense slave trade. As of 1750, the sultan's slave emporium shuffled some 3,000 captives through Stone Town's squalid holding pens. Of the Islamic slave trade, Ronald Segal comments in Chapter One of his book:

> Slaves in Islam were directed mainly at the service sector — concubines and cooks, porters and soldiers — with slavery itself primarily a form of consumption rather than a factor of production. The most telling evidence ... is found in the gender ratio. The Atlantic Trade shipped overall roughly two males for every female. Among black slaves traded in Islam across the centuries, there were roughly two females to every male [Segal 2001].

The Arabs profited from the sale of black flesh as well as from the gold, iron, ivory, rhinoceros horn, and tortoiseshell that slaves transported from the mainland. With the profits, the sultan started his own continental business in slave stations and caravan routes from Lake Nyasa. In 1800, his slaving web began routing some 15,000 black Africans through Zanzibar.

Aided by trader Tippu Tib (also Hemedi bin Muhammad el Marjebi), a Zanzibari-born Arab-Swahili opportunist, in 1821, Sultan Sayyid Said bin Sultan, called Said the Great, resided at the oceanfront Beit al-Ajaib [House of Wonders], and garrisoned Omani troops at Fort Lamu. Within months, he claimed the island for his capital. To increase his wealth, the sul-

tan created a sophisticated financial backing for trade by establishing 6,000 Indian *banyans* [financiers] in Africa to outfit caravans and to hire bookkeepers and managers to smooth out rough edges in the capture and dispersal of slaves. As the operation grew, Arab traders began moving as many as 1,000 captives from Zanzibar to the mainland in a single convoy. Resplendant in robes and turbans, the Arab masters reveled in their power and bribed the Nyamwesi with firearms to guarantee the availability of ivory, which manufacturers in Europe and America used for billiard balls, piano keys, carvings, and knife handles.

On the return trek, black coffles bound at the neck by yoke and chain carried heavy elephant tusks over the trails. Whipped, starved, and diseased, they lived in caves or out in the open. As the annual procession swelled to 50,000, many weakened and fell by the wayside to die. On arrival at coastal wharves, the hapless blacks could put down their burdens for the sea voyage. On the crossing to Zanzibar, they were so closely packed in the holds of dhows that they died of suffocation, infection, and buffeting by high seas. Before Arab shipmasters arrived in port, they culled the sickliest of the lot and tossed them overboard to avoid paying taxes on those least likely to survive.

At the Stone Town market, clever dealers cleaned slaves with seawater and dressed their wounds with tar. Oiled, fed, and freshly bathed and clothed, each black walked the circuit of the slave market while customers scrutinized teeth and eyes and prodded genitals and limbs before raising a bid. One officer of the British East India Company remarked on how casually buyers handled and felt the bodies and skin of appealing Africans. Lashed to the extremes of endurance, the weakest expired on the block. Those slaves who cried out least from whippings proved their strength and raised the purchase price.

From Zanzibar, most newly bought

slaves passed over the Indian Slave Route to Arabia, China, India, Malaysia, or Persia. On the 2,000-mile crossing, as reported by Captain G. L. Sullivan of the British ship *Daphne*, dhows were so crammed with humanity that people were stacked on laps and withered away from dysentery, exhaustion, and hunger. A lesser number remained on the island for the labor-intensive cultivation of the clove crop, introduced in 1828 by Salih bin Harmali. Ironically, the pungent fragrance of cloves blended with the stench of slave pens to give Stone Town its distinctive aroma. The demand for black African slaves — particularly boys and girls to be trained as domestics and sexual amusements — remained brisk into the early nineteenth century. Also flourishing was an international trade in attractive Abyssinian women, who helped increase the flow of German thalers into Zanzibari tills. The market was especially keen for adult males needs in Brazil as sugar plantation workers. [*See also* SALVADOR DA BAHIA, BRAZIL.]

By 1850, half of Zanzibar's people were slaves, 10,000 of whom belonged to Tippu Tib, the island magnate. Ironically, one of the most immured islanders was the sultan's daughter, Princess Sayyida Salme (also Saline bint Sa'id), who was born to Jilfidan, the sultan's Russian wife, at Mtoni Palace on August 30, 1844. At age seven, the princess and her mother moved into a town court, where the child became the first literate Arab female. She learned to write by copying Koranic calligraphy onto a camel's shoulder blade. Following her parents' deaths, the seven-year-old princess joined the struggle of her brothers Barghash and Majid and took charge of revolutionary correspondence.

At age 22, Princess Salme angered her brothers by conceiving a child, an infraction that could have resulted in a death sentence. She fled in August 1866, converted to Christianity, took the baptismal name of Emily, and bore Rudolph Said-Ruete. Under

a possible penalty of execution by stoning, she married the baby's father, Rudolph Heinrich Ruete, a merchant from Hamburg, Germany. The marriage cost her all claims of inheritance from her family.

After Salme was widowed three years later, she never regained admittance to Zanzibar society. She established the Princess Salme Institute, which supported education, scholarship, and health care for women and children. Daily journaling in *Memoirs of an Arabian Princess* (1886) made Salme the first Arab royal to write about life for secluded Islamic women. She disclosed the social and educational privations of females as well as her awareness of prejudice from native-born Omani, who snubbed Zanzibari women for being as uncivilized and barbarous as the black palace slaves. The practice of immuring wives and children that she had fled continued until the accession of Sultan Khalifa bin Harab, who abandoned concubinage in 1911.

Contemporaneous with the Princess Salme's liberation from Islamic strictures, in the mid–Victorian period, the English began to feel public pressure to end servitude. In the early 1830s, a British vice-consul, Captain James Frederic Elton, reported that Zanzibari slaves were emaciated and covered with sores. In response to such outrages to civilized behavior, colonial authorities gradually whittled down world flesh peddling at markets in India and Iran.

Chief among the opponents of slavery was Scottish missionary-explorer David Livingstone, who maintained a home at Stone Town and vilified its foul slave market by calling it "Stinkibar" (Ditmars, June 1997, p. 38). In a letter to James Gordon Bennett, he declared:

> If my disclosures regarding the terrible Ujijian slavery should lead to the suppression of the East Coast slave trade, I shall regard that as a greater matter by far than the discovery of all the Nile sources together.... This fine country is blighted, as with a

curse from above, in order that the slavery privileges of the petty Sultan of Zanzibar may not be infringed [Stanley, 1872].

Livingstone was correct about the source of the problem. Under Sultan Sayyid Majid bin Said, who came to power in 1856, slaving worsened, with 19,000 black Africans put on the block at Zanzibar and an unknown number smuggled in or imported for use by the sultanate.

In 1861, a year after the British anchored a ship off Zanzibar to monitor Arab slavers and confiscate their boats, the island liberated itself from Omani control. The change made no dent in slaving, which produced an appalling record of one dead during kidnap and transport for each one sold. Livingstone disputed that number with the counterclaim that procurement and transport of shackled slaves cost ten deaths for each living slave. According to historian Ronald Segal:

> At Zanzibar, the slaves were unloaded hurriedly. The dead were thrown overboard to drift with the tide, until they rotted in their passage. The sick and weak were left to lie on the beach, to save the customs-house tax, in case they died before they could be sold [2001, p. 148].

In 1868, one eyewitness, British sea captain Philip Howard Colomb, a Scottish vice-admiral and commander of the *Dryad*, who was engaged to suppress atrocities against black Africans, found the starvation, disease, and general wretchedness too miserable to watch. At the insistence of British Consul-General Sir Henry John Kirk and the concurrence of the British Royal Navy and U.S. and German embassies, after 1870, the island completely ended the slave trade, which had reached around 20,000 captures annually.

The cessation of slaving existed mainly on paper. The British had more interest in trade than in human rights and used slavery as a crowbar to gain entry to island politics. Moreover, the abolitionist posturing of American consuls William H. Hathorne,

John F. Webb, and Francis R. Webb, backer of expeditioner Henry M. Stanley, did little actual damage to Zanzibar's trade with New England cloth markets or to the flesh peddling of the major entrepreneur, Sultan Barghash bin Said al BuSaidi, consolidator of Stone Town's slave commerce.

In December 1873, during negotiation with Sir Bartle Frere, a Welsh diplomat and former Governor of Bombay, Sultan Barghash claimed that Arab slaving was a defensible operation sanctioned by Islamic law and custom. He feared that abolition of slavery would further damage island agriculture, which was recovering from a severe hurricane. Nonetheless, under threat of naval bombardment and under duress from Christian nations, the Church Missionary Society, and the Society for the Mitigation and Gradual Abolition of Slavery Throughout the British Dominions, which had been active for over a half century, Barghash closed the Stone Town slave market. The British forced the cessation of sea transport of captives and the liberation of slaves owned by Indian residents and negotiated for protection of former captives until they could find housing and jobs.

In 1878, Barghash also banned overland slave caravans to Africa's east coast. However, slavery flourished behind closed doors in Stone Town for several decades. At a pit in the slave cave at Mangapwani, dealers stored their human freight until they could safely move captives off the coast under cover of darkness. When blacks received a nominal emancipation, they, like the sharecroppers of the American South, entered a labor force that worked longer hours at harder jobs for minimal pay. The black bondsman and bondswoman exchanged manacles and whips for economic dependence, exhaustion, and poverty.

Architecture

For a slaving nexus, Stone Town is remarkably well stocked with mansions and houses of worship. Its blend of culturally diverse architecture owes its survival to restoration of Arab, British, East German, Indian, Portuguese, Shirazi, and Swahili buildings that include twenty mosques and two cathedrals. Originally, the town followed the layout of Portuguese colonists, who built a residential center and established a fort after their arrival in 1504. The Omani, who took control in the 1660s, refined the fortified port with attractive shoreline palaces.

In the 1800s, East German minority housing supplanted mud huts on the city perimeter at a ghetto where slaves and their descendents were forced to live apart from other ethnic groups. A blended shore population occupied whitewashed coral-rag residences built from coral chunks and other bricolage. At some homes, first-floor boutiques let out to Indian merchants sold a variety of world merchandise. At street level, a baraza or low stone bench built the length of the block provided meeting places for men to socialize. The addition of British architectural touches, harborfront dining at Indian restaurants, and native dhows in the distance completed the eclectic mix.

Enslavement was a common theme in Stone Town's architecture. Near the shore, Sultan Barghash's famed harem quarters at the Marhubi Palace, completed in 1882, held 100 women, whom he pampered with colonnaded gardens and domed pools of cool water. He summoned his Circassian beauties to bed at a steady rate of five per night. The nearby home of chief slaver Tippu Tib still stands, but the old slave market gave place in 1877 to an Anglican edifice, the United Mission to Central Africa Cathedral, built in Arabo-Gothic style with tri-foil arches and crenellations. The basilica's designer, Bishop Edward Steere, recycled the infamous whipping post as an altar and placed a font over the slop pit into which market masters jettisoned dead slaves. On church grounds, staff maintains the cramped, stale-smelling slave dungeons, where 150 captives occupied two rooms for up to four days each while awaiting sale and transport. Daily, high tides flushed the subterranean corrals of human filth. Historic spots along Stone Town streets attest to slave pens that concealed captives long after the sultan emancipated slaves. Carved rows of chains on residential portals indicate the owners' attitude toward the right to own blacks.

Currently, Stone Town is a UNESCO World Heritage Site, part of a preservation effort that encourages local initiatives to rescue historic areas. During the Zanzibari renaissance, the Aga Khan Trust for Culture sparked the conservation and rehabilitation of early buildings, particularly the ornately balconied Old Dispensary, a four-storied seafront hospital begun in 1885 by Sir Tharia Topan, an Indian-born merchant, philanthropist, and customs adviser to the sultan. Alternately known as the Tharia Topan Jubilee Hospital, the building featured stained glass, peaked gables, and intricate woodwork. A subsequent owner remodeled it into a charity, the Khoja Haji Nasser Nur Mahomed Charitable Dispensary, which remained active until 1964. In 1990, workers began refurbishing the old dispensary into the Stone Town Cultural Centre.

The Aga Khan Trust's Historic Cities Support Program also preserved Stone Town's seawall, ornate balconies, grilled verandahs, 560 double doors carved with symbols and studded with brass spikes and bosses, and teak flooring and staircases and replicated native woodcarving, stonemasonry, metalworking, and other authentic artisanal touches. Memorable examples include a nineteenth-century *hammam* [bathhouse], an Ibadi mosque completed in 1855, and Sultan Barghash's Anglo-Arab palace, the multi-pillared Beit al-Ajaib, the first dwelling to boast electricity and a small train, called the Bububu Light Railway. Additional preservation moneys came from the European Union for harbor redevelopment and from the United Nations Capital Development Fund for the rehabilitation of the Central Market.

Coastal Activities

In a city that bans automobiles from entertwining alleyways, street travel reacquaints tourists with the feet. Foot traffic preserves peace outside residences, where latticed balconies once immured Muslim women from the sight of males. A museum exhibition of Princess Salme's good works attests to the strength of a famed island feminist. Walking tours from the beach feature the fish market, stalls selling khikois and katangi cloth alongside ebony and woodcarvings, the chevron-patterned Balnara Mosque, the massive Arab fort dating to 1700, and the palace museum, which exhibits the medicine chest of Dr. David Livingstone.

In the harbor, visitors book harbor tours, take lessons at the diving school for exploration of coral reefs, watch dhow races, listen to Afro-Islamic tarabu (also taarab or tarab) music, ride motor scooters or bicycles through the alleys, or sit on benches to play *bao*, a traditional board game. At the market, banana-leaf baskets offer fragrant black peppercorns, cardamom, cinnamon, clove, coriander, cumin, curry powder, nutmeg, pilau mix, turmeric, and vanilla, all sources of wealth for early Zanzibaris. Naturalists enjoy a stroll on the boardwalk through Jozani's mangrove swamp and forest reserve just outside of town, the home of the rare red colobus monkey and the duiker, a delicate antelope.

For all its peace and beauty, the environs of the beach are not far from reminders of slavery. An excursion northwest across the bay to Changuu Island, also called Prison Island, offers sparkling waters and sugar-sand beach for snorkeling, reef div-ing, photography of frangipani and peacocks, shelling, swimming, and spearfishing for barracuda, kingfish, manta ray, shark, tuna, wahoo, and wrasse. The island is home to a giant tortoise reserve and a former slave pen where an Arab master incarcerated uncooperative blacks. In the 1890s, a British General named Matthews adapted the structure for a government prison that later doubled as a quarantine station. Like the blacks marched in from Africa's dark heart, the giant tortoises, an endangered species that lives to 100 years, are also prisoners that the sultan imported from the Seychelles or the Mascarene Archipelago in the 1800s. In another parallel, the tortoises, like black Africans, annually suffer the pilfering of their eggs and the kidnap of animals for sale as exotic pets.

SOURCES

"The Aga Khan Trust for Culture," http://www. akdn.org/aktc/hcsp_zanzibar2.html.

Andrews, Beverly, "Zanzibar: Behind the Veil," *ProutWorld News*, July 7, 2001.

Bennett, Norman R., "Americans in Zanzibar, 1865–1915," *Tanganyika Notes and Records*, Vol. 60, 1963, pp. 49–66.

_____, "Stanley and the American Consuls at Zanzibar," *Essex Institute Historical Collections*, Vol. 100, No. 1, 1964, pp. 41–58.

Bhacker, M. Reda, "Family Strife and Foreign Intervention: Causes in the Separation of Zanzibar from Oman," *Bulletin of the School of Oriental and African Studies*, Vol. 54, No. 2, 1991, pp. 269–280.

Caputo, Robert, "Swahili Coast," *National Geographic*, Vol. 200, No. 4, October 2001, pp. 104–119.

Ditmars, Hadani, "Restoration of Zanzibar," *Middle East*, June 1997, pp. 38–39.

_____, "Saved by the Constructs of Oppression," *Globe and Mail*, May 10, 1997.

Ferguson, Ed, "Value Theory and Colonial Capitalism: The Case of Zanzibar, 1897–1945," *African Economic History*, Vol. 18, 1989, pp. 25–56.

Freeman-Grenville, G. S. P., "The Portuguese on the Swahili Coast: Buildings and Language," *Studia*, Vol. 59, 1989, pp. 235–253.

Gates-Hunt, Richard H., "Salem and Zanzibar,

a Special Relationship," *Essex Institute Historical Collections*, Vol. 117, N0. 1, 1981, pp. 1–26.

Gibbons, Fiachra, "In the Service of the Sultan," *Manchester Guardian*, April 6, 2002.

"The History and Conservation of Zanzibar Stone Town," *African Business*, March 1997, pp. 34–35.

Lacey, Marc, "Tourists and Islam Mingle, Not Always Cozily," *New York Times*, March 6, 2002.

Lancaster, Pat, "Behind the Veil," *Middle East*, July 2001, p. 48.

Marozzi, Justin, "The Pot and the Kettle," *Spectator*, Vol. 288, No. 9,055, February 23, 2002 pp. 35–36.

Matloff, Judith, "Zanzibar Island, Gem of Arab Decor, Tries to Restore Heyday," *Christian Science Monitor*, August 30, 1995.

Mead, Rebecca, "Island Scene: Somewhere off the Coast of Zanzibar," *Travel & Leisure*, June 2000, pp. 80–84.

Middleton, Nick, "Totally Tropical," *Geographical*, February 2000, p. 46.

Osborne, Christine, "Mending Broken Bridges," *Middle East*, October 1997, pp. 38–39.

Patience, Kevin. *Zanzibar: Slavery and the Royal Navy*. England: privately published, 2000.

Pavlu, George, "The First Slavers," *New African*, November 1, 1999, p. 16.

Pierson, Gerald J., "U.S. Consuls in Zanzibar and the Slave Trade, 1870–1890," *Historian*, Autumn 1992, pp. 53–68.

Powell, Andrew, "Blue Lagoon," *Harper's Bazaar*, December 1994, pp. 91–92.

Renault, François, "The Structures of the Slave Trade in Central Africa in the Nineteenth Century," *Slavery & Abolition*, Vol. 9, No. 3, 1988, pp. 146–165.

Ricks, Thomas, "Slaves and Slave Trading in Shi'i Iran, AD 1500–1900," *Journal of Asian and African Studies*, Vol. 36, No. 4, November 1, 2001, p. 407.

Segal, Ronald. *Islam's Black Slaves: The Other Black Diaspora*. New York: Farrar, Straus and Giroux, 2001.

Sheriff, Abdul, "Localisation and Social Composition of the East African Slave Trade," *Slavery & Abolition*, Vol. 9, No. 3, 1988, pp. 131–145.

Stanley, Henry M. *How I Found Livingstone*. London: Sampson Low, Marston, 1872.

"The Story of Africa: Slavery," http://www.bbc.co.uk/worldservice/africa/features/storyof africa/9chapter3.shtml.

Sturken, Barbara, "Operators Once Again Are Including Zanzibar in Itineraries," *Travel Weekly*, October 27, 1994, pp. 99–100.

Whitman, Bill, "Resorts," *National Geographic Traveler*, September 2001, pp. 41–43.

Williams, Stephen, "Zanzibar: A Touch of Old Spice," *African Business*, April 1996, pp. 40–42.

"Zanzibar," *Africa News Service*, February 14, 2001.

"Zanzibar: Land of Legend and Fable," *London Times*, May 3, 1998.

Zuckerman, Jocelyn, "Ten Great Things about Zanzibar," *Gourmet*, May 2001, p. 88.

Sydney, New South Wales, Australia

Location

The capital of New South Wales, Sydney is Australia's oldest city and one of the world's largest deep-water ports. The recently cleaned twelve-mile harbor splits the city, lying on 150 miles of the island's southeastern coast at Port Jackson, east-to-west into two halves. The spot was once settled by the Eora, whose ancestors may have sailed east from Asia as early as 98,000 B.C. The hut- and cave-dwelling natives flourished along the bay on oysters and shellfish as well as lizards, birds, and roots. After the area's selection in 1788 as a reception center for felons from England's overflowing prisons, convicts carved steps into natural sandstone at the Rocks, a rugged spur overlooking Sydney Cove. The city remained active in receiving trans–Pacific whalers and sealers and in exporting the prisoner-grown flax for sails and Norfolk pines for clipper masts.

Today, Sydney headquarters cultural, financial, industrial, retail, shipping, and transportation activities and exports grain, meat, sheep hides, and wool. The coast is best known for two architectural marvels — the dramatically winged Sydney Opera House and Sydney Harbour Bridge, a $20-million tour de force that wags have dubbed "Old Coat Hanger." Long rid of its image as a primitive outpost of Oceania, the port offers a modern terminal, sophisticated art venues, miles of beach, and world-class yachting.

Contacts

Australian Tourist Commission
2049 Century Park East, Suite 1920
Los Angeles, California 90067
Email: hotline@atc.australia.com
http://www.australia.com

History

The closing of the American colonies to England resulted in increased shipping of felons to Australia. [*See also* FORTESCUE BAY, TASMANIA.] Colonial Sydney, which was built on European models, rapidly nailed together a notorious wharf district plagued by crime, epidemics, and poverty. In 1788, the port entered over a century of serious outbreaks of tuberculosis and other contagious diseases, which periodically assailed the people coming and going from global shipping lines. The first 1,500 white Australian settlers infected aborigines with smallpox or possibly chicken pox, an unknown pathogen that claimed over fifty percent of native shore-dwellers. Natives terrorized by the invisible enemy fled inland, carrying infection to more virgin-soil populations.

In November 1800, the disembarking of more English criminals aboard the *Royal Admiral* introduced "gaol fever," a general term for typhus or typhoid fever. A new wave of sickness arrived on the *Surrey* in 1814, when officers, crew, prisoners, and passengers carried a scourge of typhoid. The dreaded "plague ship" drifted offshore until one sailor aboard the *Roxberry* volunteered to steer the wandering vessel to port. Sequential outbreaks of diphtheria, influenza, measles, and scarlet fever eluded harbor quarantines and caromed about the Pacific to and from Sydney as shipping and fishing linked shores. The resultant devastation of aborigines left land open to squatters, who were quick to seize the best parcels.

Into the last decades of the nineteenth century, Sydney continued receiving outsiders, notably, passengers aboard the first American trans–Pacific steamship, the S.S. *Monumental City* in 1853, and continued to suffer waves of illness introduced at dockside. In 1860, measles and dysentery slew 270 Sydney children; seven years later, in the urban slums, Sydney's infants and toddlers suffered a six percent infection rate from measles, which killed the weakest from secondary infection with enteritis or pneumonia. Worst hit were residents of urban tenements.

In 1875, 10,000 children of the harbor city fell ill with scarlet fever, which claimed 584. In May 1881, port dwellers suffered a double blow from chicken pox and smallpox, which resulted in the construction of a port quarantine station. Racial tensions caused whites to blame Chinese immigrants and to boycott and rampage Asian businesses. The era so inundated the city with deaths that officials established a new cemetery at Haslem's Creek and built a railway to carry mourners to the burial sites of loved ones.

By 1884, passengers arriving in expectation of a tropical paradise found Sydney battling tuberculosis. Lessening the chance of survival was Asiatic flu, which arrived in 1892, felling a quarter of the citizenry and targeting those with TB-weakened lungs. In 1900, bubonic plague scourged the Rocks, striking Sydney's dock workers and port residents with a kill rate of one out of every four infected with the disease. Armed with more recent techniques of public health, the port authority dispatched a rat brigade to exterminate the disease bearers under piers, to destroy rodent-plagued slums, and to cleanse 4,000 suspect residences. The improvement in shoreline defenses helped spare Sydney in 1918, when an influenza pandemic girdled the globe.

Ecosystem

From the outset, Europeans were charmed and bemused by the variance between old world flora and fauna and the unusual specimens of Australia — the kookaburra, kangaroo, finch, flying squirrel, and parakeet. Women found opportunities to explore nature and to contribute to collections that classified species and expressed to the outside world the wonders of eastern Australia. Watercolorist Sarah Stone painted birds, reptiles, and mammals for John White of Worthing, Sussex, a surgeon of the first fleet and focal naturalist, who engraved Stone's work among 65 pictures published in *Journal of a Voyage to New South Wales* (1790). Scots expeditioner Robert Brown, the prize botanist of the century, first saw Sydney in 1801 from the deck of the *Investigator*. He collected specimen plants he described in *Prodromus Florae Novae Hollandiae* [Messengers of the Plants of New Holland] (1810). His contemporary, biologist William Sharpe Macleay, contributed observations of the region's insects and formulated a new system of classification in *Horae Entomologicae* [Entymological Hours] (1819), which revolutionized natural history. For his work, the Linnean Society of London honored him with a bust and extensive honors.

One immigrant couple, ornithologist John Gould and his wife, Elizabeth Gould, published 600 original watercolors in *The Birds of Australia* (1848), a seven-volume work that particularized species of bee-eaters, crow shrikes, finches, flycatchers, frogmouths, kingfishers, martins, musk duck, pardalotes, raptors, robins, swallows, swifts, and wrens. Another female artist, Fanny Elizabeth de Mole, captured the Sturt pea and other flowers in *Wildflowers of South Australia* (1861); her contemporary, Marrianne Collison Campbell of Wharf House, Sydney, painted the showy waratah blossom for Joan Kerr's *From Sydney Cove to Dun-*

troon, which was not published until 1982. A late-nineteenth-century fancier of South Australian wildflowers, Margaret Cochrane Scott, exhibited spare images of the caladenia and diuris with the South Australian Society of Arts. At the beginning of the twentieth century, Lilian Medland, on staff at the Austral Museum in Sydney, produced postcard views of local birds, which she collected in *Birds of Paradise and Bower Birds* (1950). Today, naturalists continue to observe pelicans, shore birds, dolphin and whale pods, and a wide variety of butterflies, including the birdwing, brown darter, fritillary, nymph, satyr, skipper, and swallowtail.

Coastal Activities

Unlike the hard-pressed immigrants and prisoners who settled eastern Australia, visitors to Sydney anticipate a clean, modern city proffering a variety of tourist attractions, including aboriginal artworks, Taronga Zoo, the Sydney Harbour Casino, and the lighthouse at Grotto Point. On the waterfront, Circular Quay, the former shipping axis, offers light rail access to five piers, a jetboat wharf, a contemporary art museum, restaurants, and shops. Preserved by the lanolin in sheep's wool, the finger piers of Sydney Cove at Walsh Bay retain ties to Australian history. The arts flourish at the Old Finger Wharf Theatre, where viewers can attend the Australian Theatre for Young People, Sydney Dance Company, Sydney Philharmonic Choir, or Sydney Theatre Company or view aboriginal stage shows by the Bangarra Dance Company.

Photographers and climbers enjoy harbor tours by ferry, water taxi, Jetcat, or seaplane to view the great-arched Harbour Bridge, one of the world's architectural icons. Erected in 1932, the structure earned the name "iron lung" because it brought life-sustaining jobs to the area during the Great Depression. Since 1998, it has accommodated twelve-member climbing teams, who scale the upper girders for a panoramic view of the harbor.

Sydney's most recognized landmark is the Sydney Opera House, a world-famous port ornament that Danish designer Joern Utzon completed in 1973. The fantasy shape of its pair of multi-leaved white ceramic roofs echoes the shapes of seashells and the full-bellied sails of European schooners that brought white colonists to Australia. The building is the setting for a variety of children's programs and cultural performances. The opera complex is the venue for the post–Christmas Sydney Festival, a gathering of international musicians, dancers, singers, and actors. Completing the aura are harbor fireworks, a New Year's Eve delight and high point of the 2000 Olympics.

At the west, the ten-story Australian National Maritime Museum, which opened at Darling Harbour in 1991, contains coastal treasures, notably, the sternpost from the *Endeavour*, the ship that bore English sea captain James Cook to Australia in 1770. Among the exhibits are a Dutch star globe, an aboriginal raft made of mangrove timbers, a bark canoe crafted by the Yanyuwa of Carpentaria, models of clipper ships, an exhibit on Arctic explorers, diaries and belongings of colonists, and the forty-foot *Australia II*, the native sloop that Alan Bond captained in 1983 to win the America's Cup. At outside berths, viewers can tour the commando raider *Krait*, the destroyer *Vampire*, the submarine *Onslow*, the lightship *Carpentaria*, the pearling lugger *John Louis*, the Indonesian trader *Sekar Aman*, and the *Tu Do* [Freedom], an unseaworthy Vietnamese boat that Tan Thanh Lu captained to bring 39 refugees to Darwin in 1977. The nearby aquarium and underwater tunnel feature rays, seals, and sharks and coral gardens.

Beach-goers can choose Camp Cove, Clovelly Bay, Tamarama Cove, or Bondi, Coogee, Manly, or Nielsen Park beach, the city's most popular strands, which are protected from sharks by a system of monitor-ing, netting, and sirens. The most active athletes can choose from inline skating, surfing, sailing, canoeing and kayaking, and scaling Bronte's sandstone headlands. Snorkelers and divers view cuttlefish, octopi, sea dragons, seahorses, sharks, and sponges. Nature lovers follow the Manly Scenic Walkway and stroll the tropical plant display at Royal Botanic Gardens, which enwrap Farm Cove and border Woolloomooloo Bay. The best in shoreline viewing are annual regattas, which assemble some of the world's fastest and best-groomed seacraft for Australia Day festivities each January 26 and for the BMW Sydney Winter Series, Hardy Cup international youth race, Hog's Breath Regatta, Mooloolaba Race each Easter, Sydney Hobart Yacht Race, and Volvo Ocean Race or Whitbread Round the World Race.

SOURCES

Armstrong, Dorothy Mary. *The First Fifty Years: A History of Nursing at the Royal Prince Alfred Hospital, Sydney, from 1882–1932*. Sydney: Royal Prince Alfred Hospital Graduate Nurses' Association, 1965.

"Attention All BMW Sydney Winter Series Skippers," *Offshore Yachting*, April 2002, p. 5.

"Australia Day Afloat," *Offshore Yachting*, April 2002, pp. 50–52.

"Australian National Maritime Museum," http://www.anmm.gov.au/inwater.htm.

"Australia's Boat People," *Economist*, Vol. 351, No. 8,122, June 5, 1999, p. 40.

Beder, Sharon, "Let the Spin Begin," *Harper's Magazine*, Vol. 300, No. 1,800, May 2000, p. 50.

Calaby, John H., "The European Discovery and Scientific Description of Australian Birds," *Historical Records of Australian Science*, Vol. 12, No. 3, 1999, pp. 313–329.

Campbell, Peter, "Rolex to Sponsor Sydney Hobart," *Offshore Yachting*, April 2002, pp. 8–9.

Cannon, Michael. *Who's Master? Who's Man? Australia in the Victorian Age*. Sydney, Aust.: Thomas Nelson, 1971.

Davison, Graeme, "The European City in Australia," *Journal of Urban History*, Vol. 27, No. 6. 2001, pp. 779–793.

Fearis, Beverley, "Four hours in Sydney," *Busi-*

ness Traveler, Vol. 15, No. 7, August 2002, p. 10.

Guild, Sara, "Urban Survival Kit: Sydney," *Business Traveler UK/Europe*, December 2001, p. 14.

Hopkins, Fred, "First to Cross: The S. S. *Monumental City*," *American Neptune*, Vol. 60, No. 1, 2000, pp. 61–72.

Hoy, Anthony, "Port in a Storm," *Bulletin with Newsweek*, Vol. 117, No. 6,189, August 31, 1999, pp. 36–38.

Hull, Jeff, "Going for the Gold, and Green," *Audubon*, Vol. 102, No. 5, September 2000, p. 16.

Jarrett, Ian, "Ante Rises in Gaming War," *Asian Business*, Vol. 33, No. 12, July 1997, pp. 12–13.

Jeffrey, Betty. *White Coolies*. Sydney, Aust.: Angus & Robertson, 1954.

"Jern Utzon," *Architecture*, Vol. 88, No. 8, August 1999, p. 23.

Karskens, Grace. *Inside the Rocks: The Archaeology of a Neighbourhood*. Sydney: Hale & Iremonger, 1999.

Moldofsky, Leora, "Venues: The Triathlon Uncovers Dangerous Waters," *Time International*, Vol. 155, No. 14, April 10, 2000, p. 24.

Myers, Peter, "Utzon's Return," *Architecture Australia*, Vol. 91, No. 6, November–December 2002, pp. 75–77.

Park, Edwards, "Around the Mall and Beyond," *Smithsonian*, Vol. 22, No. 2, May 1991, pp. 22–25.

Pearce, Robert, "Banks, Baudin, and Birds of a Feather," *Australian Biologist*, Vol. 15, 2002, pp. 1–10.

"Quintessential Experiences," *Town & Country*, Vol. 156, No. 5,260, January 2002, pp. 29–32.

Roberts, Melissa, "A Whale's Journey Down Under," *Newsweek International*, September 13, 1999, p. 71.

Rodwell, Grant, and John Ramsland, "The Maritime Adventures of Joseph Barden," *Great Circle*, Vol. 21, No. 1, 1999, pp. 16–45.

Shapiro, Howard, "Armchair Travelers, Here's What You Will See in Sydney," *Knight Ridder/Tribune News Service*, August 7, 2000.

Staub, Molly Arost, "Scintillating Sydney — Australia's New Cultural Revolution," *The World and I*, Vol. 16, No. 9, September 2001, p. 74.

Stone, Brad, "A Green Medal for the Sydney Games?," *Newsweek*, Vol. 130, No. 20, November 17, 1997, p. 16.

"Sydney — Mooloolaba Race," *Offshore Yachting*, February 2002, p. 59.

"Sydney: The Best Stopover Village," *Offshore Yachting*, December 2001, p. 59.

"Tropical Shirt Regatta," *Offshore Yachting*, April 2002, p. 34.

"Twilight Racing on the Yacht," *Travel Trade Gazette UK & Ireland*, November 4, 2002, p. 45.

Tyquin, Michael, "Going in Style: Sydney's Funeral Train System," *Journal of the Royal Australian Historical Society*, Vol. 86, No. 1, 2000, pp. 65–73.

Ulterino, Matthew, "Going for the Green," *Amicus Journal*, Vol. 19, No. 2, Summer 1997, pp. 13–15.

Waxman, Peter, "Service Provision and the Needs of Newly Arrived Refugees in Sydney, Australia," *International Migration Review*, Vol. 32, No. 3, Fall 1998, pp. 761–777.

Tintagel Head, Cornwall

Location

Tintagel Head, one of seven purported birthplaces of the legendary folk hero King Arthur, is an ancient peninsula that has eroded to a scrap of land scarcely linked to the northwestern coast Cornwall, a maritime English shire. The crumbling ridge dating to ancient times obliges visitors to cross by a footbridge. On the opposite site, the craggy, windswept spit of land perches on southwestern England's extended wand 250 feet above strong currents of the Atlantic Ocean. Amid breakers that explode into lead-colored towers of seawater capped with foam, the rocky tor juts out to sea like a faint-hearted isle clinging to the mainland by a tenuous causeway.

The island's upper plateau looks down on a stone-paved beach that contributes to the mythic aura of a princeling's birthplace. A narrow stone defile leads down the isthmus to a shingle on its west side that boasts a cave of the wizard Merlin, Arthur's cousin, protector, and mentor. The cavern, a natural tunnel open on both ends, is damp from salty spume and a tidal channel that flows through at high water. Across the beach below Barras Nose, a second cave receives the same influx of the sea. The jagged head-

Historian Geoffrey of Monmouth claimed Tintagel as the childhood home of King Arthur (courtesy of Peter Turnham).

land, favored by artists, writers, sportsmen, and literati, is warmed by the Gulf Stream, which fosters west country gardens and pastures.

Contacts

Tintagel Tourist Information Centre
Bossiney Road
Tintagel, Cornwall P>34 OAJ
Phone: 01840-779084
Fax: 01840-779084
Email: tintagelvc@ukonline.co.uk
http://www.cornwall-info.co.uk/details.
    asp?listid=1723

Tintagel Castle
Tintagel, Cornwall PL34 0DB
Phone: 01840—770328
http://www.heritage-trail.com

History

From 8,000 to 4,000 B.C., Tintagel was host to flint-armed hunter-gatherers who survived on berries, herbs, gray seals and shellfish, oxen, swine, and red deer. From 4,000 B.C., woodlands and thick bracken gave place to stone residences and megalithic tombs, ritual henges, hill forts, fields, and moor. A thriving pastoral era continued until the late 1700s, when quarrying, mining, clay removal, and enclosed farming civilized a once-wild land. The outlines of fifty small buildings and recovered glass beads and pot shards attest to early habitation by a flourishing populace.

Evidence of a Roman settlement called Durocornovium appears only in print. The first legions overcame the native Dumnoni around A.D. 50, but the isolation of the west country kept Roman involvement in local life to a minimum. Two inscribed milestones date to the reign of the Roman co-emperor Licinius from A.D. 308 to 324, when the empire's metallurgists may have dug for antimony for use in metal alloy or

medicines. The stones also suggest a well-traveled route to a significant coastal trading post. At the departure of Roman discipline from Britain in A.D. 409, Saxon invaders destroyed and looted records and largely obliterated Cornwall's early written history.

The name "Tintagel" gives clues to the headland's function. The word links to Cornish morphology, perhaps *din* [fort] plus *tagell* [constriction], suggesting a fort built at a narrow neck of land. From the Celtic era, Tintagel Head hosted a distinct pattern of residence, beginning with two small buildings west of the inner ward dating to the fifth century A.D. Within the area, walls of other buildings running north-south and east-west suggest habitation on the site of a previous defensive earthen rampart and protected residents into the beginning of the sixth century. The land appears to have passed to St. Juliot, an obscure Cornish woman who founded a monastic cell and hermitages that grew from the core residence to around twenty rooms. The encircling turf barrier testifies to the abbey's obedience to the Rule of St. Columba, who called for monks to live in a tight enclosure accessed by only one gate, a symbol of the one true God.

Archeological digs further revealed the rock stacks outlining the great hall, a ruined tunnel that may have been a meat cellar, and a 10 by 15 foot chapel of Bossiney, a Celtic abbey that, according to the *Domesday Book*, may have flourished as a pilgrim center from A.D. 500 to 850. The site suits a religious retreat for its solitude, serenity, and freedom from worldly distraction. Designers of the chapel deliberately turned priestly backs on Cornwall by placing the altar facing the sea. On the mainland, a parish cemetery and church dedicated to St. Materiana (also Madrun or Madryn), a fifth-century princess of Gwent and local evangelist, provide more palpable proof of human dwellings. From A.D. 600 to 1200, the chapel was only a shard of culture remaining on the abandoned outpost. After the Norman Conquest, at the arrival of evangelists, the Cornish monarchy may have transformed the former Celtic site into a Christian stronghold.

In 1130, when Geoffrey of Monmouth, an Oxford-trained historian, began composing heavily embroidered Arthurian lore, beginning with *Prophetae Merlini* [Merlin's Prophecies] (1135), he claimed Tintagel was Arthur's childhood home. Geoffrey perpetuated his belief in a real king named Arthur in *Historia Regum Britanniae* [History of the Kings of England] (1136), which traces the British monarchy through 75 kings dating back to 1200 B.C. Geoffrey followed with *Vita Merlini* [Life of Merlin] (1151), which answered questions raised by the earlier work concerning Merlin's kinship and relationship to Arthur. To substantiate the quasi-historical works, Geoffrey claimed to have drawn on the writings of Walter, the Archdeacon of Oxford, but no copy of Walter's text has survived to substantiate the later work.

Geoffrey may have drawn his settings during local preparations to erect Tintagel Castle, begun in 1141 and completed in 1145 by a grandson of William I the Conqueror, Reginald (or Reinald) de Dunstaville, who was the Duke of Cornwall and the illegitimate son of Henry I and a mistress, Sybil Corbert. Reginald may have intended the defense post as a military precaution during a period of baronial unrest. Geoffrey dedicated his narrative poem to Reginald's half brother, Robert Fitzroy de Cae, Earl of Gloucester, and may have chosen Tintagel as Arthur's birthplace solely for political reasons during a period of civil war led by Stephen and Matilda, claimants for the English throne. Subsequent romancers accepted Geoffrey's choice of Tintagel as the Bethlehem of Arthurian lore.

Until the building of Tudor fortifications in the 1400s, Tintagel Castle remained the stronghold of Cornish earls. A noted crusader, Richard, Earl of Cornwall and younger brother of Henry III, purchased the promontory from Robert Gervase de Hornicott, called Robert of Tintagel, and rebuilt on the old princely ramparts in 1233. To ennoble his own lineage, Richard may have chosen the site for its international fame as Arthur's birthplace. In 1236 and 1272, Richard added to the original construction, perhaps to increase headland security.

The residence passed to Edward, the Black Prince and the hero of the battle of Crécy in 1346, who adapted Tintagel Castle into a dungeon. Surviving from the 1300s is a small manor constructed of stone walls a yard thick and topped with exposed timbers and slate roof. Inside the residence, a deep hall paved with stone led to a huge fireplace. On the cliff, a church with Norman font and granite tower date to the 1400s. The eroded outlines of the church served as a navigator's landmark visible far out to sea.

Embellishments to Arthur's biography further obscured history. In the mid-nineteenth century, Tennyson's narrative poems spread Arthurian fervor among Victorians, who created the first tourist throng up the precipitous path to Tintagel Head. In 1860, Tennyson himself walked the uneven heights of the promontory and conceived a poetic line for *The Coming of Arthur* in which eight huge waves pounded the beach on a hellish night. As the sea roared, the ninth breaker produced a flaming crest that carried the naked infant Arthur to the feet of Merlin. Tennyson's lines worked their magic. By the 1900s, the town of Tintagel was overrun by the Arthur industry as hordes of visitors made the precarious trek over the isthmus to Tintagel Head.

Shoring up the history is an early twentieth-century cultural preserve, the Hall of Chivalry, in Tintagel village, a site favored by literary pilgrims. Formerly called

Trevena House, the museum was the conception of millionaire Frederick Thomas Glasscock, a retired jelly and candy manufacturer from London. In 1927, he founded the Fellowship of the Order of the Round Table, which quickly grew to 17,000 members. For atmosphere, he designed a mock round table, kingly throne, and 73 jewel-toned glass windows depicting the Knights of the Round Table. A first-class library held works on elusive, yet long-lived Arthurian lore which influenced an impressive list of English writers. In early fall 1864, English poet Algernon Swinburne joined a friend on a tour of Arthurian sites, including Tintagel Castle. In the historic environs of Celtic England, he completed *Atalanta in Calydon* (1865), an English version of Greek tragedy. In the twentieth century, authors Mary Stewart and Marion Zimmer Bradley revisited the setting as sources of novels: Stewart's trilogy *The Crystal Cave* (1970), *The Hollow Hills* (1973), and *The Last Enchantment* (1979); and Bradley's *The Mists of Avalon* (1983).

Cinema director Richard Thorpe filmed MGM's first wide-screen color movie, *The Knights of the Round Table* (1953), at the ravine on Tintagel's coast overlooking the beach, which locals call the Vale of Avalon. The two-dimensional film starred Mel Ferrer, Ava Gardner, and Robert Taylor in the roles of King Arthur, Queen Guinevere, and Sir Launcelot. The plot focused on the legendary love triangle as recorded in Thomas Malory's *Le Morte d'Arthur* (1450). The movie earned Oscar nominations for art direction and set decoration and for sound.

Legend

Although no historical manuscripts prove King Arthur's significance to the area, the oral history of Tintagel's wild, enigmatic headland links to the late A.D. 400s, when the quasi-historical king was born to human parents. According to most accounts, he was the base-born son of the beautiful and principled Queen Ygraine (also Igraine, Ygerna, or Ygerne), widow of Duke Gorlois, and of Uther Pendragon, a title meaning "foremost leader." In the version by Geoffrey of Monmouth, Uther fell in love with Ygraine upon seeing her at Uther's royal court in London at Easter. He angered Gorlois by flirting openly with her through proffered sweetmeats and eye-to-eye conversation.

Uther's affront provoked bloodshed. The duke and his retainers withdrew to Tintagel, where he immured his wife in the castle, which he assumed was unassailable. Uther gave chase on the grounds that the duke had insulted his king. A siege of Cornwall's fortified camp at Dimilioc near modern-day St. Dennis engaged the military while Uther plotted to seduce the queen. To circumvent the duke's guards posted at the isthmus, Uther called on the magic of Merlin to aid in a stealthy approach up Tintagel's seaward side. As a charm that would entice Ygraine for one night of love, Merlin provided Uther with a potion to change his appearance into Gorlois's double.

At sunset, Merlin, Uther, and a servant successfully entered Tintagel's keep. Meanwhile, the king's men killed Gorlois in battle and ended Uther's need for covert seduction. After he married Ygraine, he lived with her part-time at Tintagel and at the court of King Mark, whose lore connects him with the famed headland. A separate love story of Tristan and Isolde describes Mark's selection of Tintagel as the burial site for the tragic lovers. A lesser tale picks Tintagel Castle as the place where King Arthur died after receiving mortal wounds at Slaughter Bridge over the Camel River. From Tintagel, a burial cortege bore him to a tomb at Glastonbury Abbey.

An alternate myth interprets Arthur's emergence as a symbol of the birth of all life in seawater. The text describes Arthur as a sea god's son who washed up with the tide at an easily defensible spit of land off the Cornish coast. Alfred, Lord Tennyson, in Part 11, the "Guinevere" section, of *Idylls of the King* (1859), pictured the mage Merlin, Arthur's protector, appearing at the seaside cave that served as a hermitage. The wise old man rescued the infant Arthur from the breakers:

> They found a naked child upon the sands
> Of dark Dundagil by the Cornish sea;
> And that was Arthur, and they foster'd him
> Till he by miracle was approven King
> [Tennyson, 1949, p. 139].

In another passage, the poet described how Arthur was born two years before Uther's death and how Merlin appeared at a "secret postern-gate" to receive the infant and place him with foster parents, Sir Ector and his wife, to be reared in safety away from monarchical struggles (*ibid.*, p. 141). By age fifteen, Arthur was ready to take his place in British history.

Perhaps the first known Christian warrior, Arthur came to glory in the era when the Celts were making their most desperate stand against Saxon encroachment. Records refer to him as diplomat, *dux bellorum* [military commander], and *Riothamus* [high king], a designation that suits the saga of Camelot. Wrapped in idealism, romanticism, and the trappings of chivalry, the era expresses an heroic confrontation between a dying creed and a vigorous invasive culture destined to trounce and thoroughly eclipse Celtic England.

Appropriately, the king conceived in Tintagel's surf retreated to a watery nether world of Avalon (or Avilion) to recover from near-mortal wounds and await the time that England would need him most. Those most imbued with Arthurian belief declare that the spirit of the *rex quondam, rex futurus* [once and future king] hovers over Tintagel in the shape of a chough, a red-legged seabird now extinct except for isolated pairs in zoos. The animistic Arthur also lights the sky in Arcturus, a bright star, and in Ursa

Major, whose name replicates the feral significance of *Arturos* (bear).

Archeology

Archeologist Courtney Arthur Ralegh Radford, author of *Arthurian Sites in the West* (1975), excavated Tintagel Head in the 1930s. Sponsored by the British Ministry of Works, he continued for three decades and disclosed a number of significant, but inconclusive finds. His team located costly eastern Mediterranean pottery, which may have been the tableware and wine and oil storage of a well-to-do fifth-century household. The ceramic shards marked with Roman lettering provided the first tangible connection between Tintagel and Arthur's historical period. One possible interpretation is that the dishes, imported from Mediterranean ports, were used in a princely manor yet to be discovered, but which may have been known to Geoffrey of Monmouth through oral history.

Additional finds are highly conjectural. The Celtic site, dating to the 1100s, included a court that may have risen atop an oratory and empty tomb, which perhaps was a shrine for the founder's bones or a repository for religious relics. Radford found a total of four graves, but no human remains. At the site, he deduced that a one large building was a guesthouse that sheltered pilgrims. On the grounds, two wells, a garden, and a larger building possibly housing a library and scriptorium completed the complex and enhanced its work.

Radford surmised that additional structures overlooking the cove on the north side of the promontory offered a refectory and steam bath as well as quarters for around fifty monks. A terraced site closer to the isthmus held a three-room building constructed of substantial masonry. Designed in the Roman style, the complex rose above a hypocaust, a subterranean firing chamber that heated the stone floor. The main room was fitted with wooden benches along the walls, perhaps indicating a space where monks studied. Farther up the incline, a path entered a modest terrace that held rectangular chambers open at each end. To the east, remains of grain-drying ovens and cattle pens appear to have contributed to the monks' livelihood.

The successful excavation of Tintagel Head led historians to a wide range of surmise. One possible identification of the buildings was the lost Irish monastery of Rosnant (or Rosnat), an unidentified early medieval abbey that educated St. Eugenius, later Bishop of Ardstraw. Early parchments show that the monastery had once been a hub of religion and culture. In 1981, a scholar of Tristan lore, Oliver J. Padel, lecturer in Celtic languages at Cambridge University, come to another conclusion from analyzing Cornish legends that characterized Tintagel as a traditional seat of kings.

After a serious grass fire on Tintagel Head in summer 1983, the analysis of Tintagel Head made a radical shift from Radford's findings. Erosion of topsoil disclosed around 100 ruins of rectangular structures that were much older than Rosnant. The fire also revealed thousands of pot shards of amphorae [storage jars] from the Aegean, eastern Mediterranean, and North Africa. The cache suggested a much higher standard of living than an abbey would have maintained.

Historians considered that Tintagel may have been a trading station where Cornish merchants exchanged local tin for earthenware. Archeologists who examined the dishes began concurring with Padel that the island was the court of a king as wealthy as the legendary Arthur. He would most likely have preferred a hill fort or citadel overlooking the sea, particularly as a summer court for an itinerant household. Alternative conclusions pointed to an unusually prosperous secular community or a trade depot with ties to sea routes to the Mediter-

ranean, particularly the rich ports of Alexandria or Carthage.

In June 1998, further excavation led by Chris Morris, professor of archeology at the University of Glasgow, and sponsored by the university and the English Heritage Society (EHS) turned up a number of hearths, evidence of windbreaks anchored in the soil, and some Mediterranean amphorae, a fine domestic ware that indicates trade links between the ancient kingdom of Dumnonia in Cornwall and the Mediterranean. Rachel Harry, one of the Glasgow team, located neck fragments of a unique yellow-green glass flagon similar to sixth-century glass produced in Cadiz and Málaga, Spain. The find was the first evidence of early British trade with Iberia. The unearthing of a leacht, a common monastic monument or memorial stone in western Ireland, added weight to the argument that the buildings belonged to a religious community and that the leacht may have been the tomb shrine of the founder.

Headlines focused less on earthenware and glass than on a breakthrough made by Kevin Brady, another of the Glasgow team. On July 4, 1998, he found a slate artifact measuring 8 by 14 inches and broken on one edge. Residents may have recycled the slate from the rubble of a collapsed building to use as a drain cover on the eastern terrace. Called the "Arthur stone," it was inscribed with Latinate lettering reading "Pater/Coli Avi Ficit/Artognov" [Artognou, father of a descendent of Coll, made this]. The slate is important for two reasons: it is the first secular inscription from England dating to the Dark Ages and it establishes that literacy existed in a secular context. Some historians have connected Coll with King Cole, an historical figure from the A.D. 500s, the focus of the children's rhyme "Old King Cole." Scholars have mused that Artognou may be a Latinate form of Arthnou, a tenuous, but inconclusive suggestion of the name Arthur. Geoffrey Wainwright, head EHS archeologist and member of the Royal Commission on Ancient and Historic Monuments in Wales, acknowledged that the inscription established the existence of the name Arthur and made a case for the man's high rank in Cornwall.

Coastal Activities

Tintagel is both a starting place for fans of Arthurian lore and an ideal summering site for camping, photography, swimming, surfing, and body-boarding. For castle climbers, the rugged track leading to the stony remains suffers from attrition, particularly after the main site split, leaving one part on the mainland, the other on the promontory, and the connecting sliver of land gradually disappearing into the sea. Caving at St. Nectan's Kieve, the retreat of a Celtic hermit, draws the hearty trekker northeast up the coast to a picturesque cataract and site of an old mill. A Bronze Age carving in a nearby rock face takes the shape of an ancient maze called a finger labyrinth from the viewer's use of an index finger to trace a path from the opening to the center.

Nearby, villagers maintain a market-day atmosphere at open-air stalls selling traditional Cornish meat pasties and cider. The truly Arthur-struck visit Condolden Barrow, a hill burial mound overlooking Tintagel Head that historians connect with Cador, a sixth-century Celtic king. Literary hounds continue the pilgrimage a few miles away to Camelford, site of Arthur's final battle against Mordred, the king's son fathered unintentionally on the king's own sister.

SOURCES

Ashe, Arthur. *The Landscape of King Arthur.* New York: Henry Holt and Co., 1986.

Ashton, Graham. *The Realm of King Arthur.* Newport, Isle of Wight: J. Arthur Dixon, 1974.

Byrd, Laura, "A Place of Legends," *The World & I,* November 1, 2001.

Conlee, John, "Warwick Deeping's 'Uther and Igraine, '" *Arthuriana,* Vol. 11, No. 4, Winter 2001, pp. 88–95.

Harry, Rachel, and Kevin Brady, "Early Medieval Tintagel," *Heroic Age,* Issue 1, Spring/ Summer 1999.

"Has King Arthur Been Discovered at Tintagel?," *Current Archaeology,* Vol. 159, September 1998.

"In Memoriam," *Heroic Age,* No. 2, Autumn/ Winter 1999.

Jenkins, Elizabeth. *The Mystery of King Arthur.* New York: Coward, McCann & Geoghegan, Inc., 1975.

Lacy, Norris J., ed. *The Arthurian Encyclopedia.* New York: Peter Bedrick Books, 1986.

Morris, Chris, "Not King Arthur, But King Someone," *British Archaeology,* No 4, May 1995.

"New Evidence Suggests Legendary King Did Exist," *Hickory Daily Record,* December 29, 1982.

Reno, Frank D. *The Historic King Arthur.* Jefferson, N. C.: McFarland & Co., 1996.

Tennyson, Alfred, *Idylls of the King* in *Victorian and Later English Poets.* New York: American Book Co., 1949.

Thigpen, Ann Marie, "An Arthurian Journey in England's West Country," *Atlanta Journal-Constitution,* June 16, 1985, pp. 1F, 14F.

Walker, Amelie E., "King Arthur Was Real?," *Archaeology,* September 23, 1998

Uchinada, Japan

Location

An area known for breakthroughs in internal medicine and cardiac treatment at Kanazawa Medical University, Uchinada is also a popular beach town lying due west of Tokyo on the island of Honshu. Edged in hard-packed white-sand along the Sea of Japan, Uchinada rises at the base of Noto Hanto or Noto Peninsula, a seafood haven for crab and squid. In 1982, Kamiyamada Shell Midden was named a National Historical Site for Tachiyama, a trapezoidal heap of seashells, which Doctor Kubo discovered in 1930. Excavators along the Kahoku Lagoon probed the stratum to identify a cache of carp bones, freshwater pond snail shells, ishigai, and ocean shells that indicate the interweaving of the sea into the lives of aborigines living as early as 3,000 B.C.

Today, the thumb-shaped Nano Hanto promontory offers 500 miles of prime shoreline braced by headlands topped with gnarled pine stands. The town of Uchinada is home to one of Japan's largest dunes and one of the nation's 100 most scenic natural spots. The area and its gentle breezes suit water sports and the ancient art of kite-flying, a hobby, cultural art, and holiday celebration practiced by adults and youth.

Contacts

Masaaki Modegi, President
Japan Kite Association
1-12-10 Nihonbashi, Chuoh-ku, Tokyo 103-0027, Japan
Phone: 81-0-3-3275-2704
Fax: 81-0-3-3273-0575
Email: jka@tako.gr.jp
http://www.tako.gr.jp/eng/index_e.html

Asian Kite-Flying

Asian kite-flying has a long history dating to around 1,000 B.C., when people observed the lift of sails, banners, and bamboo hats in the breeze and attempted to harness the wind's energy. Coastal communities developed methods of applying that energy through the flying of kites. The Chinese elevated kites to muster the militia. The Balinese raised their prayers to God with kites. In Indonesia, the use of a kite trailing a fishline and hook over the surf enabled coastal fishers to lure large fish without creating a human shadow to scare them away. The Siamese decorated palaces with kites and developed kite fighting, a sport governed by 78 rules.

In imitation of elegant court kites called *feng cheng* [wind harps], Chinese hobbyists began shaping leaves and bamboo sticks into bird or tent kites flown on flax string. A millennium before kites were made from paper, the frail, buoyant shapes benefited kite makers as a means of chasing away evil spirits, acknowledging the arrival of spring, lifting thank offerings to deities, carrying lanterns aloft, startling birds from rice paddies, and forecasting the weather. For practical purposes, the Chinese believed that the act of guiding a kite turned the flier's face upward and rid the body of excess heat at the same time that tracking the kite improved eyesight. They established September ninth as the Double Ninth Festival for the ninth day of the ninth month and celebrated with a kite festival, a day of rising anticipations for success and happiness.

The invention of lightweight silk greatly advanced kite technology. Kite makers chose shapes from a long list of symbolic meanings: eagles for power, Mandarin ducks for nobility, cranes for honesty, bees for industry, and butterflies for love. Amorous youths scribbled love verses on graceful silk kites and suspended them over the homes of their sweethearts. Soldiers used kites for spreading informational leaflets, sending military signals, target practice, carrying gunpowder, and lifting observers for reconnaissance. During the Middle Ages, bands of soldiers carried a windsock variety of kite shaped like a dragon and tipped with burning tar to terrify the enemy.

The Japanese *tako* [kite] is an early art form derived from the gunny-cloth-covered kites of China and Korea. The first Japanese model recorded in history appeared in the A.D. 600s, about the time that Chinese priests brought Buddhism to the Japanese islands and flew kites as spiritual symbols. To create the kite skeleton, crafters used splits of aged bamboo and shaped them over a flame. Experts collected bamboo lengths from demolished houses and prized pieces above the kitchen stove, which grease and smoke cured and toughened. The most expensive kites employed *washi* [rice paper] for coverings and black ink for markings. Families congratulated parents of new-born boys by giving them "son kites." The ritual may date after 1558 to Hamamatsu, where Iiwo Buzenn-no-Kami announced his new-born heir with a kite lettered with the boy's name.

Japan's towns and villages developed individual shapes of kites, for example, the bees of Aichi, the beetles of Yamaguchi, and the *yakko-dako* [infantrymen] of Tokyo. At competitions, winners received a cow and elevation in a sedan chair for first place, a pig for the runner-up, and a sheep as third prize. In A.D. 1600 , the Dutch introduced a new kite symbol, the blue, red, and white fighters from India, which Nagasaki adopted as its kite emblem. In 1649, fliers formalized the martial art of *ika gassen* [kite fighting], which began as friendly competition between villages.

In addition to sport kiting, in the late 1600s, the Japanese architect Kawamura Zuiken, developer of the nation's west coast, employed *ohdako* [oversized kites] to elevate roof tiles during the construction of shrines and temples. A Japanese thief lifted himself by kite to a castle roof in an effort to steal ornamental koi made of gold. In the mid-seventeenth century, officials favored the serious side of kite-flying and limited sporting events to the Dragon Boat Festival and the Lantern Festival. In 1760, the Japanese government halted all leisure kite-flying lest people grow more interested in their hobbies than their jobs. The Chinese were even more rigid in their separation of sport and work kites. During the Cultural Revolution, which began in 1966, Mao Ze Dong's last decade of power, authorities banned kite-flying and punished offenders by jailing them and destroying their craft.

Since 1990, the Japan Kite Association has organized the Uchinada Kite Festival and other hobby events. After the election of Masaaki Modegi, a restaurateur and kite collector from Tokyo, as president of the as-sociation, he and an assistant, Teruaki Tsutsumi, director of Tokyo's kite museum, promoted the festival among international participants, bringing people from around the globe to Uchinada. At his kite museum, he began exhibiting models to instruct children on kiting history and creativity. He based his enthusiasm for kite exhibitions on the hope for domestic and international friendship through peaceful endeavors.

Coastal Activities

The Uchinada coast is a favorite of local and foreign vacationers seeking wide expanses of shore along the Sea of Japan. Young beach-goers prefer the hard-packed shoreline for windsurfing, cycling, driving, and horseback riding. Each year, Uchinada's residents celebrate Marine Day, which commemorates the Japanese navy's triumph over Russia's Baltic fleet on May 28, 1905.

Currently, the making, painting, and flying of kites is a respected Japanese art and often the hobby of Uchinada's elderly beach-goers. Traditional kite-fliers gather for regional club activities and favor Golden Week, April 29–May 5, which concludes on national Children's Day. Special kites honor children by name as tokens of good luck and future prosperity. For *ika gassen* [kite fighting], teams ready a line of models to replace those destroyed during in-air combat. To assure victory, combatants equip kite strings with ground glass, sharp sand, a porcelain edge, or *gagari* [razor blades] and maneuver the armed kites against opponents' lines to slice them in mid-air or to lasso or entangle them. Teams keep score by the number of opponents they down while their own sky warriors remain aloft.

During the spring kite festival, entrants gather at Uchinada's shores outside Kanazawa to fly streamers, single-line, oversized, art-form, three-dimensional, and fighting kites in individual competitions. Festivals begin with the smashing of the saki keg, toasts

and speeches, taiko drumming, and dancing. Crowds view and photograph a variety
of fliers — glass-coated, basket- and box-
shaped, multiple layers, warrior, and miniature models as well as gliders. Some clever
models even whistle, hum, and blink their
eyes. At the thirteenth annual festival on
May 3, 2001, the miniature kite competition
featured models from Canada, Holland,
Japan, and the United States. The winner
for the third time was Nobuhiko Yoshizumi
of Kyoto. In addition to prizes for the smallest entrant, the festival awarded the most
beautiful, the best flier, best crafted, and
most original kites.

SOURCES

Demi. *Kites*. New York: Crown Publishers, 1999.
Despojad, Ron, "Nine (or Ten) Days in Japan,"
    Kitelife, June/July 2001.
Dolan, Edward F. *The Complete Beginner's Guide
    to Making and Flying Kites*. Garden City, N.Y.:
    Doubleday & Co., 1977.
Farber, William, "Czech Kite Fairy Tale,"
    Kitelife, No. 27, Summer 2002.
Gomberg, David, "Postcards from Uchinada,"
    Kite Lines, Vol. 12, No. 4, Winter 1997–1998.
Kaboyashi, Jun, and Ryoichi Kiz, "Evaluation of
    Metal Contents in River Water Using a Sim-
    ple Fractionation Method," *Journal of Health
    Science*, Vol. 47, No. 5, 2001, pp. 460–463.
Kent, Sarah. *Creative Book of Kites*. New York:
    Smithmark, 1997.
"Kites of Japan," *Piecework*, Vol. 6, No. 1, Jan-
    uary/February 1998.
Moulton, Ron. *Kites*. London: Pelham Books,
    1978.
Newman, Lee Scott, and Jay Hartley Newman.
    Kite Craft. New York: Crown, 1974.
Pelham, David. *The Penguin Book of Kites*. Lon-
    don: Penguin Books, 1977.
Streeter, Tal. *The Art of the Japanese Kite*. New
    York: Weatherhill, 1974.
Wang Xiaoyu. *Chinese Kites*. Shandong, China:
    Shandong Friendship Publishing House, n.d.

Vizcaya, Miami Beach, Florida

Location

A National Historic Landmark on
South Miami Avenue, Villa Vizcaya graces
the shores of Biscayne Bay in northern Coconut Grove on Miami's arty South Beach,
America's largest art deco district. The
property faces out to sea toward Key Biscayne and an intracoastal waterway that parallels Florida's Gold Coast. Industrialist
James Deering began the seventy-room
project on low-lying marshland in 1914 and
completed the sumptuous residence two
years later as a winter home and exhibit hall
for his collection of antiques and art objects.
He chose a name reflecting both his taste
and Miami's topography — the Basque
"Vizcaya," meaning "elevated place." Set
across from the Miami Museum of Science
and Space Transit Planetarium among
Cuban neighborhoods in one of Florida's
rare native hammock forests, the James
Deering residence continues to draw tourists,
socialites, art and architecture students,
painters, naturalists, and historians to a remarkable beach home and its unique sea
vista.

Contacts

Holly Blount, Marketing Director
Vizcaya Museum and Gardens
3251 South Miami Avenue
Miami, Florida 33129
Phone: 305-860-8451
http://www.vizcayamuseum.org/

Greater Miami Convention and Visitors
    Bureau
701 Brickell Avenue, Suite 2700
Miami, Florida 33131
Phone: 305-539-3000
Http://www.miamiandbeaches.com

For its elegance and rich detail, Villa Vizcaya earned the nickname "Hearst Castle of the East" (courtesy of Holly Blount).

Biography

Agricultural industrialist and art enthusiast James Deering was the son of Clara Cummings Hamilton Deering and Chicago tractor magnate and philanthropist William Deering, a benefactor of Northwestern University and Northwestern Memorial Hospital. James Deering and his older half-brother Charles gained their wealth from the Deering Harvester Company, the family's farm implement company, which William Deering established in Fargo, North Dakota, in 1870 from his early experimentation on machines that reaped and bound grain. The firm, originally called Gammon & Deering, began manufacturing original farm machinery in 1880. Charles assumed the company presidency and James became the company vice president when

their father retired in 1901 and moved to Spain. The Deering brothers prospered in 1902 from the merger of their holdings with the McCormick Harvesting Machine Company under the new name of International Harvester.

In retreat from Midwestern winters, during the Gilded Age, James Deering considered settled in Egypt, on the South Seas or the Riviera, and in the tropical United States. He gravitated to the unexploited shores of South Florida to build an Atlantic Coast refuge where the sea air might relieve his sufferings from arthritis and pernicious anemia. Like his father, who developed an art center at Sitges outside Barcelona, Spain, James had a yen to combine European esthetics and art with the elements of his daily life. His plans grew into an estate grander than that of his brother Charles, who erected Deering Hammock in Cutler, Florida.

In 1912, James paid Mary Brickell $1,000 per acre for a prime parcel of wild hammock and pineland. Two years later, began reshaping the 180 acres of bay-front property by engineering a channel to Biscayne Bay. Because dredging produced three small artificial islets, he was forced to buy them back from the state of Florida for $1,230. He engaged Francis Burrall Hoffman, Jr., a 29-year-old architect educated at Harvard and L'École des Beaux Arts in Paris, to erect a four-story residence with an additional tower level on each end. Against the builder's advice, to preserve virgin forest, Deering located his dwelling at the shore on the northeast end of the tract. Amid sea grape, banyans, pines, guava, and citrus trees, he planned formal gardens below sea level.

Hoffman shared Deering's love of classic buildings devoid of ostentation. To make the Italian Baroque residence self-sufficient, Deering requested plans for a small village comprising gondolas, a garage with turntable for washing cars, farm village, livestock pens, barns and mule stable, dairy, pastures, citrus groves, and poultry complex. For the convenience of guests, lanes led to tennis courts, a subtropical forest, and a yacht basin with access to the Atlantic Ocean. A discreet service level on the mezzanine included twelve rooms for staff housing and activities that remained largely out of sight and earshot. Within eighteen months, the house was finished.

Meanwhile, with Paul Chalfin, an associate of the New York Studio of Interior Design, Deering sailed aboard the *Lusitania* to European furnishing marts. The two men scoured Florence, Venice, and London for tapestries, carpets, paneling, mantels and cornices, murals, light fixtures, ceilings, art objects, and rare friezes and paintings to adorn the beachfront manse. Much of Deering's collection came from Villa Rezzonico

at Bassano del Grappa on the Italian Veneto. From a palazzo in Palermo, a doge's palace in Venice, the Villa Gamberaia near Florence, a French chateaux on the Loire, and Spanish casas, he selected decorative items to be crated and shipped to Miami for placement in Villa Vizcaya. To create ambience, he informed Chaflin that the villa required its own orchid house to supply rooms with fresh blossoms year round.

On December 25, 1916, as cannons boomed at the shoreline, 57-year-old James Deering piloted his motor yacht into the bay, docked at the stone breakwater, and moved into his home, which admirers dubbed the "Venice of the Tropics." In ecstasy, he wrote to Chalfin: "If proportion is the highest expression of beauty, as I believe it is, I do not know where you would go to find anything more beautiful" ("The Residence," 1987, p. 38). His guest lists included the notables of his day — orator William Jennings Bryant, showman Florenz Ziegfeld, and actors Lillian and Dorothy Gish and Marion Davies. With them came reporters from *Harper's Bazaar, Town and Country, Vanity Fair*, and *Vogue*. In March 1917, artist John Singer Sargent visited Deering to paint his portrait in oils. Sargent lingered to sketch watercolors of spring flower beds, shady paths, palmetto fronds, and sea views of the grounds and beach. At times confined to an ornate wicker wheelchair, Deering wintered at his villa until his death. Ironically, at age 66, the millionaire who treasured the Atlantic Ocean for its boost to his failing health died at sea on September 21, 1925, on a voyage home from France.

Architecture

Deering chose a European decorative style for his coastal palace, which, from its inception, bore an air of understated opulence. Two towers at each end of the villa overlooked the bay. For walls and structures, he selected native cypress for beams, steel-reinforced concrete, Cuban and Florida limestone, and stucco painted to look mellow with age. Mules pulled in local limestone quarried at Vizcaya from South Florida's only stone factory. Deering roofed the building with handmade Cuban tiling retrieved from weathered island villages. Around a central courtyard, 34 period rooms replicated Renaissance, Baroque, Rococo, and Neo-classic style in furnishings, balustrades, and decor. He specified that each bath should draw water from the sea for therapeutic body soaks and refinement of the complexion.

When construction began in 1914, the builder became Dade County's major employer by hiring 1,000 master carpenters — ten percent of Miami's labor force — plus stonecutters, painters, plasterers, joiners, gardeners, and artisans from Europe. The ground plan of Deering's living quarters was simple and convenient. Sea themes marked art works, china tableware, and the tea room, where stained glass pictured a caravel and seahorse. The east loggia stood open to sea breezes, which unfortunately carried in moisture that constantly threatened delicate plaster, textiles, and paintings and the strings of harpsichord, harp, and dulcimer. Adding to the luxury of the estate was early twentieth-century technology — a central vacuum cleaning system, elevators and dumbwaiters, built-in refrigeration, fire sprinklers, master clock system, electrical call buttons to staff quarters, and a telephone switchboard.

Deering placed his swimming pool in a grotto half in and half out of doors. Over the shaded shallow end, a vaulted ceiling protected guests from too much sun and displayed his love of the sea in paintings of sea creatures, corals, and shells. Another grotto lined in native seashells welcomed incoming guests. Leading up from the sea were steps sliced from coral slabs containing fossilized brain coral and sea fans. For those arriving by land, Samuel Yellin, an immigrant Polish artist-blacksmith in Philadelphia, forged an ornamental caravel on the wrought iron front gate to extend the host's welcome and link the estate to Spanish explorers.

In the villa's interior, Deering displayed marquetry floors, chinoiserie, and historic pieces culled from his European shopping venture, notably, a tall gateway from the palace of Italian admiral Niccolò Pisani. Deering bought an ancient Roman altar and statue of the wine-god Bacchus leading babes riding sea monsters. Deering's buying jaunts also produced Egyptian urns, a chair that Paolina Borghese had owned, Sheffield silver plaques, tapestries that had hung in the home of poets Elizabeth Barrett and Robert Browning, and art objects that once belonged to Queen Isabella of Spain and Marie Antoinette. One bed featured a headboard embroidered in gilt thread for Lady Emma Hamilton, mistress of Horatio, Lord Nelson. In the master suite overlooking the bay, Deering occupied a suite with bath and sitting room that looked seaward from a private balcony. The decorator coordinated marble walls, silk paneling, carved wood overlaid with gold leaf, and a linen ceiling canopy to drape his bed in the style of Napoleon's field tent. Because of Deering's belief in the health benefits of living by the sea, he ordered gold-washed faucets shaped like swans to dispense fresh water and seawater and a bronze and black marble shaving stand oriented toward the bay.

On the grounds, Deering mapped out ten acres of formal Italian plantings, an American trend of the Gilded Age emulating Tivoli Gardens from Italy's grand Villa d'Este. For landscaping, he hired Italo-Spanish architect Diego Suarez of Bogotá, Colombia, who had studied Renaissance gardening at the Florence Architectural School. Suarez strategically placed orange jasmine hedges, oleander, American live oaks *(Quercus virginiana)* filmed with Spanish moss, and spacious lawns leading to the shore. Workers unwrapped a shipment of 265 royal palms from Havana and planted them in four rows along the causeway. To complete the plan, he had to strengthen the base with concrete pilings to assure that seasonal gales would not uproot the plantings. Because of a shortage of labor and materials during World War I, he did not complete the work until 1921.

The result was a subdued elegance that invited solitude and reflection. Suarez adorned the grounds with a fan-shaped parterre, water stairway, peacock bridge, and topiaries. He treated the garden as an outdoor room and added a central rise to hold a poo, a stone casino on a raised mount, an open-air theater garden with turf seating, a hedge labyrinth and secret garden, and paths and loggias lined with statues of classic gods and sea monsters. Framed in symmetry and authentic in style and building materials, the estate earned Michelin's praise as the finest example of Italian Renaissance architecture in America.

To harmonize with Florida's seashore climate, Deering retained native mangroves along the shore and oriented the residence toward Biscayne Bay. The villa's stone walkways led down from a coral ridge past refined gardens, coral caves, and waterfalls to overlook incoming waves of the Atlantic Ocean around a sculpted stone breakwater in the shape of a Renaissance barge, designed by Alexander Stirling Calder. It became Vizcaya's trademark and earned admiration from publicity in postcards, guide books, and a seven-page spread in the July 1917 edition of *Architectural Review*.

The landscaping was a masterpiece of adaptation that replaced traditional European boxwood and plane trees with plants and vines that could thrive in Florida's swampy terrain, humid climate, salty breezes, and seasonal hurricanes. The traditional Italian horticulture blended the dominant seahorse emblem and an antique travertine dolphin fountain with cascades,

bay-view terracing, pools, urns, and trellised bougainvillea. Flanking the stone barge, the lattice-top teahouse in the seawall and yacht landing provided guests with access to the bay. A boathouse sheltered Deering's private fleet, which included the cruiser *Psyche* [Spirit] and an eight-foot houseboat-yacht named the *Nepenthe* (Forgetful).

History

In the years after James Deering's death, a skeleton staff maintained the villa and property. The formal gardens suffered severe saltwater damage from a category four storm at 2:00 A.M. on the night of September 18, 1926, when the Great Miami Hurricane swept northeast from the Caribbean Sea. For over an hour, the "big blow," the worst in American history, produced sustained 120 mph winds that killed many livestock, devastated the University of Miami, darkened the homes of 55,000 of the 300,000 residents, and left 18,000 homeless and 240 dead. Vizcaya survived with gardens in turmoil and lower rooms under eight feet of water. The barge lost statuary; the *Nepenthe* and *Psyche* sank in the bay.

The storm and a resultant twelve-foot tidal wave on the Miami River signaled the end of the Florida boom and the beginning of the end for the Gilded Age, which vanished during the Great Depression. Like many residents surrendering an idyllic life on the Florida shore, James Deering's heirs — his nieces Barbara Deering Danielson and Marion Deering McCormack, Charles's daughters — opted to sell much of the original 180-acre tract to developers. The portion extending to the south passed to the Catholic diocese for a church, school, and Mercy Hospital. The northern end retained its value as a Miami landmark.

For its elegance and rich detail, Villa Vizcaya earned the nickname "Hearst Castle of the East." Among the dignitaries who visited the estate were Juan Carlos I and Queen Sofia of Spain, Elizabeth II of England, Pope John Paul II, President Ronald Reagan, and President Bill Clinton. In 1952, Miami-Dade County purchased the residence and the remaining fifty acres for $1 million and received from the heirs an assortment of antiques and art works as a donation. The structure required installation of a climate control system and the enclosure of the courtyard in glass to ward off humidity and corrosive salt air.

The following year, county officials relocated the Dade County Art Museum to the estate and named Robert Tyler Davis as director. Davis collected original correspondence from designer Paul Chaflin and also found time to paint views of Vizcaya's flora and seashells. Curator Doris Littlefield disseminated details of Vizcaya's style and artistry through courses at the local community college and public lectures on decorative art. Extending the value of the villa to the community was the Miami Museum of Science, which opened on three acres of the former Deering property in 1960. Six years later, the non-profit organization added the Space Transit Planetarium. In 1989, the Metropolitan Dade County Commission signed a 99-year lease to allow the museum to continue its educational exhibits, which annually drew over 250,000 visitors.

In 1970, the 54-year-old property earned international acclaim after it was listed on the National Register of Historic Sites. The Vizcayan staff and fifty volunteers who continued restoration and preservation organized annual parties to raise funds for their work. In 1979, the National Trust for Historic Preservation recognized the effort with the David E. Finley Award for maintenance of the beauty of residence and grounds. The next year, the Florida Trust for Historic Preservation presented the staff an award of merit. In 1985, the National Recreation and Park Association conferred a similar honor for their contributions to Miami's historic district.

The villa survived a late twentieth-century storm less lethal than the unnamed 1926 hurricane. In the fall of 1992, Hurricane Andrew damaged Vizcaya when 140 mph winds and torrential rains struck the Biscayne Bay area. The villa's staff erected flood barriers around the exterior to prevent a deluge from the sea and screened windows against winds and torrents. After the blow, workers began clearing debris and replanting according to the original horticultural plan. The next year, Vizcaya returned to full operation and opened its substantial library to students.

At the invitation of President Bill Clinton, 34 leaders of the Western Hemisphere gathered at Vizcaya for the Summit of the Americas conference on December 10, 1994. Against a backdrop of flute and guitar music, dignitaries enjoyed moonlight strolls and assembled for picture-taking on the grounds. Photographer Eduardo G. Galliani made the most of polite hospitality at the seaside villa for the group's poses. He contributed finished copies of his work to the National Portrait Gallery in Washington, D.C., and to Vizcaya's collection.

Coastal Activities

In the 21st century, Vizcaya Museum and Gardens continued to receive 200,000 visitors annually. A garden for the blind perfumed the air with fragrant flowers and herbs and offered statuary for touching. The grounds welcomed the Miami International Film Festival and the Florida Shakespeare Festival, which featured an outdoor performance of *Julius Caesar*. The complex served as a locus for painters and photographers, civic conferences, concerts, receptions, private occasions, and a televised tour on the Home and Garden network.

In 2000, rebirth of Deering's agricultural compound produced Vizcaya Village, a living tutorial of smithies and workshops west of South Miami Avenue that reprises South Florida's history. In spring 2002, planners for the Dade County Park and Recreation Department added the David A. Klein Orchidarium to the villa's attractions. The floral complex required construction of a twelve-foot pergola and two greenhouses, where staff tend fragrant cattleya hybrids and swan and vanda orchids.

Docents and the non-profit La Lega dei Viscayani [the Viscayan League] raise funds and public interest in the historic property by hosting annual entertainments, particularly the New Year's Eve Celebration. The October Halloween Sundowner, a two-night costume party with a spectacular buffet and a haunted mansion theme, is popular with some 2,000 young professionals for the evening's good food, lively music, and revelry. The pre–Thanksgiving Vizcayan Ball, called Festa dei Medici, is a more sedate black tie affair featuring an orchestra and catered delicacies for $500 per person or $10,000 per table. The annual White Carnaval de Vizcaya draws costumed guests for an outdoor extravaganza. For $550 each, guests anticipate a variety of white-only costumes, bay-side garden tours, dancing, and food from four distinguished restaurants. The event is the centerpiece for CARE Resource, Florida's largest AIDS charity supporting HIV/AIDS prevention and education.

In addition to in-house festivities, the financing of Vizcaya's upkeep requires the staff to rent out the house and grounds for private entertainment. Each March, the Renaissance Historical Society of Florida holds a cultural festival on the villa's grounds that draws 15,000 participants. The gala features arts and crafts, fortunetelling, royal jesters, the Masque di San Marco dancers, theatricals, buffets, and a living chess game enacted by team of costumed chess pieces placed on a life-size board.

As a balance to the villa's stress on arts and gracious living, the nearby Miami Science Museum promotes knowledge of Florida's shores, weather, and birds and interest in nature conservation. The Falcon Batchelor Bird of Prey Center researches data on raptors such as the burrowing owl and offers adoption, rehabilitation, and release of injured birds. A favorite with birders is an exhibit on the habits of eagles, hawks, falcons, owls, and condors. The museum staff has also presented an overview of shipwrecks in the Western Hemisphere and a tutorial on coastal reptiles, including alligators, crocodiles, lizards, rattlesnakes, tortoises, and vipers. In 1999, a presentation on turbulent landscapes studied the motion of water and air currents to form clouds, eddies, whirlpools, and hurricanes. Recent programs offered museum-goers a robotic zoo featuring the chameleon and platypus, a simulated underwater shark environment with live cam shots of baby sharks, and a traveling photographic display on Florida's warm-water manatees.

SOURCES

Biondi, Joann, "If You're Going to Miami," *Milwaukee Journal Sentinel*, January 10, 1999.

Boytano, Larry, and Nina Korman, "Night & Day," *Miami New Times*, October 29, 1998.

D'Addano, Beth, "Vizcaya: An Italianate Villa Set in Premodern Miami," *Boston Globe*, February 10, 2002.

Davidson, Rebecca Warren, "Past as Present: Villa and the 'Italian Garden' in the United States," *Journal of Garden History*, Vol. 12, No. 1, 1992, pp. 1–28.

"The Deering Estate at Cutler," *Florida History & the Arts*, Summer 2000.

Engel, Lisa, "Village Arising in the Shadow of Miami Museum," *Miami Herald*, December 5, 2002.

George, Christy, "Vizcaya Elevates Opulence to a New Height," *Boston Herald*, April 25, 1996.

"Greater Miami: Something for Everyone in This Eclectic Town," *Florida Travel*, September/October 1999.

"Greater Miami: The Beaches," *Meetings & Conventions*, June 1, 2001.

Handelman, Steve, "Summit of the Americas," *Time*, April 19, 2001.

Harwood, Kathryn Chapman. *The Lives of Vizcaya*. Miami, Fla.: Banyan, 1985.

"How Would an Andrew-strength Storm Affect South Florida's Landmarks Today?," *Sun-Sentinel*, August 24, 2002.

"Italy's Hollywood Sets the Stage for Vizcaya's 44th Annual Ball," *PR Newswire*, November 15, 2000.

MacDonald, Moira, "Hot Nights, Cool Sights," *Toronto Sun*, October 1999.

Martin, Laura C. *Southern Gardens: A Gracious History and a Traveler's Guide*. New York: Artabras, 1996.

McIver, Stuart, "The Blow That Broke the Boom," *Sun-Sentinel*, September 19, 1993.

Naquin-Delain, Marsha, and Rip Naquin-Delain, "What's Hot," *Ambush*, Vol. 20, No. 25, 2002.

Nicholas, William H., "Vizcaya: An Italian Palazzo in Miami," *National Geographic Magazine*, Vol. 98, No. 5, November 1950, pp. 561–594.

Pedicini, Sandra, "Future of Volusia Wilderness Rests with Secretive Chicago Company," *Orlando Sentinel*, December 4, 2002.

Perkins, Cathie, "Ready or Not," *Office of Emergency Newsletter*, Vol. 5, No. 4, June 2001.

Pollock, Philip M., "Historic Swimming Holes," *Florida Heritage Magazine*, Spring/Summer 1995.

"The Residence of James Deering's Winters," *Southern Living*, Vol. 22, No. 11, November 1987, p. 38.

Rothaus, Steve, "Video Shows White Party Excess," *Miami Herald*, November 30, 2002.

Solis-Cohen, LIta, "The Market for Samuel Yellin Ironwork," *Maine Antique Digest*, July 2000.

Spraker, Jean E., "Samuel Yellin: Metal Worker," *Minnesota History*, Vol. 50, No. 3, 1986, pp. 118–126.

"Vizcaya Miami Mansion Is Both Enduring and En-Deering," *Florida Times-Union*, July 28, 2002.

Werne, Jo, "Museum Opens Its Library of Rare Volumes to Students," *Knight Ridder/Tribune News Service*, December 30, 1993.

"William Deering & Company," *Argus*, June 7, 1894.

Winey, Marilyn F., "South Florida Offers Intriguing Cultural Sites," *Standard-Times*, May 7, 2000.

Wyss, Bob, "Vizcaya Is a 'Newport Cottage' of Biscayne Bay," *Providence Sunday Journal*, November 8, 1998.

"Yikes! It's Getting Spooky," *Miami Herald*, October 25, 2002.

Zimny, Michael, "Miami's Verdant Villa," *Florida Heritage*, Spring 1999.

Woolacombe, Devon

Location

On the southern coast of England's Bristol Channel at the north end of Morte Bay, Woolacombe is part of a marine conservation area and the locus of west-country family seaside vacations. Stretching along Marine Drive on a shallow bay due east from the island of Lundy, the white-sand beach lies at the north end of a curved shoreline reaching from crags at Barricane Beach south to Putsborough. At the end of a steep valley, the shoreline extends for some three miles and borders a line of grassy hills, pasturage, and cliffs, notably Baggy Point and Morte Point, two National Trust headlands.

Although peaceful in appearance, the coast is subject to strong breakers and erratic currents at low tide. In the mid-1940s, Allied battalions transformed the strand into a grueling testing ground for invasive tactics aimed at the Nazi occupations force in France. By June 5, 1944, Allied trainees were in place along the French coastline for the D-Day landing at Normandy. Currently, the harsh battering of the Atlantic Ocean at Woolacombe damages local strands, eroding the 96 steps of Combesgate Beach, Mortehoe, which date to the early 1950s.

As a vacation site, Woolacombe is a low-key getaway known for clean sand, risk-free water sports, and cautious lifeguards. The village features standard English fare — tidy shops, pubs, the Grand Narracott Hotel, fish-and-chips cafes, and restaurants serving local cockles and mussels. For the quality of its shore as a bathing area, Woolacombe won the 1999 England for Excellence Gold Award for Family Resort of the Year and, in October 2000, the best British Beach listed in the *Mail on Sunday*. The strand regularly earns Blue Flag and Premier Resort Awards for beach safety and cleanliness.

Contacts

Woolacombe Tourist Information
The Esplanade
Woolacombe, Devon
Phone: 44-0-1271-870553
Email: woolacombetic@visit.org.uk
http://www.holidaysinnorthdevon.co.uk/
    woolacombe.html
http://www.woolacombetourism.com/

Hannah Streatfield
North Devon Voluntary Marine
    Conservation Area
Braunton Countryside Centre, Caen Street
Braunton, North Devon, EX33 1AA
    England
Phone: 01271-817486
Fax: 01271-814149
Email: HStreatf@deon.gov.uk
http://www.devon.gov.uk/tourism/pages/
    attracts/hercoast.html.

History

The Atlantic shores of Woolacombe were occupied as early as the Stone Age by stone-tool makers and flint flakers. The *Domesday Book* reported on the site in early English history, when the area was known as Wolnecoma, which means "wolves' valley." The bay and beach took the surname of a family who owned farmland from the time of King John in the early 1200s. The seaside village lay in the shadow of the nearby town of Morthu, now known as Mortehoe, an infamous bastion of smugglers and brigands. Woolacombe did not take shape as a separate community until late in the Middle Ages. Beginning with agrarian families, the settlement grew into a village and a traditional English vacation spot favored by thousands of local and foreign visitors for its bracing salt air and pounding rollers.

World War II forced Woolacombe into new roles. In 1939, Robin Gladstone, owner of Clare House Preparatory School and Abbey School, Beckenham, chartered a train to take students from bomb-endangered Norfolk to the safety of Woolacombe. Under the supervision of headmaster Cyril Crump, the children remained for nearly a year until school authorities made more permanent arrangements at East Grinstead, Sussex. The precautions proved worthwhile after the Blitz reduced the Clare House furniture repository to rubble. Similarly, the staff of High Trees School in Surrey evacuated dormitories and commandeered four Woolacombe hotels to shelter pupils until the danger of war passed. In the absence of the student body, over the next five years, the empty school billeted members of the Royal Air Force and the Army Transport Service.

As the war grew grimmer and England's chances of survival dimmed, Woolacombe became the U.S. Assault Training Center, one of two beach staging areas for Operation Overlord, a grand plan for the liberation of France mapped out by General Sir Bernard Law "Monty" Montgomery, commander of ground forces, and General Dwight David Eisenhower, supreme commander of the Allied expeditionary force. In mid–April 1944, the 225-man 2nd Army Ranger Battalion, the only unit in training for a suicide mission, rehearsed maneuvers off Woolacombe with demolitions units and three engineer battalions in preparation for the D-Day landing at Normandy. In *Spirits of the Sand: The History of the U.S. Army Assault Training Centre* (1992), Richard T. Bass described how the amphibious crew, commanded by Lieutenant Colonel Paul Williams Thompson, developed strategies and tactics and practiced beach assaults under realistic ordnance and typical Atlantic Coast conditions.

At ten beach sites, Thompson's instruction was meticulous. Soldiers ducked under mock artillery and mortar fire and practiced at an artillery range. At a wire-cutting range, they wielded bangalore torpedoes for penetrating wire obstacles. At the infantry demolition range, they exploded satchel charges against beach obstacles and concrete gun implacements. After mastering beach landing and an obstacle-course, they practiced hurling grenades and firing flame-throwers and rockets. Ten dummy pillboxes at Baggy Point contributed to verisimilitude. One bunker bears the name A. A. Augustine scribbled in the concrete before it dried. Augustine was one of some 9,000 killed on D-Day.

By June 6, 1944, most of the U.S. landing forces, minus those already hardened by combat in North Africa Italy, and Sicily, had seen mock action on Slapton Beach or Woolacombe Beach while facing close-range fire, underwater obstacles, minefields, and tank advance. In addition to the basics of sea-to-land tactics with heavy packs, armaments, and gear, Thompson introduced new equipment for trial runs. The preparation paid off at the perilous Normandy landing, where Lieutenant Colonel James Earl Rudder and his 225-man 2nd Army Ranger Battalion, called "Rudder's Rangers," climbed the Pointe du Hoc promontory on Omaha Beach and seized it from German artillery units, losing 140 rangers in the effort. Thompson, who led the 6th Engineer Special Brigade up Omaha Beach, suffered two severe wounds at the landing and earned a Distinguished Service Cross, Bronze Star, and an Order of the British Empire. [*See also* OMAHA BEACH.]

Late in the twentieth century, Woolacombe turned to a new battle, the fight to save nature. In 1993, ecologists launched the North Devon Heritage Coast Service to preserve flora and fauna extending from the cliffs into the sea beyond. Among their projects were local walking tours and upgrading of trails and footbridges, distribution of hand tools and gloves for gardening and tree

and hedgerow planting, creation of nature reserves on salt marshes, installation of safe bird and bat habitats, and education of children on biodiversity in marine environments. The group also launched Operation Otter, a monitoring program coordinating the tracking and identification of animals by 280 volunteers.

The North Devon Voluntary Marine Conservation Area, established in May the following year and funded by the Devon Wildlife Trust, promoted sustainable shore and sea use and the preservation of marine wildlife. Stretching from the Bristol Channel, the refuge encompassed fifteen miles of shingles and sheltered coves and diverse life nurtured by the Gulf Stream, including gobies and blennies, basking shark, sunfish, cup coral, giant fan worms, star coral, and dolphins and porpoises. Among the tutorial strategies ecologists employed were tide pool field projects, celebrations of World Oceans Day on June 8 each year, and a full-color poster illustrating birds, plants, and sea animals that coexist in the North Devon ecosystem. In August 2002, the focal beach area was extended from Barricane Beach at Woolacombe to Down End at Croyde, offering citizens a 21-mile expanse on which to learn about sea birds and mammals, rare fish, and corals.

Coastal Activities

Long removed from wartime exigencies, Woolacombe is a favorite English shore for sunning and swimming as well as for surfing, boating and canoeing, bass and dab fishing, camping and caravanning, kite-flying, and pick-up games of cricket and beach volleyball. North Devon's Marine Rangers hold seaside events, including rock-pool rambles, diversity counts, and scuba-diving trails. Snorkelers locate spiny starfish, rocklings, sea anemones, shanny, and spider crabs on the rocky seabed. Strollers examine tide pools and gullies or venture north to Barricane Beach to bird-watch or beach-comb for exotic shells and fossil fish hammered from rocks. Inland activities take visitors golfing, wildflower sighting, and hill-trekking into the countryside, along the Tarka biking trial, or to 1,000 acres of sand dunes at the Nature Reserve of Braunton Burrows.

Each year since 1989, the annual U. K. National Sandcastle Championships, sponsored by Alpharma, Coca-Cola, HTML Limited, Last Chance Travel, and Wall's Ice Cream, raise money for the North Devon Hospice in Barnstable and the Green Wellie Appeal. In addition to sand-structure competitions for teams of children and adults, participants enjoy a Punch and Judy show, a children's poster contest, a kite exhibition, and a Royal Air Force air show. In July 2002, attendance reached 15,000 among observers, who witnessed the competition free of charge. The top three sand sculpting teams made likenesses of Homer Simpson, a mole, and a dragon. Earning special recognition from the 32 entries were a sculpted Noah's ark, Alexander Milne's Tigger, an igloo, a dolphin rider, Snoopy, a mermaid, and a treasure chest. The contest raised £3,000 for charity.

SOURCES

Ambrose, Stephen E. *D-Day June 6, 1944: The Climactic Battle of World War II.* New York: Touchstone, 1995.

Bass, Richard T. *Spirits of the Sand: The History of the U.S. Army Assault Training Centre.* Exeter, Eng.: Lee, 1992.

Bray, Roger, "Somewhere in Britain," *Manchester Guardian*, June 30, 2001.

"Conservation Area Grows," *North Devon Gazette & Advertiser*, August 8, 2002.

"Enter the Bucket-Spade Brigade," *North Devon Journal*, May 17, 2002.

Harrison, John, "Coast Along with Kings of the Castle," *Sunday Mercury*, July 18, 1999, p. 51.

Jones, Tim Kilvert. *Normandy: Omaha Beach.* Havertown, Pa.: Casemate, 1999.

Lewis, Adrian R. *Omaha Beach: A Flawed Victory.* Chapel Hill: University of North Carolina Press, 2001.

"North Devon Voluntary Marine Conservation Area," http://www.devon.gov.uk/tourism/pages/attracts/hercoast.html.

O'Connell, Dee, and Laura Kavalier, "Observer Best Beaches," *Manchester Guardian*, July 16, 2000.

"Steps Will Make a Welcome Return," *North Devon Journal*, 11 June 11, 2002.

Thomas, Gillian, "Surfer's Waves of Nostalgia," *Sunday Mercury*, February 15, 1998.

"Woolacombe, North Devon, Wins Best Family Holiday Resort Award from ETC," *M2 Communications Ltd.*, December 13, 1999.

GLOSSARY

aeolian — marked by soughing and moaning wind sounds

amphictyony — an association of neighboring Greek states that defended their common social, economic, and religious interests

aquifer — a permeable waterway lined with sand, gravel, or rock

archipelago — a group of islands spread over an expanse of ocean

atoll — a doughnut-shaped coral island consisting of a reef encircling a central lagoon

aurora australis or **southern lights** — an optical phenomenon caused by the sun's energy impacting earth's gases, creating colorful rays

bergy bit — a chunk of glacier that breaks free and floats in the ocean

biota — living things — plants and animals — that occupy a region

breakwater — an offshore island chain, sandbar, reef, or artificial wall or structure protecting a coastline from heavy breakers and sea currents

brough or **broch** — a Scottish term for a round stone tower

cairn — a heap of stones piled up as a landmark, grave topping, or memorial

calving — the detachment of an iceberg from a larger body of ice

caravel — a Renaissance sailing vessel featuring three masts and a high rear deck

causeway — a raised path or roadway across an expanse of water or wet ground

cetacean — a member of the family of large, hairless marine mammals that includes the dolphin, dugong, manatee, narwhal, porpoise, and whale

coaster — a merchant vessel suited to offshore trade, but not to ocean voyages

cofferdam — a tight pen or enclosure in a river or sea that is pumped free of water to expose the bottom

coral bleaching — a whitening of coral caused by a slight rise in ocean temperatures, causing the living coral to die and emit a substance that bleaches it

coral-rag — coral-bearing limestone known as oolite, a common coastal building material

corsair — a swift pursuit vessel used by Barbary Coast pirates

corvette — an easily maneuverable warship or escort vessel smaller than a destroyer or frigate

dendrochronology — the dating of wood by the examination of growth rings that identify the age of the original trees

dhow — a high-backed Arab boat fitted with lateen sails

diorite — a crystalline rock that is easily crumbled

dolomite — an expanse of limestone embedded with calcium or magnesium carbonate crystals

dolerite — coarse basalt

dune — a sandy hillock or ridge shaped by wind and held in place by coastal plants or by a fence or other artificial barrier

eco-feminism — a strand of feminist philosophy that supports preservation of the environment

ecosystem — a complex environment and the living things that inhabit it

endangered species — a particular plant or animal that exists in such small number or in so hazardous a habitat that its survival and propagation are in jeopardy

floodplain — a flat tract or plateau that floods when nearby waterways overflow

fumarole — an aperture in a volcano that allows vapor and hot gas to escape

gillnetting—snaring fish in the tight mesh of vertical nets that entangle heads and gills

gneiss—metamorphic rock striated into parallel bands or planes

Greenpeace—a non-profit organization in forty countries worldwide supporting the preservation of biodiversity and the integrity of the environment

greens—crusaders on behalf of the environment; members of pro-environmental political parties and action committees

hammock—a raised patch of vegetation and hardwood trees in coastal lowlands

headland—a promontory or steep incline that juts out from a shoreline into a body of water

hummock—a rounded knoll or hill

International Fund for Animal Welfare—an international effort to improve the welfare of wild and domestic animals by reducing commercial exploitation, protecting wildlife habitats, and aiding animals in distress

ironshore—a shoreline of rough uplifted, sharp-edged coral and/or limestone rock

karst—irregular limestone expanse pocked with caverns, sinks, and underground waterways

katabatic wind—a dense downward thrust of a cold air mass

kirk—Scottish term for "church"

krill—shrimp-like crustaceans that are the primary food of large sea mammals

loch—Scottish term for a fjord, a narrow arm of the sea forming a nearly landlocked bay

loggia—a roofed gallery with open, colonnaded side

maquis—scrubby undergrowth

merchantman—a commercial vessel

métis or **Métis**—mixed-blood Indian; when capitalized, the term refers to the offspring of an Indian and European

minster—an important or influential church

moraine—the accumulated soil and stones that glaciers push ahead of them as they advance

mudflat—a flat plot of ground lying slightly under water at high tide and left bare at low tide

ocean tomography—a method of measuring surf, tides, and temperatures by passing waves of energy through the water to generate a three-dimensional image of the ocean's mass

ozone layer—a gas belt twenty to thirty miles above the earth that blocks the sun's ultraviolet radiation

palisado—a long, flat spit of land

permafrost—a subsurface stratum of earth that remains frozen

petroglyph—prehistoric art created by carving or inscribing letters, symbols, or natural shapes on rock faces or ledges

phytoplankton—a tiny floating ocean plant that is the basis of the sea's food chain

polder—a tract of flat, lowlying land reclaimed by walling off or damming the water that once covered it

polderjongens [polder men]—Dutch workers who guard reclaimed land from flooding by repairing dikes, levees, and roads

reef—an expanse of coral, sand, or rock stretching near the surface of a body of water

rhyolite—acidic lava formed from molten granite

rutter or **routier**—a collection of pilots' sailing directions

salt marsh—a flat tract of land subject to floods of salt water

sandbar—a ridge or crest of sand pushed upward by an ocean current, particularly after a storm

sastrugi—wind-carved waves in snow

schist—layered crystalline rock

seamount—a subsurface mountain rising from the seabed

shellcrete—a coastal building material blended of sand and pulverized seashells

shoal—a sandbank or natural shallow stretch of coastline

sluice—an artificial drainage line or millstream fitted with a floodgate or dock to regulate the passage of water

sound—a broad inlet or shallow ocean expanse separating an island from the mainland

spur—a rocky ridge branching out from the side of a mountain

tell—a mound or archeological site in the Middle East that rises above successive human settlements

terp—an artificial hillock raised above flatland for the purpose of building residences or businesses

thermal plume—an elongated column of heat or hot gases coursing upward from the sea floor

tsunami—a tidal wave produced by a violent shift in the sea floor

tundra—a mossy, treeless flatland topped with black muck above permanently frozen sublevels

undertow—an offshore current coursing deep and out of sight

UNESCO—the United Nations Educational, Scientific, and Cultural Organization, established in November 1945, which allies 188

member states to foster world peace and security through the advancement of world culture

watershed — a region that drains precipitation into a watercourse or body of water

whinstone — basalt or chert, both of which are fine-grained igneous rock

World Culture Heritage List — a UNESCO project that protects monuments and buildings of esthetic, archeological, historic, scientific, ethnological, or anthropolical value

World Wildlife Fund — an international conservation effort to preserve nature through advocacy and campaigns that demonstrate solutions to environmental problems

Appendix: Selected Literary Works and Films Providing Data on Beaches and Shores

Alphabetical List of Titles

Ab Urbe Condita [From the City's Foundation] (ca. A.D. 14), Livy

Aeneid (19 B.C.), Virgil

Alexandria—The Submerged Royal Quarters (1998), Franck Goddio

Annals (A.D. 109), Tacitus

Archaeology of Elmina: Africans and Europeans on the Gold Coast, An 1400–1900 (2001), Christopher R. DeCorse

Archaeology of Kahoolawe (1973), J. Gilbert McAllister

Argonautica (ca. 245 B.C.), Apollonius of Rhodes

La Bahia de los Pinos [Bay of Pines] (1542), Juan Rodriquez Cabrillo

Basque Whaling in Labrador in the 16th Century (1993) (monograph), Jean-Pierre Proulx

Between Pacific Tides (1939), Edward Flanders "Doc" Ricketts and John Steinbeck

The Birds of Australia (1848), John Gould and Elizabeth Gould

Birds of Paradise and Bower Birds (1950), Margaret Cochrane Scott

The Brendan Voyage (1978), Tim Severin

Cannery Row (1945), John Steinbeck

Cape Hatteras Lighthouse, Sentinel of the Shoals (1991), Dawson Carr

Capharnaum: The Town of Jesus (1985), Stanislao Loffreda

Cleopatra's Palace: In Search of a Legend (1999), Franck Goddio

The Conservation of Aldabra (1968), David R. Stoddard

A Cruising Voyage Round the World (1712), Woodes Rogers

D-Day June 6, 1944: The Climactic Battle of World War II (1995), Stephen E. Ambrose

Darwin (1991), Adrian Desmond and James Moore

De Administrando Imperio [On the Governance of the Empire] (A.D. 950), Constantine VII

De Reditu [The Return] (A.D. 417), Rutilius Namatianus

Description Geographique, Historique, et Archeologique de La Palestine Accompagnée de Cartes Detaillees [Geographical, Historical, and Archeological Description of Palestine with Detailed Maps] (1868), Victor Guérin

A Description of the Cape of Good Hope; with Matters Concerning It (1726), François Valenty

A Description of the East and Some Other Countries (1743), Richard Pococke

A Description of the Island of Jamaica and Barbados (1672), Richard Blome

Diving for Sunken Treasure (1971), Jacques-Yves Cousteau

The Encantadas or Enchanted Isles (1854), Herman Melville

Ethnological Results of the Point Barrow Expedition (1892), John Murdoch

Excavations at Capernaum (1989), Vassilios Tzaferis

Finnish Folklore (1967), Otto Andersson

279

Flowers of Tierra del Fuego (1969), Rae Natalie P. Goodall

From Sydney Cove to Duntroon (1982), Joan Kerr

Galápagos: The Lost Paradise (1990), Peter Salwen

Geographia (ca. A.D. 150), Claudius Ptolemy

Geography (20 B.C.), Strabo

Gesta Danorum [Deeds of the Danes] (ca. 1185), Saxo Grammaticus

La Grèce et les Monarchies Hellénistiques [Greece and the Hellenistic Monarchies] (1921), Maurice Holleaux

Histoire de l'Expedition de Trois Vaisseaux [History of an Expedition of Three Vessels] (1737), Karl Friedrich Behrens

Historia Regum Britanniae [History of the Kings of England] (1136), Geoffrey of Monmouth

The Historical Ecology of Ofu Island, American Samoa (1997), Terry L. Hunt and Patrick Vinton Kirch

The Histories (ca. 450 B.C.), Herodotus

Hralf's Saga Kraka (ca. 1100s), anonymous

"Hymn to Apollo" (ca. 690 B.C.), anonymous

"Hymn to Delos" (ca. 270 B.C.), Callimachus

Iliad (ca. 750 B.C.), Homer

In Pirate Waters (1969), Richard Wheeler

Inuit, Whaling, and Sustainability (1998), Milton M. R. Freeman, et al.

Inupiat and Arctic Alaska (1990), Norman A. Chance

Islam's Black Slaves: The Other Black Diaspora (2001), Ronald Segal

Journal of a Voyage to New South Wales (1790), John White

Journal of La Salle's Last Voyage, 1684–1687, Henri Joutel

Journal up the Missouri (1811), Henry Marie Breckinridge

Kaho'olawe: Na Leo o Kanaloa (1995), Nelson Foster

Kitab ar-Rujari, Al- [The Book of Roger] (1154), ash-Sharif al-Idrisi

Landnamabok [Book of Settlements] (late A.D. 900s), anonymous

Laxdaela Saga (ca. A.D. 1245), anonymous

The Legends and Myths of Hawaii (1888), David Kalakaua

Library of History (59 B.C.), Diodorus Siculus

Life and Death in the Coral Sea (1971), Jacques-Yves Cousteau

Light in the Sea (1989), David Doubilet

Lighthouses of Texas (1991), Baker, T. Lindsay

The Living Sea (1963), Jacques-Yves Cousteau

Marine Shells of Southern Africa (1969), Denis Harper Kennell

Metamorphoses (A.D. 8), Ovid

Le Monde du Silence [The Silent World] (1956) (film), Louis Malle

Myths and Legends of Maoriland (1961), Alexander Wyclif Reed

Narrative of Missionary Enterprises in the South Sea Islands: With Remarks upon the Natural History of the Islands, Origin, Languages, Traditions, and Usages of the Inhabitants (1837), John Williams

Natural History (A.D. 77), Pliny the Elder

Navigatio Sancti Brendani Abbatis [The Navigation of St. Brendan the Abbot] (ca. A.D. 700)

A New History of Jamaica (1740), Charles Leslie

New Voyage Around the World (1697), William Dampier

Normandy: Omaha Beach (1999), Tim Kilvert Jones

Ocean Acoustic Tomography (1996), Walter Heinrich Munk

The Oceans, Their Physics, Chemistry, and General Biology (1942), Walter Heinrich Munk

Odyssey (ca. 750 B.C.), Homer

Omaha Beach (2002), George Bernage

Omaha Beach: A Flawed Victory (2001), Adrian R. Lewis

On the Origin of Species by Means of Natural Selection (1859), Charles Darwin

Orkney Folklore & Sea Legends (1995), Walter Traill Dennison

Orkneyinga Saga: The History of the Earls of Orkney (1206), anonymous

Othello (1952) (film), Orson Welles

Oudheid en Natuurkundige Verhandelingen [Antiquity and Physical Treatises] (1766), Rutger Paludanus

Pacific: An Undersea Journey (1992), David Doubilet

Parallel Logic: A Barrow Memory (2002), Elise Sereni Patkotak

The Peloponnesian Wars (ca. 400 B.C.), Thucydides

Periplous (ca. 350 B.C.), Pseudo-Skilakes

The Polar Passion: The Quest for the North Pole (1989), Farley Mowat

Ryan's Daughter (1969) (film)

Scott's Last Expedition (1913), Robert Falcon Scott

Sea of Cortez (1941), John Steinbeck

Seashells of Eastern Arabia (1995), Donald T. Bosch and Eloise Bosch

Seashells of Oman (1982), Donald T. Bosch and Eloise Bosch

Spanish Exploration in the Southwest, 1542–1706, Juan Rodriguez Cabrillo

Spanish Explorers in the Southern United States, 1528–1543, Pedro de Castañeda de Najera

Tales of the North American Indians (1929), Stith Thompson

La Terre Sainte [The Holy Land] (1884), Victor Guérin

Three Adventures (1973), Jacques-Yves Cousteau

Tierra del Fuego, Argentina (1978), Rae Natalie P. Goodall

Tierra del Fuego, Uttermost Part of the Earth (1948), Esteban Lucas Bridges

The To'aga Site: Archaeological Investigations at an Early Polynesian Site in the Manu'a Islands, American Samoa (1993), Terry L. Hunt and Patrick Vinton Kirch

Traditional Fishing Boats of the West Coast (2002), Charles E. Moore

The Universe Below (1997), William J. Broad

Unwritten Literature of Hawai'i: The Sacred Songs of the Hula (1909), Nathaniel Bright Emerson

Vikings of Today; or, Life and Medical Work among the Fishermen of Labrador (1895), Sir Wilfred Thomason Grenfell

A Visit to Capharnaum (1972), Stanislao Loffreda

Vita Brendani [Life of Brendan] (ca. A.D. 900)

Voyage autour du Monde [Voyage around the World] (1839), Louis Claude Desaulses de Freycinet

Voyage de Decouvertes aux Terres Australes [Voyage of Discoveries of Australian Lands] (1807), Charles-Alexandre Lesueur

Voyage Nouveau de la Terre-Sainte [A New Journey to the Holy Land] (1668), Michel Nau

The Voyage of Discovery (1905), Robert Falcon Scott

The Voyage of the Beagle (1909), Charles Darwin

Voyages Avantureux [Adventurous Voyages] (1579), Martin de Hoyarsabal Where Time Stood Still: A Portrait of Oman (1980), Suzanne Marie Adele Beauclerk, the Duchess of St. Albans

Wildflowers and Other Plants of Texas Beaches and Islands (2002), Alfred Richardson

Wildflowers of South Australia (1861), Fanny Elizabeth de Mole

Wildlife of the Galápagos (2002), Julian Fitter, et al.

With Captain, Sailors Three (1978) (film), Michael Katzev

Wonder Tales of Maoriland (1956), Alexander Wyclif Reed

Wreck of the Belle, the Ruin of La Salle (2001), Robert S. Weddle

Chronological List of Titles

Ancient Writings

ca. 750 B.C., *Iliad*, Homer
    Odyssey, Homer
ca. 690 B.C., "Hymn to Apollo," anonymous
ca. 450 B.C., *The Histories*, Herodotus
ca. 400 B.C., *The Peloponnesian Wars*, Thucydides
ca. 350 B.C., *Periplous*, Pseudo-Skilakes
ca. 270 B.C., "Hymn to Delos," Callimachus
245 B.C., *Argonautica*, Apollonius of Rhodes

Roman Era

59 B.C., *Library of History*, Diodorus Siculus
20 B.C., *Geography*, Strabo
19 B.C., *Aeneid*, Virgil
A.D. 8, *Metamorphoses*, Ovid
ca. A.D. 14, *Ab Urbe Condita* [From the City's Foundation], Livy
A.D. 77, *Natural History*, Pliny the Elder
A.D. 109, *Annals*, Tacitus
ca. A.D. 150, *Geographia*, Claudius Ptolemy

Early Middle Ages

A.D. 417, *De Reditu* [The Return], Rutilius Namatianus
ca. 700, *Navigatio Sancti Brendani Abbatis* [The Navigation of St. Brendan the Abbot]
ca. 900, *Vita Brendani* [Life of Brendan]

Late Middle Ages

950, *De Administrando Imperio* [On the Governance of the Empire], Constantine VII
late 900s, *Landnamabok* [Book of Settlements], anonymous
ca. 1100s, *Hralf's Saga Kraka*, anonymous
1136, *Historia Regum Britanniae* [History of the Kings of England], Geoffrey of Monmouth
1154, *Kitab ar-Rujari, Al-* [The Book of Roger], ash-Sharif al-Idrisi
ca. 1185, *Gesta Danorum* [Deeds of the Danes], Saxo Grammaticus
1206, *Orkneyinga Saga: The History of the Earls of Orkney*, anonymous
ca. 1245, *Laxdaela Saga*, anonymous

Renaissance

1542, *La Bahia de los Pinos* [Bay of Pines], Juan Rodriquez Cabrillo
1543, *Spanish Explorers in the Southern United States, 1528-1543*, Pedro de Castañeda de Najera
1579, *Voyages Avantureux* [Adventurous Voy-

ages], Martin de Hoyarsabal

Age of Discovery

1668, *Voyage Nouveau de la Terre-Sainte* [A New Journey to the Holy Land], Michel Nau

1672, *A Description of the Island of Jamaica and Barbados*, Richard Blome

1687, *Journal of La Salle's Last Voyage*, Henri Joutel

1697, *New Voyage Around the World*, William Dampier

1706, *Spanish Exploration in the Southwest, 1542-1706*, Juan Rodriguez Cabrillo

1712, *A Cruising Voyage Round the World*, Woodes Rogers

1726, *A Description of the Cape of Good Hope; with Matters Concerning It*, François Valenty

1737, *Histoire de l'Expedition de Trois Vaisseaux* [History of an Expedition of Three Vessels], Karl Friedrich Behrens

1740, *A New History of Jamaica*, Charles Leslie

1743, *A Description of the East and Some Other Countries*, Richard Pococke

1766, *Oudheid en Natuurkundige Verhandelingen* [Antiquity and Physical Treatises], Rutger Paludanus

1790, *Journal of a Voyage to New South Wales*, John White

1800s

1807, *Voyage de Decouvertes aux Terres Australes* [Voyage of Discoveries of Australian Lands], Charles-Alexandre Lesueur

1811, *Journal up the Missouri*, Henry Marie Breckinridge

1837, *Narrative of Missionary Enterprises in the South Sea Islands: With Remarks upon the Natural History of the Islands, Origin, Languages, Traditions, and Usages of the Inhabitants*, John Williams

1839, *Voyage autour du Monde* [Voyage around the World], Louis Claude Desaulses de Freycinet

1848, *The Birds of Australia*, John Gould and Elizabeth Gould

1854, *The Encantadas or Enchanted Isles*, Herman Melville

1859, *On the Origin of Species by Means of Natural Selection*, Charles Darwin

1861, *Wildflowers of South Australia*, Fanny Elizabeth de Mole

1868, *Description Geographique, Historique, et Archeologique de La Palestine Accompagnée de Cartes Detaillees* [Geographical, Historical, and Archeological Description of Palestine with Detailed Maps], Victor Guérin

1884, *La Terre Sainte* [The Holy Land], Victor Guérin

1888, *The Legends and Myths of Hawaii*, David Kalakaua

1892, *Ethnological Results of the Point Barrow Expedition*, John Murdoch

1895, *Vikings of Today; or, Life and Medical Work among the Fishermen of Labrador*, Sir Wilfred Thomason Grenfell

1900s

1905, *The Voyage of Discovery*, Robert Falcon Scott

1909, *Unwritten Literature of Hawai'i: The Sacred Songs of the Hula*, Nathaniel Bright Emerson

The Voyage of the Beagle, Charles Darwin

1913, *Scott's Last Expedition*, Robert Falcon Scott

1921, *La Grèce et les Monarchies Hellénistiques* [Greece and the Hellenistic Monarchies], Maurice Holleaux

1929, *Tales of the North American Indians*, Stith Thompson

1939, *Between Pacific Tides*, Edward Flanders "Doc" Ricketts and John Steinbeck

1941, *Sea of Cortez*, John Steinbeck

1942, *The Oceans, Their Physics, Chemistry, and General Biology*, Walter Heinrich Munk

1945, *Cannery Row*, John Steinbeck

1948, *Tierra del Fuego, Uttermost Part of the Earth*, Esteban Lucas Bridges

1950, *Birds of Paradise and Bower Birds*, Margaret Cochrane Scott

1952, *Othello* (film), Orson Welles

1956, *Le Monde du Silence* [The Silent World] (film), Louis Malle

Wonder Tales of Maoriland, Alexander Wyclif Reed

1961, *Myths and Legends of Maoriland*, Alexander Wyclif Reed

1963, *The Living Sea*, Jacques-Yves Cousteau

1967, *Finnish Folklore*, Otto Andersson

1968, *The Conservation of Aldabra*, David R. Stoddard

1969, *Flowers of Tierra del Fuego*, Rae Natalie P. Goodall

In Pirate Waters, Richard Wheeler

Marine Shells of Southern Africa, Denis Harper Kennell

Ryan's Daughter (film)

1971, *Diving for Sunken Treasure*, Jacques-Yves Cousteau

Life and Death in the Coral Sea, Jacques-

Yves Cousteau

1972, *A Visit to Capharnaum*, Stanislao Loffreda

1973, *Archaeology of Kahoolawe*, J. Gilbert McAllister

Three Adventures, Jacques-Yves Cousteau

1978, *The Brendan Voyage*, Tim Severin

Tierra del Fuego, Argentina, Rae Natalie P. Goodall

With Captain, Sailors Three (film), Michael Katzev

1980, *Where Time Stood Still: A Portrait of Oman*, Suzanne Marie Adele Beauclerk, the Duchess of St. Albans

1982, *From Sydney Cove to Duntroon*, Joan Kerr

Seashells of Oman, Donald T. Bosch and Eloise Bosch

1985, *Capharnaum: The Town of Jesus*, Stanislao Loffreda

1989, *Excavations at Capernaum*, Vassilios Tzaferis

Light in the Sea, David Doubilet

The Polar Passion: The Quest for the North Pole, Farley Mowat

1990, *Galápagos: The Lost Paradise*, Peter Salwen

Inupiat and Arctic Alaska, Norman A. Chance

1991, *Cape Hatteras Lighthouse, Sentinel of the Shoals*, Dawson Carr

Darwin, Adrian Desmond and James Moore

Lighthouses of Texas, Baker, T. Lindsay

1992, *Pacific: An Undersea Journey*, David Doubilet

1993, *Basque Whaling in Labrador in the 16th Century*, (monograph), Jean-Pierre Proulx

The To'aga Site: Archaeological Investigations at an Early Polynesian Site in the Manu'a Islands, American Samoa, Terry L. Hunt and Patrick Vinton Kirch

1995, *D-Day June 6, 1944: The Climactic Battle of World War II*, Stephen E. Ambrose

Kaho'olawe: Na Leo o Kanaloa, Nelson Foster

Orkney Folklore & Sea Legends, Walter Traill Dennison

Seashells of Eastern Arabia, Donald T. Bosch and Eloise Bosch

1996, *Ocean Acoustic Tomography*, Walter Heinrich Munk

Underwater Archaeology, George F. Bass

1997, *The Historical Ecology of Ofu Island, American Samoa*, Terry L. Hunt and Patrick Vinton Kirch

The Universe Below, William J. Broad

1998, *Alexandria—The Submerged Royal Quarters*, Franck Goddio

Inuit, Whaling, and Sustainability, Milton M. R. Freeman, et al.

1999, *Cleopatra's Palace: In Search of a Legend*, Franck Goddio

Normandy: Omaha Beach, Tim Kilvert Jones

2000s

2001, *Archaeology of Elmina: Africans and Europeans on the Gold Coast, An 1400-1900*, Christopher R. DeCorse

Islam's Black Slaves: The Other Black Diaspora, Ronald Segal

Omaha Beach: A Flawed Victory, Adrian R. Lewis

Wreck of the Belle, the Ruin of La Salle, Robert S. Weddle

2002, *Omaha Beach*, George Bernage

Parallel Logic: A Barrow Memory, Elise Sereni Patkotak

Traditional Fishing Boats of the West Coast, Charles E. Moore

Wildflowers and Other Plants of Texas Beaches and Islands, Alfred Richardson

Wildlife of the Galápagos, Julian Fitter, et al.

GENERAL BIBLIOGRAPHY

Abbott, R. Tucker. *Seashells of the World.* New York: Golden Press, 1962.

Adkins, Lesley, and Roy A. Adkins. *Dictionary of Roman Religion.* New York: Facts on File, 1996.

_____. *Handbook to Life in Ancient Rome.* New York: Facts on File, 1994.

Aksyonov, Andrei, and Alexander Chernov. *Exploring the Deep.* London: Collins, 1979.

Almanac of Famous People. 6th ed. Farmington Hills, Mich.: Gale Group, 1998.

Asante, Molefi K., and Mark T. Mattson. *Historical and Cultural Atlas of African Americans.* New York: Macmillan, 1992.

Ashdown, Charles Henry. *European Arms & Armor.* New York: Barnes & Noble, 1995.

Ballard, Robert D. *The Eternal Darkness.* Princeton, N.J.: Princeton University Press, 2000.

Barraclough, Geoffrey, ed. *Atlas of World History.* Ann Arbor, Mich.: Borders Press, 2001.

Bass, George F., "Cape Gelidonya: A Bronze Age Shipwreck," *Transactions of the American Philosophical Society*, Vol. 57, Part 8, Philadelphia, 1967.

_____, ed. *Ships and Shipwrecks of the Americas: A History Based on Underwater Archaeology.* London: Thames and Hudson, 1996.

_____, "25-Year History of INA Research," http://ina.tamu.edu/25yearhis1.htm.

Baugh, Albert C. *A History of the English Language.* New York: Appleton-Century-Crofts, 1957.

Bell, Robert E. *Place-Names in Classical Mythology: Greece.* Santa Barbara, Calif.: ABC-Clio, 1989.

_____. *Women of Classical Mythology.* Santa Barbara, Calif.: ABC-Clio, 1991.

Bentley, James. *A Calendar of Saints.* Oxford: Orbis Publishing, 1986.

Biography Resource Center, http://galenet.gale-group.com.

Bowder, Diana, ed. *Who Was Who in the Roman World.* New York: Washington Square Press, 1980.

"Bowhead Whales," *Beringia Natural History Notebook Series.* Washington, D.C.: National Audubon Society, September, 1992.

Breeden, Robert L., ed. *Clues to America's Past.* Washington, D.C.: National Geographic, 1976.

_____, ed. *The Ocean Realm.* Washington, D.C.: National Geographic Society, 1978.

Broad, William J. *The Universe Below.* New York: Simon & Schuster, 1997.

Brothwell, Don and Patricia. *Food in Antiquity: A Survey of the Diet of Early Peoples.* New York: Frederick A. Praeger, 1969.

Bryant, Arthur. *The Medieval Foundation of England.* Garden City, N.Y.: Doubleday, 1967.

Bunson, Matthew. *Dictionary of the Roman Empire.* New York: Oxford University Press, 1991.

Burdett, Anita L. P. *Records of Dubai, 1761–1960.* London: Archive Editions, 2000.

Burton, Maurice. *Under the Sea.* New York: Franklin Watts, 1960.

Bury, J. B. *The Cambridge Medieval History.* Cambridge: Cambridge University Press, 1957.

Bushnell, O. A. *The Gifts of Civilization: Germs and Genocide in Hawai'i.* Honolulu: University of Hawaii Press, 1993.

Business Leader Profiles for Students. Detroit: Gale Research, 1999.

Butler, Alban. *Lives of the Saints.* New York: Barnes & Noble, 1997.

Byock, Jesse, trans. *The Saga of King Hralf Kraki*. London: Penguin, 1998.

Cannon, John, and Ralph Griffiths. *Oxford Illustrated History of the British Monarchy*. Oxford: Oxford University Press, 1998.

Cannon, Michael. *Who's Master? Who's Man? Australia in the Victorian Age*. Sydney, Aust.: Thomas Nelson, 1971.

Cartwright, R. A., and D. B. Cartwright. *The Holy Island of Lindisfarne and the Farne Islands*. Vancouver: David & Charles, 1976.

Casson, Lionel. *The Ancient Mariners*. Princeton, N.J.: Princeton University Press, 1991.

Cavendish, Richard, ed. *Man, Myth & Magic*. New York: Marshall Cavendish, 1970.

Chaliant, Gérard, and Jean-Pierre Rageau. *The Penguin Atlas of Diasporas*. New York: Viking Penguin, 1995.

Champagne, Duane, ed. *Chronology of Native North American History*. Detroit: Gale Research, 1994.

———, ed. *Native North American Almanac*. Detroit: Gale Research, 1998.

Clain-Stefanelli, Elvira, and Vladimir Clain-Stefanelli. *The Beauty and Lore of Coins, Currency, and Medals*. Croton-on-Hudson, N.Y.: Riverwood Publishers, 1974.

Cohn-Sherbok, Lavinia. *Who's Who in Christianity*. London: Routledge, 1998.

Constable, Nick. *The World Atlas of Archeology*. New York: Lyons Press, 2000.

Cordingly, David. *Under the Black Flag*. San Diego, Calif.: Harvest Books, 1995.

Cousteau, Jacques-Yves. *Diving for Sunken Treasure*. Garden City, N.Y.: Doubleday, 1971.

———. *Life and Death in the Coral Sea*. Garden City, N.Y.: Doubleday, 1971.

———. *The Living Sea*. New York: Harper & Row, 1963.

———. *The Shark: Splendid Savage of the Sea*. Garden City, N.Y.: Doubleday, 1970.

———. *Three Adventures*. Garden City, N.Y.: Doubleday, 1973.

Cribb, Joe. *Money*. Toronto: Stoddart, 1990.

Crump, Donald J., editor. *Blue Horizons*. Washington, D.C.: National Geographic Society, 1985.

———. *Majestic Island Worlds*. Washington, D.C.: National Geographic Society, 1987.

———. *The World's Wild Shores*. Washington, D.C.: National Geographic Society, 1990.

Crystal, David, ed. *The Cambridge Biographical Dictionary*. Cambridge: University of Cambridge, 1996.

———. *The Cambridge Encyclopedia of the English Language*. New York: Cambridge University Press, 1995.

Davidson, Alan. *The Oxford Companion to Food*. Oxford: Oxford University Press, 1999.

Davidson, Basil. *African Kingdoms*. New York: Time, Inc., 1966.

Davidson, Linda Kay, and David M. Gitlitz. *Pilgrimage: From the Ganges to Graceland*. Santa Barbara, Calif.: ABC-Clio, 2002.

Davies, Charles E. *The Blood-Red Arab Flag*. Exeter, Devon: University of Exeter Press, 1997.

Davies, Glyn. *A History of Money from Ancient Times to the Present Day*. Cardiff: University of Wales Press, 1994.

Dictionary of American Biography, Base Set. American Council of Learned Societies, 1928–1936.

Dubin, Marc. *The Greek Islands*. London: Dorling Kindersley, 1997.

Durant, Will. *The Life of Greece*. New York: Simon & Schuster, 1939.

Eagle, Dorothy, and Meic Stephens, eds. *The Oxford Illustrated Literary Guide to Great Britain and Ireland*. Oxford: Oxford University Press, 1992.

Early Encounters in North America (database). Alexandria, Vir.: Alexandria Street Press, 2001.

East, Gordon. *An Historical Geography of Europe*. London: Methuen, 1966.

Eck, Diana L. *On Common Ground: Columbia University Press* (CD-ROM). New York: Columbia University Press, 1994.

Einzig, Paul. *Primitive Money*. Oxford: Pergamon Press, 1966.

Encyclopedia Americana (CD-ROM). Danforth, Conn.: Grolier, 1999.

Encyclopedia Britannica, http://www.britannica.com.

Encyclopedia of World Biography, 2nd ed. Detroit: Gale Research, 1998.

Explorers and Discoverers of the World. Detroit: Gale Research, 1993.

Facaros, Dana. *Greek Islands*. Chester, Conn.: Globe Pequot Press, 1988.

Farmer, David Hugh. *The Oxford Dictionary of Saints*. Oxford: Oxford University Press, 1992.

Gale Encyclopedia of U.S. Economic History. Farmington Hills, Mich.: Gale Group, 1999.

Gardner, Joseph L., ed. *Atlas of the Bible*. Pleasantville, N.Y.: Reader's Digest, 1981.

Goodrich, Norma Lorre. *Medieval Myths*. New York: Mentor, 1961.

Gosner, Kenneth L. *Field Guide to the Atlantic Seashore.* Boston: Houghton Mifflin, 1979.

Graves, Robert. *The Greek Myths.* London: Penguin, 1960.

Gray, William R. *Voyages to Paradise.* Washington, D.C.: National Geographic Society, 1981.

"Greenpeace," http://www.greenpeace.org/homepage/.

Grierson, Philip. *Numismatics.* London: Oxford University Press, 1975.

Grimal, Pierre. *The Penguin Dictionary of Classical Mythology.* London: Penguin, 1990.

Grollenberg, L. H. *Atlas of the Bible.* New York: Thomas Nelson, 1957.

Grove, Noel. *Wild Lands for Wildlife.* Washington, D.C.: National Geographic Society, 1984.

Guerber, H. A. *Myths of Greece and Rome.* New York: American Book Co., 1893.

Guide to English Heritage Properties. London: English Heritage, 1989.

Hammond, N. G. L., and H. H. Scullard, eds. *The Oxford Classical Dictionary.* Oxford: Clarendon Press, 1992.

Harwood, Kathryn Chapman. *The Lives of Vizcaya.* Miami, Fla.: Banyan Books, 1985.

Hastings, James, ed. *Encyclopedia of Religion and Ethics.* New York: Charles Scribner's Sons, 1951.

Hebbert, Antonia, ed. *Cornwall.* London: Purnell Book Publication, 1987.

Historic World Leaders. Detroit: Gale Research, 1994.

Hopper, R. J. *The Early Greeks.* New York: Harper & Row, 1977.

Horbury, William, ed. *The Cambridge History of Judaica.* Cambridge: Cambridge University Press, 1999.

Hough, Frank O., et al. *History of U.S. Marine Corps Operations in World War II.* Washington, D.C.: Historical Branch, U.S. Marine Corps, 1958.

Howatson, M. C., ed. *The Oxford Companion to Classical Literature.* Oxford: Oxford University Press, 1989.

"International Fund for Animal Welfare," http://www.ifaw.org/.

Jack, R. Ian. *Medieval Wales.* Ithaca, N.Y.: Cornell University Press, 1972.

Jeffrey, Betty. *White Coolies.* Sydney, Aust.: Angus & Robertson, 1954.

Karskens, Grace. *Inside the Rocks: The Archaeology of a Neighbourhood.* Sydney: Hale & Iremonger, 1999.

Kemp, Peter, ed. *The Oxford Companion to Ships and the Sea.* Oxford: Oxford University Press, 1988.

Lopez, Robert S. *The Birth of Europe.* New York: M. Evans, 1967.

Lyttelton, Margaret, and Werner Forman. *The Romans: Their Gods and Their Beliefs.* London: Orbis, 1985.

Mac Donough, Steve. *The Dingle Peninsula: History, Folklore, Archaeology.* Dingle: Brandon Book Publishers, 1993.

Mackay, Angus, and David Ditchburn, eds. *Atlas of Medieval Europe.* London: Routledge, 1997.

MacKendrick, Paul. *The Mute Stones Speak.* New York: Mentor, 1960.

Magnusson, Magnus. *Cambridge Biographical Dictionary.* Cambridge: University of Cambridge, 1990.

Mantinband, James H. *Dictionary of Latin Literature.* New York: Philosophical Library, 1956.

Martin, Laura C. *Southern Gardens: A Gracious History and a Traveler's Guide.* New York: Artabras, 1996.

McArthur, Tom, ed. *The Oxford Companion to the English Language.* Oxford: Oxford University Press, 1992.

McCrum, et al. *The Story of English.* New York: Viking Penguin, 1986.

Merriam-Webster's Geographical Dictionary, 3rd ed. Springfield, Mass.: Merriam-Webster, 1997.

Metzger, Bruce M., and Michael D. Coogan, eds. *The Oxford Companion to the Bible.* Oxford: Oxford University Press, 1993.

Moorey, P. R. S. *The Biblical Lands.* New York: Peter Bedrick Books, 1991.

Morrison, H. Robert, and Christine Eckstrom Lee. *America's Atlantic Isles.* Washington, D.C.: National Geographic Society, 1981.

Nash, Jay Robert. *Encyclopedia of World Crime.* Wilmette, Ill.: CrimeBooks Inc., 1990.

National Cyclopaedia of American Biography. Ann Arbor, Mich.: University Microfilms, 1967.

New Catholic Encyclopedia. San Francisco: Catholic University of America, 1967.

"National Geographic," http://www.nationalgeographic.com/

New Larousse Encyclopedia of Mythology. London: Prometheus Press, 1968.

Notable Scientists: From 1900 to the Present. Farmington Hills, Mich.: Gale Group, 2001.

Opitz, Charles J. *Odd and Curious Money.* Ocala, Fla.: First Impressions, 1986.

Paor, Liam de. *Saint Patrick's World.* Dublin: Four Courts Press, 1996.

Parker, Michael St. John. *Britain's Kings and Queens*. Andover, Hants: Pitkin, 1994.

Patterson, Lotsee, and Mary Ellen Snodgrass. *Indian Terms of the Americas*. Englewood, Colo.: Libraries Unlimited, 1994.

Pickford, Nigel. *The Atlas of Ship Wrecks & Treasure*. New York: Dorling Kindersley, 1994.

Plummer, Charles. *Lives of Irish Saints*. Oxford: Clarendon Press, 1997.

Price, Ira Maurice. *The Monuments and the Old Testament*. Philadelphia: Judson Press, 1925.

Pritchard, James B., ed. *Everyday Life in Bible Times*. Washington, D.C.: National Geographic, 1967.

Pritzker, Barry M. *A Native American Encyclopedia*. Oxford: Oxford University Press, 2000.

"The Ramsar Convention on Wetlands," http://www.ramsar.org/.

Reader's Digest Illustrated History of South Africa. Capetown, South Africa: Reader's Digest Association, 1994.

Rice, David Talbot, ed. *The Dawn of European Civilization: The Dark Ages*. New York: McGraw-Hill, 1965.

Roberts, Nancy. *Blackbeard and Other Pirates of the Atlantic Coast*. New York: John F. Blair, 1993.

Sandz, Victoria. *Encyclopedia of Western Atlantic Shipwrecks and Sunken Treasure*. Jefferson, N.C.: McFarland, 2001.

Snodgrass, Mary Ellen. *Chronology of Epidemics*. Jefferson, N.C.: McFarland, 2004.

_____. *Coins and Currency in History*. Jefferson, N.C.: McFarland, 2003.

_____. *The Encyclopedia of Frontier Literature*. Santa Barbara, Calif.: ABC-Clio, 1997.

_____. *Encyclopedia of Kitchen History*. London: Fitzroy-Dearborn, 2003.

_____. *Encyclopedia of World Scripture*. Jefferson, N.C.: McFarland, 2002.

_____. *Religious Sites in America*. Santa Barbara, Calif.: ABC-Clio, 2001.

_____. *Voyages in Classical Mythology*. Santa Barbara, Calif.: ABC-Clio, 1994.

_____. *Who's Who in the Middle Ages*. Jefferson, N.C.: McFarland, 2001.

Spalding, Mark D., et al. *World Atlas of Coral Reefs*. Ewing, N.J.: University of California Press, 2001.

Speake, Graham, ed. *Encyclopedia of Greece and the Hellenic Tradition*. Chicago: Fitzroy Dearborn, 2000.

Standish, David. *The Art of Money*. San Francisco: Chronicle Books, 2000.

Starr, Chester G. *A History of the Ancient World*. New York: Oxford University Press, 1991.

Stephen, Leslie, and Signey Lee, eds. *Dictionary of National Biography*. Oxford: Oxford University Press, 1917.

Tannenbaum, Barbara, ed. *The Encyclopedia of Latin American History and Culture*. New York: Charles Scribner's Sons, 1995.

Terras, Victor, ed. *Handbook of Russian Literature*. New Haven, Conn.: Yale University Press, 1985.

"UNESCO," http://www.unesco.org.

Van der Heyden, A. A. M., and H. H. Scullard, eds. *Atlas of the Classical World*. New York: Thomas Nelson & Sons, 1959.

Walker, Barbara G. *The Woman's Encyclopedia of Myths and Secrets*. Edison, N.J.: Castle Books, 1996.

Walker, Harlan, ed. *Cooks and Other People: Proceedings of the Oxford Symposium on Food and Cookery 1995*. Totnes, Devon: Prospect Books, 1996.

Walker, Sheila S., ed. *African Roots/American Cultures: Africa in the Creation of the Americas*. Lanham, Md.: Rowman & Littlefield, 2001.

Weatherford, Jack. *The History of Money: From Sandstone to Cyberspace*. Pittsburgh, Pa.: Three Rivers Press, 1998.

Wheal, Elizabeth-Anne, et al. *Encyclopedia of the Second World War*. Edison, N.J.: Castle Books, 1989.

Wheeler, Richard. *In Pirate Waters*. New York: Thomas Y. Crowell, 1969.

Whitfield, Philip, ed. *Animals*. New York: Macmillan, 1999.

Who's Who in America. Chicago: Marquis Who's Who, 1971.

Winters, Harold A. *Battling the Elements: Weather and Terrain in the Conduct of War*. Baltimore: Johns Hopkins University Press, 1998.

The Wonders of the World. Washington, D.C.: National Geographic Society, 1999.

Woodward, Fred. *Identifying Shells*. Seacaucus, N.J.: Chartwell Books, 1993.

"The World Heritage List," http://whc.unesco.org/nwhc/pages/doc/mainf3.htm.

World of Invention, 2nd ed. Farmington Hills, Mich.: Gale Group, 1999.

World Religions. New York: Macmillan Reference USA, 1998.

"World Wildlife Fund," http://www.panda.org.

Wright, G. Ernest, ed. *Great People of the Bible and How They Lived*. Pleasantville, N.Y.: Reader's Digest Association, 1979.

INDEX

Main entries are in **boldface**. Numbers in brackets refer to illustrations.